# FRANZ KAFKA

# FRANZ KAFKA

## A Critical Study of His Writings

**WILHELM EMRICH**

*Translated by Sheema Zeben Buehne*

FREDERICK UNGAR PUBLISHING CO.
*NEW YORK*

Translated from the German *Franz Kafka*
by arrangement with the original publisher
Athenäum Verlag GmbH, Frankfurt am Main

First paperback edition, 1984

*Printed in the United States of America*

Library of Congress Catalog Card Number: 68–12121
ISBN 0-8044-2168-4 (cloth)
ISBN 0-8044-6136-8 (pbk.)

# Translator's Foreword

In the great morality plays, Everyman undertakes an examination of his self and his life; only after viewing the purgatory and hell within himself does he die his own death, presumably to enter paradise. If one viewed the writings of Kafka as a vast canvas that depicted the inner and outer life of Everyman, one could easily be impressed and detained by smaller or larger details and be caught by the beauty, magic, or horror of aspects of the canvas. Perhaps one would fail to take in the whole; perhaps one would lose sight of the panorama of man's existence; for Kafka's view of the outer and inner life, projected on a tapestry of verbal imagery, is as lucid and luminous as the colors and the figures of, say, the Unicorn Tapestry, yet as elusive as the various meanings intrinsic to it.

Dante, like Everyman, knew of the existence of man's inner purgatory and hell; yet he needed a Vergil to guide him. But why Vergil? Was it perhaps that Vergil was a poet whom Dante trusted, and hence one to whom he could turn for explanation and justification of what he saw? The reader of Kafka also knows of the existence of inner purgatory and hell and dimly senses their presence in the Kafkaian world. Like Dante he needs a guide who, accompanying him across the tenuous bridge that stretches into the other world, will illuminate for him what he sees.

It is in the role of such a guide that Wilhelm Emrich's book can function. Casting light upon the shadowy portions of Kafka's canvas, it brings to the reader's consciousness an understanding not only of Kafka's world, but of that world as it exists within each of us.

Because this book presents an analysis of Kafka's work that is fundamental and all-embracing, any subsequent criticism of Kafka must take it into account. Since Professor Emrich's profound study is perhaps unique in that it possesses a universal overview with a classical, philosophical approach to the totality of Kafka's writings, it may well serve as the starting point for all future evaluation of Kafka's literary production.

The beginning of this book is not easy; it is not easy because it is laying the foundation for Professor Emrich's overview of Kafka's literary endeavor. The tapestry of Kafka's writings is, as it were, divided into panels, and we are conducted from one to another in a passage that spans the poet's worlds. As panel after panel is revealed, the clear white light directed upon the tapestry is refracted into the colors of the spectrum; and the whole, visible in its parts, irradiates the parts, visible as a whole. Once the reader grasps the philosophical structure underlying the analysis, he will sense a growing excitement that reaches its peak with Professor Emrich's quasi-novelistic interpretation of *The Castle*.

It is no wonder that Professor Emrich's *Franz Kafka* has been widely read and discussed in Europe. With this translation a remarkable work on Kafka is made available in English.

In translating, I have tried to do justice, above all, to the thought, preserving as much as possible of the emphasis and of the sequence of phrase. The extensive quotations from Kafka's writings repeatedly necessitated an interweaving of two quite disparate styles: Kafka's and that of Professor Emrich. Although various English translations of Kafka's works exist— and I have frequently drawn into comparison those available to me—I have in all instances made my own translation.

Needless to say, in this as in every translation there are bound to be variations in interpretation and usage. What may occasionally appear to be an inconsistency may actually be an intentional distinction. I felt it important to retain Kafka's verb tenses even at the cost of fluidity of text. At times I have varied in my translation of certain German words; for example, for German *Kampf* I have used both "battle" and "struggle," in accordance with my own interpretation of the connotations in a given passage. Except where the English equivalents of proper names seemed to me to carry the full connotations of the original I have retained the German form; for instance, Josef but Josephine, the landlady of the Inn at the Bridge, but the landlady of the Herrenhof. By employing "universal" and "Universal" in the translation, I have tried to differentiate Professor Emrich's uses of the philosophical term.

I wish to express my heartfelt thanks to Mr. Frederick Ungar, who initiated this translation, for his interest, encouragement, understanding, and patience. It was a pleasure to work with my long-suffering editor, Mr. Michael Levien, to whom I am indebted for queries and suggestions.

To my friend Lelia Brodersen I here express my deepest gratitude and appreciation. Not only her indefatigable help in typing and proofreading but her illuminating psychological insights and her aesthetic sensitivity to English made this translation possible.

S.Z.B.

# About the Author

Wilhelm Emrich, professor of German language and literature at the Free University of Berlin, has lectured as visiting professor at several universities in the United States. He was born in Nieder-Jeutz, Lorraine, in 1909, and studied Germanic philology, philosophy, and history at the University of Frankfurt am Main. His intellectual and spiritual development was greatly influenced by his teachers Paul Tillich, Theodor W. Adorno, Max Horkheimer, and Karl Mannheim, and by his father, a physician.

Professor Emrich's first important work, *Die Symbolik von Faust II,* published in 1943, and not yet translated into English, brought him recognition as an outstanding scholar in the field of philological research.

In the following years Professor Emrich widened his field of interest, conducting intensive studies in modern literature at the Universities of Göttingen and Cologne. Out of these studies there emerged his great work *Franz Kafka,* which immediately upon publication in 1958 was highly acclaimed by German critics and scholars.

Professor Emrich is the author of many books and essays, not only on notable literary figures such as Schiller, Goethe, Eichendorff, and Kafka; he has written also on various aspects of literature and aesthetic criticism and has analyzed the works of many contemporary writers, including those of Samuel Beckett. A selection of his essays, translated into English for the first time, will be issued soon by the publishers of the present volume.

# Contents

CHAPTER VII

**The Human Cosmos:
The Novel *The Castle*   365**

### CHAPTER I

# The Universal Thema

*Classical and "Modern" Beauty*

Mystery is an element of every great poetic work. It is also its humanizing element. It rescues the individual from being dominated by the universal; for "the *beautiful* is that which pleases . . . without the intervention of a concept" (Kant);[1] and "beauty can never become aware of itself" (Goethe).[2] Mystery dwells in the beautiful and begets what has been called the aesthetic charm, the magic, the untranslatable, original, or irrational quality of poetry—concepts that are quite inadequate, because they are general.

But mystery is also a dehumanizing element. Wherever it occurs in isolation it destroys contact, the basis of all human nature, spreading fear or horror in the Grotesque,[3] calling up nightmares wherever it holds itself imperviously aloof from the general understanding. Mystery that is nothing but mystery, that with indifference raises a barricade between itself and all comprehending thought, destroys beauty, of which it is an element, but not the essence. For the beautiful is "the sensuous appearance of the idea" (Hegel),[4] not its opponent. That is

*1*

what is forgotten in deluded discourse about the irrational quality of the beautiful. "The *beautiful* is that which pleases universally, without the intervention of a concept," is Kant's full definition. The beautiful is the synthesis of mystery and the manifest, of the individual and the universal. Poetry is a mode of giving form to "revealed mystery" (Goethe), concealing and revealing the universal in the individual and the individual in the universal. In this manner alone does it safeguard human nature. In this manner alone does it do away with both the tyrannous domination of the hollow universal and the desperate anxiety-dreams of the isolatedly individual: in the semblance of a reconciliation that, to be sure, remains semblance (for beauty is semblance), but that vividly conjures up and challengingly proclaims, in the illusion of such a synthesis, the possibility of a perfect, concrete, and at the same time universal human race.

Such thoughts are classical heritage. They still maintain their validity, even where they appear betrayed or abandoned in the extreme art forms of the twentieth century that explicitly effect the breach between the universal and the individual by putting on the bogy-mask of incomprehensibility.

This is a startling thesis and requires substantiation. Beauty, as it has just been defined in the classical sense, is still alive in the incomprehensible works of art of the twentieth century. This apparent· contradiction is resolved as soon as the significance of the breach between the individual and the universal, caught sight of in these art forms, is revealed. The universal from which these apparently extremely individualistic art forms are severing themselves—art forms that are very often maligned as being pathologically off-beat—is no longer the universal of classical aesthetics at all; it is no longer Hegel's "Idea," or Kant's and Schiller's "Intelligible," or Goethe's "Primal Phenomenon," or "the Infinite" of the romantic period. It has been perverted into a philosophy of life, into an "ideology," into a maxim for practical-technical behavior and action, into common sense that makes the world surveyable and puts this world at its disposal, and that misuses even the idea of freedom and the dignity of man, using it as a pretext for the exercise of power. The true universal in the classical sense has indeed become "incomprehensible" in the twentieth-century world. It has retreated into the interior of incomprehensible art works that consistently dare not and cannot any longer express this universal in the language and in the forms of older art—and this is how such works differ essentially from classical art. To express this more pointedly: since this true universal is no longer lived, believed in, and thought, there is no longer any language or art form that would be able to communicate it comprehensibly. For not only, of necessity, were the linguistics and subject matter of the classical period themselves caught in the maelstrom of perversion, as is betrayed by the twentieth-century epigonous imitators of that period; not only did the universal truth contents, given definition and form by the classical period, deteriorate into hollow ideologies, possessing merely historical status; but the true universal itself became mute and amorphous. It can no longer "appear" and can no longer "be thought."

With that, the termination of all art is reached—on the assumption that the true universal does not exist, that classical aesthetics was a fraud, that the human being represents a merely finite being, that neither "mysteries" nor "revelations" exist, that the world is a surveyable, calculable structure, and that the universal is nothing but the mental image of the world as conceived by twentieth-century society at large and its "public opinion."

If this assumption is incorrect, then art is possible in the twentieth century, though only in the form of an absolute enigmatization with reference to the universal of this century. Such an enigmatization would rescue the individual and the true universal from domination by the base general public of our time. The "mystery" of this art would at the same time be an element of humanization. This, of course, would imply that such a mystery could also be revealed; that is, it could reveal itself to the human understanding. However, if individuality—which *per definitionem* is beyond the general understanding—

as well as the true universal, can no longer enter into the language and the point of view of today's general public, how, in that case, is a revelation of its mystery still possible? That is, how then are art and beauty still possible?

Franz Kafka achieved the solution of this problem more consistently and more astringently than any other poet of the twentieth century. Not without reason is his work the most inscrutable of our age, harboring as it does the most impenetrable mysteries that have ever been immersed in a work of fiction. Not without reason does it arouse in his readers fear and horror; and not without reason has there arisen that fashionable monstrosity, the word "Kafkaesque," that betokens everything nightmarish, intricately ghostly, and absurd, not only in human thought, action, and dreaming, but also in modern bureaucracies, machines, equipment, and enslaving-institutions. But not without reason does his work belong to the most finished linguistic and artistic creations that the literature of this century has produced. Can it be that beauty has realized itself in his work? Despite all the horrors and absurdities of the contents? Is it possible that a veritable universal is included in it? If so, in what form and language? And can this language be deciphered? Can its riddles be solved?

The answer to these questions will serve to judge not only Kafka's writing but also the art of our era; perhaps our era itself, and its spiritual and intellectual direction.

## The Universal of "The Hunter Gracchus"

In order to elucidate the problem, let us examine a passage of Franz Kafka. In a fragment pertaining to "The Hunter Gracchus" (B 334 ff.)[5] this "dead" and "in a certain sense" alive Hunter Gracchus (B 102) who, ever since his death fifteen hundred years ago, has been sailing the "earthly waters" (B 102) in an old bark "without a rudder . . . driven by the wind that blows in the undermost regions of death" (B 105), is visited in a harbor by a guest who still "roams about outside" (B 335), on land, among the living, and is questioned about the inter-relationships of his story:

First tell me briefly but connectedly, how about you? To tell the truth, I really don't know how it is with you. For you, to be sure, these things are matter of course, and you assume, as it's characteristic of you to do, that the whole world knows of them. But in this short lifetime—life, you know, is short, Gracchus; try to make yourself understand that—in this short life, a person has his hands full trying to support himself and his family. Interesting as the Hunter Gracchus is—this is my conviction, I'm not toadying—a person doesn't have time to think of him, or to inquire about him, let alone worry about him. Perhaps on one's deathbed, like your man from Hamburg—I don't know. Perhaps that's when a hard-working man has the leisure, for the first time in his life, to stretch out, and then at some moment or other the green Hunter Gracchus will flit through his idle thoughts. But otherwise, as I said, I didn't know anything about you; I'm here in the harbor on business, I saw the bark, there was the gangplank available; I crossed over—but now I'd like to know something about you connectedly. (B 336-37)

To that the Hunter Gracchus replies:

Ah, connectedly! The old, old stories! All the books are full of it, in all the schools teachers put it on the board, each mother dreams about it while nursing her child at her breast. It is the whisper in every embrace, shopkeepers tell it to customers, customers to shopkeepers. Soldiers sing it as they march, the preacher calls it out in church, historians in their studies see open-mouthed what happened long ago and are forever describing it. It is printed in the newspapers and the people pass it on from hand to hand. The telegraph was invented to let it circle the earth more rapidly. It is dug up in buried cities, and the elevators race to the roofs of the skyscrapers with it. Passengers in trains proclaim it through the windows, in the countries they are traveling through, but even earlier than that the savages yell it in their faces. It can be read in the stars, and the seas bear its reflected image. The brooks carry it from the mountains and the snow scatters it again on the summit. And you, man, are sitting here and asking me for

continuity. You must have had an exquisitely scoundrelly youth.
(B 337)

To this the living guest replies:

Possibly—as is characteristic of everybody's youth. But it would
be very useful to you, I believe, if you looked about in the world
a bit. Odd as it may seem to you—and I'm even amazed at it
myself, but it's so, nevertheless—you are not the subject of the
talk of the town. However many things are being talked about,
you aren't one of them. The world goes its way and you are making your journey, but I never noticed before today that your
paths had crossed one another. (B 337-38)

The story of this Hunter Gracchus is thus the story of everything that was and is: primitive times and the present never
cease to tell the story; even the cosmos—stars, seas, mountains
—knows of his story. It is the Universal in universal significance, continually being heralded by everything. But no one in
the living world knows of it; for all the living are busy with
something else. They have "their hands full" supporting themselves and their families: "I didn't know anything about you;
I'm in the harbor on business." Only shortly before death, "at
some moment or other the green Hunter Gracchus will flit
through his idle thoughts," "when a hard-working man has the
leisure, for the first time in his life, to stretch out." "Work,"
"business," the toil and moil of life prevent one from having any
thought, any form of knowledge about the true Universal of
that-which-is. On the other hand, however, even the Hunter
Gracchus knows nothing about what activates the very busy
human world. This very man who knows everything, whose
story represents what is most universal, is helplessly at a loss
regarding the thought processes of this busy world. "But I don't
undertand the fellow's [the "hard-working" man from Ham-
burg] chain of reasoning. Perhaps you can explain it to me . . . I
need various explanations. You, who roam about outside [on
the earth], can give them to me" (B 335). But no "explanation"
is possible. The two worlds talk past one another. Neither one
can "understand" the other.

This is the pattern of all of Franz Kafka's stories and novels: the two worlds that cannot make themselves understood by one another.[6]

## Between This World and the Hereafter

The story of the Hunter Gracchus might readily suggest that one impose on the all-inclusive universal, of which this hunter speaks, some general concept or other that has appeared in the history of the human spirit, labeling that concept, say, religious, ontological, metaphysical, cosmological, mythical, or even "higher" poetic reality; and designating the opposing world as the empirical, space-time, social reality. It is precisely this, however, that would fail at the very outset to grasp the gravity of the problem and the true structure of Kafka's works. What Hunter Gracchus is here paraphrasing can no longer be made to fit into a general concept that will be adequate. For the point of the story of this hunter is precisely that he has no fixed abode anywhere, neither in a metaphysical-religious sphere, nor in a real-empirical one. It is explicitly stated that before this story of his began he had lived happily and had also died happily, with everything safely in order both in this world and in the next:

I had been glad to live, and I had been glad to die. Before I stepped on board [the death barge] I happily threw down in front of me that junk—rifle, pouch, gun—that I had always proudly carried, and I slipped into the shroud as a girl slips into her wedding dress. Here I lay and waited. Then the catastrophe happened. (B 103-104)

This "catastrophe" is described as follows:

"My death barge lost its way—a wrong turn of the rudder, a moment's inattention on the part of the guide, a distraction because of the breathtaking loveliness of my native land—I do not know what it was; I know only that I remained on the earth and that ever since my barge has been sailing the waters of the earth.

In this way I, who wanted to live only in my mountains, have been journeying since my death through all the countries of the earth." "And you have no part in the Hereafter?" asked the mayor, wrinkling his brow. "I am always on the great stairway that leads up to it," said the Hunter. "On this infinitely wide outside staircase I rove about, now up above, now down below, now to the right, now to the left, always on the move. The hunter has turned into a butterfly. Don't laugh." "I'm not laughing," protested the mayor. "Very discerning of you," said the Hunter. "I am always on the move. Even if I rush up with the utmost vigor and can already see the gate sparkling on high, I awake on my old barge, drearily stuck in some earthly waters. There, in my cabin, the fundamental mistake of my erstwhile dying grins derisively at me on every side." (B 102)

With that the problem that pervades all of Kafka's other works as well is formulated precisely as follows: The all-inclusive universal expressed in this story of the Hunter Gracchus is that this hunter has dropped out of the classifications of this world as well as out of those of the hereafter; he is universally everywhere and nowhere, can no longer be definitely placed; there is no unequivocal determinability for his existence. His "story" is the antithesis of every delimited individual story. It is the story of a being who participates in everything and yet is not absorbed in any part of the world. Hence, everyone in the story tells of him without its being possible to define or put a frame around what is told. It is nowhere to be found in the finite consciousness of the people, in their "talk of the town." Only as they face death does the green Hunter Gracchus at some time or other flit through their thoughts.

But his story implies still more: it began with a strange break with all defined order. Formerly the Hunter had enjoyed living in a clearly structured world. Now, he who "wanted to live only in his mountains" must voyage restlessly "through all the countries of the earth" (B 102). No longer is there any secure place for him in the world. He is barred even from the hereafter that he once confidently intended to enter.

Thus has Kafka clearly characterized his own historical position: It *was* at one time possible to define the earthly and the spiritual situation of man in terms intelligible to everyone—for once, fifteen hundred years ago:

"Everything proceeded in order. I . . . was dead, and this bark was to carry me to the Hereafter. I still remember how joyfully I stretched out here on this plank-bed for the first time. The mountains had never heard such singing from me as these four walls —shadowy as they were even at that time—heard then." (B 103)

Now, however, the former hunter is fluttering about like a "butterfly" among all the spheres. Now he understands neither the earthly nor the spiritual world. All empirical and metaphysical definitions break down.

Here, as everywhere else in his works and autobiographical writings, Kafka expresses this breakdown as a sudden, momentary "inattentiveness," a "distraction," a "losing" of the way, a "wrong" turn of the rudder. In the diary of 1910 Kafka speaks of the fact that he had "stepped back" "out of the time-streams," "in some kind of self-forgetfulness, in a distraction, a fright, a surprise, a weariness" (T 22). "Although up to that point we have been focused with our entire self on what our hands do, what our eyes see, what our ears hear, the steps our feet take, we suddenly turn to what is exactly the opposite, like a weather vane in the mountains" (T 20-21); that is, all the ideas that man up to this time has used to determine, interpret, and clarify his life, lose their validity.

In most cases Kafka's stories and novels begin with this kind of sudden, incomprehensible loss of any possibility of normal orientation. In an unguarded, absentminded state of sleep or distraction, their chief characters wake up suddenly to find themselves displaced into a world that they can no longer regulate or explain with their mental images; thus, for example, Josef K., in the novel *The Trial*, on awaking, in his preoccupied state, feels himself "taken unawares" (P 30-31). In the novel *The Castle*, K. "goes astray" in the strange world of the village and castle (S 10). The "country doctor" follows an ominous "mistaken ringing of the night bell" (E 153), etc.

At the root of this is a fundamental, critical questioning of cognition, the problem that had already engaged the young Kafka in his "Description of a Battle": Are our so-called normal mental images at all able to safeguard and regulate human life? The mental images determined by our understanding and our sense perceptions are designated as "flimsy" (E 14); they do not have the strength to retain the objects and inter-relationships of the world "that sink down about me like a fall of snow" (B 43) and lose "their beautiful outlines" (B 34). Already in this early work, there emerges that same image of the fluttering butterfly into which the Hunter Gracchus sees himself transformed: " ... we flutter about, uglier than bats though we are" (B 58). This impossibility of arriving at certainty led Kafka while he was still a young man to the formulation of an extremely radical critique of cognition and language that we shall deal with further on. Language and thought, indeed even sense perception, do not arrive at the true beauty and order of "objects," at the self-certainty that "reposes" in them (E 14). Even the cause of this "losing his way," of this loss of all reassuring mental images, is unknown to the Hunter Gracchus: "I do not know what it was" (B 102); that is, he does not know what it was that actually altered his safe course in the death ship.

Essentially, however, it is this: The only thing that the Hunter knows is the fact that he has remained on earth: "I know only this, that I remained on earth and that ever since my ship has sailed earthly waters" (B 102). The only certainty is that man remains bound to the earth, that even in death he cannot reach the "Hereafter." Even though he strives after that unceasingly, he "awakes" again and again on his "old ship, still stranded forlornly in some earthly sea or other" (B 103).

In this, too, Kafka has described the situation of "modern" man with precision: he has fallen completely into the clutches of the "earthly" world. The crucial element, however, in this story as well as in all of Kafka's stories—the element, too, that characteristically distinguishes Kafka from his contemporaries—is the fact that the hunter who moves in this earthly world is a "dead" person who does not belong to this earthly world at all, whom no one understands, and who, by the same token, does not understand any living person.

This "dead" person who is "in a certain sense alive, too" (B 102), embraces in the midst of the earthly world the duality of death and life. Only now can one understand why this story represents the universal in its universal significance, the totality of all that is, the All-encompassing that has crossed the borders between life and death, that is found both *above* and *within* all that is. In him the mystery of all that is has awakened: everything that all human beings, mountains, and stars, from the beginning of time to the present, have told one another and continue to call out to one another.

A twofold aspect results from this: on the one hand, this dead and, at the same time, living man possesses total perspective, universal knowledge of all that has been and is; he "could be an interpreter between the people of today and their ancestors" (B 335) and also has broken through all boundaries of space: "Good gracious, a man from Hamburg, and here in the South you know that he died today?" (B 336). On the other hand, by reason of this intermediate position of his between life and death, he no longer fits into any fixed earthly or spiritual classification; he sails "without a rudder," completely disoriented upon the earthly waters, and is, therefore, able to reach and comprehend neither the limited world of ideas of the much-occupied living, nor the "gate" of the Hereafter that "shines on high."

This twofold aspect leads not only to the heart of the objective situation concerned with the history of ideas, as it is reflected in Kafka's work, but also to the heart of Franz Kafka's subjective, personal problems. They will be sketched in, first of all.

## Kafka's Historical and Personal Position

Basically, it is the complete absence in the twentieth century of all security-giving earthly and metaphysical conceptions and systems that is the cause of the remarkable journey of the dead-living Hunter Gracchus upon the earthly waters. In this tale it is not at all a matter of a mysterious or fantastic invention of Kafka's but of the poetic description of reality for the human being in this century; perhaps it is the poetic description of a reality that is even much older in origin but that man did not become fully conscious of until the twentieth century.

Man in this century has limited himself by his "work," by his "business," by the effort of "making himself and his family successful." He is completely circumscribed and delimited; he has lost sight of "the Whole"; only shortly before his death, "perhaps" (for even this is not certain) an intimation of the Whole might flit through his "idle" thoughts disengaged from work. Basically death has been eliminated from this work-world; it has become simply bad luck or an accident at work that one quickly passes over in order to proceed with the agenda of the day. The possibility of keeping death constantly in one's mind in the midst of life, this possibility that would be the prerequisite of any truly "spiritual," completely human existence on earth, has grown "incomprehensible" to the world that has become the slave of work. Although safety and the safety devices of this work-world appear to be continually in process of being perfected, nevertheless this constant process of perfecting is just the opposite of a universal order, although at the profoundest level (without the knowledge of those who bring it about) it takes place only for the sake of universal order. "The telegraph was invented to let it circle the earth more rapidly," etc. The breakthrough into consciousness of a genuine, universal order can, therefore, take place only by man's leaping out of this limited, "normal," conceptual, and ordered world. This leaping-out has been the fate of all of Kafka's heroes, as well as his own. It is the source not only of their sufferings and despair, but also of all their "battles," of their most demanding objectives, of their clairvoyant perceptions; indeed, even of their almost hubristic hopes of creating an indestructible world—indeed, of "surviving" forever (T 545). They are constantly battling on the border between life and death, between the here and the hereafter, most strikingly perhaps in the dramatic fragment "The Warden of the Tomb" (B 301 ff.).

This leaping out of the so-called "normal" finite work-world appears in Franz Kafka's personal life as a determination to embrace uncompromising loneliness, as the will not to let himself "be deceived by the words of all the authorities everywhere" (B 294), but to break with everything that is thought, done, lived, and believed in in the world around him; that is, so to speak, to exist like someone shut off from this world, to exist alive as a "dead man." A diary entry of October 19, 1921, formulates this unequivocably:

He who does not cope with life in a living way, needs one of his hands to ward off to some extent his despair over his destiny—succeeding only very imperfectly—but with his other hand he can record what he sees amidst the ruins; for he sees differently from others and more than they: he is, after all, dead during his lifetime, and yet actually he is the survivor—the assumption being that for his struggle with despair he does not need both hands and does not need anything more than he possesses. (T 545)

The twofold aspect of this dead man who is dead during his lifetime becomes comprehensible here. On the one hand he sees differently from and more than everyone else, possesses a universal view, is indeed actually the survivor. On the other hand he is entirely disoriented, can "not cope with life in a living way," since he no longer moves in the finite securities of this life and hence must stake everything he possesses and even more, in order to master his despair.

That the figure of the Hunter Gracchus cloaks Kafka himself is not only evident through such conspicuous parallels in his writings and diaries, but can be inferred from the name "Gracchus." In Kafka the name "Gracchus" has nothing to do with the Roman Gracchi but must be translated literally from the Latin. Etymologically the Latin *Gracchus* is directly related to the word *graculus*, "jackdaw," and is derived from the stem *gracc* that imitates the natural sound, the croaking sound made by jackdaws, crows, ravens, etc.[7] The Czech word *kafka*

(*kavka*), however, likewise means "jackdaw," and Kafka would
often style himself as a jackdaw: "I'm an utterly impossible bird
[fellow]. I'm a jackdaw—a kavka. . . . Bewildered, I hop around
among people. They look at me full of suspicion. After all,
I'm a dangerous bird, a thief,[8] a jackdaw. But that is only the
appearance of things. In reality I lack the taste for glittering
things. I am grey like ashes. A jackdaw that longs to disappear
among the stones" (J 18). Also "Raban," the name of his hero
in the story "Wedding Preparations in the Country," is, of
course, a similar translation of the name "Kafka" [*Rabe*]
(=jackdaw, raven); the second "a" in the name Raban was
probably meant to suggest the sound of the analogous "a" in
"Kafka." Indeed, Kafka loved such phonetic allusions; thus, for
example, he writes in his diary about the name Georg Bendemann, the hero of his tale "The Judgment": "Georg has the same
number of letters as Franz. In Bendemann, the 'mann' is merely
an intensification of 'Bende' intended to cover all the as yet unknown possibilities of the story. Bende, however, contains just
as many letters as Kafka, and the vowel 'e' is repeated in the
same positions in which the vowel 'a' occurs in Kafka" (T 297).
Furthermore, the image of the "hunter" and the "hunt" plays a
great role in Kafka's diaries and writings. Here is one example
among many others: "This hunting gets its direction from mankind. The loneliness that was to some extent sought by me . . . is
now becoming entirely unequivocal . . . the hunt goes through
me and rends me to pieces. Or else I can . . . maintain myself,
and consequently let myself be carried by the hunt [in an] . . .
assault upon the ultimate earthly frontier" (T 552-53).

There can be no doubt about it: in all these images it is a
matter of a breaking-out from all the familiar areas of life into
the peripheral zones of existence where life and death overlap in
a paradoxical, in-between state in which the departed still lives
and the living has already departed. For only in such a state can
universality be obtained.

Thereby, however, it becomes clear that Kafka's so-called
loneliness, isolation, and despair were anything but simply a
subjective, unique destiny that can be explained purely bio-

graphically or psychoanalytically (for instance, by the famous conflict with his father) and that can, therefore, be dismissed without further claim on us. On the contrary, this loneliness was the requisite condition that made it possible for Kafka—perhaps as the only modern poet—to break through the circle of thought of his era without compromise, to press forward to the creation of a general, true universality with universal significance and thereby to achieve the heights of classical poetry. Without this loneliness, without this radical break with the conventional thinking and mode of life of his environment, Kafka·would never have become the great poet, never the great creator of a universal truth. For only by virtue of such loneliness was he able to pass beyond the limits of the conceptual world of his own century and once again arrive at the formation of an absolute reality. But the very expression "absolute" reality calls for correction. The so-called absolute position of the man who is dead in his lifetime is itself not a secure one; it is not the "Hereafter" that shines through the "gate on high." It cannot be grasped at all by the concepts of traditional religions or philosophies; it has nothing to do with the "Absolute" of, say, idealistic philosophy; even the true, infallible "law" of which Kafka speaks again and again is something other than the law of, say, the Jewish religion.[9]

As an expediency, for lack of an adequate linguistic expression (since all traditional forms of language are of necessity inapplicable), so that we may make at least some sort of assertion, we have formulated the term "the true universal"—a formulation with a minimum of content—for that which is characterized by the very fact that it cannot be systematized or put into fixed conceptual, philosophical, theological, ontological, etc., categories. That it exists is certain, as has already been shown by the story of the Hunter Gracchus, which was explicitly identified with that which is absolutely the most general and most universal imaginable, with everything that was and is. But how it is to be interpreted remains uncertain. And Kafka himself, in his own countless interpretations to be found among his writings and diaries, has done everything to retract

every possible limited interpretation or even to carry it through
*ad absurdum*. If Kafka's writing were, as many interpreters
assume to be the case, a reflected image, an expression or symbol
and allegory for certain religious concepts and matters of faith,
or for certain social and biographical phenomena (in a purely
empirical sense),[10] it would be incomprehensible why Kafka
enigmatized his works in this way at all. Merely to dupe the
reader, or to have his works appear particularly "interesting"?
Not only the seriousness of everything he produced speaks
against this, but also the simple fact that he allowed his works to
be published only with great reluctance, and in the end directed that the works he left at his death be destroyed altogether;
that is to say, his most important works, consisting of his three
novels and some very significant stories.

The enigmatic structure of his writing is, on the contrary, an
essential expression of the fact that the true universal, which is
striving to assume form here, is itself something enigmatic—
enigmatic, to be sure, only with regard to the conceptual world
of man caught in his own finite categories. In this it differs
fundamentally from the true universal of the poetry of the past.

## The Universal in the Classical Period

For the poetry of the classical period the true universal could
still be verified by human reason and hence, too, it could be
given artistic shape in the form of comprehensible compositions,
images, events, and contents. It is true, of course, that "the
Intelligible," in which the idea of moral freedom is expressed
philosophically, also, like every true universal, stands outside of
and above all natural mental images that are bound to the temporal phenomenal world. But as a postulate of practical reason
it is universally sensible and can, therefore—as in Schiller's
dramas—be expressed artistically as the victory of the moral,
ideal sphere of freedom over man's dependence on his instincts
and passions, and on the laws of nature or of the social-political
reality. What is more, this freedom can be viewed directly

within the phenomenal world in the form of "loveliness" [*Anmut*] or in the form of man's moral capacity to act against his own natural interests. There is no need here to break through the natural categories of space and time, causality, etc., as is the case later in Kafka, unless it be in the form of a "miracle" (*Maid of Orleans*) that is readily understood as inherent in certain religious ideas bound up with the medieval subject matter.

It is not otherwise in the case of Goethe: for him the "Primal Phenomenon" can be manifested directly in the space-time phenomenal world, although it oversteps the bounds of the rational, empirical world, appearing as "inscrutable" or as "tremendous and monstrous" or "horrible and dreadful," even bursting the limits of time and space as in that "immortalized" moment in which past, present, and future become "one,"[11] or in the phenomenon of the "daemonic." For the primal Phenomenon" for Goethe can still be "beheld" and given form through a harmonization of "idea and experience." Empirical science and "higher," "ideal" perception can mutually penetrate one another and produce what Goethe calls "totality."[12]

Even in the case of Kleist, who of all of Goethe's contemporaries possesses the greatest affinity with Kafka (Kafka read Kleist intensively and had a great love for him)[13]—for in Kleist the world is likewise enigmatized, no longer does anyone understand anyone else—the enigmatization can still be resolved, can be transformed into a revelation of the mystery; because the unrecognizable, absolute "feeling" that at first bewilderingly breaks into the phenomenal world governed by reason, appearing to remove every possibility of communication, ultimately turns out to be an absolute, rocklike, immutable[14] force that brings order into the situation and only now gives man's perverted legal statutes and limited intellectual ideas their true meaning; so that out of the tragic or comic misunderstandings a higher universal order arises that reconciles the finite and the infinite, reason and feeling. Even here in Kleist, the true universal can still be given poetic shape in forms and subject matter that are still generally comprehensible. Although—in contrast to the classical period—it is already expressing itself in the form of something that is not recognizable (absolute feeling), something that is an extremely discordant note in the realm of understanding and reason, and as such is apparently breaking away from the canon of classical principles of mediation, it can still be generally understood and imitated; what is more, it can even be defined theoretically and illustrated practically.[15]

Although it is a matter of a general universal in all these productions of the classical epoch, this universal is one that is determinable, one that man can grasp and understand by means of his intellectual and spiritual powers. Not at variance with this are the literary works of the romantic period; its formulation and concept of the "infinite" fit into an even more rigid philosophical systematic representation than do the productions of its classical opponents. What are the "wondrous" incidents in the writings of a Novalis—the transformations of human beings into stones, plants, animals, and spirits, or into beings of bygone epochs—if not clear and interpretable images of that universal philosophy of nature and history, that "transcendental universal poetry" which he himself attempted to substantiate theoretically in his fragments and essays and which the theories and systems of a Friedrich Schlegel, a Schelling, a Hegel develop further in manifold transformations through quite diverse mutations of the romantic fundamental idea of the identity of spirit and nature.

In the nineteenth century this heritage of the classical-romantic epochs was progressively eaten up, and in the twentieth it finally crumbled away. This is not the appropriate place to describe and interpret the process in detail. However, it may not come amiss to give some hints at the process, since only they will make Kafka's position comprehensible from the historical point of view.

## The Disintegration of the Universal
## in the Nineteenth Century

The reciprocal penetration of idea and experience (Goethe),

or the realm of freedom and the realm of necessity (Schiller, Kant), of absolute feeling and rational-empirical reality (Kleist), or spirit and nature (romanticism), gives way in the course of the nineteenth and twentieth centuries to a progressive isolation of the spheres. Natural science banishes the Idea from nature—in a sharp turn against the Goethean and romantic view of nature and the investigation of it. Natural science becomes a "strict" science that makes the observer completely subordinate to the "object" and tries to eliminate the subject in order to put the emphasis on the pure, objective laws of phenomena. This is paralleled in literature in the development from realism to naturalism, in that the subject is eliminated; the peak is reached in the theory and practice of Arno Holz: Doing away with poetic freedom, he makes the composing subject [the poet] subservient to his object [theme] which prescribes to him the "necessary" linguistic formation [literary form] that originates solely in the "thing" [theme].[16]

On the other hand, in the same era the subject acquires an unconditional autonomy, removes itself completely from the laws of phenomena and from those of the social environment and its ideological contents, and isolates itself in the movements of *l'art pour l'art,* and in their theory of "absolute poetry."[17] The poet creates for himself his own "artificial" dream worlds and form worlds, since every symbolizing "idea" has disappeared from the phenomenal world that surrounds him. Corresponding to the objectivism of naturalism is the subjectivism of "absolute poetry": the breaking-out into a completely unreal, impalpable dream world that is actually fashioned and controlled (as seen from a more precise point of view) with a very high degree of consciousness and rationalization in clear analogy with the artificial, denaturalized forms of technology. The antithesis is merely a seeming one. The "lifeless" object penetrates even the most subjective art, and the most objective art transforms the universe into the phantasmagoria of the isolated subject (Arno Holz: *Phantasus*).[18] The two conflicting movements, naturalism and formalism (i.e., absolute literature), stem historically from the same set of prevailing circumstances and develop strikingly

analogous forms.[19] These two movements, in which crassly
naturalistic configurations suddenly shift directly into surrealis-
tic constructions—and vice-versa—have dominated literature to
this very day.

The great art of the novel of this epoch makes constantly
renewed attempts, to be sure, to mediate between or reconcile
the realms that are falling asunder and isolating themselves—
from the productions of nineteenth-century so-called "poetic
realism," through increasingly tense and complicated works, to
those of Thomas Mann, Robert Musil, Hermann Broch. The
constantly increasing tensions and complications at the root of
their novelistic art correspond to the heightening tensions and
complications in the total structure of society that is delineated
in this novelistic art, a society that from the nineteenth century
to the present time has brought forth far more catastrophes
than reassuring systems.

Characteristic of the novelistic art and of the society it depicts
is, on the one hand, the fact that scientific research makes itself
master of the spiritual and intellectual life of man. This finds expression in the invasion of psychology and sociology into the
novel of the nineteenth and twentieth centuries. Man's inner life,
having been made an object of research like any other object
of nature, becomes determinable and analyzable from a finite-
empirical approach; Christianity's immortal soul, Kleist's absolute "feeling," Goethe's superempirical "Daimonion," etc., become a transparent, unmysterious natural phenomenon that,
like every material phenomenon, is subject to scientifically comprehensible laws; and the intellectual world of the imagination
becomes a product of social factors, sociologically determinable
in accordance with prevailing conditions, circumstances, interests, and traditions in which the representatives of that world
exist. On the other hand, this same novelistic art tries to postulate ethical norms, to draft valid criteria for behavior, and to
humanize society. For it is impossible to have any critique of
society—and these novels are primarily works that are critical
of society—without a positive, ethical postulate by which social
conditions can be evaluated and condemned, a postulate that

can serve as a criterion for determining such systems as may be worthier of mankind.

However, the farther the novelistic art advances from the nineteenth century into the twentieth, the more indefinable do its postulates become. Already in so-called "poetic realism," in which the aftereffects of the classical and romantic heritage are still palpable, the universal classical ideal of education, an ideal that found its most vivid and poetically most concrete realization in the richly calibrated scale of the intellectual and social orders in Goethe's novel *Wilhelm Meister,* vanishes. The reciprocal interpenetration of art and society, of absolute ethical postulates and concrete "conduct" in *Wilhelm Meister* can no longer be achieved in "poetic realism": the individuals governed by artistic, ethical, or religious "ideals" get into the fringe areas of society or are wrecked by it—they become eccentrics, cranks, oddities; whereas, conversely, in *Wilhelm Meister,* coming from the fringe areas they assimilate into society to the point where, for example, there is a fusion of art and handicraft. Or else, as in Stifter's *Nachsommer,* the reconciliation becomes a fantastically stylized, unreal utopia, one of great luminosity and beauty, to be sure, in which classical possibilities once again, before their final decline, assemble in a pure, transparent autumnal atmosphere; but it is a reconciliation clearly guarding itself against a social world rising afresh, a world hated by Stifter, that no longer permits of such a utopia.

In such a retreat the foundering artists themselves, resignedly, accept the maxims of society's "real" way of acting, as does Gottfried Keller's Green Henry in the so-called "positive" second version of the novel. The universal educational goal of the classical epoch is transformed into a limited, middle-class morality that takes its standards from the given facts of the surrounding world and the historical situation. Even though an unconditional ethical claim still exists in Keller's morality—no great moral literary work is possible without such a claim—the mediations he effects between this absolute claim and the "real" data are nevertheless either stridently dissonant, as in his grotesque figures,[20] or are determined by a "humor" that does not bring about the reconciliation (as talk about humor that "reconciles" would have it) but pushes it off into the unattainable, makes it provisional. The artist becomes the renouncing "citizen" who accepts the limits set him "with humor" but with a quietly suppressed feeling of uneasiness at having to conceal what is best in him, without its having had a chance to live, for the sake of moral reasons that he does not dictate to society (nor to himself), but that society dictates to him. With that the finitization of classical morality is achieved. In Goethe's "Renunciation," that was based upon the free decision of his "Daimonion," the absolute and the contingent were truly reconciled, not by means of humor, but rather by that "serene" freedom that can assimilate even the "monstrous" and the "daemonic." In Keller's humor, however, renunciation becomes resignation; the absolute disappears in the contingent. Not without reason was Keller an adherent of Ludwig Feuerbach who in his philosophy brings about the destruction of all absolute, superempirical value concepts, reducing morality to empirically limited, relativistic values. The unconditional ethical claim loses its metaphysical foundation. It becomes a vague claim that can no longer be defined. Since it can establish its identity only in experiential reality itself, it becomes a mere "appearance" that softly fades away into the dark and transfigures earthly realities. The humorous transfiguration of the everyday world attempted in poetic realism is the expression of the discrepancy between an undefinable absolute claim and inferior reality that is beheld in such a way "as if" it satisfied this claim—this "ideal" claim that has vanished into dreamlike unreality. The knowledge that no camouflage will succeed and that the reconciliation is a fiction is expressed as humor that imparts the appearance of a fleeting, transitory reconciliation to what is irreconcilable. The humorist is the disillusioned metaphysician who wishes to establish his lost aesthetic or ethical ideal upon the earth. While he himself sees the reconciliation as the illusion that it is (and humor means nothing other than this), he remains an unconditional moralist, but one wearing the mask of a citizen who, smilingly adjusting to the terms of existence, only now and then seriously thrusts aside the deceptive curtain and then, of course, gazes into the unfathomable.[21]

The vague, indeterminable character of the absolute realm of the ideal expresses itself further in the peculiar combination of sentimentality and realism that marks almost all of German literature of the nineteenth century (not, of course, the art of Keller, Stifter, etc.). Sentimentality is nothing but the expression of a spiritual and mental state that "senses" the absolute only in hazy outline and with its vague presentiments brings about a muddled fusion of all of reality (subjective sensations, impressions of nature, and the environmental world); that is, it prunes reality as it poeticizes it. Sentimentality, to be sure, existed even in the "sentimental" preclassical period. But the nature of this very period, too, was determined by the disintegration of an objective religious system of values. Only by making the comparison with this period can one appraise the philosophical and literary achievements of the Goethe period, that in the face of a disintegrating system of values once again forged ahead to erect universal systems of values.

Sentimentality is a characteristic of disintegrating systems of values. It does not occur in any literary period that possesses clear, absolute value principles—not in the Middle Ages nor in the sixteenth and seventeenth centuries. Even in the romantic period it appears only after the breaking up of romantic universalism in the epigonous writings characteristic of late romanticism. (The apparent exceptions, Wackenroder and Tieck, among others, belong to the school of sentimentality, not to the romantic school.)

With the ultimate complete disintegration of values, however, humor and sentimentality give way to irony and cynicism. That is the state of affairs in the twentieth century.

Even in Wilhelm Raabe's so-called "pessimistic humor"— and it is questionable whether or not that is still really humor —one catches sight of a peculiar phenomenon; in order to understand the later novels of the twentieth century as well, including those of Franz Kafka, it is essential to cast light upon this : *All* values are called in question; and the paradoxical attempt is thereby made to obtain a universal, humane set of values by playing off all these problematic values against one another in a constant reversal: value becomes valuelessness, and valuelessness becomes value. Stopfkuchen, in Raabe's novel of the same name, by playing off the isolated, ostracized individual against society, as well as society against the individual, exposes the actual valuelessness and ensuing intolerance that are inherent in every empirically limited set of values. By unremittingly establishing and abolishing all limited realms of value, he achieves genuine reconciliation and acquires universal humanity. In the rapid passage through the totality of the dynamics of tensions and conflicts humanity is born—in a state of suspension over an abyss of inhumanity, indeed even through the instrumentality of inhumanity.[22]

Raabe's *Stopfkuchen* already shows the complicated interweaving and tensions present in the later novelistic art of a Thomas Mann, a Robert Musil, etc., with respect not only to subject matter, but also, above all, to the form of the narrative, in which various levels of narration are telescoped into one another with considerable artistic ingenuity and highly enigmatic interrelations, unsurpassed, as far as stratified structure is concerned, even by the analogous narrative forms in Thomas Mann's late works, *Dr. Faustus* and *The Holy Sinner*.[23]

With the foregoing, the historical premises for Kafka's stories and novels have been basically though sketchily clarified. Absolute, universally binding values have disappeared. In as complete a transit as possible through all relative values, new binding values are sought; the negativity of all limited values is critically revealed as their tensions and contradictions are endured. The art of writing novels grows to be a critical art. It exposes the concealed inhumanity of all relative values that are lived by. It thereby creates an awareness of true humanity. This humanity, however, cannot "appear" anywhere and cannot be "defined" with generally binding force. Only indirectly does it become visible in the "ironical" annulment of all realms of value (Thomas Mann), or in "satirical" unmasking (Robert Musil). The positive ethical postulate puts on the mask of destruction. Its positiveness appears as negativeness. Negativeness becomes the world's only hope.

What answer has Franz Kafka given to this state of affairs?

*Kafka's Naturalistic Beginnings, His Intensification of Naturalism, and His Estrangement from It*

As the Hunter Gracchus tries to clarify the story of his life to his living guest—the story that is being told by all earthly beings—he says: "I am—no, I cannot; everybody knows it, and am I, of all people, to tell it to you? It was such a long time ago. Ask the historians! Go to them, and then come back again. It was such a long time ago. How am I to keep it in this overcrowded brain of mine, I wonder" (B 338). In this way he refers his guest to the "historians." He feels his lot to be a "historical" fate about which the historians could supply the best information. He himself, however, cannot keep his own story in his "overcrowded brain." For its origins, its continuities and connections, as well as its modes of manifestation, are incalculable. "Every book is full of it; in every school the teachers put it on the blackboard," etc.

The Universal of this story of the Hunter Gracchus is, hence, on the one hand, something eternal, from the beginning of time, that the whole cosmos tells of; on the other, it is something historical, and it is primarily the historians who have knowledge of it. It has gone down in history, and history could shed light upon it. It could be adequately clarified, however, only as it passes through all earthly phenomena; this is beyond the power of a single "overcrowded brain."

It is striking that the Hunter Gracchus is trying to express the Universal, the meaning of his history, in the form of cumulative enumerations: "every book is full of it," etc. His effort is aimed at achieving totality by means of a quantitative summary of absolutely everything that exists. The meaning, the significance, the "knowledge" of his universal story rests within every existing thing itself—not externally to it, outside of it.

This corresponds not only to the thinking of the natural sciences in modern times, but also to the practice of the naturalistic literature that was determined by these sciences. Through empirical investigation or through the descriptive presentation of everything that exists on earth, the attempt is made to arrive at the binding universal laws of the world and to unlock its meaning. Arno Holz, the naturalistic poet, in his *Phantasus* wishes to portray the entire world and world history from the beginning of time to the present in the form of an "extensive totality,"[24] and simultaneously in such an "extensively" quantitative configuration he hopes to be able to reveal the secret and meaning of that-which-is, about which all things unceasingly bring tidings. For him, too, all phenomena have knowledge of him, relate the same secret, and are, therefore, in the core of their being, all identical with one another; world, I, soul, thing, etc., are one: "Seven trillion years before my birth I was an iris," is how Arno Holz's poetic work *Phantasus* begins, a work that definitely is in the center of his writing and that accurately mirrors the original "nature" concept of his so-called "thoroughgoing naturalism,"[25] the natural scientific "monism" of his period.

And it must not be forgotten that the young Franz Kafka, precisely like Arno Holz and other naturalistic poets, was not only an extreme Darwinist, but was actually a follower of Ernst Haeckel, and for many years was under the influence of the scientific view of life and the psychology of the end of the nineteenth century and beginning of the twentieth, with its scientific orientation.[26]

Improbable as it may sound, Franz Kafka's earliest writing can best be understood as stemming from naturalism rather than from expressionism. The reactionary movement within it, apparently aimed against naturalism—the breakthrough into the "dream world" of a completely isolated subject who is "alienated" from the world—has its very roots in naturalism itself, in which the totality of the world is mirrored in the fantasy of a dreaming poet, isolated in his garret.[27] In the history of literature the "isms," that have been set up in opposition to one another like immovable craggy boulders, conceal the historical truth. The tensions and apparent contradictions are already present within the created works of art themselves.

Kafka is no exception. For the early Franz Kafka it is above all a matter of "description" that records, and of exact reproduction of everything that exists, precisely as it is for that "consistent naturalist" Arno Holz, for Emile Zola, and others. The concept of "description," as it appears already in the title of the earliest prose story preserved for us from the period 1904-1905,[28] the "Description of a Battle," became significant for Kafka under the influence of Ernst Mach's teachings, Franz Brentano's experimental, inductive psychology, and others.[29] In the early story "Wedding Preparations in the Country," from the period 1906-1907, Franz Kafka, like a naturalist, records accurately all the events that take place first in a street of a large city and later in a train and a taxi; he tries to seize life as it flows past and to record it with exactness by stringing the individual events along additively without their deriving a definite, recurrent significance and function in the total work through the compositional layout. The phenomena appear and disappear without leaving a trace. It is a matter of the profusion of all Being itself that has as yet not been subjected to a centralizing idea or a compositional structure. The exactness of such descriptions, the precision with which all details are graphically and concisely recorded, has become a much-admired characteristic of Kafka's work, even of his later prose.

However, there is an astonishing disparity between the exactness of such descriptions and the interpretation of what has been described. To Eduard Raban, the hero of "Wedding Preparations in the Country," all the observed events appear incomprehensible and strange. He feels it a torture to set forth into this profusion of life as it undulates meaninglessly past, and for that reason he would prefer to remain at home in bed as a "bug" and send his clothed body out into the world (H 11-12). In the "Description of a Battle" it is precisely the most ordinary events that are given the designation of that-which-is-astounding and that-which-is-most-incomprehensible.

An ordinary conversation between two women about the weather turns into an impenetrable enigma:

"Ah, but just listen! When I was a little child, not yet quite established in my life, I opened my eyes after a short midday nap and heard my mother in her natural tone of voice call down a question from the balcony: 'What are you doing, my dear? My, but this is hot weather!' A woman replied from the garden: 'I'm just having an afternoon snack in the open air.' They said this without deep thought and not particularly distinctly, as if that woman had expected the question, and my mother the answer" (B 43).

The I-narrator, upon being told this, says in reply, " ... I said that this incident was extremely remarkable and that I did not understand it in the least. I added, also, that I did not believe that it was really true and that it must have been invented for a definite purpose that I just did not see" (B 43). The ordinary world at the moment of waking from sleep, when "I was not yet quite established in my life," appears completely incomprehensible. And the whole occurrence is related as an example of two different possible ways of viewing the world. The world can be viewed naïvely and without reflection as a safe, solid world: just as those women, "without deep thought," consider their conversation as something that is quite a matter of course; its questions and answers they "expect." However, the world can appear also as an improbable and unstable one, the "real truth" of which cannot be "believed" in. Indeed, this childhood experience is related as an illustration for the sentence that precedes the narration: "And I hope to learn from you how the things that sink down around me and are lost like a fall of snow really behave; yet for others even a little whiskey glass on the table stands as solid as a monument" (B 43). Hence, even in this early story there is adduced "proof that it is impossible to live" (B 23).

Precision of description and incomprehensibility of the thing described that unceasingly sinks into, indeed even melts away into, a turbulent "stream" that bursts all space and bounds (B 59)—an image that occurs again and again in Kafka (T 20,

H 348, 287)—this disparity is, in point of fact, amazing. For how can a poet possess the interest and the doggedness to describe with the utmost exactness every detail of phenomena that are at the same time slipping through his fingers? An insoluble contradiction exists here. Either Kafka is a sceptic, or he is a religious metaphysician, who experiences all that is earthly as threatening and laments the transitoriness and futility of it; in that case, however, this vanishing world can no longer stir him to creation at all; he must take an absolute point of view— whether in the negative sense of radical religious or nihilistic despair, or in the positive sense of a world-surmounting religious attitude. Or, on the other hand, Kafka is a naturalist; but then he must resort to the world of earthly phenomena and must also creatively abstract from it a meaning that rests in this world itself.

The contradiction is indeed insoluble if one starts from the customary imagery of our world view. Furthermore, the erroneous ideas and the conflicting explanations existing to this very day in the interpretations of Kafka have come about largely as a result of such oversimplifying ideological key-images. The contradiction can, however, be surmounted if one tries to take in Kafka's own position, the greatness of which lies in its sustaining both possibilities simultaneously: letting the earthly world have its full due,[30] and at the same time inquiring into the meaning of the "whole" from an absolute, critical, lofty standpoint. "I don't want to hear anything more in bits. Tell me everything, from the beginning to the end. I won't listen to anything less than that, I tell you. But I'm burning with impatience to hear the whole story," says the hero of the "Description of a Battle" (B 22).

The "battle" that is "described" here and that is continued in the "battle" of all the later heroes of his writings,[31] is nothing other than the almost superhuman effort to master the "details," all the concrete factual data of life, as well as the "whole" of life, and to bring them into a meaningful harmony that has "life-potential"—although in all probability a harmonious accord of this kind appears "impossible."

Looking ahead, even from this point, one may note that Kafka's writing on the one hand reveals startlingly clairvoyant insights into the actual social life of the present time and describes the reality of our social-political life with bold exactitude and realism; on the other hand, however, he tries also to gain a grasp of the "whole" by inquiring what the assumptions are that underlie our apprehension of reality in general and that enable it to be "classified" and "lived" as a "whole." An interpretation that does not even include this universal aspect, but has only a biographical or only a sociological, ontological, epistemological, psychoanalytical, etc., bias, must of necessity miscarry.

But to return to our theme: at first it appeared as if Kafka's "naturalistic" description of the phenomenal world ran aground on the interpretation of what is described. The described world is incomprehensible and strange to the describer himself. The summative enumeration of everything that exists does not lead to the unlocking of its meaning and its law. To be sure: "Every book is full of it, in every school the teachers put it on the blackboard, . . . it is printed in the newspaper, and people pass it along from hand to hand . . ." etc. But what it actually is that all these books, teachers, newspapers, indeed even stars, seas, and streams, are talking about—that remains obscure. The totality of everything that is known is unintelligible.

Even in this Kafka has not yet gone a single step beyond the beginnings made and the intentions stated by the naturalistic writers and scientists of his time. The naturalist Arno Holz, who likewise wanted to reproduce, in the most exact linguistic form possible, the sum of all manifested things, in his drama *Ignorabimus* came to realize the impossibility of representing the "whole" and of being able to apprehend it. He, too, like the Hunter Gracchus, attempts to cross over the boundary between life and death, to be at home in both spheres simultaneously, and this he attempts specifically with the assistance of scientific experiments that aim at penetrating into the realm of the supersensuous, into the realm of existence after death. He, too, concludes with a sceptical *ignorabimus* "we shall not know it," precisely the same conclusion reached by the exact sciences that, of course, ever since Kant, have consciously excluded from all empirical knowledge the fundamental question of meaning, as to what things "in themselves" actually are, and have relegated that question to the metaphysicians and ontologists among the philosophers.

Nevertheless, there is an essential difference between Kafka's creations and those of naturalistic writing. The naturalists were of the opinion that they could at least give adequate form to natural phenomena, their laws and interrelationships. But precisely in this respect Kafka entertains decided doubts. The presuppositions with which man views, imagines, conceives of, and gives form to reality—that is to say, the modes of viewing time and space, the laws of logic, causality, etc.—even for the young Kafka do not reproduce reality correctly but on the contrary alter and even distort it. Already in the "Description of a Battle," it is said of things: "It really seems to me that it does not do you any good when one reflects about you; your courage wanes, and you health declines..." (B 52). "Always, dear Sir, I have had a desire to see things just as they tend to behave before they manifest themselves to me. That's when they are beautiful and serene, I suppose" (E 14).[32]

Through man's looking at things and thinking about them, they change, and indeed they change in a negative sense. They lose their original beauty, serenity, courage, health, and truth.

Here it is not so much a matter of the old epistemological insight that man cannot perceive things "in themselves," but rather the much more serious moral problem: that man's contemplation and thought schematize, limit, and mutilate the full reality of that-which-is. Through his own imagining and thinking, man blocks his access to the "whole," indeed to the primordial purity, beauty, excellence, and truth of that-which-is. As man imagines, he constructs a lie about the truth of that-which-is, a lie even in the reversible sense that the lie of beautiful appearance is spread over the true suffering of this world. In "In the Gallery" (E 154-55), that famous and frequently interpreted fragment, this becomes quite clear: what the "normal" person sees as reality and what Franz Kafka, accordingly, consciously expresses grammatically by the verb form denoting an objective fact, the indicative mood—the "happiness" of the equestrienne—is actually the lie, the illusion. What cannot be seen, indeed what appears as impossible and unimaginable in our time-space perceptual world and what, accordingly, Kafka expresses grammatically by the verb form denoting an act or state merely entertained in thought, the subjunctive mood—the equestrienne's suffering: being chased "in a circle for months at a stretch into an ever-widening grey future," constantly chased by a "pitiless boss swinging a whip" in the presence of a "public that never grows tired," whose applauding hands "are actually steam hammers"—is the truth. Since the lie of the "normal" view conceals this truth, so that the public sees only a radiantly happy artiste being thunderously applauded, help is not possible; the visitor in the gallery "cries ... without knowing that he is crying, as if he were sinking in an oppressive dream." However, if the truth could be seen, rescue would be possible, for then "perhaps ... a young visitor in the gallery ... would rush ... into the circus ring and cry out the command, 'Stop!' through the fanfares of the ever-accommodating orchestra" (E 154-55).

From this example the meaning of Kafka's peculiar estrangements grows quite clear: when he breaks through the normal time-space world of perception and imagination it makes for revelation, so that the full truth may become manifest; and simultaneously these breakthroughs have a "saving," humanizing significance, at least in the sense of an ethical postulate. They are not distortions of reality but rather a restoration or a full disclosure of reality. Kafka was a "realist" in a more universal sense than the naturalists. In a conversation with Gustav Janouch, Kafka once designated himself as "a very mediocre, bungling copier" of "commonplace" reality. He said that he was no "practitioner" who injected "miracles into ordinary occurrences," and that such an impression arose only because "people ... close ... their eyes ... and ... see ... so little" (J 38); he said that his aim was to give an undisguised "sketch" of reality; that his art represented not a suppression of naturalism but rather an intensification of naturalism.

This thesis needs to be substantiated more precisely.

If it is true that the full truth and reality of that-which-is is limited, distorted, falsified, or at least made to assume a misleading appearance by the normal world of perception and imagination, then that world must be given up or else it must be relativized and corrected from a universal point of view. And Kafka's writings, as is well known, are unceasing efforts to reveal that which is the mere seemingness inherent in certain limited perspectives, whether it is a sensuous perception that suddenly turns out to be different from what it appeared to be upon first glance (H 311 *inter alia*), or whether the most diverse and contradictory possibilities of interpreting an occurrence are developed in tormentingly endless reflections with downright pettifoggery on a gigantic scale: every opinion is given a strictly logical basis and is made reasonable; it is then challenged with equally strict logic and relativized with reference to other possible opinions. Here, too, Kafka appears to want to develop a "sum total" not only of everything that exists but also of all possible modes of thought, in order to gain a universal position. "Naturalism," the extensive, quantitative compilation of all earthly phenomena, extends not only to the "description" of such phenomena but also to interpretation that is varied in an infinite profusion of possible thought processes.

Thus, in Kafka it is not at all a matter of eliminating or fully negating the normal forms of perceiving and thinking, but rather it is a question of correcting and intensifying them, of attempting to achieve a complete presentation of all possibilities of perception and thought. The "normal" mode of seeing and thinking, as is yet to be shown, is maintained throughout his works, but it is subject to a mode that is all-encompassing.

The universal view of the whole is achieved by Kafka's allowing unlimited scope to all human possibilities. This holds true not only for the modes of viewing time and space and the logical categories of thought, but in general for man's total conscious and subconscious life. Even all of man's dreams and

visions, all the realms of his preconscious or subconscious are
set free and mingle unbroken in the turbulent "stream" of
phenomena and mental images. Crass erotic scenes, as they
occur in dreams, all the wish-images, the guilt and anxiety feelings ordinarily suppressed in so-called normal daily living,
emerge and come clearly to light; they necessarily have access
and entrance into a delineation that comprises the "whole" of
life.[33] In this sense, too, Kafka was a "naturalist." Moreover,
early in his life he was already strongly influenced by Sigmund
Freud's research on dreams.[34]

Just as in the inmost recesses of man's conceptual and dream
world places and times can be interchanged and arbitrarily
altered, so in Kafka's writing, varying with the spiritual realities
of the inner world, the chronological and spatial orders of
ordinary, normal consciousness can undergo thorough transformation according to the changing perspectives of consciousness, as, say, in the story "An Everyday Confusion" (H 74-75).
Here, too, it is not at all a matter of supernatural occurrences
but that of giving form to natural inner processes, indeed
"everyday" ones.

For all that, Kafka nevertheless differs basically from the
naturalistic poets in creative style and intention. Unlike modern
novelists who use the psychoanalytical technique of association, he does not simply imitate the processes of the subconscious in the form of "inner monologues" or so-called
"automatic dictations of the subconscious"; that is, he does not
simply register dreams as they "actually" occur or as they possibly could occur. Furthermore, he did not share the view of
psychoanalytically oriented physicans or poets that man's inner
life could be altogether clarified by means of dream analysis,
and that a radical cure of emotional and psychic disease could
thereby be effected (H 335). For him all physical and psychological disease had in turn its basis in a single disease that has
its "exemplar" in the "nature" of man whose "predicament"
consists of his being unable to "get a real footing" anywhere,
of being unable to find absolute certainty anywhere; in the last
analysis, herein lies the origin of his flight into neurosis, etc.:

" . . . all these alleged diseases, sad as they may appear, are facts of faith, man's moorings in some maternal ground when he finds himself in a predicament; likewise, even psychoanalysis finds the archetypical bases of religions to be nothing other than that which establishes the 'diseases' of the individual" (H 335). And in a letter of April 1921, to Max Brod, he writes with reference to his own disease: "That tuberculosis has its seat in the lungs is as little likely as that, for example, the World War had its cause in the ultimatum. There is only one disease, no other, and this one disease is being blindly hunted by medicine like an animal through forests that have no end."

For Kafka, therefore, the psychoanalytical illumination of man's emotional and spiritual life signifies the domination of what is subconscious by a limited, rational method and thereby gives rise to a new falsification of total human truth and reality. The psychoanalytical possibility of getting a "hold" on what is subconscious leads to the mechanical manipulation of emotional and spiritual life; that is, the last refuge that has been left man in a finitized mechanized reality is itself forfeited to technocratic control and becomes an "object" that can at option be directed, used as a pawn, and computed according to arbitrary purposes, and be made a usable organ of society.[35] The original humanization that was inherent in Sigmund Freud's research and experimentation in healing[36] turns into dehumanization. Healing becomes a polite lie. The patient, freed of his crises, becomes the empty, docile object of society to which he adapts himself without any crisis; that is, without resistance. Here, too, the semblance of "happiness" conceals the injury and mutilations that are in truth inflicted upon the human being. And this injury—herein lies the actual inhumanity—is something that the happy patient is himself no longer aware of. Only now does the superiority of Kafka's writings become impressively manifest. Only now is there divulged the meaning of the remarkable fact that in Kafka no one "understands" anyone else any longer, that crucial truths remain unknown to the very person affected by those truths, and can no longer penetrate into his consciousness. As in the instance of the young spectator in the gallery who, moved by the suffering that is hidden from him, "cries without knowing that he is crying" (E 155), so throughout Kafka's works people's most personal truths remain veiled for them. For it is precisely people's own "normal" consciousness that obstructs their knowledge of all mutilated life; but at the same time it prevents them from having access to an existence that may be unmutilated, one that is whole in "truth," an existence in which things still possess courage and health, beauty and repose (E 14, B 52).

Deluded by his normal conceptions of the nature of human courts of justice, Josef K. is unable to understand that the forensic books contain obscene pictures or old, dirty novels of the tenor of: "The torments that Grete had to endure from her husband Hans" (*The Trial*, P 67). He does not sense that the universal court that is in session every day within our own heart and soul is dealing with—and must deal with—precisely such themes incessantly, since they form a far greater part of the whole process of life than those actions that can be passed sentence upon by the paragraphs of the *Civil Law Code*. What is going on within the court officials in the novel *The Trial* remains incomprehensible to Josef K., although the same sort of thing is constantly taking place not only within his own inner being but also outside in human society, with neither him nor this very society itself perceiving what is actually going on. The scenes, images, and actions that seem odd and improbable from the normal approach, mirror, in truth, quite "common, everyday confusions," that can, however, no longer be resolved when seen in the ordinary field of vision. Franz Kafka once remarked of Picasso's pictures and of the improbable distortions of human limbs in them: "He [Picasso] merely makes note of the disfigurements that have as yet not penetrated into our consciousness" (J 88).

Thus the two worlds that in Kafka can never understand one another—Hunter Gracchus and his guest; the universal officials of the world and K. (*The Trial* and *The Castle*), etc.—are not Kafka's own arbitrary or fantastic constructs but are our own reality itself. Fundamentally they are a single world, none other than the human world itself. The divergences are merely illusory in nature, engendered by whatever limitations of "knowledge" exist at the time. The Universal is no "divine" authority; it is neither a superempirical, "Intelligible," or ideal sphere any longer, nor an absolute sphere in the sense of the classical period. It is the essence and sum total of everything that is lived, felt, thought, imagined, and done by human beings—just as in Kafka's novels the court and castle officials, constantly on the move, are noting down and entering into the official records anything and everything that people experience. "Between the farmers and the castle there is no great difference" (S 20). "Nowhere had K. ever seen office and life so interwoven as here—so much so that at times it might seem that office and life had changed places" (S 81). The castle officials come as little near to equaling divine beings as does the hero K., or as do the inhabitants of the village;[37] but in the former everything that ordinarily is kept hidden by the normal consciousness of everyday life becomes visible without restraint— one might even say, without inhibition. Their "official" existence differs from the "private" existence of K. or from that of the village inhabitants only in that it represents the universal, superindividual laws of existence that are never fully realized by private persons although these laws are undoubtedly functioning in them. With what precision and artistic mastery this interplay between the "official" sphere and the "private" one is carried out in the novel *The Castle,* will be shown in our analysis. The seemingly absurd, improbable processes within these official authorities—the officially prescribed channels that thwart and contradict one another; the peculiarly dreamlike scenes; the erotic incidents; the interminable reflections—they are all an unveiling of what occurs constantly in our private and social reality. And the power that the officials exercise reflects nothing other than the "force of life" itself (S 445), the force that reality incessantly exercises upon all living beings. The ineluctability of the official authorities is the ineluctability of life itself, of its superindividual laws that determine everything.

### Kafka's "Battle" between Law
### and Dissolution of Boundaries

Here, too, however, the "battle" that all of Kafka's heroes wage against this ineluctability of existence becomes clear. It is the battle in Kafka's earliest story, "Description of a Battle," in which the hero furnishes "proof of the fact ... that it is impossible to live." For at the moment when life opens all of its sluices, as it were, and the whole of existence comes into view undisguised, no protective order whatever, no determining "law" can be recognized any longer. Hence, man can no longer "live"; he is engulfed by an infinitely expanding "turbulent" stream (B 59), or he sees himself facing an unfathomable labyrinth of official decrees and forces of existence that are constantly crossing one another but are nevertheless always moving to and fro in "equilibrium," since "even the world in its course ... corrects itself" (S 356), and "this great judicial system remains to a certain extent eternally in a state of suspension" (P 146). At the moment when the heroes Josef K. (*The Trial*) and K. (*The Castle*) are wrenched out of their customary existence and placed before the totality of all the forces of existence, all these universal forces must appear to them as an impenetrable confusion of conflicting powers that are open to countless interpretations at variance with one another—interpretations that are, indeed, continuously "correcting" one another without the individual's understanding the correction and what it was that was corrected.

From only one finite, limited point of view was order still possible, even though it was only an "apparent" order: an order of "falsehood." However, since this order is now disrupted, and since even the absolute, divine order has sunk below the level of man's consciousness, the totality of everything-that-is crowds in upon man with bewildering profusion; every form of orientation is snatched away from him; he wavers about helplessly like a "butterfly" among the contradictions and the thousand kinds of possibilities of order and disorder. The very Hunter

Gracchus—whose "story" has become universal and is being unceasingly "told" by everything whatsoever that was or is— has become a "butterfly" fluttering meaninglessly to and fro among all the spheres, unable to obtain a footing either in the Hereafter or in this life. The seemingly universal view of this Hunter is the view of one who perplexedly "hunts" hither and yon among all the possibilities of life and thought, and consequently no longer "understands" the finite, limited orders of earthly existence.

Yet it is precisely this—to step out of every apparent order —that is the sole and necessary prerequisite for attaining to the "true law" of human existence, and for creating an unconditional, binding law code. One might even say that all of Kafka's writing can be understood as an uninterrupted wrestling to overcome the lawlessness of the human world (the "relativity" that arose in the deterioration of values in the Occident), and to gain an inviolable, true, universally binding system of administering justice.

The basic structure of Kafka's stories becomes accordingly discernible: the hero of these stories always falls out of a finite, apparently firmly established order; suddenly and terrifyingly there opens up before him the "totality" of existence through which he now reels helplessly to and fro in his search for a true, protective law that he can nowhere find but that is, nevertheless, set up immovably as the goal of his life.

The battle that he wages is a battle for a livable existence in a world in which, however, there can be no living, since there is no absolutely secure, "true" order to be found in it. Only illusory orders are possible, but these always turn out to be *dis*-orders.

Therefore, it is precisely when man glances at the total (and in this sense, the "true") structure of reality, when the falsehood of the limiting concepts is rent, that the world loses its boundaries, becoming an inconceivable chaos of multifarious focal points and movements; and truth is wholly beyond any kind of knowledge.

Yet, notwithstanding, redeeming action becomes possible

now, as is shown by the "Stop!" of the visitor in the gallery
who was to leap into the circus arena, into the circle of a
furious chase that was speeding along "perpetually... without
a pause," bring the gruesome motion to a standstill, and put
an end to the equestrienne's torture.

This apparent contradiction—or double aspect—that pervades all of Kafka's work, requires explanation. For it alone
can settle the quarrel that was kindled a long time ago:
Was Kafka merely a negative poet, a totally destructive nihilist?
Or did he have knowledge of an absolute realm, and was he
able to produce an affirmative answer to the human question of
meaning?

### *"Complete" Knowledge and Responsibility*

Let us proceed from the first aspect. Even in the early
stories, the exactly described phenomenal world, life in its
fluctuations, had already grown both incomprehensible and
astounding. Why? The answer is given in the stories themselves.
As Raban, in "Wedding Preparations in the Country," watches
two traveling businessmen in a train compartment, the story
goes:

He understood nothing of what one traveler said; the other's
reply he would also not understand. To be able to understand
would first require extensive preparation, for these people here
had been dealing with merchandise from the years of their youth
on. But if, so many times already, one has held a spool of thread
in one's hand, and handed it so many times to one's customers,
one then knows the price, and can talk about it while villages
come toward us and hurry past, while at the same time they
swerve into the depths of the land where they are bound to disappear from our sight. And yet these villages are inhabited, and
perhaps travelers are walking in them from store to store. (H 23)

The exact understanding of a phenomenon would be possible only if one made "extensive preparations," if one knew
all the prerequisites for and conditions of that phenomenon

and had thoroughly investigated them. At the same time, however, there are so many conditions and prerequisites, and there are so countlessly many other phenomena mixed in—villages that fly past that "are bound to disappear from our sight"—that an adequate understanding seems entirely impossible. Man cannot grasp *all* phenomena, but even a *single* phenomenon cannot be adequately determined; for who can get all its associations, causes, and consequences into his "overcrowded brain"?

In the same story it is stated that Raban had the "natural need . . . to observe everything exactly, at least everything in his surroundings. The result . . . was that there were very many things he did not notice" (H 34).

Franz Kafka moves within the framework of modern scientific thought and of naturalistic writing, in which the claim is made that every finite phenomenon is determined and explained by other finite phenomena. And at the same time, bursting this framework, he carries this method of knowing *ad absurdum*. However, one does not have the right to misinterpret this bursting by idealizing it. When all is said and done, man lives in this earthly world of his, and he can master it adequately only with earthly means; even "humanity," justice, love, kindness, order can be achieved by him only with the insights, the powers, and the experiences that are given him. Every truly just judgment of a fellow man—and this involves every genuine relationship with him—presupposes knowledge about him; in fact, complete knowledge. Otherwise misjudgments, misunderstandings, and conflicts are unavoidable.

To this fundamental condition of human life and of life worthy of man, Kafka clung both with respect to others and as it concerned himself. In his diary Kafka writes on January 12, 1911: "Self-knowledge might be given a definitive written form, I suppose, only if it could be done with utmost comprehensiveness, including all the immaterial consequences, and with utter truthfulness" (T 37). The impossibility of obtaining absolute completeness does not release one from the responsibility of trying for it over and over again; it does not permit a "rape of the world" from an "absolute" religious position, as Kafka once argues in a trenchant criticism against Kierkegaard.[38]

However, the more Kafka remains within the limitations of the human race, the greater the anguish with which he suffers these very limitations. The meaning of his "despair" lies in his sense of responsibility toward the world and toward himself. That sense of responsibility is the source of his only seemingly absurd writing, the source of his immense efforts ever anew to question and to account for everything seen and said amidst a thousand changing aspects. And from this sense of responsibility arose his personal suffering; his merely seeming inability to gain a clear relationship with his parents, with women, with his profession, etc.; his grotesque, suicidal proclivity to complicate with apparent lack of necessity all his relationships with his fellow men, as is exemplified in a letter to Milena describing his inner relations to her, in which he writes:

It is, say, as if a person before every single walk he takes had not only to get washed, combed, etc.—and even that is troublesome enough—but besides all that, since before every walk everything he needs is missing over and over again, he would have to sew his clothing, cobble his shoes, manufacture his hat, trim his cane to size, etc. Naturally he can't do all of that well; it will hold together for the distance of a few narrow streets, but on the Graben,* for example, everything suddenly falls apart, and he stands there naked in shreds and tatters. The torture of it then! to run back to Old Town Square! † And finally, to cap it all, he bumps into a mob on Eisen Street that is giving chase to Jews. (M 248)

Or in an analogous passage from his diary: "... theater director, who has to do everything from start to finish himself; he has to produce even the actors. A visitor is not admitted—the director is busy with important theater work. What is it? He is changing the diapers of a future actor" (T 574).

* Tr. note: The *Graben*, once the city moat, was in Kafka's time the busiest street in Prague.

† Tr. note: *Altstädter Ring*, the street on which Kafka's father lived.

Since Kafka cannot and dare not accept anything as given, neither phenomena nor the "words of all the authorities everywhere" (B 294), for they all produce only seeming, temporary, "deceptive" orders, he sees himself compelled to examine everything given [all actuality]—and, of course, he is not in possession of anything else—with reference to its stability, its conditions, origins, and contents; that is, he is compelled to break down everything into its elements and, as it were, to assemble and produce it again himself. Inasmuch as it goes beyond man's power to do this, everything falls apart in shreds and tatters, and he himself stands naked on the Graben; that is, he can no longer establish any relationship with other people, he can no longer "live" in any given system. That is the ethical meaning of his rigorous "isolation," a mode of "existing" that he himself chose, that he desired with an imperative truthfulness, and that was vital to him.

He was himself aware of the paradox inherent in this "existing." A solitary existence is a contradiction in terms, for each thing that exists already presupposes relationships with something else that exists. How did Kafka overcome this paradoxy? This question leads to the very core of his life and his writing.

## The Path to Universal Truth

### A. BEING AND RELATION

All phenomena of that-which-exists can be expressed in terms of the most manifold relations. However, these relations can never arrive at that-which-exists itself. Kafka formulated this in his diary as follows: "What one is, one cannot express, for one is just that; one can communicate only what one is not, that is to say, falsehood. Only in the chorus [of communications] may there be truth of a kind" (H 343). In another passage he writes: "There are only two [aspects, modes]: truth and falsehood. Truth is indivisible and therefore cannot per-

ceive itself; whoever lays claim to perceiving it must be Falsehood" (H 99).

This position makes it understandable why, in his writings,
Kafka is constantly compelled to retract all his assertions over
and over again, to call them into question, and to designate
them as merely "seeming"—and this applies not only to intellectual assertions but even to remarks about sense perceptions, which are always described with restrictive phrases or
called into question in every respect. "For we are like tree
trunks in the snow. They seem to be resting flat on it, and one
should be able to shove them aside with a slight push. No, one
can't do that, for they are firmly attached to the ground. But
look, even that only seems to be so" (E 44).

Even the very means by which the poet works, language
itself, falls within the scope of such doubt: "Language, for
everything outside the world of the senses, can be used only by
way of suggestion and never, not even approximately, by way
of comparison; because language, since it accords with the world
of the senses, treats only of possessions and their relations"
(H 45).

Since even language, from the very fact that it has gram-
matical systems, has its abode only in the world of relations, it
cannot express any "truth"; it cannot express what man or
the world actually "is." Only in passing through all statements,
in the "chorus" of all falsehoods, might there be "truth" of a kind.

Thereby new light is cast upon the question of why in
Kafka's works everything constantly becomes enigmatic, why
nobody is able to understand anyone else, and why everyone
talks at cross purposes with everyone else. Such "relativism,"
however, does not abide in a scepticism that frays everything to
shreds. On the contrary, it rests in a clear awareness of the
hidden "truth," of "Being" that asserts itself ineffably in and
among all relations.

B. "SUPPRESSING" AND "FORGETTING" THE TRUTH

The Hunter Gracchus already knows of this hidden truth that

rests in the "Being" of all phenomena themselves; and, justly assuming that all others have this knowledge, he accuses them of either consciously "suppressing" or of actually having "forgotten" their knowledge of the mystery that all men and things are constantly proclaiming: "There are only two possibilities present," he says to his guest who has just declared that no one in the world knows anything about the universal history of Hunter Gracchus.

"Either you are suppressing what you know of me and have some definite purpose or other in doing so. If that's the case, I tell you quite frankly that you're on the wrong track. Or, on the other hand, you actually believe that you can't remember me, because you are confusing my story with another one. If that's the case, I'll tell you merely that I am—no, I cannot; everybody knows it, and am I, of all people, to tell it to you? It was such a long time ago. Ask the historians! ... How am I to keep it in this overcrowded brain of mine?" (B 338)

The suppression of the truth takes place, on the one hand, because of "some definite purpose or other"; that is to say, man pursues goals and interests. Like the guest, he is involved in "business" that hinders him from finding out anything about the "true" meaning of everything-that-is, and from having anything at all to do with it. In other words, the "suppression" springs from the vital necessity of actually holding one's own on earth, of acquiring property, of supporting one's family, etc. Actual life itself forces man to be silent, and it prevents consciousness from voicing what is true of Being. Man deliberately suppresses his hidden knowledge of the so-called ultimate questions in order to have breath for this world.[39] The Hunter, however, sees that this is a "wrong track" and that man, in suppressing the truth, will never advance to a secure and true existence.

However, it may also be that the guest believes he can actually no longer remember the Universal, and this is so because he is confusing it with another story. What does this mean? It obviously means that the guest—man who moves in

the Finite—can never completely forget the Universal. He
"believes" that he merely "is no longer actually able to remember
me." The Universal has been lost in some ancient past, for
these are indeed "old, old stories," and it [the Hunter's story]
is "something which happened long ago," even though nowadays it is still unceasingly "racing in the elevators to the roofs
of the skyscrapers." Man, however, believes that he can no
longer remember; [and he has this belief] "because another
story" interposes itself—a story which he confuses with the
present one. Thus a "pseudo-story," an "other one" that bears
some similarity perhaps to the true one (for otherwise no confusions could arise), takes the place of the true one. And this is the
real reason for man's thinking and actually "believing" that
he can no longer remember.

The enigmatic profundity of such sentences requires interpretation of the utmost precision. In man's consciousness there
is another story that cannot be forgotten, one that he definitely
remembers, for otherwise he could not confuse it with the
genuine one. However, "because" he puts this other story in
place of the authentic one and mistakes it for the latter, in this
way interposing a substitute, he succumbs to the illusion, nay
more, to the honest, actual "belief" that he no longer has any
recollection of the genuine story. His awareness of and his belief
in a pseudo-story are, therefore, the reason why he seemingly
forgets the true story.

### C. THE TRUTH-SUBSTITUTE

To attempt an explication of the contents with respect to
what is meant here by that "other story," would be to go beyond the bounds set for the interpreter. The only thing that
issues clearly and irrefutably from the text is this: In man's
consciousness and belief some other story has anchored itself—
one that hinders him from remembering the true story.

In reference to this, the word "believe" should be—and
actually must be—interpreted in the sense of "being of the
opinion," or of "considering as true"; that is to say, it must

mean simply that another story is identical with that of the
Hunter Gracchus. Nothing further is mentioned, but that suf-
fices. Some other story—whether this story is seriously believed
or not is immaterial, and no mention of this is made in the
text—has taken the place of the true universal story of everything-that-is. That means unequivocally that people—if they do
not prefer to "be silent" altogether and to dedicate themselves
exclusively to their practical business affairs—orient themselves
to some substitute-story or other. And it is precisely *this* that
is the cause of their not attaining insight into the true universal
story. Certain substitute-ideas satisfy them, and this satisfaction
prevents their access to that which "is," which is being unceasingly proclaimed by everything that has Being.

There can be no doubt that the guest's confusion is the confusion of those people who are still letting themselves "be deceived by the words of all the authorities round about," and are
putting truth-substitutes in place of the genuine truths. This
criticism of everything on earth that is said, thought, believed,
and lived cannot be excelled.

### D. THE VEILING OF TRUTH IN "BEING"

But what then is the true story of this Hunter? It is characteristic that he breaks off with the words, "I am." "I am—
no, I cannot; everybody knows it, and am I, of all people, to
tell it to you?" The Hunter himself cannot say what he *is.*
For "one cannot express what one is." He refers the guest to
others, to the historians, for "everybody knows it." However,
exerybody's knowledge is not communicable. Each communication would convert that knowledge into "falsehood."

It is a matter of the same paradoxy that Kafka presented in
as late a story as his "Investigations of a Dog," in which the
Dog "from this world of falsehood where there is no one to be
found from whom one can learn the truth," attempts "to cross
over to the truth" (B 284). In this tale, too, "the silent ones"
are "the preservers of life" (B 256). Here, too, it is impossible
to bring to light in communicable form the knowledge hidden

within all dogs, although this knowledge and *only* this knowledge—no absolute knowledge that is beyond time, since such
knowledge no longer exists for Kafka—contains the entire truth.

For what is there besides dogs? To whom else in the wide,
empty world can one appeal? All knowledge, the totality of all
questions and all answers is contained in dogs. If only this knowledge could be made effective, if only it could be brought into
clear light, if only they did not know so infinitely much more
than they admit they know, than they admit to themselves. Even
the most garrulous dog is more reserved [about this knowledge],
more covert than is usually the case with places that have the
best foods. (B 225)

In an imaginary reply of the "fellow dogs," there are described the affirmative possibilities that would ensue if one ultimately succeeded in expressing this universal knowledge in
words.

Now, it could be said, "You complain about your fellow dogs,
about their silence with respect to crucial matters. You maintain
that they know more than they own up to, more than they are
willing to admit to in life, and this suppression, the reason and
secret of which they naturally suppress along with all the rest as
well, poisons life, making it intolerable to you, so that you would
have to alter it or forsake it. That may be, but, after all, you
are a dog yourself, you possess this knowledge about dogs. Express it then, not just in question form but as an answer. If you
express it, who will oppose you? The great chorus of dogkind will
chime in as if it had been waiting for that. Then you will have
as much truth, clarity, and avowal as ever you wish. The roof
of this mean existence, that you speak so ill of, will open up, and
dog by dog we shall all mount to freedom on high. And should
we not succeed in that, should things get worse than they were
before, should the whole truth be more intolerable than half the
truth, should it be confirmed that the silent ones, as the preservers
of life, are right, should the faint hope, that we now still have,
turn into complete hopelessness—still, it is worth trying to say it,
since you do not want to live the way you are being allowed to
live. Well then, why do you reproach the others for their keeping silent when you yourself remain silent?" The answer is easy—

because I am a dog, essentially just like the others, rigidly un-communicative, offering resistance to my own question, adamant through fear. (B 256)

The impossibility of broaching the truth that is hidden in "Being," rests in the very nature of his dogness.

### E. THE UNVEILING OF THE TRUTH

Thereupon, however, the Dog outlines "something monstrous" (B 257). First he rejects the clearly nihilistic possibility that all of dogkind "will terminate, destroy, and forsake," on the basis of his exceedingly sceptical "questions," everything that it has built and achieved through its work, all the "founda-tions of our life" (B 257). "No," as he says, "I truly no longer expect that." Instead of this he develops another "monstrous" possibility. "But it is not only our blood that we have in com-mon but also our knowledge, and not only our knowledge, but also the key to it" (B 257). But what does this "key" consist of? The Dog continues:

I do not possess it without the others; I cannot have it with-out their help. Iron bones containing the most precious marrow can be gotten at only when all dogs with all their teeth collectively bite into them. Naturally, that is only an image and is exag-gerated. If all teeth were ready and willing to bite, they would no longer have to do so. The bone would open, and the marrow would lie freely exposed, so that the feeblest little dog could seize it. If I remain within this image, my intention, my questions, and my investigations aim, I must admit, at something monstrous. I want to bring about this assembly of all dogs by force; I want to have the bone open under the pressure of their willing readi-ness; then I want to release them to the life that is dear to them; and then I, alone, entirely alone, want to lap up the marrow. That sounds monstrous, and it is almost that—as if I wanted to feed myself not on the marrow of just one bone but on the marrow of dogdom itself. (B 257)

If one were successful in gaining the cooperation and willing-ness of all dogs—the words mean nothing else but this—if one

were successful in this, the closed mystery, the "most precious
marrow" would be accessible. Biting would not be necessary
then, and this is essential, but only "the willing readiness" of all
teeth. "If all teeth were ready and willing, they would no longer
have to bite," etc. What does that mean? Obviously it means
only that neither exertion nor violence will open the bone, but
only a sincere, willing readiness for that collective task of revealing the most precious marrow, the complete truth of all
Being. This marrow would then become, of its own accord,
"freely exposed," and be accessible so that "the feeblest little
dog could seize it."

In the light of numerous parallel passages and parallel incidents throughout Kafka's writings, which we shall consider in
detail in subsequent chapters, one may safely interpret this passage as follows: An assistive and willing readiness for the full
truth means the ability to renounce all personal, limited ideas,
wishes, and efforts of will and to enter into the fullness of all
of that-which-is. This willing readiness, to be sure, includes the
renunciation of a personal "life." This follows incontestably
from the passage, "... I want to have the bone open under the
pressure of their willing readiness; then I want to release them
to the life that is dear to them." Thus the willing dogs, at the
moment of their willing readiness, were not in the life "that is
dear to them." It is precisely this life of theirs that they had to
surrender. The entire truth is revealed only when all partial
truths, all limited forms of life and their contents, go under.

Moreover, it is not enough for just one or a few to achieve
such a willing readiness. In joint assemblage they must all relinquish the life that is dear to them. Only then is insight into
the whole granted; that is, truth cannot be arrived at by an individual but only by the collective whole of all individuals. One
could conclude from this that truth cannot reveal itself in a
single actuality of Being that would be representative of everyone, but only in the "assembly of all dogs." That would imply
nothing less than doing away with the ancient metaphysical
identity of the "One" and the "All," of the microcosm and
the macrocosm. Thereby, too, the individual instance could no

longer be considered as a representative "symbol" of the whole; the structure of Kafka's writing would be separated from the poetic forms of classicism by an abyss. Kafka's works would no longer contain any symbols in the classical sense;[40] perhaps only his total work could still act as a symbol of a total described reality. However, even this would be impossible, for Kafka's total work, even then, would necessarily remain a "fragment," an endeavor that could not be consummated, because to pass through all the spheres of existence exceeds man's power. With good reason does the Dog himself designate his aim as "something monstrous."

However, the insight, that the individual can never by himself attain the whole, that he "cannot have" universal knowledge "without the others . . . without their help," has yet further causes and consequences. From the point of view of the history of ideas, this insight stems from the destruction of every unified concept of truth that is binding on everyone in the same way, no matter whether this concept has appeared in the form of metaphysics, religion, or categorical ethics; and this insight is commensurate with the situation of modern man who faces a confusing multiplicity of individual truths at war with one another. Even though in classical and older times conflicting truths likewise opposed one another, nevertheless each individual conception of truth contained in itself the rocklike conviction that it was valid for everybody, that it applied to everything-that-is; furthermore, in each case it was structured in a binding, universal sense. Modern man, on the contrary, insofar as he is "secularized" (and Kafka's works are concerned with this "secularized" man), sees, "unbelieving" and perplexed, a profusion of possibilities of truth that possess no universal binding force but that can be referred to one another in the most manifold relations, and, what is more, that can sweepingly relativize and historize themselves.

However, that same insight of the Dog, the insight that truth cannot be found without everyone else's help, has yet another meaning. What may at first be surprising in the light of Kafka's "loneliness," is that this insight accords to each reality of life and to each reality of thought its full right and takes each one seriously. This means that this insight does not become obdurately intolerant toward the life forms and life contents of others. The presupposition, then, is that the individual surrenders his own [life form], declaring that it is not the "absolutely" true one. Such a surrender, however, is possible only if *everyone* surrenders his own [life form]. The logic is consistent. The "monstrous" venture is necessary. It is the only possible way of existing meaningfully and humanely. Each one of us has to abandon his individual position.

Accordingly, humanity would realize itself if all people renounced the "life that is dear to them." Logic goes head over heels into the "monstrous." Only in this way, however, does it assert truth. Kafka once wrote, "Whoever renounces the world must love all people, for he renounces their world, too. As a result he begins to have an idea of what is the true human nature that cannot but be loved, provided that one is its equal. He who within the world loves his neighbor does no greater and no lesser wrong than he who within the world loves himself. There would be only the question of whether the former is possible" (H 46). Only renunciation of the world and of life makes it possible to feel love for all human beings, and reveals the "true human nature." For "within the world" neither truth nor love is possible; in it the true human nature remains constantly concealed.

Thus the "struggle" for that which is universally true is in no way a struggle merely for universal knowledge and understanding but, rather, a struggle for universal love. Striving for truth and striving for humanity are one and the same thing. The True and the Good are inseparably bound to one another; for if the True is that very "Being" that is hidden beneath all relations, the understanding of the True is also the understanding of true human nature, the understanding of that which man actually *is*. In such *complete*, undisguised cognition, however, only love is possible, since this true human nature "cannot but be loved." Universal truth is universal love.

Only now does the actual meaning of Kafka's striving for

the complete, ineffable truth become clear: it means the endeavor to gain a completely valid humane existence. Now, too, it becomes clear why such an unveiling of the truth not only brings about the loss of all relations to life, together with a helpless, disoriented reeling amidst all realms, between this world and the Hereafter, but also possesses a rescuing function—why that unveiling enables the spectator in the gallery to cry out his "Stop!" into the circus ring.

## The Universal Morality:
## Relation to What Is Religious

But what is the meaning of "renouncing the world" in this context? One would mistake Kafka's position completely if one conceived him to be an ascetic, withdrawn from life, or a Utopian apostle of humanity. Even his morality has a universal aspect and has nothing whatever to do with what one ordinarily understands as "morality"; "renunciation"; sacrifice; love; overcoming one's tendencies, instincts, passions, egoism, etc. This becomes clear from his concept of "guilt," a concept that is baffling and profoundly enigmatized.

The very first sentence of the novel *The Trial*—"Someone must have made a false accusation against Josef K., for one morning, without his having done anything wrong, he was arrested"—immediately removes from Josef K.'s guilt every "moralizing" element. Josef K. has in point of fact done "nothing wrong." And, furthermore, there is no mention of a false accusation by someone else. Nevertheless, Josef K. is arrested. But by whom? By public authorities who incessantly note down everything and enter in the records everything that is going on around them; moreover these authorities themselves experience uninhibitedly whatever can be experienced on earth, are themselves corrupt, hypocritical, lying, unbridled in their instincts, dirty and sordid, etc.; in other words, here life itself is the "court of justice." "Everybody, of course, belongs to the court," it is stated in the novel (P 181)—not only the corruptible officials who avidly chase after women, but also the depraved girls who pursue Josef K., etc. This court has nothing in common with either a "divine" or a human court in the sense of a juridical or a social moral code. It is the totality of all human processes and proceedings. They are all under the jurisdiction of a court, or else are present in the court. But nobody knows it. Even the official authorities do not know the "law" according to which judgment is being passed. It is, however, an "invisible court" (T 31, P 190, 272, *inter alia*) that is unceasingly passing sentence on all the acts of living, and not according to the conceptions of human morality. Life itself—the compulsion of having to exist—makes a person guilty. "But I am not guilty," Josef K. cries out to the chaplain of this court; "it is a mistake. Why, how is it at all possible for a person to be guilty? After all, we are all human beings here, each one like the next" (P 253). How, then, can man be declared guilty of being alive, of being human? This is what Josef K. thinks. "That is correct, but that is the way guilty people usually talk," is the logically consistent reply of the chaplain of the court.

Universal morality is possible only through the insight "that it is impossible to live" without guilt. The limitations of our consciousness transform every moment of our existence into guilt. Unsuspecting, we become guilty even when we resolve to do what is best. Unselfish action can bring about the most disastrous results and can be a form of guilt toward ourselves. Responsible action in the full sense of the term would be possible only in the Universal, only if all the causes, motives, and consequences of an act could be taken in at a glance. That, however, goes beyond man's life within this world. "He who within the world loves his neighbor does no greater and no lesser wrong than he who within the world loves himself. There would be only the question of whether the former is possible"; that is, whether love within the world is at all possible.

Hence, in *The Trial* it is not to the point to look for some kind of guilt in the ordinary humanitarian-moralizing sense; for example, to the effect that Josef K. "did not love" his neighbor sufficiently, that he was incapable of love,[41] and that therefore he had to perish. Even a renunciation within the world, in the sense of asceticism, or an abnegation of one's instincts, etc., can be guilt, guilt that Kafka took for granted if only because of the insight he gained through psychoanalysis.

Kafka's concept of guilt approaches most closely the religious doctrine of original sin, with which indeed he often grappled in his diaries. However, the differences between his concept and the religious doctrine ought not to be obscured. One should read Kafka's reflections on original sin, as, for example, in the following:

The expulsion from Paradise is, in the main, eternal. Consequently, although it is true that the expulsion from Paradise is final and life in the world unavoidable, yet the eternity of the event (or, to express it with reference to time, the eternal repetition of the event) makes it nevertheless possible not only that we could remain continually in Paradise, but that we actually are continually there, no matter whether we know it here or not. (H 94)

Man is thus all the time *here* in Paradise already; he merely does not know it. In complete reversal of the religious doctrine of original sin (Genesis 3:22) Kafka writes, "We are guilty not only because we have eaten of the tree of knowledge but also because we have not yet eaten of the tree of life" (H 101).

On the basis of our knowledge of good and evil, we find ourselves unavoidably in the "world," which for Kafka is a world of "falsehood," because it moves in constant "motivations"[42] and acts of cognition that can never attain to the truth of man's indwelling Being; that is, they can never attain to "Paradise." Notwithstanding, however, man lives constantly in "Paradise" and would grow free of guilt and sin if he could eat of the "tree of life." Kafka's concept of guilt is not a negation nor even a denunciation of life, but is criticism of sham life. It is a matter of gaining a "true" life through a "liberation" of the "indestructible" Being hidden in us, which for Kafka has the same significance as the image of "eternal life." Logically, then, "faith" for Kafka is nothing other than the

"faith" in the indestructible Being indwelling in man himself:
"To have faith means to liberate that which is indestructible
in oneself; or, more accurately, to liberate oneself; or, more
accurately, to be indestructible; or, more accurately, to be"
(H 89).

Herein Kafka is basically at variance with Judaic-Christian
religiosity, and, yet again, is decidedly in harmony with it.

For him there is no transcendental god who lovingly or
threateningly encounters man, face to face, as an "entirely
different" supreme being. On the other hand, that which is indestructible in man, the "Being" in man, is for Kafka too, a
realm that is removed from earthly consciousness, emotion, and
volition, a realm that is completely unattainable; and, hence, it
likewise represents a transcendence that cannot enter into any
psychic, intellectual, or "natural" area of man's imagination or
conception and, for that reason, remains continually "concealed" from him. "Man cannot live without an unremitting
confidence in something that is indestructible in himself, yet
not only what is indestructible but the confidence as well can
constantly remain concealed from him. Faith in a personal god
is one of the modes of expression for this continuing concealment" (H 44).

Unequivocally, Kafka has thus designated faith in a personal
god both as an unconscious masking of the more primary faith
in what is indestructible in man and as an expression of the fact
that this indestructible thing and man's faith in it "remain concealed" from man. Once again it is a question of that "forgetting" (of the "confusion" of the true story with an "other"
one), for which the Hunter Gracchus reproaches his living
guest: for, "what is more joyous than the faith in a household
deity!" (H 47) Nothing other than this is meant when Kafka
says that man must eat of the tree of life, which, according to
Holy Scripture, God had indeed specifically reserved for Himself, since eating thereof would make man wholly equal to God.
Divine, eternal life for Kafka rests in the "indestructible" Being
of man himself. By that, however, is meant anything but a so-
called apotheosis of man, in the sense of a modern, hubristic

"Titanism." For the rift between the concrete human being and the "Indestructible" within him is just as great as it is in the Judaic-Christian world. No mystical absorption, no spiritual effort, and no intellectual power can ever reach this Indestructible in us, let alone bring it forth. For it is beyond all earthly, psychic, or intellectual determinability; and yet, "sitting in judgment" as the true "law" that makes its claims absolutely, it determines our existence. This is what the Protestant theologian, Paul Tillich, in his defense of modern existentialism and in his exposition of traditional theology has called the "God above God"[43] who eludes every theological reification or assertion.

In other words, in his resistance to a "personal god," Kafka regains what is actually the most primordial religious experience, according to which the Kingdom of God rests within ourselves, but separated by an abyss from the empirical world of our spiritual inner self as well as of our whole nature. By removing the reification and personification of the god-concept, by rejecting as inadequate every specific definition, he restores the unconditionality of the religious claim; but he restores it on the basis of a radical, modern "Humanism"[44] that is concerned with the critical "liberation" of man from all the deceptions and all the hidden, inhumane life forms of this "world" of his in which he is enmeshed.

While Kafka, according to his own testimony, broke with every religious tradition (H 121), rejecting even the traditional humanism that believed in the spiritual powers of man, in man's so-called natural goodness, he opened up an absolute realm in which "Being" and "Law," absolute existence and absolute ethical demands, coincide: a third realm, unattainable, in which the rift between religion and humanism is closed, a realm that is unconditionally demanding and valid, but that cannot be defined.[45]

This becomes sharply clear in Kafka's novel *The Trial*. Throughout, hidden in the court authorities of this novel, there is contained "the supreme court that is completely inaccessible to you, to me, to us all" (P 190). This has no existence exterior to the negative, earthly outward forms of the court, which

Josef K. meets with: the corrupt, sensually animal-like officials, etc. It exists as the true, determining, "infallible" law that is everywhere "inaccessibly" present. For it is present in every single person, as well as in all people "taken collectively." "The Indestructible is one thing: every individual human being is that one thing, and at the same time it is common to all; hence the matchless, inseparable unitedness of all human beings" (H 47). However, Josef K. mistakes the physical, outward forms and the statements of the court for the hidden "truth" itself. He does not sense that he may consider the phenomena and the authorities of this world *merely* as "necessary," but not as truth itself. No one can, and no one may escape the "necessity" of living in the concrete, physical world. However, man ought not to succumb uncritically to this necessity, to these conditions, entanglements, and errors in which he is daily involved. Everything that is lived, thought, and believed by the court authorities of this world, whatever man does in that unending performance of living and thinking, "one must not . . . take to be true; one must consider it merely as necessary," says the "chaplain" of the court to Josef K. " 'A bleak point of view,' said K. 'Falsehood is made the world order.' K. said that in conclusion, but it was not his final judgment" (P 264).

If everything that man lives, thinks, and asserts is "falsehood," or even "evil" (and Kafka expressed this idea again and again), one is tempted to adopt the bleak point of view from which the entire world order is seen as falsehood. But this is precisely what Kafka opposes. Josef K. goes to his destruction because, among other reasons, he accuses the world order instead of accusing himself. In so doing, according to a statement of Kafka's, he commits the actual original sin: "Original sin, the old wrong that man committed, consists in man's unceasing reproach that he has been wronged, that the original sin was committed against him" (B 295-96). He does not, in that case, accept the world by a free act of his own for which he will freely assume the guilt, but denounces the world order as guilty. He does not see that the multifariously "motivated" world has resulted from his own "knowledge of good and evil" (H 49),[46] that he can overcome that world only through a free act of his own that will effect a total critique of himself and of the world. To "liberate oneself" from the world of false-hood is possible only for him who levels critical knowledge against himself as well as against the world, for the man who, while he is *in* the world, is at the same time seeking the "true" world, which is not identical with the world's individual life forms and statements, enmeshed as they are in relations.

To "renounce the world," therefore, does not mean, for Kafka, to flee from the world or to exist outside of it, but rather, while existing in the very midst of the world, to realize "the true human being," to "liberate" the Indestructible in oneself. Kafka saw an analogy, for instance, in the relation between sensual love and divine love. "Sensual love obscures divine love; it could not do so on its own, but it can do this because it unconsciously contains within itself the element of divine love" (H 48). The "element" of the divine that is "uncon-sciously" contained in that which is itself earthly, is effective in liberating the divine, in overcoming the delusions of the earthly-physical world which are as strong as they are for the very reason that they bear the element of the divine in them and with it produce labyrinthine confusions.

Kafka's critique, therefore, is leveled not only at the self-assertion of the earthly, but also at the self-assertion of the divine, insofar as it confronts man as something "completely other," extrahuman in the form of objective, determinable com-mands. In man himself both spheres exist. He is obliged to keep them sharply separated, but at the same time he has to realize his task of reconciling the two.[47]

## Thinking and Being: Kafka and Heidegger

It appears necessary, however, to establish yet another fun-damental demarcation. In Kafka's works, when "Being" is dis-cussed, when this "Being" is designated as something ineffable that "conceals" itself, that is "forgotten" by the rational-objective consciousness, one is reminded, even to details, of Martin Heidegger's modern fundamental ontology; and one is led to consider Kafka the forerunner of this philosophy and to interpret his work in connection with Heidegger. Extensive studies of this nature have already been made.[48]

From the point of view of the history of ideas, it would be possible to extend the parallels even further; for example, to link Kafka's enigmatizations with the terminological enigmatizations of Heidegger's treatment of language. In the case of both men, one might think that a secret, indirect mode of expression became necessary because of the very fact that "Being" is not "expressible." In Kafka this took the form of strange images that, breaking through the rational world of objects, refer[49] to the "Being" that is concealed. In Heidegger it appeared as word formations that bring to "light" again, from out of the "oblivion of Being," the "Being" that "originally" dwelt in the language; and these word formations, through a return to the so-called "root words," immediately conjure up linguistically the "truth" of "Being" that is behind all rational-logical relations. And even Heidegger's antimetaphysical passion, his attempt to detect "Being" even in what is concretely earthly (even on the basis of an analysis of common, everyday states of mind), his attempt to extricate "Being" from every transcending or rationalizing systematics of thought—to all this there seem to be parallels in Kafka's work.

Hence, from the historical point of view, the same situation reaches expression in both men; this situation is mastered in each case in a manner that is merely formally different: on the one hand the presentation is poetical; on the other, philosophical. And yet it is the very variation in their language that betrays the difference, the gulf that separates them. Kafka remains within the bounds of rationally logical, everyday language. He does not go back to the profound, root meanings of the words he uses. In contrast with Heidegger, he never tries to define "Being" itself linguistically, or to express it directly. It remains that which is simply void and incomprehensible; and, although it always confronts one, making claims upon one, it itself cannot be disclosed anywhere or "made clear." Therefore, for Kafka, "Being" is not something that was "closer" in pre-rational, half-mythical times than it is today; it is not something that *waes* [existed] or dwelt in very ancient forms of language and that was later disguised by the ideational thinking of occidental metaphysics. On the contrary, it is liberated from its "oblivion" by rationally ideational thought and, of course, also "made clear" by it, but in a different sense from that in Heidegger.

Since possible rational acts of thought are brought into play collectively, the limitation of these acts of thought grows clearly evident, so that an awareness of "true Being" is awakened. This true "Being" remains as absolute claim, remains "law." It lacks that mystical, or rather, mythical, component which was the predominant influence on Heidegger in his late period, from the time of his Schelling studies.[50] "Being" [for Kafka] no longer appears as a concealing ground that can "lose its attribute of concealment" as man, by demolishing his ideational, delimiting thought, renders himself accessible to the entire range of that-which-is, enabling himself thereby to become engaged in the "Being" that abides concealed within and beneath every "entity-of-being" thus disclosed. On the contrary, it is through the utmost intensification of rationally-ideational thought that existence is disclosed; that the "futility" of all representational thought and of everything-that-is is revealed; and that, at this point, in contrast to Heidegger, there emerges an absolute emptiness,[51] which makes one "free" for the "court of justice"—that "invisible court of justice," in the face of which no entity-of-being and no thinking can any longer exist, a "court of justice" that hurls man in "self-consumption" (H 105) (which is unconditionally demanded of him) out of everything-that-is, thereby threatening the very basis of everything-that-is—namely, "Being" itself. Even though in Heidegger "Being" discloses itself only through an act of "nothingizing" every entity-of-being, nevertheless through such an act merely the covering, flimsy veil of that-which-is is removed, as it were, and "Being" remains preserved in the overt and nothingized "entity-of-being." There is no question of a leap out of that-which-is.

Consequently, even the transition from that-which-is to "Being," in contrast to Heidegger, cannot be effected at all. With the leap out of that-which-is, "Being" itself is extinguished. In order to arrive at "Being," Kafka must annihilate everything-that-is, and thereby even "Being" itself. The meaning and the consistency of his unconditional ethical rigorism lie in this paradoxy. There is no sphere in which "true Being" could be caught sight of, in which it would let itself be opened up, illuminated, unveiled, etc. Indestructible "Being" is an absolute claim, a postulate that cancels out all "Being." Only as not-being can "Being" manifest itself, as pure "law" that may not be formulated, that expresses itself only as negation of everything-that-is, and thus also as negation of all "Being."

Intrinsic here is Kafka's relationship to ancient Israelitic tradition: "Only the Old Testament has vision—say nothing about it yet" (T 504).

God's rage against the race of man. The two trees, the groundless prohibition, the punishment of all (serpent, woman, and man), the favoritism shown Cain whom He tempts further by addressing him. Man is no longer willing to let himself be chastized by My spirit. At that very time there began to be preaching of the name of the Lord. And whereas he led a godly life, God took him hence, and he was seen no more. (T 502)

On the other hand, intrinsic here also is his relationship to Jewish cabala that—in contrast with Orthodox Judaism, in which God's transcendence is external to man—transferred the absolute claim to man's inner being and made man the abode of the Divine.[52]

Kafka's radical "modernity," however, lies in his having recognized the insuperable difficulties of bringing these traditions bindingly into the intellectual world of present-day man, and in having, consequently, persevered in his lonely position; in having let the Absolute of the ethico-religious claim remain, so to speak, empty, in the form of a pure postulate that critically jeopardizes all life that has been lived, with a view to producing thereby a notion of the "true human being." About his own writing, which he designated as an "attack upon the last earthly frontier," he once expressed himself as follows:

All this literature is an attack upon the frontier, and, if Zionism had not intervened, it could easily have developed into a new esoteric doctrine. Rudimentary beginnings of that exist. Of course, how inconceivable is the genius required for this! One who forces his roots afresh into bygone centuries or creates bygone centuries afresh, and does not expend himself while he is doing all this, but only now begins to spend his energies. (T 553)

Hence, Kafka's "faith" in the "Indestructible," in the "Being" in man that must be "liberated," can neither be identified wholly with a religious faith that has appeared in history, nor be equated with modern existential philosophy. For Kafka has rigorously rejected every modern attempt to make "Being" "clear" in the "entity-of-being" itself. Even Heidegger's early attempt, under the influence of Kierkegaard, to reach positive "Being" by negation of the negation, lies outside the world of Kafka's thought and belief. "I had no inherited portion in the extreme negative that topples over into the positive," he wrote with reference to Kierkegaard and the latter's dialectic theology (H 121). Accordingly, Kafka would not have been able to share Heidegger's ontological reflections about the relationship between Nothing and Being. For Heidegger "the nothingizing of Nothing is the Being of that-which-is."[53] For through the nothingizing of the void that originates through negation of the "null" entity-of-being, Heidegger attains to the "Being" that "abides" hidden in that-which-is. For Kafka, however, it is "Being" that nothingizes everything.

From this paradoxy, according to which the "Indestructible" is that which destroys everything, new, apparently insoluble contradictions arise; and these must now be given more careful scrutiny.

## *The Lethal Nature of "Being" and "Truth"*

Let us return to the passage quoted from Kafka's "Investigations of a Dog." Until now we have interpreted this passage in a positive sense, as if the Dog, through the willing readiness of all dogs, succeeded in obtaining the most precious marrow of the bone, that is to say, valid knowledge of the "truth" that "is" in all dogs. But, in so doing, we have refrained from mentioning what is most monstrous in the "monstrousness" of the Dog's "intention, questions, and investigations." The Dog wants to "bring about" the assembly of all dogs "by force." Furthermore, he says, "I want to have the bone open under the pressure of their willing readiness; then I want to release them to the life that is dear to them; and then I, alone, entirely alone, want to lap up the marrow. That sounds monstrous, and it is almost that—as if I wanted to feed myself not on the marrow of just one bone, but on the marrow of dogdom itself. But this is merely an image. The marrow that is in question here is no food: it is the opposite; it is poison" (B 257).

In other words, humane readiness on the part of everyone to forsake the life that is dear to him, and thereby to reveal the "true human being," does not come about of its own accord. It must be "brought about by force" and is, therefore, achievable only through an inhuman act. What, however, is the meaning of this coercion? Obviously this: to compel all dogs to give up, at least temporarily, the life they have led hitherto and to dedicate themselves to the Whole, or to prepare themselves to crunch the bone that contains and conceals the Whole, and do away with the obstructing barriers. The very readiness to do this opens the bone. In view of the extremely personal nature of all of the works of Kafka (his diaries often pass directly into fictional prose, in an indistinguishable mixture of autobiographical confession and literary work), one will not go wrong in connecting the "coercion" (that the investigating Dog exercises upon his fellow dogs) with Kafka's own objective of conveying to his fellow men at least a notion of the "Whole"—

and of doing this by means of his writing. There is surely no doubt that these investigations of a dog reflect Kafka's own creative inquiry.[54] Analogously, in an autobiographical confession, he writes:

Many years ago I was once sitting, sadly enough of course, on the slope of St. Lawrence Hill. I was analyzing what my wishes in life were. The most important or most fascinating one turned out to be the wish to obtain a view of life (and, of course, necessarily bound up with that, to be able to convince others of my view through my writing) in which life preserved, to be sure, its natural, hard-to-bear ups and downs but at the same time was recognized just as clearly as a Nothing, a dream, a state of suspension. (B 293-94)

## A. THE GUILT OF UNIVERSAL LITERATURE

This characteristic writing of his always appeared to Kafka as guilt. Even in an early letter, dated November 9, 1903, he writes to Oskar Pollak, "God does not want me to write; but I, I must." And even in his late period, in a letter dated July 5, 1922, he says to Max Brod that writing is "reward for service to the Devil. This descending to the dark powers; this unleashing of spirits that are by nature chained; questionable embraces and everything else that may be going on down there that one no longer knows anything about up here when one is writing stories in the sunlight. Perhaps a different kind of writing exists, too; I know only this. In the night, when fear does not let me sleep, I know only this." The writer, he continues, "is the scapegoat of mankind; he allows man to enjoy a sin without guilt, almost without guilt."

This means, therefore, that the writer who "unleashes" the Whole of human life, who "unleashes" all his spirits that are by nature chained, thereby heaps upon himself all the sins of man, which the rest of mankind, viewing his work, can enjoy "almost without guilt." And actually that itself is guilt, too—toward others as well as toward oneself.

The monstrous intention of the Dog, however, goes even further. He wants to dismiss the others to their life again, "and then I, alone, entirely alone, want to lap up the marrow"; that is, universal truth, the totality of existence, is to be reserved for him alone. In a letter written to Max Brod early in October 1917, he says analogously:

What do you think of this brilliant bit of self-knowledge...? If I examine myself with respect to my ultimate goal, I find that I am not actually striving to become a good person and to measure up to the requirements of a supreme court of justice; but, very much to the contrary, I am trying to view and assess the entire community of men and animals, to recognize their fundamental preferences, wishes, ethical and moral ideals, and, as soon as possible, to develop myself so as to be thoroughly pleasing to everyone; indeed, so pleasing—here comes the "leap"—that ultimately I, as the only sinner who will not be roasted, may openly, in full view, bring out all the mean, sordid elements intrinsic to me. And so, to sum it up, only the tribunal of men and animals is of importance to me, and, what is more, I want to deceive them —of course, without deceit. This central point of self-knowledge perhaps makes it possible to establish various conclusions and motivations.[55]

This letter illuminates the entire problem at one stroke!

Humane readiness on the part of everyone is a utopia. A utopia could make it possible for everyone on earth to lead a life worthy of man; but utopia cannot be realized, for it assumes that all people who cling to their dear lives will possess insight, knowledge, and willing readiness. Man cannot live his own life and simultaneously maintain his view of the nature and activities of the whole "tribunal of men and animals." The Universal must, so to speak, be "axiomatic" for him. It is impossible constantly to work it out for oneself anew in the midst of the trials and afflictions of this life that is already hard enough as it is. The purpose of every religion is to bestow the Universal upon man as an axiom by which he can be certain of existence and accept it as a matter of course, an axiom according to which he always orients himself. But then, religion in the present time is no longer unconditionally binding for everybody—

no longer even for Kafka: "I was not led into life, as was Kierkegaard, by the hand of Christianity, a hand that is, to be sure, already rapidly sinking; and I have not yet caught hold of the last corner of the Jewish prayer shawl as it flutters past. I am either end or beginning" (H 121).

What remains is the fullness of earthly life itself. The Universal must be brought forth from it. And *this* was Kafka's real task.

### B. THE GOAL AND THE RESPONSIBILITY OF UNIVERSAL LITERATURE

Immediately before Kafka dissociates himself from Christianity and Judaism and designates himself as "end or beginning," he defines his task as follows:

It is not laziness, ill will, clumsiness (even these are all involved to some degree, because "vermin are born out of nothingness") that cause me to fail at everything, or not even so much as to fail—at family life, friendship, marriage, career, literature—but it is the lack of ground under my feet, of air to breathe, of commandments. To create these is my task—not so that I can then recover lost ground, so to speak, but so that I'll not have overlooked anything; for this task is as good as any other. It is even the most primary task, or at least the reflection of it; just as, in mounting up high where the air is thin, one can suddenly step into the light of the distant sun. And this is a task that is by no means uncommon; it has surely often been set before, but whether in such proportions, of course, I do not know. (H 120)

The task is the same as that set for every human being who is searching for the Universal. Kafka must himself "create" the missing ground, the air,[56] the commandments. It is the "most primary" task or "at least the reflection of it." For there, up high where the air is thin, where dear life is forsaken, a reflection of the distant sun can still flare up. This sun is the "supreme court of justice"; to its pronouncements man must measure up if he "is striving to become a good person." But the sun is "distant." In the novel *The Trial* the high court has disappeared. "Where was the judge whom he had never seen? Where was the high court before which he had never appeared?" Josef K. finally asks in despair. "He raised his hands and spread out all his fingers" while the murdering hands of the hangmen seized his throat (P 272).

Thus there remains only the earthly "tribunal of men and animals." Within this court "the ground, the air, the commandments" are to be created. This gives the task "such proportions" that they exceed all former ones. And the daring venture of undertaking such a task confers upon this poet his exceptional position, of which he was fully aware and which, of necessity, had to evoke his extreme "despair" as well as his extreme "arrogance."

I battle; nobody knows it, but many a one suspects it; that cannot be avoided; but nobody knows it. I fulfill my daily duties; I may be criticized for a little absentmindedness, but not for much. Naturally, everyone battles, but I battle more than others do; most people battle as though in sleep, the way one moves one's hand in a dream to ward off an apparition; but I have stepped forth, and I battle with the most careful and well-considered utilization of all my powers. Why did I step forth from the crowd that of itself is certainly noisy but in this respect is alarmingly quiet? Why did I call attention to myself? Why am I now at the head of the enemy's list? I do not know. To me a different kind of life did not seem worth living. Born soldiers is what military history calls such people. And yet it is not like that; I do not hope for victory, and battle as such gives me no pleasure; but I take pleasure in it merely insofar as it is the only thing to be done.[57] As such, the pleasure it gives me is more than I can in reality relish, more than I can bestow; perhaps I'll be done for, not because of the battle but because of this pleasure. (H 338-39)

It now grows discernible why the "monstrous" intention of the Dog consists of his lapping up "alone, entirely alone," the "marrow" of all dogdom, and of nourishing himself on it while everyone else lives his dear life, and why, nevertheless, at the same time, this marrow is not a nourishing food but, on the contrary, "poison."

His exceptional position—which is an essential one, since life in common with others within the Universal remains a utopia—possesses, of necessity, a twofold aspect. On the one hand, it means taking upon oneself the responsibility for everyone, for the totality of the community of men and animals: "I never felt the pressure of any responsibility except that imposed upon me by the presence of other people, by their glances, by their judgments" (H 303). Or, in the sketch "At Night":

Rapt in the night. As one at times lowers one's head in order to reflect, to be so completely rapt in the night. Round about, people are sleeping. A little play-acting, an innocent self-deception that they are sleeping in houses, in solid beds, under solid roofs, stretched out or curled up on mattresses, in sheets, under quilts; in reality they have come together, as they once did in those days, and as later on again, in a desolate region, an encampment in the open—a vast number of people, an army, a nation, flung down beneath a cold sky upon the cold earth where they had previously stood—brow pressed upon arm, face toward the ground, breathing quietly. And you are awake, are one of the watchers; you find your neighbour by brandishing a piece of burning wood from the pile of brushwood near you. Why are you awake? The saying goes that someone must stay awake, must stand guard.[59] (B 116)

On the other hand, this responsibility of the sole watcher rests on principles that can be derived only from that very community of men and animals that surrounds him. Since a supreme court, to which he could answer satisfactorily, is nowhere to be found, he sees himself resorting "very much to the contrary, to viewing and assessing the entire community of men and animals, to recognizing their fundamental preferences, wishes, ethical and moral ideals." The "battler" who has stepped forth from that very community sees himself compelled to examine the community's entire world of bustle and imagination, and "then as soon as possible develop [himself] so as to be thoroughly pleasing to everyone." This is K.'s "battle" in the novel *The Castle*. He must "survey" the entire "realm" of earthly possibilities of

living and thinking, so that he can be admitted into the community of all beings as one pleasing to them all.

This sounds like "conformity," like acquiescence in the prevailing principles of society. Indeed many interpreters have
considered Kafka's total "endeavor" in this light.[60] However,
nothing would be more mistaken than this kind of interpretation. It overlooks the crucial "leap" that Kafka speaks of in the
quoted letter. Kafka wants "to deceive ... of course, without
deceit" the tribunal of men and animals. What does this mean?

By recognizing "their fundamental preferences, wishes, ethical
and moral ideals," by "viewing and assessing" the Whole, he
can, of course—acting in conformity with them—develop so as
to be "pleasing." But only in the form of mimesis,[61] camouflage, deceit. On the outside he appears virtuous. Yet this
camouflage is not deceit but its opposite. For it is in mimesis,
in the imitation,[62] in the "description" that with exactitude
simulates the Whole—*all* preferences, wishes, moral and ethical
ideals—that the contradictions, the falsehoods, the mean and
sordid elements hidden in the Whole are revealed. All of Kafka's
literary work, primarily his three novels, is in fact a unique
exposition of the contradictions and mean, sordid elements
hidden within human associations and ideals, hidden, indeed,
within the heroes themselves. Not falsehood, but the truth of
the Whole is caught sight of. However, since all others of
necessity remain rooted in these falsehoods, they are culpable.
The "only sinner who will not be roasted" is he who in the
total mimesis at the same time lays bare and lives out the mean,
sordid elements intrinsic to himself. He is not only protected
by the blindness of the others, but also protected from the
highest authority because he is, in fact, transmitting truth, making his own confession.

Nevertheless, it is true, he remains a "sinner"; this responsible work of his that transmits truth remains "reward for service to the Devil." Facing the highest authority, the only one
left him, "himself," he knows that he is guilty. He who stands
"outside" the law is "himself" the "sole law," is what is said in
the sketch "On the Question of Our Laws" (B 91 ff.). It is

this sole law that condemns him. The self pronounces sentence upon the self: [63] "We live upon this razor's edge" (B 93). The marrow that the Dog laps up is not nourishment; it is "poison."

## The Catastrophe of Creative Literature and the Cosmos

The most extreme point is reached, and, at the same time, the darkest possible eclipse. The rudderless bark of the Ḥunter Gracchus sails "driven by the wind that blows in the undermost regions of death" (B 105). The search for "Being" leads to the annihilation of Being. "For the first time" in the history of literature the daring venture of the poet Kafka breaks off "far down into all the depths . . . the music of the world that until now could at least be sensed," simultaneously marking thereby the end of all poetic writing. In *He*, the autobiographical confessions of the year 1920, there is this statement:

Although everything that he does seems extraordinarily novel to him, yet, consistent with this impossible wealth of novelty, it seems also extraordinarily dilettante, scarcely even tolerable, unfit to become historical, bursting the chain of the generations, breaking off for the first time, far down into all the depths, the music that until now could at least be sensed. At times, in his arrogance, he is more afraid for the world than he is for himself. (B 291)

Kafka's experiment, employing the most daring, alienating images, summoning up all conceivable possibilities of reflection in order to blast the full truth out of that-which-is, results in the bursting asunder of "Being" itself. The attempt to establish a "Universal" again, in the manner of the classical period, has failed. Creative literature is no longer possible, the "historical . . . chain of the generations" breaks off, the "music of the world" is at an end.

For to write creatively, to make music, to build a realm of beautiful forms, is possible only for the person who *within* the world is sustained by an indestructibly eternal law of this world.

For that reason Kafka never designated his "writing" as "creative literature." He tried, as it were, to restore the basic element needed to make creative writing possible. And this utmost effort of his "demonstrated" not only the "impossibility" of life but also of creative writing.

There has been a great deal of "creative" writing about him, and there will be yet more. But the great ones among these writers have themselves had, and do have, knowledge of this same destiny. They have done, and still do, nothing but vainly lay down the "law" according to which it would be possible to live, to write, to act. In incalculable descriptions, analyses, reflections, in running through all possible phenomena of social, scientific, historical, intellectual, and spiritual life, they, no differently from Kafka, join brick to brick in order to arrive at a structure of a lasting, universally valid order of "Being"; they pursue the same "summative" procedure: Thomas Mann, Robert Musil, Hermann Broch, James Joyce, etc. Like Kafka, they show the constant changes and contradictions of each individual "given" phenomenon, and they end in the same desperate radicality inherent in the question: Is creative literature still possible? (Thomas Mann: *Dr. Faustus*; Herman Broch: *The Death of Vergil*; *inter alia*).

Kafka is only one link in the chain they form; he is a child of his times, as all of them are. However, he has radicalized the problem as no one else has done, not only by his concern with historical contents, as in the case of the "historians" of his Hunter Gracchus, but by his attempt to give form, so to speak, to the abstract, ever-valid patterns of human life and thought (as, for example, the organizations of public authorities in his novels), and by the light he has cast in general, through poetically impressive images, upon the tension between consciousness and "Being." Thereby he succeeded in penetrating immediately from the more or less accidental, individual phenomena, as they are related to time, into what is basically general—and in this sense, of course, also "universal"; he succeeded in quarrying to the surface the universally valid conformities with natural law that are concealed in all time-relations and in all time-contents; and, what is more, he succeeded in a generally apt, impartial presentation and interpretation that do not distort the individual instance. The abstract models of existence that he created, for example, in the "universal tribunal of men and animals" of his novels, meaningfully mirror the world conditions of our times. They do not decide for or against any sphere one-sidedly, but show the "exigencies" of everything that we live and think, without making any limited position absolute. As a result, his novels have a power and significance beyond their time.

In this sense—and in this sense only, of course—the lustre of great literature is visible in his work, and "beauty" lies concealed even in the horror of what he has to say. He was unable to present the Universal in "positive" guise, but in its very negativity it assumes a form that is all the more demanding. By its absence in positive form the Universal is more actual and imperious than it is among the apparent certainties of the positive assertions with which pseudo-poets lull themselves. "To effect the negative is still incumbent upon us; the positive has already been given to us" (H 42, 83), for "he does not live because of his personal life; he does not think because of his personal thought. It seems to him as if he were living and thinking under duress on the part of a family that is itself certainly overflowing with vitality and intellect, for whom, however, he, in accordance with some law that is unknown to him, represents a formal necessity. Because of this unknown family and these unknown laws he cannot be released" (B 295).

He was consistently aware of the "necessity" of his writing, in spite of or because of his misgivings about it. He did not dare relax in his battle; he could not be "released." His writing was more than despair and hubris. It was the inescapable fulfillment of a claim imposed upon him by the community of men in accordance with an unknown supreme law, even though this community itself might know nothing of such a claim.

Even so, his writing represents for us all a "formal necessity," though it may not be that with respect to the particular contents. For this writing, as no other of our generation, leads us to the "truth" of our times and makes us aware of the formal "claim," even though that claim probably cannot be formulated in the specific contents.

## Surmounting the Catastrophe

And perhaps that is why this writing is more than merely revealing description of what exists. Perhaps on the basis of such revelation he succeeded also in mediating between the "combatants," between the absolute, all-consuming law ("Being") and earthly life ("that-which-is"). A statement of Kafka's permits of such a conjecture:

He has two opponents. The first one harries him from the rear and has been doing so ever since the very beginning. The second blocks his passage forward. He battles with both. Actually the first one assists him in his battle with the second one, for he wants to push him forward; and, likewise, the second one assists him in his battle with the first one, for he, of course, is thrusting him back. But it is only theoretically that way. For, after all, not only the two opponents are there, but he himself is there too; and who really knows what his intentions are? Yet, all the same, it is his dream that at some time, at an unguarded moment— that of course requires a blacker night than has ever yet existed —he will leap forth out of the fighting line and because of his combat experience will be elevated to the position of judge over his opponents who are battling with one another. (B 300)

This blackest night, in which the music of the world breaks off, is the prerequisite for man to be "himself" elevated to the position of "judge." Even though this is a "dream," one nevertheless catches sight of a rescuing mediation in it. There are "unguarded moments" in which man "leaps forth out of the fighting line and because of his combat experience is elevated to the position of judge. . . ." Man's liberation is sighted by way of a dream, a liberation that at the same time includes a judge's official regulating function.

One could harbor the suspicion that Kafka, in accordance

with the dialectic pattern, wants to have the negative—through its most extreme intensification—turn into the positive, possibly in the sense of the negative theology of Kierkegaard or Karl Barth. That is not the case. Following upon that quoted passage in which he describes his "most primary task" and its "proportions," comes this statement:

I have been endowed with absolutely none of the requisites for living, so far as I know, except for the weakness common to all mankind. It is a gigantic strength in this respect: with it I have vigorously taken on the negative of my era, which is really very close to me, which I never have the right to attack but which I do have the right to defend to a certain degree. I had no inherited portion in the meagre positive nor in the extreme negative that topples over into the positive. I was not led into life, as was Kierkegaard, by the hand of Christianity, a hand that is, to be sure, already rapidly sinking. . . . (H 120-21)

Here Kafka clearly admits that he will uphold his "era," particularly its "negative," and not battle against it. He has no share in the meagre positive of this era; the authorities round about him were not able to deceive him. And he has just as little sympathy for the sudden theological shift from the negative to the positive, since for him nothing positive exists into which his negative could suddenly change. His negation—and this is a crucial difference—is *not* leveled *against* the world and against his era, as was the case with Kierkegaard. In a letter to Max Brod (end of March 1918) he writes explicitly, with slashing criticism of Kierkegaard:

Kierkegaard's religious outlook refuses to reveal itself to me as it does to you, in spite of that extraordinary clarity which is so seductive even to me. The very stand Kierkegaard takes seems to prove you wrong. For, to begin with, the relationship to the divine, as far as Kierkegaard is concerned, defies any outside point of view, perhaps so much so that even Jesus would not be in a position to judge how far any follower of his had come. For Kierkegaard, this seems, to a certain extent, to be a question to be left to the Last Judgment, that is to say, answerable—insofar as an answer is still necessary—only after the end of this world. For that reason the present-day outer image of the religious relationship has no meaning. Now, to be sure, the religious relationship wants to reveal itself, but cannot do so in this world. Therefore, aspiring man must set his face against the world in order to rescue the divine in himself ; or, what comes to the same thing, the divine sets him in opposition to the world in order to rescue itself. Consequently the world has to be raped by you as well as by Kierkegaard, now more so by you, now more so by him ; the differences are merely in the aspect of the raped world.

And in a letter to Max Brod at the beginning of March 1918, Kafka writes that Kierkegaard's religious "positiveness . . . soars . . . too high; the ordinary mortal . . . he does not see, and he paints the monstrous figure of Abraham in the clouds."

For Kafka, what is at stake is the deliverance of the world, and, what is more, the deliverance of the ordinary human being who is always the subject of Kafka's portrayal. Kafka feels himself primarily responsible to his "era," strange as that may seem when one considers his extreme isolation or the (only seemingly) complicated structure of his work that contains (again, only seemingly) nothing of the actual exigencies and crises of his era. The "negative" of his era was exactly what he accepted "vigorously," without any veiling, without any attempt to represent it falsely as positive. He saw his task as that of providing this era with its "missing ground, air, and commandments." This lack of ground makes existence on earth impossible. This fact must be brought into consciousness; it must be "demonstrated." This is the purpose served by the representations of the absurdities, the falsehoods, the barbarities, and the contradictions of this world. At the same time, however, even these absurdities, etc., are "necessary." Without them one cannot "live." Nothing short of these constitutes earthly existence. He who is only good becomes guilty in consequence of his very goodness. The absolutely "pure" world is the dead, empty, sucked-out world, "purified to the very bones" ("Jackals and Arabs," E 163). Thus in Kafka "two opponents" battle with one another unremittingly. The one "from the very beginning" harries him out of the world "forward" into the Absolute, "to food that you can eat, air that you can breathe, life that is free, even though that be beyond life" (T 572). The origin of everything-that-is, "Being," aims also at doing away with everything-that-is. The other, thrusting him back into life, in the face of the absolute claim, means to affirm that-which-is concretely, and to rescue it. Both, alike, are necessary in order to establish human existence, but they cancel one another out reciprocally, and cannot be reconciled with one another.

At an "unguarded moment," however, that is, at a moment when neither of the two opponents is directing his gaze at him, when both, therefore, are, as it were, no longer existent for him—and that would mean only that both life and the absolute claim sink away, and that then a "night" sets in, "blacker than any that has ever yet existed"—at such a moment there is the possibility that he might "leap forth out of the fighting line and because of his combat experience be elevated to the position of judge over his opponents who are battling with one another."

In other words, not until *everything* is negated, not only concrete life with its contradictions and its infinite relations, but also the absolute claim that is a deadly menace to life— when the chain of the generations snaps and the music of the world itself breaks off, when man is thus no longer ruled by any allegation or pretense—not until then can the responsibility be transferred to man himself, admittedly, of course, only "because of his combat experience." That is the meaning of Kafka's enigmatic statement: "To effect the negative is still incumbent upon us; the positive has already been given to us" (H 42); it is the meaning, too, of his other statement that those who stand "outside the law" are the "sole unequivocal law imposed upon us" (B 91, 93). For "the spirit becomes free only when it ceases to be a prop" (H 48).

However, to be "judge over his opponents who are battling with one another" means being responsible in the highest degree for "doing justice" to both of them. The compulsion to live and the absolute claim continue to exist. The positions are merely shifted. Formerly, man was the victim of his opponents. He submitted to the conditions of life or to the absolute command-

ment. Now he stands above both. However, that is his true
"universal" position. He must reconcile the opponents.

Yet such a reconciliation is possible only in a "night, blacker
than has ever yet existed." Man must surmount the absolute
catastrophe. "All suffering about us we, too, must suffer. Christ
suffered for men, but mankind must suffer for Christ" (H 117).
That was Kafka's answer to the unbelief, to the "ground"-
lessness of his era. Man must himself take on the redeeming
death of Christ. Just as Christ, when farthest removed from
God ("My God, my God, why hast Thou forsaken me?"), in a
night "when the earth did quake ... and the sun was darkened,"
mediated between the earthly human race and the God of the
Old Testament, that unconditionally demanding God, so the
task remains for the man who has not been "led into life by
the hand of Christianity," to take redeeming death upon himself of his own accord.

The Messiah will come as soon as the most unrestricted individualism is possible—when nobody will destroy this possibility,
nobody will tolerate the destruction; that is to say, when the
graves open. Perhaps that is also the Christian teaching, both in
the actual demonstration of the example that is to be followed,
an individualistic example, and in the symbolic demonstration of
the resurrection of the mediator within the individual human
being. (H 88-89)

All responsibility, all suffering, and all reconciliation are en-
joined upon the "individual human being." This is Kafka's
closeness to, and, at the same time, his remoteness from our
Jewish and Christian religion—his "end or beginning."

CHAPTER II

# Beyond Allegory and Symbol

Since Kafka's writings strive to give expression to the universal story of everything that was and is, a story known to everyone and at the same time forgotten, they create a structure that no longer corresponds with any structure of the past. The universal story is related incessantly in Kafka's works. All the figures, all the people and animals, indeed, all the events, actions, images, phenomena, constantly speak of it. However, just as the living guest of the Hunter Gracchus comprehends nothing of what is being told—although he is eager to learn the "continuity" of this strange hunter's story, and finds this living dead man extremely "interesting"—similarly the reader of Kafka's works constantly has the exciting feeling that they are expressing something highly significant and, what is more, that touch on "ultimate questions" and truths, but that it is at the same time impossible to comprehend what is expressed in them, impossible to translate it into a language that consciousness can understand. The reader gropes his way as though through an alluring prophetic dream that seems to be revealing to him, with certainty and immediacy, profound truths that have hitherto been hidden. But at the very moment he awakens to the full

consciousness of day, and means to give an account to himself
of what he saw and had knowledge of in the dream, all his
ideas and verbal formulations prove impotent. Unable to communicate to his normal consciousness what he has read, he
cannot interpret it with assurance. Hence, the interpretations of
Kafka's writings are as confusing or conflicting as these writings themselves, as the interpretations that Kafka inserted in
the midst of his writings (e.g., P 257 ff.).

In the novel *The Trial*, for instance, all the characters talk
about the peculiar trial as they would about something self-
evident and real; and even the strange procedures, the judicial
hearings, the court chambers and court offices are presented as
if they were quite natural and ordinary in the midst of a
modern metropolis with banks, telephones, and tenement houses,
although all these strange procedures defy every experience and
reality to which one is accustomed. Consequently, from beginning to end the reader does not know what these peculiar
proceedings at law and these innumerable administrative authorities that are constantly being "talked about" mean, what the
trial signifies, what the charge hinges on, etc.

The amazing precision with which all the details of the legal
proceedings are clarified and worked through, and with which
the locales of this court of justice are described—this precision
is grotesquely incongruous with the cryptic quality of meaning
as a whole, a meaning that is nowhere clarified and formulated.
It is like the case of the Hunter Gracchus whose story is unceasingly being told by all teachers, mothers, lovers, historians,
newspapers, merchants, telegraphs, savages, stars, seas, and
streams, without its being possible for these very people (mothers,
lovers, etc.) to say what they are talking about; hence the
Hunter's guest has good reason to demur: "Odd as it may seem
to you—and I am even amazed at it myself, but it is so,
nevertheless—you are not the subject of the talk of the town.
No matter how many things are being talked about, you are
not one of them. The world goes its way and you are making
your journey, but I never noticed before today that your paths
had crossed one another." The "subject" of the talk of the

town is something entirely different. It is the normal content of our ordinary, everyday consciousness, or of our consciousness with the stamp of history and civilization upon it. And yet the Hunter, too, is right in believing that what the people are *really* talking about is his universal story. *Within* that which all men and objects are, go through, and express, there lies hidden the Universal as well. It cannot be found outside of human beings and objects.

### Allegory and Parable

From this may be drawn important conclusions for an understanding of the structure of Kafka's writings. These works of fiction give form to the Universal in the midst of our everyday world of reality and language. However, there exists an unavoidable discrepancy between this Universal and the specific content of our everyday reality and language, that is to say, the normal "subject" of the talk of the town. Although both are ultimately identical, they never "cross" one another in the consciousness of man while he is involved in his empirical-historical world. Man in this state will therefore feel that whatever has been given form in Kafka's writing is an "unreal" assertion and representation, since it is no longer compatible with and comprehensible in terms of his own conceptual world. In Kafka, what has been stated and given form cannot—in his view—signify simply itself, but must conceal "beyond" itself an "other," "real" meaning. Since, for example, the "trial" seems no longer to correspond to the outward forms of a conventional court case, something else must be "signified" by this trial. And the effort of the reader or interpreter is then directed at "deciphering" this real meaning that is hiding behind the unreal discussion of the trial. Consequently the work is understood as a secret "allegory" for which one needs only the "key" in order to decipher[1] the meaning (to allegorize = to say something differently from the way one means it). Or, on the other hand, analogously, it is read as a "parable," as a "parabolic"[2] work

of literature, behind the material images and events of which
there is hidden a different, more profound meaning that likewise
needs deciphering and "interpretation"—as, say, a parable of
the Bible or Lessing's parable of the three rings. And Kafka
himself has supported this view, for instance, in his parables
"Before the Law," "An Imperial Message," and elsewhere.

The surprising element, however, in these so-called parables
of Kafka's is that Kafka in his own detailed explanations, say,
of the parable "Before the Law," nowhere states or hints at
what its individual characters or events really signify, what its
more profound spiritual, allegorical, or parabolic "meaning"
consists of, who is meant in the figurative sense by the gate-
keeper or by the man from the country, etc. Kafka expounds
in detail only the behavior of the characters, their relations
with one another, their mutual hierarchic positions. The question that is posed is whether they mutually deceive themselves
or are deceived; whether they act justly or unjustly; whether
they live, act, and speak freely or under constraint, etc. And
even these questions are answered in an inconsistent manner.
*All* possible interpretations are kept open; each one maintains
a certain plausibility; none is unequivocally certain; that is, this
so-called parable merely repeats in condensed form the very
same problems, events, contradictions, and uncertainties presented by the whole novel *The Trial*. The parable provides as
little enlightenment about the "real" meaning "behind" the trial
as the novel itself. It is just as obscure, now as before, what
"the law" actually is that the man from the country wants to
fathom; what the rules and regulations of this law consist of;
what the law orders and forbids; why the trial is being conducted at all; what the charge consists of; what is guilt or
innocence, etc.

Thus it can no longer be a matter of a parable in the strict
meaning of the term. For every parabolic or allegoric representation must refer to a determinable meaning or concept, as is
the case in Lessing's parable of the three rings, in which the
rings unequivocally denote three religions. Characteristic of
Kafka's writing, however, is the very fact that it is no longer

possible to establish any unequivocally determinable meaning "behind" the phenomena, proceedings, and utterances; that is, it is precisely this Universal of Kafka's that can no longer be translated into a philosophical, theological, or generally ideological language of concepts. Allegory and parable are possible only against the background of a firmly defined religion, philosophy, or world-view. The background of Kafka's "parables," however, is a void. His "Universal" is the totality of all earthly phenomena, of the potentialities of life and thought themselves, without metaphysical basis and background. Hence, in the exegeses of his so-called parables, the issue is that of very specific earthly questions: whether our human consciousness "deludes" us or not; whether we live freely or under constraint; what reciprocal relationships we have with one another; whether there are definite, legitimate hierarchies; whether we are in any way able to understand what guilt and innocence are; when are we acting justly, when unjustly, etc.

This means that the questions raised concern the extent to which human powers of knowledge and life can in general establish a valid order of life and system of justice, can find a "law" that will give security, can distinguish truth from falsehood, certainty from uncertainty. The "trial" that is being enacted is itself mirroring the Universal, the totality of all sorts of processes of life and thought in all their conflicting, many-sided, incalculable possibilities. And only in this sense would it be possible to speak of parable or allegory.

Their vast numbers mounting incalculably to absurd, inconceivable proportions, the court authorities, who in frantic haste are experiencing and noting down everything that happens on earth, are a graphic representation of the human processes of life and thought that go on without interruption in consciousness and in the subconscious—processes that in their totality cannot be "understood" and cannot be fitted together to form a meaningful integrated whole by the limited consciousness of the individual. The court authorities are thus, in fact, a figurative representation pointing to an actual, total meaning; and in this sense they are "allegorical." However, the allegory can no longer

be defined conceptually, because the totality itself can no longer
be established conceptually but can be arrived at only in the
ceaseless passage through all individual phenomena and processes of thought, a passage in the form of "frantic haste" or a
"hunt"; that is, it can never be achieved at all. Not without
good reason is the goddess of justice in *The Trial* also the
goddess of victory and of the hunt—a goddess for whom the
steady balancing of the scales is no longer possible (P 176-77);
that is, a goddess who no longer allows any sure determinability of what is really just or unjust. Thus, although Kafka's
world of imagery and his seemingly figurative language still
appear to contain elements of the allegorical and parabolical,
no systematic conceptual interpretation can any longer be given;
that is, it is no longer a matter of allegory and parable in the
strict sense at all. Only as one passes through all the separate
images and statements themselves can the universal meaning
of the work reveal itself.

In other words, Kafka's images and statements are *themselves*
"actuality" and are not at all unreal allegorical or parabolical
representations. Each word, each image signifies, in fact, itself;
to be sure, it does so in a sense that is revealed only when all
the parts of the work are synthesized. *Because* the Universal
can no longer be fitted into the structure of any ideology, it
can no longer be directly formulated in the work, and to the
reader it always remains an incomprehensible mystery that the
writer himself cannot and dare not ever reveal; for, if he should
do so, the very Universal itself would be surrendered, betrayed,
and reduced to a determinable, historically limited form that
has already passed through the mint of traditional religions or
philosophical systems, thereby doing away with the Kafkaian
structure of the Universal. Therefore, the concepts of allegory
and parable cannot be applied legitimately to Kafka's writing.
The use of these terms creates confusion and has already produced the most pernicious and most absurd endeavors at interpretation.[3]

On the contrary, in Kafka the relationship between figurative
and actual statement and representation is structured in such a

way that he, Kafka, never loses sight of the Universal; that is, of the totality of all the processes of life and thought. However, he can describe these at any given time only in the ordinary linguistic forms, images, and conceptual possibilities that are already available; these ordinary linguistic forms, etc., he must not only extricate from their limited aspects at any given time but also simultaneously correct in the light of the Universal, by presenting different or contrary aspects, so that a constant "state of suspension" (B 294) ensues, and what has just been said or described may even fade away or be retracted; that is, a dissolution of the boundaries of both the world of objects and the world of ideas ensues. In point of fact, through this, every statement or created image becomes a figurative, temporary, or problematical one that never conveys its meaning fully and completely. But every statement, every form of image is to be taken literally as an actual one, signifying itself. It cannot, and should not, be interpreted by reference to any sort of meaning or concept that lies outside the work and that is not formulated within the work itself, as has been the case in interpreting the "castle" as the abode of "grace," etc. The "law" in the "trial" is simply the law, no more and no less. To identify it with, say, Jewish law, or with God, or with the Chinese concept of Tao, etc., is to take oneself outside of the work. Only when all the statements about the "law" have been read and interpreted in the context of the novel is it possible to arrive at a valid definition of what the law is in *The Trial*. The seemingly figurative statements and images are the actual ones. It is only the implicit interrelationship of all the statements that makes it possible to determine their actual meaning.

## Symbol

In this respect the structure of Kakfa's writing appears to resemble a form of literature that ever since Goethe's time has been called "symbolic."[4] The so-called "liberation" of literature from religious and rigid ideological commitments, a liberation that began in Germany at about the period of *Sturm und Drang,* gave rise at that time to a form of literature that no longer points to a definable metaphysical or conceptually determinable world image, but that develops a "higher" universal meaning "with immediacy" from the earthly phenomena themselves. Inherent in the poetic images and forms themselves, for Goethe, is their "ineffable" meaning that can be instinctively felt "with immediacy" and that becomes "manifest" through intuition. These images and forms are "symbols" that in the concretely particular already imply the universal, as opposed to the allegory which is still in quest of a specific image for the universal.

Goethe states that the allegorist invents images for alleged concepts; the symbolist, however, sticks to the word, in which the universal is already implied as an ineffable "manifest mystery," without its ever being possible to define it by a concept, let alone replace it by one.[5] Even here, the universal, as in Kafka, is no longer unequivocally determinable. It is manifested in the "phenomena" themselves as something "primordial-phenomenal" that remains "impenetrable," "manifesting" its mystery to intuition alone, through the many-sided "relationships" among the phenomena.[6] The phenomena, however, are the guaranty that the universal exists and can be experienced. What is more, the universal can even be directly "intuited" in them. Although, to be sure, it is no longer present as a theological, philosophical, or ideological background and cannot be defined conceptually in terms of that background, it nevertheless appears in the terrestrial forms of nature. Nature for Goethe is the theater in which the revelation of God takes place. The poet expresses the Divine in images and symbols. This he is able to do, because his quickening power, the "inner light"[7] of his own soul, itself shares in the Divine, because his perceptive "eye" is itself an organ and mirror of the Divine, so that the artist can persuade the phenomena to speak truly and openly, to reveal the eternal universal "primordial phenomena." When soul and nature are intimately related with reciprocity, the universal becomes manifest in poetic image and symbol.

It is a very different matter in Kafka. For him the phenomena no longer reveal the Universal with immediacy; for, the moment they "appear," they are already distorted by man's imagining, intuiting, thinking, and feeling. The phenomena remain true, beautiful, and serene only until they come into man's sight (E 14). Man's ideas, moods, and thoughts, constantly changing and hence themselves "flimsy," are also constantly altering things, which, moreover, never suffice for him, and which he can never have "enough of" (B 41), since in their separateness they never represent the "whole" of existence, never fill it completely. This holds true not only of things but, analogously, of man himself, who likewise can never create the whole out of "himself" alone and, hence, feels that he (as well as things) is a perpetually "foundering" creature, no longer possessing ground "to walk on," air "to breathe," and a "secure" existence. Already in Kafka's earliest writing,[8] in the "Description of a Battle," this is formulated with unusual acuteness. "There was never a time when I was convinced of my existence through myself alone. The fact is, I take in the things around me with such feeble notions of them that I always think, the things once did exist but now they are being submerged" (E 14).[9]

One fears many things. That perhaps corporeality will vanish, that people are really as they seem to be in the dusk (B 57). . . . Isn't it this fever, this seasickness on solid ground, a kind of leprosy? Doesn't it seem to you that because of sheer frenzy you can't be content with the true name of things, that that's not enough for you, and now with extraordinary haste you pour names over them at random. But quickly, quickly! Yet, no sooner have you run away from them, than you have forgotten their names again. The poplar in the fields that you have named "Tower of Babel," for you did not want to know that it was a poplar, is swaying again without a name, and you have to name it "Noah, in His Drunkenness." (B 41-42)

Thus, the poetic images and the figures of speech are interchangeable. They do not catch the essence of things at all but are "poured over" things "at random." Consequently, therefore, they no longer possess the force of symbols in the Goethean sense, for, originating in "haste" and in the rush in which human ideas, associations, and moods dash along in resistless change, they lack the power to give certainty. And, analogously, with logical consistency, even the very reality of man and object is called in question.

But what is it that you do, as if you were real. Do you want to make me believe that I am unreal, standing here oddly on the green pavement? Yet it has been such a long time since you were real, you, sky, and as for you, Ring Plaza, you have never been real! It is true, of course, you are still more than a match for me, but really only when I let you alone. Thank God, moon, you are no longer moon ; but perhaps it is remiss of me that I still continue to call you, who are named moon, moon. Why are you no longer so supercilious when I call you "Forgotten Paper Lantern of Curious Color?" And why do you almost retreat when I call you "Column of the Virgin," and I no longer recognize your menacing attitude when I call you "Moon That Casts a Yellow Light." It really seems to me that it does you no good if one reflects about you; your health fails and your courage flags. (B 51-52)

Thus, whereas in Goethe poetic intuition and symbolizing reveal the true nature of things, manifesting the universal primordial phenomenon, in Kafka intuition and poetization destroy the truth and even the reality of man and object. No longer therefore, can one talk of symbols in Kafka. His writing is neither allegorical nor symbolical. Rather, it possesses a resemblance to a kind of parable for which aesthetics and poetics have so far not furnished a designation, because before Kafka this kind of parabolic world had not yet made itself visible. Kafka's world of parable and imagery introduces a new epoch of literature. The structure of that world is revealed only in the correlation between the individual images and the universal intention.

## Destructive Consciousness

The destructive role of reflective and creative intuition and

imagination appears to have its origin in the superior strength
of man's consciousness. This is consistent, too, with Kafka's
position, as one views it from the standpoint of his intellectual
development. The great significance of the natural sciences for
the young Kafka must early on have taught him to discern
that it is the way of these sciences to destroy the vividness of
things, to reduce all their sensuous qualities to abstract quantities, such that the "true" structure of things can at best be
arrived at only by means of an incalculable series of com-
putational operations.

Multifarious features in his works point to this view of his.
To cite only a few examples: Poseidon, the sea-god, ruler of
all the oceans of the world, "sat at his desk and calculated.
The administration of all the bodies of water caused him endless
toil." He

calculated without pause.... Thus he had scarcely seen the
oceans—only fleetingly while he was hurriedly mounting Olympus
—and had never actually crossed them. He was in the habit of
saying that he was waiting for the end of the world to do that;
and then, just before the end, after he'd checked the last calculation, there would probably still be a peaceful moment when
he would be able to get in a brief tour. (B 97-98)

In order to survey the totality of his possessions on earth,
Poseidon has to calculate without stopping. "The administration
of all the bodies of water caused him endless toil." The Universal can be arrived at only if one surrenders the sensuous
phenomenal world which becomes of no consequence and
meaningless, since what is at stake is the regularity of natural
laws, of the "law" of everything-that-is; and this regularity of
natural laws, according to the understanding of modern scientists,
can be found only in mathematical quantities. Only when the
"last calculation" is concluded—and that is possible only with
the "end of the world," since only then will the world complete
the sum total of its phenomena—will there be a peaceful
moment, only then can a brief tour of the visible world be
permitted.

Analogous examples can be found everywhere in Kafka. One may consider, for instance, the sketch "The New Lawyer," in which Bucephalus (Alexander's charger of old that had once borne him to the "inaccessible" portals of India) "in the present-day social order" is transformed into a lawyer who is constantly studying "law books." For, whereas in Alexander's times at least the "direction" to the eternally inaccessible "portals of India" was still clearly "indicated" by the "royal sword" of the great Alexander, the present-day social order has become completely disoriented and lacking in direction: "No one points out the direction; many are holding swords, but only in order to brandish them, and whoever follows their movements with his eyes becomes confused" (E 145-46). Hence, whereas Bucephalus could at one time clearly adopt a course and continue in the direction of the inaccessible, he must now study law books interminably, since he is no longer given the benefit of any certainty, of anything that will guide him in the right direction.

Nothing other than that is implied in Kafka by the endless protocols and studies of records, both in the chambers of the court authorities and in the castle chancelleries. The officials, too, are no longer in touch with the "real," visible life of the external phenomenal world. Although "office and life" are inextricably "interwoven" (S 81), those in "office" are concerned with determining general lawfulness, the law of life. And this, of necessity, removes them from every "immediate" contact with the public, with life outside in its concretely visible existence. The apparent contradiction of there being, on the one hand, no "difference" between the officials and the inhabitants of the village, and, on the other, an unbridgeable chasm between them, will concern us in detail when we analyze *The Castle*. This contradiction makes itself clear in the antinomy, that cannot be set aside, of man's individual free "self" and the general, collective forces of life. Both are always inextricably "interwoven" in existence, but are at the same time separated by a chasm. Since all reflection is already subject to general laws, it can never attain to the concrete, indefinably individual phenomenon of the living "self."

Hence, however, a discrepancy arises between the physical phenomenon and law, between image and meaning; and only when this discrepancy is clarified is it possible to recognize and thereby also to interpret the Kafkaian figurative world.

Since computations or determinations of the universal regularity of the laws of nature are unbounded and can never come to an end, their meaning, too, is never fully present; man can never have "enough" and is condemned to the constant hungering of a "hunger artist." On the other hand, only through such incessant hungering does life maintain itself and remain in "suspension." If man had "enough," that is, if perfection or completion were attained, then all life too would cease and the "world" would come to an end. Fulfillment would be annihilation; and, conversely, if one let up in one's battle and one's "work," everything would sink into darkness and hopeless entanglement. "If one has the strength never to stop looking at things, never shutting one's eyes, so to speak, one sees many things; but if one relaxes for no more than an instant and closes one's eyes, everything immediately drifts away into the dark" (S 446).

Consequently, the meaning or the "law" of such regularities that are inherent in life can never be developed into a design or even be formulated in literary representation. The gap between the representation and its meaning is immense; and hence the more precise the representation, the more immense, the more inconceivable, indeed the more preposterous it must appear—in spite of the unshakable conviction that there is an unmistakable law (P 264), that in the last analysis the incalculable computations of the authorities are never mistaken. "For mistakes do not happen, you see, and even if a mistake does happen, as in your case, who may then definitely say that it is a mistake?" (S 90).

Thus, since the representation never makes sense at the time, it must constantly take on the character of new enigmatizations, new unresolvable contradictions. This is what makes it appear figurative, provisional, disquietingly impelling, endless—fragmentary, if you like. Nevertheless, the representation rests upon an infallible regularity that is free of error. Only this lends it the character of truth, of the "truly" universal. The representation *itself* in its *totality* establishes truth and universality. For, because of the very fact that the representation does not make any finite meaning an absolute one, because of the very fact that Kafka, in delineating the endless process of life and imagination, refuses to confer on any individual interpretation the status of total interpretation, he is incessantly expressing the Universal. Thus only the *totality* of the representation is the immediate, actual statement of the Universal, and could, for that reason, perhaps be designated "symbol," if one still desires to employ this concept. Even the official authoritative body, that is unceasingly computing everything, is not the representative of the Universal but is only a partial phenomenon; it, in turn, can be clarified fully only in counterplay with the physically concrete existence, say, of K., who, as he fought against it, "stood here in his earthly solidity, not to be got rid of," and was thereby actually able "to force" the official apparatus "to work" (S 433). Thereby a new problem emerges, and only as it is illuminated does the structure of Kafka's figurative world become discernible.

## The Concrete Holds Its Ground

Until now we have spoken of the supremacy of human consciousness over concrete things and phenomena, and from that we have inferred and explained the demolishing of the structure of the symbol in classical literature. At the same time we pointed to the historically ideological connection between this process and the supremacy of the quantitative-mathematical thinking of modern science. The problem thus posed had long since been voiced in Goethe's vehement, singular hatred of Newton, in whose mathematical-physical thinking Goethe must have seen a threat not only to the "truth" of natural phenomena, but also to the existence of his own writing. For, as the physical qualities of phenomena are reduced to mere secondary properties, or even to a deceptive "semblance," the vivid images of poetry, likewise, no longer contain a higher truth, no longer manifest the "primordial phenomena" with immediacy, so that, through the quantitative thinking of modern physics, poetry, so to speak, loses its inner legitimacy.

In Kafka, however, there is present also, to an equally strong degree, the contrary tendency opposing this abstract thinking that dissolves everything concrete. K.'s battle against the castle authorities can be explained only from this front-line position. "The authorities ... always had to defend remote, invisible things merely on behalf of remote, invisible masters; whereas K. was battling for something very much alive and close at hand, that is to say, for himself" (S 80). Indeed, even a certain superiority in K. over the authorities is derived from this front-line position. The officials, for example, cannot endure the sight of K. and cannot leave their rooms as long as K. tarries outside, so that K., as it were, holds sway over the field of battle even though he feels this very domination—and this has yet to be dealt with in detail—as a lack of contact with the officials and hence, too, as his own weakness and defeat. His superiority is attributed categorically to the fact that, face to face with the officials, he asserts his "earthly solidity" and is thereby in the position of forcing the bureaucratic machinery to function.

Indeed, he already understood how to manipulate this official apparatus, how to play this delicate instrument, intent as it always was on some sort of settlement or compromise. The trick consisted essentially in doing nothing, in letting the machinery run of its own accord, and in forcing it to work merely by the fact that one was standing here in one's earthly solidity, not to be got rid of. (S 433)

K., by "doing nothing," merely by maintaining his earthly solidity, "not to be got rid of," forces the machinery to work. The machinery is therefore dependent upon what is concretely earthly. The machinery, in general, is really nothing else but life that is reflected and brought into consciousness; to be sure, included are even the unconscious reflexes of instinct and dream to which the officials unrestrainedly surrender themselves. Through these reflexes, for example, Klamm the official is able to be copresent even in the amorous embraces of K. and Frieda—by reason of K.'s belief that in this embrace, through Frieda's "mediation, an almost physical relationship with Klamm, enough for communicating in whispers, had come into being" (S 444).

Since the officials represent all the laws inherent in existence (conscious as well as unconscious ideas, impulses, and sensations), they are *omnipresent*, even in man's most private domain, and hence exercise unlimited power. But, being simply laws inherent in life and not concrete life itself, they merely record and pass judgment on its events and most secret instincts and intentions. They are the expression of the ideas, wishes hopes, dreams, instincts, etc., that in man are constantly coming into being and running their course. Therefore, their appearance is constantly changing. Every person sees Klamm differently. And these "differences" in the way he appears "arise through the mood of the moment, the degree of excitement, the particular state of hope or despair—among the countless possible gradations—in which the observer ... finds himself" (S 235). However, the officials are not concrete life; they are not K. "himself." They are defending "invisible" things, whereas K. is battling for "something very much alive and close at hand," battling for "himself." As long as K. thinks, reflects, and imagines, he is in their power. As soon as he "does nothing," he is playing with them and compelling them to function simply through his heavy, earthly existence that is "not to be got rid of," that he is defending against them.

The interplay consists of K.'s needing the officials in order to gain clarity about himself and his life, to be able to "survey the land," and, on the other hand, of his being swept along by these officials into endless contradictions and reflections that now, more than ever, make a secure existence on earth impossible for him. On the one hand he must defend what is "very much alive and close at hand" in him, his existence, against the officials; on the other, he must strive to obtain the very closest contact with the officials in order to gain clarity about and knowledge of legality in general, the law specifically, and the "ground" upon and through which he can exist. Fundamentally, therefore, K. and the officials are nothing but *a single person*, the human being himself, the total human being who is in conflict with himself, or who is engaged in a battle with the two opponents harrying him. The one opponent, in a wild rush, wrenches him from the frontiers of the human race; the other thrusts him back into concrete earthly existence. Of himself Kafka at one point writes:

What else can happen but that the two different worlds separate, and they separate, or at least pull at one another, in a horrible way. There are probably various reasons for the savagery of the inner process; the most obvious is introspection that does not allow any idea to come to rest, that hunts and flushes each idea by way of becoming itself in turn an idea to be given further chase by further introspection. Secondly: this chase is in a direction away from mankind. (T 552)

The other world, however, the concrete, "external one haltingly takes its routine course" (*ibid.*). Both worlds, the world of endless reflectibility and that of physical existence, are inseparably united in every human being; there is no human life without them.

In Kafka, however, the two worlds are in conflict, inasmuch as they have developed in extreme divergence from one another in the twentieth century. The officials who protocol everything in "great haste" (S 92) are no more than these introspective observations of man that wrest him out of this terrestrial world. Opposing them is the need for "rest," for concrete earthly existence.

## The "Rebellion" of Things

Even in as early a work as "Description of a Battle," the superior power of consciousness is resisted by visible things that are true, beautiful, and tranquil before being struck by the

ray of human consciousness and intuition. Things "rise in rebellion" (B 59) against the disfigurements inflicted upon them
by human thought and creative imagination. They "avenge"
(B 32, 35) themselves on man by "thrusting forward . . . mutely
terrible walls" (B 31) against him. In other words, the visible
world, things, become dumb, impenetrable, and take on a hard-
ness that is menacing in its relentlessness. They become pure
objects, stripped bare of meaning; they no longer reveal any
mystery, no longer, like Goethean poetry, unlock a higher truth
that is accessible to the human soul.

In this, too, Kafka has "described" a modern destiny. Corresponding strictly to the radical volatilization of nature, as its
physical properties are resolved into mathematical-physical for-
mulae—the "administration of all the oceans" through endless
arithmetical computations ("Poseidon")—is the counterprocess:
the absolute objectification and reification of nature, whereby
it is merely an object emptied of meaning, a thing without any
spiritual or intellectual content. What is more, from the supremacy of consciousness, the converse arises: the superior power
of things and objects over man's living and thinking.
Things enter into human life, dominating it without making
sense. As they are described in this early work of Kafka's they
become "importunate" and "vain" (B 31); imperiously they demand attention, admiration, even service and submission; they
show curiosity and "capricious partiality for the pulp of our
brains" (B 31). Man becomes the slave of the things that he
degrades to bare objects, items. Things not only elude man's
thinking, but they actually play with it, with the "brain." However, that is merely the converse of man's power over things.
For prior to this there was a description of how the hero of
"Description of a Battle" was capable of altering nature and
its objects as much as he pleased: "The stones disappeared in
accordance with my wishes, and the wind died away" (B 25);
"I caused a high and massive mountain to appear, towering
far off at a considerable distance, facing me on the road"
(B 26). Notwithstanding, in this very landscape that he has
himself created, man feels utterly lonely in a world emptied of

meaning. Hence, in the world of things he can no longer "breathe." "But now—I beg you—mountain, flower, grass, shrubbery, and river, give me a little space, so that I can breathe" exclaims the ceaselessly "brooding" stout man, who has just had to "humble" himself before this vindictive landscape (B 32). At this moment "all things lost their beautiful boundaries" (B 32). Chaos sets in. For as soon as "breathing" is wished for, it is shown to be impossible; man can no longer assert himself as a free being in the face of the superior power of things; everything becomes futile and meaningless, since thought itself has already depreciated things, "for how often have we both attacked these things—my friend the praying man and I" (B 35). "That is the vengeance of water and wind; now I am lost" (B 35). And the stout man, who is basically pure consciousness (gnats fly through his motionless body; thorny branches pierce it without meeting any resistance), goes under in a stream rushing down "torrentially," the banks of which went on and on "without limit," while the hero of the story cries out, "What are our lungs to do . . . if they breathe quickly they choke themselves, their inner poisons choke them, if they breathe slowly, unbreathable air, mutinous things, choke them. But if they are minded to go in search of their right tempo, they perish in the very search" (B 59). That is the "proof that it is impossible to live": neither in the hurried, unceasing "chase" of his own "inner" world of ideas nor in the world of external things can man breathe. There is no form of existence, inner or outer, in which he can live. Everything loses its boundaries and "rushes" into the bottomless void.

In his early work Kafka has thus already sketched the structure of his writing. All his later work was merely further elaboration, elaboration and repetition down to the very details. For example, this same image of the double breathing, the inner and outer, reappears in *The Trial* when Josef K. finds it hard to breathe in the atmosphere of the court officials' chancelleries, and the officials find it hard to breathe in his.

Yet in this another element that is of greater consequence becomes evident.

Even the "self" of man, his solid, earthly-physical existence, loses its boundaries and is split in a strange way. When the stout man sinks in the torrential stream that flows "into the distance," the water of which "flowed ... in clots and smoke" against the "crumbling brink" of the shore (B 59), something peculiar happens to the "I"-narrator who is watching. Shouting on the shore, he formulates the cause of this sinking, invoking the image of the double breathing. His arms and legs grow to monstrous, vast proportions, while his head and his eyes become diminutively small. Indeed, the gigantic arms want to "crush my poor head."

It was really as small as an ant's egg—only it was a bit damaged, and for that reason no longer perfectly round. I executed beseeching rotations with it, for my eyes were so small that it would have been impossible to notice their expression. But oh, my legs, my impossible legs, lay across the wooded mountains and shaded the village valleys. They grew, they grew! They were already projecting into the space that was now devoid of landscape; they had long since extended in size beyond my sight. But no, it is not that—I am small, all the same, temporarily small—I'm rolling—I'm rolling—I am an avalanche in the mountains! Please, people, you who are passing by; be so kind as to tell me how big I am; just measure these arms, these legs. (B 60)

The organs with which man thinks and looks at things, his head and his eyes, are damaged and become diminutively small. They become unable to measure and to recognize the parts of the body that grow boundlessly, those specific parts with which man walks upon the earth and handles things. Arms and legs, by contrast, precisely like the space that "was now devoid of landscape," are made to lose their outlines in immense extensions, and move out of sight.

That is, the autonomizing of the world of things includes man also. One's own arms "crush my poor head." The body, like the mutinous things, takes vengeance on thinking. Man can no longer recognize himself; he can no longer determine his own "measure." He believes that he is small and surveyable, but only "temporarily" so. He is like an avalanche that grows menacingly and monstrously larger and larger, the coming "size" of which can no longer be foreseen.

What is most peculiar about this autonomizing of things is expressed in the following statement: "In the course of this, the banks of this river stretched out boundlessly, and yet with my palm I touched the iron of a signpost, tiny in the distance. Now, this was not entirely comprehensible to me. I was, after all, small," etc. (B 59). The arms and the hand, that want to crush the head, touch the iron of a "signpost." Obviously, therefore, they are able, independently of the brain, to point to a road, to give direction, actually a very definite, certain direction; for the signpost is made of "iron"—in the midst of the world dissolving in smoke and clots. Therefore, things and bodies— detached from the human consciousness that is diminutive, damaged, limited, and no longer "round"—have a power of their own that indicates direction and determines the route.

Only thereby is the problem of the Kafkaian world of images and figures of speech revealed in its full depth. The "mute" things and bodies develop unsuspected possibilities beyond limited consciousness, beyond the endless reflectibility of man's imagination. They gain a power of their own and are able to lead him into realms that lie beyond the province of what is empirically comprehensible. Here an entire complex of new questions and riddles comes into view.

The most impenetrable mysteries of Kafkaian writing are not those of the paradoxical movements of conscious or unconscious ideation at the level of reflection; they are not in the endless thought and dream processes that are constantly crossing and contradicting one another, processes that are going on, say, in the strange chancelleries and in the confusion of the juridical courts with their officials who make records of everything. On the contrary, the actual riddles emerge as one is faced with the mute things and bodies that pervade Kafka's writing in dismaying abundance and that stubbornly resist every interpretation that would provide adequate meaning.

In this category, for example, are the two bounding celluloid balls in "Blumfield, and Elderly Bachelor"; the starlike spool of thread, "Odradek," that goes on two little rods in "The Family Man's Worry"; the flying bucket in "The Bucket Rider"; the ride on a branch (T 309-310); the sword in the back (T 457); the loaf of bread that cannot be cut and that contracts and shrinks (H 381-82); the rain in the room (H 355-56); the wild brier bush that suddenly shoots up in the midst of a well-cared-for park (H 430); the balustrade of the theater box that is transformed into a man and still remains a balustrade (H 311-312); the bridge in human form that stretches across a ravine (B 311-12); the little wall cabinet without any lock or key (H 290); the stairs that keep growing in number or that appear unexpectedly (B 136 ff., H 141); the doors that turn up in impossible places (H 233, 362, P 187); the forest that shrinks and expands (H 374); the strange buildings or caravansaries in which it is no longer possible to find the way (H 269-70, 272, 349, 297).

And inseparably connected with these is the entire complex of Kafka's animal transformations and animal stories. People turn into animals, or animals turn into people, as in the stories "The Metamorphosis," "A Report for an Academy," "The New Lawyer," and in the fragments in which, for example, a dapple-grey horse turns into a lady (H 407). There are also his pure animal stories, as for example "The Burrow," "Investigations of a Dog," "Josephine the Singer, or the Mouse Nation." Animals startlingly and unexpectedly break into the human world, as in "The Vulture," as with the two "unearthly horses" in "A Country Doctor," or "the gigantic mole" in the story "The Village Schoolteacher," or the jackals in "Jackals and Arabs." In ordinary, everyday rooms or buildings there appear not only enigmatic, unexpected objects, but also dragons, snakes, storks, squirrels, dogs, martens, gigantic horses, etc. (H 103, 142 ff., 242, 282, 332, 347, 362 ff., 397 ff., 407; T 375, 396 ff., 519, 525), and they make their appearance in a thoroughly incomprehensible or empirically impossible manner.

And there are also ghosts that enter the room, as in the story "Unhappiness," or in the fragment "The Tormentor" (H 145), or in the dramatic fragment "The Warden of the Tomb." Or wild horsemen, whose language is completely unintelligible and whose behavior is bestial, threaten city and country ("An Old Folio" [E 155 ff.]).

Only in the light of these curious phenomena does it grow quite clear that in Kafka we are indeed in a realm beyond allegory and symbol. For these strangely alien things and animals actually break away from individual, determinable, allegorical, and symbolical references. They do not represent in each case definitely distinguishable, empirical, spiritual levels in man, and levels of consciousness in him; but they enter into a completely different world, one that lies outside these levels. And they can be comprehended, therefore, only from the point of view of Kafka's "Universal" thema as it has been previously described. They could at best be considered as symbols of this Universal. But, since this Universal cannot be articulated conceptually, philosophically, psychologically, etc., and since, too, the immediate physical appearance of things and animals does not itself contain their general significance, the word "symbol" in this context loses its meaning. The very fact that these things or animals are arbitrarily interchangeable betrays this.

Kafka's writing compels us, therefore, to abandon the aesthetic categories that have been in use up to now, and we are compelled to inquire into the functions of his images exclusively as they occur within the framework of his own creative works.

### CHAPTER III

# The Strange Things and Animals, and Man's "Self"

The mysteriously poetic world of things and animals in Kafka was rendered accessible to us at the outset in the examination of his very earliest literary work, "Description of a Battle." In this work things broke out "in mutiny" against the domination of human thinking, willing, and feeling. Obviously, therefore, Kafka intends to conjure up in them a realm that is not accessible to man. However, this realm must nevertheless be somehow related to man. If that were not so, why would Kafka cling so stubbornly to his effort to represent such a realm? Is he searching in it for a "forgotten," lost sphere that could perhaps be more vital for man than is the world in which he lives and to which he is accustomed? Does it perhaps contain a significance that can liberate man and give him direction, a meaning to which that strange "signpost" referred us? The answer is to be sought first of all in our analysis of what is probably Kafka's most puzzling creation, the curious "Odradek" in the piece "The Family Man's Worry."

*The Enigmatic Figure, Odradek*

The text begins with a statement about the *word* "Odradek."

"Some say that the word 'Odradek' stems from Slavic, and on the basis of this they try to trace the form of the word. Others in turn are of the opinion that it stems from German and is merely influenced by Slavic. The uncertainty of the two explanations probably justifies one's concluding that neither is correct, particularly since no meaning for the word is to be found in either" (E 170). Thus, although this word Odradek gives the impression that it stems from two known human languages, not only is the derivation uncertain in both cases, but also no "meaning" for the word can be arrived at by means of these languages. Accordingly, therefore, this word is beyond language symbols, although it appears to have its origins in human forms of language.

Nevertheless, despite all the ironical and humorous aloofness with which Kafka here plays hide-and-seek with his readers, reference may be made to the fact that the word Odradek definitely allows of a meaningful linguistic interpretation. In Czech, and generally in West Slavic, there is the verb *odraditi*, "to counsel someone against something."[1] Etymologically this word comes from German: Czech *rad* = German *Rat*, "counsel, counselor." The Slavic "influence" accordingly applies to the prefix *od* (German *ab*, "off, away from") and to the suffix *-ek* that is the equivalent of a diminutive. But the first point of view is also justified, according to which the word is a pure Slavic formation, the "form" of which can be fully clarified through Slavic. In that case, Odradek would signify a small being that counsels someone against something, or that in general always counsels negatively. The corresponding form for Odradek in German, therefore, would be something like *Abrätchen*,* a parody by analogy of formations like: Privy Councilmanikin, councilmanikin of the district, councilmanikin of the town, councilmanikin of the court, of the board of education, the school board, the administration, etc. Odradek would be the nullification or the inversion of all these councillors, their deal-

---

*Tr. note: An approximate English equivalent of this hypothetical word is a "negatively advising councilmanikin."

ings, and the concerns of their office. He can merely "advise against" everything.

Possibly the sound of yet other words plays a role in Kafka's concept; for example, the Czech word *radost*, "joy," or the adjective *rad*, "obliging" (characterizing a person who is "glad to do something"); perhaps also the German word *Rad*, "wheel," which suggests itself in the light of the "starlike" form of this spool of thread, Odradek.

The analysis of the form Odradek itself, however, shows that such meanings may indeed be in sympathetic vibration, but the first is the central and determining meaning. And Kafka's rejection of the possibility of any interpretation of the meaning corresponds with the poetic meaning inherent in the figure of Odradek itself; for primarily it is doing just this: advising against everything—even, and particularly, against interpretations of meaning. What is more, it is specifically designated as a being that appears "meaningless": "The whole, to be sure, appears meaningless, but in its way self-contained" (B 171). The meaning of the poetic little being is the annihilation of every kind of limiting meaning; its meaning is primarily "advising against." Such is the masterly manner in which Kafka has both enciphered and deciphered his work; he has formulated his statements not only "mysteriously" but also quite "openly."

The description of Odradek confirms this interpretation in a surprising manner. Kafka continues at first: "Naturally no one would engage in such studies if there were not really a being called Odradek" (E 170). This "real" being that calls itself "Odradek" (E 171), "resembles, to begin with, a flat, starlike spool of thread" (E 170). Again, therefore, it appears at the outset as if it belonged to man's world of things, and specifically as if it were a part of a thing that is of service in man's practical work. "And actually, it seems to be covered with thread, too; to be sure, it was probably only old, broken off pieces of thread of the most various kinds and colors, knotted together or else tangled" (E 170-71). Thus, the state of the thread is that of decay, it is frayed and useless; it is broken off and old. What is more, it consists of the most varied pieces knotted together or in a tangle—that is, "the most varied" pieces come together here in a tangle that in part cannot be unraveled, not unlike the "word" Odradek which is likewise a mixture of various linguistic elements. The thread that actually serves in sewing together pieces of clothing that have been torn apart, is itself something pieced together and at the same time a tangle that cannot be unraveled. "However, it is not only a spool; from the center of the star there emerges a little cross-rod, and at right angles to it is joined another little cross-rod. With the help, on the one side, of this latter little rod, and one of the points of the star on the other side, the whole is able to stand upright, as if on two legs" (E 171).

Thus Odradek appertains not only to man's world of concrete things but also to the human frame. He "is able to stand upright, as if on two legs"; what is more, he is able to run and does so "with extraordinary nimbleness"; and he is able to speak and laugh, "but it is only a kind of laughter that one can produce without lungs. It sounds somewhat like the rustling of fallen leaves." Even this human form therefore represents, as it were, a decline and an extreme, final state. The form no longer lives and "breathes"; it speaks and laughs "without lungs." The parts of its body are rigid and lifeless, "like the wood that it appears to be" (E 172).

But even this conception of the final stage of a process of decay is not accurate.

One would be tempted to believe that this thing had formerly had some purposive form or other and that it was now merely broken. However, this does not seem to be the case; at least, there are no indications of it; nowhere are there any traces of extensions or additional parts, and there are no signs of any broken places that would point to something of this nature; the whole appears, to be sure, meaningless, but in its way complete in itself. (E 171)

In other words, this "real" being Odradek is not at all something just put together, but is a whole that is complete in itself, that can no longer be grasped by the mind, and is something that therefore "appears meaningless."

As a totality that is self-contained, it is beyond any humanly possible interpretation of what it means. That is, it represents an integrated whole consisting of the most contradictory elements, now no longer in the form of endless reflections and interminable life processes but in the form of a whole that is complete in itself, removed from any human interpretation of what it means. "No further details can be given, however, since Odradek is extraordinarily nimble and cannot be caught." He remains out of reach, but he represents a totality in itself, something that is rounded off and indivisible.

In vain I ask myself what will happen to him. Can he really die at all? Everything that dies has had a kind of goal, a kind of occupation beforehand, and has worn itself out in this, fretting and chafing ; but that is not the case with Odradek ... the idea of his probably outliving me too, is almost painful to me. (E 172)

Odradek, therefore, does not participate in the hectic rush of life and thought processes. Deathless, he is out of reach of everyone and everything; and, hence, he has an "indeterminate abode." And the "family man's worry," that disquieting feeling of the man who bears the burden of responsibility for his earthly house, rests in his recognizing in Odradek the limit of all earthly existence, in his realizing that no human interpretation can help him to get at this "self-contained whole" confronting him, and that it will outlive him (and herein lies the "idea that is painful" to him), so that now even his own human goals and purposes, in the pursuit of which he has worn himself out fretting and chafing, in retrospect must appear useless and meaningless.

In Odradek, therefore, one can actually gain sight of the Kafkaian conception of life from as extreme a point of view as possible. In the midst of what is mortal there is something immortal, something that is complete within itself for all purposes. It is both thing and non-thing, human and non-human. It talks and it evades any interpreting talk. It is pure "thing" and yet removed from all things and classifications of things. Universally it spans the separation between spirit and matter, between thinking and existence; it is the two in one. But only by crossing the boundaries of both, by passing beyond the sphere of the spirit and the sphere of matter, does it become existent and "real." By relinquishing both spheres it becomes a self-contained whole. It can therefore no longer be interpreted as representing either one to the other. Its reality is no longer a symbol of something spiritual that is sense-determined. And its speech is no longer an interpretation of what is real, no longer a determination of the laws and the coherent connections of existence. True, it remains earthly and preserves elements of language, elements of what is material and human. But it does away with their definitions and determinations. It is absolute freedom in the midst of existence; it can no longer "be caught," no longer be forced into any system of things or thought. To be sure, this freedom is possible only through the surrender of life, breathing, and every volitional intention that has a definite goal. This surrender gives Odradek the "appearance" of something that has died off, been cast away, of something old and useless. Only out of the "ruins" of existence does freedom awake; only in these ruins can one "outlive" (T 545).

And even Odradek's laughter rings out from this freedom, a laughter as from another world, a laughter as if from the "moon"; that is how Kafka once formulated it to Oskar Pollak in a very early letter, dated November 9, 1903. Only through such laughter, from a world-remote distance, can that strange atmospheric and stylistic phenomenon in Kafka be adequately defined—a phenomenon that has quite inappropriately received the designation of "humor."[2] Humor is acquiescing with resignation and with a smile to "the given" and to its uncrossable limits and its ineradicable contrasts. Odradek's laughter, however, rings out "without lungs"; it is the repudiation of everything; it is "amusement" at the "proof that it is impossible to live" (B 23). The distance is so great, the humorous contrasts have moved so far away that, as it were, they disappear. The "liberating" laughter on earth becomes the freedom of the laughter on the moon.[3] For even the boundaries between life and death have fallen away. He who laughs is beyond the humorous and the tragic; that is, laughter becomes uninterpretable. That is why one never knows in the case of Kafka's so-called humor whether one is to laugh or remain serious. Neither laughter nor gravity is entirely adequate for his creative style. For this so-called humor is exempt from all relations and therefore can no longer be designated as tragicomedy and the like; for example, in the sense that "behind" the humor tragedy is hiding; or that behind the tragic humor lies concealed; or that gravity and merriment "mingle."

*The Liberating Function
of Kafka's Parabolic World*

The configuration of Odradek made evident the fact that the traditional relations of object-significance, phenomenon-essence, sign-meaning, or particular-universal, are no longer applicable to it. A particular does not guarantee a determinable universal, as is the case in allegory. No longer is the universal immediately imparted in the particular, as is the case in symbol. The parabolic image, on the contrary, is itself already beyond the sphere of the particular, beyond the sphere of interpreting discourse. In the parabolic image the particular forfeits its very particularity, and is removed from all earthly determinable categories. Odradek is a being that no longer can be known by experience. And the Universal is no longer a basic idea that can interpret or that can be interpreted. On the contrary, the parable is an image of a Universal that is "unattainable," that cannot be captured, that is beyond the relation between object and significance, substance and spirit, sign and meaning. Even its plasticity is no longer pictorial in the empirical sense; its significance is no longer meaningfully "significant" but is "meaningless." What the poet has created lives, on the contrary, beyond and above all earthly phenomena and concepts that are intellectually comprehensible. Kafka himself grasped this peculiar structure of his images and "parables," and formulated it in his sketch "On Parables":

Many complain that again and again the words of the wise are merely parables, but useless in daily life—and we have only this alone. If the wise man says, "Cross over," he does not mean that one is to walk across to the other side—this is, after all, something that one could accomplish without further ado if the result were worth the walk; but the wise man means some kind of mythical Beyond, something that we do not know, that even he is unable to describe more specifically, and that cannot therefore help us here at all. Actually, all of these parables are merely saying that the incomprehensible is incomprehensible—and this we already knew. But what we wear ourselves out with, every day— that is another matter. Thereupon someone said, "Why do you resist? If you went along with the parables you would then yourselves have become parables, and in that way already free of the daily struggle." Another said, "I wager that that is a parable too." The first one said, "You have won." The second said, "But unfortunately only in the parable." The first one said, "No, in reality; in the parable you have lost." (B 96)

The parable refers to something that is beyond all comprehension, even beyond that of the creator of the parable himself; and it is therefore, like Odradek, "useless." But whoever could go along with the parable, whoever himself became a parable, would be "free," relieved of the "daily struggle." From the point of view of empirical "reality," this is itself merely a parable and, therefore, useless talk and imagining. But "in" the parable, seen from within its sphere, is really no longer *merely* a parable but more than that, an actual "liberation," a release from all unending earthly "struggles."

Thereby the liberating function of Kafka's parabolic world becomes clear. From the point of view of the empirical "real" human being, all of Kafka's writing is meaningless, absurd, useless, incomprehensible. It cannot "help" such a person; what is more, it cannot even enlighten him, but can only confuse or torment him. If, however, empirical man were to "go along with" this literature, take it not only as a parable, not only as "literature," but as *the* reality and truth of life, he would be "free." For this poetic world of parables takes a view that is beyond any bias imparted by things and thoughts. It has become "judge" of the adversaries battling with one another; it sees the world from the point of view of a being "outside our human race" (T 21).

Only when these literary works are comprehended not simply as "literature" and fiction, but as concrete representations of our *entire* human existence, do they have liberating significance. Only then does man himself become the master and "judge" of his own existence, of the totality of his earthly and spiritual existence.

From this point of view, however, even the parabolic world of Kafka can be adequately unraveled and interpreted.

## Childhood and Old Age:
## Existence Free of Purpose

The analysis of the structure of Odradek has established that this "real" being that leaps about freely and immortally is made up of elements of ordinary, everyday things and human languages. These elements have the character of remnants. Old, torn threads that have become useless, threads of the most varied kinds and colors, are pieced together, knotted together, chaotically tangled, and the spool, furthermore, is furnished with little rods that resemble wooden human legs. And yet the whole, surprisingly, "nowhere" shows "traces of extensions or additional parts or broken places," and is a completely self-contained, intact structure.

What does that mean? Manifestly this: when people and things are no longer governed by goals and purposeful volitional impulses, when they are callously rejected as useless junk, swept aside, disposed of like "fallen leaves," when they break off purposeful connections, it is then that they become free, become healed and whole; they are then rid of all domination by thought and wish; only then are they saved. And then, in a peculiar fashion, "old age" and "childhood" merge, since both are "useless"; for the one it is too late, for the other too early, to be within the clutches of existence, systematically calculating as it is. Odradek, consisting of "old" pieces, is at the same time treated and looked upon as a "child." "Of course, he is not asked any difficult questions, but he is treated—his very tininess tempts one to do that—like a child" (B 171).

A new stratum of meaning that extends through all Kafka's writing is clarified by this interrelationship. Even in his earliest work, "Description of a Battle," Kafka displayed a distinctly clear and close connection between the world of the child and this world that we have revealed, the world of the problematic nature of "things." When the rebellious "things" have taken their vengeance on man, when the rending asunder of brain and body takes place, when head and eyes become diminutively small, and legs and arms project into the boundless, with a hand pointing to an iron signpost, when the "proof" is produced "that it is impossible to live," and man can no longer "breathe" but suffocates either because of inner poisons or because of the mutinous "things," when the world sinks into chaos, there appears in the version given in Kafka's second fair copy (without doubt, therefore, more authentic than the version that Max Brod has published)[4] the following text:

I slept, and with my entire being I wandered into the first dream. In it I tossed about in such anguish and pain that the dream could not tolerate it, but it did not dare wake me either; for, after all, I was sleeping only because the world around me was at an end. And so I ran through the dream, which had ruptured in its depths, and I returned, as though rescued (having escaped from sleep and my dream), to the villages of my native land. (B 347)

Following upon that is the scene, "Children on the Highway," which Kafka published as the first piece in his *Reflection* (E 25 ff.). Rescue from chaos and from the end of the world is thus accomplished by a return to childhood. And this childhood, structurally, has the same characteristics as those of the "child" Odradek. These children roam about on the "highway," wrenched out of the solid world of adults; what is more, they are pressing forward out of time and space. "We made a hole through the evening with our heads. There was neither daytime

nor nighttime" (E 26). "Then birds took wing like sparks flying. I followed them with my eyes and saw them as they soared
all in the same breath, until I no longer believed that they were
soaring, but that I was falling" (E 25). And the scene ends
with the child's running off, away from the community of village
and parents with their overconcern for him, running off through
the woods over toward "the city in the south, about which it is
said in our village, 'There are people there, just think! who
don't sleep!' 'And why not?' 'Because they don't get tired.'
'And why not?' 'Because they are fools.' 'Don't fools get tired?'
'How could fools get tired!' "

Children and fools here become parabolic images of a world
that defies definition both with reference to orientation in time
and space, and with respect to the laws of life. They never grow
tired; they are "extraordinarily mobile and cannot be caught,"
as is the case with Odradek. They represent the only world that
promises "liberation." In their world things and thoughts are
liberated. Existence and imagining have become a perfect whole.

Numerous developments in other works might exemplify the
same point. Only a few may be referred to here.

The piece "Unhappiness," from the group *Reflection*, begins as follows:

When it had grown to be intolerable . . . and I was running along
the narrow rug in my room as if on a racetrack, and when,
frightened by the sight of the lighted street, I turned again, and
once more, gaining a new objective in the recesses of the room,
in the depths of the mirror, I screamed aloud, just to hear the
scream, to which there is no answer, and nothing takes away the
force of my screaming, so that my scream rises without anything
to offset it, and it cannot stop, even when it ceases to sound,
then out of the wall the door opened with such haste, because
haste was needed, and even the coach horses down below on the
pavement reared, exposing their throats like horses grown wild in
battle. In the guise of a little ghost, a child suddenly appeared
out of the completely dark corridor. (E 44-45)

The situation is the same as that in the "Description of a
Battle." The reflecting "I," pursued by ever new "objectives" . . .

"as if on a racetrack," is in conflict, torn between things (the sight of the lighted street) and self-examination (the mirror). This chase, the "extraordinary haste" in which the stout man and the praying man are involved in the "Description of a Battle," must be strictly differentiated from the purposeless mobility of Odradek, from the mobility of the children and of the fools who never sleep and never grow weary. The climax of the chase is reached when he can only "scream" without finding an "answer," and the scream rings out unendingly even when it "ceases to sound." The reflection has reached its conclusion; he can only scream and become silent without receiving an answer. At the same time, the physical world erupts, precisely as in the "Description of a Battle": the horses grow "wild" as in a "battle" and expose their throats; that is, they make themselves ready for destruction. At this moment rescue comes. A child appears in the form of a phantom, a ghost that hails from nowhere, and it calms him down. " 'Quiet, quiet,' said the child in an offhand way, 'everything is really all right' " (E 46). At the same time the child is a piece of himself; indeed, it is he himself: "Her nature is mine" (E 48).

In the novel *The Castle* something similar happens with the officials. In contrast to the fools who are never weary, the officials, working in wild haste, are "tired all the time" (S 340, 360) and sleepy. In them this restless weariness likewise mounts and works itself up into unending "screams," and, what is more, into the paradoxical combination of "silence" and screaming (S 157). And in their case, too, there ensues the sudden liberating change into a childlike state. The officials' "babble of voices ... sounded like the mirth of children getting ready for an outing"; that is, they are about to break away from firmly established patterns; "another time, like the upheaval at break of day in a chicken coop ... somewhere or other a gentleman was even imitating the crow of a rooster" (S 360).

The officials become like children and animals: that is, they by no means represent merely the endless reflectibility of consciousness; in them the synthesis of a "contradiction" is effected. Of Bürgel the official, it is stated:

He was a short, good-looking gentleman whose face showed a certain inconsistency in that his round cheeks and cheerful eyes were those of a child, but his high forehead, his pointed nose, his narrow mouth with lips that would scarcely close, and his chin so receding that it almost vanished—these were not at all childlike but betrayed superior reasoning ability. (S 339)

The synthesis of this contradiction in the case of the official Bürgel will have to be considered further on. Anticipating, let us now refer merely to the fact that in the case of the officials there is, analogously, a paradoxical synthesis of the inconsistencies in their mode of life. They live in a world

...where nobody was tired, or rather, where everyone was tired, always tired, but without its doing any damage to the work; indeed, it seemed on the contrary to promote the work. From that, one could conclude that this weariness, in its way, was entirely different from that of K. Their kind of weariness was probably the fatigue that occurred in the midst of happy work, something that from the outside looked like weariness but was actually indestructible tranquillity. (S 360)

Thus, in these officials one seems to catch sight of a liberating reconciliation. Subsequent analysis of *The Castle* will show that this reconciliation, however, is bought at the price of separating off a part of the individual "self." The officials, insofar as they appear in "office" and not as "private individuals," represent the cosmic world order, the general, "official" laws of life and manifestations of life in the created physical universe. This cosmic order is in restless, continuous motion, always at "work." But this motion is simultaneously one that is at all times oscillating within itself; it is a motion that never grows "weary"; thus, in this sense, it is "indestructible tranquillity ... in the midst of happy work." Only in this way can the apparent reconciliation and synthesis of mutually exclusive opposites be explained. The decisive antithesis, however, in Kafka's world-image—the "battle" between the absolute demand of the individual free "self," on the one hand, and life's manifestations, fulfilled and effected, eternally revolving within themselves, on the other—is not resolved in the case of these officials. It is acted out as a "battle" between K. and the officials; in part also, it is presented as an analytical exposition of the officials themselves, of their "official" function and of their "private" one. However, even in the officials it becomes evident that in the "childlike state," as Kafka presents it, the antinomies are always either surmounted or separated from the whole. The conflict that is decisive for Kafka, however, becomes evident through his enigmatic "things" or "animals."

### The Totality "behind" Thinking

The analysis of Odradek led to the insight that a universal existence that is free of purpose can arise only from the ruined site of work, and that, in such an existence, age and childhood, decline and youth become one. Even in the "Description of a Battle" mention is made of the "essential walls of a house burnt out within [within man]."

There is scarcely any obstruction now to one's view. In the daytime, through the large window holes one sees the clouds of the heavens, and at night, the stars.... How would it be if ... I told you in confidence that some day all people who want to live will look like me—cut out of yellow tissue paper, so silhouettelike. (B 48)

Even in 1920 Kafka formulated this in his diary in a similar manner: "A segmentlike piece is cut out of the back of his head. With the sunlight the whole world looks inside. This makes him nervous, it distracts him from his work; also, he is annoyed that he of all people should be excluded from the spectacle" (T 541). The meaning of these sentences is clear: the Universal, "the whole world," looks inside man; he ought to succeed, as it were, in leaping behind his thinking, in rising above himself and his thinking. As long as he is still devoted to his "work," which is *in front of* him, he is excluded from the spectacle. The Universal behind him disturbs him at his work. On the other hand, he would very much like to enjoy the "entire" spectacle. Work and universality cannot yet be combined. Only if he were to look at himself from behind, see himself as a ruin, look through his thinking, only then could the heavens and the stars reveal themselves to him; what is more, he could see through himself. However, since he may not renounce his "work," both universality and undisturbed work remain withheld from him.

### The World of Work and the Things Free of Purpose: Blumfeld's Two Balls: On the Problem of Ergocentric Interpretation

With this the key has been found to an interpretation of "Blumfeld, an Elderly Bachelor," the enigmatic story in which two celluloid balls constantly bounce along behind the bachelor while he is in his lonely room. During the day this bachelor is fanatically devoted to the work in his office. But even there he is constantly disturbed by his two assistants, "pale, weak children" (B 166) who are useless and good-for-nothing, only up to mischief, and just as foolish and worthless as the old servant who is supposed to sweep the office in the mornings.

But even though the little lad is impervious to any rational consideration, at least the servant, this half-blind old man, whom the head of the firm would certainly not tolerate in any department but Blumfeld's, and who is still alive only by the grace of God and of the head of the firm, surely at least this servant could be obliging and for just a moment relinquish the broom to the young lad, who is certainly clumsy and who will immediately lose all interest in sweeping and run after the old servant with the broom in order to induce him to take on the sweeping again. (B 170)

Blumfeld would like best of all to throw out the two childish helpers and the blind old man from his place of employment. But they live by the incomprehensible grace of God and of the

head of the firm—someone who has no appreciation of Blumfeld's work and, what is more, seriously "underrates" it, to
Blumfeld's great distress, "in an obvious manner" (B 162).
However, it would be impossible to convince Mr. Blumfeld
on logical grounds that such children and old men have the right
to live, and it would be impossible to convince him of the
limitations of his own work-world; the private world of his
imaginations can no longer make him conscious of his limitations. That would be possible only if Blumfeld *himself* were
thrown out of his firmly established empirical and professional
world.

This happens on an evening when Blumfeld, returning to his
bachelor's room from the "gigantic amount of work that has
been imposed upon him" (B 162), is overwhelmed by a feeling
of bleak forlornness and loneliness. Only now does the meaninglessness of his own existence become clear to him; only
now does he feel the desire to have some kind of living creature near him, even if it be just a little dog. But even this
thought is banished, for dogs cause unpleasantness, inconve-
nience, and dirt. Preoccupied with such thoughts, he enters his
room and suddenly sees, to his astonishment, the incomprehensible "magic" of the two bouncing celluloid balls that, constantly following him "from behind," are "reporting to him for
duty" (B 146). But they are as meaningless, as disturbing,
and as useless as his two assistants in the office of the lingerie
factory. Consequently he intends, on the following morning, to
hand the two balls over to an "ugly" child who will surely enjoy
playing with such useless toys and who would be able to liberate
him from these balls. At the same time, however, these balls
affect him with deeper "concerns" (B 157). He dimly senses that
they are "something that is part of him . . . that somehow had to
be involved also in any judgment of him as a person"; indeed,
he dimly feels that it is "a matter of their accompanying Blumfeld through life" (B 157-58). Only when he goes to work again
does he manage to shake off such "concern." It is here a matter
of the same concern that the "family man" felt with respect
to Odradek: the sudden, painful presentiment that there is

basically, coordinate with his own limited and mortal existence, yet another sphere that he has forgotten or missed, and that that alone would make his life "whole." For the concept of indestructible totality emerges again in the case of these playthings, too. Despite all the force that Blumfeld uses, they cannot break, and they remain "whole" in a mysterious fashion (B 145, 150). Moreover, they obey "mechanically the law that governs them" (B 148); they are on the "alert" and always in motion.

Hence it would be a mistake to assume these two balls to be symbols for the two helpers—an interpretation that might readily suggest itself. It is true, of course, that there is some mysterious connection between the balls and the helpers. But such a breakthrough on the empirical-psychological level could in no way be justified artistically if it were to serve merely the purpose of making it clear that Blumfeld really ought to gain a greater spiritual understanding of his helpers. Psychological-empirical phenomena must be presented in a psychological-empirical way, possibly in the sense of a spiritual development in Blumfeld, from his being a hard-boiled work-fanatic to his becoming a child-loving man. But that is not the issue involved here at all. It is a matter of producing a sphere that is beyond all empiricism and psychology,[5] a sphere that is as mute and impervious as the two balls, a sphere that cannot be reached by any sentiment of adults who are "fond of children."

At the same time, in this regard one should consider the following. By contrast with Odradek, the two balls are pure things that "obey mechanically the law that governs them." They are, therefore, not free. Also, they do not represent any synthesis of man and thing; they cannot talk, as does Odradek. Only as Blumfeld's dueling opponents, or as "servants" and "companions in life" are they existent at all. It grows clear from this that it would be erroneous and disastrous in the highest degree to shift Kafka's images and figures mechanically to the same levels each time. The images, figures, characters always have different functions, according to the context of the particular work in which they appear. To be sure, their function cannot be disclosed—and this is just as important for methodical analysis—without knowledge of the *complete* works of Kafka. A so-called pure "ergocentric interpretation" that restricts itself to the framework of the Blumfeld story *alone*, is faced with the following dilemma. It will have to endeavor to determine the function and meaning of the two enigmatic balls. Necessarily, in so doing, it will come up against connections with Blumfeld's two assistants. The two balls that annoy the bachelor Blumfeld then appear, say, as symbolic representatives of Blumfeld's feeling of guilt toward the two assistants, a feeling of guilt that arises from his subconscious and that he vainly tries to repress. But that is just the kind of interpretation that would deny this tale artistic quality, since one cannot see why the two assistants should be replaced symbolically by two celluloid balls that bounce about pointlessly—balls that, moreover, cannot have their origin in Blumfeld's subconscious, since, in that case, images that were much more differentiated and much more illuminating psychologically would have had to be chosen. Within the framework of this story, taken by itself, the two balls can appear only as foolish, abstruse, artistically unsuccessful products of Kafka's fantasy. That is to say, only when the total problematic nature of Kafka's world of things and people becomes perspicuous will the artistic necessity and the general meaning of this piece of literature be revealed.

The passage, for example, where the balls "obey mechanically the law that governs them," cannot be understood at all if one does not know the significance of the law in Kafka—for what is the meaning of a "law" in the case of "magic" that breaks through all laws? Where, in any part of the story, is it at all possible, through an interpretation that is entirely ergocentric, for such a law to be disclosed and made understandable? Only if one is in close contact with everything that Kafka wrote can the meaning become lucid; for the conventional opinion that every work of art is autonomous, and hence needs no explanation by means of other works, is of course justified, but only with the qualification that the interpreter whose interpretation is "ergocentric" must himself first be at home in the specific world of expression characteristic of that work of art before he dare interpret it. Kafka's parabolic world has its distinctive character. In it the images function differently from the way in which they function in older literature. As little as a traditional interpreter of Goethe's "symbolic" figurative world is able to appreciate aesthetically the "allegorical" literature of the baroque period or that of the late Middle Ages —for he is geared to depreciate this kind of art—just as little is it possible for a modern critic who has not worked himself into the specific structure of Kafka's figurative language (on the basis of a knowledge of its make-up) to appraise the artistry of Kafka's world of imagery. The ergocentric interpretation becomes meaningful only when, for example, the much-favored custom of interpreting images as an expression of psychical states is discarded. If one puts oneself into the interior of Kafka's world of images, the work will then suddenly begin to live of its own accord; it will no longer need any explanation from the poet's other works. However, first of all, the new fundamental principles of his writing must be clarified.

Germane to these fundamental principles is the phenomenon of the Universal to which his images are keyed. However, Kafka's conception of the "law" is inseparably bound up with it. Therefore, let us first try to understand the association of assistants-balls-law from the point of view of Kafka's *The Castle*, since in the novel the connections become clear. In *The Castle* K., like Blumfeld, is accompanied by two useless, childish assistants who are constantly running "behind" him, who "disturb" him at his work, and who are subject to a law that governs them; that is, they are subject to the "office" that commands them to serve K. As long as they are performing their official duty—that is, as long as they are under the constraint of the universal Personnel Registry Office of the officials, they cannot and may not define their own significance; they are, as it were, as "mechanical" and silent as the two balls. To be sure, they do talk, but it is incomprehensible, childish stuff that K. does not understand. Only when K. dismisses them with a sound thrashing, driving them away from him in this way, are they no longer on "duty," and they can therefore enlighten him about their function and about the "orders" that they received from the authorities: to "cheer" K. at work, with jokes, jests, laughter, teasing—K., "who takes everything so seriously" (S 309). When K., amazed, asks Jeremiah, the assistant, "By the way, why didn't you talk so openly as this right away, when you first came to me?" Jeremiah replies, "Because I was on duty; that's obvious" (S 310).

As long as the assistants serve K. in the name of the ruling life powers, they do not stand before K. as free beings, and they cannot and may not interpret their own role. K. himself has the task of recognizing their meaning, their significance and function for him and for his existence, and to react and act accordingly. But he cannot, any more than Blumfeld, stand behind himself or rise above himself, and he cannot rise above seeking and searching or above his work in which he "takes everything too seriously." He cannot step out of his own limited perspectives into that realm where thought and child-like nature become universally one. The assistants were sent him by the Office to make him aware of the counterweight, the diametrically opposite pole. He is to recognize and accept them as "companions in life." In this he is as little successful as Blumfeld who, like K., furiously rejects the balls and the assistants.

In *The Castle*, by contrast with the Blumfeld story, there is no longer any need of a thing-image, because in the novel the superempirical Universal exists already in a parable of enormous scope, in the form of a castle bureaucracy that is incomprehensible to K. In the Blumfeld story, however, it is a matter of a limited empirical world that must have the awareness of its limitation blasted into it, as it were, for shock purposes, in the form of something that is empirically inconceivable; that is, in the form of absurd "things." When K. enters the village in darkness and mist, he is already outside of every limited empirical order. "Nobody comes. It's as if the world had forgotten us," remark the inhabitants of the village (S 421). And K. himself asks, "What is this village in which I've lost my way? Is there really a castle here?" (S 10). From the first, K. is confronted with the Universal in village and castle; hence, from the very beginning, he moves within a world that is inconceivable to him, one in which even chronological and spatial orders fluctuate (S 29). Not until Blumfeld has his shocklike encounter with the two incomprehensible balls does he come into conflict with another sphere that intersects the accustomed order of things. Strictly speaking, however, the encounter is the same in both cases: Blumfeld is confronted with childish, useless balls; K., with a castle that "disappointed him as he drew closer to it," for

the paint had long since peeled off, and the stone seemed to be crumbling away. With a fleeting thought, K. recalled his little home town. It was scarcely inferior to this so-called castle.... The tower up above here...was a uniform cylinder...the battlements of which—precarious, irregular, cracked in places—notched the blue sky, as if sketched by the hand of an anxious or slovenly child. It was as if a melancholy inmate of a house, who by rights should have been kept locked up in the most secluded room of the house, had burst through the roof and risen up to exhibit himself to the world. (S 18)

Thus, the entire castle is cracked in places, dilapidated, old, and at the same time childlike, sketched by a child's unsteady hand. It does not fit in K.'s normal ideational world and is disappointing to him. Furthermore, the castle is both lifeless and free:

The castle, the outlines of which were already beginning to melt away, stood quiet as always. Never yet had K. seen the slightest sign of life there.... When K. looked at the castle, it seemed to him at times as if he were observing someone peacefully sitting there and gazing before him, not, as one might suppose, lost in thought and guarding himself in this way against everything, but free and unconcerned. (S 134)

Thus, in this description of the castle, once again there emerge almost all the elements that we encountered in the figure of Odradek: brokenness, decay, old age, childlike nature, uselessness, lifelessness, freedom, being self-composed and self-contained. Evidently, therefore, extending through Kafka's total works there is a homogeneous stratum of images that, so far as meaning is concerned, are definitely related. These images represent a sphere that is not accessible and that is free of purpose, a sphere that is removed from plan-making consciousness, and even from "life" itself. The images, therefore, do not reflect any psychological states symbolically, but designate the peripheral zones of human existence. This makes it clear why Kafka is no longer bound to deal with the tension between Blumfeld and his two helpers psychologically, but, as it were, must do so absolutely. The issue is not that Blumfeld gain understanding of his assistants, but that he cross over the boundary of his world and accept that which is purely and simply "other"; this alone could make him a true human being, although the other sphere takes the form of what is apparently parahuman. The balls that "disturb" him are his true "companions in life." The disturbances caused him by his childish companions crystallize in the form of parahuman things free of purpose; at the same time, their indefatigable "bouncing" represents the eternal motion of the universal powers of existence. *For that reason* they are subject to a "law," the universal law to which Blumfeld himself is subject, without his knowing it. For that reason, too, they are at the same time "whole" and "indestructible" things. The "Totality" and the "Indestructibility" of existence become visible to them. Hence, although they represent a sphere that is free of purpose, within this sphere they are themselves "mechanical" (B 148), subject to the "law that governs them," and indeed are even Blumfeld's "subordinate attendants" who have "reported to him for duty" (B 146)—exactly like K.'s two assistants in *The Castle*, for they represent universally general law, and hence cannot be free.

Blumfeld alone, the individual human being, is charged with the task of enduring and resolving the conflict between their universal sphere and his own limited world of consciousness and work. For the issue here is this very conflict. As soon as Blumfeld turns to his "work," the balls lose significance for him; as soon as he returns from work to his private sphere, the balls come into view again. When "the thoughts about his work gradually" gain "the upper hand over everything else" in him (B 161), he forgets the balls. Outside of work, however, the balls are inseparably connected with his "person." As he goes to work he is still reflecting: "It is strange how little the balls have concerned him since his separation from them. As long as they were behind him, at his heels, they could be considered as something that was a part of him, that somehow had to be involved in any judgment of him as a person" (B 157). He must use force to separate them "from him" when he goes to work, for they are in fact a part of the essence of his "person." He can be a human person only if he absorbs the totality of his existence. It is the same conflict that Josef K. must endure, the conflict between "work" and universal judgment.

Only from such points of view can we understand and appreciate the artistic necessity of Kafka's world of imagery. The balls are poetic indications of something universal. However, since they represent something universal they cannot and may not be interpreted within the story. In fact, what they represent is precisely the uninterpretable and inaccessible. And the reader of such tales is himself shifted, as it were, into the role of the heroes of these stories. The "incomprehensibility" of these balls must strike him as inconceivable "magic," must strike him with the same sense of shock that Blumfeld experienced. Only then does the story fulfill its artistic intention. An ergocentric interpretation of the balls would not only destroy the work of art in itself but would also miss the point that in all art there remains "manifest mystery," that art can lend shape to its manifestations only mysteriously and indirectly, and that only through such manifestations does art assert its stature and truth.

## The Liberating Role of Things

Numerous parallels in other works help to complete the picture. Again and again Kafka has sharply confronted the purposeful work-world with spheres of existence that are purpose-free. In the novel *The Trial* Josef K., the bank procurist,* who is "always in the continuum of his work" (P 31), must on Sundays climb up to attics "where tenant families who themselves already belonged to the poorest of the poor were accustomed to throw out their useless odds and ends" (P 76). And these decayed, collapsing attics with breaks and holes in the ceilings are reached only by one's going through backyards in which hordes of children rove about, or through kitchens, "where one young woman with gleaming black eyes . . . happened to be washing baby clothes in a tub" (P 51).

Other examples that speak for themselves signify the universal "battle" that is always the issue for Kafka.

It sometimes happens (often one has scarcely any inkling of the reasons for this) that the greatest bullfighter chooses for his scene of action the ruined arena belonging to a little town, situated off the beaten track. Up until then the Madrid public had barely known the name of this town. An arena neglected for centuries —here with grass growing exuberantly, a children's playground ; there, burning hot with bare rocks, a retreat for snakes and lizards. Above, the upper edge of the arena long since demolished, a veritable quarry for all the houses round about—nothing left but a small bowl that will hold scarcely five hundred people. No adjoining buildings, above all no stables ; but, worst of all, the railroad has not yet been constructed this far. (H 67)

"But you have never heard of this staircase," I told myself by way of excuse, "and in the newspapers and in books everything, no matter what or where, is constantly being picked to pieces. Moreover, there was nothing about this staircase in them. . . . And now the very thing you need is what escaped you. . . ." At that point I believed I could remember once having read something about a similar staircase, possibly in a children's book. (H 141)

The desire to find a "staircase" that leads one out beyond

---

*Tr. note: The German *Prokurist* has no exact equivalent in English. The term is used to designate an employee, usually of fairly high rank, who is empowered to sign on behalf of his firm.

everything that is "given," occurs elsewhere in Kafka, for example in the piece "Advocates":

If then you find nothing here in the corridors, open the doors; if you find nothing behind these doors, there are other floors; if you find nothing up above, never fear; swing yourself up onto fresh stairs. As long as you do not stop climbing, the steps will not stop; beneath your climbing feet the stairs will keep on growing upwards. (B 138)

The victory over this world that determines and enslaves everything can be gained only as one divests oneself of the world, piece by piece; not, however, in the sense of resignation but in the sense of progressing upward.

The battle can be waged only with "toy rifles" that can themselves still be broken to pieces. Only liberation from everything leads to the freedom above everything.

In our building, this monstrous building in the suburbs, an apartment house veined with indestructible portions of medieval ruins, today, on this foggy, icy, winter morning, the following notice was circulated: "To all my fellow tenants: I own five toy rifles. They are hanging in my cupboard, one on each hook. The first belongs to me. Whoever wants to can apply for the others. If more than four apply, those over and above four must bring their own rifles and deposit them in my cupboard. For there must be unity; without unity we won't make any headway. Moreover, I have only rifles that are completely useless for any other purpose: the mechanism is spoiled; the corks are torn off; only the hammers still click. It will, therefore, be difficult to procure other rifles like these in case the need arises. But basically, at the outset, even people without rifles will be satisfactory, so far as I am concerned. At the crucial moment those of us who have rifles will take those who are unarmed and put them in the middle, a mode of fighting that among the early American farmers proved effective against the Indians—why should it not prove effective here also, since the circumstances, after all, are similar? Thus, the rifles can even be dispensed with for good, and even the five rifles are not absolutely necessary; but since they are already at hand, they might as well be made use of. If the other four tenants, however, do not want to carry them, they need not bother. Then I alone, as leader, shall carry one. But we ought not to have any leader, and, therefore, I shall break my rifle to bits, too, or put it away."

That was the first notice. In our building people have no time and no desire to read notices, let alone reflect upon them. Within a short time, the little pieces of paper were floating in the stream of dirt that starts in the attic, is fed by all the corridors, is flushed down the stairs, and there battles with the counterstream that surges up from below. After a week, however, a second notice appeared: "Fellow tenants! As yet, no one has reported to me in answer to my appeal. Except when I was away having to earn my living, I have been at home all the time, and during my absence the door to my room was always open, and on my table was a piece of paper on which anyone who wanted to could list his name. Nobody has done that." (H 60-62)

Kafka's "battle"—as in the case of the bullfighter, as here, and as everywhere in his works—is thus Janus-faced. It is indeed true that all earthly "weapons," all available means, all possibilities of thought and existence, must be utilized in order to make it possible to survey land, to obtain ground and breathable air in the battle with savages, the "Indians"; that is to say, in the battle with the menacing universal forces that burst forth unchecked, destroying all human boundaries (cf. the analogous battle against the wild peoples of the North in the "Construction of the Great Wall of China"). However, it is in this very battle that all earthly weapons prove to be useless, unserviceable, absurd. Yet the useless, rusty "toy rifles" are still the most useful weapons in such a battle. For only where existence appears to be completely purposeless, where life is completely snuffed out, where breathing no longer takes place by means of the lungs (Odradek), can one "survive." Only what is useless, what has died off, is "succor" in such a battle. For one is prompted to smash even that too, and to win the battle without any help. Hence, in Kafka, the absurd things turn into liberating means of help, or even into carriers that bear man forth out of his masked and masking existence, and that can themselves be abandoned or relinquished. Even in as early a work as the "Description of a Battle" there is the statement:

"We make engines of war, towers, walls, silk draperies that are actually of no use, and we might be very much astonished about this if we had time to be. And we maintain ourselves in suspension; we do not fall—we flutter about, uglier than bats though we are" (B 58).

The meaning of the seemingly absurd things that, as in a book of children's fairy tales, burst astoundingly into the empirical world, is the liberation of man from the "obstacles" that are put in his way by the world and by his own ideas.

Today, in a dream, I invented a new means of transportation for a steeply sloping park. One takes a branch that need not be very thick, presses it against the ground at a slant, keeping one end in one's hand, and sits down on it, as if riding sidesaddle, as lightly as possible ; naturally the whole branch will then race down the slope, and since one is seated on the branch, one is pleasantly carried along at full speed upon the springy wood. There will then turn out to be some way of utilizing the branch for traveling uphill too. Apart from the simplicity of the whole device, the chief advantage lies in the fact that the branch, being thin and supple, can be lowered and raised according to need, and it can get through everywhere, even where it would be difficult for a person to get through alone. (T 309-310)

The ride on the bucket in the story "The Bucket Rider" is to be understood analogously. "The coal, all used up; the bucket, empty; the shovel, meaningless (B 120). . . . My bucket is already so empty that I can ride on it (B 121). . . . My bucket has all the merits of a good mount; it does not have the power of resistance—it is too light" (B 122). And so his bucket carries him forth out of the world, "never to be seen again," into the regions of the glacial mountain ranges beyond the reach of human sight, where all life is extinguished. But this distance and lifelessness are not annihilation. "The Bucket Rider" was published by Kafka in the *Prager Presse* in a shortened form only. In the original manuscript the following sentences are a continuation of the published portion:

Is it warmer here [in the regions of the glacial mountain ranges] than down below on the wintry earth? Round about, everything looms white ; only my bucket is dark. High aloft though I was before, I am now far down below ; I crane my neck, looking up to the mountains. A sheet of ice, frozen white, here and there cut through by the tracks of vanished skaters. Over the deep snow that does not sink so much as an inch beneath my weight, I follow the footprints of the small arctic dogs. My riding has lost its meaning. I have dismounted and am carrying the bucket upon my shoulder. (H 55)

The meaning is clear. The earth had denied him the coal that would warm him. The bucket had borne him off, forth from the earth, up into the free realm that in Kafka is always expressed by the image of fierce, icy coldness, as our subsequent remarks on "A Country Doctor," *The Castle,* etc., will show. But this cold seems "warmer" to him than the earth. Perhaps it contains a more genuine possibility of existence than that which the earth can offer. Everything reverses itself. The liberating bucket is now "the only thing that is dark." The rider now has to carry his mount himself, for now everything is thrust upon him alone. The very "succor" of the empty, liberating things becomes a burden to him now. And he is no longer "high aloft" but "down below." He must see to conquering the "mountains" of this frozen waste and to finding a way through them. This way can be obtained only through knowledge, through full "clarity of vision," for

Only straight ahead, O hungry beast, does the path lead to food that you can eat, air that you can breathe, life that is free, even though that be beyond life. O great, tall commander, it is you who lead the masses ; lead those who are desperate through the mountain passes that you alone can discover beneath the snow. And who will give you the strength? He who gives you your clarity of vision. (T 572)

## The Healing Role of Things

Inanimate things, however, have yet another meaning. They are pure "Being" and hence represent that "indivisible truth"

that can never be reached by "perception," that separates things
into parts and is therefore always subject to falsehood (H 99).
For this reason, too, Odradek is a "self-contained whole" without breaks and without parts. And hence, too, Kafka has repeatedly described the process through which man himself,
becoming fully one with things, enters into this kind of complete and true Being that is indivisible. The most grandiose
portrayal of this is in "Prometheus" where, in terse sentences,
Kafka's entire view of life is presented.

Four myths tell of Prometheus. According to the first, he was
chained fast on Mount Caucasus because he had betrayed the
gods to men, and the gods sent eagles who fed on his constantly
regenerated liver. According to the second, Prometheus, agonized
by the eagles' piercing beaks, pressed himself further and further into the very rock itself until he became one with it. According to the third, his betrayal was forgotten in the course of the
millenia: the gods forgot it; the eagles forgot it; even he himself
forgot it. According to the fourth, everyone grew weary of what
had come about without reason. The gods grew weary; the eagles
grew weary; the wound healed wearily. There did remain the inexplicable rocky mountain range—the myth attempts to explain
the inexplicable. Since the myth stems from a foundation of truth,
it must conclude again in the inexplicable. (H 100)

The "wound" that in Kafka is again and again inflicted on
man who is searching for a sound "foundation" and who hence
betrays the secret of the gods to men, so that he must be
punished because of this offense [cf. the diaries of 1910 (T 20),
and, among others, the story of "A Country Doctor" (T 20)]
—this wound heals wearily as Prometheus becomes "one" with
the rocky mountain range, as he enters into the foundation of
truth. In a sketch, the parts of which are scattered, Kafka
writes similarly about Poseidon who is unceasingly computing
everything: "Poseidon grew disgustedly weary of his oceans.
His trident fell from his hands. Quietly he sat on a rocky coast,
and a seagull, dazed by his presence, flew about his head in
faltering circles" (H 128). Or else, conversely, man's inability
to penetrate into the sound, nourishing foundation of truth is

described, for example, in the image of the loaf of bread that no knife can cut, since it represents an impenetrably indivisible totality (H 381).

## The Lethal Role of Things

And finally, there are scenes in Kafka in which the disparity between man and thing leads to a fatal catastrophe. In the story "The Bridge" (B 111-12) a human body rigidifies to act as a bridge that "overhung an abyss," an abyss that is situated at an inaccessible, "trackless height." This human being wants to bridge opposites. However, he remains human not only in his external form and clothing but also in his nature as well. "My thoughts were always in a state of confusion and always spinning in circles." When at last the long-yearned-for wanderer, who is to entrust himself to the bridge, appears, the bridge turns out to be incapable of supporting him; and the reason for this is that this bridge constantly engrossed in thinking, now wants to *see*, to discern *who* this wanderer actually is that it has to carry across.

And I turned round to look at him—the idea of a bridge turning round! But before I had turned round completely I found myself plunging down, down, down, and there I was already torn to pieces and pierced through by the sharp-pointed flintstones that had always looked up at me so intently and peacefully from the swirling water.

Thinking man, by virtue of his thinking, can, if need be, still endure the antinomies of existence in the form of a bridge spanning the abyss; but the very moment he so much as makes the attempt to gain universal perspective (i.e., to "turn round," to reverse his existence, to set himself as it were above himself), he is impaled upon the things that until then had lain so "peaceful" beneath the "swirling" waters. In the conflict between the poisons within him and the rebellious things, man perishes "in the very search" (B 59).

That is the meaning of Kafka's visions of destruction and of death. Universality can be gained only by one's surrendering that human form of existence in which "thoughts" are "always spinning in circles." Only when man becomes open to that "peaceful" and "indestructible" form of existence that is in "Being" itself, is he himself able to be supported and to support; only then is the antinomy really resolved; only then do rest and restlessness, being and thinking, become one.

We are confronted with analogous problems in those of Kafka's works that deal with animals.

## The Animal as Liberating "Self"

### A. MODERN ALIENATION AND ITS "LAW"

It is in the early story "Wedding Preparations in the Country," from the period 1906-1907, that the process of alienation still taking place in the working and metropolitan society of today is, to begin with, reflected upon. The hero, Eduard Raban (cover name for Kafka), is standing on the street of a metropolis with the intention of going to the railroad station. It is raining. A lady on the opposite side of the street "now looked at him. She did it casually, and, besides, perhaps she was merely watching the rain coming down in front of him" (H 8). In the second version, it is said of this lady, "Without intending to, she seemed strange to all the passers-by, as if because of a law" (H 33).

By "law," the young Kafka hence understood nothing other than the force of collectively anonymous, unknown occurrences, hidden from the will and the "intention" of the individual —occurrences which alienate people from one another. This force is represented here by "one's work," by an existence in the "office," an existence that splits man off into two spheres: an official one and a private one. This point of view emerges unequivocally from Raban's immediately following trains of thought:

"Well, then," he reasoned, "if I could tell it to her, she wouldn't be at all surprised. One overworks at the office to such an extent that one is too tired even to enjoy one's vacation properly. But for all the work one does, one still doesn't gain any right to be treated with loving kindness by everyone; on the contrary, one is alone, a perfect stranger to everyone, and merely an object of curiosity. And as long as you say *one* instead of *I*, it's of no consequence, and the story can be recited, but as soon as you admit to yourself that it is you yourself, then you are actually pierced to the quick and are horror-stricken." (H 8)

Heidegger's later concept of the impersonal "one" is already apparent here. But Kafka's later transfer of the "law" to the "office" of the officials of the court and of the castle becomes evident even in this early work. The strangeness of these officials with respect to K., who wants to defend his "self" against them, rests in the fact that these officials are subject to a law of which they themselves are unaware, a law that compels them to behave indifferently toward the "I" of the "personal" existence and, what is more, even to guard themselves against this personal existence, since it would "practically disrupt" the official organization (S 354). They exert an inescapable constraint, since, indeed, *everything* is enacted amidst laws that are valid on a superindividual-collective level—*everything,* even the seemingly private emotions of love that obey universal biological and psychological laws, even the intellectual trains of thought that likewise are subject to the general conditions of physiological reflexes and to the general postulates of logic.

As Raban now grows conscious of this cleavage between the impersonal "one" and the "I," and as he inquires into this "self," he feels himself "actually pierced to the quick and [is] horror-stricken." For what else is there upon which his "I" can be grounded, since he must sacrifice everything to the "office," since everything is subject to it? It is thus by no means the case that Kafka first gave form to this predominance of official existence in *The Trial* or in *The Castle.* Even in this early work, Raban feels all the events of life as "strange," anonymously collective forces that make him shudder with dread, events that take place meaninglessly and mechanically, that are incomprehensible and alien to him, that he can participate in only with utter loathing; the climax of the hideously grotesque element of the story is reached when this loathing is directed at, of all things, his own "wedding preparations," at his journey to his bride in the country.

## B. THE "BEETLE" RABAN

From this extreme tension existing between an impersonal "one" that dominates everything and an unfathomable "I" that sees itself "pierced to the quick" there now develops the following train of thought, one that leads to the focal point of of the peculiar animal transformations in Kafka's works.

"And, what is more, can't I do what I always did in dangerous undertakings as a child? I don't even need to go to the country myself; that isn't necessary. I'll send my fully clothed body. If it goes out the door of the room falteringly, this faltering is not a sign of fear but a sign of its nothingness. Furthermore, it is not excitement that causes my body to stumble on the stairs when it travels to the country, sobbing, eating its evening meal there in tears. For I, I shall meanwhile be lying in my bed, smoothly covered with my yellowish-brown quilt, getting the breeze that blows through the room from the slightly open door. The coaches and people on the street ride and walk hesitantly over the smooth, bare ground, for I am still dreaming. The coachmen and the people walking are shy and, looking at me, they ask my permission before each step they are about to take. I encourage them, and they do not encounter any obstacle. Lying in bed, I have the form of a large beetle, a stag-beetle or a cockchafer, I believe.... Yes, the large form of a beetle. I would carry on then as if it were a matter of my hibernating—and I press my little legs against my bulging body. And I murmur a small number of words—those are instructions to my sorrowing body that is standing quite near me, leaning low over me. Before long I am through —my body bows, flits away, and will accomplish everything to best advantage while I rest." (H 11-12)

In this way, by abandoning its human existence and becoming an animal, the "self" gains superiority over bodies and things. This prehuman animal form of existence (that had already been near and dear to him while he was still a "child," as a means of rescue in the face of "dangerous undertakings") gains such superiority, however, only because it occurs while he is in a "dream" state, in "hibernation." It is then removed from all human reflections and efforts; it "rests," and in such a state of dreamy sleep it can control and direct bodies, people, even life on the street outside, and, indeed, in such a way that the people on the street no longer "encounter any obstacle." It is, therefore, no longer a question of any kind of rational control, but of an unconsciously free and weightless disposition that causes all obstacles to disappear as if of their own accord. What is hereby achieved is freedom from the domination of the impersonal "one" that makes plans, freedom from the domination of the "office," from that of the "dangerous undertakings." An analogous scene occurs in the novel *The Castle*: "K. slept ... irksome consciousness had disappeared; he felt himself free.... And it seemed to him as if with this he had gained a great victory.... In his sleep K. harried a secretary.... Was it really a combat at all? There was no serious obstacle" (S 348).

To be sure, this is only a "dreamed of" borderland possibility. In *The Castle* it does not actually lead to a real victory but, on the contrary, to K's defeat; oversleeping, he fails to utilize a most important opportunity offered him by Bürgel during this dream, because of this very sleep. True victory lies not in the elimination of consciousness but in the union of free, unconscious existence and conscious existence that arranges and plans.

Hence, in "Wedding Preparations," too, this dreamy possibility is represented merely as a passing reflection of Raban's, and is in turn abandoned. Raban has to carry his journey through in a thoroughly concrete manner. He cannot leave his self in bed in a dreamy, animal form and send only his empty body to the country. He remains a human being in unresolvable tension.

However, for Kafka this free, animal form of existence has always been a fundamental means of expressing the antinomies of human existence. Animals do not yet live in a state of consciousness that delimits, objectifies, and thereby hypostatizes everything. An animal still finds itself in the "great instinctive feeling of freedom in all directions" (E 188)—no different from the children in "Children on the Highway." For Kafka, animal existence is therefore a thoroughly positive sphere that is still present in the interior of man, even if only as a memory of the emotional world and the psychological level of the child. It appears primarily in man's "dreams," in that state in which rational consciousness is excluded. The conflict between animal existence and the rational world of work, therefore, determines many of Kafka's animal stories.

## The Beetle in the Story "The Metamorphosis"

In this story the metamorphosis takes place, likewise, in a dream. But everything proceeds in reverse from the way in which it occurs in Raban's metamorphic vision. For Gregor Samsa, the hero of "The Metamorphosis," does not at all desire such a transformation into an animal; on the contrary, it happens to him suddenly—a frighteningly incomprehensible and strange occurrence. He is far from identifying his ego with a beetle, as is the case with Raban. It is true that he too, precisely like Raban, is in a state of unresolved conflict between work and ego. But Samsa does not thoroughly reflect upon this conflict with the same consistency as Raban. Samsa vacillates between the two spheres. On the one hand he is ruled by the rational, plan-making considerations related to his work: he wants to get up and carry his business trip through. " 'Just not stay in bed uselessly,' Gregor said to himself" (E 76). On the other hand, however, he curses his work, "the irritations of business," the "plaguing torment of traveling" (E 72),

and he ponders, "What if I sleep on a bit and forget all this
foolishness?" (E 71). This "foolishness" refers to his metamorphosis in to the beetle—transformation that inwardly he
in no way accepts (by contrast with Raban), but actually wants
"to forget" in his sleep. Samsa can look upon the dream metamorphosis only as a negative phenomenon that disturbs his daily
work routine. The beetle acquires frightful characteristics; it
becomes a "monstrous verminous insect" that is of no help to
him but merely hampers him. "When Gregor Samsa awoke
from troubled dreams one morning, he found himself in his
bed, transformed into a monstrous verminous insect. . . . 'What
has happened to me?' he thought. It was no dream" (E 71).
Samsa, thus, by contrast with Raban and his vision, is in a
waking state. The transformation that had taken place in his
dream—characteristically in "troubled" dreams—suddenly overtakes Samsa upon his waking, as an incomprehensible occurrence that has "happened to him," something that he, accordingly, did not want, let alone, like Raban, long to have happen.
He shakes it off as "foolishness," and reflects for a long time
and in detail upon his strenuous career, upon his relationship
to the head of his firm; and he considers whether he can now
still catch the seven o'clock train (E 73). It does not enter his
mind at all that he could perhaps be hindered in his business
trip by his transformation. At the outset this consideration is
beyond the scope of his imagination. For him the metamorphosis is nonexistent. He remains rooted in the realm of the
impersonal "one." The "self" is a burdensome verminous insect,
a monstrous creature of a nightmare that *cannot* be reality.

Nevertheless, immediately after Samsa awakes, the meaning
of his "troubled dreams" and thereby, too, the meaning of the
dream metamorphosis becomes obvious in his very reflections.
Samsa complains of his "strenuous work," of the "irritations
of business," the "worries about making train connections, the
irregular meals and bad food," the "constantly changing human
associations that never last and never grow cordial and warm.
To the devil with it all" (E 72). Thus he feels the estrangement,
the missing "cordial and warm" associations with people, ex-

actly like Raban. What is more, he ponders on the idea that he would like most of all to "have given notice long ago." Only his concern for his parents, who have to pay back a large debt they owe the head of his firm, has prevented him until now from telling his employer his

real opinion of him with absolute honesty. He would fall right off his desk chair! ... Well, I haven't given up hope entirely yet. Once I get the money together to pay off what my parents owe him—that will probably take five to six more years—I'll do it without fail. Then I'll make the final break. But for the time being, of course, I have to get up, because my train leaves at five. (E 73)

There can be no doubt that this conflict, between his occupation and his desire to make the final break and become self-reliant and independent, was the cause of his "troubled dreams." Since the pressure of the moral obligation of his occupation prevails in this conflict, and since the fulfillment of his desire to become a "self" of his own is put off for five to six years, this desire *must* of necessity be felt as disturbing and as running counter to his work. The possibilities that offer themselves in the "dream" of simply having the "self" remain in bed and freely and independently direct all the goings-on outside in the world, without being pounded to bits in the hustle and bustle of business—the possibility of this as it occurs to Raban is not one that Samsa can accept. Hence he wards it off. But to ward something off is not to overcome it. The self remains where it is. Man can never quite become the impersonal "one." And the meaning of this terrible "metamorphosis" rests in the very fact that this "irremovable" self, the self that is "not to be got rid of," this reality of the ego that struggles against the impersonal "one," suddenly invades Samsa's concrete daily reality, too, in a shocklike manner, and cannot be simply driven away as an apparition and as a dream fabrication. The seemingly fantastic unreality of this "vermin" is that which is actually supreme reality from which no one can escape.

The boldness of this work of Kafka's lies in the resolute consistency with which it lifts the conflict out of the psychologically internal-emotional plane; on this plane it had been dealt with by other poets for centuries—as, for example, in the case of Wilhelm Meister's conflict between a business career and his "mission." Whereas in older literature the conflict takes place in man's inner, contemplative nature in the form of a clash between feelings and the demands of the world, in Kafka man's contemplative inner nature is alienated from itself. It is true that Samsa feels the conflict in himself and reflects on it, just like any normal person, but at the same time Kafka lifts these feelings and reflections out of their frame of reference and points the conflict up to the absolute antinomy between the impersonal "one" and the "self," in the course of which the two realms can no longer be reached and articulated by reflection and feeling; and the reasons for this are to be found in the history of the period.

What is new in Kafka's creative writing and view of the problem is his realization that the "law" of man's alienation remains hidden from modern man, just as in the case of that lady who appears strange "without intending to, as if because of a law." Man has become the slave of the unknown law of the impersonal "one" to such an extent that he does not even know about his own self or his inner life any longer at all; he represses it and cloaks it again and again by means of calculations. Samsa, it is true, feels extremely uncomfortable in his business life; he senses the conflict through and through, but he believes, in turn, that he can get the better of it by means of mere computations of a business nature. He calculates that when he has saved the amount of money he needs for his parents, he can then at last make the "final break" and take the leap, and get away from his business firm. But he has no idea at all of where he will actually leap, of what potential forms of existence he would like to actualize. His own inner being remains alien to him. It is for this reason, therefore, that Kafka gives it a form that is quite alien to him, the form of a verminous creature that threatens his rational existence in an incomprehensible manner. That is the meaning of the peculiar fact that Kafka, again and again, represents man's own inner

being—indeed his "actually" innermost being—either in the
form of strange objects and animals that frighteningly break
into life, or else in the form of absurd court authorities that
demand that man give account of his own self, preventing him,
likewise, from carrying out his work at the bank—and indeed,
ultimately completely ruining his professional career (*The Trial*).
One need but compare the first scene of "The Metamorphosis"
with the first scene of *The Trial* to perceive the astounding
analogy. In *The Trial,* too, the "surprise" attack upon Josef K.
by the authorities takes place immediately upon his waking in
bed after oversleeping (like Samsa) as a result of failing, in his
heavy slumber, to hear the alarm clock. Thereby, in an illuminating manner, these court authorities "gravitate toward"
Josef K.'s own "guilt" (P 15), of which he is ignorant, and
must "arrest" him; in the same manner, in the literal sense
Gregor Samsa is taken into custody by his monster and "im-
prisoned"—Gregor speaks of his "imprisonment" (E 101). And
Josef K., too, wants to shake off the entire trial by immediately
entering the world of his profession.

I was taken unawares; that's what it was. If I had ... got up ...
immediately after waking ..., if I had acted sensibly ..., everything would have been nipped in the bud. But one is so little
prepared. At the bank, for example, I am prepared for things; it
would be impossible for something of this sort to happen to me
there; I have my own attendant who serves me there; the outside
telephone and the interoffice telephone are on my desk in front
of me; there are always people, associates and officials coming
in and out; but apart from that, and above all, at the bank I am
always in the continuum of work, and hence I always have my
wits about me. (P 31)

The work-world of the impersonal "one" here, too, is meant
to cover up the alien self that, in the form of a monstrous,
gruesome court of justice, bursts in upon Josef K., just like the
horrible insect into which Samsa sees himself suddenly transformed. For this court—as our subsequent analysis will show—
mirrors the total inner imaginative world not only of Josef K.
but of all other human beings. Since the self is not the "inner

being" that is understood and that is "one's own," it must assume the form of something that is external and strange; but it must be in the form of something strange that breaks through the laws of the external, empirically-rational everyday world. This is the completely clear and artistically legitimate consequence ensuing from the modern alienating and reifying process. Kafka does not create "surrealist" phenomena but, on the contrary, creates our reality with utter artistic truth.

Furthermore, since Samsa does not accept his dream world, his subconsciously free, instinctively animal-like existence, exempt from the compulsion of calculation, is perverted in him into a "verminous insect," by contrast with Raban's dream beetle that operates "quietly," that indeed exerts a quieting and liberating influence, originating as it does in childhood's fairy-like imaginings, where animals are wont to assist the child in "dangerous undertakings" and "rescue" him, as is the case in Grimm's fairy tales where animals, "clearing away" all "obstacles," help young princes or simpletons to come through their dangerous ordeals and adventures successfully. Furthermore, in folk fairy tales, children or lovers, by instantly transforming themselves into animals or things, can rescue themselves when they are pursued by witches or evil magicians.

In their original form, Kafka's animal figures possess this affirmatively rescuing significance. They represent the subliminal dreamlike world, the state of man *before* he thinks, that part of him that is prehuman and early human, a part that is always present along with everything else within his soul. However, since modern "business" is very much more dangerous, and since man himself puts himself at the mercy of business, he disowns even his own helpers and obstructs his own "deliverance."

The most gruesome aspect of Samsa's fate is not his metamorphosis but the blindness with which everybody treats this metamorphosis. Samsa will not admit it. "I shall get dressed right away, pack up my sample case, and depart" (E 88). His parents and his sister do not understand it. The self is what is absolutely alien, void, and nonexistent, not only in the world of business but also in the world of the family. To be sure, his mother and sister love him dearly. In a touching manner they try at first to improve his condition, to surmount their feelings at the sight of this vermin, to take care of him, to protect him, to see to the comforts of life for him, to preserve or once again evoke what for them was human and lovable in him. But the terrible truth of this short story is the realization that even the "most beautiful," most tender relations among people are founded on illusions. No one knows or suspects what he himself "is," and what the other person "is." Gregor Samsa's parents, for instance, never had any inkling of his conflict, of the "sacrifice" that he was making for their sake: "His parents did not understand all that very well; in the course of many years they had convinced themselves that Gregor was provided for in this business for the rest of his life" (E 89). They had never dreamed that there was trouble brewing within Gregor, that something had been "out of order" long before the eruption of this inner sickness in the form of the metamorphosis. They did not know that the essential in man can actually be concealed, distorted, and destroyed if he is provided with no more than the "necessaries of life." Now that the distortion assumes visible features, they are at a loss and feel their son to be a "foreign body."

By the same token, however, Gregor had also been mistaken in his relations with his family.

"What a quiet life the family led after all," Gregor told himself, and as he stared straight ahead into the darkness he felt a great sense of pride at having been able to provide his parents and his sister with such a life in a beautiful apartment. But what if all the peace, all the prosperity, all the contentment should now come to a terrible end? (E 95)

He believed he had to provide his family with a pleasant, contented, secure life by sacrificing himself, by selling himself to his business. The reciprocal relationships are based upon secret calculations and compromises, the consequences of which are no longer even suspected by anyone. The semblance of an orderly system and of a "contented" world is created. However, in

Gregor's troubled dreams this semblance is torn asunder, and out of the ensuing rent truth arises in the shape of the monstrous verminous insect. Through his "sacrifice" Gregor had distorted his own self. The immolated animal now becomes visible in a merciless distortion.

The deception goes still further. In reality Gregor's parents did not need the sacrifice at all. His father possessed more money than Gregor knew about. His father, too, was able to work and was by no means so ill as it had appeared. Even Gregor was deceived. His sacrifice was meaningless. The family's whole happiness and contentment were founded on deception and covert calculation. The business world invaded even one's private life. Everything rested on "possessions" and "assets," not on "being" (cf. H 42-43). The entire idyll of the family was a lie; nowhere was there "truth." The more money Gregor had given his family, the cooler the relationship between them had grown: "They had simply got used to it, not only the family, but Gregor as well. They accepted the money gratefully; he was glad to hand it over to them—but no longer was there any special warmth in consequence" (E 102). Only now, in Gregor's deformation, does the immolated animal become visible, but that is the very reason why it must be driven away. The monster must disappear, "the stuff from the adjoining room has to be got rid of" (E 141), for only through falsehood can the world continue to survive. Gregor himself must demand this. "He recalled his family to memory with deep emotion and love. His conviction about the necessity of his disappearing was more resolute, if possible, than that of his sister" (E 136). When Gregor "kicks the bucket," the idyllic lie continues unchecked in an intensified form. "Three jobs" are in store for them, and a marriageable daughter "stretched her young body." The "terrible end" overtook only Gregor, and it came upon him for the very reason that he wanted to provide for his family.

However, his metamorphosis into an animal has a positive meaning, too. When the beetle Gregor hears his sister playing the violin, there is this decisive statement: "Was he an animal, since music moved him so? It seemed to him as if the way to the unknown nourishment he had been longing for were becoming manifest to him" (E 130). Here is where the meaning of this transformation into an animal first becomes clear. The matter at issue is the "unknown nourishment" that does not exist on earth. As an animal he is at the same time more than an animal. His alienation had the purpose of awakening in him the "longing" for this "nourishment." For Kafka, music had always been a way of sweeping man beyond all earthly limits. In as early a work as the "Investigations of a Dog" it is a matter of combining the science of music with that of dietetics, of enticing down from above, with the help of music, that nourishment that does not originate on earth, and of developing a "doctrine of singing that summons down nourishment from above" (B 289). And this doctrine is to end in an "ultimate science that made freedom valued above all else" (B 290). The final intent of Gregor's metamorphosis into a beetle is the escape into freedom, that longing for man's "unknown nourishment."

The animal, or rather the monster of this "metamorphosis," thus designates a sphere that can never be expressed, and, what is more, that cannot even be seen. For not one of the people involved actually sees the animal. In spite of all the realism in the description of this animal, the animal itself can never be understood, and a visual image of it can never be gained. It is beyond all power of human comprehension by empirical means, precisely as it is in the case of "things" in Kafka; for example, the spool of thread, Odradek, etc. It would be meaningless to interpret Samsa the beetle, as a real beetle. Kafka himself formulated this unequivocally. When the publishing firm of Kurt Wolf planned to put out "The Metamorphosis" and had Otto-mar Starke prepare an illustration for it, Kafka wrote to the publisher on October 25, 1915, saying, "It has ... occurred to me that he [O. Starke] might want to draw the insect itself. Not that, please, not that! I do not wish to restrict his scope, but I wish only to request it as a result of my better understanding of the story, as is natural. The insect itself cannot be drawn. It cannot be drawn even as if seen from a distance."

Gregor's hypostatized dream is at the same time more than a

dream, for even dream figures could, if need be, still be copied. It is the mystery that everything talks about and that is nevertheless ineffable. In a "parable," however, such a mystery is unveiled. Truth becomes manifest: " ... you would yourselves have become parables" (B 96). Samsa's "metamorphosis" is the entrance of his self into the parable. Only there does his self become "real" only there does it demolish the falsehood of the human world.

What, then, is the beetle Samsa? It is obviously something that is felt to be unbearable, alien, and frightening by *everyone,* including even Gregor Samsa. For even he, to begin with, does not identify with this beetle. Although he becomes subject to it and has no choice but to assume a beetle's mode of life, he is, at first, caught in the thoughts, ideas, and emotions of his former life, and he feels it painful to be no longer able to make himself understood. To be sure, existing as a beetle thrusts him out of everything that he is used to and makes him alien and frightening to everyone. But his attachment to the world around him is not thereby diminished, not even by the fact that his family's actual financial circumstances, hitherto kept hidden from him, are now made manifest. He would like to return to his old life, but is prevented from doing so by the incomprehensible force of his beetle-existence. Hence, even his sister, who has loved him very much and has taken care of him, finally says with justice, "He has to be removed; that is the only way, Father. You must simply try to rid yourself of the thought that it is Gregor" (E 134).

However, as his longing for music and for the unknown nourishment has already shown, Gregor finally does nevertheless free himself from his enslavement by the empirical world. His death is not merely a meaningless annihilation, but a liberating realization. Gregor says, "Yes," to his own death. He dies reconciled with himself and with the world.

He recalled his family to memory with deep emotion and love. His conviction about the necessity of his disappearing was, if anything, more resolute than that of his sister. In this state of blank and peaceful meditation he remained until the tower clock struck the third hour of the morning. He lived to see daybreak brightening everywhere outside his window. (E 136)

Nowhere within the substance of the tale, of course, is any mention of this realization made; nowhere, likewise, is there any intimation of the nature of the "unknown nourishment" referred to—whether what is meant is spiritual, religious, psychological, or even purely physical. Since we have hitherto—in conjunction with Raban's formulation that he "himself" remained at home as a beetle and sent merely his clothed body to the country—spoken of the fact that Samsa's masked "self," a self that is hidden from him, appears in his troubled dreams as a beetle, some clarification is needed.

It is no longer possible to understand this "self" psychologically as the soul, as a determinable, spiritual neutrality that can be explained in terms of the realm of feelings, wishes, hopes, dreams, strivings, etc.; somewhat in the sense, perhaps, that in the conflict with his business occupation there arise against the world of work and the world of family a series of "inner" emotions, ideals, and goals which now represent, as it were, Samsa's "actual" self that until now had been suppressed. That is out of the question. Besides, in that case, it would be altogether impossible to understand how such an inner life could assume—of all forms—the form of a disgusting verminous insect. Even in the view developed by us—that, unlike the Raban vision, it is a matter of a perversion of the self, since this self is suppressed or opposed by Samsa and must therefore assume negative characteristics—such a psychological interpretation is not possible. For, in that event, Samsa inwardly would have to come to terms with his suppressed self. This self would have to develop content and meaning that would have appeal for him, force him to adopt a point of view, and "transform" him inwardly, in either a positive or a negative sense. But no statement whatsoever is made with respect to such psychic changes and transformations. The "metamorphosis" does not take place as a transformation of spirit, mind, or character. This is what is unprecedented and incomprehensible in this story, and what distinguishes it from all former literature dealing with man's heart and mind.

Accordingly, the thesis that the beetle-animal represents the dreamlike unconscious, animal and prehuman, sphere of instinct in man must be decidedly limited or modified. To be sure, this animal is born as it were in a dream; for "when Gregor Samsa awoke from troubled dreams one morning, he found himself in his bed transformed into a monstrous verminous insect." The metamorphosis, thus, had already taken place before his waking, while he was still in the state of sleeping and dreaming. The dream—that is, the state of being freed of the pressure of diurnal consciousness—is, it is true, the prerequisite for the metamorphosis. But nothing passes over from the dream world into the metamorphosed state. Samsa's beetle-existence by no means shows any of the neutrality present in dreams; it shows nothing of a free, instinctively certain immediacy of feeling, of reacting, of experiencing—not even in the sense of its perversion in the form of anxiety dreams or in the form of immediate reactions that, perhaps threateningly, cut across rational diurnal conceptions. For in the very midst of his beetle-existence, he is still swayed by his diurnal conceptions.

Such obvious and understandable interpretations all miss fire. The beetle is, and remains, something "alien" that cannot be made to fit into the human ideational world. That alone is its meaning. It is "The Other," "The Incomprehensible," pure and simple, beyond the reach of any feeling or imagining. "It cannot be drawn even as if seen from a distance," not only in the sense of pictorial art, but also in the sense of imitative interpretation. It is interpretable only as that which is uninterpretable.

And only as such does it contain truth. For whatever "stems from a foundation of truth, must conclude again in the inexplicable" (H 100). Truth and the self are identical. The "self" is the inexplicable, pure and simple. It is beyond all our conceptions of the self. The beetle embodies a world beyond our conscious as well as our unconscious imagination. The animal, although it is nothing but man "himself," is the absolute disaffirmation of the so-called "human" world. The cleavage between the world in which Samsa lives and Samsa's beetlehood is the cleavage between "imagining" and "being." Since for Kafka the world beyond "imagining" is in man himself, since there is no "beyond" exterior to man, the "image," the "parable" of this beyond is necessarily an earthly image that is unearthly and that at the same time cannot be "drawn." The paradoxy of these circumstances is the reason why Kafka represents such a beyond in the form of things or animals that incomprehensibly break into everyday existence, causing bewilderment and fright, or abolishing all "obstacles." The perverting of Raban's beetle to Samsa's verminous insect is merely the inversion of the angle of vision.

Raban saw the world from the vantage point of the motionlessly tranquil self and of the foundation of truth. To him the world was bound to appear perverted, intolerable, and disgusting; he was seized with horror at the mere thought of exposing himself to it. Samsa, on the contrary, wishes to remain in the world. For him and for his environment, therefore, the tranquil self must appear as a terrible monster that tears him out of his beloved surroundings. *Both* positions are defensible. Only both together constitute human life. Kafka criticizes and affirms both. It would be mistaken to insist upon interpreting Kafka only through Raban's hermitry, or interpreting him only through Samsa's concern about family and career. Both cross one another in Kafka, just as the names of both, Raban and Samsa, are cover names for his own name (J 26, T 297). Only when both beetle-visions are interpreted can the full meaning be revealed.

### The Ape in the Story "A Report for an Academy"

In the story "A Report for an Academy," an ape "at liberty" (E 184), who had possessed the "great feeling of freedom in all directions" (E 188), is wounded through the "wanton shot" (E 186) of a human being and captured. Since he is "for the first time without a way of escape," and can "not live without" a way of escape, he "stops being an ape" (E 187-88) and takes on human existence. Through the utmost efforts, he succeeds in overcoming his apehood and in becoming a human being. However, this becoming a human being is a "development urged on by the whip," a development which requires the sacrifice of his freedom. The gateway of his life "grew ever lower and narrower; I felt myself more at ease and more included in the world of men" (E 184).

At the same time, as a human being he cannot make his former "freedom" or, what is more, "truth," understandable, let alone "achieve" it. For it is something "that despite my best intention I cannot express" (E 185). Only the "drift" can still be intimated. "But even though I can no longer achieve the old ape-truth, at least it is present in the drift of my description" (E 188).

No matter how comfortable and "included" he feels himself in his human existence, a breeze from afar blows cool on his heel and reminds him, as it reminds everyone, of his former freedom and truth. "Your apehood, Gentlemen," thus he reports to the academy, "insofar as you have something of this sort in your past, cannot be more remote from you than my apehood is from me. But it tickles the heel of everyone who walks on earth here, the little chimpanzee as well as the great Achilles" (E 185). The regaining of freedom would, like the arrow that once struck Achilles in the heel, cost man his life. In Kafka, moreover, the image of cool or cold air always signifies this kind of ominous freedom that robs man of his life; whereas stifling heat, by the same token, expresses the superior strength of life under bondage; this is the case in the novels *The Trial* and *The Castle*.

Furthermore, the "wound" is the basic stigma of the ape who has become a human being. He shows it in a free-and-easy manner to everyone, for "if it is a matter of truth, any high-minded person will dispense with the very best manners" (E 186). The wound is the metaphor for the condition of man who, though he lives, lives only in a disabled state in a hybrid world that represents neither complete freedom nor complete bondage. Having been locked up by human beings in a cage that had "no

way of escape," the ape, it is true, broke his way out into the
human world, but this newly acquired human freedom is no
genuine freedom: "Incidentally, among human beings one de-
ceives oneself all too often so far as freedom is concerned. And
just as the feeling of freedom ranks among the most sublime of
emotions, the corresponding delusion ranks also among the most
sublime" (E 188). And thus even this ape, who has become a
human being, lives on in a questionable, hybrid existence. "If
I survey my development and its goal up to the present time, I
neither complain, nor am satisfied." During the day he remains
human in the hustle and bustle of successful vaudeville performances. At night he sleeps with a female chimpanzee "and in the
manner of apes I enjoy myself. During the day I do not want to
see her; in her look, you know, is the madness of the bewildered trained animal, and I cannot endure it" (E 195-96).
The chimpanzee that has remained an ape lives the madness and
bewilderment of the trained animal. The ape that has become a
human being lives with a wound and with a painful memory of
his lost freedom.

In the "Report to an Academy" Kafka has described not the
metamorphosis of a human being into an animal but the reverse
process. He concludes with a resignation that is in harsh contrast to the ideology of progress. On the one hand, of course,
becoming a human being is a gain: "These strides forward! This
penetration of the rays of knowledge from all quarters into my
awakening brain!" (E 195). On the other hand, however, it is
a loss:

I, a free ape, submitted to this yoke.... Although at first the
return [to animal existence] ... through the gateway that the whole
sky forms over the earth was left up to me—as I developed, urged
on by the whip, that gateway became constantly lower and narrower ... and the opening in the distance ... became so small that
I ... would have had to scrape the skin off my body in order to
get through. (E 184-85)

That means, therefore, that the gateway to animal existence is
the universe. In the world of man it shrivels up to become an

opening that one can get through only with loss of life. But through this opening the current of air is blowing that tickles the heel not only of an Achilles, but indeed of "everyone." Thus, again, the animal is the symbol of universal freedom.

## *"A Country Doctor"*

The "unearthly horses" (E 153) in the story "A Country Doctor" have a similar function. The horses bolt out "through the crumbling door of the pigsty that had not been used for years" (E 146); that is, like all of Kafka's "unearthly" forces, things, and animals—emerging from the world of the useless, the crumbling, the cast-off, the decayed, the devoid-of-purpose, indeed the base and the filthy—they enter into the human world, and this takes place at the very moment when the country doctor is summoned to someone "dangerously ill," who is suffering from an invisible "wound" and wishes to die (E 148). With his normal medical vision, with his customary medical methods, the country doctor is unable to detect any wound. "What I was certain of has been confirmed: the boy is well . . . best to push him out of bed with one shove" (E 149). Not until the unearthly horses neigh does he discern the wound. "Oh, now both horses are neighing; the noise, ordered by the powers that be, is meant to facilitate the examination, I suppose" (E 150). Only through such orders "from the powers that be . . . do I discover that the boy is indeed ill."

Here it is not a question of a physical wound, therefore, but it is the human being's life wound, a wound that Kafka once defined in his diary in the following manner: "Symbol of the wound . . . the depth of which . . . signifies its justification" (T 529). As always in Kafka, it is a question of the justification of the whole of human existence.

Thereby it grows clear just what is meant by the "mistaken ringing of the night bell" that causes this country doctor to be wrenched from the whole orderly routine of his customary existence. In the light of his ordinary daily medical routine and duties, it was mistaken ringing, for it is not at all a case of someone's being physically ill. On the contrary, the doctor is torn from his sleep in the middle of the night by the ringing of the powers that be, a ringing that imposes upon him the duty of healing a wound that affects the total existence of man, wherein the question of the justification of human life is posed. It is the same situation that Gregor Samsa in "The Metamorphosis" and Josef K. in *The Trial* are caught in when they wake from sleep, having failed to hear the normal ringing of the alarm clock. Josef K., too, is drawn by the "powers that be," by means of an unknown tribunal, to offer justification for his life. The country doctor, too, like Josef K. and Gregor Samsa, struggles against undertaking this task.

Always demanding the impossible of the doctor. They have lost their old faith ; the parson stays at home and pulls his vestments to pieces, one after the other ; but the doctor is supposed to do everything... Very well then, as you please, I have not volunteered my services. If you are going to wear me out with tasks that are rightly the province of religion, that too I will let you do to me. (E 151)

In this way the doctor is forced against his will, in an era that has become lacking in faith, to take over the duty of the priest: to heal and save the human soul. " 'Will you save me?' the boy whispers, sobbing" (E 151). But the boy realizes that this doctor cannot heal him, since the doctor is suffering from the same wound and from the same directionlessness. The doctor is himself a "patient" and is therefore put into the patient's bed. "You too have just been dropped off somewhere; you have not come on your own. Instead of helping me, you are crowding me on my deathbed" (E 152), the sick boy says in his ear. There is some limited hope only if the doctor, in a state of complete "undress," is made to lie down with the sick boy. "Strip his clothes off; then he will cure us. And if he doesn't cure us, then kill him! It's only a doctor, it's only a doctor." Not until all earthly safety measures are abandoned does man gain a certain superiority; only then might he be able to effect a cure.

"Then I am stripped of my clothes ... I am absolutely calm, and superior to all of them, and remain that way, too, although that is of no help to me, for they now take hold of me by my head and feet and carry me to bed" (E 152). And this superiority of the physician finds expression in his being able to explain to the sick boy the deeper significance, the "distinguishing characteristic" of his wound. "Your wound is not so bad. . . . Many a one proffers his side and scarcely hears the axe in the forest, much less that it is coming closer to him" (E 152). On the basis of his rich experience in "all the sick-rooms far and wide" the doctor, by contrast with the boy, possesses "perspective" and imparts to the patient the comforting feeling that the very fact of his having such a wound differentiates him from people who go on living from day to day in unawareness, and that receiving and enduring this wound consequently confers a higher dignity upon his life. This disclosure of the meaning of his suffering reassures the patient: "And he accepted it and grew tranquil" (E 152-53).

It is true, of course, that such reassurance by no means entails a complete cure. The boy probably dies of this wound: "I have located your great wound; you will perish of this 'blossom' in your side" (E 151). Characteristically, this wound is located on the right side, "in the coxal region," precisely where the wound of the ape in the "Report to an Academy" is located—"below the hip" (E 186), a clear reference to the wound that Jacob receives in his wrestling with God. No human being can cure this wound. Hence the children's song, "Rejoice, ye patients, the doctor has been put in bed beside you!" is justifiably designated as "the new, but mistaken song" (E 153). It is a matter of the illusion of modern times to the effect that man can rescue man. It is the same illusion to which Josef K. succumbs when he constantly seeks "help" from advisers, lawyers, women, other defendants, etc. Of necessity, everyone stands alone here, just as the portal to the law [*The Trial*] is meant for one man only, the man from

the country. "If helping me were the task set," says the
Hunter Gracchus,

"every door of every house, every window would remain closed;
everyone lies in his bed, the covers pulled over his head—the
entire earth a lodging for the night. That makes good sense, for
no one knows of me, and if anyone knew of me he would not
know of my whereabouts, and if he knew of my whereabouts he
would not know how to keep me there and would not know how
to help me. The thought of wanting to help me is a disease and
has to be cured in bed." (B 104)

Indeed, the country doctor cannot help even himself: "I
am ... superior to all of them ... although that is of no help
to me." For he, of course, in contrast to the dying boy who
experiences a certain liberation and comfort in death, must
continue to exist on earth. But that has now become impossible, ever since, as swift as lightning, he was torn from his
customary life by the "unearthly horses." True, he thinks of
"escape," he wants to go back to his house. But this is the very
thing that is his undoing: the wish to escape prevents escape.
The disease of wanting to help can be cured only in bed. For
"all human failings are impatience.... Because of impatience
they [human beings] were banished from Paradise ... because
of impatience they do not return" (H 39). "But now it was
time to think of my escape," says the doctor after the patient
has grown quiet; and he quickly gathers his resources—horses,
clothes, fur coat, satchel. But his resources and aids turn into
enemies. The unearthly horses, that once in "an instant" drew
him as swift as lightning to the patient, now trot "slowly"
through the snowy wasteland "like old men." His clothes no
longer cover him. "I did not want to waste any time dressing";
the fur coat "is hanging in the back of the carriage, but I cannot reach it." His impatience to escape is what robs him of
the means of escaping. All his resources, the earthly as well
as the unearthly, fail him. "Naked, exposed to the coldness of
this most wretched era, with an earthly carriage but with

unearthly horses, I, old man that I am, am roaming about" (E 153).

It is thus a question of the same situation as that of the Hunter Gracchus who sails along, without any bearings, between this world and the Hereafter. Both were suddenly hurled out of their safe and secure course of life: the country doctor through the "mistaken ringing" of the night bell; the Hunter Gracchus through "a wrong turn of the rudder." The country doctor, suddenly compelled to heal a wound that is beyond medical aid, rushes forth, bursting the bounds of all earthly and super-earthly security. The task imposed has placed an absolute demand on him. This demand makes its appearance in the two gigantic, unearthly horses that as swift as lightning draw him to the patient before whom he must prove himself. At the same time, not only is the door of his house demolished by the savage, sensual "groom" of these horses, but Rosa, the maid, "this beautiful servant girl who had been living in my house for years, scarcely noticed by me" (E 150), is raped by him. The intrusion of the absolute demand, therefore, is not an intrusion by a divine, other-worldly power, but the outbreak of powers that dwell within man himself and that demolish the false categories and sham patterns of his ordered existence. It is significant that the horses and the groom burst forth out of a pigsty that has not been used in years. Not only unearthly but also subterranean, subhuman impetuous forces surge up, forces that, like the pigsty, have until now gone unnoticed, elemental forces that the country doctor himself had even denied in that for years he had "scarcely noticed" Rosa, "the beautiful servant girl" in his house.

Crucial for an understanding of the Kafkaian world is the fact that in that world all the forces of existence loom up naked and insist on being brought under control. It would be completely beside the mark, for example, to interpret Rosa's being raped from a purely moralizing point of view as punishment for the country doctor's former coldness toward this girl. No other-worldly power pronounces sentence on human beings; it is the life forces themselves, dwelling in people, that burst forth unrestrained and pass judgment. The horses and the groom are the country doctor's and Rosa's own inner being. As the groom crawls out of the pigsty on all fours, this statement is made: "The maidservant stood near me. 'One does not know what sort of things one has stored up in one's own house,' she said, and both of us laughed." The horses and the groom had been concealed in the doctor's house without his or Rosa's knowledge. And, unsuspecting, the two "laughed" about it until frightful reality forces her to "cry out." The unearthly horses and the sensual groom really represent the decisive contrasts of life, and hence the country doctor has to choose between them. If he follows the horses, he "sacrifices" Rosa; if he follows the groom, he will keep Rosa, to be sure, but forgo the "joyous drive" with "such a beautiful span of horses. . . . 'Unless you ride along with me,' I said to the groom, 'I shall forgo the trip, no matter how urgent it is. I have no intention of giving up the girl to you by way of paying for the trip' " (E 148).

However, the doctor has to pay the price. Rosa is forfeited to the groom's strong instinctual drives; the doctor succumbs to the force of the "unearthly" horses that misuse him "for sacred purposes" and refuse to return him to his house, with its secure and ordered patterns. No reconciliation is possible. The doctor had already made his choice earlier when he followed the "mistaken ringing" of the bell. The horses drag him forth against his will, despite his feeling of responsibility toward Rosa—a feeling that suddenly begins to awaken in him. He must obey the unconditional command, even though he suddenly realizes— and realizes too late—that he thereby, once and for all, sacrifices Rosa whom he has ignored for years. The horses and groom represent the same phenomena that appear in the novels *The Trial* and *The Castle*. In these too the women succumb to the violent carnal forces of the court, or to Klamm's brutishly savage menials. There too Josef K. tries in vain to tear the court usher's wife from the grip of these forces. There too the masters are not only invisible officials who pull the groundwork of his life from under his very feet, but they are also avid "woman chasers." And there too the court holds its sessions in dirty backyards and in filth—just as the horses lodge in the doctor's pigsty.

The court mirrors the totality of the conflicting forces of existence. Horses and groom are none other than a manifestation of the universal "tribunal of men and animals." These forces erupt when that "icy winter" (E 146) prevails, which, in Kafka, is generally an atmospheric accompaniment of such eruptions out of secure, ordered patterns. It is in cold, icy winter too, for example, that K. enters the universal world of the castle authorities, and in that world it is actually always winter, " a very long winter and unvarying," and even on the two days when the sun is shining, "even during the most beautiful day of all, even then snow occasionally falls" (S 410). It is on such a winter's day of "thick, driving snow" (E 146) that the doctor stands about in his yard, at a loss, "without purpose ... distracted, tormented," for "my own horse had died in the preceding night as a result of overexertion in this icy winter" (E 146) and other horses were unobtainable. At that point there appear the strange "unearthly" horses.

At first the doctor feels them to be "helpers" and anticipates a "joyous" drive. He is thankful even to the groom "that he is helping me voluntarily, when all the others fail me" (E 147). Originally, therefore, they are in fact those liberating, succouring powers that remove "all obstacles." But in removing these obstacles they are at the same time disposing of concrete life itself. For this reason they at the same time exercise a threatening effect on both Rosa and the doctor. For the two are by no means willing to relinquish the illusory patterns of their ordered existence. The doctor lets himself be misused for sacred purposes only against his will, and when he catches sight of the patient (E 149) he wants to "drive back again immediately," home to Rosa. Caught in the conflict between the absolute demand made upon him (the physician as priest), on the one hand, and concrete sensual existence (Rosa), on the other, the doctor goes to pieces; and, roving about in an endless wasteland of snow, "never" finding his way "home" again, he leads a life among all spheres.

The most profound cause of this going-to-pieces is that "most wretched era" (E 153), that age which is no longer cognizant of any obligatory command and law.

What, then, are the horses and that groom who is also termed "beast" by the doctor (E 147)? They designate utmost extremes in man: his "chase" into the realm of the absolute material-sensual, and into the realm of the absolute spiritual-mental. These realms reflect man's entirety, and hence basically are even identical despite their antithetical tendencies. Not only do the horses obey the groom's call, but their breaking-out is indeed identical with the breaking-out of the groom; just as, on the one hand, the "unearthly" horses come out of the pigsty, on the other they neigh upon instructions from "the powers that be" in order to get the country doctor to examine the wound carefully, and "to facilitate" the "examination" (E 150). Hence, the groom calls the horses "brother" and "sister" (E 147). They belong to him as siblings belong to one another. All three of them are as one. The retrograde movement, the desperate "avidity" for putting down roots in the realm of the material-sensual, and for having one's "fill to the point of satiety" of carnal instinct—this of necessity corresponds to the "hunt," man's "assault" upon the "ultimate earthly frontier" (T 552-53).

It is of utmost significance in *The Trial* that Josef K., on the very day he is arrested by the court of the highest instance, wrenched out of the normal confines of his profession and way of life, and compelled to vindicate himself absolutely, is seized also by an extreme craving for sexual pleasure, so that he enters Miss Bürstner's bedroom, kisses her on the mouth, "and then all over her entire face, just like a parched animal whose tongue is lapping up water at the spring that it has at last come upon" (P 42). Josef K. becomes a "parched animal." The "chase" that the goddess of justice starts off is also the hunt for earthly spring water. Both pursuits are identical, just as the court officials in themselves are a union of both: they are "judges" and at the same time greedy "woman chasers" (P 253).

Only in such an antithesis do they represent man's totality, a totality that bursts the circumscribed, illusory patterns of his ordered existence, but that *could* establish genuine patterns and categories if man himself were able to become judge over the adversaries fighting one another within himself; that is, if he assumed complete control over the span of horses and the groom. The country doctor, however, lets himself be swayed in this conflict of the contrasting powers. Through his playing them off against each other, through his not doing full "justice" to either, the two destroy him; and in the end he remains in Nowhere, roving about aimlessly, "betrayed, betrayed" (E 153).

It is characteristic of Kafka that he designated the horses as "unearthly" beings and not as "supernatural" ones. They are the negation of what is earthly, not the affirmation of a sphere that is beyond this world or that is supernatural. Indeed, they have their origin in the lowest, most useless form of what is earthly, a realm that man can no longer control. Hence, they are able "to help" the country doctor to leave with lightning speed the existence he has hitherto led. Going back is the very thing they must prevent him from doing; similarly, Gregor Samsa's metamorphosis into an insect prevents him from ever returning to his family and condemns him to an immobilized existence. The sudden change in the horses' pace from wild pursuit to slow trot is accounted for by this negation of all the modes of being that are accessible to man's calculating grasp. The horses promise liberation, but it is a liberation beyond every finalizing, purposive consciousness; in the same way, the groom in his sensual savagery promises liberation, a liberation of instinctual forces long concealed, ignored by the doctor and by Rosa, but now (like the liberation through the unearthly horses), suddenly changing into destruction, no longer permitting the servant girl Rosa and the doctor to return to the customary routines of their lives.

This too is a reflection of our "most wretched era," and its sign is that modern man (and he alone) has been given boundless opportunity and scope to develop to the full all the intellectual and sentient powers and faculties active in him, and to do so without being guided by an absolute command influencing him from above or from within. The actual content of this tale, a content that is a critique of the times, is clear beyond any doubt: "They have lost their old faith; the parson stays at home and pulls his vestments to pieces, one after the other; but the doctor is supposed to do everything" (E 151). Groom and horses are the forces that determine our age: bestial savagery and directionless spirit. The unearthly, "uncontrollable horses" (E 149) compel the doctor instead of the priest to heal the "wound." They take charge, but "if they didn't happen to be horses, I'd have to drive sows. That's the way it is" (E 150).

*Every* means is acceptable to our era. All spheres are arbitrarily interchangeable. Hierarchies have disappeared. And a surrogate healing instead of the healing effected by a priest is not possible. The doctor himself becomes the patient, the smitten victim. And the forces that he can no longer control, upon being let loose, burst the world asunder, with both physical savagery and spiritual death, with that fatal tedium and emptiness in which the horses trot along through "the wasteland of snow," the "coldness of this most wretched era." The "joyous" chase that snatched the doctor from the boundaries of mankind, making him face total responsibility, is converted into the numbness of death within a spirit that no longer sees a goal or a road ahead and that succumbs to the monotony of an endless, unchanging wasteland. The sign of the era is the wasteland, the monotony of the unchanging, that "ennui" which ever since the fin de siècle—indeed, ever since Georg Büchner, that "most modern" of poets of the nineteenth century—has become a basic theme of literature.

The literary greatness of Kafka and of his story about the country doctor lies in his having herein summarily sounded the keynote of our age, as it were, in a poetically accurate description. Since "modern" man has no binding universal order at his disposal, the erupting forces of human existence, forces that "one has stored up in one's own house," become man's master, take the lead, and overpower him. The unexpected aids and resources become his undoing; the liberating horses become trammels, hampering forces that banish the doctor irredeemably to the wasteland of snow.

Here, too, the animals are images of a realm concealed within man himself, a realm that could have the function of liberating and rescuing man if he were to become judge of that realm and not its victim; that is, if man could attain to a superior level of consciousness that would span his *total* existence. In the knowledge of the self, "totality" would also be discoverable. "He is allowed to do everything except to forget his self; and this in turn means, of course, that he is forbidden everything except the one thing necessary at the moment for totality" (B 297-98).

Gregor Samsa and the country doctor had each forgotten his "self." At the moment when what they have forgotten erupts in them, they are forbidden everything; that is, they must renounce they be able to do what is "necessary at the moment for all given reality and all security. Only upon so doing would totality"; that is to say, to take on the responsibility for totality and assume the judgeship. The "self" would then become the governing power that establishes a system for the whole. But Samsa is not capable of that; nor is the country doctor; nor is modern man, who is constantly circumscribing his existence as he makes it secure. Faced with his patient, the country doctor, with most precipitate haste, seeks his own "rescue" and security: he wants to return to his former mode of existence. The "self" appears to him, therefore, just as it appears to Gregor Samsa, to be a destructively invading bestial force, an inconsistency between the spiritually "unearthly" horses and the instinctual world of the senses—an inconsistency that tears him apart. Man perishes because he forgets his own "self," and because in so doing he perverts his own "self"—while he is seeking to preserve himself, and because he is seeking to preserve himself.

### "*A Hybrid*"

Other animal stories of Kafka's supplement and complete the picture. "I have a peculiar animal, half pussycat, half lamb. It is an heirloom that belonged to my father. But it did not really develop until my time; formerly it was much more lamb than pussycat."

Such is the beginning of the story "A Hybrid" (B 108 ff.). This animal is a composite of contradictories. It has the teeth of a beast of prey and drinks milk. It lies in wait for chickens, "but it has never yet taken advantage of an opportunity to commit murder." "It flees from cats but wants to attack lambs." To be sure, it has characteristic traits of the two animal species, but it no longer bears any relationship to either and is entirely alien to all other animals. It is an animal "that, though it has countless in-laws on earth, probably does not have a single blood relative." It is the Other, pure and simple, the incomprehensible, the self-contradictory.

With only one single being does it have close relations—with the narrator, the "I" of the story—there is "no getting it away from me at all" (B 109). It is man's undefinable self that eludes all definition, and like every human self it is an "heirloom that belonged to my father" but that does not attain to its peculiarly characteristic development "until my time." When it weeps tears, the narrator asks, "Were they mine? Were they his?" For the animal weeps at the moment "when I, no longer able to find any way out through my work and everything related to it, was willing to let everything go to ruin, and in this frame of mind stretched out in my rocking chair at home." At this moment, when the hopelessness of human existence makes itself felt, this animal weeps like a dog: "It's not enough that it is both lamb and cat, it insists on being almost like a dog, besides" (B 109).

In Kafka, a dog's existence is always an expression of that stage at which man no longer knows of a way out. At the end of *The Trial* Josef K. dies "like a dog." The dog "Never-Again is of the opinion that things cannot go on as they are, and that somehow or other a way out has to be found" (H 139). The "Investigations of a Dog" are the agonizing experiments carried out by an animal, to the point of his own destruction, an animal whose "forefathers went astray" (B 269) and occasioned an "endless wandering" of all their descendants, a desperate search for "truth, clarity, avowal" (B 256), and "sublime freedom" (B 256, 290). Thus the "Dog" no longer lives in freedom that extends in all directions, as, in the "Report to an Academy," was the case of the ape before he was taken prisoner. But the Dog, like all of Kafka's animals, knows of his loss. Hence in the story "A Hybrid," he "weeps."

The development of this singular animal thus proceeds from peaceful lamb to fighting cat to weeping dog, but not in the sense of a development in a straight line, for, even in its existence as a lamb, characteristics of the pussycat are already present. And the primary contradiction throughout is that between cat and lamb, between the fighting and the immolated animal. This contradiction presses toward the termination of existence:

For that reason he is too cramped in his skin.... Perhaps the butcher's knife would be a deliverance for this animal, a deliverance that I must deny it, however, considering that it is an heirloom. It will have to wait until its breath leaves it of its own accord, even though it looks at me occasionally with intelligent human eyes that challenge me to intelligent action. (B 110)

The contradiction can be resolved only in death; as is always the case in Kafka, the breakthrough to freedom can take place only in death, a death, however, that signifies a knowledge of the self, "an intelligent action," and that cannot therefore be identified with the death of the body, but that on the contrary denotes the surmounting of the empirically constricting boundaries, the leap into a universal existence.

This is unequivocally clear from an addendum that Kafka wrote to this story: "A little boy had a cat as the only heirloom inherited from his father, and through it became Mayor of London. What shall I become through my animal, my heirloom? Where is that gigantic city spread out?" (H 65) Only this undefinable heirloom could enable man to become mayor of the gigantic city of this world, would enable him to obtain total knowledge, a perspective of the Whole—universal existence. For even truth, the law of totality, is contained within the self.

## The Animals in Kafka's Fragments and Short Stories

This identity of self, animal, and the All becomes particularly clear in the "vulture" (B 113) that, with its beak, strikes off from man everything that the latter needs for life—boots, stockings, feet—and finally, in killing man, it at the same time, by force, exacts universal liberation for him: "Falling back, I felt liberated as it sank beyond rescue, drowning in my blood that filled every depth and overflowed every shore." In the act of liberation, animal and self go down in the All that is completely filled by man's blood ["The Vulture"].

One may bring to mind those jackals, in the story "Jackals and Arabs" (E 160 ff.), that want to purify the world to its very core—"Purity, we want nothing but purity." They, too, exist in a contradiction. Because they feel nothing but disgust for the living Arabs they are incapable of killing them and have to pass the task on to the people from the cold "far north." " 'We know,' began the oldest one, 'that you come from the north, and we are putting our hope in that very fact' " (E 161). Thus, here again there appears the image of coldness, of the north. The stranger from the north is to put an end to the "very old feud" by removing the "blood" from everything living (E 161). But the stranger still has too much "human nature" in him (E 162) and cannot, therefore, effect the "purification" of the world. Thus these jackals live on in an "absurd hope" as "fools, veritable fools" (E 164), in an eternal discord between a filthy, living, hot world with unbreathable air, and an empty desert where there is indeed "purer air" (E 162) but where life can no longer be lived. "Sir, you are to put an end to the feud that divides the world. It was a man just like you that our fore-fathers described as the one to accomplish this. We must have rest from the Arabs, breathable air" (E 163).

Kafka's animals are the expression of the self-contradiction in man. They represent extreme instances of going beyond empirical boundaries, instances in which the levels of reflection and the forms immanent in life are forsaken and the totality of human existence is caught sight of. "In amazement we saw the great horse. It burst through the roof of our chamber. The overcast sky moved languidly alongside the prodigious outline, and the [horse's] mane flew whistling in the wind" (H 103).

The door opened, and there came into the room—fine and juicy, its sides voluptuously curving, slithering footlessly forward with its entire underside—the green dragon. Formal greeting. I asked it to come right on in. It expressed its regrets at being unable to do so, saying that it was too long. And so the door had to remain open, and that was very distressing. (H 282)

This gigantic dragon that made the room uninhabitable was "summoned" by the "longing" of the occupant of the room, and offers its assistance to him. "Summoned by your longing," says the dragon, "I have crawled here from a long way off, and underneath I am chafed quite sore. But I am glad to do this. Glad am I to come; glad am I to offer you my services" (H 282).

Or, another sketch: "Sweet serpent, why do you stay so far off? Come closer! Still closer! Enough! No farther! Stay there! Alas, there are no bounds for you. How am I to gain control over you if you acknowledge no bounds?" (H 140).

Or, the fragment may be recalled in which the narrator, coming home in the evening, finds in the middle of his room "a large, an overly large egg . . . almost as high as the table." Out of the egg there creeps, "still lacking feathers, beating the air with wings that were too short," a stork. " 'What do you want in our world?' I felt like asking" (H 142 ff.). The narrator cherishes the hope that the gigantic bird may be able to carry him forth to far-distant southern countries, and he concludes a written pact with the bird; in this pact the contradiction that became evident previously in the "Country Doctor" is clearly formulated. In order to rear the bird to maturity so that it will be able to fly, the narrator must feed it with fish, frogs, and worms; he must surrender his room to defilement, abandon his comfortable way of life, and go to great expense. The flight to a remote region can be bought only at the sacrifice of his wonted existence. Furthermore, he himself must guide the bird as it practices flying, and direct it "systematically." This entails ceaseless trouble and effort, for there "was no stork mother there" that could have taught the young bird to fly.

Thus the bird is none other than man himself, who must learn to fly. There is nothing other than man that could help him to succeed in this flight. Only in man are there the powers that would be able to bear him aloft above himself and his world. The bird, like all of Kafka's animal characters, is the symbol of a realm within man that is unavailable and unattainable but that, on the other hand, can be developed only through human powers and "practice," through great sacrifice and renunciation, the sacrifices and self-denials involved, to be sure, extending beyond the bounds of what is accessible to man's thought and volition. "If the bird had not been so willing, my instruction would probably not have sufficed" (H 144). In this bird there are, thus, simply its own powers that cannot be reached by man's empirical thought and volition; similarly, man's hand, independent of brain and eye, points to an iron signpost ("Description of a Battle"). And thus, the instruction between bird and man relies upon reciprocal help and counsel, since that very realm in man that is not available to him rationally and empirically is what makes "road directions" and guidance on one's course possible but, conversely, needs "road directions" and nourishment from empirical man in order to become capable of existence in this world.

Kafka once formulated this very clearly in a sketch, as follows:

It is the animal with the huge tail, a foxlike tail many meters long. Some day I should like to lay hold of that tail, but it is impossible. The animal is always on the move, it is incessantly jerking and switching its tail. . . . Sometimes I have the feeling that the animal wants to train me. What would be the point otherwise of its pulling its tail away from me whenever I reached for it, and then waiting again quietly until I am tempted again, and then jumping away all over again. (H 332)

The following example may show how remote from all customary psychological conceptions this relationship between animals and man is. "I am here, giving a clear explanation: everything that is said about me is false, if it follows on the assumption that I, as a human being, was the bosom friend of a horse. How strange that this monstrous assertion is spread abroad and believed!" (H 293) In the case of Kafka's references to animals, it is never a matter of a psychological process, of "bosom friendships" between man and animals.

What I did was merely this: I lived with a horse for a year in the same way in which, say, a human being—if he encountered no difficulty on the outside that would prevent him from making all the necessary arrangements for achieving his goal—would live with a girl whom he regards highly but who rejects him. And so, I shut myself and the horse Eleonor in a stable and never left this joint abode except to give lessons by means of which I earned enough to pay for instruction for the two of us. Unfortunately that was, after all, a matter of five to six hours a day, and it is not at all impossible that this loss of time was the cause of the ultimate failure of all my efforts; and let these gentlemen, to whom I so often appealed in vain for support in my undertaking, and who would have had to hand over only a little bit of money for something that I was ready to sacrifice myself for in the same way in which a bunch of oats that is crammed between a horse's molars is sacrificed—indeed, let these gentlemen just take heed of that! (H 293-94)

Indubitably this sketch conceals a personal confession of Kafka's. The pursuit of the inaccessible realm is constantly endangered by the necessity of earning money during the day. For the instruction of the horse he is ready to sacrifice everything, even himself—to cram himself like a bunch of oats between the horse's molars, although this horse "rejects" his love at all times, and must reject it, since it is the Other, pure and simple. For, "Just succeed in making yourself understood by the wood louse. Once you teach it to inquire into the purpose of its work, you exterminate the race of wood lice" (H 334). Accordingly, a horse standing useless in a stable can suddenly become a wondrously great, human "madame" who helps the narrator to enter gratuitously into a world that is strange to him, and "to overcome" all "difficulties" (H 406 ff.).

Or, in a curious apothecary shop that one can enter without a door, directly through the wall, shop assistants who have squirrel tails hand the requested medicines to all the customers with lightning speed. They "climb up . . . with tearing haste but with tiny little clambering movements—one does not see what they are climbing on; one wipes one's eyes and still one does not see it—and fetch down what was requested" (H 362 ff.).

The medicines can be reached and handed down only by animals that are climbing upon a nothingness or upon an invisible something. For that here it is a matter of the true medicine for [man's] despair of existence is unequivocally clear from the situation of the person who enters this apothecary shop. In a feeling of disgust that "verges on nausea," he experiences the impossibility of any "connection" with another earthly being (H 362-63).

### The Marten in the Synagogue

One may consider as analogous that peculiar animal in the synagogue (H 397-403), the marten that cannot be caught, which, like Odradek, outlives all the generations. This marten has often been identified[6] with God Who, in the process of the dissolution of the Jewish religion, has long since been forgotten and now leads a pitiful animal existence in a decaying synagogue that is to be converted into a "granary" (H 399). Various passages in the text speak against this point of view; for example, "if they [the women] concerned themselves more with prayer, they could forget the animal completely; and the devout women would do this, too, if the others, who are in the majority, permitted it; but the latter always like to call attention to themselves, and to that end the animal is always a welcome pretext" (H 400).

Furthermore, mention is made of the fact that especially in earlier times devout rabbis tried to banish the animal from the synagogue and dedicate God's house anew. Moreover, the animal lives in constant "fear" of persecutors although at the present time it is not being persecuted at all, and the narrator continues: "And yet this fear! Is it the memory of times long since past, or the presentiment of times to come? Does this old animal perhaps know more than the three generations that are at times assembled in the synagogue?" (H 402) "It has long since come to be a matter of indifference to the men ... and even the children who see it for the first time are no longer astonished" (H 399). Only with the women and with the gleaming brass rod of the Ark of the Covenant does the marten have any connection. "Its favorite whereabouts is the grille in front of the women's section" where it tarries "with obvious relish." And, though it takes no notice of the women, they are both afraid of it and fascinated by it. "If they could, and if they dared, they would have coaxed the animal to come even closer in order to justify their being all the more frightened" and "to call attention to themselves" (H 400). Moreover, it is the women who are not devout who do this, and they are the large majority.

It may be recalled that in *The Trial* and in *The Castle* only the women have a positive and unconditional relationship with the officials of the court and of the castle; indeed the women feel a commingling of fascination and fear in this relationship by which, in turn, they strive to gain esteem and recognition in the eyes of the surrounding world. That is the case when the barmaids, fascinated, give themselves to the officials in order to gain a favored position over the village inhabitants; on the other hand, however, they try to flee from the officials (e.g., Frieda; the wife of the court usher in *The Trial*; etc.). In contrast with this large majority of women are only a few who on principle hold themselves aloof from the officials, because they feel themselves committed to an absolute "truth," an absolute moral law; among these, for instance, is Amalia, who is consequently set apart from the village community. The officials, however, represent the "universal tribunal of men and animals," and not the highest court which is unknown even to them. In the officials all the hidden forces of life and existence come to light unchecked, and it is precisely this that fascinates the women and evokes the mixture of fear and admiration; whereas the men are absorbed in their "work" and their endless "exertions"; and the children are at the point where the forces of life still lie *ahead* of them.

Just as the two horses and the groom in the "Country Doctor" represent the complete bursting forth of the universal tribunal of men and animals, the marten in the synagogue could be interpreted as the representative of this total reality of life that exists in every human being but that is ordinarily concealed. Supporting this point of view would be the paradoxical combination of its predacious teeth and its stationariness, its "somersaults" turned with lightning speed and its "extraordinary" quiescence (which exists also in the case of the officials), as well as the mixture of blue and green in its coat (the heavenly and earthly colors), and finally also the fact that this animal tarries with pleasure not only in front of the women's section, but also with strained "eyes that are always open and that perhaps have no eyelids," "tight close to the Ark of the Covenant" (that is to say, it is sitting in the antechamber of the Absolute); thus it is uniting sensuality with an "official" function in the house and antechamber of the Absolute.

The animal's "fear" could likewise be explained by this interpretation: In older, pious times, when an absolute Divine Law was still valid, the animal had been persecuted. At that time the forces of life were not yet able and not yet permitted to erupt in their totality. They were felt as a defilement of the House of God, and for that reason a new purification appeared to be necessary (cf. the excessive filth in the rooms and chancelleries of the officials in *The Trial* and in *The Castle*). Modern life, however, that "is subject to no present-day law," "is a life that is to a certain degree free and unrestrained" (B 82). In it the animal is no longer persecuted, although it has become a matter of indifference to men grown lukewarm in religious affairs, men who think more of granaries than of religion or of superrational forces of life.

Accordingly, the animal would be a parabolic image of the forces of life and of the spirit, forces active in man at all times, forces that can never be entirely eliminated—not even at times when absolute commands are valid—and that are, therefore, immortal and, like the terrifying animal, outlast all the generations.

The fragment concludes with the account that many years ago the grandfather of the present temple servant, while still a little boy, had vainly tried to capture the animal with the help of a rope, a slingshot, and a shepherd's crook; that is to say, with the help of religious emblems, just as young David made use of a slingshot to kill the giant Goliath. To interpret the marten as God is impossible if one takes into account the total structure of the text. Even the obvious interpretation that would consider the animal the self of the Jewish people, as it were, living on in conscious fear of past and future persecutions, is erroneous, since the persecutions of the animal emanate from the temple servants and rabbis. Kafka's emblems are never symbols or allegories of limited phenomena contingent on history or on the present time, but always represent aggregate human realities. To be sure, whether or not the interpretation proposed here is valid in every respect may be a matter for speculation; for even though the analogies to be found in the novels *The Trial* and *The Castle* suggest such an interpretation, it nevertheless cannot as yet be unequivocally verified within the extremely terse, enigmatic text but can be presented only in the form of a conjecture—and for that reason it was deliberately worded in the subjunctive, as a mere possibility. This is especially so with respect to everything pertaining to the identification of the marten with Kafka's universal tribunal of men and animals. For such an identification there exist no direct passages in the text itself, but only indirect references that possess no absolute cogency, by contrast with the more lucid texts of the works hitherto interpreted.

Thereby a further question arises, too: that of conveying to the empirical consciousness, as much as one can, the idea of the existence and meaning of such animals in general. Undeniably, Kafka himself pondered on this question and gave it poetic form primarily in the story "The Village Schoolteacher" ("The Giant Mole").

## The Problem of the Cognizability of the Animals ("The Village Schoolteacher")

### A. KAFKA'S CRITIQUE OF SCIENCE

In the story "The Village Schoolteacher" almost nothing is stated about the gigantic mole itself. At the heart of the story is the question rather of how the existence of the animal can be incontestably "proved." And this question has its focus in the character of the village schoolteacher. Thus it was that Kafka entitled the story as he did; this is clearly evidenced in his diaries from the end of 1914 to the beginning of 1915 (T 449-54). The title "The Giant Mole" that appears in the editions of his works stems from an error on the part of the editor.

Only at the beginning of the story is there the statement about the mole itself: "Those people, and I belong to them, who find even a little ordinary mole disgusting would probably have been killed by their feeling of disgust if they had seen the giant mole that was observed in the vicinity of a small village several years ago" (B 220). Like Samsa's verminous insect the mole is that-which-is-disgusting, pure and simple, the very sight of which is already deadly; that is, it cannot be endured by empirical life. And the narrator himself confesses to this feeling of disgust for the animal. In a passage that was stricken from the manuscript this disgust was originally modified as follows: [the feeling of disgust arises actually] "from incomprehensible causes, for the soft, dark coat, the delicate, tiny feet, the tapering, carefully fashioned nose—no part of the animal that one sees is disgusting." Thus, the feeling of disgust cannot be occasioned by what is visible but only by other "incomprehensible causes." What is unbearable in this animal is located on another level that is not understandable.

Accordingly, "the entire phenomenon" of the giant mole has also remained "completely unaccounted for"; what is more, "at the present moment" it has "once again for some time been sunk in oblivion," for "as a result of an inconceivable negligence on the part of those circles that should have concerned themselves with it, and that actually concern themselves sedulously with matters that are much less significant by far," there has "been no very great effort made . . . to account for" this phenomenon; consequently, "lacking a more thorough investigation," it "has been forgotten" (B 220). The meaning, therefore, is that precisely those phenomena that transcend[7] normal empirical existence and its orders of magnitude remain unnoticed and are not investigated. Or, on the other hand, they are leveled off by science and reduced to normal empirical conceptions. The "scholar" gives the following explanation of the giant mole:

"In your area the earth is of course exceptionally black and rich. Well, for that reason it provides exceptionally rich nourishment for moles, too; and they grow unusually large." "But not that large," cried the teacher, and, exaggerating slightly in his rage, he measured off a length of two meters along the wall. "Oh, yes, indeed," replied the scholar, who obviously thought the whole affair ludicrous. (B 222)

And even later, when the narrator in the first person and the schoolteacher believe they have "discovered" and proved the existence of this giant mole that exceeds all usual dimensions, the narrator says to the teacher, "Every discovery is immediately channeled into the sum total of the sciences and with that, as it were, ceases to be a discovery; it is merged in the Whole and disappears" (B 237).

With that, a crucial problem in the field of modern sciences is touched upon. Even where human thought goes beyond the normal experiential world and, so to speak, makes superempirical "discoveries," such discoveries are immediately made to disappear again, because they are channeled into the sum total of the sciences; they are classified in frames of reference, or they are historized and relativized, and in that way they are invalidated so far as their special quality and their stimulating, superempirical significance are concerned. This holds true for matters of the most exalted religious faith, for every philosophical metaphysics or ontology, as well as for the worlds of imagery in art and literature.[8] Each and all are sucked up by scientific thought that either derives one phenomenon from the other, or constructs historical connections that in turn obliterate every "discovery" and take it back to the level of what is comprehensible—and even more than that, to the level of what is obvious and ordinary. As a result, however, not only the threatening element of such discoveries is lost, but the rescuing element as well. At all events, the triumph of the commonplace, of empirical normality, remains forever assured.

Kafka's critique of science has, however, a yet further goal. The narrator admits that science in no way lacks the vision for such discoveries. Such discoveries are examined and discussed, the instances when the frontiers of thought are transcended are observed; but they are distorted to such an extent that they forfeit the intrinsic meanings at their very core, and sacrifice the stimulating truths that dwell within them. The narrator continues:

"Indeed, one has to have a scientifically trained vision even to recognize it [the discovery] then. It is immediately bound up with basic principles, the existence of which we have never even heard of, and in a learned argument the discovery is swept up into the clouds by these basic principles. How are we expected to understand that? When we listen to learned discussions we believe, for example, that the point in question is the discovery; but meanwhile the discussion is about quite other things; and the next time we believe that something else is the subject of discussion, not the discovery, and then the discovery is actually the very point at issue. Do you understand that?" (B 237)

In other words, science links the discovery with "other things," with basic principles or manifold historical relations, in such a way that in learned argument confusions are constantly taking place. The discovery is brought to bear upon other problems or phenomena and thereby loses its own character. No matter how scientific thinking goes on, the significance and effectiveness of the discovery become confused and are lost.

B.  KAFKA'S CRITIQUE OF SOCIETY

But even on the nonscientific level, the discovery cannot win through. Instead of those people who, because of their profession, were actually intended to ascertain and shed light upon the existence and significance of the giant mole, an "old, un-heeded village schoolteacher" has made it "his life task" (B 221) to authenticate the existence of this phenomenon. But the teacher is "without influence" (B 222), finds no understanding anywhere, meets with "insuperable prejudices" (B 222), for "one may not demand that the whole world pay constant attention to it, particularly since the mole's existence has not been estab-lished beyond question; and in any event the mole cannot be brought forward and displayed" (B 228). Also, since the giant mole does not make a concrete appearance, it is of course impos-sible to adduce convincing evidence that it does exist. In attempt-ing to do so, the teacher goes to pieces. He wants to prove something that is beyond all empirical proof.

At this point the narrator in the first person, characteristically designated as a "businessman," intervenes. In the original word-ing of the manuscript he appeared as an "official." Kafka must have had a definite, inner reason for changing the profession of his narrator. Presumably he wanted to strengthen the con-trast between him and the teacher, who is in fact also a govern-ment official. For the narrator is interested in getting the general public to accept the teacher's discovery, and in gaining a follow-ing, etc. This effort extends into the economic sphere. The dis-covery is to come into the market as a piece of merchandise; propaganda is to be made for it.

The businessman wishes to help gain a victory for the "good

intention of a man who is honest but without influence" (B 222),
a victory for the latter's "dedication to his convictions" (B 221).
That is, the issue now is no longer the "affair" itself (B 223,
226), but rather the strength of conviction, the attitude of faith,
which is to be propagated, "disseminated" (B 225). The
teacher's "main object, that of establishing proof of the
phenomenon of the great mole ... mattered less" to the
businessman "than the defense of his [the teacher's] integrity"
(B 223) and the "merited dissemination ... of the teacher's
pamphlet" (B 225).

In other words, Kafka, with a keen eye, penetrates the dilemma of every modern attempt to gain a universal mode of life
and knowledge that will break through the limited empirical
world. Such an attempt is either branded as unscientific (or, as
the case may be, absorbed, leveled, and killed in spirit by
science), or becomes the object of propaganda campaigns that,
seizing upon the urgent desires for absolute knowledge that are
present in the people at large, try to gratify those desires by a
propagandizing of "convictions" and "attitudes of faith" and
"honorable" interpretations, where what is at stake is "dissemination" rather than truth-content. Gaining adherents, fellow
believers, comrades-in-arms, is what counts. To the businessman the "affair" itself is unessential as well as incredible; for,
from his point of view, this discovery "that the teacher has
made" "is not ... so to speak, of paramount significance"
(B 235).

Consequently there are also immediate differences of opinion
between the teacher and the businessman. The latter wants to
prove the existence of the mole on his own. "Later, when I
read the teacher's pamphlet—it had a very detailed title: 'A
Mole, of Such Great Size as Has Never Been Seen by Anyone
Before'—I found actually that we were not in agreement on
essential points, even though we both believed that we had
proved the chief item, that is to say, the existence of the mole"
(B 224). What the two have in common is the fact that basically
they believe in the existence of a sphere that transcends the
customary empirical world. But their interpretations and state-

ments differ—the dilemma of every faith, the dilemma that leads to the continual formation of differing sects. A quarrel immediately arises between the teacher and the businessman about the proper line of argument and interpretation. In fact, through the very assistance of the businessman, the teacher sees himself in effect betrayed and cheated. Although the business-man actually has an unselfish desire to advance the teacher, although he intends to relinquish the glory and the priority of the discovery to him and would like to help to promote his position in society, etc., and although he even gives him money, nevertheless the businessman remains completely rooted in the domain of business and calculations; for all these offers and expedients of his are in themselves nothing but the expres-sion of this domain of business to which the entire problem is now reduced.

To be sure, not even the teacher is free from such calculating thought. He silently accepts the offers of money, harbors hopes of being esteemed by society, and of improving his family's circumstances; indeed, "he was even very ambitious and wanted to gain money, too; this, in the light of his numerous family, was quite understandable" (B 227). Like everyone else he is human and has worries about his means of existence, worries that force him into a correspondingly matter-of-fact mode of thought. Yet, in spite of this, he himself believes that he is serv-ing only the interests of the "affair": "The affair, the affair alone was of moment to him. . . . To this affair, however, I was being false, because I did not understand it . . . because I had no instinct for it. . . . It was far and away beyond me . . . he believed he could lay claim to being completely altruistic without too much want of truth" (B 226-27).

And in fact it is this old, unheeded teacher who is closest to the "affair." He knows that it cannot succeed because of all the manipulations and customary ways of thinking, because it is "far and away" beyond the "capacity" of his contemporaries. "The defense of his integrity" was unimportant to him, because his integrity "seemed self-evident . . . to him and in need of no defense" (B 223). Ultimately, therefore, he can react only "silently" and mutely. The narrative fragment breaks off with the following deeply moving scene: the village schoolteacher resignedly finds "everything quite all right," realizes that the businessman in no way intended to betray him but unselfishly wanted to help him. But, now that all their differences are clarified, the schoolteacher, instead of taking his leave as the businessman expected of him, remains seated, mute and motionless, to the businessman's "embarrassed surprise," and "saddles" the latter with "his mute presence, to no purpose" (B 239). "His sitting there in silence" becomes "downright annoying" to the businessman (B 239).

The published version of the fragment concludes with these words: "If one looked at the small, tenacious old man from behind, as he sat at my table, it was easy to believe that he could not possibly be got out of the room at all" (B 238-39). In the manuscript there is another penciled sentence in parentheses: "His long, stiff overcoat, that he never took off, stuck far out from his body in sharp box pleats, and turned him into a bulky mass."[9]

What remains is man's sheer existence, "mute" and "to no purpose." It cannot be "got rid of," and it cannot be resolved in calculations. It is there, facing the businessman, like a threatening bulky mass with sharp box pleats. This mute existence alone knows about the phenomenon of this animal, and could speak of the truth that goes far and away beyond all understanding; but it has been made speechless. In an era that disseminates such an endless amount of knowledge as to annihilate true knowledge, this mute existence can no longer make its knowledge known.

## The Pure Animal Tales and the Universal

In the story "The Village Schoolteacher" a complex of problems was alluded to that motivates also the three great animal tales of Kafka's late period: "Investigations of a Dog," "Josephine the Singer, or the Mouse Nation," and "The Burrow."

These tales are pure animal stories, no longer in the sense that
animal and man are confronted with one another, but in the
sense that the animal plane is adhered to exclusively. Everything is narrated from the point of view of the animals. The
human world makes no appearance, not even in the case of
dogs and mice that, spatially, live within a human world. On
the other hand, however, these animals experience and reflect
the problems of human beings. The animals are not described,
say, on the basis of zoological animal psychology in an effort to
give Gestalt to their inner lives. Nevertheless, it would be
erroneous simply to identify these animals of Kafka's with
human beings, and to consider them as a development of
Aesop's fables, in which animals mirror human conditions, and
moral philosophies are uttered in animal disguise. The fact that
Kafka chooses exclusively animal characters in these stories has
another significance, an artistic one.

These animals—like all of Kafka's animals—make manifest a
situation in which the masking veils of man's limited empirical
ideational world are dropped; a situation, therefore, in which
the totality of human existence erupts unveiled; thus, a situation
in which the fundamental antinomies of this existence are experienced and reflected. Kafka, by choosing animal characters as
the subject of his presentation, immediately transports the reader
to another level of consciousness and existence, where the normal human world is transcended; a similar situation is encountered in the case of the officials of the court and of the
castle, or in that of the enigmatic events in the story "The
Construction of the Great Wall of China." Hence, too, it was
possible for Kafka, in a letter to Max Brod, written at the beginning of October 1917, to speak to the "tribunal of men and
animals" and to identify it with the "whole community of men
and animals." The universal court officials in the novel *The
Trial*—that is to say, the whole "human tribunal"—are mentioned in the letter in the same breath with the animal tribunal
and the community of animals. What happens and is reflected
in the court chancelleries of *The Trial* is in fact the concern and
life world also of the animals in the three great novellas. Only

in this sense are they [the animals] human beings. And the analogy of these three novellas with the story "The Village Schoolteacher" rests in this: the problem in them is no longer the eruption into the animal world, as it is in "The Metamorphosis" or in "A Country Doctor," etc. (or, in reverse, as it is in "A Report for an Academy"); but, on the assumption that such an eruption has already taken place, the further problem arises of how a universal reality that has erupted in this fashion can now actually be understood, regulated, enabled to exist, and made capable of survival.

What has here taken place is an essential change from Kafka's middle period to his late work, a change that grows visible too in the transition from the novel *The Trial* to the novel *The Castle*. Whereas in *The Trial* the matter at issue was still the confrontation of empirical reality (bank career, etc.) with universal consciousness (court), whereas the heroes here, just as in "The Metamorphosis" and in "A Country Doctor," are also suddenly torn out of their concrete, empirical existence, and a lasting conflict between the two levels takes place, in *The Castle* K. is immediately placed altogether into the sphere of the Universal, a world that is beyond all relevance to reality, a world that was "forgotten by the world" (S 421), one in which not only the castle but also, as it happens, the village too, is included. And the problem of this "stranger," K., who has lost his way and finds himself thrust into the sphere of the village and castle, is now: How can one survey land in such a sphere? How is one able to exist? How does this sphere become comprehensible, clear and distinct, able to survive? It is this problem that dominates, likewise, the "Investigations of a Dog," "Josephine the Singer, or the Mouse Nation," and "The Burrow."

## *"Investigations of a Dog"*

### A. THE MUSIC OF THE WORLD

The old Dog in "Investigations of a Dog," looking in retrospect upon his life and his investigations, recounts that even in his early years, while living in the midst of the Dog Nation, he felt a "spot where there was a small crack" (B 240), and this he sensed because he kept asking unanswerable questions that tugged him—not otherwise, after all, than all dogs who were constantly being gnawed at by similar questions—"again and again, irresistibly . . . out of the circle of his fellow dogs" (B 242). The "heuristic impression" (B 243) for this mode of behavior was provided by an encounter with seven music-making dogs who suddenly stepped out of the darkness into the light and "magically produced" a music "out of empty space" (B 244), a music that overpowers him and, what is more, turns his entire thinking, feeling, and willing topsy-turvy, despite his most vehement resistance. It is clearly evident from the text that these seven music-making dogs have been "conjured up" through the questions and investigations of the Dog himself: "At that time I had been running through the darkness for a long while with a premonition of great things . . . this way and that, blind and deaf to everything, led on by nothing but the vague longing . . . just then—as if I had conjured them up—seven dogs . . . stepped . . . into the light" (B 243). Even this light is not a real, empirical light, for later the dogs "disappeared, with all their noise and all their light, into the darkness out of which they had come" (B 248).

The music and light of these seven dogs were conjured up through the Dogs's being blind and deaf "to everything," "with a premonition of great things." Their music, therefore, tears the Dog also out of his habitual reflections, even removes him from the "actual" music-making dogs themselves, makes him "lose his head," and even "destroys" him (B 245).

While one was still involved in such reflections, the music gradually gained the upper hand, literally clutched at one, pulled one away from these actual little dogs, and, as one struggled with all one's strength, howling entirely against one's will, as if one were being caused pain, one could not be concerned with anything but—as it came from all directions, from above, from below, from everywhere, taking the listener into its very midst, pouring

over him, crushing him, still trumpeting fanfares above his wreck-
age in such proximity that it was already remote, scarcely audible
—the music. (B 245)

Then, when he is again "released" from the music "because
one was already too exhausted, too shattered, too weak to continue listening," he is horrified to discover that the music-
making dogs were "violating the law" (B 247), and on two
counts at that: they are not answering any questions and are,
indeed, ruling out all answers; and they are walking erect "as
if they had cast all shame away"—"as if nature were a mistake"
they quickly raise their front paws (B 247). "Was the world
topsy-turvy? Where was I? What was it that had happened?"
(B 247). Indignant, the Dog wants "to instruct" the music-
makers, wants to call their attention to the violation of the law,
when he is again struck spellbound by the "noise" of their music.

Perhaps in my zeal I would even have withstood it (since by then
I was already familiar with it), if, piercing all its volume (that,
terrible as it was, could perhaps have been contended with), a
clear, austere, unvarying tone, approaching virtually unchanged
from a great distance, a tone that was perhaps the actual melody
in the midst of the noise, had not sounded and forced me to my
knees. (B 248)

There can be no doubt that in this noisy music, "from all
directions," "coming from everywhere," there is compressed
the totality of everything-that-is, a totality that no longer can
and no longer may give a separate answer to each question, because the totality itself represents the answer to all questions,
at the same time rendering void the law that has hitherto pre-
vailed, causing nature and the habitual world to be "topsy-
turvy" and invalidated.

This is incontestably shown in striking parallels in other works
of Kafka's, parallels that are at times verbatim. In the novel *The
Castle* the statement is made that in the illimitable chancelleries
of the castle there is "incessant telephoning; this of course
greatly speeds up the work. This incessant telephoning we hear

in the local telephones [of the village] as a rustling sound and as singing" (S 99-100).

From the telephone receiver came a humming sound, the like of which K. had never before heard in telephoning. It was as if from the humming of countless, childlike voices—but even this humming was not actually a humming, but the song of very remote, the remotest voices—as if from this humming, in a manner that was nothing short of impossible, a single high-pitched but strong voice were being created, that fell upon the ear as, though demanding entry to a more profound level than just one's paltry hearing. (S 32)

The superintendent of the village later explains this telephoning from the castle in the following manner: "We hear this incessant telephoning in the local telephones as a rustling sound and as singing. This, you too have surely heard. But the only thing that the local telephones transmit to us that is correct and trustworthy is this rustling sound and this singing; everything else is deceptive" (S 99-100). He says this as K. complains about the confusing remarks of the castle officials: all the separate statements and answers of the authorities are "deceptive." The only correct and trustworthy thing is this singing of countless voices that are compressed into a single loud tone. In other words, every humanly comprehensible limited statement or answer to the questions man poses is uncertain; it is never the *whole,* true answer. Every formulation in language represents only partial aspects that are exposed to a deceptive plethora of explanations and contradictory interpretations. The only thing that is correct and trustworthy is the wordless music, the countless voices of all the officials. They reflect the totality of that-which-is, and they cannot be deceptive.

But from all of them together a single loud and resounding tone is finally formed, that threateningly demands entry to a more profound level than merely that of man's paltry hearing; this tone invades the innermost part of man, forces him to his knees, or even hunts him out of his life and carries him off (B 287). In it the totality of that-which-is is, as it were, compressed; in it absolute truth that is "not deceptive" is arrived at.

Josef K. experiences something similar in the chancelleries of the novel *The Trial*: "Finally he noticed that they were speaking to him, but he did not understand them; he heard only the noise that filled everything, and through that noise a constant, high-pitched tone, as if from a siren, seemed to be ringing" (P 91). And in the piece "Advocates" this statement is made:

Over and beyond all particulars, what reminded me most of all of a court was a drone that could be heard coming constantly from far away; it was impossible to tell from what direction it was coming; it so filled all the rooms that one could suppose it was coming from everywhere; or, what appeared even more correct, precisely where one happened to be standing was the actual spot of the drone, but that was surely a delusion, for it came from far away. (B 136)

As a matter of fact, this music includes both remotest distance and closest proximity. It is "everywhere" and is at the same time the "self" of man; it rings out "precisely" where one "happens" to be standing, and, as is stated in "Investigations of a Dog," it takes one into its midst and sounds in "such proximity that it was already remote." For it is precisely that which is closest to man, his self, that is most remote and most mysterious to him. And at the same time it is the determinant "everywhere." Self-judgment and the judgment of the world seem here to become identical, just as knowledge of the self and knowledge of the world likewise become one. What is seemingly "shattering" in the music is at the same time liberation, eruption into the "open," into total "perspective."

Indubitably this interpretation ensues from the further investigations of this Dog. When the Dog, in despair, believes that he is at the end of all his investigations and wants to die, since he has not the power "to get out of this world of falsehood . . . over to the truth" (B 284), there suddenly stands before him a "strange dog," a "hunting dog" who is under compulsion to remove him. And just then the desperate "Dog, helplessly snapping at empty space," hears a singing from the depths of the hunting dog's breast—"and new life pulsed through me at that, life such as fright gives." And

I thought...I perceived that the [hunting] dog was already singing but without his yet knowing it; and, what is more, I thought that the melody, separate from him, was floating, according to a law of its own, through the air, over and past him as if he did not belong to it, and was aiming only at me, only at me.... Its swell had perhaps no limits, and now already it was almost splitting my ears. But the worst of it was that it seemed to be there only on my account—this voice, at the sublimity of which the forest grew hushed—only on my account. Who was I that I still dared to stay on here and in its presence dared to spread myself, swaggering in my filth and blood? Shakily I got up and looked down at myself: surely the likes of this will not be able to run, was still my thought when, driven on by the melody, I was already flying along in the most glorious leaps and bounds. (B 287)

This music "aims" at him, threatens to annihilate him, removes him, his "nature," and the hitherto prevailing law of the dogs; but this music itself floats through the air "according to a law of its own," and is at hand "only on my account"; it therefore represents the true law of the self and of all Being, for at its sublimity the forest grows hushed. It liberates the Dog, instills "new life" in him, and causes him to fly along in glorious leaps and bounds.

The general and the particular, the self and the Universal, have here become identical. The "law" of everything-that-is, as well as the liberation of everything-that-is, is found here. Even in his youth the Dog had already had the feeling that he himself had "conjured up" the seven dogs with their music and their light. But even then this music was also sounding "from everywhere." And the Dog had "greeted" the "light" as "a more than bright day" and "morning" (B 243), that not only issued from him but that shone forth upon him like a promise, just because he was in the "darkness" and was "blind and deaf to everything" else around him in his "premonition of great things." Now after his period of starvation and his readiness

for death he finds "new life" and the melody's "law of its own"
that liberates and carries him away.

But—and herein lies Kafka's tragedy proper, as well as that
of his era—this liberating law is "not communicable": "I told
nothing to my friends"; it "seemed to me ... not communicable" (B 287-88). The Dog, after reaching this high point, the
pinnacle of his life, after this "being completely out of oneself,"
the experience of which he has "salvaged and carried over into
this world" as "the sole ... reality ... from the period of starvation" (B 287), is unable to communicate this to anyone and
cannot impart any determining efficacy to the law. For this
"sole reality" is "also only an apparent reality." It is "also only
apparently" real, not only in the eyes of the others but also
from the "present" standpoint of the Dog who has meanwhile
grown older. "Today, of course, I deny all knowledge of this
kind and ascribe it to my overwrought state at that time"
(B 287).

The central ambiguity in Kafka lies in the very fact that he
does indeed see, and poetically conjure up as exceedingly likely,
the possibilities of ecstatic knowledge of the self and of the
world—that "being-out-of-oneself"—but at the same time, honestly and without any illusions, he confronts the more difficult
task of providing likewise, by means of this musical law, the
"nourishment" on which the dog community can actually live.

### B. THE "SCIENCE OF NOURISHMENT"

The Dog now searches for a union between the "science of
music" and the "science of nourishment"; that is, he searches
for the "doctrine of singing that summons down nourishment"
(B 289).

In so doing, to be sure, he sets out for a "border area between
the two sciences" that arouses his "suspicion." For it is questionable whether a true, incontestable union between the two
sciences is possible. Even in his earlier investigations the Dog
had tried in vain to furnish experimental proof that nourish-

ment for the dogs could be tempted down from above; and he had tried to jolt and dislodge the conventional point of view in the sciences (that all nourishment stems from the earth) with the question of where the earth, in turn, got its nourishment. He maintains that, although no doubt exists, to be sure, that the earth produces all forms of nourishment, it not only draws nourishment forth from itself, but it also summons it down from on high. Therefore, a "bipartition" of labor is necessary: first, cultivation of the soil, which remains indispensable for obtaining both kinds of nourishment (from below and from above); and second, incantation, dance, and song, which deal "less, however, with cultivation of the soil in the narrower sense," but "serve principally in drawing down nourishment from above" (B 273).

Thus Kafka is not at all concerned with securing merely a metaphysical nourishment, but with the synthesis of earthly and unearthly existence. Even the unearthly sphere can never become actual without earthly cultivation of the soil. On the other hand, however, not to be denied, for example, is the existence of those "dogs of the air" who "live separate from the nourishing earth" (B 261), spending their lives in a "floating," "absurd" state that cannot "be fathomed" by the mind—indeed, cannot even be "seen" at all. The dominant question of the Dog, "Whence does the earth get our nourishment?" (B 271) thus leads to Kafka's old essential problem: in what, in general, is all earthly existence, in the last analysis, grounded? By what is it—as a totality—nourished?

The image of nourishment pervades, indeed, almost all of Kafka's writing. Gregor Samsa, in his beetle-existence, seeks the "way to the unknown nourishment he had been longing for" (E 130) and expects to find it—as does the Dog—through music. The "Hunger Artist" accomplishes his astounding performances of starving "because I was unable to find the food that tastes good to me. Had I found it, believe me, I would have made no commotion, and would have stuffed myself full like you and like everybody" (E 267). In the novella "The Judgment" Georg Bendemann, at his death-leap into the water, clutches "the railing hard, as a hungry man clutches food" (E 67), etc.

Through his universal questioning, accordingly, the Dog in his investigations takes a position that is in opposition to all customary scientific teachings.

> I did something that is unprecedented, that contradicts all our principles, that every eyewitness of that time will certainly recall as something uncanny. In science, which normally strives for un-limited specialization, I found a remarkable simplification in one respect. Science teaches that, in the main, the earth produces our nourishment, and, having made this assumption, it then lists the methods according to which the various foods can be obtained in best quality and greatest abundance.... Whoever has been able to keep himself even just a little free of prejudice with respect to science—and certainly there are not many, for the circles attracted by science grow greater and greater—will ... easily realize that the major part of the nourishment that ... is located upon the earth comes down from above.... With this I am not saying anything against science; the earth, naturally, does produce this kind of nourishment too. Whether the earth draws the one kind from within itself, or summons down the other from on high, makes perhaps, after all, no essential difference. (B 272-73)

The assumption which the Dog is criticizing, that all-simpli-fying assumption, is, therefore, that science leaves the earthly origin of nourishment at that and then immediately goes on to the methods of procurement instead of first posing the urgent question of where in turn the earth itself gets its nourishment. In no way does the Dog thereby deny that the earth is the originating source of all nourishment. On this point he remains at one with science. The Dog—precisely like science—remains within earthly existence. But his questions go beyond scientific questions in that he is inquiring into the basis of earthly exist-ence itself. This nurturing basis can be situated in the earth *itself*, or rather it can be *up above*, "on high." There is per-haps no "essential difference" between the two possibilities; that is, the quest, as is always the case in Kafka, is not directed toward an absolutely otherworldly, transcendent sphere. Such a sphere does not contain the "source" of nourishment; on the contrary, the critical problem is whether it is possible within earthly existence to advance toward such "Being" as is determining and nourishing, that is present in the self as well as "on high," in the Universal, since basically both mean the same thing. Whether the earth draws its nourishment "from within itself" or "summons it down from on high" comes to the same thing.

The Dog now continues his reflections. The "soil"—given reality—must be "cultivated" in order that "both kinds of nourishment to be secured" (B 273). All given reality must be thoroughly explored. In addition, however, there is "the supplementary and refining work in the form of incantation, dance, and song" (B 273). Even science knows these "two chief methods of procuring nourishment." It entirely accepts the cultivation of all given reality by means of intellectual-moral, artistic, and religious-cultural activity (incantation, song, and dance). But science, by contrast with the Dog and also with the "tradition" of the "people," wants to limit itself to "serving" "only the soil" through these "ceremonies" (B 273); that is to say, it wants to remain within given reality. According to the claims of science, "they [the ceremonies] would . . . logically have to be . . . carried out completely on the ground; all whispering, all leaping and bounding, all dancing would have to be addressed to the ground" (B 273). Surprisingly, however, the people in their ceremonies have always acted very differently, "without knowing it, and without any attempt at resistance on the part of science," and the people have "corrected science." For what always happens is "the remarkable thing that in all their ceremonies the people rise up" (B 273).

In other words, the people have cherished, and always will cherish the desire for nourishment from above, and they have never limited themselves merely to given reality; they have raised their "magical incantations on high," have mournfully sung "our old folk songs into the air," and have performed "leaping dances as if, forgetting the ground, they meant to soar up on high forever" (B 274). Science, it is true, has always countenanced this; "it does not prohibit it." But if science remained true to its own principles, it would have to oppose this. For "I . . . cannot at all imagine how scholars can put up with it—that our people, with their passionate natures, raise magical incantations on high," etc. (B 274).

Unlike science and unlike the people who silently let these "contradictions" rest, the Dog is sparked to undertake his "investigations" by these very contradictions: "I made my point of departure an emphasis upon these contradictions" (B 274). As a matter of fact, therein lies Kafka's decisive purpose.

In Kafka's work is mirrored that ominous fissure which runs through our era. So-called positive science, as well as our entire social, political, and cultural life, limits itself to given reality; it leaves a vacant space where forces that are uncontrollable now break in, whether positively in the sense of forces of religion, or negatively in the sense of salvation-preaching fanatics who fascinate and ruin whole nations, since these fanatics promise the people the very thing that the latter are vainly seeking from science: a new "center" of life. The fearsome madness that seizes whole masses of people can be blamed upon science itself and its adherents, who have neglected to fill in the vacant space and who believed they could get along "without metaphysics."

Thus, as science and common sense played into each other's hands to bring about the downfall of metaphysics, there seemed to be brought into being the strange spectacle of *an educated people without metaphysics*—like a temple that is in other respects manifoldly decorated but that lacks a holy of holies. (Hegel)[10]

Strange as it is when a nation's knowledge of its constitutional law, when its sentiments and views, its moral customs and virtues have become useless to that nation, it is at least as strange when a nation loses its metaphysics, and when the mind that concerns itself with its pure nature no longer has any real existence in that nation. (Hegel)[11]

The mind itself has robbed itself of this "real existence" within the people, by no longer concerning itself with its "pure" nature, and by capitulating to "common sense" it has betrayed

its own nature. The responsibility for this rests not with the
people but with science. For science must reflect the "basis" of
its "assumptions." It cannot make excuses for itself by maintaining that here "faith" has to take the place of knowledge and
must fill the empty space. It must scientifically "establish" the
"basis" upon which it, as science, rests. It is significant that the
Dog, in all his "weird" experiments, is aiming explicitly at a
"science." Kafka *remains* within the framework of the "given"
empirical world. Kafka wants "to battle the world, and, indeed,
to do so with weapons that are more real than hope and faith"
(H 115). His "empiricism," however, is not the mutilated empiricism that is merely an inspection of the "ground" of "common sense," but the empiricism of collective human existence
about which there must be "knowledge" and not just faith; for
this empiricism is as much the experience of the simplest man
of the "people" as it is the experience of the most complex poet
or philosopher. To illumine and analyze it is the noblest task of
every true science of man.

The Dog's experiments that now ensue serve this empiricism.
The Dog refuses all food intake and "categorically" declines all
"help" from others (B 278); that is, he steps out of the domain
of the so-called "normal" experiential world, retreating completely from the surrounding world into solitude (B 277-78)—
in the hope that then, "of its own accord, nourishment would
descend from above, and, without concerning itself with the
ground, it would knock at my teeth in order to be admitted"
(B 277). For only by his eliminating all purposeful efforts of
the will, by his shunning all "other measures" (B 277), will the
unavailable nourishment from above descend "of its own
accord."

Above all, therefore, it is a matter of man's opening up, of
his becoming free and thereby accessible to nourishment. When
he is in this state, something remarkable takes place:

I heard noises everywhere; the world, that had been sleeping
during my life hitherto, seemed to have been awakened by
my hunger; I began to imagine that I would never be able to
eat again; for, by eating, I would necessarily cause the tumul-

tuous, liberated world to become silent again, and that I could not bring myself to do. (B 282)

Going hungry thus leads to knowledge! The world that has formerly been silent and sleeping suddenly "wakes," speaks, manifests itself, is "liberated." The Dog hears and sees what had been hidden from him during his normal life. The world, so to speak, is put out of joint, erupts loudly, "unmasks" itself as, analogically, in that passage in the journal: "It is not necessary for you to leave the house. Remain at your table and listen. Do not even listen; just wait. Do not even wait; be absolutely still and alone. The world will offer itself to you for unmasking; it cannot do otherwise—it will writhe before you in ecstasy" (H 54).

However, not only does the external world erupt, but the inner world also reveals itself: " . . . the loudest noise, to be sure, I heard in my belly; I often put my ear against it and must have stared in horror, for I was scarcely able to believe what I heard. . . . I began to smell various kinds of food, choice dishes —pleasures of my childhood—that I had not eaten for a long time" (B 283). The long-forgotten world of childhood emerges once more. And this world is suddenly sensed by the Dog as a tempting "dish," as a form of nourishment that leads him to a strange conflict.

The various childhood dishes are so tempting that he forgets, and yet does not forget his decision to decline all nourishment; he both craves and rejects the dishes of childhood:

I forgot my resolve to resist smells ; or, more correctly, I did not forget it. With that resolve, as if it were a resolve inherent in what I was doing, I dragged myself about in every direction, and, taking only a few steps each time, I sniffed as if I wanted the food only in order to be on guard against it. That I did not find anything, did not disappoint me: the various foods were there ; it was only that they were always a few steps too far off—my legs gave way before I could get there. At the same time, of course, I knew that there was nothing there at all. . . . The last of my hopes, the last of the temptations vanished ; I would perish there in misery. Of what avail were my investigations—childlike endeavors from a period of childlike happiness? Here, this very moment, the situation was serious; here and now, when my research could have proved its worth, where was it? Here there was only a dog, helplessly snapping at empty space. (B 283)

Thus, as in Kafka's earlier writings, the sphere of childhood is felt to be a tempting possibility, is felt as "nourishment." Nevertheless, it cannot be the true nourishment "from above" that must descend "of its own accord" and knock [for admission] at his teeth. It belongs to a lost, childlike happiness, and is therefore always present as a remembered good; but, at the same time, it is never present and is unattainable, since in the "seriousness" of the adult world and its investigations more must be demonstrated and achieved than a return to childhood. Although childhood mirrors a condition that belongs to the true nourishment from above, this condition cannot establish and carry the *totality* of human existence. It is only a guidepost pointing to the direction of liberation and rescue; it is not the goal.

The Dog is in despair and wants to die.

Had I not desired this forsakenness? True, I had, fellow dogs, yet not in order to come to my end here in this way, but rather in order to cross over to the truth, out of this world of falsehood where there is no one from whom one can learn truth, not even from me, citizen of falsehood that I am by birth. Perhaps the truth was not too far off, and perhaps I was, therefore, not so forsaken by the others as I thought, but forsaken only by myself, in that I was a failure and was dying. (B 284)

But it is precisely this self-accusation, this resolution to die, that leads to liberation. The strange hunting-dog appears and insists on chasing him away. The Dog misunderstands him. He has no inkling of the fact that his being driven forth is the very thing that means he is rescued, that the annulling of his self means the gaining of his self, that the threatening hunter is a loving being.

"You dear little dog," [says the hunter] "do you really not understand that I must? Do you really not understand what is self-evident?" I said nothing further in reply, for I perceived—and new life pulsed through me, life such as terror gives—I perceived, through elusive minutiae that perhaps no one except me could have perceived, that the dog was breaking into song from the depths of his breast. (B 286)

At the same time, this song becomes a voice at the "sublimity of which the forest grew hushed," and yet it is a song that "seemed to be there only on my account," a song by which the Dog, ready for death, is then carried off, "in the most glorious leaps and bounds."

The liberated self and the "music of the world" are connected with one another. Such a "singing" is able "to summon down" the true "nourishment" (B 289). The Dog has experienced the breakthrough to truth and freedom.

But his critical task is to substantiate this "experience" validly, to establish a scientific foundation for the "doctrine of singing that summons down nourishment." The fragment concludes with this positive postulate. The "doctrine of singing that summons down nourishment" has been obtained through an "experience," one that is not "communicable," to be sure, but that nevertheless represents an experience fundamental to human existence. The doctrine is based upon intuition, upon prototypes, and upon re-recognition within the "self" of the intuiting individual. Its very knowledge is experience; its experience, knowledge. Its conclusiveness rests within itself. Hence the fragment—if one considers it from within—is in truth already a self-contained whole. For all the basic elements inherent in the doctrine of singing that summons down nourishment are already fully displayed in this "fragment." The fragment itself contains the scientific proof of the doctrine: to translate the doctrine into the language and the reasoning of the science pertaining to the "soil" would mean its destruction. At the conclusion of the "fragment," Kafka has expressed this with acuity. "The more profound reason for my inability" to operate with the thoughts of the science of the soil "seems to me to be an instinct, and truly not a bad instinct. . . . It was this instinct that caused me, perhaps for the very sake of science (but a science that is different from science as it is

pursued today, a science that is ultimate), to value freedom
above all else" (B 289-90). Aloofness from science as it is pursued today is germane to the establishment of this "ultimate"
science. This "ultimate" science, however, remains "science," for
it rests upon the experience of "freedom." Freedom is a basis of
the science of man, even though within the framework of the
science of the soil it is nowhere "provable." The Dog, staking
his life, has furnished proof of it.

The prerequisite of universally binding law is the spirit of
self-sacrifice. This was clearly seen by Hegel. The "strange,"
modern, "educated people without metaphysics" have given up
"this science" (metaphysics)

... in exchange for emotions, for the practical and popular, and
for the erudite historical. Corresponding to this change is the
fact that elsewhere those *solitary individuals* who were sacrificed
by their people and shut off from the world in order that contemplation of the eternal and a life dedicated solely to that contemplation might exist—not for the sake of deriving a profit, but
for the sake of the blessing—disappeared; a disappearance that,
in another context, can be considered as virtually the same
phenomenon as the one mentioned previously.[12]

That is, the "disappearance" of the "solitary individuals ... shut
off from the world" is "the same phenomenon" as the "loss of
the center," so much lamented today, the same as the loss of
metaphysics, and as the present-day victory of the "emotions,"
of the "practical and popular," and of the "erudite historical."
The "center" can be found again when the "solitary individuals
who were sacrificed by their people and shut off from the world"
reappear "not for the sake of deriving a profit, but for the sake
of the blessing." Kafka's "solitude," his seclusion from the
world, is the pre-monition [sic], the lived example of a possible
new "law." It is not the endorsement of "modern nihilism" but
the victory over it.

## C. THE AERIAL DOGS

The problem of establishing such a science of man, however, is

subtly delineated and elucidated in the "investigations" of this
Dog through statements concerning the enigmatic "aerial dogs."
It is only by means of these statements that the problem suc-
ceeds in being fully clarified.

There suddenly occurs the strange phenomenon of beings that
actually exist but that, at the same time, cannot be seen. They
live "separated from the nourishing earth" in an "absurd" condition of "hovering in the air" (B 261). "In general," their
existence is "not at all proved" (B 261). On the other hand they
"contribute . . . a great deal to science" (B 262-63); and, on the
basis of the "questions" of the investigating Dog, a "beginning"
is now being made "to prove" their existence too, "to sputter
out a kind of proof; a beginning is being made, and it will of
course not go beyond this beginning" (B 261-62).

For the most part, these aerial dogs have been identified with
the phenomenon of art and artists, just as the science of music
has been flatly equated with theology or the science of the mind
and spirit, and dietetics with natural science.[13] But why cannot
the aerial dogs be seen? Are art and artists invisible beings? And
why does Kafka employ such puzzling images if they mean
something unequivocal? The fundamental inquiry into the
meaning of his enigmatizations, especially in view of the aerial
dogs, becomes illuminated in the most paradoxical manner; for
here Kafka himself appears to be lifting the veil. Here he quite
openly calls the aerial dogs "art and artists"; here, as research
has naïvely assumed,[14] he himself offers the key to an unequivocal allegorical explanation. But let the reader consider
the text carefully and thoroughly.

In regard to the aerial dogs it is stated: "As is generally the
case, here too, of course, it is not primarily their art that sets
me thinking." "For my feeling, much more astounding" than the
art of the aerial dogs

is the silent purposelessness of these individuals. In general there
is no accounting for it at all; they float in the air, and that's that;
life goes on as usual ; now and then there is talk about art and
artists—that is all. But why, O benevolent society of dogs, why,

I ask you, do the dogs float? What purpose has this occupation of theirs? Why can no word of explanation be obtained from them? (B 261)

Thus this Dog, in his investigations of the aerial dogs, is not concerned with their art at all. He cannot content himself with the customary statement made by other dogs, to the effect that it is a matter of art and artists. Disparagingly he says, "That is all." The thing that agitates and upsets him is, on the contrary, the inexplicability, the silent purposelessness of their existence, and, even more than that, the "duty to maintain silence" that is imposed upon these aerial dogs (B 262). In other words, art belongs to a sphere that cannot be "demonstrated," that cannot "speak," and that dares not let itself be translated into the dogs' normal modes of stating things unless art is willing to relinquish its own essence. Art has actually a "duty" to maintain silence. But "why"? That is the decisive question.

Furthermore, it is said of the aerial dogs that they are useless. True, they contribute a great deal to science. However, their contributions are "worthless and bothersome." Although the aerial dogs have to maintain silence and are not allowed to speak "openly," they nevertheless seek to gain "pardon" for their useless "mode of life," or to divert attention from it and cause it to be forgotten, by means of an "almost intolerable talkativeness" in the form of philosophical considerations or observations of life which they constantly have to communicate, although all their talk is basically worthless and lacking in distinction as far as the power of the mind is concerned, so that science can utilize scarcely anything of it. "In spite of that," however,

if one asks what it is, in general, that the aerial dogs purpose, again and again one will be told in reply that they contribute a great deal to science. "That is correct," one then says, "but their contributions are worthless and bothersome." Any further reply will consist of a shrug of the shoulders, or a change of subject, or annoyance, or laughter ; and a little while later, upon reinquiring, all that one hears yet again is that they contribute to science ;

and finally, before long, if one does not have oneself well in hand, upon being asked oneself, one will say the very same thing in reply. (B 262-63)

Thus, as one considers the aerial dogs, one finds oneself in a meaningless circularity. Only annoying or ridiculous answers can be given to the question of "the purpose and meaning of their occupation."

Kafka has thereby shifted the problem of art into another dimension. The issue is not at all that of the foreground phenomenon, art, nor of its aesthetic appearance, which Kafka designates disparagingly as a "handsome pelt" that cannot reproduce itself, that has no "justification for existing," but that, at most, ought merely to be "tolerated." Likewise, too, it is not a matter of what artists say in interpreting and explaining themselves, for such utterances of artists are basically empty "talk." On the contrary, it is a matter of grasping their "meaning," of understanding the "ground" in which their intention "is rooted." This intention points to an area beyond art, leaving far behind everything that is said about art and artists and everything that "shows itself" as a concrete work of art. The image of the "aerial dogs" makes this very clear. These aerial dogs, unlike art and artists, cannot be seen: "To this day, not a single one ... have I succeeded in seeing." They cannot reproduce themselves, but they nevertheless increase their number in an incomprehensible manner. It is, therefore, not a matter of concrete, living art and artists, but rather of an enigmatic sphere which has no "life" and no "purpose" yet which appears again and again without one's knowing about its origin or its goal; therefore, if one so chooses, it is a matter of an incomprehensible spirituality-intellectuality and an aimless creative genius that cannot be propagated but that nevertheless always does propagate itself, strangely and suddenly cropping up, giving work and subject matter enough to the sciences, supplying them with "contributions" in their striving for knowledge—granted, only contributions that are worthless and bothersome, that cause nothing but headaches and annoyance, since they represent a sphere that cannot be given scientific formulation at all and that can be neither "proved" nor "demonstrated."

The aerial dogs are therefore symbols of a realm that is inherent in the earthly world and that is at the same time unearthly. They live in a "foundation" without foundation: they "float" and "rest" simultaneously (B 260). Their existence is "purposeless" and yet purposeful; their existence, despite its "worthless" contributions, is felt even by science to be significant. The aerial dogs try to "divert" attention from their purposeless existence by means of their stupefying philosophical talk. The essence of their existence, however, is "silence." Only in silence are they real. While Kafka calls their foreground stage scenery "art, artists," he removes this scenery and shows the floating foundation on which rest not only these dogs but also man himself and every science of man.

The "Investigations of a Dog" is an attempt to determine experimentally the potentialities with which man is equipped in order that he may "establish" his own existence meaningfully. Unsuspected, indeed, inexplicable powers are discovered, powers that plainly are evident and simultaneously present in every dog, but of which the Dog himself cannot become fully aware. In love with their own limited abilities and thoughts, neither the aerial dogs, nor the nutrition scientists, nor yet the musicological disciplines "that were never able to penetrate deeply into the people" (B 288), had the power to transcend their limits in such a way that a universal, all-nourishing food and code of law could ever be arrived at through their abilities and knowledge. Only when all the teeth of all dogs were in readiness could the bone open, would the marrow lie "freely exposed to the grasp of the weakest little dog." Art would be true art if it were no longer merely art; science could impart true knowledge of it had knowledge of more than just itself. Nourishment could be found if the dogs gave up this "life that is dear" to them. "True human nature" that is common to everyone, that "cannot but be loved," could show itself. Individuality and "true universality" would be reconciled; the "pure" nature of the spirit could again obtain an "actual existence" in the "people." "The Investigations of a

Dog" points up the final objective of man's investigations.

### *"Josephine the Singer, or the Mouse Nation"* : *Justification and Critique of Art*

The problem of such reconciliation as is presented in "Investigations of a Dog" is subtly delineated with even greater decisiveness in the story of Josephine. "Nation" and "singer" enter into a reciprocal relationship in which the inquiry into their common "ground" is illustrated and elucidated through the mirroring of the one in the other.

The story belongs to the few late works that Kafka completed. Shortly before he died he settled upon its definitive version, and from his very deathbed supervised its going to press. He attached particular significance to its double title. "The story is getting a new title: 'Josephine the Singer—or—The Mouse Nation.' Such titles with 'or' in them are, I grant you, not very pretty, but in this instance the title is perhaps particularly meaningful. It has something of a pair of scales in it."[15] Weighing Josephine and the nation against one another fairly and justly is in fact the theme of the tale.

Josephine's singing possesses an unusual "power" over the nation.[16] "There is no one who is not enraptured by her song. That this is so has even greater significance, because our race, on the whole, does not love music," since it is too much plagued by "daily worries" (E 268). "Only Josephine is an exception to this; she loves music" (E 269). Strangely enough, however, her singing is not at all the kind of music and singing still known intuitively "from the ancient times of our people," and yet it does not differ in any respect from the ordinary squeaking of other mice. She squeaks just like everyone else, and exactly what all the others squeak. The only serious difference, admittedly, is that, in her squeaking, the squeaking of all the others becomes conscious, so that in her squeaking the "real nature [of squeaking] becomes apparent" (E 271). For all the others squeak "without paying any attention to it, indeed without noticing it"

(E 270). Josephine, however, squeaks consciously, clearly striking an attitude as she does so, for she is the "only one" who loves music; "with her passing away, music—who knows for how long—will disappear from our lives" (E 269).

In other words, Josephine's squeaking, her "art," reflects nothing else but the squeaking that all the others do unawares and unconsciously: as is generally the case with Kafka, art presents only what is constantly taking place in life, but it does this in such a way that what takes place emerges suddenly from hiding and "shows" itself in its "real nature." And it is this alone that lends to Josephine's voice such "power" over the people. "This squeaking that starts up at a time when silence is imposed upon everyone else, comes almost like a message of the nation to the individual; Josephine's thin squeaking in the midst of weighty decisions is almost like the pitiful existence of our people in the midst of the tumult of the hostile world" (E 278).

In Josephine's squeaking, therefore, the people recognize themselves; each individual of the race listens as if he were listening to a message from the entire nation; her squeaking is itself "the existence of our people." What is more, it is an existence that suddenly becomes manifest in the midst of the tumult of a hostile world. Absorbed by this tumult, this existence had been forgotten; the people could not and dared not love any music. "Squeaking is the language of our people; yet many a one squeaks as long as he lives and does not know it; but here is where squeaking is freed of the trammels of daily life, and it liberates us too, for a short while" (E 282).

This liberation is at the same time a regaining of a lost happiness that had once been present in the brief, all too brief period of "childhood." Again the sphere of childhood suddenly turns up—that sphere, so crucial for Kafka's writing, that represents a free existence. Indeed, in close connection with that sphere, even in Josephine's squeaking there is the feeling not only of an easy, comfortable peacefulness and security but also of a "gaiety that cannot be stifled." "Something of our poor, brief childhood is in it, something of lost happiness that can never be retrieved; but there is also something of our active, modern life in it, something of its small, incomprehensible gaiety that nonetheless continues to endure and cannot be stifled" (E 282). It is the same combination of childlike nature, cheerful work, and indestructible, quiet composure that we have already encountered as a happy form of existence in the officials of the novel *The Castle*.

In Josephine's squeaking the people perceive all of this. And precisely because her squeaking is *not* music and art in the old sense, because no "excitement," no "flights" occur in it any longer, because this squeaking does not attempt to lift us into another world but, instead, squeaks what everyone else squeaks —because of all this her squeaking does not "disturb us": "it suits us, we are able to take it well," whereas "musical talents ... if they existed," would of necessity be suppressed by the "natural character of our fellow countrymen ... even before these talents could develop" (E 281).

But now comes the volte-face: Josephine does not accept this point of view of the people. She believes that she is actually producing music, art, that her singing is basically different from the squeaking of all the others, and that none of the people can really understand her singing. Furthermore, she believes accordingly that it is not she who is dependent upon the nation, not she who is protected by the people, but conversely "that it is she who protects the nation. Supposedly it is her singing that rescues us from a grave political or economic predicament— nothing less than that does it accomplish; and if it does not stave off the predicament, at least it gives us the strength to endure it" (E 276).

She insists on elevating her singing to be the determinant force of the people, and, as a visible sign of the people's recognizing it as such, she demands that she be exempt from all daily work. However, fundamentally even this is merely a pretext for her actual primary goal: "what she is striving to attain is ... just such public, unequivocal appreciative recognition of her art, as would outlive her times and surpass by far everything as yet known" (E 285).

Here, however, she encounters the invincible resistance of the people. Such recognition would be possible only if

> Josephine is well-nigh beyond the law.... If this were so, Josephine's demands would then be fully understandable; indeed, in this freedom that the people would give her, in this extraordinary gift bestowed on no one else and actually confounding the laws, it would be possible, to a certain extent, to see an admission that, as Josephine maintains, the people do not understand her; that they helplessly marvel at her art and, feeling themselves unworthy of it, strive, by an effort nothing short of desperation, to compensate for this sorrow that they inflict upon her; and that, just as her art lies beyond their power of comprehension, so they place her person and her wishes, too, beyond their sphere of authority. (E 283)

Thereby the crucial problem of the overall Kafkaian interpretation of art and the world is formulated, and, what is more, in its most mature elaboration: it is precisely the point of view that Josephine's art rises above the people's power of comprehension, that it is "beyond the law"—it is precisely that view which is negated. This means, therefore, that even she who represents the "actual nature," indeed the "existence" of the people, that existence which is always "forgotten" in empirical-finite consciousness and which makes manifest an indestructible, free, happy sphere—even she is subject to the universal law and cannot be absolved from "work." "Being" is not exempt from the laws of "existence." The unrecognizable individual "self" is also the "self" of the community which recognizes itself again in what is distinctly individual in Josephine's art. The law of the universe and the law of the individual are identical. At the deepest level, art is never "incomprehensible" and is never "beyond" the people's "power of comprehension." The presumption of being superior to the sphere of "work" is inexorably rejected by "the cold judicial attitude" of the entire nation and is declared to be *hubris* and to be impossible. Against such "freedom," against such a position that makes man's "existence" absolute, the people rightly offer resistance; for such a position would mean nothing less than chaos, the dissolution of everything that exists, the rescinding of all laws. No matter that the people recognize "themselves" in Josephine's squeaking; it is, nevertheless, this very squeaking that is the squeaking of the people. What Josephine sings is sung by everyone; whatever she evokes in the way of visions of freedom is present within all mice as vision. Whatever transcends thought, transcends thought in all mice.

Kafka breaks away decisively from the past tradition of glorifying genius. Hence, therefore—and here Kafka shows his extreme, self-critical consistency—art itself can be dispensed with.

Soon the time will come when she will squeak for the last time and cease to be heard. She is a brief episode in the eternal history of our people, and the people will surmount this loss.... Was her actual squeaking appreciably louder and more vigorous than the memory of it will be? Even during her lifetime, was it really more than simply a recollection? Was it not, on the contrary, that the people, in their wisdom, esteemed Josephine's singing so highly for the very reason that in this way it could not be lost? Perhaps, then, there is not very much that we shall feel deprived of after all. (E 290)

Her art was itself nothing other than "recollection," recollection of life's potentialities that lie dormant within everyone anyway, and that, as such, "cannot be lost" in all eternity. To kindle recollection and make it conscious has been and is the actual function of art. But such recollection can be roused by other spiritual and intellectual forces also. In this sense, too, the singer is both less and more than a singer. She not only images "art" but transcends it, going beyond it into a universal, free "existence" in which everyone recognizes himself again.

In such a transcendence, however, even the demand Josephine makes for such an "appreciative recognition . . . as would outlive her times and surpass by far everything as yet known" is meaningful and justified. Only in her squeaking does there reveal itself an immortal sphere that rises far above "everything known."

This very sphere, however, cannot and may not evade concrete "work"—nor earthly existence with its irrevocable, harsh, "cold" judiciary commands. Art has no privilege on earth. It can retain for itself the true appreciative recognition of the people only if it sustains both spheres and feels itself committed to both. Josephine, in determining to obtain this recognition for herself by pertinacity and cunning, is destroying the meaning and essence of her squeaking. "It is she herself who keeps aloof from singing; it is she herself who is destroying the power that she has won over the people's hearts and minds.... Josephine's fortunes ... are necessarily on the decline. Soon the time will come when she will squeak for the last time and cease to be heard" (E 290).

In this story about the singer Josephine, Kafka launches a definitive attack upon the kind of art that perishes precisely because it insists on being only art and nothing else, and because it cherishes the belief that it represents a "lofty, noble" sphere and ought not to put itself on the same footing with the "ordinary man" (E 287). In modern times art had become a substitute—a sentimental one, or a sulkily defiant, "titanic" one, or an arrogantly aestheticizing one—for a vanishing religion or metaphysics; it professed to represent a "loftier, nobler" sphere that could not be reached by the "ordinary" understanding. Through Kafka art is reduced to its essential meaning: art pipes only what everyone pipes. It must resign itself to this and be content. That is why art is only "a brief episode in the eternal history of our nation," an episode that can be replaced by others which, in turn, can kindle recollection and make us conscious of the immortal existence of our people. The "exceptional position" that had devolved upon art in the *Sturm und Drang* period has come to an end as a result of the very fact that the essential meaning of this art has now been recognized. Kafka's own art sums up the history of that art and concludes it, even though countless works innocently continue to appear within the framework of that lapsed history.

This novella is the last story in the series of works that Kafka himself brought to publication. Everything else of his was supposed to be destroyed. The swan song of his art and of his life, it concludes with these words:

...but Josephine, delivered from the earthly trials and tribulations, which in her opinion are allotted to the elect, will cheerfully lose herself in the countless myriads of our nation's heroes, and, since we cultivate no study of history, will soon, in transcendent redemption, be forgotten just like all of her brothers. (E 291)

The question of why we "cultivate no study of history" will occupy us further in our analysis of "The Construction of the Great Wall of China." In the Universal sphere in which the animal stories take place, no statues are raised. Here nothing temporal, nothing limited is any longer immortalized. Here every pretension is unmasked, every prerogative nullified; here only the eternal forces of existence play their eternal game; here all given facts are "forgotten," and only in such a "forgetting" is "transcendent redemption" possible. For only in "forgetting" is that "free" existence present, that childlike form of existence which has become purposeless and useless, which is a self-vanquishing submission to a self-contained "whole." The "calling to mind" what has been "forgotten" was the function of art that is liberated only when it is forgetful of self and, like a child, "joyously" enters into the sphere of what has been forgotten and is now recalled. Only in this paradoxy of simultaneous recalling and forgetting is the full purpose of human art, of human existence disclosed, a purpose that fulfills itself by abandoning every empirical interpretation—like that Odradek, of which it was said, "The whole, to be sure, appears meaningless, but in its way it is complete in itself." Kafka's swan song was the true song of a transcendent redemption. In it he destroyed himself and his art in order to achieve the "Whole" upon the highest level.


## "The Burrow" and Man's Self

### A. THE QUESTION CONCERNING THE PERFECT BURROW

In the late story "The Burrow," man's true "self," the theme of all of Kafka's animal characters, is meditated upon to the ultimate limit and is given vivid, graphic formulation. No longer is it the case that the confrontation between the unrecognizable self and rational-empirical existence is central to his examination, but rather it is the rationally unrecognizable self that alone is the focal point; that is, in this story the attempt is made, so far as is possible, to unfold and reveal this self and to determine its structure, beyond human capability as this may seem.

The late notes that Kafka made contain the following remarks about the "autobiographical investigations" he had planned:

Not biography, but the investigation and discovery of smallest possible component parts. From these I then want to construct myself, in the same manner in which someone whose house is unsafe wants to construct a safe house next to the unsafe one, using, if possible, the materials of the old house. (H 388)

Kafka wants to "construct" himself from the smallest component parts of his existence in order to produce a "safe" house. Nothing short of this is being attempted by the animal in the story "The Burrow": the construction of a true, absolutely safe and sure existence in the midst of this unsafe earthly world, and, what is more, with the earthly means given us.

The animal dreams his "dream of a wholly perfect burrow" (B 192), in which indestructible peace, absolute quiet and stillness reign. One could interpret this as a revival in modern times of utopias that attempt to construct the one perfect earthly world. There are sympathetic vibrations in this story of the burrow, but this burrow is not a social utopia—although Kafka did concern himself also with social-utopian thoughts (e.g., "The Unpropertied Working Classes," H 126-27). At the heart of the story, on the contrary, is the question of whether it is possible in the midst of the ceaselessly foundering, wearing, self-destructive world, to create a "burrow," a "castle stronghold" (B 176 ff.), that renders one safe against every form of annihilation. It is the age-old question concerning the "mighty fortress" (Luther) that reappears here in a modern variant. The animal hopes "that

the strength of the burrow removes me from the war of extermination that has been going on" (B 186). That is, the bastion of
the "solitary" individual, of him who is "excluded from the
world," is here being built. Giving form to the basic problem
of his life and of his work, Kafka now, however, ponders that
problem with the intention of describing exactly the structure of
this "solitary" and "excluded" individual himself, and of determining all the means that would make it possible for such a
burrow to give absolutely "certain" safety and protection.

To begin with, such a burrow cannot be built without a knowledge of the world that surrounds it. The animal counts on the
fact that the reciprocal war of extermination that is incessantly
raging between nature and society will, as it were, rush past this
burrow of his, and will do so because the combatants are busily
engaged with one another and have no notion at all of the
existence of the burrow. It is "even better to expose oneself to
rather heavy traffic that, because of its size, is swept along by
its own momentum.... There are many enemies here ... but
they battle against one another, and thus occupied, they race past
the burrow" (B 186). The world, having grown addicted to its
struggle for existence, knows nothing of the animal's secret
stronghold.

However, in the case of this burrow it is not a matter of an
inwardness, encapsulated with reference to the outside world,
that is utopistically hiding from the struggle for power that is
taking place outside. The animal is well aware that at any time
some enemy or other could break into the burrow and in the
process destroy it and himself as well; he knows that "in its
complete seclusion" he is "at the mercy of the first comer who
would search slowly but surely and force his way in" (B 186).
The very issue that concerns him, therefore, is that of gaining
both inner and outer security.

### B.  WAKING AND SLEEPING—THINKING AND BEING

Maximum security would be guaranteed if the animal were
able to watch over and to take in at a glance both the inner

world and the outer world simultaneously. This is possible in only one position in front of the entrance to his home, for from there he is able to take in at a glance both worlds, the outer and the inner.

However, in such a borderline situation the animal must find himself, as it were, in a double existence: he must simultaneously be both entirely within himself and entirely outside himself. A state would have to be achieved which would unite in itself the highest degree of alert, wide-awake consciousness and the deepest, most tranquil sleep, thus a state in which thinking and being are synchronized. On the one hand the animal must be at one with himself, entirely without reflection, must be at rest in himself and enjoy an indestructible inner peace of mind—to signify this Kafka employs the image of profound sleep. On the other hand, in the keenest luminosity of consciousness he must take in at a glance both himself, as he sleeps, and the dangerous world. Only in this way can he be certain of a perfect existence.

I . . . secretly spy upon the entrance to my dwelling—this time from outside—for days and nights on end. People may call it foolish, but it affords me an ineffable joy, and it comforts me. It seems to me then as if, while sleeping, I were standing not in front of my dwelling but in front of myself, and as if I had the good fortune to be able to sleep profoundly and simultaneously keep close watch over myself. To a certain degree I have the distinction not only of seeing the spectres of night in the helplessness and blind trustfulness of sleep, but also simultaneously of facing them in actuality with calm discernment, possessed of the full strength of my waking state. And I find that, strangely enough, I am not in such a bad way as I have often thought, and as I probably shall again think, when I descend into my dwelling. (B 185)

From this it indubitably follows that the burrow is the "self" of the animal. The animal in building the burrow has created his self, or, to express this more accurately—since the animal cannot beget himself and since his self is, therefore, already given and present in him—has delved and searched into his self as he works and meditates, and in accordance with the possibilities of his conceptual world has constructed this self before his eyes so that it now stands like an objective structure before his conscious awareness. "Being" has been brought before itself by thinking, and in this sense it has also "edified" itself. Thus it faces itself. And that is the position of the animal in front of "the entrance to my dwelling."

But from the moment he descends into his own inner being, into his self, once again he is "in a bad way," for then he can no longer survey and keep close watch over the outside world; indeed, he can neither survey nor watch over even himself. The antimony between thinking and being cannot be resolved.

Unconscious self-certitude does not exist in the human sphere —it is at best reserved for that which is pure object, in which all certainty and all self are at the same time obliterated, since in the realm of things nothing at all is conscious any longer. Unconscious self-certitude, therefore, must be designated as self-contradictory. Unconsciousness and certainty exclude one another; but so do consciousness and certainty. As soon as the animal steps into the structure of his self that he has himself conceived, that is, as soon as he wants to be at one with himself, he can no longer survey his own self; he can no longer "keep a close watch" over himself; he finds himself in uncertainty with respect to the world within and the world without; he no longer knows what dangers threaten him from the unguarded world of his own uncontrolled emotions, passions, etc.; he is at the mercy of the "spectres of night" in the "helplessness and blind confidence of sleep"; that is, he has succumbed even by day to the half-conscious or subconscious world of his inner being; for even his daytime consciousness is unable fully to survey his inner being; even that daytime consciousness is, to a certain extent, "sleep."

Moreover, even that universal position in front of the entrance to the self proves to be an illusion.

Well, one wakes up quickly, with a start, from one's childish dreams. What kind of security is this, really, that I am keeping an eye on? Have I any right to judge the danger that I am in while I am in the burrow, according to the experiences I have while I am here outside? ... No, I am actually not observing and watching my sleep, as I believed, but on the contrary it is I who sleep while the destroyer keeps watch. (B 186-87)

The seemingly wide-awake consciousness of the animal in front of his own burrow is itself merely sleep. Indeed, the entire I of the animal is a sleeping I, and this is so for the very reason that, while he is observing himself from without, he is no longer identical with himself and can err with respect to both himself and the threatening dangers "in the burrow," so that the only one that is really waking and watching is perhaps the destroyer who sees the observing animal together with his burrow at a glance, and destroys both.

The animal existing on the "borderline" between within and without is indeed neither *in* the outer nor *in* the inner world, and hence possesses no knowledge of what either world really looks like; he cannot "judge according to the experiences I have while I am here outside," and is therefore at the mercy of any unknown destroyer who happens to be "perhaps . . . among those who saunter past paying no attention to the entrance" (B 187). For the animal that surveys himself has through that very act fallen out of his own protective burrow and hence, more defenseless than before, is exposed to the universal war of extermination. Neither in his interior castle stronghold nor on the outside is he able to assert himself, and he is in danger of falling victim to an unknown adversary who is more than a match for him in watchfulness.

For only when he is in his burrow do his enemies have his "correct," his "full" scent; consequently they do not dare to attack the burrow; the danger remains "normal" (B 187), for then the front lines are clearly demarcated. The animal, fully armed, is then at one with himself and not divided against himself, even though he may, without reflection, succumb to the unknown forces of his inner being. The enemy thereby possesses the "full scent" of the animal. "And is not the presence of the full scent often the prerequisite for normal danger?" (B 187). However, the moment the animal has forsaken himself, as it were, and observes himself from without, his self, too, is defenselessly exposed to every surprise attack, and he can no longer recognize the danger "I am in when I am in the burrow."

The issue is that very same state of disorientation which is the fate of everyone in Kafka's works, who, like the Hunter Gracchus, dwells amidst all spheres and who is neither entirely without nor entirely within. It would seem that to have a universal perspective is tantamount—as in the case of the Hunter Gracchus —to fluttering helplessly in Nowhere.

### C. THE WAY TO ONE'S SELF

The animal must, therefore, try to reach his burrow again. This would be possible in full safety, however, only if upon his descent he could look simultaneously within and without. This, in spite of all the technical "procedures" (B 187) that the animal devises (two entrances, a confidential agent who undertakes the watch outside, etc.), is impossible. That is, all external "means of help" fail or are harmful wherever it is a question of experiencing and gaining the self.

Finally the realization dawns upon the animal that, in the last analysis, it is not at all a matter of "escape" and "safety," but that "it is really impossible to descend into the burrow without patently, at least for a little while, abandoning my dearest possessions to all the foes that surround me: on the ground, in the trees, in the air above" (B 189); and that "the burrow ... is *not* just a hole for escape and rescue"; that "the thought of safety" is far removed from him,

that here is my castle which in no way can belong to anyone else, and which is so much mine that here, ultimately, I shall be able quietly to accept the fatal wound from my enemy, for my blood will trickle away here upon my own soil and will not be lost. And what else but this is really, then, the meaning of those fair hours that I am wont to spend in the passageways, half in peaceful slumber, half in cheerful wakefulness. (B 193-94)

The animal now senses that the "self" can in fact be gained only through the surrender of the self, and that only by such a surrender does he really become himself and gain a safe existence "that cannot be lost," and, what is more, gain indestructible peace, in a joyous fusion of sleep and waking, repose and activity. Only by the hazardous venture of renouncing oneself and all self-interest, by relinquishing all self-protective utilitarian thinking, can a perfect, happy existence be made possible.

The animal even recognizes that he does not need to do anything at all in order to reach his burrow, for "the burrow and I belong to one another, are so intimately connected," that it would "quite suffice if I waited passively, for nothing can separate us lastingly from one another, and somehow, eventually, I shall most assuredly get down there" (B 194).

And thus the animal does actually reach his burrow in a peculiar in-between state that is no longer a combination of extreme conscious awareness and deepest sleep but a surrender of both, a state of whirling self-abandonment that does not rationally control the empirical world nor fully withdraw from it by means of profound sleep: "And now, already incapable of thought for very weariness, dispirited, with my head bent low, unsteady on my feet, in a semitrance, feeling my way more than actually walking, I approach the entrance . . . slowly descend. . . . Only in this state, and in this state alone, can I carry out this undertaking" (B 194-95). It is the same state which we shall later on treat of in detail in our discussion of the novel *The Castle*. In that state K., incapable of thought for sheer weariness, actually gains the decisive insights into the structure of the world authorities and into the possibilities of the "fulfillment" of all his own wishes; that is to say, he gains decisive insights into self-fulfillment.

Within the interior of the burrow, however, the situation is logically reversed: "It is a new world that gives one new powers, and the weariness that exists up above on the outside is not felt as such down here" (B 195). A similar reversal takes place in *The Castle*, when in the morning K., reeling with weariness along the corridors of the officials, witnesses with amazement their entirely different kind of weariness, a weariness that in the midst of "joyous" work radiates "indestructible quiet, indestructible tranquillity" (S 360), so that K.—by contrast with his previous state, in which he had entertained despairing reflections—now suddenly feels himself "almost at home in the midst of the activity" and views "all this not only with curiosity but also with sympathetic participation" (S 362).

The animal that has descended into his burrow experiences the same cheerful weariness, Suddenly "new powers" are operating here—powers that the animal knew nothing about when he was outside, indefatigably observing himself and the outer world. In the burrow the animal has "infinite time" (B 196). He has escaped from the torment of time-consciousness that calculates everything quantitatively,

for everything I do there, is good and important and feeds and satisfies me to a certain degree [image of "nourishment"!] ... and I just toy with my work and add to it and laugh to myself and am happy.... For your sake have I come, O passageways and rooms, and, above all, for the sake of your questions, O castle stronghold; for your sake have I set no store by my life, after foolishly trembling for it for a long while and delaying my return to you. (B 196-97)

The animal is now entirely alone with himself and is happy. He is in harmony with himself and his world. But the cleavage between subject and object, between thinking and being, is nevertheless not removed thereby. The threatening world outside continues to exist, even though it be merely in the form of the "small things" that infiltrate the burrow and that must incessantly be disposed of by the animal; similarly, man is constantly exposed to the guerilla warfare of humdrum everyday life. But not even the inner world bestows assured peace—not by any means. Indeed, the very "enticement" of becoming lost in oneself is dangerous. The animal succumbs to the "enticement" of sleep. From the joyous work that he buoyantly performs as if it were mere play, against his will he sinks into "profound sleep" (B 197).

### D. THE MENACE THROUGH THE SELF

There now follows what is possibly the most deeply meaningful twist in this story. Because of the very fact that in such sleep this animal is resting in his self, completely unconscious, this self becomes the animal's mortal enemy. For in such a state of unconsciousness the self has become lawless, can no longer be defined; hence, in turn, it is also no longer able to define anything. But it is clamoring for definition; it demands to be "heard." Only by listening to itself, only by understanding and subordinating the empirical I to the self that sits in judgment, could this self attain to laws of self-government and thereby also to a binding legislation for its outer and inner existence. Hence, from out of the animal's profound slumber this voice of the self issues as a menacing, frightening "hissing" that wakes the sleeper. No matter where the animal goes, this omnipresent hissing remains the same. Nowhere does it change in intensity or in pitch. It occurs rhythmically at short intervals. It is nothing other than the animal's own breathing: the menacing voice that rings forth from within the animal himself.

However, the animal does not listen to himself. Just as at one time, up above, outside, in front of the entrance to the burrow, he confronted himself with his reified self—to be sure, at that time still knowing that what he confronted was his self—he now, down here, succumbs to the fatal delusion that his self is something outside, an enemy that is closing in upon him from without. The menacing, judgment-pronouncing voice of the self is identified with the outside world. The animal does not face the demand of the self; he does not condemn himself; on the contrary, he believes that all that is threatening, all that is hostile, every instance of guilt must be seen solely in the external course of the world—in this respect he is no different from Josef K., when the latter fails to execute judgment upon himself but instead accuses the world order of having instituted an absurd legal action against him, an innocent man.

Hence, the animal, pursued by terror of the unknown self that is "inexplicable" to him, rushes about in his own burrow as if insane. Everything that the animal had built with infinite effort, everything that he had held up to himself as a self-image—all these things were merely building blocks, elements that were to give him security, elements with which he identified and for which he was ready to lay down his life; but all this was, so to speak, merely the reification of his own will, of his work and planning. It was never the true voice of his inner being, never the "invisible court of justice" where the final, most significant decisions are reached. The animal now objectifies even this highest authority, seeking to transform it into something external, but his efforts cannot meet with success.

To the animal the "hissing" sound, with its unvarying intensity, remains incomprehensible; just so does the strong, high-pitched tone ring out in the Kafkaian courtrooms, penetrating, threatening, challenging, and summoning for the final, decisive self-confrontation. Harassed by the hissing sound the animal, in spite of himself, begins to destroy his own burrow. Everything begins to reverse itself. The war of annihilation going on outside is displaced and shifted to the inner life. The animal destroys himself. "A complete reversal of the conditions within the burrow; what was hitherto the place of danger has become a place of peace, but the castle stronghold has been swept into the turmoil of the world and into the dangers intrinsic to the world" (B 210). For the animal believes that in the hissing sound he hears only the menacing turmoil of the outside world.

What was to happen at the end of the story we do not know. Max Brod gives a twofold interpretation in the appendix. He relates that Kafka, during his illness, in his everyday conversations with his friends, often identified the animal with his own tormenting cough. This corresponds to the text of the story, too, according to which the unvarying hissing can originate only in the breathing of the animal himself, since throughout the narrative the natural conditions that prevail when an animal burrows are most accurately adhered to; nowhere in the description of the spatial particulars is there a leap into the unreal, so that the unvarying intensity of the noise that the animal hears while constantly changing his position cannot be explained as existing in an external enemy. Furthermore, Kafka never felt his agonizing cough to be merely a biological threat of death, but rather an invitation to self-justification in the face of death. "The lung injury" had always been a "symbol" for him, the "depth" of which "signifies its justification" (T 529).

On the other hand, however, Brod quotes a remark made by Dora Dymant according to which the animal is defeated in battle with another animal that breaks in on him (B 350). On the basis of her remark, the hissing sound would necessarily stem from an external opponent. It will have to be left in doubt as to whether this is an instance of Dora Dymant's erroneous interpretation of an ambiguous remark of Kafka's, to the effect that his hero was perishing of his opponent. Possibly Dora Dymant misunderstood and naïvely imagined the opponent to be a real, empirical enemy. According to the total structure of the story, and also according to the structure of Kafkaian self-interpretations, the opponent, as countless confessions reveal, can be only within the hero himself.

In proof of this only a few instances need here be cited: "You are the assignment. Not a pupil far or near" (H 83); "Should I die very soon or become totally incapacitated for life—there is a strong likelihood of this, since I have had to expectorate a great deal of blood these last two nights—I may say that I have torn myself to pieces" (H 131); "The systematic destruction of myself in the course of the years has been amazing; it has been like a slowly developing breach in a dike, a process that is full of purpose. The spirit that has accomplished this must be celebrating triumphs; why doesn't it let me participate in them?" (T 544); "Only in such extremes does one notice how every human being is irretrievably lost in himself" (T 349); "His own frontal bone bars his way; against his own brow he heats his brow bloody" (B 292).

However, both points of view can be compatible with one another. If one looks more carefully into the problem of self-vindication and self-condemnation in Kafka, one comes upon a highly remarkable and significant insight of his that must engage our thought first and foremost; for only through this insight does the animal's struggle with his mysterious opponent become comprehensible.

### E. THE WORLD AS MAN'S "MOTIVATION"

At one point Kafka writes, "The entire visible world is perhaps nothing but a motivation of man, who wishes to rest for a moment" (H 49). He writes that man wishes to evade the "knowledge of good and evil" that would compel him to act in accordance with that knowledge; man wishes to gain "rest," untroubled by that knowledge, and therefore, since he does not possess the strength for good action, he must "destroy himself" (H 49).

Total self-vindication—total knowledge of good and evil— forces man to realize that it is impossible for him to act rightly and well on earth, and, as a result, man must destroy himself in order to reach the absolute good. Therein lies "the meaning of the threat of death, when he was forbidden to eat of the tree of knowledge; perhaps, too, this is the original meaning of natural death" (H 49). Indeed, that is also, for instance, the meaning of the court's summoning Josef K., at the end of his "trial," to kill himself. But man is afraid of this self-destruction; that is, he is afraid of total self-encounter and self-knowledge, the "strength" for which is "not bestowed" upon him (H 49). There is an analogous statement in the novel *The Trial*:

K. now knew with certainty that it would have been his duty ... to take hold of the knife himself and to bury it in himself. But he did not do this.... He could not fully do what was expected of him ... the responsibility for this final shortcoming rested with the one who had denied him the last bit of strength necessary for it. (P 271)

Accordingly, man flees from absolute self-responsibility and self-knowledge.

He prefers to annul the knowledge of good and evil (the term "Fall of Man" has its origin in this fear); but once something has happened it cannot be annulled but can merely be blurred and obscured. It is to this end that motivations arise. The entire world is full of them ; indeed, the entire visible world is perhaps nothing but a motivation of man who wishes to rest for a moment. (H 49)

That is to say, man does not bring root knowledge into full play, but moves within blurred half-knowledge: he begins to "motivate" his life, his conduct, and his deeds. He asks, "Why did I act as I did? What made me do this or that? What conditions and laws prevail in the world, that evoke this or that attitude?" etc. The question of good and evil becomes an empirical question of hypotheses and possibilities of ethical action, and at the same time the question of guilt is shifted to the given circumstances, the environment, one's fellow men, to the psychological conditions, and so on.

In this way the entire visible world becomes a motivation of man; what is more, it becomes a product, a construction of man who is, indeed, constantly shaping and changing his environment in accordance with his needs, his ideals, or the direction of his will. Man strives to create a world for himself in which he might be able to live "well." But in so doing he no longer poses the radical question of the good but purports to be constantly in quest of the good. The striving for knowledge is substituted for knowledge itself. Man endeavors "to falsify the actuality of knowledge, to make knowledge into the goal instead" (H 50). In such unremitting striving for knowledge does the empirical world then run its course—in man's thinking and working.

In all this, however, he evades the root knowledge that is already "accomplished fact." To evade or to "hesitate" before ultimate knowledge creates constant "unrest," causes work, to be sure; but fundamentally this is tantamount to trying to find "rest" and not being bothered by the real, ultimate, most difficult question; it is tantamount, as it were, to ridding oneself of the "court of the highest instance." In order to achieve "rest," man incessantly rushes into unrest. This is precisely the situation of the animal in the burrow.

The animal constantly wishes to gain "rest," "profound quiet," and he struggles expressly for this rest (B 207, 210; *inter alia*). But the peculiar hissing sound, destroying the quiet, invariably makes him start up in fright. Unceasingly the animal now brings forward arguments to the effect that the outer, "visible" world is causing this hissing. The animal therefore believes that he must combat this outer world. Once he destroys the strange, unknown opponent, then absolute, paradisiac rest will be achieved. For the animal, his actual opponent has to be the world. He does not sense that he is thereby trying "to falsify the actuality of knowledge" (H 50). Hence, too, in the animal's conceptual world, his opponent can appear as an external foe, although in the last analysis it is the animal himself who is calling upon himself to know himself and to do away with himself; in like manner, in the "Investigations of a Dog," the hunting-dog demands of the despairing Dog just such extreme nullification of the self, nullification that is at the same time also liberation of the self, and he demands this to the ominous sound of that music that is directed solely at him and that seems to be present "only on my account."

From this there ensue far-reaching conclusions with regard to Kafka's view of life.

F.   SURMOUNTING OF THE SELF AND OF THE WORLD:
     THE INDIVIDUAL UTOPIA AND THE SOCIAL UTOPIA.

The antimony, as described, between consciousness and self, thinking and being, is now revealed as a moral problem: "Eating of the tree of knowledge" brings into the world both the subject-object cleavage and "sin." Both are identical: the word *Sünde*, "sin," goes back to the word *sondern*, "to set asunder." The world's "war of extermination," of which the animal speaks, the continuing battle that rages among men, originates through the fact that man is constantly objectifying himself and transforming the partner into a menacing opponent, instead of seeing in him his own "true, human essence" that "cannot but be loved" (H 46). Genuine rest could come into being among men if they affirmed and welcomed absolute knowledge of good and evil, if each one were capable of confronting himself, if each one took all guilt upon himself, if each one did not make the knowledge of good and evil into a goal but instead accepted it as an event that has already taken place. Under such conditions a "perfect burrow" would be achieved, one in which man could live free of fear, where "unwatched and unguarded" he could enter and leave. The knowledge of good and evil would become binding law that everyone imposed upon himself, whereby order and indestructible peace would come to pass. Only then would thinking and being become identical; only then would unity be found between the objective world and the unobjective-invisible self.

Kafka's individual utopia, of man rising to his highest stature, and Kafka's social utopia, of the unpropertied working classes, are here united. Renouncing ownership and "possessions" is the same as renouncing the self's turning into a confronting partner whom one thinks one is attacking and annihilating, or even owning and "possessing." Only as the self passes judgment on itself can it open to the self of everyone else; only then can self-encounter become world-encounter; only then will subject and object no longer fall asunder in threatening and unremittent reversals. The animal, in his fearful whirl between sleeping and waking, believing himself kept watch over and observed, now by himself, now by his enemies, can find rest, can escape the diabolic circle of hostile reversals only if he confronts self-knowledge.

With this Kafka demarcates himself from every system of psychology: "Psychology is the reading of a mirror-writing" (H 122), "... the description of a reflection such as we, who have sucked ourselves full of the earth, imagine;* for no reflection actually appears—it is simply that we see earth wherever we turn" (H 72). With the aid of psychology man tries to motivate his life; he "underpins" his "existence with retrospective justifications" (H 121). He sees his life determined by motives, and "retrospectively" seeks with the help of these motives to level off the given measure of his guilt and innocence.

For Kafka, however, the relationship between life and

---

*Tr. note: The beginning of this sentence in Kafka reads: "Psychology is the description of the reflection of the earthly world on the heavenly plane, or, more accurately ...."

justification is reversed. The primary thing is justification. The feeling of absolute responsibility is the first thing that makes a human being a human being. Man's existence is defined through his "eating of the tree of knowledge." "In fact, he erects his life upon his justifications" (H 121). In other words, man is delegated to establish his existence on free and total self-responsibility; he is to assume the burden of his life and being as an act of free will and thereby as existential guilt as well; and he is not to falsify and "annul" the knowledge of good and evil, but to accept it as inevitable. This he can do only by assuming the judgeship "in a blacker night than has ever yet existed," and by "himself" becoming the judge.

The subjective world and the objective world coincide and become as one in such a judgeship. The so-called objective world proves to be the motivation of the subject. The subject recognizes it, too, as his own act, an act with which he cannot saddle other subjects. Only through such knowledge can a law be found that is valid and binding for everyone; a law, however, that cannot and may not disintegrate once again into merely "objective" laws, legal paragraphs, and individual decrees but which is grounded uniquely in the free, ethical responsibility of the one who took all guilt upon himself and who is capable, solely on the basis of his "battle experience," of "being" binding law.

For all that, however, the objective world does not thereby become a mere fiction of an empirical subject. It came into being through endless historical objectifications of the human mind, and it therefore confronts every individual subject as a world that dominates him and that is ineluctable. But the animal of "The Burrow" is not an individual person; the animal is man in general, the self in its most general and universal significance. Only the self of total mankind, by levelling knowledge at itself, could transform the hostile world that it created into a friendly world.

In all honesty, Kafka has refrained from depicting a utopia of such nature. What he does represent is the prototype of the human "burrow." He has pointed out the secret law according to which human life can threaten, destroy, recognize, and raise itself to its highest level. The outside world is recognized as a "motivated" world that is projected and expediently ordered on the basis of definite states of consciousness in man; just so does the animal create corridors and walls and bastions within which he hopes to live with safety and security, with the result that he identifies this basically external, concrete burrow with himself; and he does not realize that what has been created, for the very reason that it confronts the animal as something empirical, is no longer the animal's "self."

Only when he is in the state of "sleep" in front of the burrow—that is, in a state of consciousness freed of purpose—can the animal in his imagination become at one with his burrow, since in this state the separation between internal and external is eliminated. "It then seems to me as if I were standing . . . in front of myself" (H 185). However, in this very state he must also keep watch over himself, precisely because he has systematically, in accordance with his conceptual world, "built up" his self as something other, something actually empirical, something that stands "in front of" him even in sleep and that, hence, even in sleep must be "kept watch over." This is what accounts for the paradoxical combination of sleep and onlooking consciousness.

This same situation, however, necessarily brings about fear of the superior consciousness of another, objective world, fear of an opponent and "destroyer" who keeps watch over the animal. This means that the animal, like every empirical human being, sees himself facing another, objective world that determines *him*; against that world's encroaching power-constellations the individual is helpless. In like manner every individual subject sees himself constantly surrounded and hemmed in by objective social and natural forces that he can never entirely escape. Before these he must withdraw into his "burrow"; but this, however, is possible only through danger and temporary surrender to what is always seen as the adversary—the world.

Moreover, since even within his burrow the animal is never able to emerge from his "motivations," the external world, with its threatening noise, penetrates the animal's inner being too, and the voice of the animal's self is transformed into an external enemy. Thus, the animal persists in objectifications of his self. He is never able to venture forth and bring about a reversal, a "leap" out of the "fighting line." This means that he never becomes identical with his own objectifications; he never assumes responsibility and free self-determination with respect to the world, to thought, and to existence: he is never able to integrate the world and his own inner being within his "self," and he can never reach significant decisions about them through this "self." That would be possible only if the animal were able to advance to the absolute "good," that is to say, if he were ready to pronounce sentence on himself.

With respect to what is commonly understood as "sacrifice" of the self, the animal has not yet attained to the "good." For even in his readiness to receive "the fatal wound" from his enemy gladly, and to offer up his blood for the burrow that is so inseparable from him (so inseparable that the animal's blood can quietly ooze there, because in this burrow the blood cannot be lost but still remains, so to speak, in the animal), even in such a spirit of sacrifice the self and the world are still viewed as a hostile partnership. Only if the cleavages between subject and object were set aside or clearly detected would it be possible for a "good," amicably ordered world to come into being. Peace could come upon the earth if the delusions of consciousness disappeared.

Kafka's "Burrow" reflects this delusion of consciousness in the human race, a delusion from which man never escapes. The pessimistic turn at the end, in which the animal perishes of the antagonism of his self, is the honest reply to mankind's state of consciousness. Only if mankind abandoned its "motivations" would a different answer be possible. In that event, however, mankind too would be in a different world.

### CHAPTER IV

# The Construction of the Objective World and the Binding Law

*The Construction of Mankind and*
*the Construction of the Tower of Heaven*

With his story "The Burrow" Kafka drew the ultimate conclusions from his poetic representations of the human "self." Another stratum of his representations is concerned with the construction of the objective world confronting the self. This stratum, apart from being present in the novels, is given expression primarily in those stories that deal with the "Construction of the Great Wall of China," or with the construction of the Babylonian Tower.

The fragment "The Construction of the Great Wall of China" begins with seemingly contradictory formulations. "The Great Wall of China," the first sentence states, "was completed at its northernmost point" (B 67). In spite of this completion, however, the Wall consists only of unconnected "construction sections" and many "gaps"; many "large gaps" were filled in only slowly,

after it had been proclaimed that the construction of the Wall was already completed. Indeed, there are said to be gaps that

have not been built up at all—an assertion, to be sure, that . . .
at least as far as each single individual is concerned, one cannot
verify with one's own eyes and by one's own yardstick because
of the great extent of the Wall. (B 67)

The Wall thus transcends individual man's power of comprehension. The Wall is finished and yet not finished. It is said
to have been constructed "as a protection to endure for centuries" (B 68) against the free-roaming, wild nomadic peoples
of the north. But since it is said to consist of unconnected constructed sections, it is an easy matter for these nomadic peoples
to destroy the "portions of the Wall that stand forsaken in a
desolate region"; indeed, these nomadic peoples, because of their
free, easy mobility, have "a better perspective, perhaps, of the
progress being made in building the Wall . . . than even we, its
builders" (B 68).

"Even so, it was probably impossible to carry out the construction in any other way" (B 68) for the following reasons.
There were needed for construction "men who intellectually
were far superior to their outwardly insignificant task" (B 69-
70), who were capable of being in "sympathy to the depths of
their hearts with what was here at stake" and who possessed
"an abiding feeling of personal responsibility" (B 68). It was
necessary for these men to be in the grip of "impatience . . . to see
the construction rise at last in its perfect entirety" (B 69). For
the very reason that they knew what was at stake, and because
they were intellectually superior to the insignificant part allotted
them—and only such men could be used—they could not help
being in despair over their own limited activity:

. . . the hopelessness of such painstaking labor that, in spite of
everything, would not achieve its goal even in a long lifetime,
would have made them desperate, and, above all, would have
made them of less value for the work involved. For that reason
the system of constructing sections of the Wall was chosen. In
approximately five years it was possible to complete five hundred
meters ; after that period of time, it is true, the leaders were, as
a rule, much too much exhausted and had lost all confidence in
themselves, in the construction, in the world. (B 70)

It was then necessary to remove them once more from their seclusion, that "uninhabited mountainous region" in which they had lived "hundreds of miles distant from their homes," and bring them into contact with their homes, with their people, with the "pious" who were begging for the "completion of the construction," and with the leaders in the higher ranks conducting the overall construction of the entire Wall, so that they could gather hope and courage.

The system of constructing sections thus came about as a result of the essential character of human nature itself, since human nature in the face of such an immense architectural construction despairs of itself and of the world, and driven by necessity can effect only partial structures.

Furthermore, the construction of such a wall leads to the frontiers of human existence. It is significant that the people who do the constructing can and may carry out their work only at a distance from where they customarily live. They are forced to forsake their "homes, the river with its bridges, [their] mothers and fathers, [their] weeping wives, [their] children who still need instruction" (B 75), and must do their work in uninhabited mountainous regions. This, too, is a source of despair. And for this reason too, they are unable to remain at their work uninterruptedly.

Thereby, a further level of meaning is touched upon. Generally speaking, the construction is feasible only if the command is issued to all suitable workmen that they leave the life they love; that is to say, if the construction is recognized as a great concerted undertaking, the task of all humanity. And China, indubitably, is here the symbol of all humanity, and indeed of the universe, for "our country is so immense that no fairy tale could do justice to its size, the sky scarcely spans it" (B 77). Even the free, wild peoples in the north, beyond the borders, are antithetically a part of this, as will yet be made evident.

To be working at the frontiers of this country means the same, basically, as to be working at the frontiers of human existence and making these boundaries secure. Only now does it become clear why all the construction workers—like the truth seekers in the "Investigations of a Dog"—have to forsake the life that is dear to them. In the construction of the Wall, Kafka has actualized his investigating Dog's wish to force all dogs into a *joint* cooperative effort.

The construction of the Wall was begun at a definite point in time—that is to say, when the narrator was twenty years old and, of course, after careful preparation. For "architecture," fifty years earlier, had already been "... declared the most important field of knowledge, and everything else was granted recognition only insofar as it related to it" (B 68-69). The awareness of its significance had been fixed in everyone's mind; all China was convinced of its necessity; for only in this way would the work of the individual achieve meaning and direction. "For many who formerly," before the beginning of the joint labor, "had reached the highest level of the training available to them, and for years had not known what to do with what they had learned, gadded about uselessly with the most grandiose architectural plans in their heads, and went to rack and ruin by the score" (B 69). This means, too, that the most significant knowledge of individuals', their deepest insights and most brilliant architectural plans are of no use unless work is being done according to a common plan.

There is no limit to the mind's "going to rack and ruin," so long as each individual is concerned only with himself. Hence even after the start of the work, the individual can overcome his despair only if he emerges again and again, at certain intervals, from the limitation of his part of the work and resumes contact with the whole—above all, with the chief leaders who draft the plans. Only in this way will he gain distance from himself, will he obtain a certain perspective of the whole and be made to feel that he is not working meaninglessly and in vain.

But who are the chief leaders, and how does such a collective will to build, how does such an architect's plan come into being at all? To answer this question, one must first of all follow the narrator's train of thought exactly.

The narrator remarks that "in the days when the construction was first begun" there was "in everybody's hands" a book written by a scholar that "at that time" stirred up "a great deal of confusion in people's heads, perhaps for the very reason that so many people were trying to rally together and concentrate as far as possible on one goal" (B 71-72). The narrator mentions this book after having formulated the following thought: "First of all, one obviously has to admit that in those days feats were accomplished that were but little inferior to the construction of the Tower of Babel; feats that, so far as pleasing God is concerned (at least according to human reckoning), certainly represent the very antithesis of that edifice" (B 71). The Great Wall of China is thus, by contrast with the construction of the Tower of Babel, "pleasing to God." The book of that scholar, however, sought to prove "that it was by no means for the reasons generally claimed, that the construction of the Tower of Babel was a failure," but "that the construction failed owing to the weakness of its foundation." The Great Wall of China, he said, now "for the first time within the age of man would create a secure foundation for a new Tower of Babel. Well, then, first the wall and then the tower" (B 71-72).

Thus the scholar was concerned with laying the foundation for a tower that would reach to the sky. The Wall for him is merely the basis, the secure foundation as it were, for mankind's eternal dream of storming the heavens.

In the fragment "The City Coat of Arms" Kafka developed this thought further. According to this fragment also, the reason why the construction of the Tower of Babel fails is that people shrink back from "laying the foundations" (B 94). That is to say, people had been of the opinion that "the thought of building a tower that would reach to the sky" was an eternal one that would live "as long as there are people." However, since this thought cannot be actualized by one generation, and since mankind is constantly making progress in knowledge, inventions, and efficiency of construction, it is completely superfluous to occupy oneself with this construction now, at the present moment. Much more important is the construction of the workers' city. Everyone endeavored to obtain "the most beautiful quarters" for himself. As a result, endless wars arose. In the brief intervals of peace "the city was beautified and thereby, of course, fresh jealousy and new battles were engendered" (B 95). Thus humanity limits itself here to its material existence; this leads to the unceasing battle of extermination waged by everyone against everyone. "Furthermore, even the second or third generation recognized the meaninglessness of constructing a tower that would reach to the sky" (B 95). This complete finalization of human existence, however, is intolerable. Hence the fragment concludes with the apocalyptic hope that one "prophetic day . . . the city . . . will be shattered . . . by a gigantic fist" (B 95).

Thus, neither sheer worldliness nor titanic storming of Heaven is pleasing to God.

The scholar's book, however, confuses people's minds because it is aspiring to the opposite extreme from the earthbound city. The Great Wall of China is to become the foundation of the tower structure reaching to Heaven. Making the boundaries of mankind safe and secure is to serve the purpose of storming the heavens. The construction of the Babylonian Tower had once failed because people were not concerned about their boundaries and did not lay any "foundations," but only squabbled among themselves and for that reason completely forgot the construction of the tower that was to reach the heavens. But now, if by means of the Great Wall of China the boundaries, and thereby also the foundations, of human existence are created, then mankind too can try its hand at fulfilling its age-old dream of storming the heavens.

The scholar hereby sets a goal that once again immediately uproots human beings from the safeguards they have established at the frontiers and poses for man a superhuman task. Accordingly, the narrator voices a critical statement:

At that time the book was in everyone's hands, but I confess that to this very day I do not understand precisely how he pictured the construction of this tower. The Wall that was not even in the form of a circle but merely in a kind of quarter or half circle— was it supposed to serve as the foundation of a tower? Surely that could be meant only in an intellectual-spiritual sense. But if that were so, why then build the Wall, that after all was something actual, the outcome of the lives and efforts of hundreds of thousands of people? And to what end did the book contain designs for the tower (designs that were, to be sure, nebulous) as well as detailed proposals as to how the energies of the people were to be united in this new and mighty project? (B 72)

The narrator's position is clear. When he says that the scholar, in wanting to build something "intellectual-spiritual" upon something "actual," is asking the impossible, he does not mean that the construction of the Wall is a purely materialistic and nonspiritual undertaking, for he himself had declared, of the worthy builders, that spiritually and intellectually they had to be far above their outwardly petty task. On the contrary, he means that what the scholar is striving for, in the construction of the tower that will reach to the sky, represents a "nebulousness" that transcends the given "actual" potentialities of mankind. The construction of the Wall is an "actuality," because it relies upon and deals exclusively with the temporal potentialities and powers of mankind. However, the planned construction of the tower that will reach to the sky transcends these existing potentialities; hence, the plan of such a tower cannot but strike one as "nebulous."

This plan grows all the more dangerous, however, because it presents proposals that have already been worked out in detail, with reference to the way the energies of the people can be mobilized and "united" toward attaining a "nebulous," obscure goal. It was due to the very nebulousness of this goal, juxtaposed as it was with exact proposals for mobilization, that the book was able to fascinate the masses—indeed, fascinate "everyone"—at a time when "so many people were trying to rally together and concentrate as far as possible on one goal."

The "confusion in people's heads" thus arose in an epoch when the "educated"—that is to say, those who "had achieved the highest level of education available to them"—went to rack and ruin in great numbers; for, though they had the "most grandiose architectural plans," they had no common goal. The masses, but also these "educated" people—"everybody"—long "to rally together and concentrate as far as possible on one goal." It is amid this state of affairs, one that exactly mirrors the state of affairs of the twentieth century, that the scholar's book is a hit and is in "everyone's" hands. For the fantastic book catered to an innermost, ineradicable need of human nature. "The nature of man, essentially volatile, of the order of rising dust, does not tolerate any fettering; if that nature fetters itself, it will soon begin to shake its fetters madly, and to tear its walls, its chains, and its very self apart and send them flying to the four winds" (B 72).

This means, therefore, that the two possible ways of erecting the Babylonian Tower reflect, as it were, the cross-purposes of Kafka's two antagonists: the hunt [in the self] that drives man out of his own boundaries, and the countermovement that drives him back to his concrete earthly existence, urging him to postpone the construction of the tower that will reach to the sky and to make himself comfortable here on earth first of all.

With the foregoing the assumptions necessary for an interpretation of the true meaning of the construction of the Wall and the true meaning of the chief leaders are clarified. These leaders, of course, "in arranging for the construction in parts . . . did not" leave "out of account . . . these very considerations that conflicted with the construction of the Wall" (B 72-73). This construction in parts, that represents "a pivotal question in the whole construction of the Wall (B 71), was of course decreed not only, as the narrator now recognizes, in view of the limited achievement potentials of the individual construction workers, but also because a continuous building operation, carried out by the collective energy of the entire nation, would, of necessity, have caused the entire construction to explode in all directions, in the light of man's "nature" that does not tolerate any fetters, that immediately storms into the infinite, letting itself be fascinated by fantastic aims, such as those in this book, and letting itself be carried away beyond all bounds.

"Only in spelling out the decrees of the chief leaders over again," it is further stated, have we actually "come to know ourselves" (B 73). Thus, these leaders know man's true nature and regulate the construction of the Wall accordingly. The narrator confesses "that without the leaders, neither our book learning nor our human understanding would have sufficed even for the lowly function that we played within the great whole" (B 73).

## The "Chief Leaders" of Mankind

Who then are these chief leaders?

In the leaders' room—where that was, and who sat there, nobody that I have asked knows or ever knew—in this room, very likely, all human thoughts and wishes went round in a circle, and all human aims and fulfillments circled in reverse. But through the window, upon the hands of the leaders who were drafting the plans, shone the reflected splendor of the divine worlds. (B 73)

These leaders are invisible and not in space. No one knows them. In them "all" human thoughts are revolving. Thus they represent the totality of human conceptions, and they do so in the form of two opposing circles: man's "thoughts and wishes" are in counterplay to his "aims and fulfillments." For both are constantly neutralizing one another and cannot be brought into accord with one another; but, nevertheless, in this room they are kept in a state of balanced suspension. Moreover, into the room of these leaders there shines the "reflected splendor of the divine worlds." They are not themselves the divine worlds, but they are the reflected splendor of those worlds; in a like manner Kafka often spoke of the reflected splendor of the highest court shining upon the world of men. Analogously it is stated further on that the leaders have existed "probably from time immemorial" (B 76); that is, they are beyond time also.

These leaders are therefore a symbol of the spiritual cosmos of mankind. They correspond to the officials in the novels *The Trial* and *The Castle*. Significant conclusions, however, ensue from this. The narrator offers resistance to the thought that these universal, omniscient, and all-determining leaders have designed and decreed such an imperfect construction, a construction that is full of gaps.

What is involved here is the age-old question of the perfect world ["the best of all possible worlds" (Leibniz)]; it is the problem of man's eternal wrangling with the fact of his having been born into an imperfect, wretched world and, what is more, of his having to improve upon it. The narrator reaches the "conclusion," that rings out like an accusation, "that the leaders intended something impractical," since it would certainly have been in their power to design and plan the "construction of a continuous wall" and "to overcome" (B 73) all "difficulties" that would stand in the way of its being built.

But this accusation is basically an abstract one, for actually it is not directed at any concrete, earthly beings, but at the conceptual world that exists within every human being; that is, basically, the accusation is directed at the accuser himself. Kafka expressed this in words that have often been misunderstood:[1] "Strive to the utmost to understand the commands of the leaders, but only to a certain point, and then have done with pondering upon them" (B 73). This point is carefully determined by means of a simile:

It will be with you as with the river in spring. It rises, grows mightier, nourishes with greater abundance the long stretches of land along its banks, retains its own identity to a greater distance farther out into the sea, and, the more nearly it becomes the sea's equal, the more the sea welcomes it.—To this extent, ponder upon the commands of the leaders.—But then the river overflows its banks, loses its contours and shape, slackens the speed of its downward course, tries against its destiny to form small seas inland, damages the fields and meadows, and yet, in the long run, is unable to maintain itself in this diffuseness but flows back again within its banks, and, indeed, dries up woefully during the next hot season.—To this extent, do not ponder upon the commands of the leaders. (B 74).

Thus, as long as man "keeps his own nature," it is meaningful and possible for him to ponder upon the totality of the ideas, aims, and fulfillments within him; in that event he is even able to become more nearly the equal of the sea, of the Universal, and be the more welcomed by it, and, indeed, to maintain himself in the Universal. However, as soon as man reaches beyond himself, by attempting "against his destiny" to form "seas" —the Universal—inland, he injures both the world around him and himself; what is more, he goes completely to ruin, "dries up." Man then loses his orientation; he becomes incapable of life, harming his earthly world—the inland fields and meadows —and himself as well, and he dries up, so that he does not even reach the sea. Thus again there emerges the old image of those Kafkaian beings that drift on, foundationless, between this world and the Hereafter.

When man transcends himself thus, he is no longer permitted and is no longer able to ponder upon the commands of the all-determining leaders in the inner being of the human race, for he is then no longer able to recognize any meaning or "expediency" in such commands. Perhaps this transcendence of himself was necessary; it was like destiny, as when the force of spring floods drove the river beyond its confines. Perhaps this transcendence of himself was implanted in him, in his own essence. But the catastrophic consequences of such a determination by fate or by one's own essential nature can no longer be determined and comprehended as meaningful through the act of "pondering," since they themselves effect a breach of human existence, human imagination, human nature. To be sure, the commands of the leaders include such catastrophes, for they too are a part of human universality. But the commands can no longer be understood or subsequently executed meaningfully.

The incomprehensibility of such "commands" of the leaders will be encountered again in Kafka's novels, in the incomprehensibility of the orders of officialdom. Essential, however, is the fact that the leaders, in their very planning, take into account man's boundary-crossings, for the leaders decree a structure that is full of gaps, since a fully completed structure would surely be burst apart again by man's nature.

As a consequence, however, there emerges the stimulating problem of having the commands of the leaders thwart and contradict one another, and of having the leaders plan "something inexpedient," perhaps even absurd. This problematic question stimulates the narrator as he considers the construction of the Wall, so full of gaps that at any time it could be destroyed by the wild peoples of the north, the free nomads—this Wall that, hence, offers mankind no protection, no security whatsoever, that indeed proves to be totally useless in spite of all the toilsome work on the constructed sections, for which entire lives were sacrificed. The total work of mankind merely a meaningless Sisyphean performance!

Now, too, it becomes clear why it was so "dangerous" to ponder upon the commands of the leaders while the actual work on the sectional constructions was going on. Man would be able able to bring forth anything more at all, would no longer be able to perform even his limited "work portion," if in his pondering he went beyond that designated boundary. For in that event everything, even the part that he had constructed, would seem to be meaningless. He would become unproductive. Despair would knock his pen or hammer out of his hand. For that reason even the "best" of the builders cherished the principle of not going too far in their pondering.

A highly personal experience of Kafka's speaks to us here. Kafka himself was able to complete the "work portion" allotted to him only by constantly defending himself against the kind of pondering that would go beyond the boundary. "My doubts . . . stand in a circle around every word. . . . When I sit down at my desk, I feel no better off than someone who falls down in the middle of the traffic of the Place de l'Opéra and breaks both legs" (T 27-28). "Everything is imagination: family, office, friends, the street—everything is imagination, whether closer or farther away—woman as well; but the home truth is simply that you are pushing your head against the wall of a windowless and doorless cell" (T 546).

Now, after the construction of the Wall is "completed," such questions and doubts can and may make themselves heard more loudly and more openly, for "from the long-since vanished thunderclouds there are no longer any flashes of lightning." The work is done. But now doubts are advanced even more radically. "I may . . . seek an explanation for building in sections, an explanation that will go beyond the one that satisfied people then" (B 74). Indeed, the narrator now questions the purpose of the entire construction: it was not at all a matter of protecting the people against the northern nomads, for in reality these nomads were of the substance of bogies in fairy tales and of frightful demons in legends, and no longer possessed any true power. What is more, even the decision to build the Wall was not made at a definite date but, like the leaders themselves, had existed from time immemorial. "Guileless peoples of the north who believed they had been the cause of it; venerable, guileless emperor who believed he had decreed it! We, who participated in the construction of the Wall, know otherwise and hold our peace" (B 76).

The leaders and the construction of the Wall are eternal, endless, never to be perfected, even though man may designate or assume a beginning and end. That is the actual meaning of the interminable piecemeal construction. At the root of the summons to everyone to protect himself against an external enemy lay the secret summons to create a meaningful "safe and secure" order. Although this summons went beyond the measure of human capabilities, at any rate it produced constructed sections which, to the individual person, seemed meaningful and significant for the intellectual and material life of mankind, even though those sections will again be destroyed, and even though the ultimate meaning of the commands of the leaders and that of the inevitable destructions remains concealed from the individual human being.

At the same time, the battle against the northern nomads was nevertheless more than a sham battle.

## The "Nomads" and the Problem of Freedom

For Kafka these free, savage nomads that come from the icy cold of the north always represent a sphere that is beyond the areas of security within man and beyond rational-empirical comprehensibility. This is clearly evident in other works that were written in close connection with the complex of problems inherent in the "Great Wall of China."

In the fragment "An Old Folio," which Kafka published in the collection entitled *A Country Doctor*, "nomads from the north" invade the Chinese realm and take possession even of the square in front of the imperial palace. They speak an unintelligible language, and, indeed, "they scarcely have a language of their own" but communicate with one another somewhat "like jackdaws. Again and again one hears this cawing of jackdaws" (E 156). They are removed from the sphere of human reason and volition, and unconcernedly live in accordance with their intrinsic nature. "One cannot talk with the nomads.... To them our mode of life, our institutions are as incomprehensible as they are inconsequential. As a result they show themselves to be negative even to any form of sign language." With their grimaces "they mean ... neither to say anything nor even to frighten anyone." They behave in this way only "because it is their nature. What they need, they take. It cannot be said that they use force." Unconcernedly they befoul the city. Unconcernedly they eat live animals. They are purely and simply the Other, the extrahuman, the absolute counterpoint to "motivated" life; they are Kafka's (Kavka = jackdaw) image of a peculiar possibility of being "outside of our humanity ... outside the law" (T 21-22).

Even the motif of the "uncleanness" of these beings that are excluded and set apart is constantly appearing in Kafka; for example, in his letter to Milena he calls himself a "forest animal" that is lying "somewhere in a filthy hole" (M 223, 229; *inter alia*). This implies nothing else but that in such a dissociated state *all* of man's potentialities become patently clear, but at the same time too, on the basis of this unveiled clarity, the very utmost is demanded. "Filthy am I, Milena, infinitely filthy, and that is why I raise such a clamor about purity" (M 208; cf. also the clamor of the jackals for purity [E 163]).

Hence, the wild nomads may also, in fact, be interpreted in

an extremely ambiguous manner. They threaten the boundaries of normal, "laboring" mankind, but they also represent positive demands confronting mankind. They were able to make their inroads because "we ... until now" merely "pursued our work" and did "not concern ourselves ... with the defense of our country" (B 155).

Man, having become the slave of his "work," failed to recognize his actual opponent, since he was not worried about the totality of his human existence. Because of his work he lost sight of the meaning of his human existence and is himself, therefore, the one who is really guilty. Now the unfamiliar, long-concealed, full truth of his existence breaks in upon him. Now, "to us artisans and businessmen" there is "entrusted the rescue of our country; but we are not equal to such a task ... it is a misunderstanding, and we are dying of it" (B 157-58).

Linked with this, however, is an illuminating characterization of the emperor. Silently the emperor watches the activities of the nomads, offering them no opposition, despite the fact that "the imperial palace ... attracted the nomads to it." The emperor, complain the businessmen, should have undertaken the defense of the country. But the emperor obviously fails to do so; what is more, he does not want any resistance whatsoever to be offered.

If one pursues this question more exactly, one arrives at the following enigmatical conception in Kafka: these free nomads are basically not enemies at all. Only the businessmen feel them to be enemies. And even they must admit that the nomads use no force against them; the nomads simply treat them as if they did not exist.

Therefore, the obligation is laid upon the emperor to unite both forms of existence: the one, the form that is free, aimless, unconcerned; and the other, the form that works and plans rationally. Only if both forms were united would full, true human existence to be restored. Hence, too, the nomads are attracted by the imperial palace, but they do not attack it. They themselves sense that there is a supreme authority here, to which they appertain.

Indeed, in other fragments of Kafka's these nomads appear as very soldiers and protectors of the emperor; for instance, in "The Rejection" (B 84 ff.), in which the colonel, who represents the "imperial" government in a city, is surrounded and protected by soldiers who speak "a dialect that is completely incomprehensible to us" and who "probably do not" understand the "conversations" of the people. They are distinguished by their "strong teeth" and by a frightening "flash of their small, slitlike eyes." They are aloof, quiet, serious, and unbending, with a "certain reserve" in their very mode of being (B 87). Through their mere presence in a store they cause everyone to grow silent, for "it seems as though he [the soldier] understood them; he himself says no word but looks fixedly at whoever is talking and then, in turn, at those who are listening, and keeps his hand on the hilt of the long knife in his belt" (B 88). Their mere presence has a menacing effect, representing, as it were, the negation and the unmasking of all business, goings-on, and chatter.

Thereby, too, the problem of "The Construction of the Great Wall of China" is shifted to a new level. If, in the case of the Wall, it was not a matter of protection against the free nomads, where then did its meaning lie? Obviously it was meant to produce a "reflected splendor of the divine worlds" upon earth, for it is this kind of reflected splendor that shines "upon the hands of the leaders who were drafting the plans." With that there arises the question of what relationship exists between these leaders and the Divine, and what justification there is for having the whole construction of the Wall designated as a work that is "pleasing unto God."

## "Empire" and the Perversion of Absolute Law in History

One of the very few works of Kafka's in which the words "divine" and "God" occur is the story "The Construction of the Great Wall of China."

The controversial question that has long dominated Kafka literature, the question of whether Kafka was a devoutly religious poet or a "nihilist," takes on particular urgency, therefore, in the light of this story. And the narrator's subsequent remarks about the Peking Empire have accordingly been linked with this question too. Günther Anders,[2] for example, is of the opinion that the word "emperor" is a code word for God; likewise, the fact that the intercalated tale "The Imperial Message" makes mention of a dying and even of a dead emperor, points, he considers, to that stage in his intellectual development during which Kafka elaborated, with poetic consequentiality, upon Nietzsche's words, "God is dead." On the other hand, the following passage from the text argues for a positive, religious interpretation: "The empire is immortal, but the individual emperor falls and crashes down" (B 78); or the other passage in question: "Peking is only a dot; and the imperial palace only a very tiny dot. The emperor as such, on the other hand, is surely impressive on every storey of the world. The emperor now living, however, a human being like us . . ." (B 77). Accordingly, therefore, the imperial dignity, or the emperor "as such"—that is, the emperor in his timeless function—could be identified with God, whereas the individual human emperor, living at any given moment, would be merely his changing and mortal representative on earth.

Let us examine the text more exactly. The narrator had ascertained that both the leaders and the resolution to construct the Wall had existed from time immemorial and that the construction of the Wall had been neither occasioned by the nomads nor decreed by the emperor. The leaders who have existed from time immemorial, therefore, passed the decisive resolution to construct the Wall, a resolution that has existed from time immemorial. This signifies nothing other than the fact that, within the totality of human thoughts, wishes, aims, and fulfillments, the construction of the Wall had been resolved upon from time immemorial, and indeed, so to speak, as a reflected splendor of the divine worlds that "shone upon the hands of the leaders who were drafting the plans." The construction of the Wall is thus supposed to mirror, as it were, the divine worlds, even though merely in the form of reflected splendor.

The narrator then comes to the questions about the empire. He complains that although the Chinese "possess certain ethnic and national institutions that are singularly clear," they possess others that are "in turn singularly obscure." He states that he has always been tempted "to trace the causes, particularly of the latter phenomenon ... and the construction of the Wall is also essentially involved in these inquiries. Now among the most obscure of our institutions is, undoubtedly, the empire" (B 76). The obscurity extends so far that the people do not know "who the reigning emperor is, and there are uncertainties even about the name of the dynasty" (B 79). There prevail complete confusion and reversal of chronological orders in the juridical structure of the state and, correspondingly, confusion in the legal maxims, guiding principles, and controls upon which life depends.

The atrocities that take place in the present are labeled as crimes committed long ago and are therefore disregarded: "Bygone matters, heard tell of long ago, long since past and forgotten. And although ... the gruesomeness of life spoke irrefutably in the plea of the beggar, one shook one's head, laughing, and refused to hear anything further. So willing are we to obliterate the present" (B 81). The priest, to whom the beggar delivers the news of the terrible massacre in the neighboring province, explains that it is a matter of an "antiquated" leaflet.

If just once, once in a lifetime, an imperial official comes ... to our village, makes some demand or other in the name of the rulers, checks the tax lists, observes the teaching in the school, questions the priest about our ways and doings, and then ... summarizes everything in long admonitions to the assembled community, a smile then passes over every face .... "Why!" they think, "he is speaking of a dead man as though he were alive, of an emperor who has been dead a long time." (B 80-81)

They do not think of "obeying" him. And in his stead, when

the official takes his departure, "there arises from a funeral urn already crumbled, someone arbitrarily exalted, stamping his foot, as master of the village" (B 80-81).

For

... emperors long since dead are raised to the throne in our villages, and the emperor who lives only in song recently issued a proclamation that the priest reads out before the altar. Battles that belong to our most ancient history are only now being fought. ... The Imperial ladies ... swelling with lust for power, vehement in their greed, abandoned in their voluptuousness, perpetrate their monstrous deeds again and again anew. The longer ago it was, the more fearfully do all the colors light up ; and one day, with a loud outcry of woe, the village learns of an empress who quaffed her husband's blood in deep draughts, thousands of years ago.

Thus then do the people deal with bygone rulers, but present rulers they mix in with the dead. (B 79-80)

Kafka has thereby voiced a valid, terrible truth. Man never confronts his own era. Neither the horrors nor the demands of his age does he accept as realities that apply to him. On the contrary, he lets himself be decisively influenced in his thoughts, feelings, and actions by traditional ideas which he sees as the actual realities that prevail for him now, at the present moment. For, as man seeks to "motivate" his life, he obtains all his motivations from a bygone world upon which he bases his life. The precepts as well as the terrors of the past are for him more actual and more determinative than is the reality in which he himself exists. Entire forms of government and of society are created according to past models and guiding principles, no matter how absurd they become and how much they terrorize one. "Battles that belong to our most ancient history are only now being fought": people are stamped as enemies according to traditional points of view. Laws, ideals, goals of lost eras are made the valid judicial system, while the present-day demands are dismissed with a smile as "obsolete," long "familiar" ideals that are now meaningless.

The horrors of the present time are felt to be improbable and fantastic. They cannot and dare not be actually true. They are reminiscent of horror tales of savage, primeval times long past; therefore they are suppressed from present consciousness and treated as if they were incredible fairy tales that possessed reality only in remote antiquity. However, the true, determining law of the present—as, for example, the challenge to practice renunciation—appears likewise as an improbability, as something that is submerged and lost. That law *was* once valid in those ancient times when saints and martyrs or hermits were ready to sacrifice themselves wholly and led their lives in peace, piety, and patience, resolute in their withdrawal from all violence, war, and crime.

Logically this leads to the realization that mankind in general does not obey any commandment. For the commandments of the past that are still influential are lifted "arbitrarily" out of the funeral urn: they have no true validity for the present, nor is a timeless validity accorded to them. They are the commandments of overthrown emperors and dynasties, long since perished.

Hence the narrator elucidates:

If on the basis of such phenomena one were to conclude that fundamentally we possess no emperor at all, one would not be far from the truth. (B 81-82)

The consequence . . . is now, so to speak, a free, unrestrained life. In no way immoral. . . . But, nevertheless, a life that is subject to no present-day law, heeding only the instructions and admonitions that have come down to us from days of old. (B 82)

Nevertheless, that does not mean that there is no empire and no emperor, and thus no supreme authority instituting commandments. On the contrary, "The empire is immortal," and "the emperor as such . . . is surely impressive on every storey of the world." For Kafka the problem rests solely in the fact that the empire and its law cannot be known and cannot therefore be made effective—not in fact as one might expect, because of the ill will of the people, and not, as one might expect, because the people have rebelled against their emperor and do not believe in him and his commandments. "Again and again I cannot

help saying, there is perhaps no nation that is more loyal to its
emperor than ours . . . but our loyalty is of no benefit to the
emperor" (B 82).

In Kafka, therefore, the problem lies at a much deeper level.
The point at issue is not at all the superficial controversy that
has crept up and spiraled around Kafka: Is he a devout, religious poet, or is he a nihilist? And even in the case of these
dying emperors, the issue is not the much-discussed problem of
the so-called secularization of modern man; it is not the problem
of modern man's having abandoned his faith and of his therefore no longer existing within the safety, security, and protection
of religion and of a supreme, divine authority.

Kafka's crucial and stirring insight, on the contrary, has it
that the relationship between mankind and supreme authority is
at all times, and has been from time immemorial, "not clear,"
because it lies in the nature of the concrete, terrestrial human
being to make every action of his conform to "given" norms.
No matter how devout man may be, he really *cannot* surrender
to the absolute demand made at the present moment by the
emperor or by the empire. For at that moment his entire richly
motivated world would be snatched away from under his feet
and would be lost. Certainly, if once the people were to attain
to such "power of faith" that "having reached the point of
plucking the empire out of its Peking reverie, with all the quick-
ened reality of the living moment, they press it to their humble
and submissive breasts that ask no better than to feel that touch
once and then to perish of it," it would mean snatching, from
under the people's feet, the "ground upon which we live." It is
only this very "weakness" of the people, their inability to meet
with the emperor in the present moment, that establishes the
concrete existence of the people at all, and it is this weakness
that is "one of the most important means of uniting our people."
"To find fault here justifiably and in detail would mean hammering away not at our consciences but, what is far worse, at
the very legs we stand on" (B 83). Man's conscience, to be sure,
would demand such a direct, immediate encounter with the emperor; life, however, of necessity opposes it.

The relationship between empire and dying emperors is also clarified thereby: the specific emperor in office, as representative of the highest authority of the world, is constantly threatened by his own "imperial household"; this, in turn, represents him to the concrete world. "Malice and enmity in the garb of servants and friends—the counterbalance offsetting the imperial power, ever striving with poisoned arrows to shoot the emperor down from his side of the scales" (B 78). The emperor who rests on justice, on the "scales" of the highest authority, must be shot down from this balance scale, must be overthrown again and again, since this supreme commandment in its immediacy would consume all earthly life. For this reason, even the empresses, as representatives of the earthly will to live, quaff the emperor's blood.

Those who are the very closest to the emperor and whose task it is to mediate the orders of the supreme authority, to transmit them to the people, and to guard over their implementation— they are the very ones who are not permitted to let all these orders go through except in the form of commandments of emperors, slain long ago, who already possess the character of the past, of the historical, of something far removed from the present. The people themselves have no notion of this perversion of the supreme commandment, of such an "execution" of the present emperor. Like "people who have come too late," individual members of the populace stand in a side street "while far ahead, in the center of the market place, the execution of their lord is taking place" (B 78).

Analogously, the "imperial message," too, can never reach the separate individual among the people. In the "chambers of the innermost palace," the messenger comes to a standstill, and even should he rush through the "millenia" his message would never reach man (B 79). The true imperial message that the emperor whispers directly, without any mediation, into the messenger's ear—that message can never arrive at its destination. The "world" itself, "the center of the world, full of its heaped-high dregs," intervenes between emperor and people. Only sifted, altered, perverted orders reach his subjects.

This attitude could be interpreted as a radical Protestant or Old Testament attitude of faith, according to which every concrete given commandment, every terrestrial security is condemned as a perversion of the true, Divine commandment, of the unalterable transcendence of God; moreover, man is charged to present himself for the encounter with the "entirely Other," and, in so doing, to relinquish all aids, instructions, and guiding principles obtained by means of priests or concrete statues and institutions. Indubitably, a genuine element of Kafka's writing is touched on here, an element that, according to his own avowals as well, brings Kafka close to Kierkegaard and the Old Testament.[3]

In that event, however, the conclusion of the fragment is curious, in that the people's weakness of faith is defended and set off against man's conscience. Kafka, in contrast with Kierkegaard, tries to do justice to the "simple man" and to "life." We have already referred to Kafka's pertinent letters, dated March 1918, written to Max Brod. In these Kafka objects to the "rape of the world" by means of Kierkegaard's radical, religious "positivism." And further: the emperor's message does not arrive at all. The basis of Protestant and Jewish faith—according to which God's message can at any time reach whoever in his faith is ready to open to Him and, what is more, actually overtakes man even against his own will, against his very resistance —this basis in the case of Kafka seems to have been abandoned.

Herewith, in fact, a completely different standpoint of Kafka's emerges. The emperor is unable of himself to reach his subjects, although "the empire actually has its ultimate mainstays there [in the people]" (B 77); nor can the people of themselves reach the emperor, although "our thinking" is aimed "only at the emperor" (B 77). The two are mutually dependent upon one another, but neither finds access to the other. The impossibility of an encounter results from the nature of the two, not from a lack of faith or from a deliberate break between the two. Kafka's interpretation of the world rests upon a clear insight into the nature of both spheres. It opposes not only a radical, religious nullification of the world in favor of God, but also a

radically earthbound existence. Relentlessly it unmasks the ominous consequences that every one-sidedness must of necessity
produce, in those epochs of mankind that are deeply religious
as well as in those that are weak in faith.

Epochs that are supposedly secure in religious faith pervert
the Divine message into predatory wars and battles on the
ground of alleged commandments from highest Divine authority,
no less than do opponents without religion cross weapons under
the banner of supposedly sovereign historical or natural rights
and necessities. The chaos of mankind is always produced by
motives and norms belonging to emperors long since slain. The
"present-day" law, however, must remain invisible.

## *The Attempt at Mediation: The "Nobility"*

Thereby there arises the question of a possible mediation between the emperor and the people, between absolute commandment and lived history. Only if one pursues this question does
the actual meaning of the construction of the Wall, and the
meaning of its leaders, grow transparent.

One may already have been struck by the passage where it is
said that "even the construction of the Wall . . . is essentially
involved . . . in these inquiries" about the empire (B 76). The
orders of the leaders who are drafting the plans for the construction of the Wall while there shines upon them the reflected
splendor of the divine worlds—these orders are perceived and
complied with. Since they represent all human thoughts, wishes,
aims, and fulfillments, they are therefore nothing other than
the conceptions of all people, but in a universality and timeless
duration transcending every individual conception of man. They
are extracted from the rise and downfall of all emperors; they
symbolize the totality of human existence. As such, they can, in
a true sense, also mediate between empire and people; they
possess that "overview" which for Kafka is always the main
issue. No less immortal and, like the "emperor as such," existing

from time immemorial, they constantly keep in sight both earthly life and the supreme, lawgiving authority.

The center of gravity in the Kafkaian view of life is, hence, displaced to this universal potentiality, inherent in man himself, of giving shape to the world and form to life. It is not a matter of traditional "faith," or "nihilism" (which in itself bespeaks inferior tradition), but of determining the potentialities latent in man for his achieving "present-day" legislation that is unconditionally binding and yet has the capacity to survive.

Kafka with his image of the "nobility" has further elaborated on the problem of these leaders in other stories belonging directly to the cycle of motifs and to the creative period of "The Construction of the Great Wall of China"; namely, "On the Question of Our Laws," "The Rejection," and "The Conscription of Troops."

## A. TRADITION AND LAW

In "On the Question of Our Laws" Kafka has formulated the problem with particular acuity and cogency. In this sketch it is stated that within the history of mankind all the laws and guiding principles that have arisen, according to which we "try to adapt ourselves a little to the present and future," are "uncertain" and, what is more, even bring "severe damage more often than not . . . since they" give "the people a false, illusory security that leads to recklessness in the face of coming events" (B 92). This means that, although all the given, concretely formulated laws and guiding principles of ethical, metaphysical, religious, or national-political character[4] engender the feeling of security, this security is deceptive. It is deceptive not only because these historically traditional laws oppose and contradict one another, but also because they seduce man into growing "reckless" in the face of "coming events"; that is, they make him incapable of actually recognizing the seriousness of the new decisions at the time, and incapable of acting correspondingly with full responsibility and complete adequacy.

For mankind, carried along by traditional laws with the

safety and security they bring, enters unsuspectingly into new situations that make a mockery of the old concepts and that set mankind tasks for which it is unprepared and to which it is no longer equal. Only when man no longer relies upon guarantees and securities but, as it were, gazes into the unfathomable, does he become vigilant, does his eye grow keen for what is approaching, does he have the power even to obviate what is approaching—yet he must at the same time bear within himself an un-conditional, absolute commandment, must possess a concept of the "true nature of the human being," for it is this that will prescribe for him the guiding principles of his action in the "battle" against all distortions.

Since the "majority" of the people are in no way now able to imagine such an absolute law—although they possess an infallible awareness of it—they believe that the uncertainties and weaknesses of the traditional laws do not rest in the essence of these laws themselves but "that there is not nearly enough of the tradition available and that therefore much more research must yet be done on it," and they hope "that one day there will come a time when the tradition and the research on it, with a sigh of relief as it were, will reach the end and put in the final period, and everything will have become clear" (B 92).

This in fact corresponds to the conceptual, historical-minded world of the modern era, to a historical consciousness that has been developed to such an extreme that it believes that in the "research" done in history it can trace guiding lines even of future developments; and this, at the same time, corresponds to the analogous modern transformation of the "unconditional" law into the so-called "historical" law: the meaning of all human existence unfolds, according to the modern view, solely in its history. From Hegel via Marx to Spengler, Toynbee, and others, the Absolute is historicized; "salvation" is expected in the belief that *one day*, in the passage through all historical battles, it will nevertheless be possible, "with a sigh of relief," to reach the end and put in the "final period," and for "everything" to become "clear."

Man's unconditional responsibility, however, is hereby shifted to the historical: all crimes, atrocities, or base compromises are "justified" in view of the historical future or the supposedly "unfavourable" historical conditions. An unconditional ethical action in the midst of conditioned existence is rejected as "utopia" or "suicide." The commitment to any ethics is destroyed through a historicizing approach.

But what is the Absolute commandment?

At the beginning of the sketch the statement is made that the truly determining laws are the "secret of the small group of nobles ... who rule us"; "for the nature of these laws demands, too, that their existence be kept secret" (B 91). This means, therefore, that the true laws cannot and may not be formulated. The moment they were formulated they would lose their "nature" and, what is more, their "existence." It is of their very essence that they cannot become evident in the form of comprehensible statutes.

This accounts for the paradoxical statement that they are given "exclusively into the hands" of those who stand "outside the law" and who are therefore no longer ruled by the law, but who, themselves, in a condition of freedom, have become identical with the law, "for from their very inception the laws were established for the nobility" (B 91). The nobility is itself the law. "What the nobility does, is law." Other laws "do not ... perhaps ... exist ... at all" (B 92).

What, then, is the nobility? It is that authority within man that in "liberated contemplation of the self" (H 109) assumes the responsibility for everyone and "does" what could at the same time be considered as the law for everyone. "If all responsibility is thrust upon you, you can avail yourself of the occasion and feel like sinking under the responsibility; but try it—then you will realize that nothing was thrust upon you, but that it is you yourself who are this responsibility" (H 106-107). In the "being" of man there is included at the same time the responsibility for everyone. Nothing is "thrust upon" man from the outside, but man, in comprehending himself as responsible authority, is also acting responsibly for everyone. It is just

such responsible "being," however, that is removed from all empirical determinability and all ideological fixation. It can be
realized only through renunciation of the world as it is standardized and determined by traditions, and, at the same time,
through the knowledge of the hidden "secret" law within every
human being—that law that demands "renunciation" in the
face of every secure "possession," but that only thereby recognizes "the true essence of man . . . that cannot but be loved."

This true law, in the presence of which the true essence of
man is first revealed and in which, hence, right action is also
actualized, can never be shaken off, never be "repudiated." On
this all people of the human "race" are agreed, both those in the
great "majority" and those in the "little party" (B 92).

The "overwhelming majority of our people," who are oriented
to the prevailing traditions, cherish the hope, to be sure, that,
when all historical legislation has been examined, some day
"everything will have become clear, the law will belong only
to the people, and the nobility will disappear." But that is not
said, as it were, with hatred of the nobility—not at all, and by
no one. It is more likely that we hate ourselves, because we
cannot yet be deemed deserving of the law" (B 92-93).

Thus the goal of the people is that they themselves shall become the nobility. The majority hope to be able to achieve this
through the study and knowledge of all laws; they hope one day
to gain "clarity" about the true, determining law and to be
liberated from the "torment" of ignorance. They cannot hate
the nobility itself, for it represents, indeed, the actual, true
nature of the people.

The "little party," on the contrary, questioning all historical
legislation critically, recognizes it as uncertain and deceptive.
Hence it doubts whether a binding law actually exists at all. The
"little party" represents the sceptics among the people, or, if one
wishes, the "individualists," or even the "nihilists"; for they
"believe . . . in no actual law" (B 93). Hence they see "only
arbitrary acts of the nobility" and seek "to prove . . . that, if a
law exists, the only way it can read is: What the nobility does
is law" (B 92). Thus they reduce all action to free, arbitrary

self-determination that is no longer subject to any norm, neither a historic nor an absolute one. This "little party" completely lacks commitment. The law of its action is shifted exclusively to the uniqueness of the moment. Its ideal, as it were, is what in the nineteenth and twentieth centuries has been termed "the free development of the personality."

But even this "little party" that refuses to accept any objective, alleged authority, cannot reject the nobility itself, but acknowledges "the nobility and the right of its existence completely" (B 93). For even free and, what is more, arbitrary self-determination is possible only on the basis of the "nobility," that inmost secret authority which constitutes human dignity, the essence of man himself.

This authority is at the same time always an authority that is "passing sentence," whether it is judging the people or the individual himself who is acting arbitrarily. It imposes upon man a burden of responsibility despite the fact that it disclaims all external, historically traditional laws and even all absolute laws of, say, a religious nature.

Hence, "a party that would have faith in the laws and at the same time would repudiate the nobility" would have "the entire people behind it immediately" (B 93); because then the people would be free of every responsibility. They could live their lives to the full, without restraint. "But such a party cannot come into being, because nobody dares to repudiate the nobility." To do so would mean the renunciation of man's being. "We live on this razor's edge": we live under a law that "torments" us because we do not know it. If, however, we elevate ourselves to the law, to the nobility, we waive every definable law; we grow silent; we are condemned to concealment. We can do the right thing, but the nobility passes judgment on us and on all earthly activity; like a knife it cuts through everything that is lived, thought, done, causing everything to drop away from us like an untruth, an absurdity.

In his stories "The Rejection" and "The Conscription of Troops," Kafka has given impressive form to this power of the law of the nobility, a power that judges and denies everything.

**B.**  THE RIGIDIFYING OF ABSOLUTE LAW
INTO HISTORY-LESSNESS

In the story "The Rejection" the colonel, or, as the case may be, the chief tax-collector, represents the law. "Thus he supports the law, and thus it supports him" (B 88). He is one of those nobles in whom law and person have become one. He "stands . . . there like the wall of the world. Behind him there is nothing more . . . he does, after all, signify the conclusion of the whole" (B 86). That means that at the same time he represents the law of the world itself.

In the little town that he governs "one is almost under the impression that the people are saying, 'Now that you have taken from us everything that we had, please take us, our very selves, also' " (B 86). The law demands not only the sacrifice of all possessions but primarily the surrender of the self. Hence, too, the colonel must "deny" all the requests of the population. Any mitigation of life, even though it be only "tax exemption for one year," is impossible. For in such a law it is no longer a matter of individual specific rights at all. Not while he is in office and represents the law, but only as a "private person" can the colonel grant reliefs (B 89, 90). As an official he is no ordinary "person like all of us" (B 89), but he "breathes" in another world in an "extraordinary . . . extremely clear" manner (B 88).

His government in the little town is sharply demarcated from the specific historical governments, outside in the nation and in the capital, under the constantly changing dynasties. The little town under his government is removed from historical change. He rules directly, as it were, an emperor without intermediaries, independent of the rising and falling authoritative powers.

And now it is remarkable, and I marvel at it again and again afresh, how we in our little town quietly submit to every command from the capital. For centuries no political change has taken place among us which originated in the citizens themselves. In the capital the high rulers have superseded one another ; what is more, even dynasties have been extinguished or dethroned and new ones begun ; in the past century even the capital itself was destroyed and a new one founded far away from the old one; later the new one too was destroyed, and the old one built up again—all this has actually had no influence on our little town. (B 84-85)

Analogously, the colonel rules without concrete "documents," but also without having himself seized the power; he is "no tyrant" (B 86). "Since ancient times the development has been such that the chief tax-collector is the highest official, and the colonel submits to this tradition no differently from the way we submit to it" (B 86). His office, so to speak, like the leaders of the construction of the Wall, has existed from time immemorial. For that reason, too, the impassable distance between the little town and the rest of the world is emphasized at the beginning of the story. The little town is situated, as it were, outside the known world, as is the bureaucratic government in the novel *The Castle*. And, just as the officials in the castle grant none of the requests of the parties but, inaccessible and inscrutable, reject the parties as they desperately press their claims (K., Amalia's father, and others), thus also do the inhabitants of this little town, in complete dependence upon the colonel, bring forward their requests ever anew, to experience rejection ever anew. Like the villagers in *The Castle* they put themselves completely into the hands of the officials, but they cannot, indeed dare not, count on being heard. For in the face of this law, this wall of the world, behind which there is nothing more, this wall that terminates the whole, only complete submission or complete repudiation is possible. The guilt of existence can be paid off in full only through the abandonment of life as through the tax levies unalterably determined by the government. All tax relief is forbidden. For every morsel of life that is lived, there are fixed debts to be paid. Here, nothing can be bargained down.

Only in this way, too, is that strange formulation understandable: that the supplicants, at the moment of denial of their plea, breathe a sigh of relief, since "one cannot, so to speak, get along without this rejection" (B 89-90). The fulfillment of the request would endanger or even eliminate life itself. Either it would signify a breakthrough of the require-ments and systems of laws immanent in terrestrial life, or it would precipitate a complete reversal of the conditions of government—both basically coming to the same thing: if the official were to fulfill the request in opposition to all his regula-tions, he would, as the official Bürgel formulates it in *The Castle,* go through "an elevation in rank beyond all description," would "practically tear the organization of the administrative authori-ties apart," break the law of the world to bits, act with com-plete autonomy, making the laws himself, "cease ... being an official personage" (S 354), and have the "entire responsibility" (S 352). But that cannot take place unless the supplicants, in an "unguarded moment," rush in on him; that is, without any individual motivations or individual pleas, in complete freedom and openness. Then "fulfillment" would almost be "reaching out" to the supplicants (S 355). But that, too, is impossible. For the specific living individual is fettered to the specific moti-vations and formulations of his pleas. He cannot come "un-guarded"; his own thinking guards him, and it has already been recorded and seen through in advance by the officials.

The scope of this problem will occupy us further in the analysis of the novel *The Castle.* In the story "The Rejection" the problem is already in resonance, particularly if one con-siders the concluding sentences:

There is, admittedly, as far as my observations go, a certain age group that is dissatisfied [with the rejection]; it consists of, say, the young people between seventeen and twenty. Quite young fellows then, who cannot have the remotest notion of the possible consequences of even the most unimportant thought, let alone of a revolutionary one. And they are the very ones among whom dissatisfaction creeps in. (B 90)

Youth, which still goes to all lengths, filled with revolutionary ideas that burst all bounds, is not content with a world legis-lation in which, in terrestrial life, no fulfillment is possible. Youth shakes its chains, but it is as yet unable to have a general view of the consequences of its own revolutionary thinking.

Youth still dreams in terms of utopias and does not sense that the fulfillment of a single request that would change life would be unexceptionably possible only through the sacrifice of youth's own world, a world in which indeed every fulfillment always remains merely an apparent fulfillment, since it automatically terminates itself and thereby causes new enslavements or new and worse tax collections.

Lasting tranquillity was achieved in the little town only because no requests whatsoever were granted. Only in this way did the town lift itself out of history's war of annihilation. Peace is paid for with the annihilation of all hope. It ricochets from the "wall of the world ... behind which there is nothing more." That is the terrible truth of this story.

### C. THE MODERN PERVERSION OF THE LAW

Even more dreadful is the story "The Conscription of Troops." The narrative begins with these sentences: "Conscription of troops—which is often necessary, for battles on the frontiers never cease—takes place in the following manner: the order is issued that on a certain day, in a certain district of the city, all the inhabitants—men, women, children, indiscriminately—must remain in their dwellings" (B 330). And accordingly, without exception, all of them, in their own homes, are levied for military service. No one dares evade it. But occasionally someone is missing—"always a man." However,

he never really intends to evade military service; it is just because of fear that he has not come; but it is not fear of military service that keeps him away; it is just general shyness about making an appearance; the order is literally too grand for him, terrifyingly grand; he is unable to come of his own strength. But he does not therefore flee, he simply hides himself (B 331)

and is, consequently, also immediately found by the soldiers of the "young nobleman" making the levy, who then punishes the man by beating him with his whip.

It is understandable why invariably it is only men who feel

such fear of the conscription order: they are the ones who recognize what is at stake. Of course all of them—men, women, and children—are driven to the "limits" of the human realm. But women and children obey willingly without any suspicions. Only the men are shy about making an appearance, for they know that it is a matter of their final stability or final annihilation of the "self"; whereas women and children, as well as many other men, feel such a "conscription of troops" as a natural law to which one subjects oneself as a matter of course.

The situation in question here is the same as that in Kafka's novel *The Trial*, in which only the men—and among them, too, only the "accused"—offer resistance to the court, feel afraid of it, do not have the "strength" to surrender to it, while the women exhort the accused simply to make a "confession" voluntarily (P 132) and to yield to the court without opposition. In *The Trial* even children, young girls, etc—that is to say, people who have not been accused—form a part of the court as an accepted fact. For *all* human beings are involved in the general universal tribunal of life and existence. However, only a few men, like Josef K., the defendant, are aware of the fact that they are arraigned, that they have been served with a warrant of arrest, that suddenly they must justify "themselves," with the result that they are overcome by the tormenting feeling that everyone's eyes are riveted on them out of curiosity (cf. P 9, 11, etc.).

That the issue in "The Conscription of Troops" is likewise "guilt/debt"* and tribunal becomes quite clear from the following scene, the most peculiar and stirring in the story. Occasionally there are present at the levy even more people "than appear on the conscription lists. For instance a girl, a stranger, is present. and she looks at the nobleman; she comes from another region, perhaps from the provinces; the conscription of troops has lured her here" (B 331). Many women follow this lure, but "nothing disgraceful is seen in this . . . on the contrary, it is something which, according to the opinion of many, women must go through; it is a guilt/debt that they discharge to their sex."

*Tr. note: German *Schuld*, meaning both "guilt" and "debt." The text seems to demand the connotations of both English words.

Manifestly, therefore, according to this, the meaning of the "conscription of troops" is that of paying off one's guilt/debt incurred by existing—in this case, by existing as a woman. Everything that is lived must be "paid" for. That is accomplished by everyone's being driven to the frontiers of existence.

At the same time, however, an essential difference must be noted: those affected by the conscription of troops know basically nothing whatever of such a paying off. They are simply ordered about and controlled, collectively, without exception. And even the men who are filled with fear and want to evade the conscription are quite unaware of such "guilt/debt," to as little extent as Josef K., the "accused" in *The Trial*, who denies all guilt and precisely for that reason feels horror at an execution of justice that is incomprehensible to him. To be sure, they suspect that the issue is one of extremities; yet they do not confront it, but seek to conceal themselves.

This stranger-girl, however, consciously desires to pay off the guilt/debt of her existence, of her sex, by presenting herself at a levy in a "foreign" region. Fundamentally this differentiates her from the women who attend conscriptions within their own houses. "The domestic [conscription] has an entirely different meaning" (B 331). In the domestic conscription the sacrifice is simply demanded categorically, and categorically carried out, without the individual's consent or awareness, like something in nature that takes place and blindly runs its course, into which one is helplessly incorporated. Paying off one's guilt/debt can be spoken of, then, only in the sense that life itself, as it were, automatically demands its payment of blood-money according to an inescapable natural law. Women are simply the collective sacrifice of a life process; similarly the whole conscription is decreed collectively, "indiscriminately," is inflicted and enforced upon "everyone."

However, when the "stranger-girl" hears of the conscription of troops in a "foreign" region, she departs from her house of her own accord. And this decision of hers, which after all signifies a final sacrifice on her part, that of denial of the self, as is attested by the "terrifyingly grand command," is honored by everyone, even by the members of her own family. They consent,

> ... this cannot be refused, she puts on the best clothes she has, is more cheerful than she is as a rule; at the same time she is quiet and friendly, no matter how she may be as a rule; and behind all her quiet and friendliness she is to a certain extent as inaccessible as a complete stranger traveling to his native home and now no longer thinking of anything else. (B 332)

Thus conditions reverse themselves. She who prepares herself to go to those troops, pressing forward to the extreme limits of what is human—she becomes "inaccessible" and estranged from her old home. Her true home is now for her a region away from home. In sharp contrast with the "fear" of the men who have been called up, she goes "cheerfully" and "quietly" to this conscription of troops in a foreign region. Also, even the alien household that she now enters, where the conscription of troops is to take place, even this household greets her likewise with great respect, according her an "altogether different" welcome from that given an "ordinary guest." "And, if she places her hand on someone's head, it is more than the father's blessing" (B 332).

Her readiness to pay off the guilt/debt of her existence is regarded as a mark of the highest distinction. From such a woman there radiates blessing for the entire household.

But now there comes the reversal. The nobleman does not accept her readiness, her sacrifice.

> However, she is thus honored only until the entrance of the nobleman; from then on she virtually withers. He looks at her as little as he looks at the others; and, even when he fixes his eyes on someone, that person does not feel himself looked at. This she did not expect; or, rather, she definitely did expect it, for it cannot be otherwise; but it was also not the expectation of the opposite that drove her here; it was simply something that now is certainly at an end. She feels shame to a degree perhaps ordinarily never felt by our women; not until now does she actually notice that she has thrust herself into the midst of an alien conscription; and, if the soldier has read the conscription list aloud with-

out her name's being on it, and a moment of silence ensues, hunched over and trembling she flees out the door and is given a cuff on her back by the soldier, into the bargain. (B 332-33)

The inaccessibility of the law of the "nobleman" is intensified here to the uttermost extreme, even beyond that in "The Rejection." Not only are requests for the alteration or alleviation of life rejected here, but even the greatest sacrifice that man can make is refused: the sacrifice of himself, complete surrender. The nobleman looks at no one at all. Man as an individual being, as a free "self" that is prepared to pass judgment even on himself, does not exist for the nobleman. The girl has achieved the highest that man can achieve. It is stated specifically that in her "it was also not the expectation of the opposite that drove her here"; this means that she did not carry within her the expectaion of being gazed upon by the nobleman. She was free from any feminine egotism or hope of being particularly noticed by the nobleman, let alone of being marked out for his special favor. She was pure in every respect. And even the "allurement" of being present at a conscription in a "foreign" region cannot be interpreted as sheer instinct, as impairmen of a pure, self-less, voluntary resolve. The allurement is designated emphatically as "nothing disgraceful." On the contrary, the girl is here obeying a direct call to pay the guilt/debt of her sex; that is to say, to render the utmost in expiation. If she yields to this allurement she will be under coercion, it is true, but it is a sacred coercion, a selfless readiness to follow a sublime command, and it is accordingly honored by all human beings; what is more, it is felt to be an almost holy act that radiates "blessing."

Of this there can be no question: the girl wishes to consecrate herself to an ideal. She wishes to step out of her existence with quiet, joyful, composed bearing. Her home becomes a foreign region to her; the region away from her home, that of the conscripted troops, becomes her homeland. She wants to enter into an existence in which everything earthly becomes null, an existence in which she pays off the "guilt/debt of her sex"; that is, an existence in which she becomes holy and "pure." And this resolve is honored by everyone—even by the family she leaves behind. The "respect" for such a resolve is still alive in every human being.

Nevertheless, she is repudiated. This monstrous deed can be comprehended only on the basis of the characterization of this "young nobleman." The "whip" forms "his total equipment." He is "slender, not tall, weak, carelessly dressed, with weary eyes; constantly subject to fidgets, as a sick man is to shivering with cold. Without looking at anyone he gives . . . a signal . . . with a whip" (B 330). He forces those whom he whips "to pick up and hand him" the whip that he has carelessly dropped, "half in exhaustion, half in disgust. . . . Only then may he [the whipped man] fall in line with the rest" (B 331).

The young nobleman represents the final dehumanizing of the law. Behind such a wall there is really "nothing more." But for that matter in front of such a wall there is nothingness. "Even when he fixes his eyes on someone, that person does not feel himself looked at." He looks straight through people into absolute emptiness. He is "constantly subject to fidgets, as a sick man is to shivering with cold." The law has become diseased in him, as to become the law of Hell—no! as to become the law of an age in which there are only natural laws, mercilessly and automatically coming off the conveyor belt, laws to which there are no longer any exceptions. In this young nobleman there emerges the determining law of our time.

It should not be argued that a higher purpose may be at work in the inhuman nobleman, to the effect, perhaps, that the repudiation of the girl took place because she had not received the call and was not of the elect. One cannot evade the harsh text of this fragment with such predestination-theses without sinning against the meaning of religious pre-destination itself. A predestined god, sick, shaken by shivering restlessness as if by the ague, swinging his whip, staring into the void, staring through people as if through nothingness —these theses condemn themselves.

What becomes visible is not predestination but the catastrophe of the classic tragedy. Schiller's "Maid of Orleans," Kleist's "Käthchen of Heilbronn" are driven away by soldiers' fists. The last residue of modern times, the triumph of moral will or pure feeling through unconditional sacrifice, the affirmation of freedom or purity in the very face of ruin, even that remotest phantasmagoria of hope which irradiated the atrocities of modern times and which, in the "tragic" decline and downfall of man, still let meaning and purpose shine forth—even that hope is now shattered in a world in which a self of one's own is no longer perceived and contemplated, a world in which enactments and decrees deal only with masses of people according to laws that tolerate no exception.

The "shame" that the stranger-girl feels is not the shame that stems from a feeling of guilt or from a wound to her womanly nature; it is the boundlessly all-surpassing shame at having her readiness considered as nought, at having her innermost self, as it were, expunged, since even the unshakable, joyful, quiet certainty of her self has betrayed her. The absolute "feeling," that unwavering, rocklike basis of man's being—it was this in particular that Kafka always loved and revered in Kleist's writings—even this absolute, most positive certainty in man is betrayed. For that reason, and only for that reason, she feels "shame to a degree perhaps ordinarily never felt by our women." She has been struck at the very root of her being. Her sudden, frightened alarm at having attended a conscription in a different region could stem only from the feeling of a senseless rejection. Knowledge of guilt could put fresh heart into her, could make expiation possible. And expiation was the very thing for which she was absolutely ready. But what took place here is beyond all concepts of guilt and expiation. She is being driven away not because she obeyed a false voice, but because there is no longer any voice that still speaks to man. She is being repudiated not because she was not of the "elect," but because no elections whatever occur any longer, because no god calls upon an immortal human soul any longer, because only mass conscriptions take place, eliminating every responsible indi-

vidual self and even forcing the punished to pick up the whip
after their punishment and hand it to the punisher. The
penalty inflicted upon man, instead of inwardly restoring him
and liberating him from guilt, becomes the cause of his
breaking up.

Throughout his writings, "shame" for Kafka was always an
expression of man's meaningless foundering on objective,
inscrutable misfortunes; "shamelessness," however—strange and
incredible though it sounds—was an expression of the victory
of the free, discerning self over the "void"—nothingness. In
the novel *The Trial*, Josef K., after successfully enduring
Titorelli's "shameless smiling . . . directed into the void"
(P 294) and not allowing himself to be "led astray" by it,
is guided by the ever cheerful and healthy Titorelli to liberation and rebirth. But when Josef K. perishes "like a dog"
because an unknown power has "denied" him the "necessary
strength" to commit suicide, "it was as if the shame were
destined to live on after him" (P 271-72). As man crumbles
to pieces, there remains alive in him only shame, the moral feeling of a meaningless failure in the face of inscrutable forces.
The "void," however, is overcome by "shamelessly" smiling
knowledge; just as Titorelli, with reference to the court, is
one who knows, an initiate.

Therewith, however, the story "The Conscription of
Troops" takes on a gruesome meaning. The law of the "young"
nobleman is the extirpation of the law, the destruction of the
"self" in which the true, "secret" law of the nobility rests. The
"young" nobility abolishes nobility itself.

The mediation of the absolute imperial law through the
nobility—that is, the mediation between emperor and world—
in the story "The Rejection" had already led to the identification of the law with the "wall of the world." The world
itself, representing the absolute law, congealed into the immutable regularity of the natural laws inherent in everything
earthly. In the "young nobleman" the radical expulsion of
the "self" from the world is consummated.

Since the self could be given poetic form in Kafka's

"animals" only as an extrahuman monstrosity, because no "idea" and no personally determinable sphere of an inner "feeling" could assimilate this self any longer, and since the metaphysical and ethical meaning of free self-determination had disappeared from the sphere of any ideal or personal comprehensibility, the collapse of the classical "world of ideas," in which the free self was at one with the universal moral idea, was bound to bring with it the collapse of classical tragedy as well. Kafka's indefatigable, ever-renewed attempt to unite free self-determination and world law meaningfully is now frustrated here by the "world law" itself, which suddenly reveals itself as an unapproachable extrahuman law of Satan. This disclosure does not originate in any arbitrariness or personal despair of the poet. It simply depicts unsparingly what exists in our world and what has long since been practiced law. Moral sacrifice is "seen" here no longer (B 332); self-conquest is no longer perceived; "shame" is understood no more; sacrifices are no longer accepted. Victims are merely slaughtered.

Every detail confirms such an interpretation. It is characteristic that the nobleman is "young." Whereas the "nobility" in the other short pieces and the "leaders" in "The Construction of the Great Wall of China" still stemmed from ancient times, had existed indeed from time immemorial and truly united in themselves Universal law and the responsible free self; and whereas the colonel in "The Rejection" is still an "old man" who "grants minor requests ... on his own authority as a powerful private individual" (B 89-90) and sustains the tension between holding office and being a private individual,[5] the "young nobleman of "The Conscription of Troops" is a modern, "carelessly dressed," decadent snob who, existing in nothingness and in no place, whips the masses, although even this he does only with loathing.

The "law" of the nobility is perverted and diseased in that the nature of the nobility, the true human self, has become inoperative. But even historical laws are no longer determinative here. The law that this young nobleman represents remains inscrutable, now as ever, to those ruled over; hidden beneath all historical and natural relations, it is the law of a "world" behind which there is "nothing more." In this sense the law is still a "mystery" of the nobility. And only in such a sense can and may one speak of a "nobleman" at all; that is, in the sense of the absolute incomprehensibility and obscurity of his law. But his mystery is the mystery of Satan. The nobility upon which once there shone the reflected splendor of divine worlds has become a nobility in which there is the blazing flash of Lucifer's sun. The divine world has become the victim of the fallen, sick angel. The troops that he levies are dragged along to Hell. But even then there would still be hope. For contrasting with and opposed to a hell there is always a heaven. The nobleman and his troops, however, no longer know anything about hells and heavens. They are themselves only Hell, since what they still represent is only the "wall of the world," in front of and behind which there is "nothing" more. Twentieth-century mankind, that is nothing now but "world," that sees everything only as world out into which it swarms without limit—mankind does not know that such a world is merely another word for what was once called Hell. Salvation, however, has not been promised anyone who does not himself suspect that he is in the hands of the Devil.

Kafka always identified such a world with Hell. "There can be a knowledge of the diabolical, but no belief in it; for more of the diabolical than is there, does not exist" (H 116). The diabolical is not anything invisibly transcendental that could be "believed in" or not believed in; in our world it is "there" in its entirety as a reality.

That in "The Conscription of Troops" no genuine, aloofly supreme court is holding sway is evident not only from the story—above all, from the characterization of the young nobleman—but from the totality of poetic representations and theoretical definitions of the law and of the judicature in Kafka's works. The inscrutable rejections of the court officials or of the doorkeeper in the novel *The Trial* are instances not of the inaccessibility of the supreme "law" but of intermediate juridical procedures, of "mediations" that represent the law of the "world" and thereby obstruct access to the true law. These mediating authorities and channels, as will be clearly seen, definitely originate in modern, topical, social phenomena. Even in Kafka's first novel, *The Man Who was Lost Sight Of* (*America*), a similarly inhuman inaccessibility becomes manifest in the gigantic mediating channels of modern industrial society, in Messrs. Green and Pollunder, or in the figure of the gigantic hotel doorman whose phenotype resembles that of the "doorkeeper" in *The Trial* even to specific individual features.

The parallels that we have drawn between the young nobleman and the inhuman law of our present time are no arbitrary constructs on our part but are anchored deep in Kafka's work. The sharp criticism of society presented by this work is of vast magnitude. After all, even the Universal, man's break with his world of "business" and "work," originates in a clear-sighted critical knowledge of the inescapable conformities of an era that no longer tolerates any universal existence that is meaningfully free of purpose, and that consequently forced Kafka to the poetic form of his empirically incomprehensible world of animals and concrete things. The "nobility" that in the days of old was meant to mediate between the emperor and the people has, by turning into an autonomous in-between authority, relinquished its "in-between" position also, and, rendering itself independent, has become itself the controlling authority. However, it is precisely this that is the "law" of our society, the intermediary authorities and apparatus of which have become the all-controlling power, extending in front of the true law in the form of incalculable decrees, sucking up all reality into itself, representing itself as the sole law-making reality.

Almost every scene of the novel *The Man Who Was Lost Sight Of* (*America*), for instance, could be substituted as a typical example of the behavior of the nobleman: the interrogation of the ship stoker whose claim to his rights, alleged or actual, cannot penetrate in any way through the automatism, the bulwark of society's tactics ("discipline") in proceedings; Karl Rossmann's expulsion from the country villa near New York, an expulsion created first and foremost by Mr. Green who "acted the part of one who was not involved" (A 91) and whose role mounts to "gigantic" proportions; the suites of rooms in which Karl Rossmann loses his way in this country villa; the head doorman of the Hotel "Occidental" etc. All of this is repeated in the court rooms and offices in *The Trial* and in *The Castle*. And only in the supreme court is there an inkling of the true court procedures; and of such true legal procedure Josef K., of course, can see nothing at all.

It is only this supreme court that is without inhuman inaccessibility. "The Court... receives you whenever you come, and it releases you whenever you go," says the "chaplain" of the court to K. (P 265). This court knows no instances of "predestination"; these, in any case, are out of the question in Kafka's view of life. The court is not "inaccessible." Only the intermediary authorities are inaccessible; only the doorkeeper before the law is inaccessible, although he can be bribed; the countless inscrutable echelons in the court offices are unapproachable and bribable. Only the human world is inhuman.

### "In the Penal Colony"

The last statement is clarified in a truly horror-striking manner in what is probably Kafka's most gruesome story, "In the Penal Colony." Turning all of our accustomed, cherished, harmless concepts of what is "humane" topsy-turvy, the story attacks and grapples with the subject of man's truth. Also, like no other story of Kafka's, it radically reveals the contrast between the "old" and the "new" rules of court, between the old laws and today's law; it lends poetic representation, specifically and thematically, to the problem of the historical shift to modern times—the question of the absolute and of the modern "humane" legal procedure. The story must, therefore, be interpreted in conjunction with "The Conscription of Troops," since it is from the latter story that the depth and contemporary historical significance of Kafka's concept of guilt first becomes lucid and the innermost causes for the "disease" of the law in the "young" nobleman are laid bare.

In a letter, dated October 11, 1916, to his publisher Kurt Wolff, Kafka himself formulates the relations between this story and the present age, as he writes: "In explanation of this last story, I shall add merely that it is not only the story that is painful, but it is rather this general era of ours, and my particular era, that was and is very painful as well."

## A. THE OLD LAW AND "REDEMPTION"

A European explorer comes to a penal colony in the tropics and becomes acquainted with an inhuman criminal procedure devised and established by the old commanding officer who has meanwhile died. Every offense—even the apparently most harmless—is punishable by death. The condemned man cannot defend himself; there is no trial; no sentence is pronounced. "He does not know his own sentence ... it would be useless to pronounce it to him. He comes to know it in his own body, to be sure" (E 205). By means of a machine of subtle invention, his offence is inscribed deep into his body during the course of twelve hours of torture. He "deciphers" the text of his guilt "by means of his wounds" (E 213). The judge decides in accordance with the "principle": "Guilt is always indubitable. Other courts cannot act upon this principle, for they comprise numerous points of view and are subject to the judgments of still higher courts" (E 206).

This court is thus the supreme court. In it, judgment is not passed according to opinions, according to the pros and cons of arguments. For the court does not comprise numerous points of view. The former commanding officer who "at one time combined all functions in himself" (E 205), or the colonel, who is now his successor as "judge," adjudges sovereignly. But even their decision has already existed from time immemorial. The accused is always indubitably guilty. There is no need for a decision to be reached at all. And the proceedings themselves are always the same. The offender must identify himself with his guilt. He is himself his guilt. Guilt and being are identical. Only with his wounds, his sufferings, does he recognize his guilt. In twelve hours—symbol of his entire life that ends at the twelfth hour—he must come to know himself, to realize his existential guilt, as a result of which all his individual offenses also arise; that is, guilt is traced back to its root.

At the zenith of life endured, in the sixth hour, after sense-less, futile screaming and resistance, there is the beginning of knowledge: the reading of the inscription. "Understanding dawns on even the most stupid imbecile" (E 212); for "he who ... does not recognize ... the law" that leads to "inner freedom" and "redemption ... will be dragged, bullied, and flogged into knowledge of it" (J 100-101).

In the sixth hour "we all absorbed the look of transfiguration in the tortured face ... lifted ... our countenances into the light of this justice, achieved at long last and even now fading away" (E 218). In this old legal procedure "justice is done" (E 218). "Man voluntarily limits his own self, divests himself of his most precious and real possession, his own person, in order to be redeemed. Through outer subjection he wants to attain inner freedom. That is the meaning of subordinating oneself to the law" (J 100).

The old commanding officer's legal procedure is the procedure that every person must go through who wants to attain valid knowledge of his existence, inner freedom and redemption. For that reason, too, execution in the days of the old command-ing officer was still a demonstrative spectacle in which everyone took part, in which everyone looked at the image of his own road through suffering to salvation. It was not a matter of par-tial guilt; it was a matter of the total guilt of existence. Each individual lapse was merely a ray of this total guilt and therefore could also be validly expiated through knowledge of the total guilt. In this way it is possible to explain the inhumanity and absurdity of this procedure which, moreover, on a reduced scale is an accurate representation of the legal proceedings in the novel *The Trial*, where guilt is likewise established as a fact from the start, and no sentence is passed, etc.

Accordingly, the colonel does not consider this procedure inhuman, but "on the contrary... the most human and most worthy of human dignity" (E 221). But he realizes that nowadays no one can understand this any longer: "I know it is impossible to make those times understandable today" (E 219).

For the times have become more humane, "more lenient" (E 216). The new commanding officer is no longer interested in such executions but in "harbor constructions, over and over again, harbor constructions!" (E 224). He wants to abolish the old legal procedure and replace it with a humane one in which the hearing and defense take place in due order, and arguments are advanced for and against.

The old commanding officer, on the other hand, wanted to create an enduring, valid system, removed from time as it were. His "organization of the colony" was "so self-contained... that his successor, even if he had a thousand new plans in his head, would be unable to alter anything of the old state of affairs, at least for many years to come" (E 201). This corresponds precisely to the sovereignty of the "colonel" in the story "The Rejection." Now, however, in the new order of things, man takes over, since he no longer condemns himself, but, as it were, lets himself enter into a free, unrestrained life, a more humane but also a more anarchical form of life that is carried on in a clash of opinions and a nexus of interests.

The European traveler decides in favor of the new commanding officer, for the traveler then was "in no doubt about the injustice of the procedure and the inhumanity of the execution" (E 215).

B. THE NEW SATANIC LAW OF
   THE "HUMANE" INDUSTRIAL SOCIETY

With that, the old procedure has come to an end. The colonel executes himself. The new laws condemn him. Hence the text that he intends to have the machine inscribe on his body is: "Be just!" But in the course of this execution, contrary to the colonel's will, the machine falls apart. "The harrow was not writing, it was only stabbing" (E 233). Such a text cannot be written. Justice, which "is done" by means of this machine, negates itself in such a text that declares what is just to be unjust. Hence the machine can now only "murder" the executed man. Accordingly, on the face of the dead man there can be seen "no sign of the promised salvation. . . . It looked as it had looked in life . . . the lips were pressed tight together, the eyes were open and had the look of life" (E 234). The eras of redemption are past. The dead man survives in life. He can no longer cross the boundary into the liberating Hereafter. Man has fallen completely into the hands of the earth.

The new "humane" system of justice, however, is immediately reflected in the condemned man, now set free, in whose place the colonel had lain down for execution in the machine. The condemned man believes he is being "avenged" through the colonel's execution: "So this, then, was revenge. Although he had not suffered to the last, he was nevertheless being avenged to the last. A wide-mouthed, soundless laugh now appeared on his face and never left it" (E 231).

The new, "lenient" system of justice is concerned only with the categories of interpersonal requitals, advantages and disadvantages. It never condemns man; hence, too, it never condemns the nexus of interests to which man with his motivations has banished himself. In its courts it pursues only the battle of mutual extermination. Its humanity is the source of its inhumanity, in the same way in which the inhumanity of the old law represented a procedure that was "the most human and most worthy of the dignity of man."

In logical consequence, at the end of the story there remains only the vague hope that the old system of justice may rise again. And it is strange but true that the adherents of the old commanding officer, who long for his "resurrection," are characterized as "poor, humbled people" (E 235), longshoremen without jackets and with torn shirts. Only these people, who are the victims of the "humanity" of the upper classes, can expect liberation of a legal system which the judicature imposes upon everyone. For, only where everyone declares himself guilty can the victims still hope to attain real humanity. But they do not even dare admit to possessing such hope:

There are still many [adherents of the old commanding officer], but no one admits to being one. If you go to the teahouse today, that is to say on an execution day, and keep your ears open, it may be that you will hear only ambiguous remarks. These remarks are made by adherents who, though genuine enough, are, under the present commanding officer and in the light of his present views, entirely useless to me. (E 217)

And in this way even these adherents, play-acting when face to face with the traveler whom they suspiciously consider a "foreigner," declare their own hope for a resurrection of the old commanding officer to be a "ridiculous," crazy notion (E 236). Redemption becomes ridiculous in a world that is left to its own devices.

However, those who are liberated through the new humanity are themselves seized by horror. The condemned man and the soldier want to flee with the traveler. The latter threatens them, however, and leaves them behind.

Kafka himself was not satisfied with his story. On September 4, 1917, he wrote to Wolff: "Two or three pages shortly before the end of the story are contrived; the presence of these pages points to a more profound defect; there is a worm there somewhere that is making the story hollow even where it is full and whole." Almost exactly a month earlier, in his diary entries of August 5 and August 9, 1917, he had been laboring at new versions of these pages that come shortly before the end of the story. For instance, according to these the traveler lies down near the grave of the dead colonel and cries out,

"I'm a dirty dog if I let that happen!" But then he took his own statement literally and began to run about on all fours. Only occasionally would he spring up, virtually tearing himself away, rush up to one of the men and fall on his neck, crying out amidst tears, "Why does all this have to happen to me!" and then he would hurry back to his post. (T 525)

The traveler, having in fact caused the annihilation of the old law, is spellbound at the place of his guilt and turns into a "dog" like Josef K. at the end of *The Trial*, who likewise lacks the strength to pass judgment upon himself.

Even more sinister and revealing for Kafka's central intention in this attempt of his to express the "full and whole" content of the story is the subsequent sketch [in the *Diaries*]:

"Our ever cheerful commanding officer," the new, humane commander, then shouts to his workers, "Pave the way for the serpent! . . . Pave the way for the great Madam. . . . Get going! . . . get going, you serpent-fodder!" (T 525-26). Thereupon "we pioneers, we much-lauded stone-pounders" picked up

" . . . our hammers, and for mile upon mile there began the most diligent pounding. No pause was permitted, only a change of hands. The arrival of our serpent had already been announced for the evening; by that time everything had to be pounded to dust—our serpent cannot endure even the tiniest little pebble. . . . We fail to understand, we regret that she still calls herself serpent. She ought always to call herself 'Madam' at least. . . . But that is not our business; our business is making dust." (T 525-26)

With unceasing toil the cheerful, humane world crushes everything to dust in order to pave the way for the serpent, for evil; what is more, that world becomes itself the "fodder" for the serpent. For "the point is, too, that this is a unique serpent, incomparably pampered by means of our labor, and hence already of an incomparable nature." She is "naturally incomparable, too, as Madam" (T 526).

The total "labor" of this new era of the commanding officer goes toward pulverizing existence into nothingness, toward feeding Satan with a world crumbling to dust. The serpent is called Madam in view, perhaps, of her famous appellation as "the old aunt";* perhaps also, however, in continuation of a thematic chain, for in this story it is the "ladies" of the new commanding officer who have wanted the abolition of the old law and who have tried with seductive means to put through the new law (E 216, 221, 224, 225). However, it is the opinion of the workers that she should discard her old designation of "serpent." Evil is not allowed to be called by its name in this world that is cheerfully working without pause, that has become humane. But even that is not "our business; our business is making dust." Ethical questions are actually eliminated completely. The "work" is more important. By means of such labor, however, the serpent is "incomparably pampered." Nowhere does she thrive better than where there is no longer any inquiry into good and evil.

The new law is the law of the Devil. The old order, for the sake of redemption, sacrificed man; the new order, for the sake of man, has sacrificed redemption. Both orders are barbarous. Neither one can be played off against the other, for neither can be lived.

With the promise of redemption the earthly world turns to stone. If all men are guilty, the world must remain as it is. Since it is fundamentally bad, changes are senseless. The best thing that can be achieved in this world is an immutable order, a lasting tranquillity, by one's leaving the world as it is, unchanged. That is the old order. Every earthly hope bounces off, ricochets from a world of "pure" skeletons.

With the promise of a "cheerful" earthly life, however, the earth crumbles to dust. The world becomes the prey of the serpent. The absolute commandment has been banished. The restlessly changing world that manifests its vigorous life in revolts and "strides of progress" grinds itself down to nothing. Man's earthly self-assertion turns into mankind's self-annihilation in the illimitable progress of "work" and in the battle of everyone against everyone. Can both orders be reconciled? That was the cardinal question in Franz Kafka's three novels.

*Tr. note: So called by Mephistopheles in Goethe's *Faust* I, 1.335. The German word *Muhme* may mean "aunt," "cousin" (female), or any "elderly female relation."

CHAPTER V

# The Modern Industrial World:
# The Novel *The Man*
# *Who Was Lost Sight Of (America)*

The modern work-world that grinds everything to dust, that permits of no pauses save those necessary for a change of hands, was described in detail by Kafka early on, in his first novel *The Man Who Was Lost Sight Of*, which he was writing during the period 1911 to 1914. The novel is one of the most clear-sighted poetic exposures of modern industrial society that exist in world literature. In it the hidden economic and psychological mechanism of this society and its satanic consequences are mercilessly laid bare. Moreover, this novel is prerequisite for an understanding of both *The Trial* (1914), which chronologically follows immediately upon it, and *The Castle* (1921-1922). For, within the framework of a narrative style that is still seemingly realistic, the decisive phenomena that occur in the later novels are already developed in this early novel and can be related to an interpretation compatible with Kafka's view of life.

The novel was published by Max Brod under the title, *America*. Kafka himself, in his diaries, calls the novel *The Man Who Was Lost Sight Of* (T 453). We shall therefore use the title used by the author.

## The Nonstop Labor of Modern Times

In this novel, all work is carried on without break, in mad haste. The shipping traffic in New York harbour is "an endless stir, a restlessness communicated by the restless element to the helpless human beings and their labors!" (A 25). Man is not master of his work-world, but is "helplessly" exposed to it just as primitive people in the dawn of history were exposed to the forces of nature, the "elements." Without realizing it, the industrial world is effecting a return to archaic antiquity, an antiquity from which mankind, developing itself laboriously in the course of many thousands of years, had striven to rise to a form of free, individual self-determination; in the same way the free, individual self in Kafka's writings relapses into the pre-human, archiac-mythical animal. The dehumanization of modern man is clearly grasped and characterized by Kafka as a throwback to the archaic, early human world of collective hordes, of animal-mythical atavisms, and monotonously cycle-like recurrences of eternal sameness where all history, all individual time-consciousness, and all personal responsibility are extinguished. In *The Trial* and *The Castle* we shall again meet with a description of this modern global monotony. It emerges already in *The Man Who Was Lost Sight Of,* with this limitation: the labor of modern times, by contrast with that of the archaic world, represents an unmeaning, unaccented monotony in which there no longer exist any qualitative differences in the sense of, say, successions of seasons, festive highlights, but in which everything is turned uniformly into dust; similarly, the determining "restless element" here equates with the monotonously uniform rise and fall of the waves. Accordingly, for the "port officials . . . the pocket watch they had lying in front of them was . . . more important than everything that was going on in the room and that might yet take place there" (A 40): that is to say, more important than the human encounter between Karl Rossmann and his uncle; and more important than the argument as to whether the stoker was in the right or in the wrong. Later Karl Rossmann is regarded reproachfully by the head doorman of the Hotel Occidental as "a watch that keeps bad time" (A 220).

The compulsion to work without stopping switches off everything that is human. In the uncle's telephone hall one sees "in the flashing of electric lights, an employee, indifferent to every noise of the doors, with his head clamped into a steel strip that pressed the receivers against his ears ... and only the fingers that held the pencil twitched with inhuman regularity and speed" (A 58). It is pointless and superfluous for the operator to ask questions of his own or to raise any objections to the messages from the person telephoning, for

... certain words that he heard forced him, before he could carry out his intention, to lower his eyes and to write. Also, he did not have to talk ... for the very messages this man received were received by two other employees simultaneously and then compared, so that, as far as possible, errors were eliminated.... Through the middle of the hall there was constant traffic of people being rushed hither and thither. No one said a friendly hello; friendly greetings had been abolished; everyone, falling into step with the person walking ahead of him, kept his eyes on the floor over which he wanted to make headway as rapidly as possible. (A 58-59)

Everyone is shunted into grooves already marked out for him and, keeping his eyes rigidly fixed on the floor over which he is at the moment walking, wants "to make headway as rapidly as possible" in his professional career. Everyone is replaceable by everyone else: "In this way everyone here is forever filling in for everyone else. Otherwise such a large business operation would be unthinkable" (A 226).

In the Hotel Occidental inquiries are answered "without the slightest interruption" (A 222). "Just talking would not have sufficed for their task; they rattled on" (A 221), for one "knows ... pretty much all the questions that are asked, and as for the rest, well, one doesn't have to make any reply" (A 224). Through "a scarcely perceptible shake of the head" one throws the unanswerable question back to the person who asks it and forces him "to formulate the question better" (A 222); that is, in such a way that it fits into the conventional pattern.

In keeping with this is the flow of traffic on the street

... where automobiles, as they had already been doing during the entire day, kept on hurrying past one another effortlessly, as if an exact number of them were being constantly dispatched from afar over and over again, and as if far away in the opposite direction that same number were being awaited. During the entire day, from very early morning on, Karl had not seen a single automobile stop or a single passenger get out. (A 131)

Driving in automobiles thus goes on for its own sake, anonymously, as it were, as a rushing from remoteness to remoteness without any visible beginning or end.

An analogy may be seen in the economic background. In this autonomized work-world the question is no longer primarily one of production and consumption but of procurement of goods and underhand marketing that will net far more profit than direct manufacture of goods and direct sale to the consumer. The business of the uncle, who "has a hand ... in all matters" (A 109) pertaining to American economic life (with the exception of distant San Francisco),

... was a kind of commission and forwarding agency, such as, to Karl's best recollection, was perhaps not to be found in Europe at all. The business consisted of a wholesale trade which did not negotiate for goods, say, from the producers to the consumers or perhaps to the dealers, but which provided for the supply of all goods and raw products to the large manufacturing syndicates. Hence, being a business that included at one and the same time purchases, storage and warehousing, transport and shipping, and sales, all on a gigantic scale, it necessitated highly accurate and unceasing communication with clients by telephone and telegraph. (A 57-58)

Just as the automobiles mediate only between immensely distant points, without any visible evidence of a "stop" or of even a human "passenger," the uncle's business represents in the same way merely connections that multiply in number automatically and that yield enormously increasing profits. Even the gigantic business undertaking in the Hotel Occidental—symbol of Western civilization—is based upon pure middleman procedures that expand in number and size automatically and incalculably.

## Modern Intermediary Agents in Analogy with The Trial *and* The Castle

In this kind of senseless pursuit of sheer intermediary labors there no longer exists any individual person who acts directly and independently, and correspondingly there no longer exists any supreme legislative authority that has immediate effectiveness. The intermediary organs, autonomizing themselves, become anonymous powers. These govern everything, and, multiplying endlessly, they determine the lives of human beings who are at the same time thereby degraded to the state of anonymous masses blindly controlled in accordance with laws which the executive organs themselves do not know and cannot understand—what is more, laws that disregard these executive organs and control them as well. Those that rule become the ruled.

The apparatus of business and of the economic system in *The Man Who Was Lost Sight Of* thus already contains the pattern for the apparatus of the official machinery in *The Trial* and *The Castle*. These likewise depict mere intermediary bureaucracies that do nothing but rush reports, in mad, incessant haste, from one prescribed channel to another, without anyone's having final jurisdiction over a single report, and without anyone's having the responsibility of authorized signature. The vast hierarchy of "judges" in *The Trial*, of minor and chief justices, clerks, etc., that are unable to terminate a case in court but keep each case pending unremittingly, since they themselves, being dependent upon further supervisory and control boards, etc., lack the power of making final decisions—that hierarchy is a picture of today's go-between procedures that automatically multiply without limit. The officials in *The Trial* and *The Castle* mirror not only man's unceasing inner reflection and dream consciousness, but also the external social life of our time.

The following examples may show how close the ties are between *The Man Who Was Lost Sight Of* and *The Trial*. In *The Man Who Was Lost Sight Of* the longshoremen already wear "black" uniforms (A 19), as do the court officials in *The Trial*. They do not listen at all to the accusatory speeches of Karl Rossmann; in exactly the same way the officials in the courtroom scarcely pay any attention to Josef K.'s speech. The head doorman conceals his sadistic brutality from the public by means of "black curtains"; he stifles the "screams" of the tormented young man by "stopping his mouth" (A 225, 227). One may compare this scene with that of the whippers in *The Trial*. While with one arm the head doorman is tormenting Karl "with pleasure," with the other he embraces Karl's friend Therese and draws her "amiably to himself" (A 206). Sexuality and brutality are here identical, as they are in *The Trial*, where, at the very moment of Josef K.'s desperate accusatory oration, the officials are relishing a sexual scene in the background of the courtroom. The connection between sadistic sexuality and the meaningless work automatism of today presents a problem that must yet be dealt with. Already in *The Man Who Was Lost Sight Of* it plays a determinative role.

However, the tie-ins with *The Trial* lie at an even deeper level. While Karl Rossmann is on the balcony, "in downright captivity" (A 285), in the violent embraces of the singer Brunelda, a woman who exercises a sexual power over men, he catches sight of preparations going on in the street below for the election of a "judge" for that particular city district. What is involved here is the selection of a judge who will be responsible for justice in this district. And basically the entire novel *The Man Who Was Lost Sight Of* is really a singular coming to grips with the problem of "justice"; in vain does the hero Karl Rossmann constantly search for justice. In the same way *The Trial* circles round the problem of justice and of a supreme court with proper jurisdiction. But what does this election of the "judge" look like in *The Man Who Was Lost Sight Of*?

In a "general clamor" (A 277) the masses roar out an "unintelligible name" (A 279), and while so doing they "applaud
like machines" (A 281), until finally a "signal that seemed unending ... stifled ... every human voice" and "the crowd that
had obviously been coached to do so" brought the opposing
party to "complete silence" (A 281-82). The masses are bribed
with free beer: "the leaders ... organized ... the distribution
... which took place as everyone paraded past the door of the
restaurant" (A 284). The candidate for the judgeship, however,
does not get a chance to be heard at all. Nothing of what he says
is understood, particularly since so many other speakers keep
interrupting with loud shouts.

Finally everything is reversed. Although the speaker and his
party had previously been in control of the crowds and had
"organized" them, it is now the mob that takes over anarchic
command: the speaker and his porter had "not the slightest
freedom of movement any longer" (A 286). The ruler becomes
the prisoner of his own system. He

... could no longer take a single step of his own volition; it was
no longer possible to think of ... influencing the crowd.... The
multitude surged forward aimlessly, everyone supporting himself
on his neighbors, no one standing upright any longer ... the
nominee kept talking all the time, but it was no longer quite clear
whether he was explaining his political platform or calling for
help. (A 286-87)

Karl observes all this "in breathless confusion" (A 287).

With this, Kafka has trenchantly criticized the structure of
modern large-scale industrial society. The mob, lacking purpose
and plan, becomes autonomous and controls even the judge
that it has set over itself; similarly, in reverse, the leaders who
on the face of things are in control are ruled anarchically by the
mob that they have organized. To reach the summit of satirical
truth, Kafka then adds the words of the student:

"The man ... does not have the remotest chance of being elected.
I happen to know everything about him.... He is not an incom-
petent man, and according to his political views and his political

background he would be just the right judge for the district. But not a soul thinks he could possibly be elected; he will lose out in the election with as glorious a lack of success as possible; he will have wasted his few dollars on the election campaign, and that will be all." (A 302)

Just as the economic middleman system, following a law of expansion of its own dynamics, automatically excludes any personal intervention, the politico-juridical executive organs are overpowered by the self-evolving laws of industrial expansion, and even with the most beautiful "platform" they can no longer prevail against the mounting technological inventions and refinements. Every individual stands helpless in the face of an irresistibly onrolling movement that is no longer governed by any real "plan" but that merely brings forth pseudo-plans, only to devour them again; since every plan at the very moment of its birth is being superseded by a new advance that will no longer tolerate any true "freedom of movement," but either forces both the "leaders" and the led, alike, into downright captivity, or exterminates them without leaving a trace. Every hope, every repeatedly attempted purposeful intervention, seen from the viewpoint of the total picture, turns out to be a utopian beacon, briefly flashing up and dying out again:

And in the morning, as in the evening and in the dreams of the night, there passed on this street a constant flow of crowding traffic that, seen from above, appeared as a blend of ever-fresh elements, an intermingling of distorted human figures and roofs of vehicles of every sort ... and all of this was caught and penetrated by a powerful light which again and again was scattered by the multitude of objects, carried off and assiduously regenerated; and to the dazzled eye the light appeared palpable, as though above this street, covering everything, there were a pane of glass being shattered to bits every instant, repeatedly, with might and main. (A 49)

The monotony of work that whisks everything off, distorting human figures, ultimately becomes also the monotony of hope that again and again dawns and dies away.

## Justice and Discipline

However, such montony of work in which progressive differentiation turns actually into undifferentiation, now becomes
visible also in the psychical and ethical behavior of its seeming
individuals. Everybody reacts with the same basic attitude. The
graduations are only apparent or quantitative in nature. Karl
Rossmann, the only one whose behavior is qualitatively different, is with logical consistency "killed as a punishment" or
"pushed aside" (T 481).

It is not without tragic irony that, of all things, Karl Rossmann wants to become an "engineer" and that he sincerely tries
with all his might to be accepted into America's engineering
world. He is not in the least a "critic" of the modern system of
labor. On the contrary, he wants to gain a firm footing in that
system and become a good worker, not unlike his spiritual
brother K. later on in *The Castle*.

However, his goodness of heart, his "innocence" (T 481),
keeps him from being accepted. His struggle for man's "rights,"
for true justice, renders him useless for this world, in spite of
his tireless labor and honest diligence. For, all his kind, unselfish
actions, in the eyes of the world around him, change into evil,
since a good action in the eyes of this world seems absolutely
incomprehensible, unthinkable, or foolish. This sixteen-year-old
lad, who remains an innocent "child" even while he is dominated by Brunelda (A 258), was cast off by his Prague parents,
in order to avoid a social scandal. A poor servant girl, prey to
her instincts, had seduced him and had a child by him without his
having been in any way aware of this seduction. In spite of his
parents' repudiation of him, he remains devoted and loyal to
them, and for the photograph of his parents he is ready to sacrifice everything he possesses. As he looks at their photograph, he
"tried from various angles to catch his father's eye. But no
matter how he altered his view by placing the candle in various
positions, his father would not come to life" (A 117). His
father remains lifeless; he is no longer a human being; he has

succumbed to society's inhuman, mendacious moral code. His mother, however, is a suffering victim of society: "His mother, on the other hand, had certainly been better photographed; her mouth looked awry, as if she had been hurt and were forcing herself to smile" (A 117).

Without misgivings he believes that his parents know what true right and wrong are. On board ship, as he battles for the stoker's rights, the thought goes through his head: "If only his parents could see him as he stood up for the right in a foreign country before distinguished personages ... would they revise their opinion of him? Set him between them and praise him? One day, one day look into his eyes, so full of devotion for them?" (A 31).

However, the inner certitude of justice founders on society's "discipline" (A 42), a discipline that is impervious to every human impulse. And indeed this holds true for members on the lowest levels of this society as well as for those on the highest: for the stoker and the servant as well as for the uncle. It is because the stoker gives vent to his indignation, instead of keeping matter-of-factly to ship discipline and its regulations, that his words strike deaf ears; what he says creates the semblance of injustice; he "disturbs" the authorities at their "important tasks" and inspections of the records, and he makes "impatient" all who expect and desire a quick, orderly judicial procedure (A 24, 27). And even the attendant—who at first remained "calm and ... unaffected ... by the atmosphere of distraction that was setting in, who, sympathizing in part with the troubles of the poor man being held at bay among the rich, nodded earnestly to Karl" (A 25)—even the attendant "once again" gets "completely into the realm of his masters" (A 28). Nobody is spared the automatism of prescribed, officially standardized regulations, not even the stoker.

"Don't misunderstand the situation," said the senator [Karl's uncle] to Karl [who is still championing the "cause of justice"], "perhaps what is at issue is a matter of justice, but at the same time it is a matter of discipline. Both, and most particuarly the latter, are subject here to the judgment of the Captain." "That's about the size of it," muttered the stoker. Whoever noticed this and understood it, smiled, somewhat taken aback. (A 42)

Even the senator, who is in the highest echelon of society, bows to conventional discipline. He apologizes to the Captain for having interrupted official business with a personal family scene, the unexpected meeting with his nephew Karl. Karl feels this apology as an incomprehensible "self-abasement on the part of his uncle"—all the more so because the Captain accepts it unhesitatingly and without any polite phrases of protest. In the consciousness of these people, whatever is official takes precedence over anything private—"His politeness stops at discipline." And consequently Karl realizes with horror that he can do nothing more for the stoker "without insulting everybody" (A 43). Weeping desperately, he can do nothing further but kiss the stoker's hand and exhort him: " 'But you must offer resistance, say yes and no, otherwise people really will have no notion of the truth' " (A 44). However, even this anguish of Karl's is interpreted by his uncle in the following way: " 'The stoker seems to have cast a spell over you,' he said, and looked knowingly over Karl's head at the Captain. 'You felt yourself deserted, then you found the stoker, and now you are grateful to him—that is of course quite commendable. But, just as a favor, don't carry things too far; learn to understand what your position is' " (A 44). Hence "doubts arose in his [Karl's] mind whether this man [the uncle] would ever be able to take the place of the stoker" (A 47). Karl senses that it is in fact the "position," the "splendid career" (A 33) being offered him through his uncle's patronage, that precludes every genuinely human feeling, that rules out all striving for justice and truth.

In the "Stoker" chapter Kafka has displayed, in compressed form, the structure of his novels: the unresolvable antimony between "private" and "official" existence; the impossibility of realizing private existence within a society that is governed exclusively by the "office and officialdom" and that levels away even class distinctions on the basis of this schematization and regimentation of thought.

This is not contradicted by the apparently liberal, independent character of the uncle. Even he, who represents the American "self-made man," is trapped in the "discipline" of his intermediary agents. He can no longer think and act freely; he, of all people, who is bent on *only* free and independent action and judgment, who "advised ... Karl for the present not to become seriously involved in even the most trifling matter. He ought to examine and observe everything, of course, and not let himself be caught up in anything" (A 49), but to make his judgments independently.

Although the uncle grants Karl the opportunity of developing himself freely, of cultivating his personality as it were, pursuing his inclinations and exercising his talents, he nevertheless warns him against dreamy, solitary inactivity, against looking down, from high up on the balcony, upon the swarming, bustling stir of traffic below. "That was bound to confuse a person in any case. This solitary idleness that led one to lose oneself in gazing at a busy New York day might be permissible for a tourist ... but for someone who would be staying on here, it was fatal" (A 50). He therefore urges [Karl] to learn something practical soon and to adjust to his new circumstances. He fears that a complete overview of the work-world, as gained from a dreamy, solitary distance, can bring only corruption and confusion.

## Technology as Free Play

The "child" Karl, however, still hopes that his dreamy, free play will lead to a true shaping of life for him. In this passage one cannot help hearing the echoes of Kafka's conception, with which we are familiar, of childlike and purpose-free existence and of the rescuing function of "music" and play: "In the early days Karl entertained high hopes of his piano playing and, at least before falling asleep, was not ashamed of thinking it possible that this piano playing would have a direct influence upon his situation in America" (A 53).

Thus it is here a matter of the breakthrough into "direct" existence as opposed to all mediations—the breakthrough to direct "influence" upon even concrete life by means of a piano playing that does away with all obstacles. But that remains merely a dream, possible and thinkable only in the proximity of "sleep." "But if he then looked out upon the street, it was unchanged and remained merely a small portion of a great circular course, a portion that, by itself alone, could not be brought to a standstill unless one knew all the forces operating in the circle" (A 53). Life, racing madly along in a monotonous "circle," cannot "by itself alone" be brought to a standstill. Karl must enter into life, become acquainted with all its forces, and, owing to these—fail.

In like manner Karl construes the "latest invention" of his desk as a plaything, indeed, as a felicitous reminder of the nativity play of his childhood. The subtle mechanism of this desk becomes a plaything for him. A last, supremely utopian hope reveals itself here: if all technology could be transformed into purpose-free play, mankind would once again be free of the spell of monotonous work-enslavement. Childhood and Karl's childlike wish to become an "engineer" are here linked in such utopian play as to form an enchanting, meaningful, integrated whole.

But the uncle "by contrast with Karl, was not at all pleased with this desk" (A 51), and gave his consent to the piano playing only "reluctantly" (A 52). He can no longer respond with immediacy. Even his final judgment of Karl is determined by middlemen, his ostensible friends. This man who thinks for himself is the very man who fails to form an independent judgment of the moral qualities of the nephew he loves.

The decision as to whether Karl loves him truly, obeys him honestly, and trusts in him, or whether he can be seduced and corrupted by other people to act against his uncle's wishes—this decision concerning Karl's ultimate repudiation the uncle places in the hands of middlemen who outrageously misuse this confidence of his.

## The Intermediary Agents and
## Kafka's "Doorkeeper" in The Trial

These middlemen, foremost among them Mr. Green, are the actual rulers and figurants of the time. Just as the mediating apparatus in the business-transportation-communication world is constantly increasing without check, and assuming monstrous and gigantic proportions, so do these middlemen grow into immensities before Karl's frightened eyes: "At the sight of Green's gigantic figure—Karl had already grown accustomed to Pollunder's great size—that gradually emerged before them as they ascended the stairs, every shred of hope did indeed depart from Karl" (A 70); "Mr. Green, perhaps even slightly stouter than Mr. Pollunder ... appeared to be a great gymnast, a gymnastics demonstrator" (A 98). And finally, shortly before the crisis, there is this statement: "In this corridor Green assumed a size that was by this time ridiculous, and Karl pondered, for the fun of it, whether he had not perhaps devoured good Mr. Pollunder" (A 106).

Green's figure grows progressively in the course of subsequent events. At the same time, he is a "gymnastics demonstrator"; that is, he determines the line of march of the age; similarly, in the uncle's telephone hall, everyone blindly follows the person walking directly in front of him.

Again the parallels with *The Trial* are striking. The doorkeepers that bar immediate entrance to the Law increase incalculably: " ... one mightier than the other. The very sight of the third one is more than even I can endure" (P 256; E 158). The intermediaries are involved in the unceasing process of growth. Possibly that is also what underlies the peculiar fact that, for example, the Hotel Occidental in *The Man Who Was Lost Sight Of* swells out increasingly from page to page of the novel. At first it consisted of only six storeys (A 139), then there are over eight, "since a lady had fainted on the eighth floor" (A 183). On page 152 the hotel has at least 536 rooms, for Room 536 is mentioned (A 152), and finally the hotel is a gigantic complex of buildings, scarcely assessable any longer, with "five thousand guests" (A 195) and "countless" entrances (A 227).

Although these inconsistencies may be explained by the fact that the existing fragment of the novel derives from a manuscript that had not as yet been intended for publication, nevertheless this growth in the size of the hotel building is characteristic of Kafka's poetic fantasy in which such intermediary systems mount into incalculability. And, just as the doorkeepers in *The Trial* are actually the "mighty" (P 256), so too is the head doorman of the Hotel Occidental: "Besides, in a certain sense, as head doorman I am in a position above everyone, for all the portals of the hotel are in my charge—this main entrance, the three middle entrances, and the ten side entrances, to say nothing of the countless little doors and the exits without doors" (A 226-27).

The seemingly most insignificant and lowly figure in a public building, the doorman, is turned into the dominating character because everyone is geared to mediation, and no one dares any longer to enter directly and to assert himself freely.

Kafka's doorkeepers and mediating authorities and channels that grow to colossal dimensions are the picture of an age in which complex systems of apparatus, incessantly and automatically increasing, wrest all decisions from the hands of individuals, who are decision-makers only in appearance. The uncle—who thinks for himself, who is immensely rich, who indeed determines almost the whole of American economic life—puts himself into their power and sacrifices his beloved nephew in preference to cutting these intermediaries to shreds.

*Sadism in* The Man Who Was Lost Sight Of
*and in* The Trial, *and the Perversion*
*of the Conditions of Ruling Power in Society*

These mediating authorities and channels are at the same

time corrupt and sadistic. Every contact with a fellow man becomes an act of violence. Mr. Green carves pigeons "with sharp thrusts" (A 72) and unscrupulously, "with the energy of a man who has eaten his fill" (A 74), grabs at Pollunder's daughter Klara, whose "extremely lively eyes" thereupon take on a heightened "sparkle" (A 75). For Klara herself can conceive of love only in the form of taking possession and of an athletic "wrestling match" (A 83). Self-inflicted pain becomes pleasure. In the world of mere possessions, of "having and holding," love too is only a brutal taking possession.

And even the "country house," symbol of "freedom," peace, and relaxation (A 92)—even it turns into a "fortress" with "endless corridors," "empty rooms," and "darkness everywhere" (A 87, 92). Work, never ceasing, rushing madly, penetrates to the very core, to the innermost dwelling of the owners, forcing them constantly to take measures to safeguard and protect what they possess, even forcing wrestling matches into their private lives, and thereby cutting off the fortressed house from "chapel" and "church," the refuge for true peace (A 86, 88).

But, where no one has any real or secure ownership any longer, where wealth is altogether a fiction, where only intermediations still take place, where everyone is the hunter and the hunted, in the offices of the doorkeepers, of the head doorman, and of the ordinary doormen who rattle off information ceaselessly with lightning speed—there the agonizing pleasure of the sadist, unchecked, makes its inveterate abode. For he who is tormented can remain alive only if he torments others. Only in this way can he abandon himself to the pleasurable illusion that he dominates where he is dominated.

Sadism is the desperate mode of compensation for the lack of love relationships, for the failure to meet one's fellow man on a human basis in the rush of this work-hectic existence Sadism is the gruesome form of contact that our estranged mass society takes on. Long after he had written *The Man Who Was Lost Sight Of*, Franz Kafka had the following conversation with Gustav Janouch:

"The Marquis de Sade, whose biography you have lent me, is the virtual patron of our times."

"You don't really mean that, do you?"

"Oh, yes! The Marquis de Sade can get his joy in life only at the expense of somebody else's suffering, just as the luxury of the rich is paid for by the misery of the poor." (J 78)

It is characteristic that the "tall," burly, head doorman always feels the need to be greeted and addressed by even the most insignificant elevator boy as "Head Doorman," and this "each and every time" the elevator boy goes through the doorway in the course of the day (A 198). He can be sensible of the dignity of his position only through the obsequiousness of his subordinates, since he himself no longer possesses any inner dignity or feeling of self-respect. Inner justice is replaced by outer discipline; the emptiness of the person is masked by

. . . his sumptuous, resplendently decorated uniform—golden chains and ribbon-braid were intertwined even on his shoulders, making their serpentine way down along his arms. . . . Moreover, as a result of the weight of his clothing, the man could as a rule move only with difficulty, and never took up a position without planting his feet wide apart, in order to distribute his weight properly. (A 192)

He becomes the prisoner of his alienated mode of existence. And finally he goes so far as to rob Karl, emptying his pockets and appropriating even his personal jacket while Karl is desperately wrenching himself free from him.

Here too there exist analogies to the officials and guards of *The Trial*—for example, the scene when the black-uniformed, burly guards steal Josef K.'s underwear. The parallels exist down to details. It is said of the head doorman of the hotel: "His glossy black mustache, its ends twirled into long points as is the fashion in Hungary, did not stir even with the most rapid movement of his head" (A 192). And of the examining magistrates in *The Trial*: "Tiny little black eyes flitted to and fro; their [the magistrates'] jowls hung low as in drunkards; their long beards were stiff and sparse, and putting one's fingers into such a beard would seem like merely clawing at it and not like running one's fingers through a beard" (P 62). And when, in "Before the Law," the "man from the country" sees the "doorkeeper," the following is stated: ". . . but as he now more carefully inspects the doorkeeper in his fur coat, with his large pointed nose, his long, thin, black, Tatar beard, he decides, on the contrary, that he would rather wait until he receives permission to enter" (P 256). Likewise, there is repetition of "the stale odor . . . that came from the head doorman" (A 227) in the offices of the courts. And in the same manner in which the head doorman calls Karl "suspicious . . . because I so choose" and because "I" want "to enjoy you" (A 227), the lawyers and court officials enjoy the torment of the defendants who have been accused arbitrarily without manifest grounds (Lawyer Huld vis-à-vis Block, the merchant), or they take delight in the "screaming" (P 61) of the student trying to rape the court usher's wife who finds the court "so disgusting" (P 66).

Torture, however, strikes back at the torturer. The torturing guards are themselves tortured and whipped incessantly in the lumber room; likewise, in *The Castle,* in the officials' rooms and offices "screams" are heard that are at the same time hopelessly "mute" (S 157). For by its nature the torture of the restless work-world cannot be abolished and is unavoidably bound to intensify. Even the savagely sadistic head doorman is in reality himself a tortured man. The head cook has knowledge of this:

"Whatever the head doorman may have told you, you must not take it very seriously. He is of course an excitable man, and no wonder with his duties; but he has a wife and children besides, and he knows that a young fellow who is entirely on his own must not be tormented unnecessarily; the rest of the world will see to that all right, with good measure." (A 207-208)

Everyone is ensnared in the labor system. Basically, everyone is tortured by everyone else. The differences in the respective social "positions" are specious.

Even Karl's uncle, who is enthroned upon the peak of this

industrial work-world, is tortured by his own "principles" regarding work. They are "unpleasant" to him and "depress" him, and he fears a "general attack" (A 107). These "principles" compel him to deny his personal love for Karl and to cast aside the being with whom he desires contact and whose love he sadly longs for in a world without close relationships. Because of the very fact that he so urgently yearns for contact with his nephew, he is bound to be all the more deeply wounded at the slightest sign of Karl's seeming indifference. The search for a close relationship, however, is self-defeating. "Guarding" his nephew leads to repudiating him.

Karl really loved his uncle. Even in the hour of decision at the country house he dreams of surprising "his dear uncle . . . whom until now he had known only completely dressed and all buttoned up to the chin," in his room the next morning and dreams of breakfasting "together" with him in sincere, frank friendship (A 76). Karl, too, longs for a genuine, humanly warm relationship with his uncle. Such a relationship, however, becomes impossible through "lack" of "frank discussion" (A 76). The uncle had given Karl "permission" to drive to Pollunder's estate only "reluctantly" (A 64). He was justified, therefore, in concluding on that account that Karl, of his own accord, obeying his immediate instinct, through love for his uncle would necessarily decline Pollunder's invitation. However, he makes no effort to ascertain the actual state of his nephew's feelings but leaves the decision about that to Mr. Green, of all people! He believes that Karl should always and unconditionally guess and fulfill his secret wishes, and that only such behavior as this is an indication of love. Thereby he unconsciously treats Karl as an object in relation to those wishes and robs him of his freedom. For, from his uncle's statements, which were full of "inconsistencies" (A 63), Karl, in no way able to determine immediately what his uncle's emotional state was, could not yet suspect that a crucial human decision was at issue. At heart the uncle knows this: he postpones the decision until midnight, a time when Karl was bound to have reached a state of clarity about where the center of gravity of his inner life rested—with

Pollunder and his daughter Klara, or with him, his uncle. Karl had long ago decided in favor of his uncle; indeed, there was no need of a decision at all, since he had always craved for contact with his uncle. But now their personal relationship had long since been in the hands of Green, who victimizes both. The immense figure of Green destroys the genuine, human encounter The uncle inflicts a wound upon himself by inserting a third person between himself and his nephew, by not allowing for a "frank discussion" and a free opportunity for his nephew to reach a decision, although he labors under the delusion that Karl did make his own free "decision" by having "gone away" from him "against" his [the uncle's] "will" (A 107).

This liberal uncle who has structured his life and his business thinking on the "freedom" of the "personality," on the private initiative of the "individual," capable man, this very uncle succumbs inevitably to the inconsistencies of that same free enterprise, the "principles" of which have their roots in making everyone into an object for everyone else, in handing everyone over to everyone else's free enterprise, unrestrictedly, and in so doing annihilating every true human freedom. The ostensibly free decision is dictated by others. The differences in personal character or in social class among the members of this mass society are merely flimsy illusion. In truth they are all identical with one another, including the good chief cook and Therese, who, likewise allowing themselves to be deceived by the external "appearance" (A 214) of Karl Rossmann's supposed guilt, consider the innocent guilty and at the same time fall victim to the mechanism of their need for that contact that they all lack.

For both the chief cook and Therese are seeking a close relationship. By the headwaiter's erotic overtures and arguments the chief cook lets herself be beguiled into prejudice against Karl, whom the headwaiter, out of jealousy, wishes to get rid of. And Therese, who strives for nothing other than contact with Karl—indeed, on the very first night she is powerless to resist visiting him in his bedroom, although he is a stranger to her—is actually happy when Karl escapes with no more than a black eye. She wants to secure for herself nothing else but his life and his proximity. The question of whether he is treated "justly" or "wronged" is unimportant to her: "In Therese's eyes there shone purest joy, as if it were wholly immaterial to her whether Karl had committed some wrong or not, whether he had been justly judged or not, if only he were allowed to get away, in disgrace or honorably" (A 218).

## The Perversions of Love

In other words, these women who are so kind and ready to help do not see through the mechanism of the naked, sadistic terrorism in which everyone is entangled. They succumb to their only seemingly "immediate" feeling and need for human proximity, and in so doing, without misgivings, they accept the injustice that is inflicted upon everyone and constantly repeated in everything.

Here light is first shed upon the fact, so deeply shrouded in mystery, that in *The Trial* as in *The Castle* the women are "in bondage" to the officials and surrender themselves unconditionally to them. In a masculinist world of absolute separateness— the officials are all men—there are only either mannish women (Klara, the athletic wrestler; or Gisa, the cruel teacher in *The Castle*, who, revealingly, is also the only woman of the village who controls even the castle officials: *viz.*, Schwarzer, the castellan's son); *or* feminine and maternally devoted women who submit to the system that abuses them. Their "help," their "pity," that they afford the "defendants"—in this regard, Karl is of course also a defendant—consists of a recommendation to the defendants that, without any will of their own, they accept the system after all, make their "confession" (cf. P 132), and submit to the self-glorifying and self-admiring officials. The women find all the defendants "handsome" (P 221) for the very reason that the defendants too are helpless and in need of contact; therefore, the women take them under their care. However, this espousal and help mask the truth, and indeed often signify a covert sadistic lust for power. For example, Leni in *The Trial* kisses Block, the merchant, and at the same time degrades him to the state of a cringing dog; without restraint she lets herself be "exchanged" by the defendant Josef K. for his mistress Elsa, and with the same lack of restraint she takes possession of him (P 135).

Love is itself only the reflection, the confirmation of the all-pervading social system based on power and violence. Poor Therese, whose mother was rejected and destroyed by a cold world in the most cruel manner, is, like all women, a victim of the male system, but she accepts her debasement without misgivings, and her eyes light up in "pure joy," if only the victims are just allowed to "get away." Individuality, the right of free self-determination, has disappeared.

This perversion of love into violence or submission, a perversion that encompasses all classes, is most mercilessly laid bare in the extended Brunelda episode. In it Kafka reached what is perhaps the culmination of his critical investigations of society. For in this episode the cycle of ruler and ruled, of wealth and poverty, as well as the assimilation and, what is more, the monotonous, undifferentiated identicalness of all seemingly different spheres—all this becomes manifest in its most flagrant but, at the same time, most veracious form.

Brunelda, the rich singer who can apparently go on living free from care, relieved of the hustle and bustle of work, "completely independent" (A 264)—she, of all people, subjects herself to Delamarche, the strong man, the unemployed and antisocial vagabond who impresses her when he slaps his comrade Robinson in the face. For, just because her own husband adores her abjectly, humbling himself before her to the point of masochism, just because she dominates him unrestrainedly and can, when enraged, throw anything she pleases at his head with no opposition on his part, because between them love is only a relationship between mistress and servant, a relationship based on a purely possessory ideology, just because of this she must long to be subjugated by a man who comes from the lowest stratum, who is outstanding for sheer brute strength, but, at the same time, whom she in turn, through her wealth, has entirely in her hands and whom she makes dependent upon her sexually. No matter how the conditions may be reversed, what it comes to is always a matter of reciprocal possession and subjugation. Her humiliation before Delamarche is itself of course domination over him in turn. Delamarche's physical superiority is at one and the same time tantamount to his financial as well as sexual dependence and enslavement. Thus each is chained to the other in unbounded mutual torment, in a perversion of all emotions. Wealth or poverty—in both spheres the struggles for power that are taking place are always the same.

### Capitalism as "A State of the World and of the Soul"

Once, when Gustav Janouch showed Kafka a drawing by George Grosz, in which capital was represented by a fat man sitting on the money of the poor, Kafka said that the picture did not hit the truth quite accurately, since it advanced a partial for the general view:

"The fat man in the top hat is sitting on the poor man's neck. That is correct. But the fat man is capitalism and that is no longer quite correct. The fat man rules the poor man within the framework of a definite system. But he is not the system itself. He is not even its ruler. On the contrary, the fat man is also wearing shackles that are not shown in the picture. The picture is not complete. That is why it is not good. Capitalism is a system of dependences that go from the inside to the outside, from the outside to the inside, from top to bottom, and from bottom to top. Everybody is dependent; everybody is shackled. Capitalism is a state of the world and of the soul." (J 90)

Capitalism as a state of the world and of the soul, reaching into the most intimate erotic impulses and into all interpersonal encounters—that is the actual theme of *The Man Who Was Lost Sight Of*. But even the designation *capitalism* is permutable. The "system of dependences" extends over the total industrial mass society of modern times; what is more, it extends over all past and present social forms in which one rules or is ruled in accordance with a purely utilitarian or possessory ideology, in which a supreme and personal law, free of purpose, is no longer glimpsed.

Mankind becomes a grey, formless, and hence nameless mass only through defection from formative Law. Then there are no longer top and bottom ; life grows shallow and becomes mere existence: there is no drama ; there is no struggle ; there is only the attrition of substance, decay. But that is not the world of the Bible and of Judaism.... The Jewish people have never ... been ... anonymous ... nameless. On the contrary! They are the Chosen People of a personal God, a people that can never sink to the low level of an anonymous and hence spiritless mass if they adhere to the fulfillment of the Law. (J 102-103)

And following on this Kafka paraphrases the task of the poet: "To shrink back from one's own mission is sin. Misunderstanding, impatience, and indolence—these are sin. It is the poet's task to lead what is isolated and mortal onward to eternal life, to lead what is contingent onward to what is in accordance with laws and principles. His is a prophetic task" (J 103).

Kafka always felt this prophetic task as his charge, his mission. He sought the formative law that would once again bestow a personal, eternal life upon an anonymous, aimless multitude. Hence, with all his unsparing, truthful exposure of the present-day state of the world and of the soul, in the subsequent novel *The Trial* he intended to make evident the infallible, true Law —in the midst of the perversions of the law that take place incessantly among the court authorities, in the court offices and chambers, in today's mediating channels. The officials of this court are themselves no "godlike" beings; to assume that they are would be the height of modern delusion and demoralization of values. In a ghastly way they reflect everything that is being lived today. But behind them, behind the gigantic doorkeepers, the "radiance" of the supreme Law (P 257) remains "inextinguishable." How to break through the barriers of the doorkeepers and of the earthly mediating channels that increase incalculably—that was the problem in his novels *The Trial* and *The Castle*.

However, even *The Man Who Was Lost Sight Of* would also have remained incomplete and, seen from within the work, also a fragment, if there were not disclosed, at least at the conclusion, a vague hope, a possibility—albeit a utopian one—of leaping out of the "system of dependences."

This possibility is developed or at least envisaged fragmentarily in the so-called "Nature Theater of Oklahoma."


## The Nature Theater of Oklahoma

This Nature Theater has often been interpreted as a landscape in the Hereafter, to which Karl Rossmann comes following his death. His trip to Clayton in the subway would then signify a death-journey, his admittance to Clayton (=town of clay) would be his admittance to the realm of the dead, and Oklahoma (=beautiful country) would be Paradise.[1]

With this interpretation, too, Max Brod wished to unite two contradictory statements of Kafka's. According to one of Kafka's diary entries, "Rossmann and K. [in *The Trial*], the innocent man and the guilty one—in the end both, without distinction, are destroyed as a punishment; the innocent man, with a rather gentle hand, more pushed aside than struck down" (T 481). And according to an oral statement of Kafka's to Max Brod, "the present, unfinished chapter on the 'Nature Theater in Oklahoma'" was supposed "to be the final chapter and to end in a conciliatory vein.... In enigmatic language Kafka intimated with a smile that in this 'almost unbounded' theater his young hero would find a career, freedom, support, and, what is more, would recover even parents and homeland again as though by paradisiacal magic" (A 356-57).


### A. THE ARTIST AND SOCIETY

A careful examination of the text will reveal that the highly artificial thesis that equates the journey in the subway with a death-journey, etc., is superfluous, and that the apparent contradiction between Kafka's two remarks can be resolved in a much more analogous manner. Karl Rossmann, within the American work-world, is in fact pushed aside and destroyed as a punishment; he finds no footing in that world and is bound to go to pieces in it, disappearing like someone who "is lost sight of" without there being any need of an explicit act of violence. He is silently, automatically as it were, "with a rather gentle hand ... pushed aside" and eliminated. Innocent, he is "destroyed as a punishment," because within this society all the innocent are in any event punished, by being deprived of their basis of life. For according to Kafka, in the "world" everyone is "punished," not only he who is guilty, but also he who is innocent. Hence, too, "being destroyed" does not have to be a physical death, and during this trip in the subway for which Karl Rossmann totals up the necessary fare, portioning it out from his slim amount of ready cash, there is nowhere any mention, not even the slightest suggestion, of Karl's dying. The events take place quite naturally within the framework of modern traffic conditions.

The placard that he sees at a street corner, however, reveals a possibility outside the system of dependences. It proclaims: "Everyone is welcome! Apply if you want to become an artist! We are the Theater that can use everyone, everyone in his proper place!" (A 305). In this theater, the "largest theater in the world," one that is "almost limitless" (A 311), everyone without exception can play the role for which he is suited, only on the condition, of course, that he really wants to become an "artist." The placard, nonetheless, does not have much appeal, for " ... nobody wanted to become an artist, whereas everyone wanted to be paid for his work" (A 305). But on the placard there "was not the faintest hint about pay" (A 305).

This "Nature Theater" of Oklahoma is thus outside the work-world that is enmeshed in calculating, utilitarian thinking. However, it is also outside what is normally envisaged as a theater for or of "artists" or actors. For everyone is engaged according to his intrinsic abilities and desires and thereby ranks already as an actor. "For what position do you feel yourself qualified?" is the question put to Karl Rossmann. " 'I was admitted as an actor,' said Karl hestitantly, in order to make the gentleman understand the difficulty in which he had been placed by the last question," for not knowing in the least whether he was "qualified for playacting" in the customary sense, he consequently fears difficulties. " 'That is correct,' said the gentleman," and thereupon he enrolls Karl as a technical worker, since Karl had stated originally that he wanted to become an engineer (A 322-23). Thus everyone has already been admitted as an actor in accordance with his inclinations. This "Nature Theater" is truly a "World Theater" in the old cosmic sense of the baroque period—albeit the premises are new. It is "indeed the largest theater in the world . . . almost limitless" (A 311). The role each individual plays here is his original life role, rooted in him, as it were, by his own "nature." And wanting "to become an artist" means nothing other than playing this life role as perfectly and naturally as possible according to man's inner nature.

The statement "Nobody wanted to become an artist" can be explained in this way too. Nobody in the modern work-world wants to play the role which he is equipped by nature to play; on the contrary, he thinks primarily of pay and outward success in the world. For that reason also, the only ones who apply for admission to this theater are society's outcasts, "unpropertied and suspect people," without luggage (A 330), or a poor man and his wife, with their baby in a baby carriage, who are also admitted as actors. Only those who have been excluded from society fulfill the requirements for such a "Nature Theater" at all; this, however, in no way signifies that these people are already good, or are able to play their roles perfectly, or even really cherish the wish to become artists. For as yet they have in no way comprehended what it actually means to become an artist, or what the significance of this theater actually is; they simply wish to find refuge somewhere or other, since, as things are, they no longer see any possibility of finding a place in conventional society. Therefore, too, they are not people who "died a pious death," as one interpreter has it.[2] On the contrary, they have all the bad habits and even the brutality of living beings; for example, there are the fellows on the trip to Oklahoma who "pinched" Karl Rossmann's and his friend Giacomo's "legs with all their might" (A 331). It is not a good world, let alone a world in the Hereafter, that reveals itself here; on the contrary, it is a very "natural" world with all the weaknesses and vices that dwell in natural man. Moreover, in the "nature" of these people there is still a great deal of society's cruelty, ruthlessness, and sadism. The transition from the work-world to this Nature Theater does not take place abruptly; it does not, as if miraculously, transform those who are admitted.

Nevertheless, the placard is undoubtedly written in the style of a religious summons, a summons to *conversio*, in the style of a proselytizing treatise with a slight touch of caricature and charlatanry: "The great Theater of Oklahoma summons you! It summons you today only, once only! Whoever forgoes his opportunity now, forgoes it for evermore! ... hasten, that you may be admitted before midnight! At twelve o'clock everything will be closed and opened no more! Accursed be he who disbelieves us! Arise, onward to Clayton!" (A 305).

In the case of this attempt to break away into the "world of the artist," what is involved is a single, irrevocable opportunity offered until twelve o'clock, until midnight only, under the appeal to "faith," clearly echoing analogous threatening statements in the Bible (cf. the parable of the ten virgins, among others).

What is demanded here is faith in the extremely remote and incredible chance of man's being able to realize himself, to realize what is "indestructible" in him, the "being" that is within him. Indeed, Kafka defined "faith" in this very way (H 89). In the midst of a world of advertising, a world of business efficiency that posts bills about everything, there is here conjured up a sphere in man that withdraws from this very kind of advertising world. Hence, even this placard appears "improbable" to everyone: "There were so many placards; nobody believes placards any more. And this placard was even more improbable than are placards ordinarily" (A 305).

The tone, reminiscent of religious language, emphasizes this incredibility of the placard. The demand is made for faith in that indestructible truth of the self, ever forgotten and suppressed by man, a truth that transcends all human power of comprehension. This summons signifies only this. It takes on the pathos of religious language because what is in fact involved is the power of a supreme faith that bursts the bounds of all normal thinking. And the caricaturing persiflage of this pathos—the "grandiloquence" (A 306) of this placard, its ballyhooing affectation—is at the same time a reflection of the sphere in which a demand for such faith exists. By outbidding the world's offers to a grotesque and incredible degree, and at the same time taking thereby a leap out of the sphere of these offers, since there is no longer any talk of "payment," the ballyhoo really does become "folly" in the eyes of the world; the message becomes nothing but a message in the form of a servant;* and hence it can be accepted only by the wretched, the outcast, the "unpropertied," and the "suspect"—similarly, in the Bible parable of the great supper† the vagabonds and street-corner loafers are invited, because everyone else, enmeshed in the "world," has deaf ears for Christ's invitation.

### B. THE SPIRITUAL DIN OF THE WOMEN

The religious character of the offer is confirmed by the very nature of the reception in Clayton by means of female trumpeter-angels and male drummer-devils. However, just as the placard does not allude to a life in the Hereafter but summons whoever wants "to become an artist," so too do these trumpeting angels, who welcome the arrivals, offer a foretaste, as it were, of what is actually to be understood by art and the pursuit of art in this Nature Theater.

These angels here are not real angels, of course, but quite ordinary women—Karl's former friend Emily is among them—who, on being engaged at the Nature Theater and then dressed

---

*Tr. note: *Knechtsgestalt*, cf. Philippians 2:7.
†Tr. note: Luke 14:15–24.

up as angels, now stand on separate pedestals at varying heights and blow trumpets. What is more, their trumpeting is "a chaotic noise—the trumpets were not in tune with one another, they were being sounded without regard for one another" (A 306). Thus, each of these women blasts away at her trumpet, just as she pleases, paying no attention to the trumpeting of her neighbors. They all blow "without regard for one another."

Unquestionably, these angels are following their actual "nature," making a ruthless spiritual din as it were. Whatever the emotion present in them, it is simply being blasted out meaninglessly. This trumpeting "disconcerted" the new arrivals (A 308). Karl has the feeling that this display of angels and devils is frightening rather than attractive. The ten young fellows—who seem small by comparison with the large, indeed to some degree gigantic, female figures—as well as the older man seeking admission with his wife and small child, do not dare to make their way through these heedlessly trumpeting angels. And since there is "nowhere a placard to be seen," and "nowhere a barker, or anyone who could supply information" (A 308), these men stand helpless before the noisy female bulks who, by the "hundred" (A 307), seem to bar their way to the actual admission office that cannot be seen from the front, since it is located behind the angels' platform. In order to take up their own roles in the theater, these men and young fellows must first make their way through the spiritual din of the women.

All the details of the account bear witness to the fact that what is going on here is indeed a vehement, inconsiderate spiritual din. The women wear "white draperies with large wings at the back"; "each one stood on a pedestal, which could not be seen, however, for the long, flowing draperies of the angelic raiment enveloped it completely" (A 307). The angelic garb and wings are described as "very beautiful" and "costly" (A 311). Undoubtedly there is present an element of the ancient conception of the soul as a white garment that veils everything; it is possible, too, that there is attendant some influence from the quite similar costume of Mignon in Goethe, whom Kafka read intensively of course, and whom he venerated deeply and mar-

veled at all his life. But also, quite apart from such possible prototypes, "dress," particularly in Kafka's writing, possesses an
extraordinarily important symbolical significance, especially in
the characterization of the female soul. We shall discuss this in
great detail in our consideration of the women in *The Castle*
(Frieda, the landlady of the Inn at the Bridge, Pepi, Amalia,
etc.).

As an illustration, only one detailed and peculiar conversation between K. and the landlady of the Herrenhof Inn need be
mentioned. On the basis of this landlady's "dress," K. states,
"You're not just a landlady, as you pretend to be." At this the
landlady, taken aback, exclaims, "Well, what do you know! The
things you find out!" (S 413). This dress, as a matter of fact,
has already figured significantly in the relations between K. and
the landlady of the Herrenhof Inn:

The landlady gazed at him as though in a dream. Also, because
of that gaze, K. was kept there longer than he really wanted to
be. Now she smiled a bit, too, and only at the sight of K.'s
astonished face was she wakened, in a manner of speaking; it
seemed as if she had been expecting an answer to her smile, and
only now that no answer was forthcoming was she awaking. "You
had the impudence yesterday, I believe, to say something about my
dress." K. could not remember. (S 411)

A mysterious, dreamy, spiritual relationship, originating in the
landlady, develops between her and K. as a result of K.'s intui-
tive knowledge of the significance of the dress for her inner life;
and she, who is "aiming only at dressing beautifully" (S 415),
finally shows him an enormous number of dresses that she has
supplied herself with, because she wants to appear in new
clothes every day—clothes that K., however, considers "out of
fashion, ornate, often altered and made over, shabby," unsuitable for her years, her figure, her position, although the clothes
in question are always "expensive" and "of good material"
(S 414).

In *The Man Who Was Lost Sight Of* there is also an analogous discrepancy, although of different nature, which arises be-

tween the angelic costume of the women and their actual figures and spiritual maturity. These angelic robes make the woman appear "gigantic," since the draperies entirely cover the individual pedestals that often sweep up to enormous heights, thereby making it seem as if each female figure shot up to this height from the ground itself. In contrast with this, however, "their small heads detracted somewhat from the impression of great size; also, their hair, hanging down loose between their large wings and at their sides, was too short and almost ridiculous" (A 307).

Their small "heads" and their short, "loose" hair are incompatible with angelic raiment. The women, therefore, make a "ridiculous" impression. And furthermore there is a sorry contrast between their relentless trumpeting and the trumpets themselves. Karl "had thought that it was a crudely wrought trumpet, meant only for making a noise, but it now became apparent that it was an instrument capable of producing almost any subtle nuance. If all the instruments were of similar quality, they were being grossly misused" (A 310).

These women thus misuse the fine instruments that were given them. They are not yet artists. In senselessly blasting forth everything they feel, they destroy the opportunities of subtle expression that were entrusted to them by this theater of "Nature." They are still far removed from their "true" selves. With amazement they hear innocent Karl play the trumpet. Although he plays a very primitive song "that he had once heard in a taproom somewhere or other" (A 310), in his joyous mood he plays so beautifully that many women stop their blowing and listen. " 'You really are an artist,' said Fanny, as Karl handed her her trumpet again" (A 310).

At all times Karl had felt music to be the counterworld to the frenzy of work and ruthless emotions. He had cherished the hope that his piano playing would have an immediate effect upon the American scene; he believed it would enable him to check the maelstrom of street traffic and alter the "circular" dynamic forces outside. And while he is in Klara's room, in the face of this brutally erotic, ruthless female wrestler, as he is awkwardly

playing that old, beloved soldier's song of his native land, he becomes aware of the profoundest sorrow of his life, the abysmally
deep chasm that separates him from all human beings; and in
vain does he seek by means of this song for a different, more
remote "end," in which everything could perhaps be solved. "He
felt a song arise within him that sought a different end, an end
beyond the end of the song, and could not find it. 'I really can't
do anything,' said Karl upon the conclusion of the song, and
he looked at Klara with tears in his eyes" (A 104).

Karl Rossmann's music is not "art" in the usual sense; it is
deliberately described as primitive and imperfect, lacking in execution and masterly skill. But it is a kind of music that seeks
beyond its "end" a "different end" in which the sorrow of this
world might be able to fall away. For that very reason, however, this music is sustained by sorrow. For that very reason
Karl, weeping, says, "I really can't do anything." The helplessness of true art in the face of the sorrow of this world—this is
what was actually the most profound and intrinsic reason for
the painful self-abnegation that Kafka practiced at all times in
the disparagement of his own art, calling himself a dilettante
and a bungler (B 291; J 38; *inter alia*). Kafka's art grew great
because he himself did not consider it as art.

## C. THE PRIMORDIAL WORLD AND
## THE MOTIVATED WORLD

In what manner, however, is this "artist" Karl now admitted
to the Nature Theater?

All the others have "identification papers" and are enrolled in
the theater in accordance with what up till now they have
achieved professionally. Of course, it is expressly stated that
everything will be checked and verified again in Oklahoma
(A 324). Therefore, it is quite uncertain whether the role that
they are to play in this theater will be identical with their role
in society hitherto. But Karl has no identification papers. For
he never received a reference from any position he had held,
since he had been thrown out of all of them.

In his last positions he concealed even his true name and had himself called "Negro." In the admission offices at the Nature Theater he gives this false name, for "he had an aversion to giving his real name and letting it be written down. As soon as he obtained even the most insignificant position here and filled it satisfactorily, then let them learn his name, but not now; he had kept it secret far too long to give it away now" (A 318).

Karl, then, senses with a nicety of feeling that he ought not to identify himself and his true name either with a position that he cannot really fill entirely and satisfactorily or with one that is perhaps abominable and degrading. For, as it happened, his last position in an office had been so humiliating or so morally unsavory that, had he been questioned about it, he would have had "to lie" (A 322). By reading the concluding sentences of the fragment "Brunelda's Departure," one may surmise the depths of human depravity to which he had to descend in his last positions in the unfinished parts of the novel: of "Operation No. 25," to which Brunelda is journeying, it is said:

On closer inspection one saw that it was no tangible dirt. The stone floor of the entrance hall was swept almost clean, the paint on the walls was not old, the artificial palms were only slightly dusty, and yet everything was greasy and repulsive; it was as if everything had been put to bad use, and no cleanliness would ever be able to make up for it again. Whenever Karl went anywhere, he liked to think of what could be improved upon and what joy it would be to pitch in, regardless of the perhaps endless work this would entail. But he did not know what could be done here. (A 355)

In the diary entry of December 25, 1910, Kafka at one point speaks of a theater of human society in which all inner dirt becomes visible on the outside, "as if ... the most visible part of the theater ... were ... reserved for the most sordid people, for old profligates whose inner dirt gradually comes to the surface" (T 33).

The alteration that Karl Rossmann makes in his name in such a society, by having himself called "Negro," is, so to speak, the "black" mask with which he disguises himself and adapts himself outwardly to society; it is the mask with which he is forced to conceal the white of his "innocent" soul, in order to be able to exist at all.

In the "Nature Theater of Oklahoma," however, such a disguise would strictly speaking be unnecessary. And Karl senses this the very moment he is taken on and the inscription "Negro, technical worker" is hoisted high on the announcement board: "Since everything here was taking an orderly course, Karl would no longer have minded so much if his real name had appeared on the board for everyone to read" (A 324).

Karl gains confidence in this Nature Theater. For even the admissions procedure, to which he has to submit himself, is unusual and outside the framework of customary admissions procedures in society. The fact that he has no identification papers does not in the least prevent his being taken on: "There is no need to worry. We can make use of everyone" (A 317). To be sure, the enrollment in his case takes longer than it does in the case of all the others who, so to speak, identify themselves immediately by means of their documents. In his case the inquiry concerning his qualifications must be pursued to their point of origin. "What was it that you actually wanted to study originally? ... I mean, in Europe," is the crucial question that tips the balance (A 323).

Accordingly, he is registered in the office "for European high-school students"; this is where his "last refuge" is (A 317). For from such a place, from a European high school, he had set off into the world. His original vocational wish, the wish he had cherished there, is now the criterion for his classification in the Nature Theater. Even though this classification may not be final—for in Oklahoma everything will of course be checked once again—even though this point of departure, therefore, may not yet be really the most natural and life-determinative one, it is nevertheless, for the present, the only fixed point in the chain of professional catastrophes that Karl has experienced hitherto. First and foremost, however, Karl always did and still does identify himself with his earliest vocational wish at high school. And it is characteristic that this identification is immediately expressed emotionally as well, in the startling "similarity" between the head of the office for European high-school students and "a professor ... who in all likelihood was still teaching at the nonclassical secondary school at home." With "amazement" Karl observes this similarity (A 317-18). The head of the office suddenly, as it were, actualizes an emotional memory-image of Karl's.

And, at the same time, light is thereby shed upon the significance and function of these admissions officials. That is to say, they see through all masks and trappings into the truth of the human soul. They cannot be deceived. The head of the office immediately knows that Karl's name is not Negro; he therefore wants Karl's correct name to be registered; and even earlier he wanted to slow down the enrollment procedure by means of further questions, since Karl's identification papers were missing. But, in a peculiar reversal of social hierarchies, in this office "the secretary" has "the whip hand" (A 318). And this secretary, after Karl's obvious lie, looks at him "searchingly for a while" (A 319) and then abruptly declares him enrolled. The professorial head of the office, however, "could not do anything against his conscience" (A 319). He wants to prevent the registration of the incorrect name of Negro. But the secretary has a deeper insight: for him Karl is not a liar and the name Negro is not false, even though the external facts of the case proclaim otherwise. In the conflict between the head of the office and the secretary a genuine conflict between "conscience" and more profound psychological knowledge is brought to a head and resolved in favor of the more profound knowledge.

The same spiritual superiority is shown in the chief leader of the recruitment group, who, from the "judges' stand" at the "race track," makes the final decision about every admission. Upon the race track of the world—now grown lonely and still—he is a true judge by contrast with the perverted judges whose election was described in the Brunelda chapter. It is said of him that "he takes everything seriously," apparently even Karl's "ridiculous" answers (A 323). His "delicate but nevertheless powerful, long, quick-moving fingers occasionally attracted Karl's attention" (A 321); thus he combines sensibility with resoluteness and agility. He puts his questions forcefully and with the utmost attention to the emotions and moods of his partner:

... by the way he articulated [his questions] with wide-open eyes, by the way he leaned the upper part of his body forward, observing their effect, by the way he let his head sink upon his chest, listening to the answers and repeating them from time to time in a loud voice ... he ... knew how to endow them ... with a particular significance, the intimation of which made one wary and embarrassed even though one did not understand it. (A 321)

Thus Karl clearly feels that these questions have a "particular significance," and that regions are being touched upon here which he can only dimly "intuit."

However, the embarrassment and wariness this rouses in him prove to be groundless. For the questions that Karl fears would follow upon his specific answers are the very ones that the leader does not ask. The leader does not ask what kind of office it was that Karl was last employed in; he does not ask why Karl did not feel content there, etc.; that is, he does not inquire into the outer or inner motivations in Karl's previous living conditions, but he inquires solely about his actual social situation and about Karl's actual spiritual state and desire. "You have been unemployed?" "Where were you last employed? Last!" "Were you satisfied there?" "For what position do you feel yourself suited?" "What was it that you actually wanted to study originally? In Europe, I mean."

All the so-called explanations are immaterial to him. He is concerned solely with what "is" in Karl's outward as well as in his inward life. He actually penetrates into Karl's "being," and ultimately, what is more, into his origin, through the very fact that he is asking seemingly very simple, basic questions, that he is not asking the whys and wherefores, the pros and cons of opinions and points of view, that he is not venturing into the labyrinth of possible interpretations. He stands beyond motivated life. His interrogation is the exact opposite of every interrogation that Karl has previously had to undergo and in which he has broken down hopelessly. For example, it is the opposite of that interrogation in the Hotel Occidental, of which it was stated: Karl "knew that everything he could say would later on look altogether different from the way it had been intended, and that it depended only on the way one viewed a situation as to whether one would come upon good or evil" (A 213). The knowledge about Karl's soul operates outside the realm of any motivating "psychology."

This Nature Theater erupts from not only the business thinking of capitalistic society but also the inner spiritual motivations with the help of which society is constituted. For the emergence of a society that is based on free competition coincides historically, too, with the emergence of modern psychology, whose methods competitors usually employ to criticize one another, as well as to gain power, to justify themselves, and to denounce others. "For the last time, psychology!" These words, that appear repeatedly in Kafka (H 51, 107), have a serious ethical significance, critical of the times.

The "Nature Theater" is free of psychological "judgments." The human soul is here seen in its original state.

Therefore, in this Nature Theater it is quite possible that innocent Karl, who has been pushed aside by society with a gentle hand and destroyed as a punishment, "will find a career, freedom, support, and, what is more, will recover even parents and homeland again as though by paradisiacal magic." Hence it is that, early on, the professor from the school Karl had attended in his native land seems to turn up suddenly in the admissions office; for the premises given in this "almost limitless theater," which is "constantly being enlarged" (A 311), are such that every person once again comes to know his intrinsic spiritual sources, pure and undisguised; and therefore he once again encounters his parents and his native land in their unmasked natural forms, free of the disfigurements inflicted upon everyone, upon Karl Rossmann as well as upon his parents, by society's distorting modes of life and ideas of morality.

### D. THE UNMASKING OF THE WORLD

Actually, this Nature Theater appears to have the function of unmasking as well as of liberating. Just as the women in their angelic raiment and in their trumpeting have unconsciously unmasked themselves and could perhaps, nevertheless, slowly turn into real artists who no longer misuse the instruments of their souls, similarly, too, the pictures showing "views of the Theater of Oklahoma" emphasize the unmasking import of this theater.

Although Karl gets to see only one of these pictures, it is nonetheless enlightening enough. It "represented the theater loge for the President of the United States" (A 327). This loge "projected . . . into open space . . . in such a wide sweep" that "one could think it was not a loge but the stage" itself. The omnipotence of the nation penetrates far into open space, almost as if it itself were the stage of the world.

But what does this stage look like?

White but soft light laid bare, as it were, the foreground of the loge, while far within—behind red velvet, many-tinted in its folds draped down along the entire periphery and controlled by looped cords—the depths appeared like a dark, reddish-shimmering emptiness. One could scarcely imagine human beings in this loge, so absolute did everything look. (A 327)

Offsetting the soft white foreground is a menacing, reddish-shimmering, "empty" background in which what is human is blown away, as it were, by the "absolute" pomp of the nation.

The novel comes full circle. At the beginning, Karl caught sight of the Statue of Liberty in New York Harbor, but the Goddess of Liberty is "so high," so beyond reach for him, the little lad, who is immediately swept away from the sight of this Goddess by the "ever-swelling sea of porters" (A 9). And, furthermore, this Goddess of Liberty, instead of holding the torch of truth, holds her "sword" aloft in the "free breezes" (A 9), just as, toward the end of the novel, in the Nature Theater of Oklahoma, the symbol of this freedom-proclaiming nation is the blood-red color that projects far into open space, blotting out everything human and enclosing an "empty" space without human beings.

There can be no doubt about it: this Nature Theater is a theater that is presenting the truth of the world, truth in every sense, as a critical unmasking[3] and as a positive liberation.

Like every true utopia, the utopia that shines forth at the end of this novel is ambiguous: it is a criticism of the distorted life; it is a hope of an undistorted life in freedom. No deceptive ideal image is presented. Inhumanity continues to exist even in this theater. The "din" of the angels and devils, the ten "envious" fellows, the grotesque ovation for the newly enrolled who have been "won over" by the "abundant food," the blood-red, "absolute" loge of the nation's representative, etc. But through all the human weaknesses and inhuman terrors there shines the image of a life unmotivated and free of purpose, a life in which play and work, theater and reality, childhood and vocation unite and become reconciled in a world-play, in which "everybody," taken on and enabled to play his natural role, could express his true being that "cannot but be loved" (H 46).

### CHAPTER VI

# The World as Court of Justice:
# The Novel *The Trial*

## *The Concept of Guilt*

In contrast with Karl Rossman who is "guiltless," Josef K. in *The Trial* is "the guilty person" (T 481). Nowhere in the novel is the purport of his guilt formulated. For what is at issue is not a single, empirically determinable offense committed by Josef K. However, his guilt is defined indirectly. As early on as the occasion of Josef K.'s arrest, Franz the warder says, "Well, I declare, Willem, he admits that he doesn't know the Law, and in the same breath he insists that he's innocent!" (P 15).

Josef K.'s guilt is his ignorance of the Law.

Furthermore, it is Josef K. himself who has unknowingly brought about his arrest: "It's not as if our officials ... searched for guilt among the population, but, as it is stated in the Law, they gravitate toward guilt and have to send us warders out" (P 15). And the inspector says to Josef K., "Think less about us and of what will happen to you; better think more about yourself. And don't make such a to-do about your feeling of innocence" (P 21).

Josef K.'s guilt rests in him or in the very fact that he considers himself innocent. He later says to the chaplain of the court, "But I am not guilty, it's a mistake. How is it really possible for a human being to be actually guilty? After all, we are all human beings here, each one like the next" (P 253). How is it possible, then, he thinks, for a man to be pronounced guilty just because he is a human being? " 'That is correct,' said the chaplain; 'but that is how guilty people usually talk' " (P 253).

Here the difference between Josef K. and Karl Rossmann grows clear. Karl lives his life completely on the basis of his instinctive sense of self, and he also trusts his fellow men's inner feeling of justice. He does not consider himself innocent: "I'm guilty, it's true," he says when he is interrogated (A 211). He knows about the "law" that is within the being of man and he obeys that law steadfastly in spite of all his disappointments and in spite of all the consequences that make it impossible for him, just because of his loyalty to the law, ever to be accepted into the work-world of the human race. Josef K., on the contrary, has concealed his self, has devoted himself completely to the work-world, holds a respected position at the bank; indeed, his mother is even of the opinion that he is the president of the bank (P 280). He is in the habit of spending his evenings with a companionable group of men at a regularly reserved table, going once a week—with carefully considered self-discipline—to his mistress Elsa. To be sure, he possesses "from former days some knowledge of the history of art" and had "been a member of the Association for the Preservation of the Municipal Works of Art," but this too, "by the way, only for business reasons" (P 239); what is more, he treats even his "trial" like a business transactions:

There was no guilt. The trial was nothing but a big business deal such as in the past he had often closed advantageously for the bank, a business deal in which, as was ordinarily the case, there lurked various dangers that simply had to be warded off. With this end in view, one certainly ought not to play with the thought of some sort of guilt or other but hold as tight as one could to the thought of one's own advantage. (P 152-53)

By contrast with Karl Rossmann he has succumbed utterly to the sphere of business and the impersonal "one." He represents the average citizen of modern society. For that very reason he is guilty without knowing it. And also, for that very reason he harps on his innocence. For not one of these average citizens would ever charge himself with any sort of guilt that could not be established legally or in accordance with the conventional moral code. Not one of these citizens suspects that it is just this ordinary citizen's existence of his that constitutes his real guilt.

Hence, too, Josef K.'s guilt should not without qualification be identified with original sin in the religious sense. For in that case there would be no "innocent" people like Karl Rossmann at all, and, properly speaking, all the court authorities and officials in *The Trial* would have to be arrested. But that is out of the question. Only Josef K., Block the "businessman," and other people, "most" of whom "belonged to the upper classes" (P 80), are arrested and involved in court trials. In an original version there is even the statement that the interrogating officials, whom Josef K. is made to confront on the sixth floor of a dirty tenement house, had the appearance of people at a "socialist meeting" (P 306).

In Kafka, who for many years was very closely associated with socialistic and anarchistic trends of thought,[1] the element of social criticism ought never to be completely overlooked, even though the structure of this court exceeds and bursts the bounds of political ideologies.

Also, in the "trial"* it is not simply a matter of a "biological" process of life and disease that must at some time automatically end in death, as must any mortal life; that is to say, must end negatively.[2] Even though, according to Josef K.'s feeling, a "single hangman could replace the entire court" (P 185), and even though "actual acquittals" occur only in legends (P 186), there are nevertheless also trials that have "come to a good

---

*Tr. note: German *Prozess* means both "trial" and "process." The author plays with the word in both meanings here and elsewhere. See also note 2 below.

end" (P 147). Notwithstanding that the court is universal, for "everybody, of course, belongs to the court" (P 181), not everyone is arrested or arraigned: not everyone is standing "trial."

Total earthly existence is a "vast judiciary system" that "in a manner of speaking is eternally trembling in the balance" (P 146); but those involved and ensnared in a trial by this judiciary system are only the "guilty"—that is to say, those who know nothing of such a court, who "do not know" the inner "law," and who consider themselves guiltless. They can never be "really" acquitted, because they constantly want to "prove" their innocence, and the court is "impervious to arguments" (P 184). Arguments are what prove guilt with a vengeance. The truly "innocent...man...needs no help in court" (P 184). And an actual acquittal is therefore identical with an abrogation of all motivations. "The records of the case...disappear completely from the proceedings; not only the charge but also the litigation, and even the acquittal, are destroyed—everything is destroyed" (P 190-91). This means that total motivated life is "destroyed."

Logically, this kind of actual acquittal is unrelated to "authentic" legends of "former times" (P 185-86), because modern man can no longer possibly give up his motivations: he builds his life upon them; that is, by means of them he conceals his inward infallible law and his self that passes judgment. These motivations are actually the proof of his ignorance of the Law; that is, proof of his guilt. And to a "good end" come only those proceedings that were destined "from the beginning to turn out well" (P 147). In these cases, man trusts in his infallible self from the start; although he is involved in judicial proceedings, inasmuch as he cannot live as a finite being without motivations, he nevertheless, like Karl Rossmann, does not let himself be completely determined and deceived by the "aid and assistance" of these motivations; therefore from "beginning" to "end" he leads a "good," guiltless existence.

In this way light is shed upon the seeming contradictions and absurdities of this novel.

## Life as a Court of Justice

If actually "everybody" belongs to the court, then man's total life reality has been a court of justice all along.

When Josef K. at a later stage of his trial wants to dismiss his lawyer and take over the defense of his case himself, it is borne in upon him that the petition he plans to submit to the court would be meaningful and effective and could lead to his complete exoneration only if in it "his entire life down to the minutest actions and events" could "be recalled to memory, described and examined from every angle" (P 154-55). He senses that in this court it is a matter of justifying one's total life.

Such a petition, however, is beyond human power. For no one can survey his "total life" and "examine it from every angle." Besides, the written formulation of such a petition would consume such an endless stretch of time that Josef K. would lose his footing in life and would have to give up his bank career and his private life entirely. A complete motivation of life cancels out life itself.

On the other hand, man cannot live unjustifiedly but is responsible for everything that he lives and that he is. It is this contradiction that is Josef K.'s undoing. His entire trial is a single demonstration of that sentence of Kafka's that we have already analyzed: "The entire visible world is perhaps nothing but a motivation of man who wishes to rest for a moment," who wishes to blur and annul the ominous "knowledge of good and evil" that destroys existence, who longs to have some peace from [that knowledge] by interposing a motivated life between it and himself, making that knowledge his goal instead of accepting it as an inevitable, accomplished fact (H 49-50). The "knowledge of good and evil" is warded off by Josef K. as knowledge that is past endurance. Hence he flees into motivations and aids offered him by the visible world, and at first considers the entire court as "of no consequence whatsoever" (P 30), believing himself capable at any time of "smashing it to bits instantly" (P 72).

And then later he makes knowledge his "goal," as he thinks of describing and justifying his entire life in written form.

However, if the court facing him represents nothing but total life reality, then this earthly court of existence is also incapable of possessing absolute knowledge of good and evil, and is therefore also unable to pass final judgment, but, on the contrary, exists itself in a profusion of endless cases at nonterminable stages and in a profusion of official channels where in each case only partial proceedings can be undertaken, without its ever being possible to obtain a complete view, since they move in unceasing motivations themselves, in the course of which "the various opinions about the proceedings multiply to the point of impenetrability" (P 236). "The hierarchy and gradation of the court," Huld the lawyer explains,

"...are endless and incalculable even for the initiates...the minor officials...are therefore scarcely ever able to trace completely the subsequent course of matters they have processed; the case thus appears on their horizon often without their knowing where it came from, and it passes on without their learning where it is going.... They are allowed to deal with only that portion of the case which is defined for them by the Law; and of further particulars, hence of the results of their own work, they usually know less than the defense which, as a rule, remains in contact with the defendant until almost the close of the case." (P 144)

This court is thus nothing but an image of the countless, constantly clashing, changing "opinions" that people have of one another at various times. And even the "high judges" are, as it is stated, "in reality" quite ordinary people who, for example, sit "on a kitchen stool on which an old horse blanket is folded" (P 132). They have never sat upon a judicial "chair of state" —"that's all a fiction" (P 176). In addition they are "absurdly vain" (P 132, 176), "always vindictive" (P 146), and are always making advances to women—a striking continuation of the statements Kafka had made long ago, in his early work "Description of a Battle," about the "things" seized by the praying man and the stout man, "things" that—no differently from these officials—show a "capricious partiality for the pulp of our brains" (B 31).

In fact, these court officials represent the same incomprehensible power of life and sensuous reality as do the natural phenomena in the early work. The judges are just as impervious as the phenomena that push "mutely terrible walls" in front of man. In the officials, sensuous-earthly life runs its course unchecked. Their power is the power of life itself, that no bold, reflective thinker can escape, but that no thinker can ever really fathom or penetrate. This is what constitutes their irresistible power of attraction for women. Like the phenomena of nature, they represent, as it were, sheer sensually lived life. At the same time, however—and their full paradoxical totality lies above all in this —they are involved almost incessantly in their work of reviewing and recording; and they live, so to speak, in an abstract, life-alienated sphere of continuous judgments. "The officials lack relationship with the people ... in the very simple cases ... they are often at their wit's end; and because they are constantly compressed into their law, night and day, they do not have the right sense for human relations" (P 143).

Thus in them the reaches of human existence grow visible in the extremes: sheer physical life and sheer incessant consciousness or subconsciousness; all this, however, in terms of general conformity with the law, the "law" into which they are "compressed." In this sense they are not individuals, not private persons, but the embodiment of the laws of life and thought that pervade man; hence they do not have any "right sense for human relations."[3] Their "law" is not the supreme "Law"— that, they have no knowledge of (P 190).

And as previously in "Description of a Battle" body and thought fall apart, so too in these court officials suddenly the normal bounds of human imagination and life seem alarmingly shattered. Both their vitality and capacity for reflection transcend individual man's power of comprehension. Both characteristics emerge in them unchecked. This becomes immediately clear, early on, when Josef K. views his warders at the time of his arrest.

In the presence of these people, however, he [Josef K.] was not
even able to think ; over and over again the second warder's belly
... bumped him in a downright friendly way, but on looking up
he perceived a face completely incongruous with this fat body, a
dry, bony face with a large, lopsided nose, a face that was communicating past him with the other warder. What kind of people were
they? What were they talking about? (P 12)

## The Court as Reflection of Kafka's Psyche

Strictly speaking, however, the point here is that in Josef K.
himself, at the onset of his arrest, sensuality and consciousness
fly apart. The court and its officials are nothing but reflections of
that process that sets in in every human being who is suddenly
compelled to master and justify his life completely. For at this
moment the rules of normal consciousness and life, rules by
means of which human existence has been leveled, smoothed,
and secured, are breached. The semblance of order crumbles,
and the totality of human existence emerges first of all as a
frightening mystery that proceeds in irreconcilable extremes and
unresolvable antinomies, that can no longer be mastered and
understood by thought, that can no longer be penetrated by normal consciousness and dynamic emotion—and that is why even
the court authorities and all that surrounds them must remain
forever unintelligible to Josef K.

However, that this court is in truth the expression of his own
inner state, is something that Josef K. senses dimly on the
very occasion of his arrest, for "it seemed to him for a moment
as if he were bearing all of them upon his shoulders" (P 23).
All the antinomies and enigmas of the court have their basis
in Josef K. himself. In this court he has to come to terms with
himself alone, he has to attain to clarity "about himself," as the
inspector has previously explained. The apparently absurd, inscrutable court authorities are nothing but Josef K.'s own
earthly life reality that has hitherto been alien to him; and

hence, as he now suddenly catches sight of it, he sees it with terror as an alien presence.


## The Temporal Court and the Supreme Court

A sharp distinction is made, however, between these concrete, temporal court authorities—Josef K. can, for instance, still see the office directors (P 128 ff.)—and the "supreme" court, "the court that is completely inaccessible to you, to me, and to all of us. What it is like there we do not know, and, incidentally, we do not even want to know" (P 190). Only in this supreme court does the infallible Law prevail, that is "outside the sphere of all human judgment" (P 264).

The court authorities who represent the totality of life are thus encamped, as it were, in front of this supreme court. They themselves do not know the absolute Law. It is said of the officials, "They themselves know nothing" (P 148). But they manifest the irreversible, inherent laws of the earthly world, laws that are alterable or breakable only if one "takes the ground away from under one's feet" and "falls headlong." "Changes for the better," such as every defendant demands, are consequently impossible and absurd. It is necessary

...to realize...that this great judicial system remains to a certain extent eternally in a state of suspension, and that if one makes any change independently at the spot where one is, one does indeed take the ground away from under one's feet and can even fall headlong, whereas the great system easily compensates itself, at another spot, for the slight disturbance—everything, of course, is interrelated—and remains unchanged, if it does not perhaps grow—and this is likely to be the case—even more uncommunicative, even more observant, even more severe, even more evil. (P 146)

This judicial system, therefore, is by no means good or even divine. It is the "evil" world. And hence it is absurd to designate its officials as divine beings and to interpret their demands and instinctive sexual desires as higher religious commandments that rise above all morality on this earth.[4]

### *Freedom and World Law ("Before the Law")*

These minor authorities of the court grow much less ambiguous upon comparison with the "doorkeeper" who stands "before" the Law and not *in* the Law. For when Josef K. complains to the chaplain about the court which appears to him like a venal pack of woman-chasers, the chaplain replies, "You are deceiving yourself about the court; in the preambles of the scriptures on the Law it is said of this illusion: Before the Law there stands a doorkeeper. To this doorkeeper there comes a man from the country asking for admission to the Law," etc. (P 255). The minor authorities of the court are thus compared here with the doorkeeper. And Josef K.'s illusion, the illusion of the man from the country in relation to this doorkeeper, lies in the fact that they both consider everything the doorkeeper or the lower court says and presents to be "true" instead of considering it "only necessary." "A bleak point of view," Josef K. replies. "Falsehood is made the world order" (P 264). The doorkeeper with his statements thus unequivocally represents the "world order" which, though necessary, is not absolute truth itself.

On the other hand, however, the chaplain rejects Josef K.'s interpretation that the doorkeeper deceived the man from the country; and even Josef K.'s opinion that in the doorkeeper falsehood was exalted to the level of a world order was not the opinion he held in his "final judgment." The doorkeeper and the minor authorities of the world court in no way deceive man. They are both appointed by the Law, are servants of the highest Law, and therefore cannot lie. The individual, of course, can lie, but not the natural law pervading him, not life itself that is lived; and, as long as these officials are in "office," they represent nothing other than this conformity with natural law. The officials apparently are able to make contradictory statements and issue orders. But these contradictions result only from the various aspects under which life is lived and judgment is made. Even "lies" have their origin in definite necessities of life and thought, and in this sense are a true expression of universal laws. "Errors" do not occur and never can occur in that world organization in which "no record is lost"; in which there is "no forgetting" (P 191); in which all apparent mistakes, illusions, and lies prove to be correct and free of error when seen under aspects of totality; in which there is a continuous revision and control of everything-that-is and hence, too, a perpetual justification of everything-that-is.

But a decisive argument raised by the chaplain is that it is the doorkeeper himself who is "mistaken," because he really "does not know the interior of the Law but knows only the stretch that he must pace again and again in front of the entrance" (P 260-61). Actually, the doorkeeper, in contrast with the man from the country, has no desire at all to enter into the Law; he is even afraid of such an entrance. "From all this one concludes that he knows nothing about the appearance and the significance of the interior and is under an illusion about it. But he is said to be under an illusion about the man from the country, too, for he is subordinate to this man and does not know it" (P 261), because the man from the country is "free," whereas the doorkeeper is bound. Since the doorkeeper does "not know" all this, he is "simple" and "conceited." His statements are "clouded through simplemindedness and arrogance" (P 259).

Thereby the chaplain has in fact clearly formulated the nature of these minor officials of the world court. Early on, at the beginning of the novel, the two warders who arrest Josef K. appear simpleminded and arrogant. They set themselves up as Josef K.'s masters. And the entire world of these officials is correspondingly vain, arrogant, vindictive, etc. For it represents a rigid, self-contained world system of laws, strictly determinated, never able to go beyond itself, possessing no "freedom" and consequently also afraid of surrendering to the supreme court; for the supreme court, based on freedom and therefore able to rescind this system of laws, would tear the bureaucratic organization practically to bits, as is later stated analogously in *The Castle.*

The man from the country thus has the full opportunity of freely entering into the Law through that door which is expressly intended for him alone. For "the entrance into the Law is forbidden him ... by one individual only, the doorkeeper" (P 262). That is, only the world and its systems bar man from entrance into the Law, from entrance into "truth," and that only "now" —that is to say, as long as man lives. The moment he set this prohibition at nought, that is, the moment he was able to renounce the world, he lived in the Law.

For all that, the statements made by the chaplain must be carefully weighed. The doorkeeper, it is said, by no means remains "in his official role at all times. In the very first moments he jokingly invites the man to enter in spite of the strictly maintained prohibition" (P 260). He "laughs" as he says, "If it tempts you so, try to enter in spite of my forbidding it. But bear in mind: I am powerful" (P 256).

This distinction between official role and private person is quite essential for an understanding of the whole of Kafka's bureaucracy. The officials themselves want to break out of the strict conformity of their officialdom and therefore long for the free entrance of that very human being for whom they have basically been appointed. Hence, by no means are they *merely* arrogant, simple, vain, unapproachable, and unfriendly; on the contrary, they too feel their inferiority in facing the "free man," and are indeed often like "children," who "joke" and "laugh," and would like to live a light-hearted, unmotivated existence, liberated from all incessant "work." In *The Castle* they try to help K. by sending him comical, cheering, childlike helpers, etc. And even in *The Trial* they are occasionally like "children," with whom one is able to achieve a great deal by means of a "little joking" (P 147).

On the other hand, with their "power" they also threaten the man who is free and superior to them without his knowing it, and are also in fact "superior" to him from the point of view of this power.

"One must not then believe that the doorkeeper is subordinate to the man. To be bound through his service, even if only to the entrance to the Law, is infinitely superior to living at liberty in the world. The man is only now coming to the Law; the doorkeeper is there already. He has been appointed by the Law to this service; to be in doubt about his worth is to be in doubt about the Law." (P 264)

From this point all seeming contradictions in *The Trial* and *The Castle* are clarified. In both novels K. is set above the officials as well as being subordinate to them. As a "free" man he alone has a chance to break through the conformity of the world and attain to the interior of the true Law. He alone, not the doorkeeper, sees the inextinguishable radiance that shines forth from the interior of the Law. On the other hand he is subordinate to the officials; as long as he tries to exist on earth he stands in a relationship of dependence on them, and indeed he even believes that with their help he can penetrate to the Law. For they have been appointed by the Law itself as guardians; they serve the Law; their conformity to law has been ordained by the highest authority. Hence they are superior to the free, "lawlessly" living human being. And hence, conversely, this lawlessly living, free and alien being seeks to obtain a footing within the world organization, to enroll himself in it, to understand its meaning; he curses his freedom, strives in spite of his "battle" against the officials to gain their sympathy and assistance. The difficulties of both novels lie in this ambiguity, but therein also lies their inner truth.

Bue yet another essential aspect emerges from the chaplain's exegesis. Although the doorkeeper forbids entrance into the Law "now," he holds out the "prospect of his being able to enter at a future time" (P 258); and since the "portal of the Law is always open . . . always, that is, irrespective of the duration of life of the man for whom it is ordained, the doorkeeper will not be able to close it" (P 262-63). Although the doorkeeper means to close the portal, since as far as he is concerned everything is concluded upon the man's death, he finds himself very "gravely mistaken" in this (P 262). In reality he cannot close the portal at all (P 263).

In this there is an intimation of the possibility that the man from the country can enter after his death; what is more, consideration is given to the possibility that the man could have entered even during his lifetime, had he asked "earlier" for whom the entrance was actually intended, instead of waiting until he was dying. Then he would have received "the redeeming message" (P 258). This means, therefore, that the liberating breakthrough or the world system of laws is always possible—possible, that is to say, when man inquires into the determination of his own existence instead of staring, as if hypnotized, at the menacing "power" and superiority of the world. Then liberation from the "world" would be possible even during life on earth.

This sheds light on the basic principles of the intellectual and spiritual structure of *The Trial,* which can consequently be better understood in all its details.

## The Meaning of the Arrest

Josef K., on the morning of his thirtieth birthday, while he is still lying in bed, is arrested. Hence he is still in that state of absentmindedness, self-forgetfulness, freedom from work, and half-dream, that state in which all of Kafka's heroes are thrust out of their normal, everyday world and placed, as it were, "outside of our people, outside of our human race" (cf. T 20-22). In a deleted passage (P 304-305), express reference is made to this "most precarious moment" upon waking from sleep. This passage was probably deleted in order to avoid having the entire novel falsely construed as dealing with disconnected dream visions to be interpreted, so to speak, from a purely psychoanalytical point of view. Throughout, Kafka removed from the novel almost all sections suggestive of mere "dreams"; for example, the magnificent section "A Dream" (E 181 ff.), and a dream in the fragment "The House" (P 293 ff.). He would have

the break-in of the universal powers pervading normal consciousness understood not as mere unreal dream visions but rather as
extremely "common confusions" and realities. In this vein is the
statement made of Gregor Samsa's "metamorphosis" into an
insect: "It was no dream."

Josef K.'s arrest is an inescapable reality, not a monstrous
product of a dream, even though the arrest became possible only
through Josef K.'s dreamy slipping away from empirical, rationally ordered existence. For he says:

> "I was taken unawares, that's what it was. If I had . . . got up . . .
> immediately after waking . . . I would have behaved sensibly, and
> nothing further would have happened . . . . At the bank, for example,
> I am prepared for things; it would be impossible for something
> of this sort to happen to me there . . . above all, at the bank I am
> always in the continuum of work, and so I always have my wits
> about me." (P 30-31)

Furthermore, the morning of one's thirtieth birthday is a particularly outstanding occasion. It is an obvious time to attempt,
as it were, to justify the life one has led and the life one is still
to lead. Similarly, Block the businessman is arrested "shortly
after the death" of his wife (P 207); that is, at a moment when
his customary, normal life is disturbed, conscious awareness of
life and death wells up in him.

Crucial, however, is the fact that Josef K. feels this conscious
awareness as a strange, disturbing "power," and therefore it is
portrayed as happenings confronting him objectively, not solely
as inner reflections. The universally spiritual is itself hypostatized
in the modern work-world; indeed, Josef K., at first designating
it flatly as a "nothingness," wards it off, although he must con-
cur with Mrs. Grubach's opinion that it has to do with something very "learned," perhaps even with his "happiness" (P 30).
This "old woman" is an initiate, one who knows; she is like the
old women in Kafka who as a rule possess a secret knowledge
of such inner processes. One may call to mind the sketch
"Advocates" (B 136 ff.), in which only "old women" are in
the court building; or the role of the old women in *The Castle*—

the landlady of the Herrenhof Inn and, above all, Gerstäcker's mother.[5]

Even the "senile curiosity" of the old woman who watches Josef K.'s arrest from a window opposite is related to this aspect of old women. Having lived their lives, and surveying everything in retrospect, they possess a deeper understanding of the whole of life even though by contrast with reflective men they are scarcely able to articulate that understanding. It is not without good reason, therefore, that the examining officials who ponder the whole thing through are "grey-haired old men." Accordingly, too, later on when the actual negotiations with the warders are taking place, a grey-haired old man appears at the window beside the old woman.

And finally, when these negotiations are taken up by the inspector and shifted to the room belonging to Miss Bürstner, whose bedside table becomes the table for the negotiations and whose white blouse hangs at the open window, the two old people at the window opposite are joined by a man with a powerful physique, who, with his shirt open over his chest, was squeezing and twisting his reddish, pointed beard with his fingers" (P 19-20, 23).

There can be no doubt that all this is the objectified reflection of Josef K.'s own subconscious ideas and instinctual desires. The breakout from work-standardized existence is not only a break-in into "something learned," something spiritual, but also into an erotic "happiness," and indubitably the landlady's word intimates this. For it is on the evening following this break-in of the court into Miss Bürstner's room that Josef K.'s actual, savagely "thirsty," indeed animal-like embrace of this young lady takes place. Counterbalancing both the negotiations at Miss Bürstner's "bedside table" and the sight of her blouse at the open window is the man at the window opposite, with his powerful physique, his open shirt, and his "reddish, pointed beard" which he "squeezes and twists." The sexual sphere could hardly be manifested more clearly. And naturally Kafka's knowledge of psychoanalytical insights is involved here. Kafka did not reject psychoanalytical knowledge as such, but he refused to accept its

claim to being a panacea (H 335). Psychoanalytical interpretations of his writings are possible and indeed necessary, but they
are meaningful only within the framework of Kafka's more
universal themes.

The three subordinate bank clerks who examine Miss
Bürstner's photographs are not recognized by Josef K. until he is
requested to go to the bank. Even these clerks are thus reflections of subconscious ideas: he finds them disagreeable; he has
never liked them; he is afraid that through them his private life
could become common knowledge at the bank. The conflict between career and trial is heralded here, at this early point. For
the very reason that he finds these three clerks disagreeable,
they appear here. Everything that has not been mastered within
himself becomes tormentingly visible in this trial. His career
at the bank, his problem of guilt, his eroticism—everything is
inextricably intertwined and overlapping to the point where it is
actually visualized; thus, for example, the statement is made:
" ... the inspector had obliterated the three clerks from his
awareness and now the clerks in turn obliterated the inspector"
(P 27).

## The Ambiguous Interplay between Josef K. and the Authorities

Analysis of the so-called parable "Before the Law" has revealed a peculiarly ambiguous reciprocal relationship between
the man from the country and the doorkeeper. The same kind of
reciprocal relationship has already appeared in the scene of the
arrest. Although Josef K. is "arrested," is thus under the authority of the warders, and even obeys their commands, on the
other hand "He was playing with them," "felt himself more
and more independent of all these people," "it seemed to him for
a moment as if he were bearing all of them upon his shoulders"
(P 23, 24). He is both free and unfree as he faces them. He is
in a towering rage at the arrest, feeling it to be "terrible" (P 38),

and at the same time he yearns for it: "He harbored the intention ... of offering himself up to them for arrest" (P 24). They are merely mirrorings of his inner self, yet nevertheless they have an alien quality that subjugates him. "Wasn't he always at liberty to smash the entire court to bits instantly, at least insofar as it concerned him" (P 72)—this is said later, at a time when he is becoming increasingly dependent upon the court.

He considers the total situation as "comedy" (P 13), as a joke or a game, and, at the same time, as a destructive reality that at the very moment of his arrest implants in him the thought of suicide (P 17). This incongruity, comedy and suicide, is retained until the very end of the novel. On the walk to his execution, which, as he tells himself, he must actually perform "himself," he asks his murderers, "At what theater are you playing?" " 'Perhaps they are tenors,' he thought as he looked at their heavy double chins. He felt nauseated by the cleanliness of their faces. One still saw, as it were, the cleansing hand that had wiped the corners of their eyes, scrubbed their upper lips, scraped out the folds at their chins." "Old, second-rate actors they send for me" (P 266-67). Their "loathsome politeness" (P 271) as they prepare to execute him is repellent to him. And in one version, what is more, the two murderers are described as puppets: "Their eyebrows seemed fastened on, and wagged up and down with no relation to the motion of walking" (P 311).

Thus the entire court is equivocal: theater as well as terrible reality. It is a comedy with marionettes and puppets that dull-wittedly execute commands, puppets to which Josef K. is definitely superior. At the same time, however, they seize him mercilessly and take firm hold of him with their "regulation, practiced, compelling grip" (P 267). Everything in this world theater of authorities is fixed, learned by heart, orthodox—it is the eternally same play of this world, puppetlike, something fundamentally "lifeless" (P 267).

These "tenors" of the music of the world are theater supernumeraries. Even their cleanliness is disgusting; so too among

these authorities there is a constant "washing" and cleaning
going on; there are washtubs everywhere, with laundry drying
on clotheslines, while at the same time "filth" accumulates
everywhere, and soot and smoky air fill the court offices.

The earthly world court, mirroring all the processes of life,
has the constant desire to cleanse and is itself constantly submerged in filth.

This likewise is germane to the ambiguities of these authorities, and is part of Kafka's clairvoyant criticism of the world.
There is repetition of this in *The Castle*. "I've had enough of
this comedy," K. says at the beginning of *The Castle* (S 11).
The "Nature Theater of Oklahoma" is continued in *The Trial*
and in *The Castle*. But, whereas the man who has lost sight of
is accepted at the Nature Theater—indeed, "everyone" who
wants to become an artist is invited to join—in the theater of
the authorities of the trial and of the castle no man who is free
and a stranger is accepted at all. At this theater, freedom is out-
lawed. The utopia [of the early novel] has given way to a pitiless
world comedy in which man can no longer "breathe" (cf.
P 91-92). To be sure, this world comedy too has in itself an
ambiguous form. It appears possible for the officials in the midst
of their incessant work to indulge in purpose-free play. However, the utopian possibilities of a breakout from the determinated world would have to be paid for with the destruction of
the world apparatus itself, as Bürgel remarks; the officials would
have to become private individuals, and this dual role is actually
assigned them. By contrast, the Theater of Oklahoma is pure
"nature" theater in which everyone is able to play his role freely
and naturally. It is more positive but also more utopian. The
theater of *The Trial* is more negative but truer. The loss in
hope is a gain in truth. The negation of the "world comedy"
leads to the knowledge that there is only a spiritual world, and
that everything visible is our own motivation. "The fact that
there is nothing else but a spiritual world deprives us of hope
but gives us certainty" (H 46).

The acting out of the comedy, however, passes over to Josef
K. On the evening of the day of his arrest, he re-enacts the

entire scene of the arrest for Miss Bürstner. He himself becomes an actor. At the same time the play is in terrible earnest. He "shouts" his own name as he takes on the role of the inspector: "And now it really begins. The inspector shouts as if he had to wake me, he actually screams, unfortunately I'll have to scream too, if I am to make it clear to you . . . 'Josef K.!' " (P 39-40). In this "play" is is really a matter of "waking" his own self. And so the comedy becomes menacingly serious, for upon the scream there follows profound terror (P 41).

Analogously, all the ambiguities of the authorities are within Josef K. himself. He, too, constantly wants to cleanse himself, not only in that he protests his innocence but in that, for example, the thought passes through his head "that the warders had forgotten to make him take a bath" (P 19). Furthermore, he believes that Miss Bürstner's room was "defiled" by the presence of the warders and the inspector (P 58). He wants to put it in order again, for "once . . . this order was restored, every trace of those occurrences would be wiped out, and everything would resume its former course" (P 28).

On the other hand, he has the feeling that he himself is defiling everything. "If you want to keep your boardinghouse clean and decent, you'll have to give me notice first," he says to Mrs. Grubach (P 33).

Accordingly, he feels himself innocent and guilty at the same time, even on the same count. To Miss Bürstner he says, "Your room was thrown into disorder a bit this morning, through my fault to a certain extent—it was done by strangers, against my will, and yet, as I said, through my fault" (P 36). Expressing himself to the examining authorities, however, he says, "I had to look on and see how this room, on my account but through no fault of mine, was defiled to a certain extent by the presence of the warders and the inspector" (P 58). During this court session he calls the two warders "demoralized scoundrels" who are corruptible and who intended to trick him out of his underwear and clothes. When the warders are whipped by order of the authorities, an order that results from this accusation of Josef K.'s, he cries out, "I do not consider . . . them to be guilty at all; it is the organization that is guilty; it is the high officials that are guilty" (P 106). What is more, he thinks it would "have been almost simpler if K. had taken off his clothes and offered himself in place of the warders" (P 109). But he rejects this thought, and on the following day simply slams the door to the lumber room where the warders are whipped, hammering against it with his fists as if it would be shut tighter that way.

What is horrible must not penetrate to the outside. Josef K. is afraid that the whole affair may become known at the bank and possibly do damage to his prestige there. What he would like best is simply to have the entire lumber room cleared out. for "I tell you, we're being drowned in filth!" (P 111).

These self-contradictions in Josef K. have their origin in the conflict of the "two opponents": the one wants to force him to the unconditional knowledge of good and evil, to complete self-responsibility, and this would be tantamount to an annihilating confession of guilt; the other wants to keep him on earth, wash him clean, guarantee him prestige in the eyes of the world. The feeling of guilt, constantly repressed, emerges abruptly again and again at decisive points, above all in his private life: in front of the landlady, and in front of Miss Bürstner whose very name has symbolical significance.* In court, however, he denies all guilt to the very end.

Since he does not take over complete responsibility, he seeks "help from others ... particularly from women" (P 253), but also from Huld the lawyer and Titorelli the artist. Ways of surviving on earth are put in place of a free decision.

Of necessity woman is the focal point, for she seems to possess a more intimate contact with life than does man: it might be possible for her to unlock the secret of life for him; that is, she could initiate him into the nature of that obscure court, the judicial structure that is eternally in a state of suspension, a structure in which, for Kafka, life itself is given symbolic expression.

---

*Tr. note: German *bürsten* "to brush," used also with sexual connotations.

## The Role of Women

Three women come Josef K.'s way: Miss Bürstner, the wife of the court usher, and Leni. They represent three possible attitudes of woman as she relates to the court: (1) standing outside the court, (2) living in conflict with it, and (3) succumbing completely to its power.

Miss Bürstner is the free, independent woman. She is therefore of paramount importance to the whole of Josef K.'s trial.

She has little "experience in legal matters," but she "would like to know everything, and legal matters, particularly, interest me very much. A court of justice has a peculiar attraction, don't you think?" (P 37-38). But precisely in relation to her, Josef K. fails. Properly speaking, *he* would have to take her to court. But "what it is all about," in this matter of his prosecution at court, he himself "does not know." Miss Bürstner is "inordinately disappointed" about this (P 38). Since Josef K. does not move freely toward his self, toward his own court of justice, it is not possible for a genuine love encounter to take place with another free self, one who would like to "know everything" about the "peculiarly" attractive court. As long as Josef K. flees from himself, there exists no bridge between him and someone with whom he could be on intimate terms; and the two cannot open their hearts to one another, mutual "knowledge" cannot be passed on from one to the other, love cannot spring into being. This unmarried Miss Bürstner, on the threshold of the secret of life and love, full of expectation but still lacking in "experience," could attain to a genuine encounter with Josef K. only if he were himself already a person in the full sense of the word; that is, if he were already in and at the same time *above* the court, and did not remain entangled in the mysterious powers of life. He succumbs to these unknown and uncontrollable powers instead of defeating them decisively.

In relation to the girl, Josef K. becomes a "thirsty animal" that avidly seeks "water at the spring." With that, he has pronounced his own death sentence. "Finally he kissed her on the

neck, low on her throat, and here he let his lips linger long"
(P 42). His kiss is a deadly threat to his partner; it is the catastrophe of love, and it prefigures the scene of his destruction,
that scene with his murderers, in which "hands ... were placed
on K.'s throat" (P 272).

Josef K. knows this himself. When he catches sight of "Miss
Bürstner" on the night of his execution, he becomes "aware of
... the uselessness of his resistance." He intended "not to forget the admonition that she [Miss Bürstner] signified for him"
(P 268). This admonition is to the effect that "it has been left
up to me to tell myself what is needed" (P 269); that is, to
execute sentence upon himself, to commit suicide. "K. now
knew with certainty that it would have been his duty ... to take
hold of the knife himself and bury it in himself" (P 271). But
even for that he does not have the strength. He has to be executed by theater supernumeraries and puppets, together with
whom he constitutes "only something lifeless." Where a spiritual
free love encounter is denied, only rigid lifelessness can prevail.

However, this positive "admonition," signified for him by
Miss Bürstner, has yet another meaning. After their first nocturnal encounter Miss Bürstner had definitely turned away from
and consistently blocked Josef K.'s every attempt to resume contact with her, no matter if it was only an attempt to talk things
over with her. In this way she referred him to himself. And this
very denying him any help was the true and only help. This was
the "admonition" that he "did not forget" and that, even on his
way to execution, shows him where his help lies: in his decision
"to tell myself what is needed."

In contrast with Miss Bürstner, who is unmarried, the usher's
wife is in the very midst of matters of the court. When she
directs Josef K., as he goes to the courtroom for the first time,
she appears as "a young woman with gleaming black eyes, who
happened to be washing baby clothes in a tub" (P 51). But she
lives in conflict with the court. "It is really so disgusting here,"
she says (P 66). She has to give herself to the student attached
to the court and to the examining judge, if her husband is not to
lose his "position" (P 65). For the court is "powerful." She

hopes she will be liberated through Josef K. "If you'll take me along, I'll go wherever you wish ... I'll be happy to be away from here for as long a time as possible—best of all, forever" (P 72). From Josef K. she expects an "improvement" of the entire judicial system (P 66). And even her own husband believes that "only a man like" Josef K. could destroy the student's "power," could dare to give him a thrashing and wrest his wife away from him. And his reason for believing this is that Josef K. is "being prosecuted" (P 79). Only the defendants are free in relation to the court and not within the sway of this judicial organization.

Naturally Josef K. is unable to understand this. For in his opinion it would be particularly the defendants who would have to fear most from the power of the court, since the outcome of each trial depended on the court. " 'Yes, of course,' said the court usher, as if K.'s point of view were just as correct as his own" (P 79).

Here again is an instance where two mutually exclusive points of view appear as truth. And even the court usher's wife exists in a state of self-contradiction. While the student, at the order of the examining judge, is dragging her away, Josef K. cries out, " 'And you don't want to be set free?' ... 'No,' cried the woman and warded K. off with both hands, 'no, no, not that at all, above all, not that! What can you be thinking of! That would be the ruin of me' " (P 74-75).

However, Josef K. clearly feels that he should nevertheless have set her free. He is "raging with disappointment ... he realized that this was the first indubitable defeat that he had suffered at the hands of these people" (P 75). The antimony is of course unresolvable. The liberation of the woman would actually be her ruin. But, by not daring to set her free, he comes all the more profoundly into the power of the court instead of receiving the anticipated "help." Deliverance, in the opinion of the court usher, is possible only in one's " ... dream ... I wouldn't know of any ... other help" (P 78). Reconciliation is a "dream," dreamed in a "night darker than has ever yet existed." Reconciliation takes for granted the renunciation of any kind of help, the hazard of "ruin," the courage to be moved by a love that is no longer "within this world."

The third attitude is represented by Leni, who identifies completely with the judicial system and who urges Josef K. "not to be so unyielding—one cannot really defend oneself against this court; one has to make a confession" (P 132). She does not want to be liberated; on the contrary, she wants to make every defendant subject to her and to the court. Josef K. is "pulled down" by her. " 'Now you belong to me,' she said" (P 135). There "issued from her a bitter, provocative odor, like that of pepper." Her hand, of which she is "proud," gives the impression of a "pretty claw," because the connecting web of skin between her third and fourth fingers extends almost to the uppermost joint of her short fingers (P 134-35).

Claw and web—these are the aids afforded by a total engagement with life. To swim with the current, to drag down to her with her claws anyone who is unyielding—that is her recipe for life. For there can be no doubt that this is what lies behind the image of the web. Repeatedly in his works Kafka has developed the antinomy between swimming and nonswimming. Those who, like Hunter Gracchus, have stepped out of the stream of life, Kafka designates as "erstwhile swimmers" (T 22). And the truly "great swimmers" are for him the "nonswimmers" as well (H 319 ff.). Leni, however, is one who is unhesitatingly swimming in the stream of life.

Her kisses are at the same time bites. Her "love," so far as she is concerned, is an "exchange." She wants to be exchanged for Elsa, Josef K.'s mistress, but of course only when she learns from him that Elsa could never sacrifice herself for him. The ancient fairy-tale motif of being freed by a loving, self-sacrificing maiden from an evil enchantment and imprisonment crops up here, but the motif is in reverse.[6] No hope of deliverance is possible for a defendant who is seeking aid from the outside. This acts as an incentive to her to carry off the hopeless man as booty. For Leni does not think in terms of sacrifice. Her "kiss, undirected, landed on his back as he was leaving" (P 135). She brings under her sway only the defendants; these, one and all without exception, she finds "handsome" for the very reason that they are outsiders, branded with the mark of Cain—this is what makes the lost ones extremely attractive; this is what promises exceptional pleasure in domineering them. Moreover, she long ago became expert at the entire erotic play with these "handsome" devotees, having had excellent practice with Huld the lawyer, to whom, for his "entertainment," she relates her conquests. When Block the businessman is forced to humiliate and exhibit himself masochistically in the presence of the two of them, "K. felt as if he were hearing a rehearsed conversation that had already been often repeated, that would yet be often repeated" (P 232). She plays a part in the monotonous world comedy of this court; she has "a doll-like, rounded face" (P 122).

Not until he is in the presence of such enslavement, however, is Josef K. able to gain the insight that now, finally, he must conduct the trial himself, renounce outside help, and give notice to the lawyer as well as to the latter's strange "nurse"—must shake them both off.

However, the significance of Leni and of the lawyer is by no means exhausted with this characterization. On the contrary, they represent a stratum of our existence that, if the ultimate intention of Kafka and of the novel is to be understood, requires elucidation.

## The Perversion of Religious Grace in Huld the Lawyer

Huld the lawyer, who possesses profound insights into the swarming authorities and multitudinous official channels of the court, formulates his role as follows:

"I once found in a document, very beautifully expressed, the difference between acting for the defense in ordinary lawsuits, and acting for the defense in these lawsuits. It was stated there: The one lawyer leads his client up to the verdict by a thread; the other, however, lifts his client on to his shoulders at once, and, without setting him down, carries him up to the verdict and even beyond that." (P 226)

Josef K. is carried by this lawyer entirely; at the beginning, conversely, he felt that he was carrying the entire court upon his shoulders. The lawyer completely replaces Josef K., as it were, who is himself set aside. Whoever once comes under the sway of a lawyer, Huld believes, can no longer "maintain himself ... alone," and can therefore no longer withdraw his case from the lawyer (P 148). As representative of his client, the lawyer, bearing the entire burden of the case, is consequently described as a constantly sick, overworked man whose legs tremble with cold.

His "mistress," the "nurse" Leni, must warm him and nurse him tenderly. For he is on the threshold between the defendants and the court, and he must mediate between the two [parties]. In carrying the defendants he takes over, as it were, their own position in relation to the court. His feeling of cold corresponds to the image, that crops up in Kafka again and again, of the glacial cold into which man is cast adrift when he becomes engaged in total responsibility vis-à-vis the Universal; whereas, conversely, in the chambers of the court—where the processes of life are vibrating in themselves—an intolerable heat prevails even in winter and even with the furnaces turned off (P 186 ff.).[7]

Who, then, is this lawyer Huld?

Quite openly he points out to his client all the difficulties, the labyrinth of ways in which the defense could go astray and waste its efforts. He leaves him in no doubt about the enigmatic nature of this world or the "impenetrability" that of necessity ensues from the confusion of self-contradictory possibilities of life and thought (P 236). He reveals the limits of every kind of volitional or imaginative planning that still sways Josef K. in his desire to "withdraw the defense" from the hands of the lawyer and prepare an "organized and supervised" methodical attack upon the court (P 153), in order to protect his "interests," on the same basis as a "big ... business deal for the bank." Indeed, Huld drives his client to downright despair at the hopelessness of finding any way out of the situation involving the court.

The lawyer thus represents that entire sphere of the human spirit in which the powerlessness of consciousness is recognized, where faith takes the place of knowledge, and submission to fate takes the place of indignation and rebellion. He refers his clients to the mystery of "grace,"* to the unimaginable favor that can be bestowed, the assistance that can be rendered, if the client surrenders, if he resigns himself to his destiny, if he relinquishes his "unyieldingness."

Even the client and consequently Leni as well are thus given ambiguous form. Block's "doglike" submission, which is put on exhibit by them before Josef K.'s horrified eyes, is the very thing that is required and is proclaimed as the only meaningful assistance. "Grace" [Huld] demands the clients' unqualified and "necessary trust" (P 236). Only by trusting in this way, Huld asserts, can man maintain himself on earth and gain a meaningful life.

Yet, from this point on, Huld seems to represent a vicarious "sacrifice." His illness is a symbol of his suffering for others. And only he who accepts this sacrifice and submits to the sacrificer, experiences that "grace," that "favor" which only the sacrificer has the power to grant. Submission to the sufferer is tantamount to certainty of grace. The vicarious sufferer really does then carry the guilty man up to the verdict, and, what is more, carries him mysteriously even beyond that terrible verdict, forth to a land where there is no longer any judging, no longer any punishing.

Strange are the contours traced here: religious hope in the form of doglike submission, coupled with sexual masochism with reference to the "nurse" Leni (=Magdalena)! [8]

Kafka's interpretation of the world here assumes frightening proportions, all the more frightening because this demonstration of grace takes place in the form of a ceremony that is constantly

*Tr. note: The German word *Huld* "grace" is also the lawyer's name. Consequently a double entendre occurs whenever the lawyer's name or the word "grace" is mentioned.

and monotonously repeating itself. Once there is even mention
of the word "litany" (P 213). And reference is made to the fact
that the lawyer's petitions contain "primarily a great deal of
Latin that I don't understand" (P 212).

Leni's question whether Elsa is ready to sacrifice herself,
and her subsequent offer that Josef K. exchange Elsa for her,
henceforth acquire a new meaning, albeit a hideously perverted
one: for the exchange that Josef K. makes here means submission to sexual favor or disfavor, to grace or lack of grace
in the sexual sphere. Leaving oneself at the mercy of grace is
here identical with leaving oneself at the mercy of the compelling force of biological life. Nothing of the "liberty of a
Christian" is visible any longer;* the children of God appear
as the humiliated children of the world.

No matter how one judges of the settings for the Huld-Leni
figures, one thing remains certain: in these characters Kafka
has delineated the consequences of leaving any decision in the
hands of mediators representing the authorities; and he has set
forth his undeviating rejection of every kind of help from outside, no matter the source. He prefers to engage in "battle." It
is characteristic that Josef K. is taken to Huld the lawyer by
his "uncle," that tactless, importunate uncle who complains
that Josef K.'s trial is bringing 'disgrace" upon the entire family,
that "all our relatives will be dragged into it or at least be mor-
tally humiliated" (P 116, 119). Relevant to all this are not only
Kafka's own arguments with his family—against whom he always closed off his inner world, and in the face of whom, conversely, in self-critical despair at what was going on within
himself, he felt his poethood, etc., as a "disgrace" and a threat
to the family existence—but also his critical insight into the
fact that these very members of the family never do know any
better advice to give than that one consult some socially recognized mediating authorities or suchlike, who as mediators can
themselves recommend nothing but acquiescence in "reality as
it exists."

*Tr. note: Reference to one of Luther's missives, commonly translated as
"On Christian Liberty."

The only right thing to do is to resign oneself to existing conditions. Even if it were possible to improve on details—but to
think so is nonsensical superstition—what one might achieve would
at best be for future instances, but one would thereby inflict im-
measurable harm upon oneself by having attracted to oneself the
special attention of the ever-vindictive bureaucracy. One should
under no circumstances attract their attention! One should hold
one's peace no matter how much it is against one's liking. One
should try to realize that this vast judiciary system is, in a manner of speaking, eternally trembling in the balance.... One should
leave the work to the lawyer instead of interfering in it. (P 146-47)

This is Huld's advice. It is the advice of all consolidated powers;
it is also the advice, to be sure, of a man who sees into the
heart of the inalterability and "evil" (P 146) of the world, and
in this sense deals with reality by no means uncritically.

Huld's perversion lies in his belief that, on the basis of his
insight, he can assume responsibility for his clients and plead
their cause in court. Thereby he robs them of their personalities,
absorbing their freedom into himself as it were, transforming
them into slaves who obey him in spite of their knowing him
to be a human being like themselves, in spite of their differentiat-
ing him from the "great lawyers" dreamed of by every defendant, but beyond reach and never "to be seen" (P 215). Notwithstanding his own mortal limitations, Huld the lawyer pre-
sumes to be able to "carry" others, even beyond the verdict. The
questionable element in Huld lies in this ambiguous, opalescent
hovering between weakness and pride, between readiness to
suffer and hubris. He is, so to speak, the modern substitute for
the mystery of the unconditional vicarious sacrifice, and he dis-
torts this mystery into earthly trivia. Only in this way can one
understand his connection with Leni, in whom, likewise, the
compassionate "nurse" who cares for all the outcasts and
defendants is perverted to the life-engaged woman who wants
to liberate men from all conflict by supplying them with a
reckless, immediate *joie de vivre.*

For this reason too, one would be going completely astray if
for instance one were to see in Huld and Leni a criticism of the

sublime mystery of the Divine vicarious sacrifice. When Josef K.
wants to go to the cathedral, Leni seeks to prevent this (P 244);
and the true chaplain of the court rejects all help from women,
indeed any outside help whatsoever. In the cathedral Josef K.
catches sight of the painting representing "The Entombment of
Christ." This painting is inseparably linked with the serious, all-
enlightening words of the chaplain. He draws Josef K.'s attention to the only true help: to execute sentence upon oneself in
the presence of the Supreme One who died for the world. "The
Entombment of Christ," seen by Josef K. at a moment of deepest
"darkness" (P 245 ff.), is an admonitory image confronting him
with his own task, in the sense of that statement of Kafka's:
"All the suffering around us must be suffered by us as well.
Christ suffered for mankind, but mankind must suffer for Christ"
(H 117). To be sure, Josef K. is not yet ready for this admonition. Just as he misunderstands the chaplain's words, even wanting "to rid himself" of them (P 264), in the same manner he
still looks at this picture with the conventionally disinterested
eyes of a modern art historian viewing the "city sights" (P 252);
and in this painting he sees purely and simply a "rather modern
picture" painted in the "customary conception" of the subject
(P 246). But what Kafka's criticism is aimed at is this very
neutralization of the true content of the picture, at this flatten-
ing of the original, menacing challenge into a "customary conception" in a "rather modern" style of portrayal.

The role and function of both Huld the lawyer and Leni his
nurse consists of this and this alone. They transform vicarious
suffering for "all the suffering around us" into an aid to life for
their clients, into one of those many offers of help and comfort
that promise to make life easy and that thereby rob life of its
worth and meaning. This aid turns into the client's humiliation
and degradation; the lawyer's vicarious suffering turns into a
monotonous, ordinary, ever-recurring ceremony.

Only from this approach do Huld and Leni acquire a significance beyond limiting, particularistic interpretations: Leni
mirrors quite generically that type of women who surrenders
herself to the immediacy of her vitality and feeling for life, and

in this sees salvation also for men undergoing spiritual crises. Such women "heal" by unscrupulously supplying men with life as an immediate gift. Theirs is the most widely circulated offer of help in our times.

And Huld mirrors quite generically all the efforts of the times to deprive the individual of his self-responsible thought, volition, and action, and do all his thinking, wishing, and acting *for* him. He too is one of the most widespread phenomena of our times.

The two of them, Leni and Huld, form an inseparable pair. Their offer of help is basically the same. It is a matter of offering man earthly aids to life, no matter in what form, whether in the shape of erotic happiness or within the framework of powers that make it unnecessary for man to do any questioning or searching, and that pigeonhole him in associations—political, social, or ideological—that promise to carry him and take the "burden" of all work and responsibility upon themselves.

Huld the lawyer, like all of Kafka's characters, cannot be identified with any definite, given, historical doctrine or religious community or philosophy of life. On the contrary, his is the image, emerging everywhere, of temporal authorities having jurisdiction over life, authorities substituting for the unattainable court. It is significant, for example, that Block the businessman consults other lawyers besides Huld, who promise him the same thing. In the purposelessness of our age, help and substitute solutions—now this, now that—are sought indiscriminately. The supply of sects, ideologies, churches, associations, and organizations is indeed unlimited, and the number of "lawyers" incalculable. Each lawyer, however, is jealous of the next. In fear Block is obliged to keep his connections with the other lawyers secret from Huld. No one tolerates the help given by the next. Each is a monopolist and wants to carry his client alone.

And it is equally significant that Huld compels his clients to read his eternally same documents, "the same page, the whole day long" (P 234), to the point of insensibility. He knows with certainty that his client will never really understand these documents. "The documents that you have lent him are probably hard to understand," says Leni.

"Yes," said the lawyer, "that they are, to be sure. I really don't believe that he has any understanding of them. They are supposed to give him just an inkling of the difficulty of the battle I am waging in his defense. And for whom am I waging this difficult battle? For—it's almost ridiculous to utter it—for Block. What that means, he'll have to get to understand as well. Has he been studying uninterruptedly?" (P 234)

The lawyer himself does not believe in the value of his documents. Essentially, they are immaterial to him. Their sole purpose is to bring his clients to heel and give them some inkling of the fact that everything in the world is impenetrable and incomprehensible anyhow, and that nobody can know at what stage the trial is—whether it has "begun" at all, or even whether, perhaps, the final judgment has already been made (P 235-36). In this state of fear and perplexity that is instilled in him, the client is to gain the "necessary trust" (P 236) in the lawyer and surrender to him completely and without reservation.

Huld the lawyer is the representative of all those earthly powers that propose to get at the riddles of existence by simply demanding faith and trust, in a drastic short circuit, regardless of whether their "documents" can be understood or not understood, whether they are credible or incredible, whether they present intellectual arguments or a lack of them. Doubt is cut short while it mounts endlessly, "to impenetrability" (P 236). Within this paradox there lies in fact the essence of modern mass ideologies. They deprive man of thinking by cynically demonstrating the limits of all thought. Every intellectual deviation must be "punished" as a "breach of trust." For how can anyone deviate? —since thinking always errs as it is, and since the only guarantee for the preservation of national existence or the existence of the human race lies solely in the person, in the concrete existence of the party or organization, etc., through which alone the individual can be carried forth, past all dread verdicts, into a better future.

In fact, the power of this lawyer Huld is of such tremendous scope that it can hardly be surpassed. For no human being can live without mediation. Yet to take upon oneself total responsibility for the world, to gain a complete "view"—that is impossible. For Josef K.'s "trial" points to his assuming the responsibility not only for himself but for everyone: "Had he existed in the world alone, he could easily have ignored the trial, although of course in that event the trial would certainly not have come about at all" (P 152).

However, how is Josef K. to conduct and endure this trial alone? Justifiably, Huld the lawyer stresses the fact that without him Josef K. would be totally unable to maintain himself and survive in the world. He is bound to collapse under the burden of the arguments and proofs he attempts, the statements and petitions he formulates. He cannot possibly "give notice" to the lawyer without ruining himself. Josef K. himself recognizes this: "The decision to take the defense into his own hands presented itself to him as of graver consequence than he had originally supposed.... Now... he was obliged...to lay himself open to the court absolutely"; that is, he must dedicate his entire life to the trial, abandon all other work, and, in so doing, necessarily wreck his existence (P 159-60).

Thus, either he puts himself in the hands of the lawyer, in which event he will be able to live, albeit in the form of subjection; or, alternatively, he assumes the responsibility himself, in which event he will not be able to live.

Josef K.'s intention to "give notice" to the lawyer, an intention which is not carried out in the [extant portions of the] novel itself—the chapter [involved] breaks off before any notice is actually given—is the decisive step he takes toward his self-liberation, but it is the step he takes toward his self-annihilation as well.

The antinomy between freedom and concrete existence is unresolvable.

A third possibility results from Josef K.'s encounter with Titorelli the painter. In the latter, one has a glimpse of how the antinomy may be surmounted.

## The Possibility of Liberation through Titorelli

### A. FREEDOM IN THE COURT

Titorelli is "a confidant of the court" (P 178). He paints the portraits of the judges who are frequent visitors at his studio, which leads directly into the court chambers. In it the same heat and stifling air prevail as in these chambers. Titorelli has close "personal relations" with the judges, and it is through such relationships that the judges are "easy to manage" (P 182). On the other hand, he is a "private person"; that is, he does not hold office and is not "compressed" into legal regulations and into the work of the court. Furthermore, he does not possess any kind of judicial function: he is not an attorney for the defense, nor a defendant, nor is he an usher, a warder of the court, or suchlike. His profession as a painter, as also his situation of trust at court, constitutes no "publicly recognized position" and for that very reason is "more influential than the recognized ones" (P 178).

Because Titorelli is a "private person," Josef K. feels free and unconstrained in his presence—not under suspicion, observation, or surveillance. "Answering this question gave him sheer pleasure, particularly since his reply was made vis-à-vis a private person and therefore without any risk on his part" (P 179). He feels himself "not so much at the mercy" of the painter as of the lawyer, and "could have got rid of him without much ado whenever he chose"; this was not possible in the case of Huld the lawyer (P 290-91).

Here, then, help is offered him that does not bind him to the helper. Josef K. and Titorelli face one another as free and equal men in a balanced, reciprocal relationship. For it is not Titorelli alone who gives, helps, and counsels; on the contrary, Josef K. is Titorelli's "benefactor" and his "close acquaintance" (P 291). A genuine relationship of friendship between them is under way. The help that Titorelli offers him does not consist of his "carrying" him or of his writing petitions for him, but rather "that I conduct you in person to him [the judge]. And then of course you'd have to come along" (P 189).

Thus, Titorelli is a central, key figure. He lives in the court and nevertheless maintains himself as a free "private person." He is neither an ignorant outsider like Josef K., nor one of the officials who are "often at their wits end ... because they are constantly compressed into their law, night and day" (P 143); that is, into the legalities that they incessantly enact and record but that they themselves cannot fathom. Hence all the results of their work are constantly being shifted from one authority to another, without its ever being possible to make a final decision —that final decision is of course reserved for the supreme court, inaccessible to everyone.

## B. THE JUDGES AND THEIR PORTRAITS

In consequence of his freedom in the midst of the court, Titorelli has ample opportunity to "paint" the portraits of the judges. However, he does not paint the judges as they actually are or appear to be; what he paints, rather, is their exalted, judicial significance and function, "as the great judges of old were painted" (P 183). Earlier on, it is said of the judge's portrait hanging in the study of Huld the lawyer, a portrait that is "strikingly similar" (P 175) to Titorelli's portrait of the judge, "The portrait dates from his [the judge's] youth; but he can never have had even the slightest resemblance to the portrait, for he is a little man, almost tiny." In reality, too, he never sat upon a "chair of state" but "on a kitchen stool" (P 132). Titorelli expresses himself similarly about the judges whose portraits he has painted. Their dignified judicial attitude, he says, is pure "fiction" (P 176, 132); "I've seen neither the figure nor the chair of state" (P 176)—"You would lose every feeling of respect for judges if you heard the curses with which I welcome him when he climbs over my bed early in the morning ... [to be painted]" (P 188).

It becomes clear from this that the judges in their "reality" are quite ordinary people, for, according to Titorelli's statement, "everybody" in fact belongs to the court (P 181). The painter, however, has the task of giving visible artistic expression to what in everyday life is invisible—the intrinsic nature, function, and significance of the judicature. That is to say, it is he who first imparts to the judges actual awareness of their office and their dignity; it is he who first makes clear the actual meaning of the unconscious life processes that even in reflection are often profoundly perplexing.

Moreover, it is of moment that Titorelli in painting may not alter the so-called real appearance of the judges according to his own individual free will. On the contrary, he must paint them "as the great judges of old were painted." "It is prescribed to each [judge] exactly how he may have himself painted." For this he requires "permission from a superior." And even Titorelli the painter "was . . . informed as to what I am to paint. . . . In that I yield to my clients" (P 176).

This means that the nature and function of the judicature are premised. They are buried deep within the scheme of the universe and cannot be arbitrarily altered; and, what is more, they remain forever a constant. For in all the pictures the judges are delineated in the same attitude, variations occurring only in the form of the body, in the media, and in the "official ranks" (P 175, 183). The painter does not himself possess absolute authority to alter the nature of the judicature or to project it in any form different from what it is and has been from time immemorial. Hence one "cannot use new people" for the "position" of "court painter." On the contrary, this position is "always inherited." "My father was court painter before me. . . . Of course, such various, manifold, and above all secret rules have been laid down for painting the various official ranks, that these rules do not become known at all outside of certain families." Knowledge of how the great judges of old were painted is in the possession of Titorelli alone, and for that reason his position is "unshakable" (P 182-83).

C. KNOWLEDGE OF THE COURT

In other words, Titorelli, in accordance with ancient tradition, has been initiated into the juridical system of the world. By contrast with the "new people," who paint anarchically and arbitrarily, he knows the binding hierarchies and the eternal nature of the "old" judicature. The freedom that is his as a private person must not be confused with the freedom of the outsiders who, like Josef K., without misgivings rebel against a juridical organization that they do not know. That, too, is the very reason why Titorelli can be a confidant of the court.

Here there emerge analogies with previously described trains of thought concerning the "old" nobility and the "new" arbitrariness, references to "The Rejection," "On the Question of Our Laws," "In the Penal Colony," etc. Titorelli's freedom depends upon his superior "secret" knowledge of the "old" determinative law that recurs in its relentlessly "menacing" power in all of Titorelli's pictures; for instance, whenever the judges "arise menacingly" (P 175), or with an "indignant gesture, leap up in order to say something decisive or even to pronounce judgment" (P 131), or when the goddess of justice appears as the goddess of victory and of the hunt. According to the ancient, absolute commandment, as instanced in "In the Penal Colony," justice always has an annihilating character. Here man is always guilty.

This is precisely what Titorelli proclaims to Josef K.: "Never can the court be dissuaded" from the conviction that the accused is always guilty (P 180). "Actual acquittals" exist only in legends. Whereas Huld the lawyer described only the official channels with their impenetrable confusion, and in the course of his description issued "empty admonitions," constantly alternating between "humiliation" and "encouragement" (P 138), despair and consolation, again and again asking for renewed "trust," Titorelli tells the full, annihilating truth without mincing matters.

Josef K. must surrender to the truth. Titorelli knows the ultimate mystery of the court; he knows of the verdict itself, of "acquittal" and "nonacquittal." The lawyer, on the other hand, was merely in the antechamber of knowledge, in the position of one who, in wishing to "defend" his client, roused hope in him of "grace," which in spite of—or because of—the inscrutability of all earthly means of help, could at some time, perhaps, incomprehensibly enter in and carry one forth beyond every verdict. In that way Huld made his clients submissive to him, constantly whipping them up into a state alternating between hope and fear, plunging them into ghastly uncertainty, and even deriding this uncertainty. Huld and his clients are the embodiment of mankind as it wanders astray in the labyrinths of existence, seeking help and hope now here, now there, and in so doing submitting and succumbing to the labyrinth more and more profoundly. Titorelli, on the other hand, bestows clarity of vision; he sets man free.

On the basis of the conversation with him, Josef K. *himself* realizes that every possible procedure on earth "prevents . . . the actual acquittal." " 'You have grasped the core of the matter,' said the painter quickly" (P 195). With that, Josef K. reaches the state of maturity in which he can freely and voluntarily pass sentence upon himself. For "the spirit becomes free only when it ceases to be a prop" (H 48).

This maturing, however, cannot be effected suddenly. Only after his conversation with Titorelli does Josef K., with logical consistency, reach the decision to dismiss Huld the lawyer once and for all (P 200 ff.). In the significant fragment "The House" (P 290 ff.) a further possibility of liberation through Titorelli is disclosed. Clarification of this requires first that the figure of Titorelli be examined with even greater care.

### D. THE ARTIST'S POWER AND HIS OPEN DETACHMENT FROM LIFE

Titorelli sees the annihilating truth. For that very reason he is more human than Huld. He is "a light-minded person, easily won over, lacking in a strict sense of duty; and it was inconceivable that the court had had any dealings with such a person."

Josef K. "knew" that with Titorelli he "would finally win through in everything" (P 294). "He liked best of all to think of Titorelli" (P 293).

Titorelli is gay and cheerful. He "laughs" with the girls, is on "friendly terms" with them, although these little "mischievous brats" are a "real burden" to him and "disturb" him at his work (P 172-73). These girls, exactly like the judges, all want to be painted by him, for they "also belong to the court" (P 181).

The reason why they all urge him to paint them is clear. They stand at the threshold between childhood and sexual maturity, and indeed they present both stages in their extremes: child-likeness to the degree of childishness, even silliness, and sexuality to the degree of abandonment and open shamelessness. "All the faces" of these girls "represented a mixture of childlikeness and depravity" (P 171). Caught in the conflict of these extremes, the girls long for a presentation, a portrayal, a clarification of them-selves. This only the "male" can mediate for them—the painter Titorelli, who himself runs about freely in a nightshirt open at the chest. All the proceedings within the court take place in flagrant openness. Here nothing is any longer concealed as it is in normal social life. Hence, too, the openly sexual scenes; hence, the many half-clothed people in Kafka's novels, who emerge undisguised as if from dreams and rise to the light of day.

The eroticism of these girls, however, must be strictly dif-ferentiated from, say, Leni's. Titorelli has no sexual relations with them: "You probably noticed just now that I don't try to entice them to me" (P 173). "Laughing," he faces the girls in an open and cheerful manner. Later on the statement is made, "Why they push and crowd their way to me. I do not know" (P 173). Thus, he is neither stimulated by them erotically, nor does he understand their emotions and wishes—which are "bothersome" to him. Just as, cursing, he paints the ordinary men who intrude upon him in his bedroom or sit on kitchen stools like judges seated upon chairs of state, painting them on orders from the powers that be, according to prescribed, general rules with which he complies without knowing their meaning and without even trying to fathom it—in the same way he paints these girls also, without any desire to delve into their inner life and emotions.

Thus he confronts the lives of these men, girls, and women—for women, too, are painted by him—with complete detachment. They do not touch him. Hence he gives the impression of a person who is "light-minded, lacking in a strict sense of duty." He is not at the mercy of life, with its emotions, wishes, aspirations. He faces life with complete openness, "frankly, chest bared." He neither battles life nor becomes its slave. Only for that reason can he paint this life. His "art" is possible only on the basis of such frank, relaxed detachment. He lacks even the desire to penetrate to the sublime, ultimate mysteries of the tribunal of life. "What it is like there"—in the "supreme court, completely inaccessible to all of us, we do not know, and, incidentally, we do not even want to know" (P 190).

Well does he know the terrible truth of the court, the impossibility of an actual acquittal. But he accepts it as a datum of reality, just as he accepts the secret rules of his art that he inherited from his father, rules that he did not discover himself. This means therefore that, being completely uninvolved, he paints life as it always has been and will be without any individual nuance or alteration on his part. Moreover, wherever he paints purely "privately," so to speak, uncommissioned by the court, all those differentiations in the form of the "various official ranks," differentiations that are prescribed by the court, fall away. The pictures that he sells, that is to say, those that do not belong to the court, represent merely mute virgin landscapes, heathscapes that are all "exactly alike.'"

Titorelli himself, to be sure, believes that his heath paintings are merely "similar" to one another and not identical, or that the pictures in question are matching "companion-pieces": " 'Here is one that matches this picture,' said the painter. It might have been intended as a companion-piece, but not the slightest difference could be seen between it and the first picture." And even the third picture "was ... exactly the same heathscape" (P 196-97). The painter, living in the midst of the court, can no longer paint anything but eternally same pictures. For "the artist loses his verve to a great extent" through the "uninterrupted relations with the gentlemen of the court," the painter declares resignedly (P 182). Whoever sees into the heart of the inescapable regularity of the inherent laws of all-that-is of this earth, of the utter determinism that allows of no "actual acquittal," can no longer create any individual nuances.

And perhaps even the heathscape painted by him can be interpreted as a symbol of "all" existence upon earth. "It represented two feeble trees standing far apart from one another in dark grass. In the background there was a multicolored sunset" (P 196). Facing the splendor of sunset colors, two beings, separated from one another, standing in the "dark" grass—that is the "court judgment" upon all life: in the face of death, that is inescapable in spite of all splendor of color, each one stands alone in the "dark" grass of the earth. For "what is decisively characteristic of this world is its transitoriness. In this sense the centuries have no advantage over the present moment. The continuity of transitoriness is therefore unable to provide any consolation; that new life blossoms afresh from the ruins of the old, proves the tenacity not so much of life as of death" (H 115).

## E. EROTICISM AND THE COURT

Thereby, too, light is shed on the relationship between the painter and the girls constantly swarming about him. They appear on the scene in troops, are not individuals. Titorelli is able to see the female sex only collectively, in its eternal mixture of naïveté and sexuality.

The leader of the girls is a "hunchback," hence already marked by suffering, but avid for life; she paints "her lips red with the paintbrush" (P 173). "She did not smile ... but looked at K. earnestly with a keen and provocative glance" (P 170).

Josef K., who appears on the scene as a "battling," searching individual who has fallen out of the grip of life, must, therefore, be felt as repellent and ugly by all these girls who are greedily pressuring to be introduced into life—"Please don't paint him! such an ugly person" (P 180). He is a foreign body in the collective course of life.

The contrast between these girls and the other women of the court is drawn in sharp outline. The wife of the court usher wants to be liberated from the collective erotic pressure. Hence she loves Josef K.'s "beautiful eyes," his glance (P67), as she hopefully looks to him for rescue and individualization. Conversely, Josef K. believes that he can gain access to the court through her. Consequently there exists a reciprocal emotional relationship between them: each needs the other, and from this need, of course, arise their mutual misunderstandings.

The "puppetlike" Leni, on the other hand, loves all accused men collectively, for she is already right in the 'heart of the erotic forces of life. It is characteristic of her that what she finds beautiful is not the defendants' glance, not their eyes, but their helplessness. The "proceedings instituted against them" make all accused men handsome and attractive to her (P 221). Whereas the girls still behave unconsciously and in a childlike fashion under the collective erotic pressure—that is, they are not yet able to perceive anyone as an individual partner—Leni is alive to her role as the woman whose craving it is to seduce and whose belief it is that she must perform a succouring act of love by initiating helplessly reflective men into the mysteries of life's erotic immediacy. Deliberately she hurls "a plate against the wall" in order to "get" Josef K. "out" of his dealings with the lawyer and the chief clerk of the court (P 130).

This means that even the defense actions her own lawyer undertakes appear to her to be fundamentally meaningless efforts and nothing but idle talk. And even the entire court, with its endless proceedings, summonses, inquiries, is absurd to her. "They're badgering you," she says to Josef K. (P 244). The only effective way out, from her point of view, is to confess unconditionally and simply submit unquestioningly to the powers of life. Only in this sense does she too represent the court, the inescapable compulsion of life. She feels herself to be, so to speak, the gateway to the court, the mediatrix who brings all the outsiders in. And in this sense she is justifiably an assistant of the lawyer, who also wants to carry all outsiders into court on his shoulders.

Kafka has thus portrayed the erotic varieties of life with marked differentiation. Definite, typical forms of love are evidenced, varying in nature from that of Miss Bürstner to that of Leni and of the girls. However, the entire wealth of human love relationships in their most enigmatical reaches is not fully displayed until *The Castle*. Nevertheless, even in *The Trial* the blatantly erotic images and the form taken by the presentation of the erotism—a form seemingly undifferentiated, poor in nuance, and coarse—all of which initially causes the reader to recoil in shock, should not blind one to the fact that in reality extremely subtle phenomena are being dealt with. By no longer psychologizing; by no longer sounding the entire scale of individually shaded emotions; by no longer venturing into the plexus of slow-starting erotic preludes, camouflages, spiritual developments, etc.; by no longer presenting, subtly and sensitively, the play of love in those countless disguises and in shifting waves of emotion with which the soul and its romancers customarily operate—Kafka, on that very account, penetrates into the great, hidden "laws" of love.

In this context Titorelli's significance likewise grows. Whereas Josef K. has yet to run through the gamut of women, and must become emotionally affected and entangled by love in all its varied possibilities, without in any way gaining greater clarity thereby, Titorelli maintains an unemotional, uninvolved and yet open, dedicated detachment both within life and beyond it. [His dual aspect] can be expressed only in the form of such paradoxical statements as these: He lives and does not live. He detaches himself and at the same time does not detach himself. He is free and yet does not see an acquittal anywhere. He is the confidant of life and yet a private person. He strictly follows the instructions of those who commission his work and is yet lightminded and "lacking in a strict sense of duty." He is standoffish and yet "easy to win over" (P 294). He "torments" Josef K. with his inscrutable reserve, acting "as if he did not know" "what K. was striving for," and yet at the same time he is "friendly" and "ready to grant his request" (P 294). On this account, along with the chaplain, Titorelli becomes the most positive character of the novel. "K. realized that here, if anywhere, the breakthrough was possible" (P 294).

### F. BREAKTHROUGH AND REBIRTH

This breakthrough is accomplished as follows. In his association with Titorelli, Josef K. acquires a similarly paradoxical attitude, Josef K. "finally ... was able to torment Titorelli, for his part, and quite well too," by means of guarded reserve (P 291); and on the other hand he "fawned upon him in every way" (P 294). His requests are earnest: "He persisted in his request and went so far as to caress Titorelli's cheeks with both hands." And yet "he did not exert himself overmuch; he was almost languorous, he prolonged the situation through a craving for pleasure, he was certain of success" (P 294).

Thus Josef K. achieves a dedicated detachment similar to Titorelli's. His struggle loses the subjective blindness, the dogged vehemence, and the foolish directness of his previous phases. He is more prudent now as he confronts himself and his request, although he clings persistently to this request. Indeed, he feels that this request could be granted only through "languor," only through playful, effortless ease, not through any effort. This ease itself, it alone, was already certainty of success. "How simple it was to outwit the court!" (P 294).

This ease, however, should not blind one to the immensity of terror that must be overcome by it. Following immediately upon Josef K.'s "realization" of the "breakthrough" is the appalling statement, "He did not let himself be diverted by Titorelli's shameless smile which the latter, with head raised, directed into the void" (P 294).

Titorelli's detachment is the detachment of one who has laid aside everything human. Perceiving the truth, painting monotonously the eternally same court, standing beyond all human emotions, he "smiles" "shamelessly" into "the void." He "smiles" = he is conversant with the comedy of existence. Titorelli's shameless smile into the void—that is the true definition of Kafka's reputed "religious humour."[9] Behind it are heard "Hell's paroxysms of laughter" over which "the dear Lord weeps bitterly."[10]

Titorelli's "shamelessness" is the exact opposite of that unthinkable "shame" felt by the girl who sacrifices herself to no avail in "The Conscription of Troops," the exact opposite of that shame that "outlives" Josef K., who, at the end of his trial, is slaughtered like a "dog" in a senseless comedy.

Only by such shame can man who has turned dog still be rescued. Only in such shame does human feeling yet remain preserved. It can still fill "empty space," warm with human sentiments a world turned into an icy wasteland, even though it can express nothing more than the comfortless feeling of the uselessness and weakness of all human existence.

Titorelli's shameless smile, however, is itself only emptiness. In it there is no longer any feeling, any indignation, any grief, any despair. Here, unmoved and its equal in power, man sustains the void. Here alone is he truly the equal of the "court" of this world.

Josef K., however, does not let himself be "diverted" by Titorelli's shameless smile into the void. He holds his ground against him. For Titorelli is not the "young nobleman" of "The Conscription of Troops." Titorelli still represents the "old" law. He is like the colonel in "The Rejection," but at the same time a private person to an even higher degree. Because Josef K., persisting in his request, going so far as to caress Titorelli's cheeks, resolutely withstands Titorelli's rejecting, shameless smile, Titorelli can no longer offer resistance. "As if he were obeying a law of nature, Titorelli finally bent down toward him; a slow, friendly closing of his eyes indicated that he was ready to grant the request; he gave his hand to K. with a firm pressure" (P 294).

A most remarkable possibility becomes manifest here. The determinism and the monotony in which Titorelli lives, as he paints or smiles into the void, are converted into help just at the time when Josef K. is enduring this very monotony and trying to overcome it. As if under the compulsion of a natural law,

Titorelli *must* now grant Josef K.'s request. For this request implied an extreme in itself: the bursting asunder of every determinism, the "breakthrough." This bursting asunder now itself becomes law. Whoever dares the utmost and overcomes emptiness, forces help into being. Liberation becomes the command of the court itself.

Titorelli ... clasped K. and drew him along with him as he went. Instantly they were in the courthouse and were speeding over the stairways, not only upward, but up and down, without the slightest expenditure of effort, buoyantly like a light craft over the water. And as K. noticed his feet, reaching the conclusion that this beautiful mode of motion could not be related to his hitherto mediocre life, that very instant, above his bowed head, the transformation took place. The light that until now had come from behind them shifted and suddenly streamed, dazzling, from in front of them. (P 294-95)

Josef K. is liberated, lifted out of his hitherto mediocre life. Transformed, he is in a higher form of existence. Light strikes him from in front. He *sees*. This glimpse lasts only for the twinkling of an eye: it cannot last longer. But it has changed him as a person completely: Titorelli " ... turned him around. Again K. was in the corridor of the courthouse, but everything was quieter and simpler. There were no conspicuous details. K. took in everything at a glance, disengaged himself from Titorelli, and went his way" (P 295).

Josef K. now possesses perspective; " ... he took in everything at a glance." The confusing labyrinths of the courthouse of the world have become comprehensible. Josef K. becomes independent. He "went his way," "disengaged himself from Titorelli."

He is reborn, he has entered a new life; this is symbolized by his change of clothes—in Kafka clothes always express a definite spiritual form of existence.

Today K. wore a new, long, dark garb; it was comfortingly warm and heavy. He knew what had happened to him, but he was so happy about it that he did not yet want to admit it to himself. In a corner of a corridor, in one wall of which there were large

windows standing open, he found his former clothes in a pile—
the black jacket, the pinstriped trousers, and on top of those the
shirt with outstretched, fluttering sleeves. (P 295)

From this passage, light is shed in retrospect upon Josef K.'s
putting on different clothes early on, at the time of the arrest,
when the warders order him to change. At that time he balked
at doing this. Now at last he has truly found a "new" garb.


## Self-sentence as Redemption

However, Kafka discarded this scene of rebirth. Furthermore,
the scene occurs as a dream that Josef K. has while he is asleep
on a "sofa" in his office at the bank. Only as a dream could the
scene be given form, since the bursting asunder of our mediocre
existence on earth can be made understandable only by means
of a visionary illustration. Yet even this dream was eliminated
by Kafka. Why?

The answer is given by another dream of Josef K.'s, one that
was not stricken out by Kafka, but that, on the contrary, was
actually published by him. This piece, "A Dream," and the so-
called parable "Before the Law" are the only parts of the novel
that Kafka in his lifetime considered ready for press. The two
segments appeared in the collection *A Country Doctor* and contain the spiritual kernel of *The Trial*.

In this dream, too, a "redemption" is being delineated. It
takes place when the name Josef K. appears on a gravestone
and Josef K. himself lies down voluntarily in his grave. "The
first small stroke" that the artist made in writing Josef K.'s
name "was a deliverance for K." As "up above, his name, in
mighty flourishes, raced across the stone," Josef K., "filled with
delight at the sight of this, awoke" (E 183).

This dream is the pure visionary equivalent of the conclusion
of the novel: the sentence Josef K. passes on himself. The
dream of rebirth had to be dropped, since there would have had
to be, corresponding to it, a regenerated life on earth, a life that

could not be given form [in the novel]. Inclusion of the dream
would have gone against Kafka's conviction that in phenomenal
existence on earth every truth is perverted to a lie.

Truth and redemption become visible only in death, at the
sight of the self upon the gravestone.


### Abortive Death

However, even such a redeeming death must remain a vision.
Even phenomenal death on earth is no true death. "Our deliverance is death, but not this one." "The lament at the deathbed
is actually a lament that dying in its true sense did not take place
there. Still must we content ourselves with this mode of dying.
... Still do we play the play.... The development of mankind
—a growing in the strength to die" (H 122-23).

Josef K.'s actual death is a wretched "play" put on by puppetlike "tenors" and "supernumerary actors" who glisten with disgusting cleanliness. Only questions accompany the end:

Like a sudden blaze of light, the casements of a window flashed
open there; a human being, faint and tenuous in the distance and
at that elevation, suddenly leaned far forward and stretched his
arms even farther out. Who was it? A friend? A good person?
Someone who was concerned? Someone who wanted to help?
Was it a single individual? Was it everybody? (P 271-72)

The questions of the dying man are directed at every "single
individual" and at "everybody." Will the meaning of this death
be understood some day by mankind? Will that "high court, to
which he had never gained entrance," some day appear?

Kafka's incorruptible sense of truth forbade any other ending.

Josef K. has gained the knowledge that it is his "duty" to
execute justice upon himself. That is the utmost that can be
achieved on earth.

### CHAPTER VII

# The Human Cosmos:
# The Novel *The Castle*

The battle between free self-determination and the alleged forces of life and consciousness, intrinsic to the terrestrial world organization, acquires a new accent in *The Castle*. Whereas in *The Trial* the question of absolute justification was central to the novel and, with logical consistency, led to the progressive annihilation of all the specific bases of life and of profession, and finally to the execution of sentence on the self, conversely, in *The Castle*, the problem at issue is whether and how it is possible, within the given forces of existence, to survive as a concrete individual and at the same time exist freely.

Accordingly, the situations of the heroes of both novels are characterized at the outset as opposed to one another. At the beginning of *The Trial* Josef K. is in a secure, bourgeois, respected professional position which is then progressively undermined. In *The Castle*, on the other hand, K. is a "stranger" without a residence permit and without a definitive, unequivocally formulated right to practice his profession of land surveyor. He has left "wife and child" (S 14), has made great "sacrifices" in order "to get away from home," has undertaken a "long, difficult journey," is now "completely without means," and sees no possibility of "finding some other suitable position at home" (S 102). Thus from the very beginning he leads an existence that lacks any foundation in society.

As a result of this there emerges his dual, only seemingly self-contradictory "struggle."


## *K.'s "Struggle" between Freedom and Obligation*

On the one hand, K. wants to obtain a footing on earth and find shelter and employment; this he can do only by subjecting himself to obligations. On the other, he wants to assert his free self-determination: "I am afraid, too, that life up there in the castle would not appeal to me. I want to be free always" (S 15). He is constantly struggling to reach the castle, and at the same time he is battling for his independence from the castle and indeed even battling against the castle.

His very decision to abandon his former security in society and travel to the castle as a land surveyor is ambiguous.

The letter [Klamm's], moreover, did not conceal the fact that, should it come to hostilities, K. had had the temerity to take the initiative; there was finesse in the wording, and only an uneasy conscience—an uneasy one, not a bad one—could perceive it: it was in the three words "as you know," with reference to his being employed. K. had reported for duty, and ever since then he had known, as was stated in the letter, that he had been taken on. (S 38-39)

His very reporting for duty and his being taken on—to be sure, only apparently so—in the seignorial service at the castle are designated here as temerity on his part, as a result of his free decision to "take the initiative" in a battle against the authorities. He himself has chosen foundationlessness in society so that he may independently take up his stand against the totality of life's involvements, and be able to challenge them to combat. It is expressly stated that he fought "of his own volition, for he was the attacker" (S 80).

Max Brod's widely disseminated view that K. "is motivated not by longing for mankind's final goals and supreme knowledge, but by the need for the most primitive basic requirements of life: becoming deeply rooted in one's profession and home, being integrated into the community" (S 482), is false. K. gave up those very ancient securities of society, "wife and child," etc., for his struggle. And in the novel it is said of this struggle that he had to "gather all his strength in order not to be concerned about anything else, not about food, lodgings, the village authorities, not even about Frieda ... the succession of life's perpetual minor afflictions—that was nothing by comparison with what K. was striving after, and he had not come here to live his life respected and at peace" (S 203).

Immediately, from the very beginning of the novel, K. is aware of his self-willed battle against the world authorities: "K. sat up and took notice. Well, then, the castle had appointed him land surveyor. That ... indicated that everything one needed to know about him was known in the castle, that their relative strengths had been gauged, and that battle was being entered with a smile" (S 13). At the same time, of course, K. knows that he is dealing with a "powerful" opponent who, being already familiar with K.'s free decision to do battle, and perceiving what is behind that decision, includes K. in his infinite records and in his infinite controls of consciousness; because everything that any human being thinks and wills is immediately codetermined and cothought by these all-embracing control systems, so that, if one considers these authorities, there can strictly speaking be no thinking, no acting, no struggling at all that is free.

Hence too, conversely, this free decision of K.'s appears to him elsewhere as nothing less than a lure on the part of the castle, as an offer from the officials, which he has accepted injuriously to himself. He says that he was "lured here [by the officials] for an evil purpose" (S 101). Accordingly, even his calling as a land surveyor is most ambiguous. K. feels that his ostensible appointment by the castle as a land surveyor is actually a sign that this "employment" of his is considered an independent "battle" against the castle, and that would mean, of course, against the castle employers as well. Employment turns into rebellion against employment. On the other hand, he maintains that the authorities have lured him to this employment; thus they have themselves tried to force him, as it were, to do battle against them. The paradox of such statements becomes comprehensible only if one pursues the meaning of this land surveying.

## Land Surveying as a Revolutionary Act

The village overseer explains to K., "We do not need any land surveyor.... The boundaries of our little farms are marked off, everything is properly recorded. There is hardly ever a change of ownership, and minor disputes over boundaries we settle ourselves" (S 82-83).

Land surveying would therefore mean examining and checking the land and ownership conditions currently prevailing. This would be a revolutionary act. And in fact this is what the village understands by land surveying. Many years ago, when the overseer, upon receipt of an order from the castle authorities that a land surveyor be summoned, had replied that the village did not need one, and when Sordini the official, to whom the file on the incident had erroneously been passed on without the letter of reply, had the matter thoroughly investigated through daily "recorded interrogations of respected members of the community," it turned out that, although the majority of the village decided against engaging a land surveyor, "several" became "suspicious" nevertheless.

"The question of land surveying is one that a farmer takes to heart; the farmers suspected secret arrangements and injustices of one sort or another; moreover, they found a leader, and Sordini could not avoid gaining the conviction from their statements that, if I [the overseer] had brought the matter up in the municipal council, not everybody would have been against the appointment of a land surveyor.... In the course of this a certain Brunswick made himself particularly conspicuous ... he is probably not a bad man, but stupid, with wild ideas ... a shouter ... in all this time the matter has not quieted down, partly because of the conscientiousness of Sordini who, by means of the most scrupulous inquiries, tried to ascertain the motives of the majority as well as of the opposition, partly because of the stupidity and ambition of Brunswick who has various personal connections with the authorities whom he was always stirring up anew with fresh fabrications of his imagination." (S 92-94)

The appointment of a land surveyor is thus demanded by the opposition itself, which is dissatisfied with the prevailing social order in the village. In the nature of land surveying there exists a revolutionary element. Accordingly, K. later on thinks of obtaining "Brunswick's resources of power" in his struggle, and of finding an ally in him, for Brunswick "had been ... the leader of those who, albeit for political reasons, had demanded the appointment of a land surveyor" (S 199).

The limitation, "albeit for political reasons," reveals, it is true, the gulf between K. and Brunswick. Brunswick happens to be one of the two men who throw K. out of the first farmhouse he enters as he seeks help. Furthermore, it was Brunswick who seized the considerable property of the Barnabas family, originally highly respected but now segregated from the village and scorned by it; and it is this family that to begin with is the only family in the village to offer K. shelter and a night's lodging. To Brunswick and his opposition party, land surveying signifies only change of ownership. K.'s universal struggle against the collective authorities can impress him only as pointless, incomprehensible, or even menacing; similarly, Amalia's amazing and total opposition to the castle presents merely a welcome opportunity for him to enrich himself with her family's property, a family in whose cobbler's workshop he had originally been hired as a "journeyman," and whose house and flourishing workshop he now takes over unscrupulously after having "given notice" to Amalia's father; for he was "a shrewd fellow who knew how to take advantage of the moment" (S 268); he rose in the social scale and even now continues to entertain favorable "personal connections" with the castle—which clearly maintains a neutral attitude toward the political power struggles in the village, attempting to do justice to both parties, the majority and the opposition.

But the castle maintains a neutral attitude even toward K. The authorities regard this very struggle of K.'s against them as his function, as the meaningful and necessary business of a land surveyor, as appropriate to the nature of a truly free person, as part of his life "work." K., having deprived Klamm the official of Frieda his mistress, having intended actually to accost him in front of his sleigh at the Herrenhof Inn, having prevented him for hours from using the sleigh, and having resisted the protocol and interrogation of Momus, Klamm's village secretary—then, of all times, he receives from this very Klamm a letter stating: "The work that you have done so far in land surveying meets with my approval.... Do not relax your efforts! Keep up the good work to the very end. Any interruption would make me very angry. As for the rest, be assured, the question of remuneration will be decided in the near future" (S 160).

Naturally, K. considers this to be a "misunderstanding": "The gentleman is misinformed. I am really not doing any surveying" (S 160-61). K. has no idea that these very struggles of his against Klamm, as well as his efforts to get through to Klamm and into the castle, are already a part of his work as land surveyor. They are attempts to demarcate the land on which man exists, to gather experience, to gain knowledge, knowledge in the most varied areas, social, erotic, moral, etc. How diverse and complicated this land-surveying activity of he is, to what profundities of human life reality it leads—this will necessarily concern us later on.

We are here primarily concerned with the view that this activity of land surveying is in itself ambiguous. It is a battle that K. wages to speak "freely before a mighty man" (S 71), before Klamm, and to demand of the mighty rulers who are always "invisible" his "right" to fight "for something very much alive close at hand ... for himself" (S 80). And it is at the same time K's attempt to obtain a conclusive, definitive residence permit;

that is, to obtain a concrete phenomenal existence on earth, even though it means he must submit to the all-powerful officials. For instance, when K. replies to Klamm's letter he requests permission for a personal interview with him, accepting from the start every condition that could possibly be attached to such permission, and subjecting himself to every limitation as to time; he sees himself compelled to make such a request because all intermediaries have so far failed him completely:

"...in proof of this he cites the fact that to the present moment he has done no surveying whatsoever and, according to the information forthcoming from the overseer of the community, he never will do any; with desperate embarrassment did he therefore read the last letter of the director [Klamm]; only calling on the director personally can be of any help here." (S 164)

In the castle's life powers which universally govern everything, K. as a finite human being must see something that both hinders his free, concrete existence and at the same time renders such an existence possible; he must combat these forces as well as submit to them: this is the source and explanation of all the seeming self-contradictions and even absurdities of this novel.

What is more, it is in the very nature of this struggle that K. cannot possibly realize that his struggle is already land surveying. For he must carry on this battle in an unheard-of situation. Every experience that he gathers, every position that he assumes must in such a universal struggle turn out to be brittle, untenable, provisional, forcing him in turn to seek other, new positions in endless succession. Since he cannot, as a finite human being, survey the infinity of possibilities of existence, and since, on the other hand, he is compelled to make such a survey—if a true, valid, "free" position is to be achieved—his own activity must to him appear as a nothingness; he cannot see it and evaluate it as actual land surveying, and, indeed, may not regard it as such at all. The "land" that he surveys must remain hidden from him, for it cannot be measurable land with definite boundaries. And his most urgent craving must be to gain "in person" a direct, "free" glimpse of that most mysterious, never-attain-able life potency incorporated in Klamm, and to deal with it face-to-face, in order to be able to attain to final clarity about the essence, meaning, and compass of his own human existence.

Freedom in the presence of this life power and submission to it are here not mutually exclusive. They are merely two necessary sides of the *one* battle that K. wages: his struggle to be free within the all-determining life powers.

## The Ambiguous Relation between K. and the Village

The foregoing clarifies, too, the peculiar behavior of the village inhabitants toward K. The farmers of the village all have "veritably tortured faces—the skull looked as if it had been smashed flat on top, and as if the facial features had taken form during the pain occasioned by the blows" (S 35). They are the victims of the ruling powers. For that very reason they look hopefully to K., the land surveyor, for help and liberation, but cannot express this wish of theirs at all, since they are completely unfree and apathetic, trapped in their dead-end existence, and since the desire for freedom can be felt by them only dimly and ineffably. They are incessantly "approaching" K., attempt "to run after him always," and one of them says, " 'There is always something new to hear,' and he licked his lips, as if what was new were food" (S 39).

From a land surveyor something "new" is to be expected—inspection and modification of unjust and rigidified property and ownership conditions; for, as the overseer of the community said, "The question of land surveying is one that a farmer takes to heart, the farmers suspected secret arrangements and injustices of one sort or another." But perhaps they catch the scent of even more, of "food," that unattainable "nourishment" to which Kafka's works testify again and again.

Hence the farmers "stared" at K. as if hypnotized, and even "pursue" him importunately. K., however, cannot comprehend them: "Perhaps they really did want something from him and were simply unable to express it" (S 40). The goal that they dimly seek cannot be formulated. Moreover, so rigorously are they held captive by their work that they grow incapable of voicing their own hopes; to such a degree is their will, their originally free nature "smashed flat." Indeed, they feel a downright fear of K., and the very fact that the castle telephonically confirms his position as land surveyor, causes him to take on an uncanny and powerful aspect in their eyes. "They all crowded their way out, with their faces averted, perhaps in order not to be recognized by him the next day" (S 14).

These farmers have fallen so deeply under the spell of lifelong habits and existing social patterns, seemingly taken for granted, that they can no longer express their own wishes; they only dully sense an impulse toward what is new, and they feel downright fear of someone who is "strange" and is at the same time in the "employ" of the omnipotent castle authorities.

This grows quite evident in the case of Gerstäcker the wagoner who takes K., helplessly wading through the snow, and drives him in his sledge to the Inn at the Bridge. Gerstäcker, too, has a "stooped figure, maltreated, as it were" (S 28), is "visibly ill" (S 27), etc. He, too, is afraid of K., his behavior giving the impression that he is making a "very selfish, anxious, almost punctilious effort to remove K. from in front of his house" (S 27). He drives K. without charge to the Inn, because K. is a "land surveyor" and belongs "to the castle" (S 26). K. asks Gerstäcker whether he is driving him "on his own responsibility" and whether he might be punished on that account. Gerstäcker gives him no answer. At that K. hurls a snowball directly at his ear, in the belief that with this cruel maneuver he might be able to wake him up, so to speak; but then he feels compassion for this humbled figure of a man. Gerstäcker, however, submits to everything patiently, offering no defense, and simply asks "uncomprehendingly," "What do you want?" (S 28).

Like all the farmers, Gerstäcker has become a spineless, indeed "maltreated" object of the ruling life powers. So far as concepts like "one's own responsibility" are concerned, he is completely "uncomprehending." There is no freedom in the village. But an intimation of freedom lives in everyone. It is precisely this in

K. that fascinates and at the same time frightens the farmers.
Even Gerstäcker has an inkling of K.'s significance. In the final
portions of the extant fragments of the novel he offers K.
help and even shelter at his home, for, so he says, "Only now, as I
see you in your predicament, you, a land surveyor, an educated
man ... come down in the world, so that it goes to one's heart
... only now has what my mother once said come to mind:
one should not let this man go to rack and ruin." At the same
time he hopes that through K. he will be able to "accomplish"
something for himself with Erlanger, Klamm's secretary (S 495-
96).

Furthermore, almost all the other village inhabitants of significance to K. show this kind of ambiguous attitude toward
him. Frieda wants to be liberated through K. from Klamm's
influence, and yet at the same time she gravitates toward Klamm
again. Pepi designates K. as a "rescuer of maidens" and a "hero"
(S 381), and tries to bind him to her again, to confine him to her
"maids' room" for months. The youngster Hans Brunswick looks
down on K. just as a "teacher" (S 190), an "energetic, intelligent,
far-seeing man" (S 191), looks down upon a "younger" person "whose future extends further than his own, the future of a
little lad" (S 201). And at the same time he looks to K. not
only for help for his mother but also for a fabulous, "noble
development." Just as in a fairy tale an insignificant, ill-clad
creature suddenly soars to the role of a rescuing prince, a liberating hero, so too will K. one day rise from his present "low"
and "repellent" position and "eclipse everyone" (S 201).

Similarly, Barnabas and Olga are on the one hand far superior
to K.: with swift, sure steps they carry K. through the snow
where he bids fair to founder helplessly, and Barnabas seems to
him like a higher being from a bright, free realm. At the same
time, however, both, excluded from the village, are in reality in
a desperate, indeed hopeless position, and look to K. for their
rescue and liberation. And even Amalia, who appears to turn
away from K. haughtily and coldly, awaits his visit with agitation and sinks "in a faint" after K. has left the house (S 472).

Even Gardena, the landlady of the Inn at the Bridge, that

"powerful" figure, K.'s enemy, who designates him disparagingly as a wretched "blindworm," as a person who is "with regard to the conditions here, terribly ignorant" (S 78), even she becomes literally ill and weak because of K. (S 104 ff.), when, on leaving her, determined to get through on his own to Klamm the "eagle," he calls out to her, "But surely you aren't afraid for Klamm, are you?" (S 79). The overseer of the village offers K. a position as school janitor through fear that K. might "do something rash on his own" (S 124), etc.

K.'s position in the village is thus by no means so weak as it might appear to be upon superficial reading. It is true that he does not belong anywhere, is turned away almost on all sides, and treated like a cipher, an insignificant and ignorant "stranger"; but it is this very position, foundationless, fixated nowhere, that is also his strength. His will to be "free always" is the bastion from which he wages his battle; it is what awakens hope and fear in the village. It establishes his exceptional position and even his superiority over the officials who cannot endure the sight of him and whom he, through his sheer presence as it were, keeps pinned to their rooms and dominates (S 373-74).

His will to be "free always" is also, of course, the basis of his inferiority to both the village and the castle. For this freedom of his is also an empty, untenable freedom with which one cannot live alone:

...it then seemed to K. as if all ties with him had been severed, and as if he were now truly freer than ever before...as if he had won this freedom for himself in a battle such as almost no one else could wage, and it seemed to him as if no one had the right to touch him or to drive him away, or even so much as to address him; however—and this conviction was at least equally strong—it was also as if, simultaneously, there were nothing more meaningless, nothing more hopeless than this freedom, this waiting, this inviolability. (S 145)

Accordingly, not only is the behavior of the villagers toward K. self-contradictory, but also, by the same token, is K.'s behavior toward them. He complains about the "ejection" that falls to his lot everywhere (S 101). On the other hand, he would rather suffer such ejection than be obligated, say, as a result of accepting the offer of the Barnabas family to stay the night with them. When K. is clearly told in Lasemann's house, "You cannot remain here ... we have no use for guests," he is glad of the frank words. "He moved about more freely ... he was also, incidentally, physically the biggest man in the room" (S 23). By contrast, when he comes to the hospitable Barnabas family the following thoughts go through his head:

> The people of the village who sent him away or who were afraid of him seemed less dangerous to him, for fundamentally they merely referred him to himself and helped him to keep all his strength gathered; such ostensible helpers, however, who ... took him to their families, distracted him, whether they intended to or not, and served to destroy his strength. A shout from the family table, inviting him over, he took no notice of at all. (S 47)

On the other hand, however, he feels himself drawn to the Barnabas family again, since he senses and later also clearly recognizes that they are engaged in a battle "similar" to his own (S 235).

## *"Worker Existence" and Free Existence*

Thus K. clearly sees that both forms of human existence, obligation and freedom, endanger his struggle and can make it impossible for him to lead an existence worthy of a human being.

The first possibility is "the worker existence." It can give him support and security in his struggle.

> Only as a village worker, as far removed as possible from the rulers of the castle, was he in a position to accomplish anything in the castle; these people in the village, no matter how distrustful they were of him, would begin to talk as soon as he had become, if not their friend, at any rate their fellow citizen; and once he was indistinguishable from Gerstäcker or Lasemann ... then all avenues would surely be revealed to him at one stroke. (S 38)

Through close ties to the community, he thinks, the purpose and meaning of human life, work, and existence will dawn upon him; as a "fellow citizen" he can penetrate into the mysteries of the life powers represented in the castle, acquire a sure and secure position on earth, and gain both experience and that "knowledge" which the worldly wise, capable, powerful landlady so misses in him.

But K. knows, too, the enslaving effect of the human community in itself: " ... the pressure exercised by the disheartening environment, by the inurement to disappointment, the pressure of the imperceptible influences of every moment—these he did indeed fear" (S 38).

It is that pressure of inurement to which fundamentally every human being succumbs: the slowly progressive apathy toward every absolute questioning, the routine of everyday life, the resignation to the given, the mechanical affirmation of what is and of what is lived, the imperceptible dulling with reference to the crucial demands of the present, the lack of awareness of the injustice that is constantly being inflicted everywhere and that is reflected also in the faces of the farmers and in their brutish instinctual life, injustice noticed by none of the villagers, but accepted—even by the landlady who is supposedly so "knowing," and by Momus, Klamm's village secretary—as a "customary, natural phenomenon," and accepted without condemnation, while the two of them, "leaning back into the mass of people," surrender to the "current" (S 449).

It is precisely those seemingly worldly wise people, so excellently informed about all concrete existence, that unsuspectingly and unhesitatingly have become slaves to what is "customary" for the "mass" community. The knowing are in truth the ignorant. K.'s criticism of such a community and of such expertise in efficient living reveals the cowardice of a world that surrenders to every "current" in order to be able to live "He who is ignorant ... dares more ... too," he says to the landlady (S 79).

However, the opposite position, freedom, is also dangerous

and impedes the struggle. The authorities, by never intervening directly but by letting K. "slip through everywhere" and permitting him every liberty, "spoiled and weakened" him, and

...eliminated...struggle altogether and displaced him instead into private, unofficial life, completely unsurveyable, bleak, foreign. In this manner, if he were not always on the alert, it could well happen that one day...hoodwinked by the seeming favor shown him, he would conduct his other life so incautiously that he would collapse here.... And what was it actually, that other life here? Nowhere had K. yet seen office and life so interwoven as here—so much so that at times it might seem that office and life had changed places. What was the significance, for example, of the merely formal power that Klamm had until now exercised over K.'s position, compared with the power that Klamm had in reality within K.'s bedroom? (S 81)

Thus, at the very time when man withdraws into his free private life, his intimate, personal love life, he subjects himself to the power of Klamm who, even in his apparent loss of Frieda, is triumphant and delivers the struggling man to the anonymous powers and laws of life that he [Klamm] represents. In the semblance of freedom and a private sphere of life, withdrawn from public community life, there too the universal system of life's natural laws prevails; there too the most intrinsic "self" of man, that self for which K. is expressly fighting, perishes. Freedom and obligation are entangled with one another to such an extent that a clear, unambiguous position cannot be achieved at all.

With this the central problem of the novel is formulated: How is it possible to assert the free "self" in the midst of the all-inclusive and therefore ultimately collective life powers and instinctual forces that encompass us?

This question leads to the focal point of the love problems that dominate the novel, and thereby at the same time to the focal point of what are probably the most remarkable and enigmatic developments in the novel: the roles of Klamm and of Sortini; the extended, much-discussed Amalia episode; in general, the varied function and significance of the strange castle authorities in their totality.

## The Proteus Nature of Klamm the Official

Let us first ask: Who or what is Klamm? For Klamm is at the point of intersection in the encounters and discussions between K., on the one hand, and Frieda, the landlady of the Inn at the Bridge, and Pepi, on the other. Moreover, he is that functionary to whom K. is officially assigned, who forwards his messages to K. by way of Barnabas, and who requests K.'s interrogation by his village secretary Momus, or by his secretary Erlanger. Although K.'s assistants are assigned to him by Galater the official, Galater is acting only in his official capacity as Klamm's representative (S 309).

Of Klamm the official it is stated:

"He is said to look quite different when he enters the village, and different when he leaves it, different before he has drunk beer, different afterward, different while he is awake, different while he is sleeping, different when alone, different when in conversation, and—understandably, in these circumstances—almost entirely different up there in the castle. And even within the village itself, rather marked differences have been reported: differences in height, carriage, stoutness, beard.... Well, naturally, none of these differences have their origin in any magic, but are very understandable; they arise through the mood of the moment, the degree of excitement, the particular state of hope or despair, among the countless possible gradations, in which the observer finds himself—and he, moreover, is allowed to see Klamm only momentarily as a rule." (S 234-35)

Accordingly, Klamm is therefore not an unambiguously identifiable person, but a constantly changing being, altering according to the frame of mind of the people who see him. People's hopes, despairs, emotions, etc., alter him continuously. Consequently he represents a sphere that is forever encircled by all people in their emotional life and that gains for each a different shade of meaning or purpose, dependent upon the mood in which the person happens to be. He may really be seen only "momentarily," and then he disappears from one's sight again. These rare moments, living on in people's memory as high points in their lives, are for them indelible; of such nature are the three encounters that the landlady of the Inn at the Bridge was permitted to have with him.

In one respect only does Klamm remain ever the same—in his "clothes." "Only in regard to his clothes are the reports fortunately consistent: he always wears the same clothes, a black frock coat with long skirts" (S 235). In spite of all changes he thus possesses a definite, uniform function that is uniformly seen by all onlookers, a function which is represented in his "clothes," the token of his officialdom. In Kafka dress is always the symbol of a definite level of existence within the total cosmos or within the spiritual, intellectual, and vital development of the individual human being. This will become clear in the significance that clothing assumes for Pepi and Frieda, as well as for Barnabas, Amalia, the two landladies, etc.

Klamm's "black frock coat with long skirts" is strikingly reminiscent of the "long, dark garb" that Josef K. in *The Trial* wears after his liberating rebirth and that envelops him, "comfortingly warm and heavy"; but it is also reminiscent of the "black jacket"—without long skirts, though—that he once wore in his "mediocre life." It is from Klamm that the landlady of the Inn at the Bridge receives a beautiful "shawl" that frees her of "all suffering" whenever she wraps herself up in it completely (S 106, 108).

From that, one could conclude that Klamm encompasses a lower life as well as a higher one, but certainly what this lower or higher life is in the first place would remain completely problematical. Moreover, the transfer of images from one novel of Kafka's to another may rouse justifiable misgivings. Furthermore, for the time, the question as to why Klamm's clothes are "black" cannot be answered. However, several considerations can at this stage be introduced.

## The Death Proneness of the Authorities:
## Count Westwest and the Castle Architecture

In *The Trial* the "blackness" of Josef K.'s dress and of the court officials' clothing alluded to the death proneness of the entire earthly world apparatus. Does anything similar present itself in *The Castle*?

One is led to conjecture something of the sort, through the figure of Count "Westwest," owner of the entire castle. The name points to the domain of death but is likewise iridescent with ambiguity. It could designate the total end, death's domain behind the sunset; but it could also designate the Hereafter beyond death, the victory over death. The gloomy and, even more than that, nastily macabre or even hellishly obscene aspect, it is true, seems to predominate, as for example when the teacher, frightened at K.'s mentioning the count, calls out to K. in French, "Bear in mind that you are in the presence of innocent children" (S 19).

Even the characterization of the castle buildings themselves emphasizes this negative view. K. compares the "church steeple" of his native village with the castle tower and observes that this church steeple, "tapering" toward the top, had a loftier purpose than the flat, "uniform cylinder" of the castle tower, the "small windows" of which, flashing in the sun, have "something insane" about them. "It was as if a melancholy inmate of the house ... had burst through the roof and risen up to exhibit himself to the world" (S 18).

Although, as we have already pointed out, this castle tower, with its combination of dilapidation and childlike design, may represent a purpose-free sphere, and, although the castle rises "light and free on high" (S 17), it is still a matter of a sketch "by the hand of an anxious or slovenly child," and lightness and freedom prove to be merely an impression from afar, an impression that, upon one's coming closer, disappears and turns into "disappointment." The village church near the castle, furthermore, is merely a "barnlike" little chapel that has been enlarged (S 18).

Obviously, therefore, the religious, transcendent aspect is the very one that is banished from this castle and village, or at least sharply restricted. It is a matter of a world resonating in itself, and, although this world has the power to promise vitality, child-likeness, freedom, joyfulness, etc., it ultimately flows into the monotony of an ever-unchanging life music that is bound to death: for instance, when the myriad voices of the officials, singing afar in a childlike manner, are compressed into a single, menacing tone; or in Klamm's case into "muteness" and "screams" (S 157); or when the "joyously pulsating" tone of the bell rings out from the castle and "made his heart throb, as if he were threatened—for painful, too, was the tone—with the fulfillment of what he falteringly longed for," and that ringing tone soon dies away and is replaced by "the faint, monotonous sound of a little bell" (S 27-28), thereby creating a musical counterpart to the architectonic "uniformity" of the castle-tower "cylinder."

Thus, to interpret the castle as the castle of "grace," as Max Brod in the epilogue to his first edition (S 484) attempts to do (and many interpreters along with him),[1] does not seem feasible unless all the signs of negative, deadly monotony in the castle are interpreted as reversals occasioned by blindness on the part of K. or the villagers, and having nothing to do with the nature of this grace-bestowing, religious castle. But why must the teacher protect the children from the name Westwest if this Westwest is God, the center of all grace? Kafka cannot be intensifying the blindness of the people to such an extent that in their imagination God is identified with an obscene sphere from which innocent children must be guarded!

In order to gain complete clarity in this matter, all statements and images of the novel must as far as possible be examined in their reciprocal connections.

Let us return to Klamm, and for the time let us leave open the question of the meaning of his suit which always stays black for everyone, a question that can be adequately answered only when his role and its significance reveal themselves.

### Klamm as Superpersonal Love Power

Klamm's Proteus nature, which is accounted for by the eternally changing moods, the fluctuating states of hope and despair of the people who see him, is described with the greatest variety of expression in the novel.

The power that Klamm had in reality within K.'s bedroom" emphasizes that Klamm is copresent in K.'s and Frieda's amorous embraces. Through his love encounter with Frieda, K. has as a matter of fact gained the

... belief, which he found it impossible to give up entirely, that through her mediation an almost physical relationship with Klamm, one close enough for communicating in whispers, had come into being, a relationship which perhaps only K. knew of at the time, but which needed only a slight manipulation, a word, a glance in order to manifest itself, first of all to Klamm but then to everybody, as something which, though incredible, was nevertheless, through the force of life, the force of a loving embrace, self-evident. (S 444-45)

Accordingly, Klamm is not identical with the force of life, of a loving embrace; but a self-evident relationship with him can be established through this amorous embrace. At the same time, however, a "slight manipulation, a word, a glance"—that is to say, a spiritual-intellectual expression of one's own, even a slight manipulation on one's own, an intellectual feat—would be needed in order that this relationship with Klamm (which of course only K. knew of at first) be made "manifest" to Klamm himself and to everybody, as an incredible, certainly, but nevertheless also a self-evident fact.

It is of essential significance here that Frieda is designated as an intermediary for an involved third party, Klamm. Klamm thus represents a superpersonal sphere within the personal love

encounter. Frieda herself senses that he does so. "Her gaze
wandering afar, her cheek against K.'s chest, Frieda said . . .
It is true, I do believe it is his [Klamm's] doing that we came
together there under the counter; blessed, not cursed, be the
hour' . . . sweet were Frieda's words, he [K.] closed his eyes for
a few seconds to let her words seep through him" (S 72-73).

Accordingly, then, Klamm is the "power" that brings the
lovers together as well as the power which, bestowing happiness
and bliss, is present within love itself. K. seeks contact with this
power, sensing its proximity in love, a proximity great enough
for communicating in whispers; but he must "manifest" such
communication and contact with this power itself through a
spiritual-intellectual expression of his own; this means that, as
an independent spiritual-intellectual being, he must confront this
power eye to eye, as it were; he must "manifest" to this superpersonal power his own understanding, his own relation with it,
a relation "known" only to him at the present time; that means,
he must make this relation known to the power as well.

In other words, K. has to and wants to transform the superpersonal power into a personal power with whom he, as a "free"
man, stands face-to-face on an equal footing. This in fact is
exactly what K. is striving after. Again and again he insists on
confronting Klamm, not simply in his, Klamm's, official capacity—as Klamm the "official"—but as a "private person." K.
wants to transform the officially impersonal into a personal relationship. "But now I am duty bound to talk with him [Klamm]
as with a private person. . . . That, incidentally, I'll then have the
official facing me too, I'll welcome gladly, but that is not my
prime objective" (S 118).

## The Personalization of Eros

Hereby definite knowledge is gained for understanding the
entire novel and its complications: K. undertakes the colossal
venture of conquering the superpersonal power that "invisibly"
(S 437), mysteriously, and in protean manner is active in all love

encounters and indeed perhaps in everything that is alive; he undertakes to conquer it, eye to eye, as a personal power, and, what is more, to bring this power to awareness of his "self" and of his relationship to it. For only in so doing can he assert his freedom before this power and not turn into the complaisantly subjugated, passive object of an instinctual world or a super-personal sphere collectively controlling everything; moreover, he can reach even beyond this power to higher and more distant levels of human existence. This is formulated unmistakably when K. disdainfully rejects all official mediation with Klamm through the latter's village secretary Momus. "It was not Klamm's proximity in itself that was worth the effort to him, but it was that he, K., he alone—no one else the herald of his wishes, no one else the herald of the wishes of anyone else—should reach Klamm; reach him, not in order to rest in him but in order to get past him, to continue on, into the castle" (S 151).

Only from such a line of approach can it grow clear that Kafka is using the strange, poetic technique of delineating as "persons"—possessing concrete names and phenomenological forms—the superpersonal and invisible powers that are active at the core of our human existence.

Moreover, it is this very distinction between "official" and "private person" that is the determining factor in these characters. As "officials" the rulers of the castle are in fact purely superpersonal powers that can never come in direct, visible contact with the concrete, earthly self of the person. Klamm's letters to K. are letters from a private person and not official documents, as the village overseer observes. Also, Barnabas, Klamm's messenger, has not been officially employed. And all the strange misfortunes and the misunderstandings between K., on the one hand, and the landlady, Frieda, and Pepi, etc., on the other, stem from the fact that the women love and understand the officials not insofar as these officials are private persons but insofar as they are invading, superpersonal powers.

The landlady declares explicitly:

"Klamm as a private person! Who has ever seen Klamm as a

private person? Who can even conceive of him as a private person? *You* can, you will protest—but that is just the trouble. You can, because you cannot imagine him as an official, because you cannot imagine him at all. Because Frieda was Klamm's mistress you think that she saw him as a private person; because we love him, you think we love him only as a private person. Well, of a real official it cannot be said that he is now more of an official, now less of one; on the contrary, he is always, completely and thoroughly, an official.... Never was he more of an official than in those days, the days of my happiness; and Frieda and I are agreed about this: no one do we love as we love the official Klamm, the high, the exceedingly high official." (S 437)

The women, who are more directly in the emotional currents of life and more safely so, as it were, than reflective man, feel this world of emotion as a life potency that determines and carries them, that "bestows gifts" upon them, a life potency that cannot have personal features.

This does not contradict the statement that the landlady and Frieda, in the days of their happiness, were Klamm's "mistresses." For this love was indeed not a love between person and person. This love, the landlady explains, is of a completely different nature from, say, her love for her husband, and is therefore not in conflict with it. Hence, too, Klamm was actually seen neither by Frieda nor by her.

"You are really entirely incapable of actually seeing Klamm; that is not presumption on my part, for I myself am also incapable of doing so. Klamm is to talk to you! but he does not so much as talk to the people of the village, never yet has he himself talked to anyone from the village...not even to her [Frieda] did he talk. And that he occasionally called out, 'Frieda,' need not have at all the significance that people would be glad to attribute to it...that he point-blank summoned her cannot be claimed." (S 70)

Not only "will" Mr. Klamm never talk to K., but, says the landlady, Klamm "can" not talk at all (S 69). It is impossible for Klamm the "official" himself to establish a personal relationship with a human being. And Frieda voices the same opinion.

Klamm will never talk, "not with you, not with me, that is absolutely impossible" (S 68).

With this we come nearer to comprehending the meaning of Klamm. Conceptually, of course, this meaning cannot be defined univocally—for were that the case there would have been no need for the far-reaching poetic imagery. But by the very means of this poetic figuration the meaning of Klamm can be paraphrased and made understandable. However, Kafka's extremely fine, discriminating use of language and figures of speech demands a correspondingly discriminating interpretation.

## The Superindividual Love Emotions

The landlady once says to K., "You have snatched Frieda away from the most rapturous state ever granted her" (S 76). And this most rapturous state of Frieda's while she was Klamm's mistress is characterized immediately prior to this by Frieda, herself: "But I cannot describe it, I cannot even imagine it, everything has changed so since Klamm left me" (S 76). Her state, during her service as barmaid for Klamm, had been such that the indifference, dissatisfaction, and annoyance which possessed her then—for example, because of the insults and impertinent advances either on the part of Klamm's wild servants or on the part of the guests at the bar—appeared not to have affected her self at all. "It seemed to me as if it had happened many years ago, or as if it had not happened to me at all, or as if I had merely heard it spoken of, or as if I myself had already forgotten it. But I cannot describe it," etc. (S 76).

This most rapturous state thus consisted of being encompassed, enveloped by emotions that she did not feel as her own, that acted within her without having been determined, produced or consciously controlled by her individual self. This is in keeping with Olga's remarks:

"Klamm is, after all, like a commander of women, ordering now this one, now that one, to come to him, tolerating no one very long; and, as he gives orders to come, he gives orders also

to go.... But we know that women cannot do anything but love officials, once the officials turn to them ; what is more, they love the officials even beforehand, much though they wish to deny it."
(S 260-61)

The women's love for the officials is thus an immediate certainty through emotions that are operative before as well as after the encounter with the officials; for, even after such encounters, both the landlady and Frieda, for example, feel this love for, or, as it may be, dependence on Klamm the official, despite the fact that it may be, as in the landlady's case, in the form of nothing but a memory that accompanies her all her life and that makes it just possible for her to endure life. The love encounter with the officials themselves, however, is a happiness that comes over the women incomprehensibly, as it were, dependent not on their will but solely on Klamm's superpersonal power, and that happiness lives on in their memory as an "elevation in rank that can never be lost" (S 115).

### The Conflict between Superindividual and Personal Love

It was from this state of bliss that Frieda was snatched by K. But this too she feels as happiness, though happiness because K. encounters her as a free, distinct personality to whom she wishes to surrender herself completely. And it is precisely through this individual encounter with K. that the reversal takes place in Frieda with respect to her relationship to Klamm —this in contrast to the landlady who, now as ever, is attached to Klamm, since her husband Hans is neither loved nor regarded by her as a partner who is her equal.

"You think I'd miss Klamm?" said Frieda [to K.]. "There's more than enough of Klamm here as it is, too much Klamm ; it is to escape from him that I want to leave. It's not Klamm that I miss, but you ; for your sake I want to leave ; because I cannot get enough of you for myself, here where everyone is pulling at me. I'd rather have this mask of a pretty face ripped from me, I'd rather have my body suffer, just to be able to live in peace with you . . ." (S 184)

since "I don't know any greater happiness for me than to be with you forever, without interruption, unendingly" (S 185).

Thus, through her individual love for K. Frieda now feels an incompatibility with Klamm's sphere. For her this sphere of Klamm's is now bound to her body's emotional world, to her beautiful face.

The complications that ensue from this, for her and her relationship to K., will concern us later on. For an understanding of Klamm, what is essential here is that, at the moment of an individual love encounter, the superpersonal world mediated by Klamm is felt by Frieda as a sensuous, emotional world and is warded off by her so that she may be able to belong to K. completely and exclusively.

However, that does not mean that Klamm actually represents the sensuous sphere purely and simply. Nor does it mean that sensuousness appears in Kafka's novel as a negative sphere. It is a matter of the transformation of the superindividual into the individual sphere, since perfect happiness is possible only through such a transformation.

For Frieda's conception of happiness in her individual love for K. can be realized only in the "grave." She dreams about the fact "that here on earth there is no peaceful place for our love, not in the village and not elsewhere, and for that reason I picture a grave, deep and narrow; there we hold each other in our arms, clamped as if in a vise. I bury my face against you, and you yours against me, and no one will ever see us again" (S 185-86). Thereby even individuality is extinguished. Each buries his face against the other. The one no longer sees the other.

The figure of Klamm, however, stands above the antinomy between sensuous and individual happiness, or, rather, he embraces both spheres. This emerges from a multitude of supporting passages. Let us first consider one illustration from Kafka's poetic imagery.

## Klamm's Cognac

As, in front of the Herrenhof, K. gets into Klamm's sleigh in which, characteristically, despite the wide-open door and the bitter cold that prevails outside, it remains comfortably warm, he takes hold of Klamm's cognac bottle, opens it, and smells it. "The bouquet was so sweet, so caressing—as when one hears praise and kind words from someone whom one loves very much and does not exactly know what it is all about, and does not even want to know and is just happy in the knowledge that it is he [the loved person] who is speaking in that way" (S 141).

In the bouquet of his cognac, in its essence, Klamm mediates the happiness of sweet, individual love. Happiness through caressing, sweet emotions, that is to say, sensuous emotions; and happiness through him, solely through him, the lover, who "speaks," that is to say, makes himself known as an unmistakable, unique individuality—these coincide in the essence of this draught of Klamm's. But this essence, this fragrance of the draught, must be preserved. K. "took a sip out of curiosity." "How it was transmuted, in the course of his drinking it, from something that was little more than a conveyor of sweet fragrance, into a coachman's drink! 'Is it possible?' asked K. of himself, as though in reproachful self-accusation, and drank once again" (S 141).

K. feels it as guilt, as a reproachful "self-accusation," that he drinks the cognac out of curiosity instead of preserving its essence. His "self" must resist the temptation of incorporating the draught which now "burned" like a coachman's drink. By drinking he has sinned against himself. It is the same process that is present in the love encounters between K. and Frieda, when both reciprocally, in their "burning" bodies (S 60), "frantically ... sought ... something ... desperately ... helpless, frustrated, in order to catch the final taste of happiness" (S 66). This happiness that they seek is for K.—even in the embraces with Frieda—that contact with the Klamm's third mysterious power, which would have to "manifest" itself to everyone and to Klamm himself through a glance, a word, a slight spiritual-intellectual manipulation. Conversely, Frieda vainly seeks in K. the "glance" she once caught in Klamm's eyes as he looked at her (S 187).

Without overinterpretation one may view Klamm's draught as a resumption of the ancient fairy-tale motif of the love potion; indeed, time and again, Kafka delighted in reading fairy tales and introducing fairy-tale motifs into his literary work, often imperceptibly, but very often quite clearly.

In Klamm's draught, too, Klamm's significance grows discernible. In the image of the love potion, form is given to the insight that love is a power that suddenly attacks a person and conquers him magically, a power that permeates him against his will, a power that determines him. Hence Klamm is "the commander of women." They must follow him when he calls, and go when he sends them away. But this call, this encounter with Klamm, is always brief and very rare. It is a supreme, inconceivable, "unbelievable" happiness. For in it "momentarily" there flashes up the notion of that essence in which individual love and the superpersonal emotional sphere permeating the person are magically one. That is why the women, although they can never see or talk to Klamm himself, nevertheless feel him as a person, as a definite being, as precisely that exceedingly high official "Klamm," and not as a merely indefinite universal, which as a universal would of course have to be present in them *always.* To be sure, the encounter would be truly perfect for them only if the official and the person Klamm could become one for them.

Justifiably, K. once says to the landlady of the Inn at the Bridge, with reference to her unhappy marriage: "The blessing [Klamm's] was above you, but there was not enough understanding to bring it down," for they had neglected to "ask" Klamm (S 116); that is to say, there had been no personal encounter with Klamm, K. remarks, but simply Klamm's official signature at the bottom of the marriage certificate (S 434). Hence, K. knows very accurately—and in this he is far superior to the worldly-wise landlady—that man's decisive achievement consists of his personally overcoming and "questioning" the anonymous power of the emotions; that means gaining clarity *before* contracting a marriage, about whether happiness in love can be anticipated with respect to the chosen future partner, and whether it can be actualized and preserved; that is, whether Klamm can say yes to the marriage. Only then is there a "blessing" upon it.

Although the landlady gained an intimation of what love is through her three brief encounters with Klamm, she did not manage to lift this intimation, by means of personal "questioning" of Klamm, into the clarity of consciousness, and to actualize this intimation in her marriage with Hans. She contented herself with the superpersonal, collective currents of emotion that lead to an "official" marriage registered in the marriage-license bureau. Her marriage was only an imperfect substitute for what had been promised her in Klamm's essence. Consequently she subsists only on her memory of Klamm.

Thereby it becomes understandable why all human beings, not only women, can see Klamm only "momentarily" and also why this view of theirs is always a variable, determined by their moods, their states of hope and despair. The happiness in love promised by Klamm flashes up for a moment as an intimation; and, through the comparison with the concrete situation in which man, in his determined human relationships, finds himself at a given moment, that intimation is experienced in the form of hope, despair, longing, etc.

Thus Klamm appears here as the determining power in all interpersonal encounters. But this determining power would in turn have to be determined by man himself. Only then would true human existence, true happiness, be possible. That is the meaning of the statement that no relationship with Klamm would have to become "manifest" not only to Klamm but to "everyone."

Klamm's ambiguous Proteus nature becomes understandable through this, likewise. Just as the essence of his draught is transmuted into a coachman's drink by one's drinking out of curiosity, so Klamm's servants, once they are released from their master's discipline, break out in the village tavern like a pack of wild animals. Within the universal, natural, cosmic order—in other words, in "office"—the servants are dignified and are subject to the fixed laws of nature. Only in the human world do they erupt uncontrolled. Only in the human world does the noble animal of nature become "animal" in the negative sense; only in the human world do the instincts in their intrinsic meaning become "unchained." For in Klamm all the possibilities of human encounter are contained, the highest as well as the lowest.

And now it becomes understandable, too, why the women with whom Klamm has any dealings are always landladies or barmaids; and why Klomm's servants or the village customers reach avidly for the beer that the barmaids distribute, so avidly that they deprive themselves of enjoying the beer (S 449). It becomes understandable why K. and Frieda at their first meeting wallow in beer puddles. What is involved is the "draught." And the crucial problem consists of the form in which this beverage appears and how it is used by people. In the barroom of the Herrenhof, immediately after K.'s experience with Klamm's cognac, K. asks Pepi for cognac. He "sipped . . . at the cognac and pushed it away because it was unpalatable. 'All the gentlemen drink it,' said Pepi curtly. . . . 'The gentlemen have better cognac too,' said K. 'Possibly,' said Pepi, 'but I don't.' With that she disposed of K." (S 147).

It is striking that even the gentlemen, the officials, drink Pepi's unpalatable cognac, or drink beer, as does Klamm. Klamm's Proteus nature by no means lives on the essence alone, but on very coarse drinks as well. Since, as Frieda says, he is present everywhere, he is present even in the most sensuous expressions of existence, at all the stages of youth as well as those of decaying age. K. himself sees Klamm as a stout, ponderous gentleman, "with the weight of age" (S 53); the landlady sees him in that way too, perhaps; but as a young girl she was fascinated, at her first encounter with him, by the photograph of Klamm's young messenger doing a high jump, the messenger whom Klamm had sent to her and whose photograph she then immediately requested from Klamm and now preserves as a cherished memento.

## Klamm as Official and as Private Person

Since Klamm is the determining power in all interpersonal encounters, of all the officials of the castle he performs "the greatest amount of work" (S 358). Nobody "can hide anything from Klamm" (S 156). He knows everything. But as this invisible determining power he can never make an appearance directly, and also he can never himself protocol, list, register, and read the concrete events of life and acts of consciousness that take place in interpersonal encounters. This is taken care of by his secretaries; that is, the intermediary organs between his concrete existence and his invisible one. These organs record the actual empirical substance and the proceedings of what takes place among people, and the secretaries are therefore, as is the opinion of the worldly-wise landlady, indispensable for K.'s journey to Klamm. However, K. rightly points out the fact that their protocols can be deceptive, and that they by no means lay bare the truth of these relationships. Hence he refuses to subject himself to the interrogation by Klamm's village secretary. He wants to confront Klamm himself face-to-face. On the other hand, naturally, K. must reach avidly for these protocols, for they of course are part of concrete land surveying. However, it is with good reason that he disappointedly lays the protocol aside again, since it merely quotes one-sided interpretations made by the landlady.

Klamm himself does not "even read" such protocols (S 156). For him, too, they reflect only relatively partial aspects. For that reason Klamm is always "mute." All statements merely disguise the true relationships among people.

When he intervenes directly it is always in his capacity as a "private person," as in the case of his "private [unofficial] letter" to K. in which he praises the latter's work in land surveying. For, indeed, K.'s land surveying concerned itself with the search for the true meaning and purpose of interpersonal relationships and, what is more, with the search considered as a thoroughly individual achievement on K.'s part.

As the determining power that embraces* everything, in K.'s imagination Klamm resides, with logical consistency, in an "impregnable dwelling." The existence of Klamm's "downward-piercing, steady gaze" can "never be proved, never disproved" (S 157). He is beyond all rational interpretations and reflections, since he actually incorporates the immediacy and hence, too, the inscrutability of the most intimate mysteries of life and love.

## Klamm and the Limits of Earthly Love

But therewith, also, Klamm's limits are presented in outline. As an ever-mute determining power he can himself never enter the spheres of the mind that move outside of interpersonal encounters or that manifest themselves within the heart of these interpersonal relations as separate, independent spheres. To bring Klamm to speak is an achievement of man, who must "manifest" his personal relationship by means of "word," glance, sign, etc. It is characteristic that in the essence of his draught the beloved does indeed speak to the lover, but the content of what is spoken is of absolutely no consequence; what is more, the lover "does not wish to know exactly" what the beloved says. The feeling of happiness in love, of the good fortune that it is *"he"* who speaks, that is to say, the relationship between the lovers—this is what is essential.

Hence Klamm in no way whatsoever represents the totality of man's intrinsic being. Besides him there are numerous other important officials in the castle; for example there is Sortini, who represents an extremely intellectual type, and who lives very much alone and withdrawn. His brow is a whole fan of wrinkles, etc. The different and new complications that inevitably ensue,

*Tr. note: The word play on Klamm, *um-*"*klammern*," cannot be conveyed properly in translation. English "clam" and "clamp" are singularly inappropriate.

will concern us in our consideration of the Amalia story. In the light of these limits of Klamm's, K.'s decision not only to get to Klamm no matter what, but also to advance beyond him, and indeed penetrate into the castle, is also understandable.

And from the consideration of these same limits of Klamm's it becomes clear why Klamm's constant muteness is interrupted only by "screams such as K. had never heard before" (S 157). Klamm's "circlings, unalterable from K.'s depth, circlings which he described on high in accordance with incomprehensible laws, visible only for moments" (S 157), force the all-commanding and all-determining Klamm into his own laws, as it were. The destiner is also the destined. It is as little possible for him to enter into lasting relationships with people as it is for them to enter into lasting relationships with him. His impregnable dwelling locks him in, too. Only if a free human being in an "unguarded" moment were to seek him out and confront him face-to-face, could he burst the fetters of his officialdom, become truly a private person, and thereby experience an inconceivable "elevation in rank" (S 354). The "incomprehensible laws" within which he moves would become lucid to him as he set them aside. But, naturally, within the "world" that is eternally kept in "equilibrium" (S 356), this can never happen. And thus he simply remains an official ever in office, trapped ever mute in the same unalterable circlings.

Not without reason does he sit, ponderous, stout, dully silent, before the beer that is served him, having little in common with the essence of his own draught. Of course it is only K. who sees him in this way. And K. is barricaded off from Klamm's "sparkling" yet "simple," childlike "glance" that so fascinates Frieda and that "thrills" her (S 187) when she sees K.'s assistants, Klamm's "messengers" (S 186). "Glittering pince-nez, put on askew, covered his [Klamm's] eyes," when K. observed him through the keyhole (S 53). In the castle Klamm may look quite different. And momentarily, to be sure, Klamm's sparkling glance flashes up for his "mistresses," promising happiness, beguiling. But this happens only momentaneously. And at such moments Klamm himself cannot "manifest" himself to his mistresses, cannot show any inclination toward them, and cannot of himself bestow any "gifts" upon them. The human being must himself entreat Klamm for everything (S 109).

In spite of all the possibilities of happiness, individual love, and freedom that flash up in Klamm, and in spite of his ability to write "private [unofficial] letters," Klamm is bound to the system of laws that he himself represents and manifests. Knowledge of the fact that there are possibilities of breaking out may from time to time burst forth from out of his muteness as "screams." On the whole, like all earthly happiness, he, even he, the "high, the exceedingly high official," remains in the grip of the world system of laws. This may be the reason for his black frock coat that is always the same. It may be the reason, too, why this "eternal worker" (S 373), in spite of his so to speak earthly immortality, feels the intimations of dying, feels the "weight of age" heavy upon him, so that he himself appears usually as an old man; and only his messengers, young and radiant, approach people—Barnabas, for example (S 35), or Klamm's messenger to the landlady, or K.'s assistants who have Klamm's sparkling and simple glance and whose gleeful, childish "friskiness," together with their manly "reaching out with their arms," enchants Frieda against her will (S 187).

## The Symbols of Death and Life

Accordingly, both village and castle are constantly surrounded by an icy, deadly cold, a wasteland of snow. "To us there [inside], everything that is outside the room seems cold" (S 409). "Winter with us is long, a very long winter and unvarying ... in my recollection, now, spring and summer seem so short, as if they were not much more than two days, and even on these days, even during the most beautiful day of all, even then snow occasionally falls" (S 410).

It is the same unvarying snow wasteland which the country doctor gets into when he is snatched out of his limited life and confronted with the Universal of existence. And that this snow

in *The Castle* is a symbol of death, of the freezing of living
water, becomes clear when K., plowing his way laboriously
through the deep snow in the village, suddenly feels "aid" and
encouragement as he recalls that long ago, as a young boy in his
native village, he had conquered the high wall of an old cemetery. At that time, he had once succeeded "with surprising ease"
in climbing the smooth, high cemetery wall:

He glanced down and around, and over his shoulder as well, at
the crosses sinking down in the earth; there was nobody, here
and now, who was greater than he.... The feeling of this victory
seemed at that time to give him a support that he could hold
onto for as long as he lived; that feeling had not been entirely
foolish, for now, many years later, in the snowy night, on Barnabas'
arm, it came to his aid. (S 44)

That means, only if death could be conquered could this heavy
snow, pressing upon him, really be conquered.

Even the (only apparent) telescoping of time that K. experiences upon the snowed-up, deserted village street is understandable from here on. Just as spring and summer shrink to two days
—and even on these it occasionally snows—so does the light of
day in the village last "only one or two hours." In the remaining
time it is usually "completely dark" (S 29). What lies before us
is not a suspension of the laws of time; it is the predominance
of the night that is being symbolized. For, obviously, since
morning K. has in fact spent only one or two hours in the
village; his being without "need for food" brings this home to
him. "'Short days, short days,' he said to himself" (S 29). In
this world of village and castle belonging to Count "Westwest,"
the sphere of night and death clearly prevails. It is the outer
frame which embraces everything, and into which flow all life
and thought.

In the image of the cold snow and the warm water Kafka has
vividly symbolized the relationship between death and life. On
the village street, laden with piles of snow meters deep, there
reigns "desertedness" (S 21); indeed, there is no traffic there at
all: "Here there is no traffic" (S 26). Traffic exists only on the

"approach roads" between castle and village: all the carriages of the officials "speed madly there" "at a gallop" (S 286-87); and life and warmth exist only within the village cottages or inside the officials' sleighs and offices.

Considering this, one begins to comprehend the strange proceedings that K. meets with in his first laborious trudging through the snow-covered village street: in the first cottage he enters he sees before him a gigantic wooden vat, the size of two beds, in which two men are bathing; they squirt the warm water at him and at the jubilant, screaming children there, while a young woman, "in youthful plumpness," washes clothes in a washtub near the door. One begins to understand, too, why K., "as if there were no other means of communicating, in silence but with might and main was pulled to the door" by the two men and thrown out while the "woman washing clothes laughed with the children who were suddenly in a wild hubbub" (S 24). K. is a disturbing foreign body in this life that is vibrating uninhibitedly in consonance with itself.

It is of significance, however, that within this same room that is bursting, as it were, with steaming life, there is a "girl from the castle" (S 24) who appears "not to belong to them" (S 22), and who is "weary" and "ill." This "woman in the armchair lay as if lifeless; she cast no downward glance even at the child at her breast, but looked vaguely upward. K. had looked at her for quite a long time, at this unchanging, beautiful, melancholy picture" (S 23). He feels himself strongly drawn to her. She is the wife of Brunswick, one of the bathing men, and the mother of Hans Brunswick, the boy who sees in K. a future liberator. She thus belongs to the sphere of the castle where all life is recorded, spiritually assimilated, and officially controlled in accordance with prescribed laws. Exactly like the officials, she is always weary, cannot endure the village air; like Klamm, who sits motionless in his study, she is "lifeless."

The sphere of the castle thus rises above the boisterous life of the village into a more spiritual, "higher" world which, to be sure, is also more lifeless and diseased. This harmonizes, down to the very details, with the descriptions of the outer phenom-

enological forms of the castle; as for instance when it is
stated: ". . . moreover, up above on the mountain there seemed
to be much less snow than here in the village" (S 17); "The
castle . . . lay quiet as always, never yet had K. seen the slightest
sign of life there" (S 134). However, this does not mean that
what is present here is a gradation or even a dualism of life and
spirit. Kafka's work is far removed from these traditional divi-
sions. In Kafka "office and life" are constantly exchanging
"places" (S 81). And "between the farmers and the castle there
is no great difference" (S 20). The officials who make records of
everything are in no way, say, "purer" or more spiritual than the
villagers whom they govern. In their official chambers there prevails such filth as "not even a deluge . . . could wash clean"
(S 384). They make a great deal of noise, screaming and shouting like children, indeed even like roosters. The determining
powers are not a jot better than the life realities determined
by them. Even the relationship between the state of determining
and the state of having been determined is an interchangeable
one. Fundamentally, the work of the officials is determined and
dictated by life itself: K. "indeed, already understood how to
manipulate this official apparatus, how to play this delicate instrument, intent as it always was on some sort of settlement or
compromise. The trick consisted essentially in doing nothing, in
letting the machinery run of its own accord, and in forcing it to
work merely by the fact that one was standing here in one's
earthly solidity, not to be got rid of" (S 433).

In the face af this ineluctable gearing in which official duty
and life are meshed, this weary woman in the armchair, who
belongs both to the castle and to the village, actually holds
everything in contempt—castle, village, and the land surveyor as
well. K. asks her, "Who are you?" Disparingly—it was not
clear whether her contempt was intended for K. or for her own
reply—she said, 'A girl from the castle' " (S24).

This, too, is indicative of her peculiar, hybrid position. From
the point of view of the castle she is a "girl," and yet in the
village she is also a mother and wife. Hence, curiously enough,
in support of the religious interpretations inaugurated by Max

Brod, she has been considered a symbol of the Holy Mother of God, affiliated with the "castle" as the site of "grace."[2] But then why is her "disparaging," "contemptuous" reply over-looked? All such religious interpretations are basically blasphemies, insults to religion itself.

The mother of Hans Brunswick is not a saint but an unhappy woman who, though she tries to escape from the power of "life" and of the "spirit" of life, must nevertheless inevitably remain a slave to that power. That is her tragedy. And that is also the meaning of the desperate efforts of her son Hans to secure K. as her "physician" (S 194) and her liberator. For K. is the only really free person in the village. Hence, K. might possibly be the source of help for Hans's mother. On the other hand, K. himself is bound to be magically attracted by her and to expect help from her, for she does come from the castle and possesses—he dimly senses this—more knowledge than all the others just because of her aloofness, her "contemptuous" reply.

Only in conjunction with Kafka's total world of imagery can his characters be interpreted satisfactorily. This "lifeless" woman must be viewed as inseparably related to the situation in which she exists. At Lasemann's cottage she presents a sharp contrast to the animated activity that goes on there in the "steaming" water. With what awareness Kafka turned water and snow into symbols of life and death becomes evident through numerous, often minute, details; for example, there is the remark that the village overseer's wife, who piously folds her hands when she first catches sight of Klamm's letter (S 97), [later] "lost in dreams, was playing with Klamm's letter which she had made into a little boat" (S 102). The name Klamm and his letter, by association, evoke in her, as if in a dream, the picture of a ship and water—indeed, the erotic sphere in real dreams is for the most part linked to the element of water. And Kafka himself very often designated life as a current in which mankind is swimming, but not less truly, on the other hand, against which man must swim incessantly if he wishes to preserve the freedom and clarity of his vision: "To maintain one's composure; to stand very far off from that which passion desires; to know the current and therefore to swim against the stream; to swim against the stream for the pleasure of being carried" (H 287). In this formulation of Kafka's, K.'s goal is sharply outlined: to swim against the stream and, at the same time, to be carried by it: to unite freedom and obligation.

K's complications in his relationship with women follow as a result of this. To understand these complications one must first carefully expand upon the position and significance of these women.

### From Maid to Society Lady: Frieda and Pepi

Frieda, primarily the most important woman for K., has worked herself up from stablegirl in the service of the landlady of the Inn at the Bridge, to a position as chambermaid at the Herrenhof, to barmaid at the Herrenhof.

The landlord of the Herrenhof, who is a "polite man and, through his constant and relatively unconstrained associations with those by far his superiors, a cultivated, well-bred man," speaks "with Frieda ... in a particularly respectful way" (S 58-59). Throughout the entire village a barmaid at the Herrenhof enjoys high prestige.

This can be understood only if one considers Frieda's antecedents and the entire structure of the relationship between the "gentlemen" (officials) and the village. As a stablegirl at the Inn at the Bridge Frieda had to perform her work without having the least consideration shown for her "delicate," "small" hands (S 55). As a chambermaid at the Herrenhof she, like all chambermaids, was purely and simply an object in the hands of the all-determining powers. "The maids, of course, have no belongings" (S 384). The "commissioners" of the officials can at will and at any time rummage through the maids' beds in their search for documents which the maids have supposedly mislaid, lost, or not properly forwarded; whereas in reality the maids anxiously hand over to the landlord every piece of foolscap they find.

This, therefore, means that at this stage the maids, with no will of their own, are surrendered to the objective, all-controlling life powers and do not confront these life powers as independent beings. Mechanically they assimilate what is said, thought, willed, and mechanically too they pass it on. Although they are searched for significant documents of one sort or another, never are such documents found in their possession. The maids have only to perform their function; and their task consists—naturally, without their ever being able to succeed in it—of cleaning up and clearing away everything unpleasant, the boundless filth which the gentlemen and their servants leave behind them. For "not even a deluge" could "wash clean" the gentlemen's rooms (S 384). Tacitly it is premised that little maids make the world pleasant and beautiful. And therefore the gentlemen themselves and their servants lurk covetously around the maids' rooms. "Constantly the prowler is heard before the door" (S 385). But actual contact is obviously not possible. The differences between the worlds and levels of consciousness of the "gentlemen" and those of the maids are too great. "All [the maids] would of course be happy if he came in after all, but nothing happens, nobody comes in" (S 385). For "actually, one is not even acquainted with the gentlemen, one has scarcely seen them" (S 385).

Accordingly, these girls live in a state of indeterminate, betwixt-and-between emotion. They would like the encounter with the gentlemen, yet have a "fear" of it.

This is altered at one stroke if, like Frieda and Pepi later on, they are called to be barmaids for the gentlemen. Suddenly, outwardly, in the eyes of the gentlemen and in the eyes of the village, they are to represent "beauty," and through that beauty "power" as well; and they are to remain careful of the general social "prestige" they have thereby acquired. "And so Frieda, all of a sudden, became a great beauty, of exactly the kind needed in the tavern, yes, almost too beautiful, too powerful" (S 388). As long as a girl "is pretty, if no special unfortunate accident occurs, she will be a barmaid" (S 389).

The transition from chambermaid to barmaid is thus the transition from being a little maid who jogs along mechanically, to being a conscious, representative beauty, a respected lady, who is to allure everyone and yet keep a tight rein on everyone, who promises happiness and apportions the "draught." The tavern is a place "where one was always under the eyes of people, among them very fastidious and attentive gentlemen, and where for that reason one always had to look as refined and pleasant as possible" (S 386).

This change from chambermaid to barmaid takes place suddenly and unexpectedly, "because the gentlemen lack the patience to wait until one is developed, but immediately, without transition, they want to have a barmaid, a suitable one, as is proper, otherwise they turn away" (S 386). In this there is an enigmatic truth and criticism of life. There is no waiting for the maturing into a truly superior, conscious woman. The gentlemen demand a representative lady immediately. They take no pains and are unconcerned with the "development" of their "sweethearts." To this state of affairs the women react disastrously.

### The Adaptable Society Lady

Pepi must quickly borrow a piece of sumptuous "expensive material" from a friend and make up a dress for herself from it, for this dress "seemed" to be "the guaranty of success" (S 393).

What does this dress look like? ". . . it can be tightened or loosened again, above and below, to suit oneself, so that though it is of course only a dress, it is so adaptable—that is a distinct advantage and was actually her [Pepi's] invention" (S 393-94). Thus she stitches together a dress that will meet all the gentlemen's wishes, a dress that can be altered at will. Pepi works herself into the role of the adaptable society lady. Everything about her is calculated for effect, and only from this viewpoint can she see and judge all other women. For her, Frieda too is no more than a calculating, artful creature who, in the guise of love and self-sacrificing devotion, lured K. to her at a time when her prestige at the tavern was on the wane, then "raised a hue and cry" to make people curious and draw attention to herself, and utilized even her departure with K. from the Herrenhof and her apparent degradation at the village school merely as a means of spinning new threads surreptitiously, like a "spider," so that she could return triumphantly to the tavern and oust Pepi (S 390 ff.; 398 ff.).

Accordingly, Pepi gears herself to the inclinations of the gentlemen's secretaries and guests.

Pepi was friendly to everyone and everyone repaid her with friendliness. Everyone was visibly glad of the change; when the overworked gentlemen may at last sit down for a little while to a glass of beer, they can be transformed, as it were, by a word, a glance, a shrug of the shoulders. So ardently did everyone run his hands through Pepi's curls, that at least ten times a day she had to do her hair again. (S 395-96)

In this respect she differs from her predecessor Frieda, who sought to maintain her genuine emotional world and, as Pepi scornfully remarks, "supposedly saved [herself] entirely for Klamm, and considered every word said, every advance made by someone else, as an insult to Klamm" (S 395).

Consequently Pepi introduces the following "innovation" (S 395): she no longer concerns herself with the supervision of Klamm's wild servants, but hands over that task to the "cellarmen ... who are much better suited for that anyhow" (S 395). Whereas Frieda kept the instinctual world of Klamm's servants within bounds and controlled it, Pepi lets herself drift along in it without being able to offer any resistance: "The mob could not control itself and deprived itself of the pleasure which all coveted so greedily. Incessantly, the crowd, swaying back and forth, shoved the little maid [Pepi] around with it" (S 449). "There were tears ... running down her cheeks, her lovely braid of hair was disheveled, her dress even torn in front at her breast ... but without concern for herself ... she worked tirelessly at the beer taps" (S 452).

Pepi has no "self" of her own, as has Frieda, with which to oppose the masses. Moreover, she is "without concern" about her self; she merely endeavors to serve everyone with the desired draught. She thinks the "cellarmen" would be able to dominate the masses. For these cellarmen, who have to carry out all the coopering. and who are therefore familiar with the storage of the drinks and know their effects as well, would have to know how to make these wild servants exercise reason, moderation, and discrimination in drinking. Pepi thus relies upon possible, would-be regulating powers in her environment. She does not set the bounds herself and is consequently pulled against her will into this instinctual world, a world that is regarded even by the landlady of the Inn at the Bridge and by Momus the secretary as self-evident, as a "customary, natural phenomenon" to which they yield as to a "current," "leaning back into the mass of people," and in so doing they try "to protect themselves solely against excessively violent jolts" (S 449).

With that, however, even the artificial world that Pepi has precipitately constructed for herself collapses. In the long run, the means that were calculated purely for effect fail to work. The role that Pepi wants to play, the strange, borrowed dress that she has slipped on, strike K. as "ridiculous." For Pepi "had obviously dressed in accordance with her exaggerated notions of the significance of a barmaid" (S 136). Moreover, this very dress that is seemingly so alterable, so adaptable to all needs, is in reality "a dress very little suited to her, of glossy grey material that hung straight down; at the bottom it was gathered together clumsily in a childlike way, by a silk ribbon ending in a bowknot, so that it was too tight for her" (S 135). In the "current" of the actual instinctual powers, the dress tears.

## The Disappointed Woman

The result of this, however, is the sudden change in Pepi: she is in despair. She feels herself as a "sacrifice, and everything is stupid, and everything is lost; and whoever had the strength to set fire to the entire Herrenhof and burn it up, burn it up utterly, so that not a trace remained, burn it up like a piece of paper in the stove—he would this day be the man of Pepi's choice" (S 382). The only one who, in her opinion, would be capable of this is K., "a hero and a rescuer of maidens" (S 381).

Despair, however, is not insight. Despair is the reverse of egotistic blindness. It springs from the feeling of defiance at not being accepted, appreciated, understood by the world. And Pepi's will to be freed by K. is therefore also arrogance. She wants to show him, the fighter against the authorities, who she is: "And she had figured it out for herself, she would renounce everything and stoop to him and teach him true love, which he could never experience with Frieda and which is independent of all honorary positions in the world" (S 382).

Suddenly Pepi wants to make the leap out of everything and manifest to the fighter her supposed inner worth. But she has never really confronted herself and hence, too, has never given birth to and developed her real inner worth. She lacks the "free" quality that K. is drawn to in Frieda's "nature" (S 59), that "triumphant glance" of Frieda's (S 54) which "took him by surprise" in his first encounter with her, a "glance of particular, distinctive superiority. As this glance fell upon K., it seemed to him that it had already disposed of matters that concerned him, whose existence he himself had not yet known of at all, whose existence he was convinced of, however, by her glance" (S 52).

To be sure, K. is affected by Pepi, too. "Avidly he looked at her" on first encountering her (S 137), for he "had . . . to say to himself that had he met Pepi here instead of Frieda, and suspected that Pepi had any sort of relations with the castle—and she probably had such relations, too—he would have tried to clasp the secret to himself with the same embraces—just as he had had to in the case of Frieda" (S 438). "Then was it perhaps no different from the way it was with Frieda? Oh, but it was, it was different. One had only to think of Frieda's glance in order to understand that. Never would K. have touched Pepi" (S 137).

Pepi, too, like all women, embodies Klamm's "secret." But Pepi never was Klamm's mistress, as was Frieda. In spite of her desperate efforts to meet him, Klamm has never summoned her to him. And also, "Klamm did not come down" to her (S 398), whereas he came "down voluntarily" to Frieda (S 406). Frieda *knows* about Klamm's secret—hence her "glance." Pepi wants to obtain that secret "by weeping, by scratching, by tearing" (S 407), to exact it by artificial means.

What the "love" that she intends to "teach" K. looks like, she herself formulates. This love is a "stooping" to K., as if he stood below her. For, after all, she does have ground under her feet, but he does not. Her readiness "to renounce everything" is for her purely a renunciation of "honorary positions in the world" which she has lost anyway and which she had never captured validly but only through calculated tricks. She would never have been prepared, as was Frieda, to live with K. outside the village and castle in Nowhere or even merely to live with him in his humiliating situation as janitor at the village school. Despite or just because of her desperate outbreak of hate for Herrenhof and castle, which she would like best of all to see burnt to the ground, she has never made herself aware of what castle and Herrenhof really are, of what powers set the world and life in motion. Her glance is turned consistently backward.

Since for her everything has collapsed, she seeks refuge in oblivion and indifference, in that—apparently safer—neutrality in which women are objects, compliant tools of the authorities of the world. She strives to return to that girls' world in which what is wished is done mechanically, in which it is "warm" though hampering, while the whole "world" outside (even the tavern) is now bound to appear "cold" to her in her disappointment (S 409).

Kafka has here portrayed the resignation of those women who escape into the inward warmth of the nest after the "world" has disappointed them. There she intends to love K., there he is to belong entirely to her, and be himself protected, then, from the hostile world, from endless winter. Flight into a marriage which is outwardly shielded, in which the beautiful "dress" will be put aside, the "ribbons" snatched "from her hair," "and everything" stuffed "into a corner where it will be well concealed and not remind her needlessly of times that are best forgotten" (S 402)—that is her goal. And she is willing to resume even the daily troubles of such a confined life: "Then she will take the big bucket and the broom, clench her teeth, and get to work" (S 402). K., however, will gain ground under his feet, find "shelter," finally obtain the desperately sought "domicile" in the village—to be sure, only secretly, concealed from castle and village. For he is to see to it that he does not expose himself to new problems, questions, possibilities, he is to "show [himself] nowhere that we do not consider safe, and in general follow our suggestions" (S 410).

### Flight into Collective Marriage

These wishes and demands of Pepi's can be regarded only as slashing and thoroughgoing criticism of Kafka's against very widely disseminated forms of love. In K., her "hero" and "rescuer of maidens," Pepi sees her "helper and protector" (S 409), and at the same time subjugates him thereby to her own world that is in need of protection. In surrendering to him as to a superior (with the best of intentions), she at the same time makes him into a "docile" pupil of her so-called "love," keeps him away from world and spirit, and puts him at the mercy of her own well-meaning advice and suggestions.

This criticism becomes even more slashing—but more cogent, too, unfortunately—if one bears in mind that Pepi's love for K. shows itself as a collective love. K. is to live in the comfortably warm maids' room with three maids. Love has in this situation lost all personal uniqueness. What is being loved here is quite generically the collective being "man," the "man as helper and protector" (S 409). It is not a matter of K., the individual, but of the security, the protection that he offers. Hence, too, the woman is not an individuality but a collective being, representative of a species, optionally interchangeable with every other representative. Only quite general differences in sex prevail here. "Man" as such confronts "woman" as such, and, into the bargain, in an association purely utilitarian and in their own interests: he is to "protect" her; she is to offer him a warm nest.

There can be no doubt that in what seems to be a fantastically monstrous demand on Pepi's part there is revealed—as always in Kafka—a very real, everyday truth: the truth that any marriage that is contracted solely because of a need for protection, felt by a woman who has been disappointed by the world, is consciously or unconsciously bound to take on a collective character. This can never and must never be admitted publicly, for it conflicts with the official nature of marriage. But nevertheless it remains true. "That we'll now have a man as helper and protector will make them happy, and they'll be simply delighted that it all has to remain a secret, and that through this secret we'll be even more closely bound up with one another than before. Come, oh, please, come to us!" (S 409-410). It is the obscure collective secret of these women which links them with one another most closely and which in an elemental form inhabits this very "maids' bedroom," where the maids do not yet have any "belongings" of their own and where they have not yet awakened to independent spiritual individuality. As "supplicants" they gladly and "delightedly" subject themselves to the strong, protecting man so that he may thereby be delivered over to them without misgivings.

Scarcely any other interpretation can be given to this demand of Pepi's. If Kafka had represented Pepi's wish to enter into a love or marriage contract in the so-called "normal" form in which such wishes are expressed and realized, if he had thus had Pepi ask K. to come to her and to her alone, he would have evoked in every reader the idea that perhaps in Pepi's case it really was a matter of genuine, individual love—as it was, indeed, according to Pepi's actual consciousness. However, since Kafka wants to show that Pepi is deceiving herself in this; that her apparent love for K. represents in truth only a completely general, female need for protection; that the female in her loves the male in him ("the hero")—then he had to have recourse to the striking figuration (which is absurd when considered empirically) of having Pepi try to induce K. to bind himself to three maids instead of to her alone. Only through this shocking presentation does the hidden truth become immediately visible and obvious.

For the distinctive characteristic of Kafka's images is that they correspond not to the outwardly visible truth but strictly to the truth that is "hidden." For Kafka it is not enough, as it is for other poets, to remain within the framework of the empirically visible and to hint in general intellectual terms at the truth concealed therein, òr to express it in vague feelings or visions; on the contrary, he transforms this truth immediately into a vivid image that appears as empirical reality in itself, and then of course hits the reader like a hammerblow, does not let him go, makes hedging impossible, but forces him to take a definite attitude toward the unadorned *factum brutum.*

This *factum brutum* here means that in such a marriage or love relationship as Pepi desires—and that numerous women desire along with her—there secretly exists only a collective relationship, although in the couple's consciousness and also in their concrete mode of life the marriage may seem completely normal.

Pepi, however, represents only one extreme, borderline form of love, although this form is a very widely distributed one. There are opposite positions that are just as extreme, as, for instance, Amalia's. Frieda, by contrast, is a woman who tries to bridge the extremes. Hence, justifiably, she is at the center of K.'s love experiences.

## Frieda's Battle for Personal Fulfillment in Love

From a superficial consideration, Frieda, by contrast with Pepi, is not at all suited to be a barmaid. Only under the aspect of Klamm's mistress does she appear beautiful to the others as well: "But what satisfies Klamm, how could the others help admiring that! And so Frieda, all of a sudden, became a great beauty, of exactly the kind needed in the tavern" (S 388). Seen from a normal, dispassionate point of view, Frieda is not beautiful, but "an inconspicuous little blonde girl with sad eyes and thin cheeks" (S 52). She is not even strikingly dressed. She wears a "thin, low-necked, cream-colored blouse which clothed her meagre body as if it did not belong there" (S 54), and which is accordingly derided by Pepi (S 394). "Only her silk petticoat, the only thing that she spends money on, rustles" (S 398). This corresponds to the fashions of the time before World War I, when really elegant women in high society would wear rustling taffeta petticoats beneath outer garments that were often very plain.

This sort of petticoat, then, is what Frieda wears beneath her inconspicuous outer garment, whereas, contrariwise, it is Pepi's undoing that she is unsuccessful in obtaining good underclothes. "It was much more difficult to obtain lingerie and shoes, and here is where [Pepi's] failure actually begins. . . . It was, in spite of everything, just coarse underwear that she gathered together and patched up, and, instead of trim little high-heeled shoes, it had to be low-heeled slippers" (S 394). Against her will Pepi remains in the sphere of a petty-bourgeois world of maids and housewives.

Frieda, however, "does battle." In her superior, knowing glance, which "had already disposed of matters that concerned him [K.], whose existence he himself had not yet known of at all," there "speaks not so much the struggle of the past, but the struggle of the future" (S 56). In this battle she is K.'s equal, and this also brings the two together in love.

Frieda, just like K., does not want to stay put in any specified position. In this respect, too, she differs from Gardena, the landlady of the Inn at the Bridge, in spite of her inward and outward dependence upon this worldly-wise "mommy" of hers who originally employed her and would employ her yet again, and who would like to alienate her from K. This landlady herself says of Frieda, "Frieda, who has been intimately associated with Klamm for such a long time, possesses no momento [of Klamm]; I have asked her; she is too rapturous and also too insatiable" (S 109).

As a matter of fact, Frieda, even as Klamm's mistress, has greater aspirations than has the landlady. Frieda, just like K., does not want to entreat Klamm for any "presents." K. states, "I want no presents from the castle given as acts of grace; I want only what is mine by right" (S 102). Frieda, too, in no way wishes to relax in Klamm but wants to go on, upward into the "future battle." Even though later on, in retrospect, her position as barmaid for Klamm may appear to her as a most blissful state, even in that position she was in fact already "insatiable." Even in her first conversation in the tavern with K., "in her tone, this time against her will, there seemed to be the vibrant ring, not of the victories of life but of the infinite disappointments" (S 56); indeed, she is actually raging with "anger" against Klamm, because "again and again" he brings "this rabble" along, his servants, the instinctual world, whose "presence agitates me . . . they are the most contemptible and most repellent creatures I know, and I have to fill *their* glasses with beer" (S 57). Klamm "could show consideration for my feelings, but all my pleading is in vain" (S 57).

As Klamm's mistress she lived in a "dissatisfied" state: "I was indifferent to almost everything" (S 75-76). For it is precisely that indefinite, girlish feeling of happiness in Klamm's proximity that makes her indifferent to her environment and, what is more, fills her with hatred for the bestial advances made by the men. She cannot yet sense that in Klamm's essence there must necessarily exist all the elements of Eros, and that his servants belong to him inseparably.

Not until the moment when she wins K., when she succeeds in breaking through the Herrenhof landlord's strict, official regulations, when she knows that K. will belong to her completely and that she intends to give herself to him—not until then does there enter into her "nature" "something joyous, free . . . which K. had not even noticed before" (S 59). And when Klamm calls to her, she "laughed quietly" in K.'s arms "and said, 'You don't suppose that I'm going to go! I'll never go to him.'" And then "she clenched her fist, and pounded on the door" between her and Klamm "and cried, 'I am with the land surveyor! I am with the land surveyor!'" (S 60-61). Thereupon K. cries out in horror, "'What have you done? . . .

We are both lost.' 'No,' said Frieda, 'only I am lost, but I have won you' " (S 60-61).

This points up a further difference between Frieda and the landlady. It is true that both women have some knowledge of Klamm; both feel the "happiness" that he bestows; both were close to him. Frieda, what is more, even knows, although she knows it only "with her gaze wandering afar," that her love for K.—that is to say, her tearing herself away from Klamm— was the work of Klamm himself (S 72). Her repudiation of Klamm was not a repudiation of the highest, most enigmatic happiness that Klamm was able to promise in his essence. But it was the repudiation of everything that appears on earth as a visible sign of this happiness: prestige, honor, beauty, property, the torrential current of the instinctual forces that she hates in Klamm's servants, etc. She wants to gain only one thing, and that is K. himself. She was "indifferent" to her whole environment. Only through her love for K. does she become "free." This freedom appears to the concrete upper level of her consciousness as a farewell to Klamm, as a renunciation of what is considered happiness in the customary sense. She wants to go away with K., go anywhere, at random, with him alone, and she wants to create a mode of existence for him, no matter where, no matter how. Hence she says, "Only I am lost, but I have won you."

## The Idols and the Resignation of the Married Woman

The landlady, on the other hand, who had requested and obtained from Klamm visible tokens of her happiness, persisted in her vague general feeling for Klamm, who was invisible to her. For her, too, everything external had become a matter of indifference because of Klamm: "Everything else [except Klamm] was a matter of indifference to me" (S 112); and when Klamm no longer called her, "I was very unhappy" (S 111). As a seventeen-year-old girl she sat in her garden for hours, doing nothing. In this state, "thinking of the Inn and the new work that would perhaps make me forget a little, I gave Hans my hand" in marriage (S 112).

Work, housekeeping, marriage, are for her anaesthetics, a substitute for the unattainable, lost happiness with Klamm. For that very reason she pitches into everyday life all the more strenuously, achieving astounding success through diligence, efficiency, and prudence. However, she does not love her husband; at night she raves to him about Klamm, who is far away, and inquiries into the inscrutable "reasons for his [Klamm's] change of mind" (S 111), so that Hans "really feels lost," and is unable to become "independent" and "manly" (S 116).

That is the picture of marriage as it is lived in thousands of cases. The wife develops into a practical, efficient housekeeper and housewife, takes the lead, and puts the husband out of the picture, as a rule unwittingly; for, so far as she is consciously aware, the landlady loves her husband and even carries on numerous conversations with him about Klamm.

The three presents, the mementos that she once obtained entreatingly from Klamm, are illuminating so far as her state is concerned. The first memento is a photograph that represents Klamm's young and handsome messenger, as he is suspended in midair in a high jump—the messenger whom she cannot forget. "It was the messenger through whom Klamm called me to him for the first time" (S 107). He aroused in her the first ecstatic experience of her girlhood. Meanwhile, however, the photograph has grown so faded that at first K. is able to distinguish only a young man lying "on a board, stretching and yawning" (S 107).

The second memento is a long shawl that completely envelops her. In it she finds safety and peace when she is overwhelmed by crises. As she lies in bed, sick and breathing hard, tormented by K.'s criticism of her life, of her "official" conception of love and marriage, she is strengthened and comforted by this shawl: "All suffering seemed to be taken away from her" (S 106). It is, as it were, the protective covering for her psyche, and gives her the strength to overcome all the hardships of existence and all her doubts. It is Klamm's most precious present. It validates her certainty of a continuing relationship with Klamm. It cannot fade and pass away. It is the token of an immortal, indestructible sphere that despite every mistake and every illusion remains preserved in all human beings. "It is a beautiful shawl" (S 106).

By contrast, Klamm's third present is quite different. It is a "small cap" of "delicate, lacy fabric," which is "too small," "quivered on her hairdo," makes "pitiful" the "ravages" visible in her face, although at the same time she looks "much younger in bed than in her clothes" (S 105). The small cap, which according to time-honored national custom indicates the change from maidenhood to wedlock, was the last present that she begged of Klamm. It is no longer suitable for her "gigantic" figure (S 66), indeed it makes the decline of her powerful body clearly "pitiful." The discrepancy between the life she has lived and the former meaning of this present—the symbol of a true marriage—grows relentlessly manifest. For the gigantic size of her body, of her "figure that almost darkens the room" (S 66), is of course in Kafka always the sign of those earthly powers that render themselves independent, that obstruct the path to the true law of existence. This "powerful" landlady is exactly like the gigantic mediating authorities in *The Man Who Was Lost Sight Of* and in *The Trial*: the head doormen, Mr. Green, Mr. Pollunder, the doorkeepers—symbolic of forces that work unremittingly, that are ever on duty, in "office," that only impersonally direct the universal machinery of existence, that only "mediate."

This landlady, too, wishes to mediate. But even she knows only of official mediations between K. and Klamm (S 118). And ultimately, when K. cannot promise her that he will "undertake nothing on his own" (S 118), she even becomes malicious. Thereupon she absolutely refuses K. lodgings in her inn; of course she is also deeply wounded because she has allowed herself to be swept away into confiding in K. and has exposed her private weaknesses to him.

At the same time it grows clearly evident from this that K., who compared to her seems to be so powerless, is in truth far superior to her inwardly.

## K.'s Criticism of Female Resignation in Love: Klamm's Disregarded Summons

It is K.—not the landlady and not even Frieda—who recognizes the true relationship between humankind and Klamm. The landlady's life complaint that Klamm called her only three times but then finally forgot her and left her—this very sorrow that interferes with her whole existence is branded by K. as a "legend," as a disastrous self-deception, as a weakness in faith, indeed as a "trite fiction." " 'Klamm forgets right away, you said. That seems to me highly improbable in the first place; but in the second place it cannot be proved, and is obviously nothing but a legend, invented by the girlish minds of those who happened to be in Klamm's favor. I am amazed that you believe such a trite fiction.' 'It is no legend,' said the landlady, 'on the contrary it comes from general experience.' 'Well then, it can also be refuted by new experience,' said K." (S 117).

The landlady relies upon "general experience" according to which happiness in love can be experienced only while one is young and in a state of emotional ecstasy and idealistic enthusiasm; the practical life of adults, however, has to resign itself and be content with its lot. For K. these are paltry legends to be refuted "by new experience." For K., man *always* has the chance of getting to Klamm. He has only to confront him and not let himself be frightened off by the general, "official" rules of life. True life, which is constantly being "forgotten" by the concrete human being, can in reality never forget us. It always confronts our existence as a possibility and a breathtaking promise. K. says the same thing with respect to Frieda's "mourning" over the fact that "Klamm left me" (S 76). "For Klamm not to summon Frieda any more—that, in a manner of speaking, did not happen at all," says K., "on the contrary, he did call her, but she did not heed his call. It is even possible that he is still waiting for her" (S 117).

K. thus stubbornly persists in his conviction that man can at all times freely penetrate to the high powers of existence; that the alleged "general experiences" of mankind are to be refuted and can be overcome by "new" ones. K. does not give up in the face of stupefying customs. For him the landlady's suffering is a doom of her own making, a doom that had its origins in unbelief, in the inability to engage the entire free self of the human being.

The landlady, on the other hand, feels that even to establish a merely official connection between K. and Klamm is already a "shameless" thing (S 118), so enraptured, inviolable, and sacred is that emotional state which Klamm represents to her. And this gigantic woman becomes ill at the thought of K.'s victory over Klamm—victory in his relationship with Frieda, and victory because of his tireless efforts to reach Klamm personally. This means that the landlady sees K.'s attack as a threat to the entire safe world structure by which she is supported. Land surveying in point of fact is a revolutionary act.

## In Conflict between Sensuous and Personal Love

Thereby, however, light is shed on the complications between Frieda and K.

K. is determined, before his marriage to Frieda, to speak personally with Klamm "about Frieda"; this the landlady absorbs "uncomprehendingly" (S 72). This means that K. wants to bring down upon his marriage the "blessing" that the landlady "neglected" to bring down by failing "to ask Klamm." This, however, even Frieda can never understand. "That is absolutely impossible," she declares (S 68). For Klamm, to her as well as to the landlady, is a purely impersonal, invisible, official power. Indeed, it was for that very reason that she fled from Klamm to K., fled into individual, personal love—by contrast with the landlady, who actually, all her life, remained within the framework of only impersonal, general emotions; and by contrast, too, with K., who is striving to reach Klamm and wants to question him and talk with him personally. For Frieda Klamm is the representative of an affective love that is absolutely super-individual and sensuous: "There's more than enough of Klamm here as it is, too much Klamm; it is to escape from him that I want to leave" (S 184). But she is nevertheless also "sad" that Klamm left her. The contradictions seem to become unresolvable, both between Frieda and K., and within Frieda herself.

These contradictions result from the nature of human love itself. Love is always an encounter with a unique, noninterchangeable individuality; that is to say, with a personal phenomenon. At the same time, however, love is always determined by superpersonal, sensuous powers of nature; that is to say, a collective phenomenon. In the concrete love encounter both phenomena can mask one another reciprocally. As the saying goes. "Love is blind" to the true nature of the beloved. Lovers can live with one another for years, blind about themselves and about each other, led by inclinations and feelings that govern them omnipotently and that cover over or even fail to touch at all upon what is distinctive and unique in their individualities.

However, love can also make manifest the individual self of the lover and that of the beloved; indeed, through love the self is actually discovered for the first time, brought forth and realized. In the self of the beloved the self of the lover is born as well, brought to quickening reality, brought to "consciousness." That is the meaning of the "glance" that falls upon K. at his first meeting with Frieda. Through this glance K. is as it were first made acquainted with his self. He penetrates levels of his nature hitherto unknown to him, and he illuminates these levels immediately; what is more, he masters and solves with incredible ease everything related to them. "As this glance fell upon K., it seemed to him that it had already disposed of matters that concerned him, whose existence he himself had not yet known of at all, whose existence he was convinced of, however, by her glance" (S 52).

But conversely, too, Frieda is transformed by K.'s glance, for

K. sees to the heart of her "battle" as well. Through K., Frieda's "nature" takes on something "free, joyous."

But this very glance into the "self" can fail to discern the superpersonal powers that likewise determine love and that must be individualized if a perfect fulfillment of love is to become possible.

This is the unresolved tension in the first love encounter between Frieda and K. " 'My darling! my sweet darling!' she whispered, but she did not touch K. at all; she lay on her back as if faint with love, and stretched out her arms; time was indeed infinite in the presence of her blissful love; she sighed, rather than sang, some little song or other" (S 59-60). In the blissful feeling of her lover's closeness, time and space, as it were, sink away for her, she is "faint" with love, "did not touch K. at all," sighed a little song out of happiness. She is infinitely close to K.'s self, but this very closeness is remoteness from the real K., who likewise "remained still, lost in thought," and in his spirit is bound to her with infinite closeness, and yet for that very reason is infinitely far away. Each is within himself, and, although each is psychically close to the other, neither is really open to the other; each is in his own sphere: she in a song, he in quiet thought.

With logical consistency the reversal then takes place: "Then, startled, since K. remained still, lost in thought, she began to tug at him like a child, 'Come, it's stifling down here!' They embraced one another, her small body burned in K.'s hands; they rolled about in a state of unconsciousness that K. kept trying to get free of all the time, but in vain" (S 60).

The state of spiritual closeness was no open state in which one could breathe freely; one was in danger of stifling in it. The spell is broken by Frieda. Like a "child" she tugs at him. Klamm's superpersonal powers assert their rights: The childish assistants, Klamm's delegates, who in Klamm's "employ" (S 61) are copresent, without K.'s knowledge, in this embrace, are justly designated by K. as the actually operative forces. After the embrace, when he catches sight of them, he has the feeling that "they were to blame for everything" (S 61). These powers transport Frieda and K. into the state of "unconsciousness." Although these powers bring the two physically close to one another, there is an accompanying loss of "self" in each. In vain does K. try to "free" himself from this state of unconsciousness.

Hours passed, hours of shared breathing, of shared heartbeat, hours in which K. continually had the feeling that he was going astray or that he was far away in another, an alien region, farther away than anyone had ever been before him, an alien region where even the air had no element of the air at home, where one was bound to stifle with the strangeness of it, and where one could do nothing but continue in the absurd allurements there, continue going astray. (S 60)

Even in this unconsciousness one is in danger of stifling. In neither of the two spheres can man really "breathe." That is the meaning of this image which occurs again and again in Kafka—that the individual human being is unable to breathe in the atmosphere of the officials, and the officials in turn are unable to breathe in the atmosphere of individuals (cf. P 90-91; *inter alia*). Only both worlds, that of the officials and that of individuality, constitute a full human existence. But the two spheres cannot be united.

Accordingly, from this first love encounter there result opposing aspirations and emotional states in Frieda and K. As Klamm's voice rings out in their embraces and calls to Frieda, at first she wants "to leap up ... in virtually innate obedience ... but then she thought better of it ... laughed quietly, and said, 'You don't suppose that I'm going to go! I'll never go to him'" (S 60). The moment she "thought better of it," and becomes "still," she once again is aware of the uniqueness of her love for K., wants to belong to him unconditionally and exclusively, and to break the spell of the superpersonal powers that bind her to Klamm. She terminates her "virtually innate obedience" to Klamm, having at first been in danger of succumbing to him again at his call. Her "change of heart" makes her consciously free of Klamm.

However, her isolated awareness is powerless and is deceived about the real forces of life. In her actual existence Frieda remains bound to Klamm. In the last analysis it was Klamm, of course, whom she obeyed when she broke the isolating spell of her individual love, impotent with happiness, and embraced K. Klamm had brought the two together. Hence she will always remain under the spell of Klamm and his two assistants. And she has to remain under his spell as long as she is a woman who loves.

K. feels exactly the opposite. Coming as he does from an unheard-of situation, having had the feeling in his embraces with Frieda that he was going astray, losing himself in an alien region, betraying himself and his struggle to anonymous powers unknown to him, he actually experiences a "dawning of comfort when a summons for Frieda issues from Klamm's room in a deep, commanding, aloof voice" (S 60). Klamm's call is comforting to him, because for the first time it lends a voice to the powers that are unknown to him but that tempt and at the same time alienate him. To get into conversation with that voice would mean gaining sensuous along with spiritual existence. As Frieda refuses to obey the voice, K. then "wanted to object, wanted to urge her to go to Klamm" (S 60). On the other hand, however—and this is the inner contradiction in K.—"he was far too happy . . . to have Frieda in his possession, far too anxiously happy, too, for it seemed to him that if Frieda should forsake him, everything he had would forsake him" (S 60).

Frieda's individuality is for him the only thing that he possesses. Moreover, she is the only thing that sustains him, grants him access to life, to the determining powers of existence. Therefore, on the one hand he must, "anxiously happy," keep her entirely and solely for himself. On the other hand, however, he must understand her also as a mediatrix to Klamm, and must send her to Klamm, that ruling power on which his existence depends and without which no land surveying is possible. If, however, she "forsakes" him, she will once again become completely the slave of Klamm—and in that case he himself is also lost. Sensuous unconsciousness and thoughtful, individual knowledge would have to be united in love. That is the problem

The formulation once used by the landlady to express this is quoted by Frieda in the following way: K. does not love Frieda herself at all, but he uses her only as a "pawn" (S 207), as a means to an end, in order to gain ground under his feet and to forge ahead toward Klamm. And, accordingly, when she hears from K. that he had wandered astray in the village before he knew her, Frieda is frightened too (S 206). From that she must conclude that K. loves her only so that through her he may gain space to exist in. Frieda explains,

"But then—this is what the landlady said at the end—when you see that you were mistaken in everything, in your assumptions and in your hopes, in your notion of Klamm and his relations with me, that is when my hell will begin ; for then, more than ever, I'll be the only thing you own that you still depend on, but at the same time I'll be a possession which has proved worthless and which you'll treat accordingly, since you have no feeling for me but that of ownership." (S 208)

With this, a terrible borderline possibility of human love and marriage is formulated by the worldly-wise landlady who knows what disappointment means : every love wakens hope for a new, happier chance of existence. Hence, when such a hope is frustrated, this love can change abruptly into a hell. K. himself recognizes this : "Everything you say is correct, in a certain sense; it is not untrue; only hostile. They are the thoughts of the landlady, my enemy. . . . But they are instructive—one can still learn a good deal from the landlady" (S 211).

Then, however, K. formulates this saving insight :

"But then, Frieda, consider! Even if everything were exactly the way the landlady says it is, it would be quite dreadful in one respect only, and that is if you did not love me. Then, only then, would it really be a case of my having won you by calculation and trickery, in order to capitalize on my possessing you . . . . But if it really isn't so dreadful as that, and it wasn't a sly beast of prey that clutched you to him that night—if, instead, you came toward me as I went toward you, and we found one another, both putting thought of self behind us—tell me, Frieda, what is the situation then? In that case I would be pleading my cause as

yours ; in that case there is no difference here, and only an enemy
could draw a distinction." (S 211)

K. realizes that in his "battle" both are involved, Frieda as
well as he, and that here no distinction can or should be made.
Love is reciprocal clarification and perfecting. The one partner
must never be played off against the other.

### The Tragedy of Love That Is Unthinkingly Trusting

Nevertheless, neither Frieda nor K. can sustain this love;
neither can overcome the existing conflicts.

Frieda wants to realize her individual love for K. in a worldless freedom; this is possible only in her "dream" of a "grave"
—that is to say, it is impossible in reality. At the same time,
no matter how she struggles, she cannot resist the fascination of
Klamm's official messengers, the assistants. "With her face distorted with friendliness toward the assistant and with beseeching
helplessness toward K.... [she] remained ... with ... a rigid
smile" (S 215), locked in her conflicts.

Frieda cannot independently and spiritually penetrate and
control the sensuously alluring sphere of the assistants, nor can
she really understand the individuality of K., whose private
walks to the Barnabas family are totally strange, incomprehensible, and even distasteful to her. Without reflection she surrenders herself to the "happiness" of K.'s proximity as well as
to the happiness that radiates from Klamm's superpersonal
powers. Just as, "faint" with happiness, she felt K.'s nearness,
so too, like a "child," she turns to the happiness of sensuous
embraces; in these embraces she does not have the feeling, as
does K., of "going astray," of an "alien region," a threatening
overwhelming of her self by anonymous forces. Directly and
without a breach, she unites both and appears able to realize
true love thereby; she believes—justifiably, from her point of
view—that she can become happy with K.: "My love for you

would have helped me over everything, in the end it would have advanced you too, if not here in the village, then elsewhere; it had already given one proof of its power: it rescued you from the Barnabas family" (S 209).

But that is precisely her error. She has no inkling that K.'s persistant efforts in the direction of the Barnabas family are necessarily a part of his battle, so that in this respect K. is obeying the inner law of his individuality. For Amelia is the only woman in the village who actually breaks with the officials and, what is more, does so out of clear knowledge: She alone has vision. "Face-to-face with truth she stood, and lived and endured this life, then as now" (S 278).

The ostracism of this family, on the basis of Amalia's clear, conscious break, is therefore of the highest significance for K. In it an extreme possibility of genuine battle can be caught sight of.

Frieda, however, breaks with Klamm without spiritual realization. Purely and simply, she obeys an impulse that she trusts, a magical force impelling her toward K., to whom she surrenders, faint with happiness. In truth, therefore, she cannot actually break with Klamm at all, and remains under his spell. Conflicting within her are two instincts, not two realizations.

Her dream of resting with K. alone in the grave expresses the desperate and unreflective element of her longing for K. The fascination exercised over her by the assistants, and likewise her desperate attempts to ward off that fascination, are in turn forms of expressing that same spiritual impotence.

In other words, Frieda's love is the love of every normal woman. Integratedly, harmoniously, without reflective effort, obeying only her immediate, genuine emotion, she thinks that she can love K. and establish a household with him.

Only when K., disregarding her, strives, in a way that is incomprehensible to her, to achieve a personal encounter with Klamm, and finally even visits that Barnabas family from which she intends actually to "rescue" him—only then does she become disturbed and discordant. For in Amalia and her family no immediate happiness whatsoever exists any more, and every bond with life and love is severed. In the Barnabas family, according to Frieda's opinion, K. can become only unhappy.

## The Normal Middle-class Household as an Absurd Form of Existence

Even the household that she establishes with K.—strange as it at first sounds—is reflective of quite normal middle-class housekeeping. K. submits to his occupational duties as school janitor; Frieda with touching devotion tries to make her dwelling comfortable, pleasant, attractive, and clean. However, by the very channels of K.'s occupation and Frieda's domestic tasks the outside world constantly intrudes upon their private life.

The seemingly absurd, empirically unreal presentation of their bed-sitting-room as simultaneously a public schoolroom with gymnastic equipment, a room which must be relinquished every morning for the public school instruction, is the figurative expression of a truth that remains concealed under outward middle-class life—the truth that, in fact, usually without the family's being aware of it, publicness incessantly invades the family, making any genuinely private life illusory. So-called domestic happiness is middle-class self-deception. State and society are constantly influencing the family, no matter whether through the husband's occupation or the domestic activity of the wife who is dependent upon her environment, or whether through the decrees of the authorities.

## The Terror of the "Respectable" Woman

It is characteristic that it is Gisa, the prudish and "stiff" teacher, who disturbs the private life of the lovers: "A school-janitor's family that lolls about in bed until late in the morning! Ugh!" she exclaims (S 173). And K. resignedly observes, "Indeed one did not have a moment's peace" (S 173). "Not yet fully dressed, K. and Frieda, leaning against the parallel bars, looked on at the destruction of their meagre belongings" (S 174).

Gisa the teacher is one of those women who "set great store by respectability" (S 458). Whenever she leaves her room in the company of Schwarzer, who loves her, the light is on, but generally she keeps the door locked to him (S 218). She is a woman "whose sluggish nature, it is true, occasionally was roused to a savage passion that knew no bounds; yet she would never have tolerated anything similar in others at other times" (S 217).

Hence, by virtue of her perversely dishonest prudishness, she is also the only woman in the village in whose case the relationship between village and castle is reversed. She has made Schwarzer, the son of a castellan, subject to her; and, hopelessly in love with her, he roves about in the village. Through her the determining powers are perverted and regimented. Similarly, too, the "girl from the castle" is forced into a way of life incongruous with her by Brunswick the shoemaker, who wants to turn the village regulations topsy-turvy in a purely possessive, egotistical manner.

The rape of the natural instincts and patterns by the rules of etiquette actually brings it about that the base, earthly forces dominate the spiritual, reflective, and controlling organs represented in the castle. The rules of etiquette exercise a terroristic domination and behave arbitrarily, although they are incapable of truly shaping the instinctual world; this becomes clear in the schoolteacher Gisa's "savage" discharges of emotion that "knew no bounds." It is characteristic that it is this very Schwarzer, in bondage to her, who, upon K.'s entrance into the village, in a "ridiculous" outburst of "official arrogance (S 218-19) wants to dispute K.'s right to remain in the inn and the village. In reality he is in no way authorized by the castle to confront K. with such impudence. In Gisa and Schwarzer one catches sight of the illegitimate claim made by external rules of etiquette and by norms, a claim to domination over the total spiritual and physical life of man. Hence Gisa is also the actual mistress of Frieda's and K.'s private middle-class life. She penetrates directly into their family life and destroys their household. For her rules of etiquette really determine all middle-class existence. Into Frieda's and K.'s nights Gisa's power penetrates in the shape of her old, fat, indolent cat, with whose claws she, Gisa, wounds K.

## K.'s Assistants and the World of the Elemental in the Cosmos and in Society

However, even Klamm's official messengers, the two assistants, disturb K.'s and Frieda's private life.

They are the "old" assistants whom K. brought along to the village from his earlier existence, and are nevertheless the new assistants whom Galater, substituting for Klamm, sent to K. (S 29-30, 34). That is not a contradiction. For they represent vital, unthinking, elemental forces that are always present in every human being, forces that K. must encounter here again and that he must become aware of anew. Since in their case it is a matter of superindividual, collective forces, they are as indistinguishable to him "as snakes. . . . I see you only with my eyes, and with those [my eyes] I cannot distinguish you. For that reason I shall treat the two of you as one man" (S 30). Their "most important" duty consists of cheering K. up a little (S 309). K. is bound to feel this to be annoying and distracting from his battle. Their amusing diversions would force him into Klamm's service and rob him of an unhampered encounter with Klamm. Hence, they are in fact as seductive "as snakes" whose enticements he must withstand.

On the other hand, they seem to represent precisely that purpose-free, childlike, happy life form without which human existence is not possible. However, K. must guard his freedom against even such a purpose-free sphere, for it tempts one to abandon consciousness. Furthermore, the assistants feel their duties to be "hard work" (S 309). The seemingly joyous, childish quality of their nature is strangely under coercion. That very childishness entails a great exertion on their part, whereas conversely, they consider K.'s serious struggling as something quite irrational and childish. They declare that it "is very unjust" of K., "malicious, almost childish, to make the work so much harder for the worker" (S 309).

That is as much as to say that in no way do the assistants belong to a truly purpose-free, childlike, spontaneous sphere. In reality, as will be shown later, they are old (S 308-309), and indeed their "not very appetizing" figures consist of "flesh that occasionally gave the impression of being not quite alive" (S 311). Their cheeks are flushed, "but look as if they consisted of excessively loose flesh" (S 334). Thus their youth, childlikeness, joyousness, the manly way in which they stretch out their arms after her, etc., that so enchant Frieda, can be seen only as long as they are performing their "duty" at K.'s. Off duty they are old, worn, indeed not even vigorous men. "After all, I am not young any more!" says Jeremias, as he complains about his being mistreated by K. (S 309).

However, they grow old only if they are separated, each on his own, without any contact with his coassistant. " 'It is because I am alone,' said Jeremias; 'if I am alone, then my cheerful youthfulness is gone too' " (S 308). Only as a collective being do they remain healthy and young.

They come originally from the castle where they were servants. All the servants in the castle resemble one another: "One servant looks like the other" (S 291). In contrast with their masters there, they have only very "light duties" (S 291).

"They are mostly quiet people basically, spoiled and made phlegmatic by their light duties. 'May you have a servant's life,' is a benediction used by the officials; and actually, so far as good living is concerned, the servants are said to be the real lords in the castle—they know how to appreciate this, too, and in the castle, where they go about subject to its laws, they are calm and dignified." (S 291-92)

That means, therefore, that in the castle they represent immediate, unreflective life within the framework of unbroken, natural, extrahuman laws and regulations. Hence, in the castle they are calm, quiet, phlegmatic, and have light duties.

That is altered as soon as they enter the human sphere. There, like Klamm's servants, they are, in one case, transformed into a "savage, insubordinate crew, dominated by their insatiable instincts instead of their laws. Their shamelessness knows no bounds" (S 292); for only then, when the instinctual forces, which are under strict natural laws, erupt into the sphere of free human consciousness, then, indeed, is a sudden change into "insatiability" and "shamelessness" possible. Or else, like K.'s helpers (who watch him consciously doing battle as, in contradistinction to the villagers, he refuses to succumb to the instinctual powers), they become "a little excited and astonished" (S 170). They cannot empathize with his "duties," his will, his purposes, which they do not understand; and they think that they can serve him by learning everything from him almost like automatons, by observing him incessantly through their fingers, using their hands as telescopes, and by being constantly at his heels. They are like man's elemental, involuntary instincts and reflexes that assert themselves repeatedly against his will and without his knowledge, that "divert" him from his conscious "battle." This is where their fascination lies for Frieda; but this is also where their danger exists for her, with respect to her love for K.

Since they serve adults, they retain only remnants of the childlike, joyous, or quiet, calm manner they formerly had at the castle (S 332-33). They are now constrained by duties, of which they are consciously aware. "Our job is really not easy," they tell K. at the very outset, when he catches sight of them in the tavern after his first love encounter with Frieda (S 61). As long as they are on duty they have no awareness of its meaning, and cannot and may not explain to K. what its significance is (S 310). They are then completely lost in their task, which essentially personifies a natural, unthinking sphere that would itself be nullified through reflection and interpretation. However, even within this role, they really do not feel their occupation to be play, but rather hard work, a coercion, since they are under the domination of an awareness that constantly irritates and goads them on.

The foolish and erotically attractive element of their nature is a forced artificiality that has become almost mechanical. The "assistance" that the castle contributes to the land surveyor by way of these cheery, amusing fellows is thus extremely ambiguous in character, to say the least. In that assistance there may be seen in a very sharp criticism by Kafka of the efforts of the adult world to furnish itself—by means of cheerfulness, high spirits, and buoyant spontaneity of living—with an air of animation that must long since have ceased to be genuine, since adults are no longer children and could acquire true cheerful serenity only through a more mature level of consciousness where spirit and life interpenetrate reciprocally, and where wisdom and joy become one.

Everywhere in Kafka can be found self-critical remarks against the possibility of pulling oneself out of crucial "miserable" states by means of artificial high spirits and creating the impression of living. The following is but one example: "To lift oneself out of a miserable state, even by a deliberate effort, is bound to be easy. I tear myself away from my easy chair, run round the table, exercise my head and neck, bring a sparkle to my eyes, tense the muscles around them" (E 33).

In these assistants, too, one may perceive an image of the death-proneness of all earthly things, of the domination of Count Westwest, to which their "flesh, not quite alive" alludes. In any case, completely without reflection, they are at the mercy of the master who controls them, to the point of self-annihilation. K. notices this with amazement when he catches sight of his assistant Jeremias, whom he had chased out into the freezing cold and who is now "tired to death," clinging to the fence. " 'His stubbornness is exemplary,' said K. to himself, though he had to add, 'a person would freeze to death from it at the fence.' " (S 214-15). Jeremias remains faithful to his duty, even if he is to perish in it.

Nevertheless, the assistants can by no means be interpreted univocally as positive aids that K., by virtue of his obstinate battle, cannot understand and evaluate correctly; nor can these assistants be interpreted as aids that K. should have emulated, say, even as exemplars for his behavior and in his love for Frieda. For K., too, is irritated by them.

Even Frieda sees the hybrid character, the equivocal dubiousness, and, what is more, the macabre sinisterness and "blackness" of their nature.

"Klamm's official messengers, to be sure," said Frieda, "that they may be; but at the same time they are also silly boys that still need a beating to teach them good manners. What ugly black boys they are! And what a revolting contrast there is between their faces, that suggest adults, yes, almost university students, and their childishly silly behavior. Do you think I do not see that? I am actually ashamed of them. But that is just the trouble; they do not repel me, but I am ashamed of them. I have to keep on looking over at them. Whenever one should be annoyed with them, I have to laugh. Whenever one should have an urge to slap them, I have to stroke their hair." (S 186)

In her immediate, womanly feeling Frieda is thus thoroughly conscious of the fact that the fascination that emanates from the assistants is not something that is truly spontaneous, naïve, and genuine. It is a matter of "adults," indeed, even "almost university students," who should, therefore, already be delving into spiritual regions, but who repeatedly lapse into uncontrollable "silliness." Hence it follows that, fundamentally, these assistants represent nothing but a mixture of erotic seduction-artists (this finds expression in their molestations of Frieda) and harmless jokesters who play purely and simply "the way a hungry dog plays, yet without daring to jump up on the table" (S 329).

The artificial, automatous liveliness with which they want to lighten K.'s life, is thus at bottom only a reflection of vital residues that are present in K. as in every normal human being. They are merely residues, for the intact naïveté of the child life or of the cosmic-elemental life is no longer present in man who has tasted of the tree of knowledge. This primordial vitality shows itself on the one hand as instinct erupting turbulently (as in the case of the villagers), or, on the other (as in the case of K. and Frieda), in those involuntary reflex actions or high spirits laboriously and artificially produced by the assistants, high spirits that are supposed to lighten and enliven workaday life.

Thus, even in these assistants Kafka has given form to quite "normal" phenomena of our life. Therefore, too, it is no wonder that Frieda, with her normal womanly feeling, on the one hand understands the behavior of these cheerful seduction-artists and is ashamed of it, and yet on the other, repeatedly, against her will, is affected by their jokes and by their foolish, "sparkling" glance and is never able to withdraw *entirely* from them. They are so much more enticing then the tenacious "battle" of a K., a battle that in the last analysis remains incomprehensible to her.

## The Break between Natural Love and Spiritual Demand

For what K. is *really* striving for, Frieda, in spite of her genuine love for him, can never fully understand. Her natural feelings are too much under the influence of Klamm's world. K.'s demands simply aim too high. One may call to mind Kafka's letters to Milena, who from available autobiographical information is of course the model for Frieda. In one letter to her Kafka writes: "I cannot make it clear to you or to anyone how things are in me... the most important thing is plain: within my sphere it is impossible to live, to live humanly. You see that and you still are unwilling to believe it?" (M 251). In another letter to Milena, he writes:

If you then... were willing to give up the whole world in order to descend to me, so far down that from where you were one would see not just very little but nothing more at all, you, for this purpose—strangely, strangely—would need not to descend but to reach beyond you, in a superhuman manner, reach up high *above* you, *above* you, so powerfully that in so doing you would perhaps have to split apart, plunge down, disappear (and I then, of course, with you). (M 117)

Frieda cannot measure up to K.'s demand in spite of that superior glance which pierced K. to the core and bound him to her forever—in spite of this glance which similarly fascinated Kafka in his encounter with Milena (M 42). But because of this very glance K. must fight for Frieda as if for air to breathe. Even when she leaves him with Jeremias the assistant and returns to the tavern, he still hopes to be able to win her back (S 311), never altogether relinquishing this hope (S 333, 407), not even when Frieda appears to be turning definitely to Jeremias the helper, in her belief that K. loves Olga or Amalia and has been unfaithful to her (S 336). And yet Frieda loves K. now as before. After her return to the Herrenhof she says to him: "If only we had emigrated right away, that very night— we could have been in safety somewhere, always together, your hand always near enough for me to grasp; how I have need of your nearness; ever since I have known you, how forlorn I have been without your nearness; truly, your nearness is the only dream I dream, there is no other" (S 334).

But in the long run Frieda cannot sustain K.'s sphere. She must enter into the Klamm world again. When she returns to the tavern she "gazed at him fixedly" (S 323). In vain K. "looked searchingly into her eyes." He no longer finds that former glance in her eyes. "But her rigid bearing scarcely relaxed.... It was as if she had forgotten how he looked and wished to summon him back to mind in this way [by running her hand over his brow and cheeks]; even her eyes had the curtained look that goes with intense effort to remember" (S 323).

The complications that prevent the actualization of this love result from Frieda's and K.'s disparate levels of life and consciousness. Frieda is bound to leave K. for two reasons: first, K. threatens life itself. There is profound significance in the fact that, to begin with, Frieda sees it as her primary task to take care of and heal Jeremias, the sick assistant who has been beaten by K. and chased out into the cold. To her feminine sensibility, K.'s repulse of the assistants is a sin against life itself— in spite of all the reservations that she herself has in regard to the assistants. K. destroys the naïve, immediate emotional world without which she, as a woman, cannot live. For in the assistants she loses, above all, the safe world of childhood—everything that sustains man from the very beginning: "I was drawn to him; he is a playmate I had in my childhood—we used to play together on the slope of the castle hill—lovely days—you have never asked me anything about my past" (S 329). Even his seeming attempts at seduction, she thinks, were actually "only a game" (S 329). He never seriously dared or wished to tear her away from K. In fact, K. is to blame for the severe ill-treatment accorded the assistants. He slights and even does violence to a sphere in man that must never be left out of consideration if human existence is to remain natural and vital. On the other hand, this guilt is inevitable, for the elemental sphere creates a dissonance with K.'s struggle. Only on a very high level, were K. to gain full insight into the castle, would a reconciliation with the elemental sphere become possible.

Second, K. allies himself with the dregs of humanity: with Olga who, like a prostitute, "for more than two years, at least twice a week" (S 292) has surrendered herself, in the stable of the Herrenhof at night, to Klamm's bestially disorderly servants, whom Frieda so hates; and with Amalia, the "most shameless of all" (S 325), who has severed all relationship with the officials. Obviously, therefore, Frieda finds the ostracized Barnabas family so objectionable because it is in a double sense outside any "natural" world, any human world in her sense: in Amalia the family no longer participates in the normal human world of heart and spirit—Amalia's break with the officials implies nothing else but this—and in Olga the family surrenders to the most unrestrained and depraved instinctual powers of existence. Even Barnabas and his father appear despicable to Frieda, because in desperate, futile, even humiliating petitions they constantly beg for the favor of the officials and for access to them, whereas all the villagers, including Frieda, have a quite matter-of-course, unreflective relationship with those powers of existence represented by the officials. The Barnabas family has, as it were, fallen out of mankind's normal frame of mind and spirit, and either endeavors, by all possible means of manipulation and every variety of self-humiliation, to get into that framework again, or remains defiantly on the outside, like Amalia, the "most shameless" of all.

Consistently, then, Frieda can look upon K.'s exertions gravitating toward this family only with loathing and believes that she must "rescue" K. from it. To her natural, instinctive way of feeling, K. is utterly lost if he associates with such people. By so doing he betrays his own better self, and thereby also the most sacred part of him, the part that Frieda loves. "Everyone in some general way will want to show that he despises us," says Olga; "obviously he would have to despise himself if he did not do that" (S 471). That in fact is also Frieda's attitude. For her, K.'s relationship with the Barnabas family is tantamount to a betrayal of himself and of his love for her.

That is the real reason for her return to the tavern. She cannot do otherwise; thereby she is merely obeying the sacred law of her love. Her parting from K. is the very justification of her love for him. By giving him notice of her leaving, she remains loyal to him in the most mystical sense. She loves him eternally, even though his behaviour is impossible, even though his actions prevent any love for him from being fulfilled in reality.

K. feels exactly the opposite. For the very reason of his love for Frieda, he must go to the Barnabas family: "I must go there because of our common future, as you know" (S 325). Of course she does not know this at all, but he must assume that she does. He cannot imagine that Frieda is unable to comprehend the final, innermost mystery of his struggle and thereby the mystery of his self. He must overcome the powers of existence personally, freely, and judiciously. Only in this way can his love for Frieda also reach perfection. The petitions and tireless endeavors of the Barnabas family in their attempts to get through to the castle hierarchy reflect his own efforts. And even Amalia's radical break with the officials is germane to his revolutionary land-surveying activity, and is an element, at any rate a borderline contingency, of his battle. Olga and Amalia represent the extreme poles of his ambiguous battle: infinitely painstaking (not unreflective) devotion, and dispassionate, uncompromising aloofness and breaking off with the officials. These two tendencies, if united, could lead to the complete clarification of human existence. Therefore K.'s turning to Olga and Amalia is in fact no betrayal of Frieda but the prerequisite for his attaining a perfect "common future" with Frieda.

K. recognizes "that here he found people, who, at least externally, felt very much as he did, to whom he could attach himself, with whom he could communicate in many ways, not merely in some, as was the case with Frieda" (S 235).

It can be clearly seen from this that Frieda's range of understanding, according to K.'s view, is more limited than that of the Barnabas family. Olga and Amalia see more than Frieda sees for the very reason that they are unhappier than she and no longer have the security that she has: "To be sure, he gradually lost hope of success for the Barnabas mission, but, the worse off Barnabas was up there, the closer he grew to him down here; K. had never thought that it was possible for such an unfortunate endeavor as that of Barnabas and his sister to come from the village itself" (S 235).

Hence, too, Olga and Amalia are not his goal. They merely deliver weapons to him in his battle. Now as before, his goal is Frieda, perhaps a Frieda who is to be transformed and elevated by means of new understanding, a Frieda who, as it is stated in the letter to Milena, could reach out, in superhuman manner, beyond and high above herself. But that Olga and Amalia could then become his goal, without his being aware of it; that, as Amalia bluntly tells him to his face, he has already been in love with Olga for a long time without being aware of it (S 224) —that is understandable and complicates the problem. At all events, K. consciously believes that he loves Frieda unswervingly and that he will always love her.

In summary: The antinomies between Frieda and K. are the antinomies between, on the one hand, a woman who loves directly and genuinely, who unreflectively would like to welcome and reconcile the powers of existence, who naïvely wants to restore harmony between individual love and the superpersonal natural forces; and, on the other hand, a man aspiring to the absolute, who attempts personally and freely to overcome all the powers of existence, encounters them objectively, and hopes to be able to bring about the harmony between devotion and judicious detachment, but only through the fullest understanding and through an endless experience of life and "battle," and to accomplish this in a state in which thought and emotion, knowledge and feeling, waking and sleeping, are completely interpenetrated.

The further roads that K. takes to reach this goal must at this stage be of concern to us. Primarily it is a matter of K.'s encounter with the Barnabas family and with Bürgel the secretary.

## Amalia's Unconditional Demand

### A. RELIGIOUS MISINTERPRETATION

Formerly, only three years earlier, the Barnabas family had belonged to the most highly regarded families of the village. The family was ostracized because Amalia had rejected the letter written by Sortini the official, a letter couched "in the most vulgar terms" (S 254), bidding her go to him immediately. Filled with "indignation" (S 255), she had torn Sortini's letter to bits and thrown the shreds into the messenger's face (S 254); and even later on she did not attend the official interrogations at the Herrenhof for "hushing up" the matter (S 256-57).

This scene has posed one of the most controversial problems of the novel ever since Max Brod, in his epilogue to the first edition, gave the following interpretation:

If the relations (experienced and assumed by K.) between the women and the "castle" (that is, divine guidance) should prove to be puzzling and inexplicable, particularly in the Sortini episode where the official (heaven) evidently makes some immoral and filthy demand of the girl, reference may be made to Kierkegaard's *Fear and Trembling*—a work, besides, that Kafka cherished, read often, and commented upon with profundity in many letters. The

Sortini episode is almost a parallel piece to Kierkegaard's book which has as its point of departure that God demands no less than a crime of Abraham, the sacrificing of his child; and this paradox in the book is of assistance in arriving at the triumphant conclusion that the categories of morality and those of religious belief are not to be represented as identical with one another. (S 488)

This interpretation has meanwhile met with various rejections.[3] Moreover, from the very letters that Kafka wrote to Max Brod it appears that Kafka was extremely critical of Kierkegaard despite all his admiration and veneration for him; and, more than that, once he even terms Kierkegaard's works "detestable, disgusting" books.[4]

No matter how Kafka's relationship with Kierkegaard may be interpreted in its details, an accurate interpretation of the Amalia-Sortini episode must be oriented primarily to the actual text of the novel *The Castle*. From the novel an entirely different view emerges. Brod could never have arrived at his interpretation had he but been alive to the sentence about Amalia: "Face-to-face with truth she stood, and lived and endured this life"; or to the other sentence: "But Amalia not only endured her suffering but also had the understanding to see to the heart of it; we saw only the consequences—she saw into the cause" (S 278).

This can never be said of a girl who in conventional error confuses "the categories of morality with those of religious belief." However, if one considers her vision into the truth and into her own depths as the knowledge of one whom God has smitten and in whom understanding dawns too late, then the ostracism to which she is constantly subjected would be less valid than ever from the religious point of view. For in that case she would indeed be ripe for "grace."

However, even were one to concede such a monstrosity as a "heaven" that demands immorality and "filth," even if one ventured to put God's demand of Abraham (a demand so completely different in nature) on the same level with Sortini's request, and, finally, even if one wanted to go so far, perhaps, as to construe Amalia's perception of the truth as a defiant decision to oppose this truth—that is to say, to pervert the truth and, persisting in an ostensibly antigodly, human morality, undergo the "suffering" of God's anathema in indignant rebellion against God—even then, if one considers the story in the novel in its entire context and continuity, it is impossible to see where any support can be found in the text for such an antireligious "religious" interpretation, for such an absurd concept of sin and grace, a concept that mocks every religious tradition of the Western world.

It is once stated with reference to Amalia that "there exists no disparity at all" between her and Sortini, and "nothing has to be bridged over" (S 260), that there exists no essential difference between village and castle—a thought that of course runs through the entire novel.

The unbridgeable transcendence, in the relationship of God with the world, the very transcendence that Kierkegaard rips wide open, is not present in *The Castle*, however critically Kafka turned against Kierkegaard's "positive" religiosity which "raped the world," and however critically he rejected Kierkegaard's attempt to paint the "monstrous figure of Abraham in the clouds" and to disregard "the ordinary mortal."[5]

And how is one to reconcile Sortini's ostensible godliness and "heavenly" loftiness with the remark that Sortini "had to look up to [Amalia], for she was much taller than he" (S 253)? It is such details that are much more essential and illuminating than general, overhastily conceived comprehensive interpretations. Only from consideration of such details in the course of a scrupulously careful study of the total poetic fabric can one arrive at an unassailable interpretation.

What, then, actually goes on in the enigmatic Amalia-Sortini episode?

## B. THE FATEFUL GARNET NECKLACE

Olga, from whom we learn about the preceding events, declares that the morning on which Amalia tore up Sortini's letter had been "decisive" for the ostracism of her family; however, she goes on to say, "But every moment of the preceding afternoon was just as decisive" (S 254). Let us, therefore, first consider these "decisive moments" of the preceding afternoon.

On this afternoon, on a meadow outside the village, the fire department was having a big carnival in which "officials and servants" from the castle were also participating (S 249). For the castle had "donated a new fire engine" (S 248) which was to be dedicated. Also, "sweet wine from the castle" (S 253) had been supplied, wine that "stupefied" the villagers. Furthermore, the castle had presented the village " ... with several trumpets, unusual instruments on which with a minimum of effort—even a child could sound them—the wildest blasts could be produced; when one heard that racket, one thought the Turks had come" (S 252). All the prerequisites for a turbulent, intoxicated public festival are thus on hand.

"For weeks" Amalia and Olga had been looking forward to the celebration (S 249). "Amalia's dress was particularly lovely" (S 249), for Amalia actually "knew how to make very beautiful clothes—of course, only for the first and foremost families" (S 275). That in itself is essential for Amalia's characterization. She makes very beautiful clothes but only for the first and foremost families. In the light of the highly symbolical significance that in Kafka is always attached to clothes, this can mean only that Amalia is on an exceptionally superior spiritual and intellectual plane. Also, she "made" her brother Barnabas' "jacket ... before he was a messenger" (S 230), that jacket that so delights K., since it had "the delicacy and the holiday air of a silk garment" (S 35). K. "had let himself be captivated by Barnabas' tight jacket with its silken lustre" (S 46), and he painfully senses the contrast between this jacket, that seems to him like the token of a free, higher sphere, and the "coarse, much-darned shirt, grey with dirt," that Barnabas wears under this jacket and that expresses his depressed state within the framework of the ostracized family (S 46).

Olga, however, "was at that time," before the fire department carnival, "jealous of Amalia's lovely dress," and "wept through half the night before the celebration." Interestingly, then, on the morning of the festive day the landlady of the Inn at the Bridge, of all people, turns up to "inspect" the two girls, Amalia and Olga, for at that time she was "on friendly terms" (S 249) with the highly respected Barnabas family, whereas later, like Frieda, she speaks of this family only with contempt. The landlady of the Inn at the Bridge "had to admit that Amalia had the advantage, and for that reason, in order to comfort me, she lent me [Olga] her own necklace of Bohemian garnets" (S 249)—that is, of blood-red gems.

This garnet necklace is of the highest significance. For the subsequent, fateful letter to Amalia from Sortini the official "was ... addressed ... to the girl with the garnet necklace" (S 254) without any salutation by name.

How did Amalia come to have this garnet necklace?

Olga relates: "But then, as we were ready to go out, Amalia standing before me, and all of us admiring her dress, Father said, 'Remember what I am telling you: today Amalia will get a husband'; then, I do not know why, I took off my necklace, my pride and joy, and, no longer at all jealous, put it on Amalia" (S 249-50).

Thus, the garnet necklace is not Amalia's property but belongs to the landlady of the Inn at the Bridge, who had merely lent it to Olga. And Olga in turn had impulsively put this necklace on Amalia when their father announced that Amalia would that day obtain a husband. Unquestionably, therefore, the red garnet necklace belongs in the sphere of the erotic, in Klamm's world, the world by which the landlady is completely enslaved.

However, this necklace does not belong to Amalia's sphere. Olga relates that the moment she put the necklace on Amalia and their father spoke of Amalia's future husband, Amalia's "melancholy glance, which she has had ever since ... passed high above us and beyond us, and one really almost bowed down before her involuntarily" (S 250).

Nor did Amalia participate in the revels. She is the only one not to drink of the sweet wine from the castle (S 253). Even the fire engine, beyond question an erotic symbol that Kafka con-

sciously chose, does not interest her. "Only Amalia paid no
attention to the engine, as she stood there erect in her beautiful
dress, no one daring to say anything to her; I ran over to her
now and then and put my arm through hers, but she remained silent" (S 251).

While she is in this state, the eye of the official Sortini lights
upon her.

## C. THE SPIRITUALITY OF SORTINI THE OFFICIAL

Who is Sortini?

He is described as a "man unversed in the ways of the world"
(S 260), who leads a "completely secluded life" and "who, at
least as far as is known, has no relationship with women"
(S 261). He is a "small, frail, pensive gentleman; something
that struck everyone who so much as glanced at him was the way
his brow was gathered up in wrinkles—all the wrinkles (and
there were a great many of them, although he is certainly not
over forty) extended like a fan, as it were, across his brow
straight down to the root of his nose—I have never seen anything like it" (S 249).

Sortini is thus an extremely spiritual, reflective being. Like
Amalia, he too attends the public festival "without participating." He "pays no attention to us" (S 252), and "with his silence
scares off anyone who tries to approach him with a request or
a flattering remark of one kind or another" (S 253)—exactly
like Amalia. Indeed, he obviously has almost a loathing for
people. He "glanced at them one by one in turn, wearily; it
was as if he were sighing over the fact that beside the one there
was always yet another and another" (S 253). He is bored and
wearied by the eternal repetition of sameness, the monotony of
ever-recurring, insignificant faces until, yes, "until he then paused
at Amalia, whom he had to look up to, for she was much taller
than he. At that moment he gave a start, and leaped over the
shaft in order to be closer to Amalia" (S 253).

"That was all," for, when they all misunderstand him and,
led by the father, try to approach him, he wards them "off with

raised hand and then motioned to us to go" (S 253). "But Amalia was more silent than ever. 'Well, she has fallen head over heels in love with Sortini,' said Brunswick, who is always slightly coarse and has no understanding of anyone of Amalia's nature; but this time it seemed to us that his remark was close to being accurate.... We then teased Amalia a great deal by saying that now she had really found a husband" (S 253).

And Sortini as well, from this moment on, becomes even more silent. He actually forgets his official duties completely (S 255); with his arms folded across his chest, he sits on the shaft without saying a word, until late at night, until the castle coach comes and fetches him. "He did not even go to the fire department's practice drill" (S 253-54).

The only conclusion that can be drawn from all of this is that this glance, in the case of both of them, Amalia as well as Sortini, has pierced to the depths of their souls, and that they love each other. Olga is convinced of this, too (S 261). For Amalia and Sortini are each other's equal: Sortini in his extreme spirituality, and Amalia in her "loftiness" (S 226). Even before they see one another, they both show the same disdainful, silent aloofness from the activities of the crowd. Both meet in a sphere that is *above* the sensuous fascinations to which all the others succumb.

### D. THE PERVERSION OF THE SPIRIT

But then, how is one to explain Sortini's coarse letter, couched "in the most vulgar terms"?

Olga, who has read the letter herself, says, "It was no love letter, there was not a word of flattery in it; on the contrary, Sortini was obviously angry that the sight of Amalia had affected him and had kept him from his duties" (S 255).

At the same time, without doubt, the request that Amalia come to him "immediately" at the Herrenhof, "for in half an hour" he had to drive off (S 254), was formulated in the sense of an aggressive sexual degradation. For "whoever did not know Amalia and had read only this letter was bound to consider that a girl to whom someone had dared to write in that way was dishonored, even though she might not have been so much as touched" (S 255). The letter has not been dictated by "love"—not even in its lowest form—but by anger, loathing, aggression against "the girl with the garnet necklace." Olga assumes something similar when she says, "Later we explained it to ourselves by saying that Sortini... had written the letter in a rage at having been unsuccessful in forgetting Amalia even during the night" (S 255).

Manifestly, therefore, Sortini is affected negatively by the garnet necklace which really does not belong to Amalia but comes from the landlady of the Inn at the Bridge, that is, from the Klamm sphere. This sphere disturbs Sortini in his duties. He becomes "angry" and wants to get rid of it speedily and immediately by summoning to him "the girl with the garnet necklace." This conclusion follows from the statement that this official—who is unversed in matters of the world, who lives in seclusion, who is not known to have any relationship with women—could not possibly react otherwise if he were suddenly deeply stirred by love for a village girl. Such a letter was, then, no sign of brutal insensibility. On the contrary, "When Klamm writes a tender letter, it is more embarrassing than the coarsest letter from Sortini" (S 260). "When the gentlemen get up from their desks, this is how they are, they do not find their way about in the world, and then in their absentmindedness they say the very coarsest things—not all [the gentlemen], but many of them. Why, the letter to Amalia may have been jotted down on paper while he was lost in thought, in complete disregard of what was actually written" (S 259).

Thus the girls of the village, who are influenced primarily by the Klamm sphere, by no means feel Sortini to be brutal, but have respect for him. For Sortini, absorbed as he is in work that is so remote from the ways of the world, cannot be brutal at all. "Of Klamm it is known that he is very coarse.... Of Sortini that is not known" (S 259). "Also, he is probably being confused with Sordini and taken for the fire-department expert—Sordini is the actual expert and exploits the similarity in

their names, especially when it is a matter of making representative appearances, so that by shifting these duties to Sortini he
can remain undisturbed at his work" (S 260). Even the practice
drill of the fire department was irksome to him; he really did
not fit into the picture there.

The fateful letter thus seems to have been determined by the
fact that Sortini, in this emotional state, was confused by the
garnet necklace into believing that in Amalia, to his anger, he
/had merely an ordinary village girl before him—in spite of his
first impression—and therefore, in the manner of Klamm, he
treats her as such, so that "somehow or other" he may in this
way "bridge . . . the disparity . . . between an official and a cobbler's daughter" (S 260); that is, in approaching what seems to
be the sensuous sphere of such a girl, there need exist, ordinarily, "no disparity whatsoever" (S 260).

Because of this confusion, Sortini himself, in his absentmindedness, falls out of his true official sphere. He cannot meet
Amalia as an equal on a purely spiritual plane, the only plane
where "love" would be possible for him. For that reason his
letter is no love letter.

However, the conflict may lie at an even deeper level. Amalia's
lofty, "melancholy" gaze aroused love in him, the feeling of
encountering a similar nature, even perhaps a superior one, since
he had to look up to her. In his spiritual compass, however,
love is possible only if its sensuous components are excluded;
but, in that case, it is no longer a matter of love in its full
sense. Hence he must entirely extirpate this love from himself,
or, if he yields to it, shift to the opposite extreme, shift to a
sphere that he does not know, that he can express only in the
form of vulgar insult, since this sphere is alien or odious to him.

Therefore, [on this level] no special importance need be
ascribed to the garnet necklace. Even without this external sign
the sudden change in Sortini is comprehensible. It is intrinsic to
the nature of such an abstract spirit as Sortini's that, if he is
suddenly seized by love for a village girl, an inversion must take
place in him. The garnet necklace is purely and simply the impetus, the affective element that gives him the right to shake

off his love in a manner so "dishonoring" to the girl. The conflict in Sortini is one that cannot be resolved. Within his abstract official world, he *may* not love any person whatsoever. If in spite of this he is emotionally moved by a girl who equals him in spirituality, he in turn may not love her as a person, as an individuality, but only in the universality of spiritual values. He must take no account of her person; that means, he must return immediately to his "duties."

In this, however, he is hampered by her personality. From this comes his "anger" at Amalia, anger at himself, too, because of his inability to forget her. From this, too, comes a form of letter that can give only negative value to everything connected with "love," and that is, consequently, the very opposite of a love letter. The letter has in fact been composed "in complete disregard of what was actually written"; Sortini himself does not know what he is writing, because the entire world to which this written matter is related is alien and unknown to him. The letter is not a sign of brutality but of an extreme spirituality that, to be sure, because of this extreme, is inhuman, and hence is brutal notwithstanding. Subjectively, within his own sphere, Sortini is not brutal. But objectively, seen from collective human reality, he is brutal. Wherever spirit is only spirit, appearing as an isolated, abstract sphere, it is a perversion of the human spirit.

Justifiably, Amalia is wounded to the very core and "indignant" because of such a letter (S 255). Her world collapses. The high spiritual sphere in which she lives is perverted and shattered by none other than the high official whom she loves and who himself represents this sphere within the world apparatus. This is not only a personal, individual disappointment in love. Not only her world but the world in general collapses for her. For in these castle authorities the officials guarantee the world system. Sortini is the guarantor of the spiritual world, indeed is the spiritual world itself. That is the meaning of the sentence that all women always have to love officials, even if they do not know it. That was also the meaning of Frieda's perception that her departure from Klamm would at the same

time be a departure from the world, an entering into the grave,
so that she will be "lost" if she does not belong to Klamm any
more but only to K.

As a result of Sortini's letter, therefore, the scheme of the
universe becomes invalid for Amalia. She steps out of the
sphere of her existence. And this is accomplished as a necessary,
ineluctable destiny. She no longer *can* do anything but stand outside. Her exclusion comes to pass inevitably, because for her
the world in which she lives is itself shattered. The castle hierarchy becomes meaningless for her. This is clearly evinced in
the few words that we hear her utter. She says to K. and Olga,

"So you are telling castle stories? Are you still sitting together?
. . . Are you really concerned about such stories? There are people
here who feed on such stories, they get together the way you are
sitting here, and treat each other, taking turns . . . I once heard of
a young man who was preoccupied with thoughts of the castle,
night and day, and neglected everything else ; people were afraid
for his everyday wits because his whole mind was up above in the
castle. But finally it turned out that he had actually been thinking
not about the castle but only about the daughter of a cleaning
woman in the offices ; well of course he got her, and then everything was all right again." "I think I should like that man," said
K. "I doubt that you would like the man," said Amalia, "but perhaps his wife." (S 271-72)

This scorn of Amalia's shows unambiguously that the spiritual
world has revealed itself to her as a mendacious world determined by instincts and vital needs, and that all spirituality is to
her merely self-deception, ruled throughout by powers that she
loathes, since that very official who appeared to be withdrawn
from such powers unmasked himself so dreadfully to her.

For this reason she has to break off every connection with the
Herrenhof and *can* no longer live in the systems that govern
our existence.

### E. TRUTH AS ANNIHILATION OF LIFE

With that, the reason and meaning of Amalia's so-called

ostracism also become clear. It was, properly speaking, not her rejection of Sortini that was "the decisive" factor leading to this ostracism, but rather the fact that she "did not go to the Herren-hof" (S 256-57). She thereby withdrew from all the determining laws of existence and no longer fitted into the village and world community.

Basically, as is pointed out extensively, no reproaches can be cast upon her because of her attitude toward Sortini. Neither her parents (S 273) nor the people of the village can censure her on that account (S 275). Though it is true that her rejec-tion of Sortini's message is later given prominence in village gossip, nevertheless there is great reluctance to discuss these matters that deal with the Amalia-Sortini relationship, and people prefer to maintain an embarrassed silence: "No one will tell the story straight out" (S 247).

The primary reason why everyone withdraws from Amalia and her family is that Amalia no longer visits the Herrenhof. By not going there, Amalia takes the ground from under her feet and those of her family. In the course of three years her parents are transformed from a prosperous married couple, exuberant with life, into trembling, helpless, grey-haired old people. Vocation and work are taken from them—not explicitly, not with evil intent, but silently, or in great "fear" (S 274), or out of a sense of matter-of-course "duty" (S 275), and by no means because of "hostility" (S 275). Brunswick is the only one who now and then ventures to place small orders with them, by means of which they live, but even he does this surreptitiously.

In other words, in these proceedings, which from an empirical approach are impossible and scarcely imaginable, Kafka gives expression to his conviction—frequently formulated and devel-oped in his diaries and letters as well as in his literary works —that the human being who reaches out far and high above himself in a "superhuman manner," must then necessarily split apart, plunge down, and disappear. As life and spirit become meaningless to Amalia, the springs of life and spirit run dry. Her parents, the original source of her existence, grow feeble and waste away. The empirical foundation of their life, vocation, and work sinks into the earth. What is more, even Amalia's spirituality is threatened. She takes on a "somewhat dull" and "cold" (S 48, 273), though, it is true, "clear" look (S 223). Although she is knowing, and "had the understanding to see to the heart" of her sorrow and its "cause" (S 278), nevertheless she is at the same time "entirely without hope" (S 280); hence the "dullness" of her glance. This means that she is one of those figures of Kafka's that are already dead while they are still alive —for the very reason of that absolute "solitude" of theirs (S 223)—and "beneath the ruins" of existence see "more" than all others (T 545). Their absolute aloofness makes them both lifeless and clairvoyant, both dull and serenely clear, simultaneously. "She has the timeless look of women who hardly age but who also have hardly been really young" (S 273).

In the light of Kafka's total work and thought, one cannot shut one's mind to the view that the statement "Face-to-face with truth she stood" (S 278) is meant quite seriously and literally. She does in fact see to the heart of the truth of this world : the enduring, inextricable, mysterious nexus of spirit and instinct, the unbreakable chain between the cognizant person and his vital interests. The sudden fall of Sortini the official into the instinctual sphere does not derive from confusion alone but is inherent in the core of the human spirit, whose heights are bound to become depths suddenly and ever anon, since pure spirit can never be existent upon earth. To be sure, Sortini and Klamm seem to inhabit separate offices. But all the offices are interchangeable. Any official can "substitute" for Sortini; even this highly spiritual official can appear as a "fire-department expert," deputizing for Sordini the official "who is the actual expert." Spirit and sensuousness can exchange roles. Everyone is responsible, and no one is responsible. Justifiably does Amalia refuse to enter any offices whatsoever.

No explanation on a spiritual level can set one free. For it is here that spirit has failed. All stipulations, all negotiations, have become meaningless for Amalia. Silent, completely without hope, she remains dependent upon herself alone. She grows stonelike. She becomes one of those women-turned-stone that turn up over and over again in the true myths of mankind. Women are more knowing than men. But they are also more powerless. For they are unable to give voice to their knowledge.

## F. FUTILE COMPROMISES

However, Amalia's family wants to live. "We betrayed Amalia, we tore ourselves free from her silent command, we could no longer continue living that way, we could not live completely without hope, and we began, each in his own way, to entreat or assail the castle with requests that it pardon us" (S 280). But there was nothing there to be pardoned. The castle remains unmoved and uncommunicative, eternally circling within itself. " 'But what was he to be pardoned for?' was the answer given him; so far there had been no charge received against him . . . and if nothing had happened, what was it that he wanted? What was there that he could be pardoned for? At the most, for his bothering the authorities now to no good purpose, but that was the very thing that was unpardonable" (S 281-82).

All of them, the father, Barnabas, and Olga, want to clear up Amalia's fate, get to Sortini or his messenger, and come to an understanding with the castle again. But there is nothing here to be cleared up. Amalia sees the situation correctly: " . . . we saw only the consequences—she saw into the cause" (S 278). Barnabas, Olga, and the father seek to move within the concrete phenomenal forms of existence, and to regain the lost contact and ground. But whoever has once lost it can never find it again of his own power. For the laws of life are inscrutable. Only he who stands within them beyond all question is also carried by them beyond all question.

There could be a way out—but only one: if it should prove to be that the entire affair was the result of an error or misunderstanding or oversight. In that case, Amalia's rejection of Sortini would not represent any breakout from the world system of laws but would fit into that system without Amalia's knowledge.

"If one day we had suddenly come with the news that everything was now in order, and that, for instance, it had been merely a misunderstanding which had meanwhile been completely cleared up, or that, although it had been an offense, it had already been made amends for by the action taken, or—and even that would have been enough for the people—that we had succeeded, through our connections with the castle, in putting an end to the matter ; we should then most certainly have been welcomed again with open arms—there would have been kisses, embraces, celebrations —I have experienced this sort of thing several times in other cases." (S 275-76)

It is possible that Kafka even considered utilizing such a clarification of a misunderstanding for later portions of the novel, in the unwritten final chapters of the book. The matter of the garnet necklace warrants a conjecture of this nature. In the light of Kafka's tendency to hedge with every sentence in such important official letters, it would be conceivable to have it turn out in the end that actually it was not Amalia who was intended by "the girl with the garnet necklace," since after all the necklace did not belong to her. Sortini had made a slip in his letter. Amalia ought not to have felt herself addressed in this letter at all, etc., etc. But we cannot be certain about this. In the extant portions of the novel, all such attempts at clarification are futile. This is in keeping with the inner truth and form of Kafkaian works.

In Kafka there are no longer the possibilities of the old type of novel, where the reader is led through many involvements, along labyrinthine paths, to a final "clarification" of all the strange destinies. For even if finally—as is stated in the text —everything were to turn out as a "misunderstanding" or an "offense" long since "made amends for by the action taken," what would have been gained? Amalia would be justified, and so would Sortini. But can the positions be reconciled? The tragedy would continue to exist. Sortini's perversion remains perversion. Amalia's silent accusation cannot be set aside. Within the human cosmos, person and world law are separated from one another by a gap that cannot be bridged. Only the semblance of a reconciliation could be successful from the point of view of the unsuspecting villagers, from the point of view of the human being who lives empirically. For indeed, reconciliation is being lived incessantly. Person and superindividual universality are intertwined in life, constantly and inextricably—but at the cost of "clarity of vision." The antinomies are perpetually masked. Amalia really does stand "face-to-face with truth." In the most profound sense, therefore, there can be no "misunderstanding that is completely cleared up." A clarification that would bring about reconciliation would itself be a misunderstanding. "Complete clarification," however, would be annihilating. For only he who lives "completely without hope" possesses "certainty" (H 46).

Logically, therefore, all attempts at compromise are bound to fail. In vain does the father attempt to speak with the officials. Similarly, Barnabas tries to hire himself out as a messenger, in order to obtain access to the determining powers. He is a moving, unforgettable figure, the eternal image of youth that is hopeful ever anew, youth that despite all reverses and perplexities means to find, in endless spiritual struggles, the clue to the mysteries of incomprehensible existence. Still fired by the spirit of an ideal buoyancy, he believes that he can solve the riddle in numerous conversations with Olga, who is spiritually vigorous and likewise searching; he is prepared to dedicate and sacrifice himself, sparing no pains; in his conflict between vocation and spiritual mission he has grown mature with surprising rapidity (S 300)—an enchanting image of hope for K. himself, and at the same time a shattering image of the powerlessness and helplessness of all youth. He is one of those young people toward whom Kafka always had the feeling that he once described in the following diary entry of March 13, 1922:

The feeling of one who is in distress, and who, when help arrives, then feels joy, not at being rescued—he is not really rescued—but at having fresh young people come, optimistic, ready to take on the battle, ignorant, to be sure, of what lies in store for them, yet with an ignorance that does not deprive the onlooker of hope but causes him to marvel, to rejoice, to weep. (T 576-77)

And from the coign of vantage of this hoping, seeking, erring youth the strange figure of Olga—Barnabas's fellow combatant and comrade—becomes understandable.


### G. THE TRAGEDY OF THE SPIRITUALLY VIGOROUS WOMAN : OLGA

Inquiring, searching, Olga surrenders herself to the elemental powers of existence, to Klamm's unruly servants whom she hates; but it seems important, if she is to achieve clarity, that she gain their hidden knowledge of the castle hierarchy. Olga is anything but a prostitute. In her case, too, the portrayal that shocks the reader must not obscure the core of her being. "With pleasure" K. looked "into these blue, unalluring, un-domineering, but shyly quiet, shyly resolute eyes" (S 228). By contrast with Amalia's proud, brusque, and absolutely intrepid, "heroic" nature (S 257), Olga is "shy." She is more exposed and more open to life than her sister. But her shyness is quiet and resolute. She knows her goal and pursues it undeterred, calmly and deliberately. She is neither alluring nor domineering. Her surrender to the servants does not mean that she becomes their slave or that she wants to have a deep effect on them, or that—like Frieda—she seeks to dominate them. On the con-trary, she is determined to confront the vital powers of existence, "quietly resolute," with the goal of seeing to the heart of them and of gaining clarity about what it was that took place between Amalia and Sortini. She is called "unselfish and intelligent" (S 469).

Thus she is the independent, spiritually vigorous woman who wants to meet, experience, and control all the possibilities of existence, and who faces every encounter without fear. However —and here again there are echoes of a slashing criticism of life and society—she is never really taken seriously by the men whom she meets, but is treated merely like a "toy that they madly made every effort to smash to bits" (S 297). "Not a single intimate word have I spoken with any of them during the two years, it has been only furtive actions or lies or crazy nonsense; well, the only one left for me was Barnabas, and Barnabas was still very young" (S 297).

From these male servants of life she can never obtain real information. By entering into life reality she can of course procure the means of existence for her family; but, by her making contact in such a way, the actual mystery surrounding Sortini and the officials is deepened rather than unveiled. For basically the servants themselves know nothing of the foundations and fathomless depths that constitute their sphere.

Consequently Olga remains a seeker. But her restless inquiring is really not completely futile, as is shown by her penetrating interpretation and clear presentation of the whole of the extensive Amalia episode. Reflectively, with all the tools of the mind but also with empathy, she tries to plumb the mystery. As a counterpoint to her stony sister, her enlightening, expressive consciousness is significant and necessary. Without consciousness of this kind, spiritual life will perish completely. Even though she goes astray, even though she does not advance to fundamental, mute knowledge, to her sister's "truth," nevertheless she remains an inalienable, positive element within the sphere of the human spirit. Hence at first K. feels himself drawn more strongly to Olga than to Amalia. For in his endeavor that is a search like hers, in his "battle," she is an appropriate partner for him.

But Barnabas and Olga remain unsuccessful. Nothing is clarified. The castle and the servants remain inscrutable.

At that point K. makes his appearance. And this means the turning point in the life of the Barnabas family, a turning point even for Amalia. Only a "stranger" can understand the outcasts. "You have an amazing overview ... it is probably because you come from another region," Olga says to him (S 467). Barnabas and Olga hope to secure new connections with the castle through him, either in consequence of the messenger-mediation arrangement between Klamm and K., or by way of K.'s own land surveying.

### H. K. AND AMALIA: K.'S NEW TASK

The decisive problem lies in the relationship between K. and Amalia.

Amalia appears always to turn away from K. with brusqueness and pride, scarcely noticing him. However, that is so only in appearance. Early on, even after K.'s first brief stay with her family, she has her brother give him her regards quite "specially" (S 165). Also, she has quite special expectations of him. At his second visit she invites him "to come to us more often" (S 225). Her brusqueness toward him can be explained first of all by her contempt for all "castle stories." She attaches no value at all to the efforts of her sister and brother to penetrate the castle and obtain explanations there. And correspondingly absurd and even contemptible does she find K.'s analogous attempts and endless conversations with Olga about the castle.

She does not want to be let in on the mistaken ways of K. and of her sister and brother. "Don't worry," she says to K., "I'm not in on his affairs, nothing could induce me to be let in on them, not even consideration for you, and I would do a good deal for you" (S 227).

This last expression of hers makes one sit up and take notice. And then there is her statement, "So you are telling castle stories? ... There are people here who feed on such stories ... but you do not seem to me to be one of these people" (S 271). With lightning speed and accuracy Amalia recognizes K.'s primary aloofness from the castle and the stories about it.

To be sure, K. asserts himself and declares, "But I am, I really am one of them; by comparison, people who are not concerned with such stories and only let others be concerned, do not impress me much" (S 271). Even this protest of K.'s is justified. For the battle against the castle cannot be carried on without one's being concerned with the castle and its labyrinthine stories and misleading paths. However, Amalia is right too. Of what use is any battle if one is not absolutely aloof from the whole, if one does not maintain a position outside this whole, if one allows oneself in the course of the battle to be drawn by one's opponent into his labyrinths and delivers one-self unsuspectingly into his hands? And K. himself, after Olga's long narrative, understandingly says, "Without her [Amalia] everything is hopeless ... without her we are neither here nor there, and remain in uncertainty"; and Olga confirms this, say-ing, "Without Amalia, it is as if we were building a house without foundations" (S 472-73).

K. must gain Amalia's "clear" vision into the "cause," and must lift the mystery that surrounds her. Otherwise all his effort will be in vain. Conversely, however, Amalia must be liberated from her hopeless rigidity, indeed her "dullness," by K.'s ani-mated knowledge, his "battle experiences."

However, the problem is that such an encounter can never be achieved through any conversation or any rational mode of thought, and that, on the contrary, only a complete transforma-tion, or a breakthrough to a new level of consciousness and life, could make reciprocal liberation and enlightenment possible. K. himself is close to this. He is already at a level far above that of Olga or of Barnabas. When Olga describes the constant, vain exertions of her brother, K. formulates this decisive insight —perhaps the most significant insight of the entire novel: "If a person has his eyes covered, no matter how much you may en-courage him to stare through the blindfold, he will still never see anything; only if the blindfold is removed will he be able to see" (S 245).

It is K.'s task to remove the blindfold from Amalia's eyes; but it is Amalia's task to do the same for him.

Amalia possesses the fixed look that stares into bottomless depths. K. must endure that look and withstand it. He himself is still staring at the labyrinths of the castle. Amalia must ven-ture to enter these labyrinths. K. must free Amalia of hopeless-ness; Amalia must rob him of his false hopes. Amalia must learn to live; K. must learn to see Amalia's "truth." Amalia's solitude and K.'s many-sided battle experiences must con-solidate.

There is no question but that Amalia loves K. She waits the entire day for him, "unable to do anything else" (S 463). "The

more she rebuffs a person, the more gently does she have to be
treated. She is as weak as she seems to be strong" (S 463). But
no word can blast open the stoniness of her love. "Don't you
want to call her?" K. asks as he senses that without Amalia
nothing can be known as it really is. To this Olga replies,

"That would be the end. You would learn less from her than from
me. She would reject every bond and would not tolerate any stip-
ulation. She would even forbid me to give any answers; she
would force you, with an adroitness and inflexibility that you do
not yet know in her, to break off the discussions and go ; and then,
then, to be sure, as soon as you were outside, she might collapse
in a faint." (S 472)

Amalia's absolute, lifeless spirituality can really never be reduced to words. She could be led back to life only if K. himself represented a spirituality that could no longer be perverted,
a spirituality in which love and spirit unite.

In Olga and Amalia there is a repetition, on a higher level,
of K.'s struggle to obtain Frieda. Amalia has attained to that
"superhuman" height that remains denied to Frieda. Shyly
quiet and resolute, Olga conquers Klamm's servants—whom
Frieda had controlled only by force, with the whip, "with a
single, high, slightly uncertain leap" (S 57).

Amalia knows that K. loves Olga. Her clear vision sees
through everything. "K. shook his head and reminded her of his
engagement [to Frieda]. Amalia seemed not to waste much
thought on this engagement; her immediate impression of K. was
decisive for her, since, after all, he was there, alone" (S 224).
K. knows nothing about his own love, although it becomes increasingly manifest: "Almost more important to him than the
messages" from Barnabas is "Olga herself" (S 306). He knows
even less about his love for Amalia, whose "cold" indifference
frightens him off.

Only if he became aware of his love could Amalia and Olga
be rescued, only then—and this is something that he explicitly
fends off—could he become their "good-luck charm" (S 467).
For him to mature to such consciousness of love, however,

would be possible only if he were to mature to the level of Amalia's spirituality and achieve the gentle, quietly resolute sensuousness of Olga, who neither allures nor domineers. Formerly he was in danger of being stifled by the "allurements" of Frieda's embraces. In order to preserve his spiritual self, he had chased the helpers away and abandoned Frieda, defenseless, to her hopeless conflict, without his being able to help her and lead her to a superior (and not merely naïvely immediate) harmony. Frieda was the sacrifice to the conflict between life and spirit. Olga and Amalia have conscious awareness of life and spirit. For that reason they are thrust out of them, are outside the powers that determine them, are no longer carried naïvely by them, can no longer "live" in contact with them without question. For living in the spirit can also be naïve if the spirit has no critical understanding of itself.

K. has the task of leading Olga and Amalia back into life without sacrificing their higher, critical level of consciousness. Only then could his unconditional love for Frieda, who is still determinant for him so far as his consciousness is concerned, be fully realized; only then would it also be possible for Frieda, liberated again from Klamm's tavern sphere, to raise her unconscious harmony into a conscious state.

Frieda, Olga, and Amalia are necessary levels in the course of K.'s development. They represent spheres of love without which no true human happiness can be achieved.

### K.'s Encounter with Bürgel the Official

Through his encounter with Bürgel K. gains the prerequisites for this kind of superior, mature level of consciousness. For in this encounter the possibilities of a "personal" discussion between K. and the authorities are analyzed and clarified to the last detail.

At the heart of the Bürgel episode is the problem that runs through and determines the entire novel: K.'s problem as to whether it is possible as an individual to conquer the universal powers of existence, to individualize them, and thereby over-come the insoluble contradiction between personal freedom and collective bondage. In the subsequent chapters the new level that K. achieves through Bürgel—in spite of his apparent failure with Bürgel—results, with logical consistency, in many surprising new aspects which reveal new possibilities for the solution of the love problems.

Bürgel is a key figure. For he is a "liaison secretary":

"You do not know what that is? Well, I constitute the strongest liaison"—at this he quickly rubbed his hands in involuntary mirth —"between Friedrich [the official] and the village; I constitute the liaison between his castle secretaries and village secretaries; I am, as a rule, in the village, but not constantly; I must be ready to drive up to the castle at any moment." (S 341)

In order to comprehend the significance of the "liaison" that Bürgel brings about, the nature of the entire castle bureaucracy must be considered again more carefully, although in the earlier sections of our treatise the significance of this bureaucracy has been discussed repeatedly. For only upon the most scrupulous interpretation and illumination of even the most detailed mani-festations can their enigmatic nature really be fully clarified.

A. THE NATURE OF THE CASTLE BUREAUCRACY

As early on as in the extensive conversation between K. and the village overseer, a sharp distinction is made within the castle bureaucracy between what is "unofficial" or "private," and what is "official." Klamm's letter to K. had been a "private letter" and "not an official communication" (S 98). Official de-cisions—this is expressly stated—are in the last analysis com-pletely indeterminable. They are never definite. One cannot reach for them the way a sick man reaches for a bottle of medicine that heals and saves him:

"After all, an official decision is not anything like, say, this bottle of medicine on the little table here. If one reaches for it, one has it. An actual official decision is preceded by innumerable minor investigations and deliberations; years of work on the part of the best officials are required for that, even in cases when these officials know, perhaps from the very beginning, what the final decision will be. And is there really such a thing as a final decision? To prevent there being any, there are of course the official boards of control." (S 426-27)

In other words, the work of the officials consists of exploring all the premises of a given case by means of "investigations," of accounting for them and passing judgment on them by means of "deliberations," so that a decision can be brought about. Even though one of these officials may understand the case so clearly that he believes he knows the final decision in advance, he is nevertheless duty-bound, for the sake of accuracy in the decision, to check everything and consider everything. And even if he may assume, on the basis of his investigations, that he has reached complete clarity in the case, there are other official boards of control that will in turn see the same case in different perspectives, with different practical knowledge and different insights, and hence in turn can and must annul the decision pronounced by one official. For the premises and judgments in a case are innumerable. This makes clear "the ridiculous muddle ... which ... passes judgment on the existence of a human being" (S 88).

In these bureaucracies Kafka has created an image of everyday experience: the incalculable accidents, connections, motives, influences, judgments, points of view, etc., that determine the life of each human being, with and without his knowledge. Everyone is in the power of this ceaselessly and restlessly working world apparatus. And each individual agent of this authority corrects and necessarily controls every other agent, for they are all connected with one another. Hence the village overseer declares: "You ask whether there are control authorities! There are *only* control authorities" (S 90). Their function, however, is to "prevent" there being any final decisions. For every decision within this world apparatus can be only a provisional one and must therefore be nullified or corrected. On the other hand, no matter how many mistakes and misunderstandings may occur because of limited, one-sided ways of looking at things, from the point of view of the whole there can be no mistakes; for every erroneous view is in turn itself based on definite premises and necessities associated with existence, and must therefore in turn prove to be a justified, correct view. "For mistakes do not happen, you see, and, even if a mistake does happen, as in your case, who may then definitely say that it is a mistake?" (S 90).

Thus the official machinery reflects the infinite relations of earthly existence, relations that are in perpetual motion, with their constellations incessantly altering in unremitting change. Hence the officials are always working at a furious, headlong pace, even when they are weary or sleeping or apparently doing nothing.

However, these officials can *never* pronounce a final decision. Hence K., in the face of these infinite relations, justifiably declares,

"But I believe that two things must be distinguished here: first, what goes on among the authorities and can then be officially interpreted one way or another; and second, my real person, I who am outside the authorities and am threatened with encroachment by them.... What you have related with such extraordinary, amazing, expert knowledge, Mr. Mayor, is probably valid for the first; but then, I should like to hear a word about myself too." (S 91)

The "person," the "I" of man, can never be understood through the disclosure of all the conditions, relations, and accidents that determine this "I." No judgment of a human being comprehends his core, his "real person." In the last analysis, the "real person" stands "outside" the authorities.

B. PERSON AND OFFICE

On the other hand, man must nevertheless "hear" something about his "I" from the authorities. The "I" can become concrete and existent only through a spiritual declaration, a personal judgment, which in turn can be expressed only in the form of relationships. For every formulation exists in references. It is of no use to the land surveyor to be told all the correlations in his life; what he wants is to obtain clarity about his person, about the actual course of his life, about his own work. "My ambition does not aim at having skyscrapers of documents concerning me rise and collapse, but at working quietly at a small drawing board as a modest land surveyor" (S 92). Hence the officials must confront him as "persons" who can give him specific answers to his specific questions. The anonymous general powers must take shape as concrete spiritual persons.

That in fact is the meaning of Klamm's "private letters." In these letters Klamm takes a personal interest in K. He encourages K. in his work, saying that he is satisfied with it, that an interruption would exasperate him, and that he will take care of the matter of remuneration; that is, he will supply information about the value and meaning of K.'s activities, etc. Here Klamm behaves like a person—since genuine spiritual declarations can gain significance for a human being, in the last analysis, only in the form of personal, sympathetic interest and appreciation. Therefore it is with good reason that the village overseer says, "A private letter of Klamm's naturally has much more significance than an official communication" (S 99). A nonofficial deposition from the castle was precisely what was valuable. "On the other hand, their private significance, in the sense of being friendly or hostile, is very great, greater as a rule than their official significance ever could be" (S 101).

However, since even a personal notification can be expressed only in relationships, every official is always a private person as well as an official. Official and nonofficial functions can never be strictly differentiated. The village overseer says that even of himself. His own explanations of the castle, as he metes them out to K., are half official and half unofficial in character: " ... I have not spoken with you officially—though, perhaps one might say, semiofficially" (S 426).

With that, however, the problem arises of how such personal evaluations on the part of an official—evaluations that can again and again be relativized by other official control boards, or even completely depreciated by being dismissed as "nonofficial"—can establish contact with the individual troubles, worries, and demands of the human being. Or, to state it more precisely: Is it at all possible to unite man's individual demands with universal judgments and relationships? How is the "real person"— K.'s "I," that is actually "outside" the authorities—possible and conceivable within the authorities? Or, stating it in another way: How is it possible to resolve the contradiction between the "private person" and the "official person" in the nature of the officials themselves?

The answer to this is given in the Bürgel episode.

Bürgel constitutes the strongest connection between, on the one hand, the village secretaries who protocol the statements, opinions, and wishes of the people directly, and, on the other, the castle secretaries who officially process these statements, have them take their course through the official control boards, and present them for judgment and decision to the official in charge of the appropriate protocol office—in the course of which, admittedly, the ever-swelling files keep being shuttled on again to fresh official control boards, etc.

This means that Bürgel has to mediate between the personal statements and the omnipresent universal correlations. Hence he possesses the clearest vision into their reciprocal relationship. His statements revolve primarily around the problem of the so-called "night interrogations."

### C. THE NATURE OF THE "NIGHT INTERROGATIONS": THE INTERCHANGE OF SUBJECT AND OBJECT

Bürgel, explaining this, says, "It is a standing complaint of the secretaries that they are forced to conduct most of the village interrogations during the night" (S 344), "because it is difficult or downright impossible to maintain the official character of the proceedings fully.... At night one involuntarily tends to judge matters from a more private point of view" (S 345).

Why, however, do most of the interrogations have to be conducted at night? To be able to understand this, one must make an important distinction: these nocturnal interrogations take place at the Herrenhof, in the rooms of the gentlemen; in these rooms the parties concerned (villagers), instead of dealing with the village secretaries, come in direct contact with the castle secretaries, who are in bed. On the other hand, the planned interrogation of K. by Momus, Klamm's village secretary, took place in the tavern and not in the room of one of the gentlemen. And this protocol contained statements of the landlady, and was to incorporate K.'s statements as well. It was prepared exclusively for this purpose, "to obtain an exact description of this afternoon for the Klamm village record office" (S 154).

Thus this protocol proceeded along the channels of everyday, empirical life, of rational, daylight consciousness. But for that very reason it has and maintains a purely official character, for it reflects people's conceptions only insofar as such conceptions are present on the level of universal human experience and reason. Accordingly, Momus has his "official headquarters" neither in the castle nor at the Herrenhof but in the "village"; he "attends to that part of Klamm's written work that has to be done in the village, and is the first to receive all the petitions from the village that are addressed to Klamm" (S 150). He has to do the preparatory work and strictly maintains his official character as he does so; indeed, that is also the reason why K. refuses to be interrogated by him, since "he, K., he alone—no one else the herald of his wishes, no one else the herald of the wishes of anyone else," wants to reach Klamm in person, and sets no store by interpretations and descriptions of visible proceedings, seeing in them only distortions caused by, say, the landlady's common sense.

Although the protocols of Klamm's village record office reproduce the villagers' personal opinions, whatever they happen to be at the moment, they do so on the level of everyday waking consciousness which is not even individualized in the strict sense, but moves in general relations and is, therefore, purely official by nature.

The nocturnal interrogations in the castle secretaries' rooms at the Herrenhof are entirely different.

Only when a specific investigation of a specific matter has already been fully terminated by an official up in the castle, and has thus already moved through all the possible critical examinations and judgments by that official—only then do these nocturnal interrogations take place. Only then—but then of course immediately—the petitioner in question (that is, the person whose affairs are concerned) *must* be interrogated: "The regulations to the effect that the hearing of the parties concerned must take place only after the complete termination of the other investigation, but that the hearing must then take place at once—all this and other things as well have made the night interrogations an unavoidable necessity" (S 347). For the issue now is the specifically personal attitude of the individual. Without it a decision cannot and may not be reached.

But why is it that a personal interrogation of this nature can in most cases take place only at night? The reason for this is that only at night—or only rarely during the day—can the petitioners confront the secretaries in their "private aspect."

Their "troubles and worries" (S 345), their "miserable lives," their "futile demands" (S 354) emerge completely and undisguisedly only at night, when the distracting pressure of everyday work, everyday ideas, illusory securities, etc., is lifted from them. Only at night do the individual "futile demands," all the secret troubles and worries, burst forth elementally and imperatively from man's inner being. In Kafka night is the sphere in which the human being is directly confronted with the totality of his existence and must take his stand in relation to that totality. At this point may be recalled the pertinent explanations to which we were led in our earlier analysis of Kafka's stories "The Metamorphosis," "A Country Doctor," and others; in them, similarly, night or sleep represents the determining prerequisite for man's encounter with himself.

Accordingly, even the secretaries are afraid of these nocturnal interrogations. The official character of their investigations is jeopardized:

"At night one involuntarily tends to judge matters from a more private point of view; the utterances of the parties involved gain more importance than is their due; completely irrelevant considerations of the situation of the petitioners in other respects, considerations of their troubles and worries, interfere with the judgment; the necessary barrier between the petitioners and the officials, though it may exist unbroken on the surface, gives way, and, where formerly—as is proper—only questions and answers went back and forth, at times a peculiar, totally unsuitable interchange of persons comes about." (S 345)

The normal relationship between the objective and subjective spheres, presenting itself in the form of rational communication or as a question-and-answer game, is suspended. An "interchange of persons" takes place. What otherwise appears as an objective-official sphere is suddenly changed into an immediate-subjective world.

That is the exact definition of a dream. In a dream, what is experienced by the dreamer as objectively seen images and proceedings is a world that rises up from his own inner being, a world that is himself, but which has become for him a different world, one that confronts him; he experiences it either as something "frightening," nightmarish, or as a pleasant thing —but it is always something that he sees, that is facing him, surrounding him, or determining him, and not something that he himself is or is producing. The experiences of the everyday world, rising and falling in his dreams as remnants of memory, are completely subjectivized—transformed and shaped by the "troubles and worries," hopes and fears of the dreamer; they themselves appear as images and as the expression of all these hopes and fears, without the dreamer's even knowing that fundamentally it is himself at whom he is looking.

Thus this means that whatever else is recorded by the official authorities in the way of the personal requests of the petitioners, is felt by the dreaming petitioner as an alien thing. The petitioner turns into the recording official. The secretary becomes identical with the person of the petitioner. Office and person change places. Now, suddenly, the petitioner sees his own inner being as an objective, universal, enveloping, impersonal sphere.

This, however, would mean that the secretary must fulfill all the demands of the petitioner, since he is really identifying himself with the petitioner and his demands. This is what the secretaries fear. They then lose their official function, and are at the mercy of the private petitioner; are "defenseless" (S 354), and without reservation must yield to the petitioner's every wish "for which the fulfillment is already prepared, indeed, to which fulfillment is already reaching out" (S 355).

In order to strengthen themselves against their own "nocturnal abuse of official power" (S 354) the secretaries "schedule the proceedings for either the beginning or the end of the night only, and avoid the in-between hours" (S 347). This means that they seek the time before or after deep sleep, when complete interchange of office and private person cannot be successfully managed; because in such half-sleep the demarcations of the daytime world are still operative. Or else

"...they authorize interrogations only in issues where in every sense as little as possible is to be feared; they test themselves carefully before the proceedings, and, if the result of their test requires it, even at the very last moment they will call off all hearings ... they are fond of having, as their deputies, colleagues who do not have jurisdiction over the case under consideration." (S 347)

Only with this inquiry into the admission of issues and of "proper jurisdiction" does the actual meaning of these night interrogations and of their gravity for the officials become clear.

### D. DETERMINATION AND FREEDOM

The fulfillment of all of the private demands of the petitioners is possible only when "the petitioner comes unannounced in the middle of the night" (S 349). For then the official is also unprepared and cannot take any preventive measures. That the arrival of the petitioner should be unannounced, however, is impossible, since the secretary authorized to deal with the petitions of the party in question already knows in advance everything that goes on inside the petitioner. Therefore, this authority that records all the conscious and unconscious ideas of the person can summon the petitioner to appear before the petitioner himself knows anything about his petitions. "As a result of the flawless continuity of the official organization ... everyone who has any kind of petition or who for any other reason is to be interrogated by us, receives the summons immediately, without any delay, usually even before he has explained the matter to himself, indeed even before he himself knows about it.... It is no longer possible for him to come unannounced" (S 349).

With this Kafka has given expression to the rigid determination of all earthly events. In man there are no conscious or subconscious ideas that are not determined by universal laws. Everything that goes on in man is subject to psychological, biological, logical, etc., laws, and is therefore understood and recorded by the omniscient officials before the person in question is himself aware of it. Freedom is not possible. The flawless continuity of the world laws is absolute. No one can break free of these laws. Everything that is seemingly personal always proves to be an official matter after all, and is subject to universal laws.

Basically, not even the dream sphere is excluded from this rigid determination; as, for example, when a "properly authorized" secretary deals with the petitioner—for then of course the secretary already knows the desires that figure in the petitioner's dreams, and is able to ward them off, treat them like general desires, and forestall any identification with them and with the person. The summoned petitioner is no longer able to come unannounced—

" ... at most, he can come at the wrong time ; well then, his attention is merely called to the date and time of the summons, and, if he then returns at the right time, as a rule he is sent away ; that presents no further difficulty ; the summons in the hands of the petitioner, and the entry in the records—for the secretaries, to be sure, these are not always adequate counterweapons, but they are

nevertheless very powerful ones. All this naturally pertains only
to the secretary who actually has jurisdiction over the matter ; you
see, everybody would still be free to approach the other secretaries unannounced, at night." (S 349-50)

### E. THE SYNTHESIS OF FREEDOM AND LAW

This "freedom" to approach, by surprise and at night, the
other secretaries "who have no proper jurisdiction over the case"
thus means only that the person, the petitioner, with sudden
immediacy, without previously notifying the official in question,
breaks into the latter's sphere. The barriers behind which the
competent official could entrench himself by treating the personal requests of the petitioner from the start as official, general
requests, and by relegating them to fixed categories, as it were—
these barriers are no longer present. Before the eyes of the
official stands the *person*, and only the person, with all his
actual presence and insistent immediacy.
  He cannot withstand this sight.

"There sits the petitioner whom he has never seen, but whom he
has always awaited, awaited with true longing, and whom, from a
rational point of view, he has always considered unreachable. The
very fact of his mute presence there invites the officials to penetrate
into his miserable life, to search about there as if they were on their
own property, and to sympathize with the petitioner's futile requests.
This invitation in the silence of the night casts a spell. As soon as one
accepts that invitation, one actually ceases to be an official personage. Once one is in that position, it soon becomes impossible
to refuse a request. Strictly speaking, one is desperate ; more
strictly still, one is very happy: Desperate, since the defenseless-
ness in which one sits here and waits for the petitioner's request,
knowing that once it is uttered one must grant it, even though (at
least so far as one can oneself take in the situation at a glance)
it virtually tears the official organization apart—this is probably
the worst thing that one can meet with in practice. Primarily,
apart from everything else, because it is also an elevation in
rank defying all description, a promotion that here for the
moment one lays claim to by force. According to the scope of

our position, we are indeed not even authorized to grant requests such as are in question here, but through the proximity of this nocturnal petitioner, in a manner of speaking, our official powers grow ; we commit ourselves to matters that lie outside our province ; and, what is more, we shall carry out these commitments ... but what the situation will be like afterward, when it is all over, when the petitioner, satisfied and unconcerned, leaves us and we stand there, alone and defenseless in the face of our abuse of official power—that is scarcely imaginable! And for all that, we are happy. How suicidal happiness can be!" (S 353-54)

In this scene the synthesis between personal freedom and universal world law is achieved : the official, as guarantor and representative of this world law within a definite sphere, identifies himself with the demands of the person and fulfills them by bursting asunder his own province of jurisdiction and increasing his "official powers" to an unimaginable degree, thus completely satisfying the wishes and actualizing the goals of the petitioner.

In other words, man can fully actualize his personal purposes provided he does not subject these purposes to subordinate, general realms of jurisdiction or to limited categories of existence, but, uncommitted, unannounced and unguarded, wagering his entire person, takes up a position with reference to the totality of existence; concretely this is possible only if he opens fully to the sphere of existence in which he happens to be at the moment, without reservation, and without himself being bound and predetermined by this sphere of existence. Only then is a complete integration possible between his person and this sphere of existence; only then will this sphere of existence, completely permeated by his person, be able to open up to him all the other spheres of existence that the person needs in order to be able to realize himself fully. The official without pertinent jurisdiction will then be able to develop official powers "outside" his "province" and usurp the "pertinent jurisdiction" over everything that concerns the person—this the official can do for the very reason that, possessing no authority over the person, he has not subjected that person to his official jurisdiction. For, in the last analysis, as Bürgel points out, everyone has jurisdiction over everything (S 351-52).

Categories and demarcations are of illusory nature. They originate in the limits fixed by our consciousness and our experiences—necessary limits without which no official organization, no concrete world order is possible, but nonetheless artificial limits that cannot do justice to the totality, to the full reality of human life, a reality that always penetrates simultaneously into all realms of that-which-is and of the spirit, a reality that cannot be entirely encompassed or determined by any limitations.

"It is not, of course, and in such an immense living organization it cannot be, that for each case there is only one specific secretary with jurisdiction over that case.... Who, were he the most diligent of workers, could unassisted keep all the interrelationships of even the slightest occurrence together on his desk? ...Is not full jurisdiction implied in even the smallest particle of jurisdiction? And is not the decisive factor here the passion with which the case is taken up?" (S 351-52)

Man's being in chains, his determinateness, thus has its origin in the fact that he lets himself be put into a limited, defined position and allows himself to be bound and committed thereby. The moment man insists upon the totality of his existence, upon what we have called the Universal, he too bursts asunder his determinateness, achieving a free, universal relationship with himself and his environment: he is then able to move within his limited existence and yet at the same time keep in sight and preserve the totality of human existence and of the world content. Universality and the person become one. Although the empirical-rational or irrational limitations are not destroyed or invalidated, they have nevertheless lost their spellbinding power. Man stands above them and is at the same time within them.

To be sure, though it may seem that such a personal universality "virtually tears the official organization apart," that is so only from the point of view of individual limitations. The rupture occurs, "at least so far as one can oneself take in the situation at a glance"; this means that only the official who is unexpectedly approached by the petitioner feels the trespass against the sphere of his jurisdiction as a rupture of the organization.

But he himself states that by virtue of this trespass he receives an "elevation in rank defying all description"; hence, he continues to remain in office, but now in a universal sense: swayed only by the wishes of the person with whom he has identified, he is free to trespass upon all the other spheres of jurisdiction within the world organization. It is not simply the person of the human being that becomes free, but the official being, the counterpart of the realm of existence itself; the latter too, gains a universal, free aspect. Hence the official is "happy" beyond all measure, although, on the other hand, he ought to be "desperate" because he has relinquished the specific characteristic of his sphere. Breakthrough to freedom is at the same time abandonment of the limited sphere of being in which man and world exist: "How suicidal happiness can be!"

One catches sight here of a sphere in which the empirical determinations are both overcome and preserved. The official, having accomplished the breakthrough, upon the departure of the person continues in his sphere as official, though with the feeling of his "abuse of official power," and yet, too, with the feeling of a liberating happiness.

### F. THE SYNTHESIS OF SLEEP AND WAKING, BEING AND CONSCIOUSNESS

Such a breakthrough, however, is very rare. The "opportunities" for such a breakthrough are actually "never taken advantage of" (S 343). Why?

1. The petitioner always orients himself to the secretary having jurisdiction over his case, since he believes that the others have nothing to do with his case, much less could cope with it. This means that the human being is always bound to his limiting and limited conceptual world: "Also, of course, the petitioners are kept fully occupied if, in addition to their other pur-

suits, they wish to answer the summonses and be at the beck and call of the proper authorities" (S 351). Thus man is always occupied not only with his vocation but also with the spheres of life and spirit that fall to his share; he walks in their paths, obeys their beck and call and summonses, but never dares to set his affairs at nought,* as Goethe states it, never ventures into a completely unknown, incomprehensible dimension. He entrusts himself only to worlds that he knows.

2. Such a breakthrough is rendered "virtually ... harmless," in that one "proves—and this is very easy—that there is no place for it [the petitioner's case] in this world" (S 353). Thus a faith is demanded that soars above experience, above the arguments of reason.

3. The human being, when he faces the official who is unknown to him, must set forth his request personally. The petitioner has "nothing else to do ... but somehow or other to present his request for which the fulfillment is already prepared, indeed, to which fulfillment is already reaching out." The official "waits" for this request (S 355). That is actually the crucial difficulty.

It is not only a matter of freely leaping out of all the alleged powers of consciousness and existence, but also of consciously "setting forth" one's own personal purpose and request. Thus a spiritual level is required on which man, free of all limiting acts of consciousness, must nevertheless retain complete awareness of what the central issue for him as a person, as a "self," really is, what the "futile demands" are that he wants to and must make in order to realize himself as a person.

Consciousness and freedom from consciousness must paradoxically become one. Hence, when a little while ago we spoke of the fact that in the "night interrogations" man finds himself in a dream sphere in which subject and object, person and office, exchange roles, we did not mean that man here simply plunges into an unconscious, irrational sphere. For then he would indeed come into the power of the forces of existence by

*Tr. note: The reference is to the first line of Goethe's poem "Vanitas! Vanitatum Vanitas!"

which he is subconsciously determined. Even in the dream he must preserve his individual consciousness.

He must, as it were, remain awake while he sleeps. It is the same antinomy that we met with in Kafka's late story "The Burrow," and that we analyzed in detail.

Thereby, however, an almost superhuman effort is demanded:

"One's physical strength reaches only to a certain limit; who can help it that this limit happens to be significant in other respects as well? No, nobody can help it. In this way even the world corrects itself in its course and maintains its equilibrium. Indeed, that is an arrangement that is excellent time after time, unimaginably excellent, even though in other respects it is bleak." (S 356)

### G. ILLUSIONS IN SLEEP: THE EASY VICTORY
### IN THE UNCONSCIOUS STATE

Thereby Bürgel formulated K.'s failure. In a completely overtired state, K. wanted to go to Erlanger, the secretary who has jurisdiction over his case and who had summoned him. Because of this weariness, he fails to reach Erlanger's room and accidentally gets into the room of Bürgel, who does not have jurisdiction over his case. Thereby K. satisfied all the requirements for the breakthrough, and for the fulfillment of all his requests. For, as a result of this overtiredness, all responsibilities of jurisdiction and all limitations had become meaningless for him. Suddenly he stands, as a person, directly before Bürgel, who, "taken by surprise," gives utterance to this surprise with a "faint cry" (S 338).

In an intermediate state between sleep and waking he hears Bürgel's message, that is so full of significance. "K. was asleep. True, it was not a real sleep; he heard Bürgel's words even better, perhaps, than during his previous, dead-tired, waking state—word after word smote his ear" (S 348). However, in this state he does not take in Bürgel's words with conscious awareness, for immediately following them comes this statement: "But his annoying awareness had disappeared, he felt himself free; it was no longer Bürgel that held him, yet at

times he still groped his way toward him; he had not yet
reached the depths of sleep, but he was immersed in it. No one
was to rob him of that any more. And it seemed to him as if
with this he had gained a great victory" (S 348).

As K. becomes free of his annoying consciousness, all objective world law also loses power over him. K. has the feeling of
having gained an easy victory over the officials. In his dream
he closes in upon a secretary who looks "naked, very like the
statue of a Greek god" (S 348)—the secretaries, of course, like
the Greek gods, represent specific realms of existence. But this
god is naked, defenseless, at K.'s mercy. In vain does he seek
to cover the "naked parts of his body" against K.'s attacks.
"Was it really a combat at all? There was no serious obstacle,
only an occasional squeal from the secretary. This Greek god
squealed like a girl being tickled. And finally he was gone; K.
was alone in a large room" (S 348).

Victory in the unconsciously free sphere is too easy. In truth,
it is neither combat nor victory at all but, on the contrary, a
continuous state, since unconscious freedom represents a lasting
dependence upon all the determining powers of existence. Hence
in this dream K.'s victory is celebrated even before the combat
takes place. All boundaries of time and space disappear.

Even prior to K.'s harassment of the secretary it is said:

And it seemed to him as if with this [the sheer, free uncon-
sciousness] he had gained a great victory; and, to celebrate it,
here was a social gathering as well, already on the scene, and
he or someone else raised the glass of champagne in honor of
this victory. And so that everyone might know what it was
all about, the combat and the victory were repeated, or were
perhaps not repeated at all, but were taking place only now
instead, and had already been celebrated earlier; and there was
no letup in celebrating it, because the outcome was fortunately
certain. (S 348)

And finally K. is completely alone in a large room. There is
absolutely nothing facing him. K. is in a worldless freedom, a
freedom that is accordingly dubious.

For this freedom is not founded on consciousness of self, but on mere unconsciousness. The sentence, "It was no longer Bürgel that held him, yet at times he still groped his way toward him," was telltale. K. has no secure awareness of self; on the contrary, he "gropes" toward Bürgel as if in search of something that he needs, although it no longer holds him and no longer exercises any power over him. The dreamed battle and victory were empty illusions. The object-world has not been vanquished, nor has his own subjective position been raised into clear consciousness. Although in the dream he sees his own "combat" as an observable event, he nevertheless does not register this dream objectively like an official; identification between him and the official has not taken place.

Accordingly, Bürgel in no way immerses himself in K.'s dream but, unperturbed, continues telling K. things that are vital and crucial for him, things which, however, K. in his unconscious state cannot immediately assimilate consciously. On the contrary, K. is like a "child" asleep, at the mercy of his own illusory victory that logically, even in the dream, is converted into defeat.

For, of all things, the glass of champagne with which the victory was celebrated "lay shattered upon the ground. K. crushed it to bits underfoot. The glass splinters, however, pricked him; wincing, he awoke again, feeling sick like a little child when it is being wakened" (S 349). K. has descended to the unconscious sphere of a little child, a sphere from which he now awakens again with a feeling of nausea.

To be sure, at this moment of awaking he has a sudden, brief insight into the opportunity offered him at Bürgel's: "In spite of that [his nausea], at the sight of Bürgel's bare chest, there skimmed through his mind from out of his dream the thought: All right, then, here you have your Greek god! Yank him out of bed, why don't you?" (S 349). But even that would be pure aggression and not an "expressing of the request," the primary issue in a true victory.

It never comes to the point of a personal, man-to-man encounter. Bürgel continues, unperturbed, with his detailed instructive remarks about the possibilities that open up to K. in

this night interrogation. But K. finally sinks altogether into
deep sleep. "K. slept, shut off from everything that was happening" (S 355).

### H. THE OPPORTUNITY FOR THE HOPELESS

K. is incapable of presenting his request to Bürgel, who is
waiting for it—that request, the fulfillment of which is reaching
out toward K. K. would have to combine the unconscious freedom that he found in his dream with the awareness of his own
purpose, and this he would then have to formulate as he confronts Bürgel.

After K., on entering Bürgel's room, had resignedly said, "I
am not working as a land surveyor" (S 342), Bürgel revealed
prospects to him. " 'That is amazing,' said Bürgel, jerking his
head briskly, and he drew a scratch pad from under his cover-
let in order to make a note of something. 'You are a land surveyor, and you are not working at land surveying!' " (S 342).
With this the central request, the "petition" of K. the petitioner,
is actually conjured up by way of suggestion. Bürgel the secretary, who does not have jurisdiction over K.'s case, begins to
concern himself with K. " 'I am prepared,' continued Bürgel,
'to pursue this case further. After all, things are surely not in
such a state with us that a specialist should be allowed to get
by without being fully utilized' " (S 342).

But K. considers Bürgel completely lacking in authority over
this case, since Bürgel could have no "inkling" about it (S 343)
and would know nothing "of the circumstances ... under which
K.'s appointment had taken place" (S 342). In his readiness to
be of help, Bürgel points out to him in a long speech the
unique possibilities that would accrue for him through the present encounter with him, the secretary without proper jurisdiction. However, at the crucial moment, when everything has become clear, when the only other thing that K. needs to do is to
express his request—at that moment K. is asleep.

Bürgel must lead K. on to this furthermost point of realization—hence his long speech. For he himself, the official,

wants to become a "private person," to burst his own limitations and gain universal freedom. The two of them, Bürgel and K., stand in an inseparable reciprocal relationship with one another. In the last analysis neither can exist meaningfully without the other. Only through their union could free and universal, personal and official existence, be happily united. Hence Bürgel waits for K. And hence, too, he has to point out the opportunity to K. in such detail. For the petitioner "of his own accord scarcely notices anything, of course. Indeed, in his opinion, it is probably only for some inconsequential and accidental reasons that he—overtired, disappointed, inconsiderate and indifferent because of overtiredness and disappointment—has got into a different room" (S 355).

This means that the human being generally has no notion of the fact that, when he is in those very states of despair, hopelessness and disappointment, resignation and weariness, he is closest to the liberating breakthrough. For in such states he is freed from an illusory securities. It is precisely when he is in these states that unsuspected possibilities of help reveal themselves. He need only reach out a hand to have it for the asking —of course, with a clear, conscious formulation of his ultimate goal in life.

However, K.'s failure is also inevitable. In his state of hopelessness K. cannot suddenly express the most improbable of all improbable hopes, and ask help from the very one who knows nothing at all about him. He remains the victim of his "indifference" and resignation, of his "overtiredness."

I. INEVITABLE FAILURE

The union between consciousness and dreamlike liberation from consciousness is bound to be unsuccessful. K. can do only one of two things: he can sleep or wake; he can live completely without hope or he can set his hopes upon realms of existence which he knows and to which he has access. He cannot sustain, to the end of Bürgel's explanations, the intermediate state between sleeping and waking, that state in which con-

sciousness becomes one with liberating weariness, wiping out all
boundaries; he cannot lift into consciousness the opportunity
being offered him. "One's physical strength reaches only to a
certain limit." There are "opportunities that in a certain sense
are too great to be seized; there are things that fail because of
nothing but themselves" (S 357).

This "failure" of K.'s has its cause in the limited nature of
man himself. It is necessary, inevitable. Only through this failure
does "the world . . . maintain its equilibrium," do its systems
and limitations continue to exist. For Bürgel this is an "excellent
arrangement" in the world, but one that is in equal measure
"bleak."

Nevertheless, in the midst of the limit-defining systems there
is the knowledge of a free, universal existence, a knowledge that
cannot be lost. It survives even in K. The words that he heard
even "better" in his sleep than in his waking state he has
thoroughly absorbed and preserved, even though, because of his
boundless weariness at the time, he was yet unable to assimilate
and realize them consciously. For in an undeleted fragment it is
reported that K. later relates this encounter with Bürgel in all its
details and "with all the signs of deadly despair" (S 425). Thus
he possesses knowledge of the reasons for his failure, of the
unique opportunity that he let slip past him. And it is just this
knowledge that raises man to a higher level—that is the meaning of all tragic failure—and lifts him spiritually above the antinomies that evoke failure of this nature.

Kafka could not, and should not, have represented the encounter with Bürgel in any but a tragic form, with all the
elements of tragedy as they have been known to us since antiquity: the tragic irony of K.'s being asleep at that moment of
all others, when a supreme mode of rescue is revealed to him;
the blindness of the hero; the ambiguous powers of destiny that
topple him just when he thinks he is conquering them (the
"Greek god"); the ironic, sorrowful-merry resignation that overcomes this fate-determining god in the form of Bürgel the
secretary, when all his offers of help are futile; the rescue and
elevation in rank that even the powers of destiny themselves

vainly hope for from the liberating act of the hero; and so forth. All these are immortal elements of genuine tragedy.

However, it remains a question whether this tragedy changes into a catharsis for K., too, becoming liberation and clarification through a higher consciousness that rises in him out of his failure; it remains a question whether the tragic antinomies in the spirit of the foundering hero can be reconciled.

## Surmounting the Tragic Antinomies

After his deep sleep at Bürgel's, K. again falls into the intermediate state between waking and sleeping. He is roused by the sound of knocking, "hard pounding" by Erlanger the secretary, in whose province of jurisdiction he belongs, and who calls him to his interrogation. But K. is still "desperately in need of sleep" (S 357). In a state of "uncontrollable weariness" (S 360), indeed in a kind of drunkenness" (S 376), half awake and half absentminded, he experiences both his ensuing encounter with Erlanger and his observation of the distribution of files along the corridor of the gentlemen's bedrooms in the morning.

In his own consciousness this weariness is the cause of two diametrically opposed effects and consequences. It makes him subject to the officials and at the same time places him in a position high above them.

At first he has no desire to go to the secretary having jurisdiction over his case: "He probably would have gone past Erlanger's door with the same indifference if Erlanger, standing at the open door, had not motioned to him" (S 358). He does not reply to Erlanger's demand that he return Frieda to Klamm, but merely thinks to himself: "The orders were given, without regard for him," sounding "like derisive laughter" (S 359). Erlanger had declared, "No consideration can be given to personal feelings in the course of this (S 359). Erlanger remains purely official; K. struggles against this. He wants "to have his voice heard" (S 360). But he cannot speak, because of his "uncontrollable" weariness. And for that reason, in despair, he has the feeling that he is the helpless object of official commands, and that he is "in far too low a position to interfere with them or to silence them altogether, and to have his voice heard" (S 360). Because of his weariness K. is unable to win through in the case of the officials.

However, even in the state of clear, daytime consciousness he would not have been able to achieve anything. For Erlanger states categorically that it is "self-evident" that personal feelings are given no consideration; "therefore I shall not engage in any further discussion of the case at all" (S 359). In every respect, K. is powerless in the face of this secretary with jurisdiction over him. For through Erlanger the objective powers rule without limitations. Erlanger can attain to [*erlangen*] everything; but in the same way Bürgel vouches for [*bürgt*] person and office, taking upon himself the responsibility, the guaranty [*Bürgschaft*] for both.

It is striking, however, that Erlanger, as he goes "rapidly" down the corridor, walks with "a slight" limp (S 359). Obviously he is really not entirely certain of his ground; he is sensitive, vulnerable—at all events, handicapped.

It is with logical consistency that the sudden change ensues. Because of his very weariness and indifference toward all others, K. is superior to the secretaries who have no jurisdiction over him.

As a matter of fact, he enviously establishes, first of all, that unlike his own weariness the weariness of the officials "was actually indestructible quiet, indestructible peace," and that their work promoted more good than harm (S 360).

And it was very much in harmony with this that now, at five o'clock, activity started up everywhere along each side of the corridor. This babble of voices in the rooms had an extreme cheerfulness about it. At one moment it sounded like the mirth of children getting ready for an outing; at another, like the upheaval in a chicken coop, like the joy of being in complete harmony with the dawning day—somewhere or other a gentleman was even imitating the crow of a rooster. (S 360)

The officials thus live "in complete harmony" with nature. Entirely embedded in the objective laws of the cosmos, embraced and determined by these laws, they even live them and are themselves representatives of these laws. Accordingly, however, they are also completely powerless, and, what is more, extremely "sensitive" (S 373) to the individuality of K., who, with all his worries, troubles, and futile demands, faces them in the corridor, in the bright light of morning, as if he were a "ghost" (S 371)—but, strictly speaking, a ghost should disappear in the morning, just like a "nocturnal moth" (S 372) which is supposed to retire during the day and "flatten out" in a quiet corner (S 372). By remaining in the corridor K. cannot entirely "prevent . . . the coming of the day," but can probably "delay it and render it more difficult" (S 372).

What they [the officials], by means of the night interrogations, have been happy to get over and done with, the sight of the petitioners, whom they find it so hard to endure, they do not want to have burst in upon them now in the morning afresh—unheralded, suddenly, and completely true to life. They are simply not up to that. What sort of person must it be who does not respect this! Well, it has to be a person like K., someone with that flat indifference and sleepiness of his, who disregards everything, the law as well as the most common, ordinary, human consideration, and to whom it does not matter in the least that he is making the distribution of the files and records almost impossible. (S 373-74)

### A. K.'S VICTORY OVER THE OFFICIALS

With that the relationship between K. and the officials is clearly formulated. K. represents all the secret sufferings of man, all the demands that man has to make on the world laws and on the cosmos. The officials, however, move harmoniously within these world laws. They are seriously disturbed if man's demands intrude upon them while it is still bright daylight. The quietness and matter-of-factness of their "eternal" work (S 373) are threatened. Their "indestructible quiet," their "peace," suffers shock and is pierced. Desperately the officials finally cry for help. K. "brings about ... what has never happened before ... that the gentlemen, driven to despair, begin to defend themselves and, after bringing themselves to the point—inconceivable as it would be for ordinary people—they reach for the bell and call for help in order to drive K. away, since he cannot be moved in any other way! They, the gentlemen, call for help!" (S 374).

For K. has disregarded "everything," even the "law" of the world. All other people go to work again in the morning, fit themselves into the general scheme of things, and would never dare to importune the world laws with their nocturnal despairs and demands, let alone delay the coming of day. Cheerfully they give themselves over to the moods and joys of the day again. Their night has become submerged. Through K., however, the coming of day is, as it were, disturbed; the world order becomes confused; the distribution of the files is made almost impossible; no one rightly knows any longer which file belongs to which gentleman; strife and battle about the correct apportionment arise among the gentlemen; the clear overview is lost; the world is in danger of being put out of joint.

This is the same process that takes place in Kafka at the beginning of *The Trial*, "The Metamorphosis," "A Country Doctor," etc. The analogies extend even to details, as for instance when it is said that K. drifts about in the corridor "like an animal at pasture" (S 371). Metaphorically K., like Samsa, has turned into an animal that has fallen out of the [normal] categories of existence and is now seeking "nourishment." In contrast with everyone else, his "self" no longer fits into purported existence, but is a hungry extrahuman being.

At any rate, this animal, here in the corridor of the Herrenhof, is already located "at pasture." This is decisively different from the catastrophic beginning in the earlier works of Kafka's. K. has accumulated much experience by now; he is no longer outside the Herrenhof but in the heart of it, in front of the doors of the seemingly omnipotent gentlemen. He can observe the distribution of the files accurately, and it is stated explicitly at this point: "K. observed all this not only with curiosity but also with sympathetic participation. He felt almost at home in the midst of the activity and looked this way and that" (S 362). Although by his very observing all this he causes disorder, and upsets the distribution of the files, he nevertheless has the feeling of belonging to it, indeed of feeling almost at home in it. In a paradoxical unity of contradictory elements, he is both free and at the same time included in the "activity." Through this he exists on an essentially higher level than Samsa or the country doctor or Josef K. at the beginning of *The Trial.*

He is *in* the world activity and is at the same time superior to it in the following way: without his presence the distribution of the files could take place "quickly and easily and without error" (S 373), for the gentlemen could immediately step out of their doors and "in the twinkling of an eye come to an understanding with one another, whereas negotiations through the servants require as much as hours, can never be carried on without complaints, afford constant torture to the gentlemen and the servants, and probably have deleterious effects even on their subsequent work" (S 373). What does this mean?

The gentlemen are incapable of enduring K.'s gaze. They let him see "only faces that are almost entirely masked" (S 364), as, with doors open, from "up above, along the top rail of the wall partition," they watch the distribution of files. For "in the morning, soon after their sleep, they are too shamefaced, too sensitive . . . to be able to expose themselves to the eyes of strangers; and, no matter how completely clothed they may be, they feel virtually too exposed to let themselves be seen" (S 373).

Obviously they are ashamed of the secrets of the night that they think they have happily put behind them through the night interrogations. For it is expressly stated: "Perhaps they are ashamed, these eternal workers, only because they slept. But perhaps they are even more ashamed of seeing strange people than they are of letting themselves be seen" (S 373). For they cannot have the petitioner whose worries they examined during the night "burst in upon them now ... afresh ... and completely true to life" (S 374). They are unable to bear the inconsistency between their diurnal "cheerfulness" and the nocturnal worries of the petitioners. In the face of these petitioners they cannot help feeling "ashamed" of themselves, even though they are fully clothed. They feel the nakedness of their "weak points"; in very similar manner the naked secretary in K.'s dream tried vainly to cover his weak points, his nakedness. Night reveals the weaknesses of the objective world order. The gentlemen are thoroughly aware of this.

However, the "eternal" work must nevertheless continue. As a result of their being disturbed by the shamefaced awareness aroused in them at the sight of the petitioners, everything would now have to come to a standstill. At this point the "servants" step in.

### B. HELP FROM THE ELEMENTAL POWERS

These servants who are, so to speak, the embodiment of unreflective, elemental life, obstinately oppose all intrusions of consciousness. K. marvels at the "unyieldingness" with which the one servant, despite all resistance, accomplishes the distribution of the files (S 365). True, the servant makes frequent mistakes, for "the files were not always distinguishable for the servant" (S 362). He has no overview and occasionally directs files to gentlemen for whom these files were not meant. There is a virtual hailstorm of complaints. The servant is driven hither and thither. He has to "exchange the objections of the previous holder [of certain files] for new counterobjections" on the part of the gentleman who now lays claim to those files (S 363), etc. But with obstinacy and "trickery" he finally does succeed in properly delivering all the files.

The disturbances, created by K.'s presence, lead to confusion in matters dealing with the distribution of responsibility for jurisdiction. Each secretary greedily wants to seize as many files as possible for himself, and angrily returns files given him in error, simply hurling the scrambled files far out into the

corridor in great heap, so that the servant must laboriously re-
arrange them (S 364).

## C. COSMOS AND INDIVIDUALITY

The disturbed and disrupted order leads to chaotic antagonism among all the gentlemen. The matter-of-course relations
that normally exist among all of them are suspended. Each sits
isolated in his room. No understanding with one's neighbor is
possible.

Although none of them is thinking in terms of his "individual
advantage" (S 372), without contact with the whole it is not
possible for anyone to comprehend what belongs to his province
of jurisdiction. To be sure, there are mediations available
through the servants, but they are laborious, circuitous, perpetually conducive to new questions and counterquestions, and
are "a constant torture for the gentlemen and the servants."

In other words, through the presence of K. the individual,
the world order has, as it were, lost its matter-of-courseness. It
no longer functions faultlessly and without friction. For every
act—that is, for every occurrence—in life, considerations must
be raised about where that act really belongs. The servant, performing his duty obediently, is indeed mediating valiantly and
doggedly. But he is constantly driven back and forth by messages and fresh objections of the gentlemen. He overworks himself almost to the point of exhaustion (S 365), and the gentlemen themselves begin to scream.

This means, therefore, that the moment the problematic aspect
of all earthly existence visibly appears in the form of an individual human being, the petitioner K., everything becomes
laborious. Life and spirit then have a very hard time with and
among themselves. Nothing functions any longer. And, furthermore, this has a fateful and "injurious" effect, too, upon the
subsequent processing of the files. Although everything does
take its course—the "servant" sees to that—nevertheless, progress is slow, halting. "The coming of day"—access to the
joyous, matter-of-course naturalness of all happenings—is "de-

layed" and "rendered more difficult," although not "prevented,"
for that is not possible.

It is characteristic that the night interrogations take place
"by artificial light" (S 371), in contrast to the natural sunlight
which the gentlemen in the morning welcome with shouts of
joy and even with crowing. The gentlemen have but one urgent
desire: "after the interrogation ... to forget all the nastiness"
and to meet the day with song. They do not want to have the
"morning, their favorite time ... made bitter" (S 372).

In the dispute about the files, exception is made of only one
gentleman, and that is Bürgel. The door to his room remains
closed for the entire time. No files are distributed to him
(S 364). Bürgel, of course, is the liaison secretary between village and castle, person and office. He is concerned with translation from one sphere into the other. Hence he cannot immerse
himself in either one: he cannot swim in the stream of files;
nor can he be caught in the confusion of the distribution of
the files.

### D. THE QUESTION OF THE DESTRUCTION OF K.'S FILE

At last all the files have been properly distributed. Only one
exception is noted by K. "It was probably the first irregularity
that K. had seen here in the office activity" (S 368). The servant, who kept looking over "at K. angrily or impatiently, with
a nervous jerking of his head" (S 367), rips up a "single file,
actually only a little piece of paper, a scrap from a scratch
pad" that had, "through the fault of the helper, remained in the
little cart" (S 367)—rips it "into little pieces and stuck them in
his pocket." "With his forefinger at his lips he signaled his com-
panion to be silent" (S 368). In the course of this the thought
flashes through K.'s mind, "That could quite well be my
file. The overseer of the community always did talk about this
very, very smallest of cases" (S 367).

We do not know whether this is a purely subjective idea of
K.'s or whether Kafka did in fact thereby mean to indicate a
destruction of K.'s file, and, in that case, to confirm and moti-

vate it in later portions of the novel. The fact that both the servant and his helper are "angry" with K. allows one to suspect that what is involved in the destruction of this scrap of paper is really the revenge the elemental forces take on K.— the destruction of K.'s file.

However, even if the whole incident is merely a momentary idea of K.'s, without any objective justification, it is nonetheless extremely illuminating for K.'s inner life and for the level of consciousness on which he now finds himself. To be sure, the idea seems "arbitrary and ridiculous" to him (S 367), but, nevertheless, for that reason he approaches the servant, although to no avail. And when the servant has torn the scrap to shreds and stuck them in his pocket, K. tries to "excuse" this irregularity by thinking that "the stored-up annoyance, the stored-up disquiet" in the servant had necessarily to "break out" at some time; and this was "still harmless enough," since, after all, it was just a matter of a little scrap of paper (S 368).

K. himself does not take the matter too seriously otherwise. He seems to have gained greater detachment with regard to the proceedings with the files and with regard to his own file. Obviously it would cause him no great concern if the whole file pertaining to him were to disappear completely from the castle bureaucracy. He seems to face himself and the bureaucracy with greater inner calmness as a result of the deeper insight he has gained into the organization of the authorities; indeed, he has begun to feel almost "at home" in it.

The actual reason for his behavior—and hence, probably, for his superiority as well—is the condition in which he happens to be, the condition of excessive weariness that transports him to a peculiar, intermediate state between absentmindedness and waking consciousness. On the one hand he observes accurately what is taking place in the corridor during the distribution of the files; and on the other, he feels himself caught in a "kind of drunkenness" that in turn puts him at a distance from everything. Indeed, while he is in this state of weary drunkenness he himself sees as the cause of that state his remaining in the corridor and upsetting the distribution of the files. He himself

never *knew* what he was occasioning with it. He had no idea
that through his sheer existence he controlled the gentlemen,
and that they were obliged to call for help because of him, etc.
All this he learns through the landlord of the Herrenhof and
the latter's wife; and he makes his apologies to them on
the basis of his excessive weariness and drunken condition
(S 376).

### E. K.'S SUPERIOR POSITION

It is, however, this very state of drunken weariness, this state
between sleeping and waking, that is of the greatest significance
for an understanding of the possible outcome of K.'s battle. In
this state a glimpse of the "solutions" at which the novel is
aiming is provided.

It is a matter of the bridge between waking, daytime consciousness and nocturnal, hidden, unconscious knowledge. Only
the union of both could bring about the union of free existence and bondage. Because K. did *not* know that like a "ghost"
he controlled the gentlemen and disturbed the world order with
his nocturnal worries—only because of his not knowing this
was he able to exercise his power over them at all. Knowledge
of what he was doing would have prevented this domination.
And consciously he does not even consider causing any disturbance, but apologizes and wants to work at his desk as a
simple land surveyor.

However, working quietly this way is the very thing that is
impossible unless man's self, with its inevitable, futile demands,
is confronted with the world totality vibrating within itself,
unless office and person meet one another, unless general, daytime consciousness can be united and reconciled with nocturnal
knowledge and suffering.

However, as K., unaware of his own power, looks into the
"activity" entailed in the distribution of the files, he gains a
higher, superior knowledge as well. Although he knows nothing
of his own mysterious power, he is nevertheless well aware of
his "battle" and knows of his own futile demands. And the

"activity" becomes clearer to him, step by step, so that he feels himself actually "almost at home in it."

Of course, a personal encounter with the officials, in the sense of the confrontation in the Bürgel episode, is not possible here. The faces of the secretaries remain "masked." The worlds do not touch one another. What is more, Kafka intensifies to the utmost the impossibility of such an encounter: the world itself cannot continue under the scrutiny of a person like K. It prefers to disappear rather than show itself, expose itself, "lay itself bare" in his presence. "K. had remained there with his hands in his pockets, as if, since he had not gone away, he expected the entire corridor with all the rooms and gentlemen to go away. And that would have happened, too—of that he could be quite sure—if it had in any way been possible, for the gentlemen's delicacy of feeling was infinite" (S 371).

The sheer presence of K. signifies the unmasking of the world That is a genuinely Kafkaian thought (H 124).

An unmasked world, however, is no longer capable of existence. For "whoever renounces the world must love all human beings. . . . The fact that there is nothing else but a spiritual world robs us of hope and gives us certainty" (H 93).


## K.'s Maturation toward Death

K. is close to such a transformation. Bürgel had given it clear formulation: a personal encounter between K. and the officials would abolish the very "equilibrium of the world." It is impossible within the earthly, visible world. It is an "opportunity" that fails "of itself." The encounter between K. and Bürgel *had to* end tragically. But it is the "equilibrium" of the world that K. shatters. Nothing other than this is meant by his upsetting the distribution of the files, an unheard-of act that had never occurred before. He must take the consequences and withdraw from the world.

There was surely an indication of this in his lightninglike sensing, in the course of his disturbing the equilibrium of the officials, that it was possibly his own "file"* that had just been destroyed. It is primarily this that is pointed to in the scene immediately following, K.'s encounter with the landlady of the Herrenhof.

### A. THE LANDLADY OF THE HERRENHOF:
### HER CLOSENESS TO DEATH

All along, this landlady of the Herrenhof has been on a very remote plane of existence. She wants to drive the concrete, earthly world out of her Herrenhof and not permit any "petitioner traffic" in the Herrenhof. In future the petitioners are to stay in a special building beyond the Herrenhof. She would like it best if she could transfer the interrogations of the petitioners to such a building, since "in her by-this-time abnormal striving for refinement" (S 317) she does not want to have the Herrenhof constantly "dirtied" (S 318). She is not successful in this, of course, because the gentlemen have no desire to shift their interrogations outside and shuttle incessantly back and forth between their rooms and a village building.

Nevertheless, the landlady of the Herrenhof stubbornly pursues her goal, and exercises, "by virtue of her unflagging and yet womanlike gentle zeal, a kind of petty tyranny" (S 318).

Between this landlady of the Herrenhof and K. there now ensues a strange, dreamlike encounter.

The landlady is disconcerted by the gaze that K., in his drowsiness, directs at her: "The way he is looking at me! Do send him away, won't you!" K. "said, 'I am not looking at you, only at your dress.' 'Why my dress?' asked the landlady in agitation. . . . 'He is drunk, of course, the loafer!' " (S 377).

It is possible that there are several reasons for her agitation. In the first place there is ostensibly an external reason: at the officials' cries for help, she had come running excitedly to K., with her husband, in order to drive K. out of the corridor. In

---

*Tr. note: Here as elsewhere the similarity between *Akt* (deed, action) and *Akte* (deed, file) is being played on.

so doing she tried hard to maintain her poise: "her steps were short and mincing, and K. thought she would come too late" (S 369). When she then stands with her husband before K., takes K. to task for his upsetting the distribution of the files, and "directed childishly angry looks at K." (S 375), "she rested her head, as if crushed, against her husband's shoulder" (S 375). Something has snapped in her. In vain does she try to adjust her "dress, whose disorder she had just become aware of" (S 377). She wears a "silklike, rustling, wide-skirted, brown dress, somewhat carelessly buttoned and fastened" (S 375); and K. asks her in amazement where, in the early morning, she "had hurriedly searched out" (S 375) this very "beautiful evening dress" (S 412). She is annoyed because of his remark about her dress, attributes the remark, justly, to his drunkenness, and bids him sleep off "his intoxication" in her tavern (S 377), although shortly before this—before his remark about her dress—she had "clearly" expressed herself against K.'s so spending the night in her tavern (S 377). Furthermore, of course, K.'s staying overnight like this in the tavern had been strictly forbidden by the authorities (S 59).

On awaking after a very long sleep, K., meeting with the landlady of the Herrenhof again, is at first unable, in his waking state, to recall his remark about the dress. However, the landlady, in an exact reverse of the situation, sinks into a dreamy waking-sleep just as K. "said he had had the impression that the landlady had something further she wanted to say to him" (S 411).

The landlady gazed at him as though in a dream. Also, because of that gaze, K. was kept there longer than he really wanted to be. Now she smiled a bit, too, and only at the sight of K.'s astonished face was she wakened, in a manner of speaking; it seemed as if she had been expecting an answer to her smile, and only now that no answer was forthcoming was she awaking. "You had the impudence yesterday, I believe, to say something about my dress." K. could not remember. (S 411)

In spite of her initial seeming hostility against K., there thus arises in her inner being a dreamy relationship with him on the basis of his "knowledge of clothes" (S 412). Extremely agitated anew, she is in conflict between resistance to K. and inclination toward him, particularly so when K. discovers an inconsistency between her life as a landlady and her dress. He says that she wears dresses that "are more beautiful than any he has ever seen before" (S 411). And later he tells her to her face, "You're not just a landlady, as you pretend to be" (S 413). Heatedly she cries out: " 'Anyhow,'—and as she said this it was as if a cold shudder had seized her—'you are not to concern yourself with my clothes at all, do you hear?' And, as K. was about to turn away again in silence, she asked, 'Where *did* you get your knowledge of clothes?' " (S 412).

The "cold shudder" that seizes her at the thought of her clothes points to the realm of death. Also her "head, as if [she were] crushed," resting against her husband's shoulder, suggests analogues. This woman had in fact long since ceased being a "landlady." She no longer distributes the "draught." She has stepped out of the sphere of Klamm, out of the world of erotic love relations. She wants to banish the earthly world from her Herrenhof in an "abnormal striving for refinement" and purity. She adorns herself with "beautiful" clothes, and, indeed, even specifically in the morning, with "evening clothes." She is at the evening of life.

But only in a dream state between waking and sleeping do both she and K. have knowledge about the dress. And in such a state, too, K. had the lightninglike impression that the official deed of his life was being ripped to pieces.

The landlady is still in a state of self-contradiction. Agitated, she wanted to keep K. from upsetting the distribution of the officials' files. On the other hand, she senses an inner relationship with him and becomes "excited" by his knowing, dream-intoxicated gaze. And finally she wants him to give her his considered opinion of her clothes. She leads him to her "private office," shows him an enormous number of her dresses, and asks him, "Well, then, what kind of clothes are they?" K. replies: "You insist on knowing. Well, they are of good material, quite expensive, but they are out of fashion, ornate, often altered and made over, shabby, and are not suitable for your age, nor for your figure, nor for your position" (S 414).

Various interpretations of this are possible. Her husband is described as a cultivated gentleman. She herself shows an "abnormal striving for refinement." She detests the coarse life of the villagers. She would like to appear every day, if possible, in a different, particularly "beautiful" dress. In Kafka clothes are symbols of psychical-spiritual states of the human being. Accordingly, then, this landlady would possess no stable psychical-spiritual substance whatsoever. She constantly changes her costume. She adorns herself with trappings, as it were, of the soul and of the spirit, trappings that are already worn and old when she puts them on. She makes a fancy dress ball of all the spiritual and psychical traditional attitudes available to her, in order to be able to show herself as "distinguished" and refined. This is tantamount to a satire on the cultivated society lady who is acquainted with everything that is intellectual and is ready to offer for display all the traditional cultural goods without her really identifying with a single one, a single dress. The satirical emphasis is accented here by "the petty tyranny" that she exercises over men in her "womanlike gentle zeal," by the affectation of her short steps, and by the low esteem in which she is held. She is "laughed" at for her futile efforts at dislodging the petitioners, efforts that merely necessitated new commotions, new conferences, and new petitioner traffic (S 319).

Her spirituality is far removed from the proud, inviolable "loftiness" of, say, Amalia. Even her sensitivity to K.'s harsh criticism of her ornate, outdated clothes gives evidence of the fact that she possesses neither maturity nor superiority, a fact further demonstrated by her "childishly angry look."

Involuntarily she unmasks herself. When K. says that she is not just a landlady but is aiming at something else, she replies, "I am aiming only at dressing beautifully, and you are either a fool or a child, or a very evil, dangerous person. Go, do go now!" (S 415). Without possessing a sense of beauty, she wants "only" to be beautiful. And, in spite of her resistance to this evil, dangerous K., in her vanity she cannot refrain from calling after him, "I am getting a new dress tomorrow; perhaps I shall send for you" (S 415).

However, it is possible to interpret this in another way. Everything that she once wore in her life has now become shabby and old. She is close to her end. Although she wants desperately to offer resistance, in her heart of hearts she feels that K. is right.

Both interpretations are possible. And the two need not contradict one another; rather, they complement one another. Her costumes have been shabby and unsuitable for her all along. Now, however, as she is seized by a "cold shudder," everything becomes mercilessly clear. Accordingly, her final word to K. may have an ambiguous ring: "I am getting a new dress tomorrow; perhaps I shall send for you." This need not be merely foolish vanity but can have its origin in a presentiment that she really "is aiming," as K. says, at something else, at a supernatural sphere; she may be hoping that her "new dress" will become her true dress, the dress that is suitable for her, the dress which "tomorrow"—that is, in the proximity of death —she will put on, and she will perhaps send for K. afterward, a K. who was the first human being to dare disturb the uninhibited matutinal life of the officials, and to whom she feels herself, in a state of dreamy clairvoyance, to be mysteriously related.

However, the latter interpretation is venturesome. It cannot be adequately supported by the text, and is, therefore, formulated solely as a problematical hypothesis, without any pretension to conclusiveness.

### B. WAYS IN WHICH THE NOVEL COULD BE CONTINUED

Even the thesis that in the corridor K. watched the destruction of the file on his own life is of course quite problematical, as we have shown. And even if it really were a matter of K.'s file—and this remains doubtful—this need not mean that his life itself is coming to an end. It may be that his "official" existence is being endangered. But office and person are not the same thing. K. can continue to live in the village. It is possible for new official files on him to come into being, etc. The novel could have been continued in a multiplicity of ways, and it displays ever-new possibilities of continuation: Pepi's offer, about which K. has as yet reached no final decision; K.'s visit with Gerstäcker, who invites him to live with him and take care of his horses (S 494 ff.). The Frieda episode remains inconclusive, for it is by no means certain that Frieda actually breaks definitively with K., and it is also true of K. that he still courts her. There is urgent need for a solution of the Amalia-Olga episode. And, finally, even the assistants are not entirely disposed of, for we know nothing about the outcome of the charges that Artur prefers against K. in the castle.

Nevertheless, there is bound to arise the important question as to why Kafka left the novel at precisely the stage in which it now exists and turned to others of his works. To be sure, the answer to this question, too, remains necessarily hypothetical. And the same question could be asked with equal urgency in the case of many other fragmentary works of Kafka's. However, after having had almost all of Kafka's literary productions pass by before our mind's eye, the attempt at a clarification must be ventured.

### C. K.'S SUPERIOR POSITION
#### BETWEEN FREEDOM AND LAW

The novel has reached a level at which person and office, individuality and universal world laws, reciprocally undergo, in a manner of speaking, tensile tests of extreme nature. K. has severely disturbed the order of existence. The officials scream for help. He himself was able to achieve this only while he was making a tremendous effort. He had to sleep "far more than twelve hours" in order to recover (S 379). It need not be argued that this effort, after all, meant only a lasting battle between sleeping and waking, and that the victory over the officials was in fact no "conscious" victory but one that he achieved by reeling unintentionally into it. It is the very ability to maintain a balance between sleep and waking that in Kafka always presupposes the utmost in effort; it is also the only chance one has of reconciling the contradictions between freedom and world laws, as Bürgel's forcible, detailed explanations showed.

In unconscious sleep, only an empty, worldless freedom is possible. In the state of full wakefulness man is always inferior to his officials. In the waking state he can never come free and "unannounced." Only in an "unguarded moment, and that of course requires a blacker night than has ever yet existed" (B 300), can man leap forth out of the fighting line and become "judge" over his two opponents who are battling with one another.

If K. had stood in a fully wakeful state before the officials in the corridor, had he consciously pointed out to them his misfortunes, his nocturnal worries, and his futile demands, he himself, together with his demands, would have become the property of "motivated" life; that means that he would have become an official documentary procedure, among countless others—a record that could be put on file, to be fitted into universal laws. He could equally well have been "interrogated," as when Erlanger, on the same corridor, had wanted to interrogate him somewhat earlier—and as the petitioners are forever being interrogated, put on record, and snatched up by the secretaries. However, since he stood there—uninterrogable, in a dreamlike, twilight state between sleeping and waking, incapable of having "his voice heard," in a condition of uncontrollable weariness—his "irremovable" self, his "indestructible" being, bore down upon the officials elementally and frighteningly.

At the same time, however—and this was indeed the effort that he exerted in his weariness—he was able to observe the proceedings exactly, gained an insight into the way the files worked, showed "sympathy" with it, and penetrated into the official atmosphere, feeling himself "almost at home" in it. He remains *in* the world of the officials, and yet at the same time confronts that world as a threatening, inescapable individuality. In so doing he has in point of fact accomplished all that is humanly possible: to live freely and yet participating sympathetically in the Universal.

On this highest of levels, however, life and death come into violent collision. Here the organization of the officials is in danger—as Bürgel said—of "being veritably torn apart." Daybreak is delayed. Life begins to come to a standstill. Were K. not to yield, the whole corridor with all the gentlemen would disappear—so far as that would be possible and imaginable (S 371).

For even if the ultimate, unthinkable, that for which there is "no place in this world" (S 353), were to happen, that is, if an official were to identify completely with the petitioner, penetrating into his "miserable life, to search about there as if on [his] own property" (S 354), if he thus lifted the unmotivated, undefinable "self" of man-as-official into a universal consciousness, even then, and then with a vengeance, the official organization would be torn apart. For there would come about a paradoxical reversal of all relationships.

An anarchical, indefinable freedom would become the law of the world, burst all restrictive systems, invalidate all jurisdiction, and an unimaginable "abuse of official power" would persist. The individuality would win through, but it would be at the cost of that-which-is, which would of course itself be individualized, but which would then elude all objective, universally binding determinations. Complete chaos would be the result.

Although the indeterminable law of the free individuality is the "true" humane law, it must remain "secret" and can never assume visible, definable form. For that very reason there is "no place in this world" for its realization. Only as a demand, as a postulate, can it and must it keep its efficacy. That means, at the same time, that a winning through on the part of the free individuality would be nothing other than entrance into death. Only by shedding life can free individuality be attained.

*That* is the actual reason why "excitement" and later a "cold shudder" seize the landlady of the Herrenhof when K. looks at her dress. For, indeed, this landlady of the Herrenhof *knows*

what is happening in the corridor. She knows the stoppages of
life that K.'s presence has occasioned. She knows that this very
dreamlike ignorance of K.'s, his clinging to his undefinable self,
signify a terminal state of all life.

With this, however, additional and more important relationships become clear.

### D. FINAL POSSIBILITIES OF LIFE: THE "SECRET" EXISTENCE IN THE MIDST OF OFFICE

As we have stated, K. is unmotivatedly free, and yet he sympathetically participates in the bustle of life. However, a new
and completely different form of existence could result from
this. He could "secretly" assert his individualized, free law in
the midst of the Universal of existence.

This possibility follows from Pepi's offer, which now, considered from this point of view, acquires an entirely different
aspect.

From the compositional point of view it is quite striking
that Pepi's offer takes place very late—not in fact until immediately after K.'s experience with Bürgel; that it takes place in
the corridor; and, furthermore, that it is described in great
detail. K. is to live "secretly" in the midst of the Herrenhof,
concealed in Pepi's room. And this very "observance of secrecy"
with reference to K. fills the maids with enthusiasm. He, the
"hero and rescuer of maidens," hence the free man, whom
Pepi seems to credit with the ability to set the whole Herrenhof
on fire, he, of all people, is to exercise this freedom of his, this
manly "protection" that he affords the maids, within the interior
of the Herrenhof—secretly.

Without question, a genuine possibility of existence is being
touched upon here. K. would escape from interrogations relat-
ing to the files and from the protocols, be removed from the
power of the officials, and would "nowhere show" himself
(S 410); he would conceal the law of his individuality in the
midst of the Universal. In this way, too, he would escape from
the "cold," from death, and would keep himself warm. He would

be able to exist individually. The contradiction between freedom and world laws would be surmounted as if by a stroke of magic.

Furthermore, even Pepi and her friends would be helped. They, who as chambermaids are delivered over, helpless, into the clutches of all the officials and their servants, find protection in the free, superior man, and gain the feeling of a personal sphere that is their own, a secret that belongs to them alone. At the same time they can keep their protector safe from all that is threatening. For, through their work as chambermaids in the gentlemen's rooms, they are indeed familiar with the dangers that will be coming his way. Therefore, Pepi says, it is in his own interest for K. to take her advice:

"... when you are with us, you will naturally have to be careful in other respects, too, and show yourself nowhere that we do not consider safe, and in general follow our suggestions; that is the only thing that binds you, and that must be of just as much concern to you as it is to us; but otherwise you are completely free."

"When spring comes around, and you find a position somewhere else, and you no longer like it with us, you can certainly leave; but the secret, *that* of course you will then have to keep too, and not possibly betray us; if you did, that would be our last hour in the Herrenhof." (S 410)

At the center of Pepi's considerations is the matter of keeping strictly secret K.'s sojourn with her in the Herrenhof. For according to the laws of the gentlemen, absolutely no un-official person or outsider is permitted to spend the night at the Herrenhof. With their offer the maids are consciously breaking the official law, and would be lost were their transgression to become known. Their risk is very great. What is more, they do not encroach upon K.'s freedom; he can leave again when the cold outside has passed.

The role of Pepi and her friends can accordingly be interpreted in the following manner: Pepi is not an actual individuality. She does not possess Frieda's "glance." But at one time she had "broken through" (S 409), out of her girlhood existence, to the tavern, out "into the cold" (S 409) of the great world where the battle rages for the "draught," where there must constantly be reconciliation of the wishes of the officials, their servants, and the village guests. That is where she failed. Resignedly she returns, though at the same time filled with fear of the "wretched life" in the maids' chamber (S 409), the warmth of which, it is true, offers protection, but not protection against the anonymous, invisible powers that "prowl around" the room. K. alone, the free, knowing man, is able to help here; he can provide the feeling of sure safety, but he can do this only if everything is kept "secret." By the same token, K. would enjoy safety and secret freedom here.

This, however, means that Pepi—in contrast with Frieda, whose conflict is her struggle between Klamm and K., between collective, sensuous commitment and individual, worldless freedom—represents a realm that, though nonindividual, is nevertheless a sheltering, cherishing, warming, psychical-sensuous sphere—a living protective sheath, as it were, without which no free man can live, without which no feeling of matter-of-course, self-reconciled existence is possible.

For the very reason that Pepi's emotions are in this sense not individualized, she makes no personal demands upon K., does not encroach upon his freedom, does not want to possess him as a person absolutely and forever. So far as she is concerned, conflict between person and instinct, between unconditional and conditional love, *cannot* arise at all. Furthermore, no jealousy of her friends can quicken in her. The girls from a self-contained, psychical-sensuous-intellectual triad, as can be seen from the fact that one of them had unhesitatingly presented Pepi with a piece of "expensive material," her "treasure" (S 393), and that all three together, joining in "joyful, cheering work" (S 393), made Pepi's dress.

In these three girls K. could thus find a counterpart, a female vis-à-vis that hitherto he had lacked. The endless, debilitating conflicts with Frieda would cease. He would be liberated from Olga's hopeless efforts to reach the castle, liberated from her extravagant conversations as well. And Amalia's cold loftiness, after all, could be overcome only through a supreme struggle; she confronts him like a hostile, mocking realm. Pepi and her friends, however, unquestionably afford him safety in the midst of the activity of the officials. He could exist freely and at the same time safely with them, provided that the "secret" remained guarded.

Thus, not only is a trenchant criticism of certain middle-class marriage forms contained in the treatment of the Pepi figuration —that criticism is implicit there *as well*—but, at the same time, in that figuration a possibility of love is caught sight of, suddenly emerging at the very time when K. is in a highly crucial state.

After K., within his concrete life in the village, passed through and came to know the most heterogeneous conflicts of love in the zone of tension between vital and spiritual, collective and individualized powers, he was placed on a new plane through his encounter with Bürgel and the episode in the corridor of the Herrenhof. He experienced and overcame the fundamental conflict between individuality and universality, between person and office. The antinomies were made manifest to him in their tragic insolubility. In a kind of clairvoyant dream knowledge the incompatibility between his existence and the machinery of the officials became clear. K. now knows that a personal encounter with Klamm, an encounter that at one time he stubbornly sought in his relationship with Frieda and with the landlady of the Inn at the Bridge, is impossible in itself, and that such an encounter would cancel out the world order or obliterate him from the phenomenal world.

With that, however, his struggle between personal love and superpersonal love, whether sensuous or spiritual, has become illusory. Moreover, there can no longer be any determining, directive significance in either the striving of Olga, who likewise seeks personal encounters with the officials through the mediation of the servants, or in the position of Amalia who, in her worldless loneliness, scorns the collective castle authorities.

K. is now *above* the antinomies, in a strained and exhausted state, in which consciousness and unconsciousness pervade him.

For someone in such a position, an unquestionably trusting,
undemanding female atmosphere can acquire a new, significant
meaning. Such an atmosphere keeps him alive by carefully,
shelteringly guarding his "secret," and by preventing him from
further appearance outside. An "unmotivated" life, free of
registrations and conflicts, becomes possible. It can no longer
take place in the village, in the conflict zones of the world.
Only in the interior of the Herrenhof—where life in its most
generalized aspect runs its course—and only in a state of concealment even there, can freedom and obligation be reconciled.

Such an existence, however, is mute. It is worldless security in
the world. It is freedom, but freedom in the form of an invisible
secret that puts up no struggle. And it is captivity, imprisonment, and isolation from existence—yet in the form of quiet
comfort. Free, one is captive; captive, one is free. Such a life is
in truth the veriest death. The illusory warmth is cold. Love
has turned into a twilight state, into a living grave. It is "as
if nothing could really happen outside the room; it is warm and
snug there, and we squeeze even tighter together, squeeze up
to one another even more snugly" (S 408).

Such an existence, too, is untenable. K. will renounce it with
thanks.

### E. GERSTÄCKER'S MOTHER: CLOSENESS TO DEATH

K. goes with Gerstäcker to the village. Gerstäcker offers
K. lodging and employment as "helper with the horses" (S 494).
K. "resists" and says that "he really did not understand anything about horses. Gerstäcker said that was not even necessary"
(S 495). K. does not want gratuitous help. Only when he hears
Gerstäcker say that he needs K. in order to have him prevail
upon Erlanger to do something for him [Gerstäcker], does K.
laugh and go along. In a deleted passage, when Gerstäcker
states that his mother once said that K. ought not to be
allowed to go to rack and ruin, K. declares, "A kind word.
Just for that I am not going to you" (S 496). K. wants neither
pity nor help.

According to the undeleted text, K. now goes "through the darkness" to Gerstäcker's cottage.

The room in Gerstäcker's cottage was dimly lighted only by the hearth fire and by a candlestub, in the light of which someone, bent over in a nook beneath the projecting, slanting rafters, was reading a book. It was Gerstäcker's mother. She extended her trembling hand in greeting to K. and had him sit down near her; she spoke with difficulty; it cost some effort to hear her, but what she said.... (S 495)

With that the manuscript of the novel breaks off.

In the village, K. is confronted with a very old woman who is sitting by the fire reading a book by the fading light of an almost spent candle. As has already been pointed out by Ronald Gray,[6] this aged woman gives the impression of being a "norn" or sibyl. It is Gray's conjecture too, accordingly, that Kafka was thus giving expression to K.'s own proximity to death.

This remains a hypothesis. However, on the basis of the total structure of the novel, it is a hypothesis possessed of a high degree of probability.

## The Inner Completion of the Novel

We ourselves, it is true, argued that there are too many threads in the plot of the novel that have not been tied up. However, if one looks into the depths of the problems themselves, what was there that could be brought to a conclusion? What would the regaining of Frieda have meant? Continuing the insoluble antinomies and "battles"—indeed, in the last analysis, merely repeating them. For Klamm's rule and K.'s indefinable "self" can never be united on earth harmoniously and integratedly, unless one gives shape to an unshapable utopia, without truth and without the possibility of poetic expression. This is also valid for Olga, and, above all, for Amalia. The repatriation of Amalia in life—true, that faces K. as a challenge.

But how could that be developed concretely in a creative literary form? Amalia would have to expect reparation, "enlightenment," from the castle and from Sortini. And she herself would have to correct her "truth," her extreme unconditionality. But, at bottom, was all that capable of being set right? Could her "solitude" be reconciled with the castle's world laws revolving in themselves? K.'s insights into the rooms at the Herrenhof permit a reply in the negative. Amalia, repudiated by castle and village, dead while she is still alive, guards her "secret" (S 248 ff.). K. acquires his "secret" between the castle and the village, in the Herrenhof, and likewise is dead while he is still alive. They are well matched. A bridge between them, however, would be a betrayal of the secret. It can be built only "beyond life" (T 572), where nothing more can be said, nothing more betrayed, and where everything can become manifest.

This may well be the reason why the manuscript breaks off just at the point where the crucial words of Gerstäcker's old, norn-like mother were to be formulated or to have their significance defined and illuminated. Kafka's poetic greatness lay in the hidden messages of his poetical *images*, not in the formulation of general words of wisdom, let alone in the formulation of summaries of outcomes that lift the mystery of the poetic work.[7]

For the same reason, Kafka may have shrunk from giving final, definitive features to the "outcome" of K.'s battle, an outcome that can remain true only in the preservation of the contradictions.

### The Right to Life in Death

According to Max Brod's testimony, the novel was to conclude as follows:

The alleged land surveyor obtains at least partial satisfaction. He does not slacken in his battle but dies of debilitation. The community gathers around his deathbed, and just then the decision comes down to them from the castle to the effect that, although K. had no legitimate claim to live in the village, nevertheless in consideration of certain accessory circumstances, he was being permitted to live and work here. (S 481-82)

This is exactly the tragic-ironical situation that Bürgel set forth in K.'s presence. The fulfillment of K.'s request is possible only when K. departs from this life. He may legitimately love and work on earth only if he has "battled" to the point of fatal debilitation. A claim to life does not exist as long as man submits to life. Only "clarity of vision" makes one free (T 572). Such freedom, however, is beyond this life. The right to live can become manifest only in death.

# Biographical Notes on Kafka

Franz Kafka was born in Prague on July 3, 1883, the son of a German-speaking Jewish merchant family of Czech origin. His father, Hermann Kafka, who came from the little village of Wossek near Strakonic, worked himself up with dogged effort from quite humble circumstances to become a rich merchant, the owner of a wholesale business in Prague.

The family moved several times, and the changes Franz experienced in their mode of life bore witness to his father's increasing financial success. The latter's robust physical and emotional constitution, as well as his purely practical and economical orientation, came to rouse not only admiration but also insuperable antipathy and agonizing alienation in the sensitive and delicate Franz. His mother, Julie Kafka (neé Löwy), belonged to a highly esteemed and distinguished Prague family of pronounced spirituality and intellectuality, a family whose emotional world was psychologically refined and discriminating. Among her kindred we find scholars, originals, eccentrics, endowed with an extravagant fantasy and a penchant for solitude or adventure.

It would be difficult to imagine greater contrasts than those that existed between Kafka's father and mother. However, since Kafka's mother subordinated herself completely to her husband, little Franz, whose tendencies and talents came to him predominantly from his mother's side, was thrown almost entirely on his own resources, particularly since the difference in age between him and his three younger sisters was too great for close association with them. Not until he was a grown man did he come into more intimate spiritual contact with Ottla, his youngest sister, who had inwardly freed herself from her father's sphere of influence.

From 1893 to 1901 Franz attended the German academic secondary school on the Old Town Square in Prague, where he was one of the best students in his class. When he was about fifteen or sixteen years old he became absorbed in reading Spinoza; with great enthusiasm he then read Darwin, Haeckel's *Welträtsel* [World Riddle], and Nietzsche, and subsequently professed atheism and socialism. There was a complete absence of religious atmosphere or upbringing in the home of his emancipated parents, who had no interest in religion. At school the instruction in Judaism consisted of arid moral theory and an elective course, which Kafka did not take, in the Hebrew language, given from a purely philological point of view. Through the philosophy course in his senior year Kafka became acquainted with Fechner's *Psychophysik* [Psychophysics] and his theory of the mathematical measurability of psychical quantities. It is a matter of fact that in 1903, while still a student, Kafka was engrossed in studying Fechner's inductive psychology.

Ties of close friendship bound Kafka during his high-school years to Oskar Pollak, who became an eminent art historian before his death in World War I. With Pollak and other students he founded the "Free School," a club with oppositional, anticlerical tendencies. His favorite writers were Goethe, Kleist, Grillparzer, and Stifter.

Just before graduating from high school Kafka stated that he next intended to study philosophy at the university level. However, after auditing two weeks of chemistry and signing up for one semester of German literature and philology at the University of Munich, he attended the German University of Prague, where he studied law from 1901 to 1906. He was strongly influenced by the sociology courses of Alfred Weber, who was then teaching at the University of Prague, and whom Kafka later chose as official faculty representative at his doctoral examination. Alfred Weber's analyses of late capitalistic industrial society and its inherent dangers impressed Kafka deeply and were of vital concern to him. Further, he took courses in philosophy given by Anton Marty, a pupil of Franz Brentano, and attended the meetings of the so-called Brentano circle at the Café Louvre. The influence of Franz Brentano's philosophy was strengthened by Oskar Kraus, a university instructor with whom Kafka was fairly closely associated. As Klaus Wagenbach's biography of Kafka has shown, one essential root of Kafka's ethical rigorism and his "analytical" method of forming moral judgments is to be found in Brentano's philosophical theory in regard to arriving at moral judgments.

In 1903 Kafka had been working on *Das Kind und die Stadt* [The Child and the City], a novel that has since vanished. To his friend Oskar Pollak he sent portions of this novel as well as poems and prose sketches, some of which had probably been written at an earlier date; all of these have likewise been lost sight of. During the period 1904-1905, in part under the influence of Hugo von Hofmannsthal's "Gespräch über Gedichte" [Conversation about Poems] and "Der Brief des Lord Chandos" [The Letter of Lord Chandos], he wrote the most significant sections of his work "Description of a Battle."

From that time on he read by preference diaries, memoirs, and correspondence, particularly the diaries of Hebbel, Grillparzer, Byron, Amiel; the memoirs of Kügelgen, Lord Clive, Macaulay; Flaubert's *Vita*, etc. Further, he became absorbed in Marcus Aurelius and Meister Eckhart; in the writings of Hamsun, Hofmannsthal, Thomas Mann, Flaubert, Stendhal; in the works of Kassner; in Johann Peter Hebel, Stifter, Hermann Hesse, Emil Strauss, Wilhelm, Schäfer; and later also in Carossa, Dostoevsky, Tolstoy, Strindberg; and from approximately 1909 on, in Robert Walser, above all in Walser's *Jakob von Gunten*

[Jakob of Gunten]. The avant-gardists of that era, the poets of "decadence" or of the "daemonic"—authors like Huysmans, Oscar Wilde, Frank Wedekind, or the early Heinrich Mann—were rejected by him; likewise the poets of the gruesome, the fantastic, and the grotesque (Gustav Meyrink, for example) were all rejected by him. The connections or analogies that have been made between the poetic structures of Kafka and those of Meyrink are erroneous. Actually it was the simple, "natural" poets and works of literature that Kafka loved all his life: for instance, Stifter's *Nachsommer* [Indian Summer], Johann Peter Hebel's *Schatzkästlein* [The Treasure Box], Grimm's fairy tales, etc.

His lifelong friendship with Max Brod began in 1902, while they were both students at the university. Also, he was on intimate terms with Felix Weltsch and with Oskar Baum, the blind poet. During his student days Kafka had already been introduced by his old schoolmate and friend, Ewald Felix Přibram, into the highest society in Prague.

In June 1906, after receiving his doctorate in law, Kafka spent one year in practice in the criminal and civil courts of Prague. In 1907 he worked in insurance for the Assicurazioni Generali, and in 1908 he took on a civil service position at Prague in the Workers' Accident Insurance Institute. Here he remained until the onset of his illness, tuberculosis of the lungs, in September 1917; and here, even after that, he continued to work actively at intervals, with rather long interruptions due to his illness, occupying a respected senior position in the department of accident prevention. Held in high esteem by both superiors and subordinates, he distinguished himself by his devotion to duty, his knowledge of his special field, and his friendliness. He was outstanding in suggesting and carrying out technical improvements and safety measures for the prevention of accidents to workers. Clinging tenaciously to his conviction that he ought not to shirk the demands of civilian employment, he suffered deeply because of the conflict between his profession and his poetic mission.

He maintained contact not only with the educated circles in

Prague society but also with the common people. By contrast with other Prague poets like Rilke or Werfel, Kafka cultivated close associations with the Czechs. He frequently attended the political meetings of the Czech National Democrats, Socialists, and Anarchists, but he always went alone, since the German poets of Prague who were his friends stood aloof from the political life of the Czechs or were completely uninterested in it.

Kafka participated regularly in the scientific lectures and discussions that for many years took place in the Brentano circle and at the home of Bertha Fanta. Included among the guests and speakers at her home were Albert Einstein, G. Kowalewski the mathematician, Christian von Ehrenfels the philosopher, as well as the physicists Philipp Frank, Freundlich, and Hopf (a friend of Einstein). It was here that there were revealed to him, in part by way of successive courses or lecture series, Einstein's theory of relativity, Max Planck's quantum theory, Cantor's theory of transfinite numbers, and Sigmund Freud's theory of psychoanalysis. Furthermore, the members of the group studied and discussed together Hegel's *Phänomenologie des Geistes* [Phenomenology], Fichte's theory of knowledge, and Kant's *Kritik der reinen Vernunft* [Critique of Pure Reason]. In 1911 Rudolf Steiner gave a course of lectures at the home of Bertha Fanta, who had a taste for theosophy. Kafka followed Steiner's arguments with lively interest and later paid him a personal visit.

In that same year, 1911, influenced strongly by the Yiddish plays that an Eastern European Jewish theatrical troupe were performing in Prague, Kafka began to develop an intense interest in the history of Judaism and in Yiddish literature. He became absorbed not only in Hasidic tales, but probably in Mendele Moscher Sfurim's Yiddish novels as well. These may have had a stimulating effect upon Kafka in the writing of his animal stories, since in Sfurim too, people appear in animal disguises, although, to be sure, in a rationally didactic, allegorical form that is essentially different from Kafka's mode of characterization. Although Kafka maintained a highly critical stand on Zionism in its orthodox form, he was nevertheless keenly

interested in the Zionist pioneer movement of the *halutzim**
This is tantamount to saying that he was interested in the idea
of Jewish colonization in Palestine on the basis of socialist
*kolkhozy* [collective farms].

As long as he lived, he evinced a decided preference for
naturopathy and related matters such as exercises in deep
breathing, reform measures in dress, physical culture, uncooked
food, etc. He was a vegetarian, a marathon swimmer, a good
oarsman and horseman, and a keen hiker. During his vacations
he undertook journeys to Switzerland, Italy, Paris, Berlin,
Hungary; and in 1912 he journeyed to Weimar in order to
acquaint himself with the world of Goethe, whom he had always
loved. Immediately thereafter he went to "Jungborn," a sanatorium in the Harz Mountains.

Among those with whom he associated on friendly and personal terms were Martin Buber, Franz Werfel, Otto Pick, Ernst
Weiss, Willy Haas, Emil Utitz, Rudolf Fuchs, Wolfenstein, Gustav Janouch, and Ludwig Hardt the recitalist.

Three times he became affianced and broke his engagement,
twice with the same woman (1914 and 1917). He broke off his
relations with other women as well, for instance with Milena
Jesenská Pollak with whom he had been associated from 1920
to 1922. Only in the last year of his life (1923-1924) did he
have a happy union, with Dora Dymant (Diamant), a woman
who came from a distinguished Eastern European Jewish Hasidic family. It was only through his positive relationship with
her that he was able to free himself inwardly from his parental
ties in Prague, establishing a modest household with her in
Berlin during the difficult period of the inflation.

The crises of his previous love affairs were induced by the
unconditionality of the demands that he made on himself and
on marriage. He felt his case to be "similar" to that of Kierkegaard (T 318), and, to some extent, to that of Strindberg,
whose works he was then studying intensively.

*Tr. note: "Jewish immigrants to Palestine who work in the Jewish settle-
ments at tasks contributing to the development of the country as a Jewish
homeland" (*Webster's Third New International Dictionary*).

The chronology of his writings is as follows. In 1906-1907, immediately after the conclusion of his studies at the university, he wrote the fragment "Wedding Preparations in the Country." In 1909, in the periodical *Hyperion*, he published two conversations from the "Description of a Battle," which he had written earlier in 1904-1905. In 1910 he began making diary entries; these records became a vital means of self-clarification, self-discipline, and self-development, a means that took the form not only of reflections but primarily of creative literary work: images, parables, tales.

In January 1913 he published his *Reflection*, a compilation of short pieces from the "Description of a Battle" and other sketches that he had written in the period 1910-1912. From 1911 to 1914 he worked on his novel *The Man Who Was Lost Sight Of (America)*, the essential portions of which he wrote between 1911 and 1912. On September 12, 1912, he wrote the story "The Judgment," which he felt was a breakthrough to a new creative literary style, a style contrasting with that of his novel *The Man Who Was Lost Sight Of (America)*, in which the narrative form was still under the influence of Dickens. To be sure, in 1915 Kafka still cherished the hope of being able to combine the two narrative forms (T 463). Immediately after "The Judgment," in that very same year 1912, he produced the story "The Metamorphosis." In October 1914, probably influenced by the outbreak of the war, he wrote the story "In the Penal Colony." In his opinion "In the Penal Colony" exemplified his new mode of expression more definitely and markedly than anything he had written since his first utilization of this style in "The Judgment" (T 463). Almost at the same time, in the autumn of 1914, he began working on *The Trial*, the cardinal portion of which—the exegesis of the "legend" "Before the Law" (T 448)—was written on December 13, 1914. Work on *The Trial* was continued during 1915. Concurrently, on December 19, 1914, and in January 1915, he wrote the short story "The Village Schoolteacher" ("The Giant Mole") and "Recollections of the Kalda Railroad." In 1915 Kafka was awarded the Fontane Prize for the fragment "The

Stoker" (Chapter I of his novel *The Man Who Was Lost Sight Of [America]*, published in 1913). In 1916 and 1917 Kafka wrote most of the stories that later, in 1919, he published under the collective title *A Country Doctor*. Presumably in 1917 Kafka worked on the fragment "The Hunter Gracchus" (cf. H 439).

In 1918 and 1919 he wrote "The Construction of the Great Wall of China," and probably at the same time, or possibly later (1920-1922), the related compositions "The Rejection," "On the Question of Our Laws," etc. The four stories that Kafka published in 1924 under the collective title *A Hunger Artist* were written between 1921 and 1924; the last story, "Josephine the Singer," was written in March 1924. It was probably in this period (1919-1924) that he wrote the "Investigations of a Dog." Not until the very last year of his life did Kafka write "The Burrow." In 1921 and particularly during the period of crisis with Milena in 1922, he worked on *The Castle*.

The years following the onset of his pulmonary disease in September 1917, Kafka spent by turns in sanitoriums and in Prague, but the last year of his life he lived in Berlin. He read Max Scheler, religiosociological studies by Troeltsch, as well as Martin Buber, Maimonides, and Hasidic tales; but likewise he read "zealously" (cf. his letter to Max Brod, dated the beginning of October 1917) anti-Semitic authors like Hans Blüher, since he obviously wished to meditate on the problem of Judaism from as many points of view as possible. In the last period of his life he studied Hebrew assiduously, especially in conjunction with Dora Dymant who had a superior command of Hebrew. Toward the end of 1917, and particularly at the beginning of 1918, Kafka occupied himself intensively with Kierkegaard. It was then that he first became acquainted with Kierkegaard's chief works: *Either-Or, Fear and Trembling, Repetition, Stages*, etc. An earlier fleeting allusion in his diary entry of August 21, 1913 (T 318), to Kierkegaard's *Book of the Judge*, dealt simply with Kierkegaard's analogous, complicated position with regard to the problem of marriage. His actual quarrel with Kierkegaard's religiosity began early in 1918.

On June 3, 1924, when Franz Kafka, at the age of forty-one,

succumbed to his disease at the Kierling Sanatorium near Vienna, his doctor and friend Robert Klopstock wrote: "His face is as inflexible, stern, and aloof as his spirit was pure and stern—a regal countenance of noblest and oldest lineage." Kafka wished his entire literary estate to be burned.

# Notes

*Explanation of Abbreviations*

All quotations are from the eight-volume edition: Franz Kafka, *Gesemmelte Werke* [Collected Works], ed. Max Brod (Frankfurt a.M.: S. Fischer; copyright by Schocken Books, New York). The references for the quotations do not appear in the *Notes* but are cited in parentheses in the text immediately after the quoted passage; the abbreviations used are as follows:

A = Franz Kafka, *Amerika* (Frankfurt a.M.: S. Fischer, 1953 [1–8000]).

B = Franz Kafka, *Beschreibung eines Kampfes: Novellen, Skizzen, Aphorismen aus dem Nachlaß* (Frankfurt a.M.: S. Fischer, 1954).

E = Franz Kafka, *Erzählungen* (Frankfurt a.M.: S. Fischer, 1946 [1–8000]).

H = Franz Kafka, *Hochzeitsvorbereitungen auf dem Lande und andere Prosa aus dem Nachlaß* (Frankfurt a.M.: S. Fischer, 1953 [1–6000]).

J  = Gustav Janouch, *Gespräche mit Kafka* (Frankfurt a.M.:
      S. Fischer, 1951 [1–5000]).

M = Franz Kafka, *Briefe an Milena* (Frankfurt a.M.: S. Fischer,
      1952 [1–6000]).

P  = Franz Kafka, *Der Prozeß* (Frankfurt a.M.: S. Fischer, 1953
      [14,000–21,000]).

S  = Franz Kafka, *Das Schloß* (Frankfurt a.M.: S. Fischer, 1955
      [9000–13,000]).

T  = Franz Kafka, *Tagebücher* 1910–1923 (Frankfurt a.M.: S. Fi-
      scher, 1951 [1–5000]).

The numbers following upon any one of the above letters in the
text indicate the page numbers in the volume in question.

Kafka's letters, as edited by Max Brod and Klaus Wagenbach
in *Franz Kafka: Briefe 1900-1924* (Frankfurt a. M.: S. Fischer),
appeared after original publication of the present work. However, through the gracious kindness of Mr. Wagenbach, I was
able to have a look at the galley proofs of the letters. In my
present volume, therefore, I identify the quotations from those
letters by giving the date of the letter in question and the name
of the recipient.

As a supplement to the German edition of Kafka's *Diaries*
(T), the fuller American edition should be consulted: *The
Diaries of Franz Kafka 1910-1913*, edited by Max Brod, trans-
lated by Joseph Kresh (New York: Schocken Books, 1948),
and *The Diaries of Frank Kafka 1914-1923*, edited by Max
Brod, translated by Martin Greenberg with the cooperation of
Hannah Arendt (New York: Schocken Books, 1949).

## Textual Criticism

The lack of a historicocritical edition of Franz Kafka's works
has often been justly deplored by scholars, inasmuch as the

edition provided by Max Brod presents various shortcomings
and has repeatedly been subjected to slashing criticism, from
Friedrich Beissner, Fritz Martini, Gerhard Kaiser, Hermann
Uyttersprot, among others (cf. the appended bibliography of
works on Kafka). That I am nonetheless venturing a panoramic
presentation and interpretation of Kafka's works on the basis of
the controversial published texts is for the reasons given below.

On examining photostatic copies of Franz Kafka's manuscripts,
graciously placed at my disposal by Klaus Wagenbach, I found
the wording of the texts as given by Max Brod—apart from
matters of punctuation, orthography, and a very few incorrect
renderings resulting from mistaken reading of the handwriting—
to be on the whole quite accurate. Nowhere has there been any
deliberate tampering with or alteration of the text; that is, the
substance of the work itself has in no instance been affected.
There is need, however, of a thorough, critical revision, above
all with reference to the dating and the order of the texts. Such
critical verification will be most difficult in the case of the fragments; in "The Hunter Gracchus," for instance, it will scarcely
be possible to determine unequivocally the sequence of the
handwritten texts and the points of juncture. The present and
future quarrel among philologists is therefore sparked primarily
by the question of the order of the texts, a question with which
Uyttersprot has already concerned himself in his effort to establish a different sequence of the chapters in *The Trial*. Thus,
writings like the "Description of a Battle" and "Wedding Preparations in the Country," as well as, for example, the diarylike
"Octavo Notebooks" (H 55 ff.), stand in need of a new edition
that will restore the correct textual sequence or the original
arrangement of the separate drafts, as the case may be; the
original arrangement has become obscure as a result of Brod's
combination of various drafts. Further work is necessary, not
only in order to separate clearly those passages stricken from
the text by Kafka and those left unstricken by him, but also to
give complete renderings of all the passages; in Brod's edition
of *The Castle*, for instance, this is not carried out consistently
or with sufficient thoroughness (cf. S 494 ff.). Ideally, of course,

a critical edition would contain, as well, all the different and miscellaneous text variants that afford telling glimpses into Kafka's workshop. But where can one find critical editions of twentieth-century poets? And how many poets of bygone epochs have been denied a critical edition of their works to this very day!

If in the study of literature one were to forgo interpreting the writings of an author whose works have not yet appeared in a critical edition, such an author might cease to be studied altogether. Textual errors that distort meaning exist everywhere, even in the case of authors who, during their own lifetime, personally supervised editions of their works.

The present volume is concerned with the laws of the artistic structure of Kafka's writings and with their inherent spiritual intention. These can be established beyond question from the texts that are presently available, for the structural principles and the spiritual intention are unaffected by subordinate inquiries into, say, the order and grouping of particular works. The meaning and force of what Kafka has to say, for instance, in "The Hunter Gracchus," that fragment which is structurally so opaque, hold good regardless of how this story in itself was planned from the compositional point of view. The fact that the statements in this fragment are inseparably linked to everything that Kafka wrote, legitimates interpreting them in a presentation such as this, which is concerned with the spiritual relations and the fabric of meaning in his total literary production. This holds true likewise in interpreting *The Trial*; no matter what the outcome of the controversy over the correct sequence of the chapters, the intention and the symbolical fabric of the work itself will remain unchanged, for even eventual shifts in emphasis will not alter the fundamental thesis and structure of the novel.

In many respects Max Brod's procedure may have been uncritical, since by his own confession he is not a philologist conversant with problems of editing. However, no one can question his sincere endeavor to furnish clear texts. That, on occasion, he commits errors or even allows distortions of individual words to slip in, should lead one to call to mind the words of Thomas Mann:

I know that the German editions of my books are full of mistakes, and I have often tried to eliminate at least those mistakes that I myself was able to note down and list. I have never been successful, and mistakes like "part of necessity" instead of "vale of necessity," at the end of "The Law," or "cremation blocks" instead of "cremation sites," in *The Transposed Heads* (to mention only two instances), continue to be handed down to posterity from one printing to the next. I have given up, and I no longer protest.*

As little as such distortions call in question the spiritual identity and form of Thomas Mann's work, as little too can the shortcomings of the texts of Kafka's works prevent the interpreter from venturing to reveal their secret.

## Annotations

### CHAPTER I

1. Immanuel Kant, *Kritik der Urteilskraft* [Critique of Judgment], ed. Karl Vorländer, *Philosophische Bibliothek*, XXXIX (Hamburg, 1954), 58.

2. Goethe, *Maximen und Reflexionen über Literatur und Ethik* [Maxims and Reflections on Literature and Ethics], Weimarer Sophienausgabe, I. Abt., Bd. 42, 2. Abt. (Weimar, 1907), 139.

3. Cf. Wolfgang Kayser, *Das Groteske, seine Gestaltung in Malerei und Dichtung* (Oldenburg: G. Stalling, 1957).

4. G. W. Fr. Hegel, *Vorlesungen über die Ästhetik* [Lectures on Aesthetics], I; repr. in *Sämtliche Werke*, ed. H. Glockner, XII (Stuttgart, 1927), 160.

5. The editor has placed this fragment in the "Appendix" of Volume B (*Beschreibung eines Kampfes, Novellen, Skizzen, Aphorismen aus dem Nachlaß*) (B 334 ff.), and has thus separated it from "The Hunter Gracchus" which he places in the same volume (B 99 ff.). However, a comparison of the manuscripts indicates that such a separation is not possible and that both sections belong together in counterbalance.

6. Attention has been called to this model as giving the basic structure of Kafka's epic form as well, above all by Martin Johannes Walser, "Beschrei-

---

*\**Wissenschaftliche Annalen*, V, No. 9 (Berlin: Akademie, 1956), 695.

bung einer Form. Versuch über die epische Dichtung Franz Kafkas" (diss., Tübingen, 1952). He speaks of two patterns in Kafka's writing that cancel each other out.

7. Cf. A. Walde, *Lateinisches Etymologisches Wörterbuch*, 3rd newly rev. ed. J. B. Hofmann, I (Heidelberg, 1938), 615, 284. Also: A. Walde, *Vergleichendes Wörterbuch der indogermanischen Sprachen*, rev. ed. Julius Pokorny, I (Berlin-Leipzig, 1928), 592–93. Further: A. Ernout and A. Meillet, *Dictionnaire Etymologique de la Langue Latine. Histoire des Mots* (Paris, 1951), p. 497.

8. That Kafka here designates himself as "a thief and a dangerous bird" is related to his basic conviction that this kind of bird, one that does not fit into any category, also robs the surrounding world of its "dear life." Cf. our subsequent comments on the "Investigations of a Dog" and on the ever-recurring concept in Kafka that coming of age as a human being—which means recognizing the Universal—requires the abandonment of everything that is concretely of this world. Hence, here too Kafka differentiates himself from the jackdaw in its ordinary thieving aspect, in its partiality for "glittering things."

9. On Kafka's simultaneous closeness to and remoteness from Jewish and Christian tradition cf. our comments in the following sections of Chapter I. Cf. also our analysis of Kafka's concept of the "law" in Chapter IV, "The Construction of the Objective World and the Binding Law."

10. Hitherto, research on Kafka has repeatedly attempted to reduce him to this kind of empirically determinable phenomena and thereby to elucidate his enigmas absolutely. Three chief currents of such research can be distinguished, although of course they overlap in many varied ways:

1. The theological trend. It seeks to interpret Kafka's work from the Jewish, Christian, or Manichaean tradition of the Occident. However, this trend can also veer round to an existential or even nihilistic interpretation by trying to prove, say, that Kafka's work represents the negation or the perversion of this tradition. Furthermore, too, it can be furnished with psychoanalytical underpinnings (identification of Kafka's "father image" with Kafka's concept of God) and can be combined with biographical and sociological investigations.

2. The psychoanalytical trend (see above).

3. The sociological or sociocritical-political interpretation that can likewise be combined with the first two. I cite the following as the chief representatives of these three groups, with the reservation that the boundary lines cannot be clearly drawn in individual instances:

a. The theological trend: Max Brod, W. H. Auden, Roger Bauer, Neville Braybrooke, Albert Camus, René Dauvin, Jacques Delesalle, Ronald D. Gray, Clement Greenberg, Wilhelm Grenzmann, John Kelly, Werner Kraft, Josef Mühlberger, Edwin Muir, André Nemeth, Wladimir Rabi, Marthe Robert, Robert Rochefort, D. S. Savage, Hans Joachim Schoeps, Walter Stumpf, Herbert Tauber, Jarvis Thurston, Jean André Wahl, T. Weiss, Felix Weltsch, Ignaz Zangerle.

b. The psychoanalytical trend: Angel Flores, Kate Flores, Erich Fromm, Paul Goodman, Frederick T. Hoffman, Hellmuth Kaiser, F. D. Luke, Charles Neider, Mark Spilka, Joachim H. Seypel, P. D. Webster.

c. The sociological or sociocritical-political and cultural-historical trend: Theodor W. Adorno, Günther Anders, Hannah Arendt, Edwin Berry Burgum, Michel Carrouges, Peter Demetz, Paul Eisner, Rudolf Fuchs, Erich Heller, Max Lerner, Roy Pascal, Heinz Politzer, Paul Reimann, Harry Slochower, Parker Tyler, Franz Carl Weiskopf.

11. With reference to Goethe's doing away with the empirical boundaries of time and space, cf. the detailed discussions and numerous examples given in my book *Die Symbolik von Faust II, Sinn und Vorformen*, 2nd ed. (Bonn: Athenäum, 1957).

12. Cf. *ibid.*, pp. 44 ff., 116 ff., et al.

13. Cf. T 142, 341. Further: Klaus Wagenbach, "Franz Kafka: Eine Biographie seiner Jugend (1883–1912)" (diss., Frankfurt a.M., 1957 [this has since been published: Bern: A. Francke, 1958]), p. 50; Max Brod, "Infantilismus, Kleist und Kafka," *Die Literarische Welt*, III, No. 28 (1927), 3; Max Brod, "Kleist und Kafka," *Weltstimmen*, XVIII, No. 12 (1949), 8–11; Heinz Friedrich, "Heinrich von Kleist und Franz Kafka," *Berliner Hefte für geistiges Leben*, IV, No. 11 (1949), 440–48; Hermann Pongs, "Kleist und Kafka," *Welt und Wort*, VII, No. 11 (1952), 379 ff.; also Hermann Pongs' book *Im Umbruch der Zeit* (Göttingen, 1952), pp. 85–87. Works of Kleist and of Kafka are compared and analyzed by Siegfried Walter in his dissertation "Die Rolle der führenden und schwellenden Elemente in Erzählungen des 19. und 20. Jahrhunderts" (diss., Bonn, 1951).

14. Cf. Kleist's words in "The Duel": "Exalt the feeling that dwells in your heart, and let it rise like a tower of rock . . . ."

15. For example, in Kleist's essay "On the Marionette Theater."

16. Cf. the examples cited and the careful analyses given by Hans-Georg Rappl, "Die Wortkunsttheorie von Arno Holz" (diss., Cologne, 1957).

17. H. Bremond, *La poésie pure* (Paris, 1926); E. Howald, "Die absolute Dichtung im 19. Jahrhundert," *Trivium* (1948); Hugo Friedrich, "Die Struktur der modernen Lyrik," *Rowohlts Deutsche Enzyklopädie*, XXV (Hamburg: Rowohlt, 1956).

18. See Hans-Georg Rappl, *op. cit.*, pp. 37, 77 ff.

19. See Wilhelm Emrich, "Die Struktur der modernen Dichtung," *Wirkendes Wort*, III, No. 4 (Düsseldorf: Schwann, 1952–53), 213 ff.

20. See Wolfgang Kayser, *op. cit.*, pp. 13 ff., 112 ff. (see note 3, above).

21. *Ibid.*, p. 118.

22. See the detailed argument in Renate Heuer's "Individualität und Allgemeinheit bei Wilhelm Raabe" (diss., Cologne, 1957).

23. I owe this reference to Miss Gertrud Middelhauve, who at the time of original publication was working on a dissertation on "Die Rolle der Erzähler-figur in W. Raabes *Stopfkuchen* und Thomas Manns *Der Erwählte*."

24. This term was coined by Hans-Georg Rappl in his above-cited dissertation on Arno Holz (see note 16, above).

25. Arno Holz regarded the concept of "nature" quite critically in the Kantian sense, but he subjectivized, relativized, and at the same time altered the meaning of that concept, following the example of the monistic theories of evolution (see H.-G. Rappl, *op. cit.*, pp. 37–50).

26. Klaus Wagenbach, "Franz Kafka. Eine Biographie seiner Jugend (1883–1912)" (diss., Frankfurt a.M., 1957), p. 53. It is owing to the very careful investigations of Klaus Wagenbach that light has been shed on the intellectual and spiritual development of young Kafka, as well as on the influences exercised upon him, etc. According to Wagenbach's research, Kafka was influenced very early by Darwin, Haeckel, and Fechner's rationalistic psychology, and professed atheism and socialism. During his university days he was vitally interested in the "insights into the mechanism and problems of industry" as Alfred Weber presented them (p. 131). In the circle around Bertha Fanta in Prague, Kafka became acquainted relatively early with Albert Einstein's and Max Planck's newest discoveries in physics, discoveries that were then creating a sensation (pp. 177 ff.), as well as with Sigmund Freud's theory of psychoanalysis (p. 178). Contrary to widely held opinions, Kafka showed no interest in religious problems during his youth. "Until then," that is, until about 1911, when he was twenty-eight years old, the religious world was "almost completely buried," since he had grown up in the household of parents who were uninterested in religion (p. 178). Rudolf Steiner's lectures at the home of Bertha Fanta initiated Kafka's concern with religious questions (pp. 177–78); a further impetus was given him by the Yiddish theater per-formances in Prague (pp. 182–83). As late as 1922 (in his letter to Max Brod, dated July 31, 1922), Kafka writes about the "lack of any solid Jewish ground under my feet." Not until the beginning of 1918 did Kafka read the chief works of Kierkegaard. Their effect upon him "in 1917 is therefore scarcely of any significance" (that is, during the period when he wrote the greater portion of "Reflections on Sin, Suffering, Hope, and the True Way") (p. 114). By then Kafka had long since developed the mature artistry of form and content characteristic of his writing. Kierkegaard's influence and the influence of the Jewish tradition upon Kafka's poetic world have been vastly exaggerated. For, as we shall subsequently show, within his early work "Description of a Battle" (1904–1905) there is to be found the germ of almost every subject matter and, to a partial extent, of every form and symbol in the later writings.

27. Such is the case in Arno Holz's *Phantasus*, and indeed it is so in his earliest stages, as may be seen in as early a work as *Buch der Zeit* [The Book of the Present Time].

28. Klaus Wagenbach has demonstrated that, contrary to the dating given by Max Brod (B 345), the genesis of the essential portions of the "Description of a Battle" is to be placed in the period from the autumn of 1904 to the spring of 1905. To be sure, Kafka occupied himself with this work over a very long

stretch of time, having published sections of it in 1909 and 1913 (cf. E 9–22, 25–29, 34, 40, 44, 319–20), and, even in 1910, in the *Diaries* (T 17 ff.), there are further literary elaborations of scenes from this work.

29. Klaus Wagenbach, *op. cit.*, pp. 45 ff.

30. Even in his late period, this is Kafka's chief argument in his trenchant criticism of Kierkegaard. Thus he reproaches Kierkegaard and Max Brod, saying that they "rape the world" (letter to Max Brod, end of March 1918); or, opposing Brod's picture of classical antiquity, he declares that the ancient pagans "were . . . after all, an eminently humble people in regard to religion—a kind of Lutheran sect. Anything that was absolutely Divine could not be imagined far enough away from themselves; Olympus was merely a means of keeping categorical absolutes at a distance from one's mortal body, of having air to breathe as a human being" (letter to Max Brod, dated August 7, 1920).

31. See K.'s "Struggle" in our discussion of the novel *The Castle*.

32. From the "Conversation with the Praying Man." This was a part of the "Description of a Battle." In 1909 Kafka published it together with the "Conversation with the Drunken Man" in the periodical *Hyperion*.

33. Walter Benjamin, "Franz Kafka. Zur 10. Wiederkehr seines Todestages," *Schriften*, II (Frankfurt a.M.: Suhrkamp, 1955), 196–228. In this article Benjamin calls attention to the fact that archaic elements emerge in Kafka, elements long since forgotten by modern man's consciousness.

34. See Klaus Wagenbach, *op. cit.*, p. 178.

35. Cf. Theodor W. Adorno, *Minima moralia, Reflexionen aus dem beschädigten Leben* (Frankfurt a.M.: Suhrkamp, 1951), pp. 96 ff. ("Die Gesundheit zum Tode").

36. Cf. Thomas Mann on Freud's position in modern intellectual history (1929).

37. It was Max Brod, in his epilogue to the first edition of the novel (S 488), who gave birth to the notion that the officials of the castle were divine or heavenly beings. At first this point of view was accepted by many interpreters uncritically, but later it was also rejected with incisiveness (Charles Neider, Heller, etc.). Actually, however, it has never been established clearly just what the officials are. In most cases Brod's critics expressed the view that the castle bore greater resemblance to a perversion of "Heaven" the site of "grace," and from this view they derived an aspect for Kafka that was daemonic-Manichaean or nihilistic (Heller). Even the latest work of greater magnitude dealing with the novel, Ronald Gray's *Kafka's "Castle"* (Cambridge University Press, 1956), in spite of its precise interpretation of individual sections and its careful examination of possible interpretations, labors and is lost in vague compromises. For Gray too the castle is still the seat of grace, but with this qualification: the reason why K. does not succeed in attaining to grace is that he believes he can obtain it through his own power and, what is more, compares the castle with grace, insists on identifying the two, and thereby confuses the Divine with the mortal (see Gray, pp. 79 ff.). Nowhere in his book,

however, has Gray really succeeded incontestably in clarifying (from the context of the work itself) the function and the nature of the enigmatic officials. A clarification of this kind is an essential objective of our own efforts. The extensive final chapter of the present work is concerned with that objective.

38. Kafka's letter to Max Brod, end of March 1918.

39. Kafka's letter to Max Brod, August 7, 1920 (see note 30, above).

40. See the detailed explanations in Chap. II, "Beyond Allegory and Symbol."

41. It is from this point of view that *The Trial* has been reinterpreted in the dramatization of the novel by André Gide and Jean-Louis Barrault, *Le Procés: Pièce tirée du roman de Kafka* (Paris: Gallimard, 1947).

42. Cf. H 49–50. This problem will be considered in greater detail in our analysis of "The Burrow."

43. Paul Tillich, *Der Mut zum Sein*, 2nd ed. (Stuttgart: Steingrüben, 1954), p. 134.

44. Tillich, p. 109.

45. Herein, too, was perhaps the basis for Kafka's strong leaning, from about 1911–12 on, toward Eastern European Jewish Hasidism and toward Jewish mysticism in general, in which ethical rigorism was inseparably combined with the conviction that the divine essence, or the absolute claim of God, is within man himself. Cf. Gershom Scholem, *Die jüdische Mystik in ihren Hauptströmungen* (Frankfurt a.M.: Alfred Metzner, 1957).

46. Cf. the explanations given in our analysis of "The Burrow."

47. The struggle to achieve such a reconciliation of incompatibles pervades all of Kafka's writings and is intensified to the utmost, primarily in "Investigations of a Dog," "The Burrow," and in the Bürgel episode in *The Castle*; this will be shown in our subsequent analyses.

48. For example, Max Bense, *Die Theorie Kafkas* (Cologne-Berlin: Kiepenheuer und Witsch, 1952); *idem*, *Literaturmetaphysik: Der Schriftsteller in der technischen Welt* (Stuttgart: Deutsche Verlagsanstalt, 1950); *idem*, *Aesthetica: Metaphysische Beobachtungen am Schönen* (Stuttgart: Deutsche Verlagsanstalt, 1954). Further: K. H. Volkmann-Schluck, "Bewußtsein und Dasein in Kafkas *Prozeß*," *Die Neue Rundschau*, LXII (1951). Of special significance is Heinz Ide's article "Existenzerhellung im Werke Kafkas," *Jahrbuch der Wittheit zu Bremen*, I (Bremen, 1957), 66–104. By virtue of excellent, penetrating analyses of the texts, he arrives at insights to which I am indebted for valuable suggestions, primarily with reference to the interpretation of "Investigations of a Dog" and "On the Question of Our Laws."

49. Cf. Max Bense's explanatory comments on the theory of "Odradek," *Die Theorie Kafkas*, pp. 63–67 (see note 48, above).

50. Reference should be made here to the intrinsic relations that exist between Heidegger's essay "Der Ursprung des Kunstwerks" [The Origin of

Works of Art], *Holzwege* (Frankfurt a.M., 1950), pp. 7–68, and Schelling's treatise "Über das Wesen der menschlichen Freiheit" [On the Nature of Human Freedom], 1809.

51. The following may serve as an illustration of the numerous instances of this:

> Before entering the Holy of Holies you must take off your shoes, and not only your shoes, but everything—divest yourself of your traveling clothes and belongings, and your nakedness underneath, and everything beneath your nakedness, and everything hiding beneath that, and then the core of you, and the core of the core, then the rest, and then the residue, and then even the light of the everlasting fire. Only the fire itself will be absorbed, can be absorbed by the Holy of Holies; and neither can offer resistance (H 104–105).

52. Gershom Scholem, *Die jüdische Mystik* (see note 45, above), pp. 117 ff., on the "Immanence of God."

53. Martin Heidegger, *Was ist Metaphysik?* (1929).

54. Note Kafka's frequent and recurring tendency to designate himself as a straying, searching, inquiring animal; e.g., in his letters to Milena (M 223–24), where he calls himself an "animal gone astray," and a "forest animal." Analogously, the Dog in the "Investigations of a Dog" tosses about in despair upon the "forest litter" (B 282), and there too mention is made of the dogs' "endless wandering" (B 269). In his letters to Milena Kafka speaks of the "horrible sound" of a threatening "voice" (M 40). Similar statements occur in the "Investigations of a Dog": B 245 and 286–87. And in this way various parallels can be drawn between Kafka's personal experiential reality and his work.

55. The text of this letter appears repeatedly; e.g., in Kafka's *Diaries* (T 534), where it is designated as an excerpt from a letter to his fiancée F. (Felice Bauer). The contents must have been of particular importance to Kafka, since he commits this letter verbatim to Max Brod, his fiancée, and his diary.

56. The image of the lack of air (the search for "breathable air") pervades almost all of Kafka's writings, beginning with the "Description of a Battle" and continuing through *The Trial* and *The Castle*. It designates the search for life that has survival potential. In a similar way too the image of the lack of "ground" is cardinal for Kafka (cf. K.'s "land surveying" in *The Castle*.) Ground, air, commandment are in substance the same. The search for "nourishment" likewise belongs to this sphere.

57. A clear echo of the Bible (Luke 10:42).

58. With reference to the image of "nourishment," see note 54 and our subsequent comments *inter alia* on "The Metamorphosis," on the dogs' "science of nourishment" in the "Investigations of a Dog."

59. Reminiscent of the Bible (Psalms 121:4; Matthew 26:38–41, *inter alia*). According to a statement by Manfred Hausmann, author of the book *Einer muß wachen* [Someone Must Stand Guard], during World War I this expres-

sion was often used by soldiers and in circles connected with the Youth Movement; it is possible that this is Kafka's source for the expression, since it is not to be found verbatim in the Bible.

60. E.g., Günther Anders, *Kafka pro et contra* (Munich: C. H. Beck, 1951); Edwin Berry Burgum, "The Bankruptcy of Faith," *The Kafka Problem*, ed. Angel Flores (New York: New Directions, 1946), pp. 298–318.

61. On this see Theodor W. Adorno, "Aufzeichnungen zu Kafka," *Die Neue Rundschau*, LXIV, No. 3 (1953), 325–53, particularly p. 351.

62. Cf. Kafka's sketch "The Silence of the Sirens" (H 78–80) and my comments on the subject in my essay "Die Bilderwelt Franz Kafkas" [Franz Kafka's World of Imagery], to appear in a miscellanies, ed. Friedrich Gerke, *Sammelband der Mainzer Gesellschaft für bildende Kunst*.

63. Cf. Franz Kafka's "A Dream" (E 181 ff.).

CHAPTER II

1. Thus in Norbert Fürst, *Die offenen Geheimtüren Franz Kafkas, fünf Allegorien* Heidelberg: Wolfgang Rothe, 1956). Also, Augusta Walker, "Allegory: A Light Conceit," *Partisan Review*, XXII (New York, 1955); and elsewhere.

2. Clemens Heselhaus, "Kafkas Erzählformen," *Deutsche Vierteljahrsschrift für Literaturwissenschaft und Geistesgeschichte*, XXVI, No. 3 (1952), 353–76; Werner Heldmann, "Die Parabel und die parabolischen Erzählformen bei Franz Kafka" (diss., Münster, 1953).

3. Thus in Norbert Fürst, *op. cit.* (see note 1, above). Fürst constructs most fantastic allegorical meanings; e.g., "the Inn at the Bridge [in *The Castle*] is probably the stronghold of Protestantism, just as the Herrenhof is the stronghold of Catholicism" (p. 23). If that were the case, why would there be an image of a saint in the guest room at the Inn at the Bridge? Further, he maintains, "Amalia = Eastern European Jew; Olga = Western European Jew" (p. 23); the village = the "Kierkegaard, the village with a church, the village with a castle" (p. 33); etc.

4. The definition of the term "symbolic," as developed here, came into being through Goethe and has since then been a matter of common knowledge in aesthetics. On the other hand, before the time of Goethe, and even during his lifetime, "allegory" and "symbol" were often interchangeable, synonymous ideas in the conceptual language of aesthetics. Cf. Curt Müller, "Die geschichtlichen Voraussetzungen des Symbolbegriffs in Goethes Kunstanschauung," *Palästra*, CCXI (Leipzig, 1937).

5. Goethe, *Maximen und Reflexionen über Kunst* (Weimarer Ausgabe, I. Abt., Bd. 48, 205–206); and *Maximen und Reflexionen über Literatur und Ethik* (Weimarer Sophienausgabe, I. Abt., Bd. 42, 2. Abt., 146).

6. Cf. Wilhelm Emrich, "Das Problem der Symbolinterpretation im

Hinblick auf Goethes *Wanderjahre*," *Deutsche Vierteljahrsschrift für Litera-turwissenschaft und Geistesgeschichte*, XXVI, No. 3 (1952), 331–52; *idem*, "Symbolinterpretation und Mythenforschung, Möglichkeiten und Grenzen eines neuen Goetheverständnisses," *Euphorion, Zeitschrift für Literaturge-schichte*, XLVII, No. 1 (1953), 38–67.

7. Cf. the conception of the inner light in Goethe's *Faust II*, Act V, 1, 11500, and in his *Wahlverwandtschaften* (Weimarer Sophienausgabe, I. Abt., Bd. 20, 224), *inter alia*.

8. See note 28 above for the dating of this.

9. In the "Conversation with the Praying Man," which belongs to the "Description of a Battle."

CHAPTER III

1 For this information I am indebted to my colleague, Professor Reinhold Olesch, Professor of Slavic Philology at the University of Cologne. With reference to the problem of Odradek, see also Max Bense, *Die Theorie Kafkas* (see Chap. I, note 48), pp. 63 ff.

2. Felix Weltsch, *Religion und Humor im Leben und Werk Franz Kafkas* (Berlin-Grunewald: F. A. Herbig, 1957); parts of this work are repr. in Max Brod's *Franz Kafkas Glauben und Lehre* (Winterthur: Mondial, 1948; and Munich: Desch, 1948). Further: A. G. Toulmin, *Humor in the Works of Kafka* (Somerville College, Oxford, 1951). See also the section on "Das Komische bei Kafka" in the book by H. S. Reiß, *Franz Kafka, eine Betrach-tung seines Werkes* (Heidelberg: Lambert Schneider, 1952), pp. 152 ff.; and his article "Franz Kafka's Conception of Humour," *Modern Language Review*, XLIV, No. 4 (Cambridge, 1949). Further: Marthe Robert, "L'humour de Franz Kafka," *Revue de la Pensée Juive*, No. 6 (Paris, 1951).

3. Cf. Kafka's letter to Oskar Pollak, dated November 9, 1903, in which, to be sure, there is no liberating laughter resounding from the moon; on the contrary, through the moon's laughter everything on earth becomes strangely humorous and uncertain. But here too laughter itself is liberation from the earth, and as the moon laughs, the earth becomes aware of its own nullity. In the letter written to Max Brod at the beginning of April 1918, Kafka speaks of a journeying forth and emigrating to the moon: ". . . the earth, which has shaken off the moon, has been holding on since then with a tighter grip; but we have lost our way for the sake of a home on the moon." Thus humor comes into being because of a break with all given reality by means of a journeying forth from that reality. Consequently, however, as there is no longer any humorous contrast between a normal person and an abnormal one—since whoever lapses from normality safely can no longer be measured by a reliable "norm"—humor is no longer present as it is traditionally defined in aesthetics; for instance, as the term is developed by Emil Staiger, *Grundbegriffe der Poetik* (Zürich: Atlantis, 1946), pp. 208–218. For no longer is there any unequivocal standard that is violated by the strangely humorous

or ridiculous person; there is no longer any "frame of reference" for something that has fallen out of its frame, that is "out of place" (Staiger, p. 208).

4. Cf. Max Brod's comments (B 346–47).

5. Cf. the caustic rejection of all psychology, repeatedly met with in Kafka's works: "For the last time psychology!" (H 51).

6. E.g., Marthe Robert, "Zu Franz Kafkas Fragment 'In unserer Synagoge,'" *Merkur*, No. 7 (1948), 113–14.

7. Possibly Kafka was familiar with the Czech and German popular belief that moles possess the gift of prophecy and bestow miraculous powers on man. Cf. the book that appeared in Prague in 1862, written by Josef Virgil Grohmann, *Apollo Smintheus und die Bedeutung der Mäuse in der Mythologie der Indogermanen*. In it the following statement occurs:

> That moles were generally considered to be mysterious beings is evident from the fact that moles were believed to be capable of understanding human speech and would flee on hearing themselves talked about (Plin. X, 88). In German and Slavic popular belief the mole is likewise a prophetic animal; it foretells death and birth; its heart, if eaten or carried on one's person, bestows miraculous powers (p. 50).

According to Grohmann, mice and moles were incarnations, originally of the Divine, and later on of a daemonic fire. Hence, in many fairy tales and legends mice appear as incarnations of the human soul (cf. Goethe's *Faust* in which a red mouse leaps forth from the mouth of the young witch). Thus, according to Grohmann, in popular mythology a giant mole would signify a monster of divine or undoubtedly supernatural origin. In his investigations Grohmann draws heavily on Bohemian popular belief.

8. Cf. note 7 above.

9. See Fritz Martini's article on Kafka's "Village Schoolteacher," *Jahrbuch der Deutschen Schiller-Gesellschaft*, II (Stuttgart: A. Kröner, 1958).

10. Hegel, "Vorrede der ersten Ausgabe," *Wissenschaft der Logik, Sämtliche Werke*, ed. Georg Lasson, III (Leipzig: F. Meiner, 1948), p. 4.

11. *Ibid.*, p. 3.

12. *Ibid.*, p. 4.

13. Norbert Fürst, *Die offenen Geheimtüren Franz Kafkas* (Heidelberg: Wolfgang Rothe, 1956), pp. 9 ff.; Hans Joachim Schoeps, "Theologische Motive in der Dichtung Franz Kafkas," *Die Neue Rundschau*, LXII, No. 1 (1951), 22 ff.; H. S. Reiß, *Franz Kafka, eine Betrachtung seines Werkes* (Heidelberg: Lambert Schneider, 1952), pp. 121 ff.; and elsewhere. The first really convincing refutation of these allegorical interpretations was presented by Heinz Ide in his careful analysis, "Existenzerhellung im Werke Kafkas," *Jahrbuch der Wittheit zu Bremen*, I (Bremen, 1957), pp. 85 ff.

14. Norbert Fürst, *op. cit.*, p. 12.

15. Max Brod, *Franz Kafka, eine Biographie*, 2nd ed. (New York: Schocken Books, 1946), p. 250.

16. Possibly Kafka was influenced here too by Bohemian folk tales. According to Bohemian mythology as reconstructed by the Prague scholar Josef Virgil Grohmann (in the traditions of the romantic school of nature mythology), mice were originally spirits of lightning and storm. From this hypothesis he traces connections with Bohemian legends:

> In their original character of storm spirits, the elves love music; they themselves sing wonderful songs, and in the *Rig-Veda* (I, 85: 10) the Maruts [ = storm spirits] are represented actually as flute players. Likewise, in Bohemia, not only do the mice themselves sing but they are lured in hordes by beautiful music and driven off by bad. One says to a singer who has a poor voice, "You will sing all the mice out of the house." Furthermore, the belief prevails that there are people who by whistling can lure mice and rats out of a house as well as into it (Grohmann, *op. cit.*, p. 26).

In the light of Kafka's great interest in fairy tales, legends, and myths, it is likely that he was acquainted with this publication of the Prague scholar. In all events, however, Kafka was familiar with Bohemian legends and proverbs. This, of course, should not lead one to the short-circuit conclusion which would simply identify Kafka's "Mouse Nation" with such mythological ideas. It may be purely a case of stimulating suggestions that Kafka completely transformed into his own poetic conceptions—as a matter of course.

CHAPTER IV

1. Cf. Günther Anders, *Kafka pro et contra* (Munich: C. H. Beck, 1951), p. 34. This statement is quoted in support of the author's basic thesis that Kafka's completely disoriented spiritual world could in its consequences—consequences indeed not intended by Kafka, but intellectually a foregone conclusion—lead to submission to worldly political powers,· and to blind, slavish obedience of a fascist character. A similar statement is made by Edwin Berry Burgum, "The Bankruptcy of Faith," *The Kafka Problem*, ed. Angel Flores (New York: New Directions, 1946), pp. 298–318.

2. Günther Anders, *op. cit.*, p. 85.

3. Cf. T 502 and 504. Also, the letters to Max Brod written at the beginning and at the end of March 1918 (about Kierkegaard).

4. Cf. the excellent comments by Heinz Ide, *op. cit.*, p. 80 (see Chap. III, note 13).

5. Cf. the analogous tension in *The Castle* and the detailed analysis presented in Chap. VII.

CHAPTER V

1. Norbert Fürst, *Die offenen Geheimtüren Franz Kafkas*, p. 54. See also

Max Brod, "Zur Deutung von Kafkas *Amerika*," *Neue Zürcher Zeitung* (Fernausgabe Nr. 85, Blatt 13: March 27, 1958). *Idem*, "Zu Franz Kafkas Roman *Amerika*," *Die literarische Welt*, III, No. 3 (1927), 3. *Idem*, "Kafkas *Amerika*," *Jüdische Rundschau*, XXXIII, No. 44 (1928), 3. The religious, optimistic interpretation presented by Max Brod and others (Tauber, André Nemeth, et al.) has recently been strenuously opposed; e.g., H. Uyttersprot, *Eine neue Ordnung der Werke Kafkas? Zur Struktur von "Der Prozeß" und "Amerika"* (Antwerp: C. de Vries-Brouwers, 1957), pp. 66 ff.; Lienhard Bergel, "America: Its Meaning," *Franz Kafka Today*, eds. Angel Flores and Homer Swander (Madison: University of Wisconsin Press, 1958), pp. 117–25.

2. Norbert Fürst, *op. cit.*, p. 54.

3. Lienhard Bergel, *op. cit.* (see note 1, above), emphasizes the satirical accent, but does so to the exclusion of too much else.

CHAPTER VI

1. See the references in support of this in Klaus Wagenbach, "Franz Kafka. Eine Biographie seiner Jugend," p. 68.

2. *The Trial* has been interpreted as the biological "process" of Kafka's illness by Charles Neider, H. Uyttersprot, N. Fürst, and others. The simple fact controverting this thesis is that the novel was written before the onset of Kafka's tuberculosis.

3. The problem is framed and developed on more general principles by Kafka in *The Castle*. Cf. our subsequent comments on the relationship between "office" and "person" in *The Castle*. Yet the problem is quite analogous in *The Trial*.

4. This conception, widely disseminated through Max Brod's epilogue to the first edition of *The Castle*, has been echoed repeatedly even by critics who (in contrast to Brod) derive therefrom a perversion of the religious element or a daemonic-nihilistic ideology in Kafka (G. Anders, Erich Heller, Robert Rochefort, et al.).

5. Excellent comments on this in Ronald Gray, *Kafka's "Castle"* (Cambridge University Press, 1956), pp. 132 ff.

6. Cf. Clemens Heselhaus, "Kafkas Erzählformen," *Deutsche Vierteljahrsschrift für Literaturwissenschaft und Geistesgeschichte*, XXVI, No. 3 (1952), 356 ff. Heselhaus has rightly revealed a form in Kafka, the "antifairy tale": in the antifairy tale people who have been transformed into animals can no longer (as in a fairy tale) be saved and changed back into human form.

7. Cf. the more detailed comments on heat and cold in our analysis of *The Castle*. The symbol of icy coldness appears in Kafka in numerous writings ("A Country Doctor," "The Bucket Rider," *The Castle*, *inter alia*).

8. The allusion to the great sinner, Mary Magdalen, and to the Order of the Magdalens, which was originally established to save and give nursing care to fallen women, is patent.

9. Felix Weltsch, *Religion und Humor im Leben und Werk Franz Kafkas* (Berlin-Grunewald: F. A. Herbig, 1957); Marthe Robert, "L'humour de Franz Kafka," *Revue de la Pensée Juive*, No. 6 (Paris, 1951), 61-72; and others (see Chap. III, notes 2 and 3).

10. Kafka's letter to Oskar Pollak, dated August 23, 1902. This letter was published in *Franz Kafka: Tagebücher und Briefe* (Prague, 1937), pp. 255, 247.

CHAPTER VII

1. Cf. works interpreting Kafka from the theological approach (see Chap. I, notes 10 and 37).

2. Ronald Gray, *Kafka's "Castle"* (Cambridge University Press, 1956), p. 18. Gray refers to the possibility of such an interpretation but limits it critically by emphasizing the ambiguity of this scene and of similar ones in Kafka. He compares the scene with "hidden-picture puzzles" that befool the reader. Unfortunately an exact analysis is not offered, since Gray does not exercise sufficient rigor in examining the functions of the individual characters, of the various ranks of the officials, of the servants, etc., and hence is forced to share Albert Camus's contention that a clear definition of the Kafkaian characters and events in the novel is impossible. Notwithstanding, we believe that our present interpretation furnishes proof that Kafka's novel *The Castle* has an extraordinarily strict and consistent form artistically, and that every character, every event in the novel—far from fading away in ambiguities—possesses a fixed and clearly defined meaning.

3. Primarily through the sociological and psychoanalytical trends in research (see Chap. I, note 10).

4. In Kafka's letter to Max Brod, dated the end of January 1918. To be sure, this remark refers only to Kierkegaard's *Either-Or* and to two works by Martin Buber. However, in his letters to Max Brod, dated the beginning and end of March 1918, Kafka himself speaks critically of Kierkegaard's *Fear and Trembling*; to be sure, with admiration as well, and with partial agreement. A careful analysis of Kafka's complicated attitudes toward Kierkegaard would require a separate investigation. In any case, it is evident from his letters to Max Brod that Kafka specifically disagreed with Kierkegaard's interpretation of Abraham—that very interpretation that Max Brod uses as the basis of his interpretation of *The Castle* (particularly in the Amalia episode); hence, Brod's conception is without any biographical support.

5. Kafka's letter to Max Brod, dated the beginning of March 1918.

6. Ronald Gray, *op. cit.*, p. 133.

7. Cf. the similar reluctance of Goethe upon the conclusion of *Wilhelm Meister's Apprenticeship*. In the course of his correspondence with Schiller, Goethe, in his partly dramatic statements, resisted the former's demand that the philosophical content of the novel be formulated at the end. Goethe also concealed the meaning of his novel in poetic symbols and sought to preserve its "mystery" in them.

# Bibliography of Literature on Kafka

*Bibliographies*

Flores, Angel and Homer Swander, eds. *Franz Kafka Today.*
Madison: University of Wisconsin Press, 1958. [Kafka bibliography is given by Angel Flores on pp. 251-85].

Hemmerle, Rudolf. *Franz Kafka, eine Bibliographie.* Munich:
Robert Lerche, 1958. 140 pp.

[Earlier bibliographies may be excluded since they have been
superseded by the two cited above]

*Works on Kafka*

On the basis of the above-named bibliographies, a complete
list of the writings on Kafka may be waived. Only those works
that are important for research, contain interesting points of
view, or are lacking in the two bibliographies, are listed in the
following pages.

Adorno, Theodor W. "Aufzeichnungen zu Kafka," *Die Neue*

Rundschau, LXIV, No. 3 (1953), 325-53 ; repr. in his Prismen: Kulturkritik und Gesellschaft. Berlin-Frankfurt a.M.: Suhrkamp, 1955.

Albrecht, Erich A. "Zur Entstehungsgeschichte von Kafkas Landarzt," Monatshefte, XLVI, No. 4 (1954), 207-212.

Anders, Günther. Franz Kafka: pro et contra: die Prozeßunterlagen. Munich: C. H. Beck, 1951.

Arendt, Hannah. "The Jews as Pariah: A Hidden Tradition," Jewish Social Studies (New York), VI (April 1944), 99-122.

————. "Franz Kafka, von neuem gewürdigt," Die Wandlung (Heidelberg), I, No. 12 (1946), 1050-62.

————. Sechs Essays. Heidelberg: Lambert Schneider, 1948. [pp. 99-109, 128-49 deal with Kafka]

Auden, W. H. "Kafka's Quest," The Kafka Problem, ed. Angel Flores. New York: New Directions, 1946.

Barrault, Jean-Louis. Une troupe et ses auteurs. Extraits et commentaires à propos de Shakespeare, Molière, Marivaux, P. Claudel, A. Gide, Kafka, etc. Paris: 1950.

Bataille, Georges. "Franz Kafka devant la critique communiste," Critique (Paris), VI (October 1950), 22-37.

Bauer, Roger. "Kafka à la lumière de la religiosité juive," Dieu Vivant (Paris: Editions du Seuil), IX (1947), 105-120

Baum, Oskar. "Erinnerungen an Franz Kafka," Witiko (Kassel-Wilhelmshöhe), II, No. 3 (1929), 126-28.

————. "Recollections," The Kafka Problem, ed. Angel Flores. New York: New Directions, 1946.

Beißner, Friedrich. Der Erzähler Franz Kafka. Stuttgart: Kohlhammer, 1952.

Benjamin, Walter, "Franz Kafka, zur 10. Wiederkehr seines Todestages," Gesammelte Schriften, II. Frankfurt a.M.: Suhrkamp, 1955.

Bense, Max. Literaturmetaphysik. Der Schriftsteller in der technischen Welt. Stuttgart: Deutsche Verlagsanstalt, 1950.

————. Die Theorie Kafkas. Köln-Berlin: Kiepenheuer und Witsch, 1952.

————. Aesthetica. Metaphysische Beobachtungen am Schönen. Stuttgart: Deutsche Verlagsanstalt, 1954.

Bergel, Lienhard. "Blumfeld, an Elderly Bachelor," *The Kafka Problem*, ed. Angel Flores. New York: New Directions, 1946.

———. "The Burrow," *ibid.*

———. "Max Brod and Herbert Tauber," *ibid.*

———. "*America*: Its Meaning," *Franz Kafka Today*, ed. Angel Flores and Homer Swander, Madison: University of Wisconsin Press, 1958.

Blanchot, Maurice. *La part du feu*. Paris: Gallimard, 1949.

———. "*The Diaries*: The Exigency of the Work of Art," *Franz Kafka Today*, ed. Angel Flores and Homer Swander, Madison: University of Wisconsin Press, 1958.

Blöcker, Günter. *Die neuen Wirklichkeiten*. Berlin: 1957.

Boden, Gérard. *Franz Kafka. Aspects de son oeuvre*. Algiers: Chaix, 1947.

Braybrooke, Neville. "Celestial Castles: An Approach to Saint Teresa and Kafka," *Dublin Review* (London), CCXXIX, (1955), 427-45.

Brod, Max. *Diesseits und Jenseits*. 2 vols. Winterthur: Mondial, 1947. [contains comments on Kierkegaard, Heidegger, and Kafka]

———. "Kleist und Kafka," *Weltstimmen* (Stuttgart), XVIII, No. 12 (1949), 8-11.

———. *Franz Kafkas Glauben und Lehre*. Winterthur: Mondial, 1948.

———. "Zur Textgestaltung der 'Hochzeitsvorbereitungen auf dem Lande,'" *Die Neue Rundschau*, LXII, No. 1 (1951), 18-20.

———. *Franz Kafka als wegweisende Gestalt*. St. Gallen: Tschudy, 1951.

———. "Bemerkungen zu Kafkas 'Schloß,'" *Eckart* (Witten-Berlin), XX/XXI (1951/52), 451-53.

———. "Bemerkungen zur Lebensgeschichte Franz Kafkas," *Die Neue Rundschau*, LXIV, No. 2 (1953), 232-44.

———. "Neue Züge zum Bilde Franz Kafkas," *Merkur*, VII, No. 6 (1953), 518-30.

———. *Franz Kafka, eine Biographie*. 3rd imp. Berlin-Frankfurt a.M.: S. Fischer, 1954.

——. "Uyttersprot korrigiert Kafka. Eine Entgegnung," *Forum* (Vienna), IV, Nos. 43/44 (July/August 1957), 264-65.

——. "Zur Deutung von Kafkas 'Amerika,'" *Neue Zürcher Zeitung* (March 27, 1958).

——. *The Castle*: Its Genesis," *Franz Kafka Today,* ed. Angel Flores and Homer Swander. Madison: University of Wisconsin Press, 1958.

Brück, Max von. "Versuch über Kafka," *Die Sphinx ist nicht tot.* Köln-Berlin: Kiepenheuer und Witsch, 1956.

Buber, Martin. *Zwei Glaubensweisen.* Zürich: Manesse, 1950.

——. *Schuld und Schuldgefühle.* Heidelberg: L. Schneider, 1957.

Burgum, Edwin Berry. "The Bankruptcy of Faith," *The Kafka Problem,* ed. Angel Flores. New York: New Directions, 1946.

Busacca, Basil. "'A Country Doctor,'" *Franz Kafka Today,* ed. Angel Flores and Homer Swander. Madison: University of Wisconsin Press, 1958.

Camus, Albert. "Die Hoffnung und das Absurde im Werk von Franz Kafka," *Der Mythos von Sisyphos: Ein Versuch über das Absurde.* Düsseldorf: Karl Rauch, 1950.

Carrouges, Michel. *Kafka.* Paris: Labergerie, 1948.

——. *La mystique du surhomme.* Paris: Gallimard, 1948.

——. "La machine-célibataire selon Franz Kafka et Marcel Duchamp," *Mercure de France,* CCCXV (June 1952), 262-81.

Caspel, P.P.J. van. "Josefine und Jeremias. Versuch einer Deutung einer Erzählung Franz Kafkas," *Neophilologus,* XXXVII, No. 4 (1953), 241-45.

——. "Totemismus bei Kafka," *Neophilologus,* XXXVIII, No. 2 (1954), 120-27.

Collignon, Jean. "Kafka's Humor," *Yale French Studies,* No. 16 (1955/56), 53-62.

Daniel-Rops [pseud. of J. Ch. Henri Petiot]. "The Castle of Despair," *The Kafka Problem,* ed. Angel Flores. New York: New Directions, 1946.

Dauvin, René. *"Le Procès* de Kafka," *Études Germaniques,* III (1948), 49-63.

————. "*The Trial*: Its Meaning," "Franz Kafka Today, ed. Angel Flores and Homer Swander. Madison: University of Wisconsin Press, 1958.

Delesalle, Jacques. *Cet étrange secret*. Lille: Desclée de Brouwer, 1957. [pp. 60-97 deal with Kafka]

Demetz, Peter. "Zur Interpretation Franz Kafkas," *Plan* (Vienna), II (1948), 370-78.

————. "Kafka in England," *German Life and Letters*, n.s., IV, No. 1 (1950), 21-30.

————. *René Rilkes Prager Jahre*. Düsseldorf: Diederichs, 1953.

————. "Kafka, Freud, Husserl: Problem einer Generation," *Zeitschrift für Religions- und Geistesgeschichte* (Köln-Leiden-Heidelberg), VII, No. 1 (1955), 59-69.

Edel, Edmund. "Franz Kafka: 'Die Verwandlung.' Eine Auslegung," *Wirkendes Wort*, VIII, No. 4 (1957/58), 217-26.

Eisner, Pavel. *Franz Kafka and Prague*. New York: Arts Inc., 1950.

Emrich, Wilhelm. "Franz Kafka," *Deutsche Literatur im 20. Jahrhundert*, ed. Hermann Friedmann and Otto Mann. Heidelberg: Wolfgang Rothe, 1954.

————. "Zur Ästhetik der modernen Dichtung," *Akzente*, I, No. 4 (1954), 371-87.

————. "Die Literaturrevolution und die moderne Gesellschaft," *Akzente*, III, No. 2 (1956), 173-91. [on Kafka, Rilke]

————. "Die poetische Wirklichkeitskritik Franz Kafkas," *Orbis Litterarum* (Copenhagen), XI, No. 4 (1956), 215-28.

————. "Formen. und Gehalte des zeitgenössischen Romans," *Universitas*, XI, No. 1 (1956), 49-58.

————. "Franz Kafka," *Die großen Deutschen* (Berlin), ed. H. Heimpel, Th. Heuß, B. Reifenberg, IV (1957), 486-96.

————. "Die Weltkritik Franz Kafkas," *Abhandlungen der Klasse der Literatur der Mainzer Akademie der Wissenschaften und der Literatur*, No. 1. Wiesbaden: F. Steiner, 1958.

————. "Die Bilderwelt Franz Kafkas," *Akzente*, VII, No. 2 (1960).

Flores, Angel, ed. *The Kafka Problem*. New York: New Directions, 1946.

Flores, Angel, and Homer Swander, eds. *Franz Kafka Today*. Madison: University of Wisconsin Press, 1958.

Flores, Kate. "Franz Kafka and the Nameless Guilt: An Analysis of 'The Judgment,'" *Quarterly Review of Literature* (New York), III, No. 4 (1947), 382-405.

————. "'The Judgment,'" *Franz Kafka Today*, ed. Angel Flores and Homer Swander. Madison: University of Wisconsin Press, 1958. [identical with the above-named article]

Florman, Samuel C. "American Criticism of Franz Kafka (1930-46)." M.A. thesis, Columbia University, 1947.

Fraiberg, Selma. "Kafka and the Dream," *Partisan Review* (New York), XXIII, No. 1 (1956), 47-69.

Friedrich, Heinz. "Heinrich von Kleist und Franz Kafka," *Berliner Hefte für geistiges Leben*, IV, No. 11 (Autumn 1949), 440-48.

Frey, Hermann. "Rudolf Steiner und Franz Kafka," *Blätter für Anthroposophie* (Dornach), III, No. 12 (1951), 432-40.

Fromm, Erich. "Symbolic Language in Myth, Fairy Tale, Ritual and Novel: Kafka's *The Trial*," *The Forgotten Language*. London: 1952.

Fuchs, Rudolf. "Social Awareness," *The Kafka Problem*, ed. Angel Flores. New York: New Directions, 1946.

Fürst, Norbert. *Die offenen Geheimtüren Franz Kafkas: Fünf Allegorien*. Heidelberg: Wolfgang Rothe, 1956.

Giesekius, Waltraud. "Franz Kafkas Tagebücher." Diss., University of Bonn, 1954.

Goodman, Paul. *Kafka's Prayer*. New York: Vanguard, 1947.

Goth, Maja. *Franz Kafka et les lettres françaises (1928-1955)*. Paris: Corti, 1957. [deals with Kafka's influence on French literature]

Grangier, Edouard. "Abraham, oder Kierkegaard, wie Kafka und Sartre ihn sehen," *Zeitschrift für philosophische Forschung* (Meisenheim/Glan), IV, No. 3 (1949), 412-21.

Gräser, Albert. *Das literarische Tagebuch: Studien über Elemente des Tagebuches als Kunstform* (Schriften der Universität des Saarlandes). Saarbrücken: West-Ost Verlag, 1955.

Gravier, Maurice. "Strindberg et Kafka," *Études Germaniques*, VIII, Nos. 2/3 (1953), 118-40.

Gray, Ronald. *Kafka's "Castle."* Cambridge University Press, 1956.

Greenberg, Clement. "The Jewishness of Franz Kafka," *Commentary* (New York), XIX, No. 4 (1955), 320-24.

———. "At the Building of the Great Wall of China," *Franz Kafka Today,* ed. Angel Flores and Homer Swander. Madison: University of Wisconsin Press, 1958.

Grenzmann, Wilhelm. "Franz Kafkas Werk und geistige Welt," *Universitas,* VIII, No. 8 (1953), 797-803.

———. "Franz Kafka an der Grenze zwischen Nichtsein und Sein," *Dichtung und Glaube, Probleme und Gestalten der deutschen Gegenwartsliteratur.* Bonn: Athenäum, 1950. See also the enlarged 3rd ed. (1957), pp. 141-61.

Groethysen, Bernard. "À propos de Kafka," *La Nouvelle Revue Française,* n.s., XL, No. 4 (1933), 588-606.

———. "The Endless Labyrinth," *The Kafka Problem,* ed. Angel Flores. New York: New Directions, 1946.

Gruenter, Rainer. "Beitrag zur Kafka-Deutung," *Merkur,* IV, No. 3 (1950), 278-87.

———. "Kafka in der englischen und amerikanischen Kritik," *Das literarische Deutschland,* II, No. 12 (1951), 6.

Haas, Willy. *Gestalten der Zeit.* Berlin: Kiepenheuer, 1930.

———. "Auslegung eines Aktes der Freundschaft," *Dichter. Denker. Helfer. Max Brod zum 50. Geburtstag.* Mährisch-Ostrau, 1934.

———. "Prague in 1912," *Virginia Quarterly Review* (New York), XXIV (1948), 409-17.

———. "Immer noch kein Ende mit der Kafka-Mode? Zu den neuen Interpretationsversuchen des holländischen Philologen Uyttersprot," *Die Welt,* No. 193 (August 21, 1957), 9.

Hajek, Siegfried. "Die moderne Kurzgeschichte im Deutschunterricht. Franz Kafka: 'Der Nachbar,'" *Der Deutschunterricht* (Stuttgart), VII, No. 1 (1955), 5-12.

Hatfield, Henry Caraway, and Jack M. Stein, eds. *Schnitzler-Kafka-Mann.* Boston: Houghton Mifflin, 1953.

Heldmann, Werner. "Die Parabel und die parabolischen Erzählformen bei Franz Kafka." Diss., University of Münster, 1953.

Heller, Erich. "Die Welt Franz Kafkas," in his *Enterbter Geist. Essays über modernes Dichten und Denken.* Frankfurt a.M.: Suhrkamp, 1954.

Hermlin, Stephan. "Franz Kafka," *Die Fähre 1946: Ein Almanach.* Munich: Weismann, 1946.

———. "Franz Kafka zu seinem 65. Geburtstag," *Ansichten über einige Bücher und Schriftsteller.* Berlin: Volk und Welt, 1947.

Hermsdorf, K. "Briefe des Versicherungsangestellten Franz Kafka —Zu den Briefen F. Kafkas," *Sinn und Form* (Berlin), IX, No. 4 (1957).

Heselhaus, Clemens. "Kafkas Erzählformen," *Deutsche Vierteljahrsschrift für Literaturwissenschaft und Geistesgeschichte,* XXVI, No. 3 (1952), 353-76.

Hodin, J. P. "Erinnerungen an Franz Kafka," *Der Monat,* I, Nos. 8/9 (1949), 89-96.

———. "The Fate of Franz Kafka," *Literary Guide* (London), LXIX, No. 11 (1954), 5-7.

Hoffmann, Frederick J. "Franz Kafka and Mann," *Freudianism and the Literary Mind.* Baton Rouge: Louisiana State University Press, 1945.

———. "Escape from Father," *The Kafka Problem,* ed. Angel Flores. New York: New Directions, 1946.

Hoffmann, Leonard R. "Melville and Kafka." Diss., Stanford University, 1951.

Ide, Heinz. 'Existenzerhellung im Werke Kafkas," *Jahrbuch des Wittheit zu Bremen* (1957), 66-104.

Jens, Inge. "Studien zur Entwicklung der expressionistischen Novelle." Diss., University of Tübingen, 1954 [pp. 80-108 deal with Kafka's "Description of a Battle"]

Kahler, Erich. "Untergang and Übergang der espischen Kunstform," *Die Neue Rundschau,* LXIV, No. 1 (1953), 1-44.

Kaiser, Gerhard. "Franz Kafkas *Prozeß*: Versuch einer Interpretation," *Euphorion* (Heidelberg), LII, No. 1 (1958), 23-49.

Kaiser, Hellmuth. *Franz Kafkas Inferno: Psychologische Deutung seiner Strafphantasie.* Vienna: International Psychoanalytischer Verlag, 1931. Repr. in *Imago,* XVII, No. 1 (1931), 41-103.

Kaßner, Rudolf. *Der goldene Drachen, Gleichnis und Essay.* Erlenbach/Zürich and Stuttgart: Eugen Rentsch, 1957. [contains an essay on Swift, Gogol, and Kafka]

Kauf, Robert. "Once Again: Kafka's 'A Report to an Academy,'" *Modern Language Quarterly,* XV, No. 4 (1954), 359-65.

Keller, Fritz. *Studien zum Phänomen der Angst in der modernen deutschen Literatur.* Winterthur: 1956.

Kelly, John. "*The Trial* and the Theology of Crisis," *The Kafka Problem,* ed. Angel Flores. New York: New Directions, 1946.

Klossowski, Pierre. "Introduction au Journal Intime de Franz Kafka," *Cahiers du Sud* (Marseille), XXII, No. 270 (1945), 148-60.

———. "Kafka Nihiliste?" *Critique* (Paris), VII, No. 30 (1948).

König, Gert. "Franz Kafkas Erzählungen und kleine Prosa." Diss., University of Tübingen, 1954.

Korst, Marianne Ruth. "Die Beziehung zwischen Held und Gegenwelt in Franz Kafkas Romanen." Diss., University of Marburg, 1953.

Kraft, Werner. "Über Franz Kafkas 'Elf Söhne,'" *Die Schildgenossen* (Augsburg), XII, Nos. 2/3 (1932), 120-32.

———. "Über den Tod: Zu Franz Kafkas 'Ein Traum,'" *Der Morgen* (Berlin), XI, No. 2 (1935), 81-85.

———. "Kafka und das Religiöse," *Die Fähre* (Munich), II, No. 1 (1947), 13-19.

———. "Franz Kafkas Erzählung 'Das Ehepaar,'" *Die Wandlung* (Heidelberg), IV, No. 2 (1949), 155-60.

Kuhr, Alexander. "Neurotische Aspekte bei Heidegger und Kafka." *Zeitschrift für psychosomatische Medizin* (Göttingen), I, No. 3 (1955), 217-27.

Kyler, Ingrid E. *The Pilgrimage of Franz Kafka.* New York: Columbia University Press, 1949.

Landsberg, Paul. "'The Metamorphosis,'" *The Kafka Problem,* ed. Angel Flores. New York: New Directions, 1946.

———. "Kafka et 'La métamorphose,'" *Problèmes du personnalisme.* Paris: Editions du Seuil, 1952.

Lange, Victor. "Franz Kafka," *Modern German Literature 1870-1940.* Ithaca, N.Y.: Cornell University Press, 1945.

Lawson, Richard H. "Kafka's 'Der Landarzt,'" *Monatshefte*, XLIX (October 1957), 265-71.

Lerner, Max. "Franz Kafka and the Human Voyage," *Ideas for the Ice Age*. New York: Viking Press, 1941. Repr. in *The Kafka Problem*, ed. Angel Flores. New York: New Directions, 1946.

Luke, F.D. "'The Metamorphosis,'" *Franz Kafka Today*, ed. Angel Flores and Homer Swander. Madison: University of Wisconsin Press, 1958. Also in *Modern Language Review*, XLVI, No. 2 (1951)

Madden, William A. "A Myth of Mediation: Kafka's 'Metamorphosis,'" *Thought, Fordham University Quarterly* (New York), XXVI, No. 101 (1951), 246-66.

Magny, Claude-Edmonde. *Les sandales d'Empédocle. Essai sur les limites de la littérature*. Neuchâtel: Edition de la Baconnière, 1945. [pp. 173-266 deal with "Kafka ou l'écriture de l'absurde ; Procès en canonisation"]

———. "The Objective Depiction of Absurdity," *The Kafka Problem*, ed. Angel Flores. New York: New Directions, 1946. Also in *Quarterly Review of Literature* (New York), II, No. 3 (1945), 211-27.

Maier, Anne. "Franz Kafka und Robert Musil als Vertreter der ethischen Richtung des modernen Romans." Diss., University of Vienna, 1949.

Martini, Fritz. *Das Wagnis der Sprache. Interpretationen deutscher Prosa von Nietzsche bis Benn*. Stuttgart: Klett, 1954. [pp. 287-335 deal with *The Castle* and offer a linguistic analysis of Chap. 8]

———. "Franz Kafka," *Denker und Deuter im heutigen Europa*, ed. Hans Schwerte and Wilhelm Spengler, I (Oldenburg-Hamburg: G. Stalling, 1954), 191-201.

———. "Ein Manuskript Franz Kafkas: 'Der Dorfschullehrer,'" *Jahrbuch der deutschen Schiller-Gesellschaft*, II. Stuttgart: A. Kröner, 1958.

Meidinger-Geise, Inge. "Franz Kafka und die junge Literatur," *Welt und Wort, Literarische Monatsschrift* (Tübingen-Bad Wörishofen), VII, No. 6 (1952), 189-94. [deals with Kafka's influence on current German literature]

Michael, Wolfgang. "The Human Simian," *Library Chronicle*

(Philadelphia), XIX, No. 1 (1952/53), 35-44. [deals with "A Report to an Academy"]

Middelhauve, Friedrich. "Ich und Welt im Frühwerk Franz Kafkas." Diss., University of Freiburg i. Br., 1957.

Molitor, Jan [pseudo of Aimé van Santen]. *Asmodai in Praag, Franz Kafka, zijn tijd en zijn werk.* 's Graveland: De Driehoek, 1950.

Motekat, Helmut. "Interpretation als Erschließung dichterischer Wirklichkeit. Mit einer Interpretation von Franz Kafkas Erzählung 'Ein Landarzt,'" *Interpretationen moderner Prosa,* ed. Fachgruppe Deutsch-Geschichte im Bayerischen Philologenverband. 3rd imp. Frankfurt a.M., Berlin, Bonn: Diesterweg, 1957.

Mounier, Guy-Fernand H. "Étude psychopathologique sur l'écrivain Franz Kafka." Diss., University of Bordeaux, 1951.

Mühlberger, Josef. *Hugo von Hofmannsthal—Franz Kafka. Zwei Vorträge.* Esslingen: Bechtle, 1953.

Muir, Edwin. "Franz Kafka," *A Franz Kafka Miscellany,* ed. Harry Slochower. 2nd ed. New York: Twice a Year Press, 1946. [cf. Muir's introductions to his and Willa Muir's joint translations of Kafka's works into English; naturally these have had an important influence on the English and American image of Kafka]

Musil, Robert. *Tagebücher, Aphorismen, Essays und Reden,* ed. Adolf Frisé. Hamburg: Rowohlt, 1955.

Neider, Charles. "The Cabalists," *The Kafka Problem,* ed. Angel Flores. New York: New Directions, 1946.

———. *The Frozen Sea: A Study of Franz Kafka.* New York: Oxford University Press, 1948. Published also as *Kafka: His Mind and Art.* London: Routledge & Kegan Paul, 1949.

Nemeth, André. *Kafka ou le mystère juif.* Paris: Jean Vigneau, 1947.

Pascal, Roy. *The German Novel.* Manchester: University of Toronto Press, 1956. [pp. 215-57 deal with Kafka's novels]

Pearce, Donald. *"The Castle:* Kafka's Divine Comedy," *Franz Kafka Today,* ed. Angel Flores and Homer Swander. Madison: University of Wisconsin Press, 1958.

————. "Dante and *The Castle,*" *Northern Review* (Montreal) (June/July 1947), 2-8. [identical with above-named article].

Politzer, Heinz. " 'Give it up!' " *The Kafka Problem,* ed. Angel Flores. New York: New Directions, 1946.

————. "Problematik und Probleme der Kafka-Forschung," *Monatshefte,* XLII, No. 6 (1950), 273-80.

————. "Jenseits von Joyce und Kafka. Zu Hermann Brochs *Die Schuldlosen,*" *Die Neue Rundschau,* LXIII, No. 1 (1952), 152-59.

————. "Franz Kafka's Letter to His Father," *The Germanic Review* (New York), XXVIII, No. 3 (1953), 165-80. Also in *Franz Kafka Today,* ed. Angel Flores and Homer Swander. Madison: University of Wisconsin Press, 1958.

————. "Franz Kafka: Metaphysical Anarchist," *Renascence* (New York), VI (1954), 106-111.

————. "Prague and the Origins of Rainer Maria Rilke, Franz Kafka, and Franz Werfel," *Modern Language Quarterly,* XVI, No. 1 (1955), 49-62.

Pongs, Hermann. *Im Umbruch der Zeit: Das Romanschaffen der Gegenwart.* 2nd ed. Göttingen: Göttinger Verlagsanstalt, 1956.

Pratt, Audrey E. (McKim). *Franz Kafka und sein Vater: das Verhältnis der Beiden und dessen Einwirkung auf Kafkas Werk.* Thesis, McGill University (Montreal), 1949.

Pulver, Max. "Spaziergang mit Franz Kafka," *Erinnerungen an eine europäische Zeit.* Zürich: Orell Füssli, 1953.

Rabi, Wladimir. "Kafka et la néo-Kabbale," *La terre retrouvée* (Paris), XXIV, No. 10 (February 1955).

————. "Kafka et la néo-Kabbale," *La table ronde, Revue mensuelle* (Paris), No. 123 (March 1958), 116-28.

Reimann, Paul. "Die gesellschaftliche Problematik in Kafkas Romanen," *Weimarer Beiträge, Zeitschrift für deutsche Literaturgeschichte,* III, No. 4 (1957), 598-618.

Reiß, Hans Siegbert. "Franz Kafka," *German Life and Letters,* n.s., I, No. 3 (1947/48), 186-94.

————. "Frank Kafka's Conception of Humour," *Modern Language Review* (Cambridge), XLIV, No. 4 (1949), 534-42.

————. "Zwei Erzählungen von Franz Kafka," *Trivium,* VIII,

No. 3 (1950), 218-42. [deals with "The Knock at the Manor Gate" and "The Test"]

————. "Zum Stil und zur Komposition in der deutschen Prosaerzählung der Gegenwart," *Studium Generale,* VIII, No. 1 (1955), 19-31. [deals with Thomas Mann, Kafka, and Robert Musil]

————. "Eine Neuordnung der Werke Kafkas?" *Akzente,* II, No. 6 (1955), 553-55. [deals with the author's position on Uyttersprot's theses]

————. *Franz Kafka: Eine Betrachtung seines Werkes.* 2nd ed. Heidelberg: Lambert Schneider, 1956.

————. "Recent Kafka Criticism—A Survey," *German Life and Letters,* n.s., IX, No. 4 (1956), 294-305.

Robert, Marthe. *Introduction à la lecture de Kafka, suivie de "L'épée," "Dans notre synagogue," "L'invité des morts," "Lampes neuves."* Textes et commentaires. Paris: Edition du Sagittaire, 1946.

————. "Zu Franz Kafkas Fragment 'In unserer Synagoge,'" *Merkur,* II, No. 7 (1948), 113-14.

————. "L'humour de Franz Kafka," *Revue de la Pensée Juive* (Paris), No. 6 (1951), 61-72.

————. "La lecture de Kafka," *Les Temps Modernes* (Paris), I, Nos. 84/85 (1952), 646-78.

————. "Dora Dymants Erinnerungen an Kafka," *Merkur,* VII, No. 9 (1953), 848-51.

Rochefort, Robert. *Kafka, oder die unzerstörbare Hoffnung.* With preface by Romano Guardini. Vienna-Munich: Herold 1955.

Rohner, Wolfgang. "Franz Kafkas Werkgestaltung." Diss., University of Freiburg i. Br., 1950.

Rubinstein, William C. "Franz Kafka: 'A Hunger Artist,'" *Monatshefte,* XLIV, No. 1 (1952), 13-19.

————. "'A Report to an Academy,'" *Franz Kafka Today,* ed. Angel Flores and Homer Swander. Madison: University of Wisconsin Press, 1958. Also in *Modern Language Quarterly,* XIII, No. 4 (1952), 372-76.

Sarraute, Nathalie. "De Dostoievski à Kafka," *Les Temps Modernes* (Paris), III, No. 25 (October 1947), 664-85.

Savage, D. S. "Faith and Vocation," *The Kafka Problem*, ed. Angel Flores. New York: New Directions, 1946.

Schaufelberger, Fritz. "Kafkas Prosafragmente," *Trivium*, VII, No. 1 (1949), 1-15.

Schoeps, Hans-Joachim. "Franz Kafka oder der Glaube in der tragischen Position," *Gestalten an der Zeitenwende* (Berlin: Vortrupp, 1936), 54-77. Published in English translation in *The Kafka Problem*, ed. Angel Flores (New York: New Directions, 1946), pp. 287-97.

———. "Theologische Motive in der Dichtung Franz Kafkas," *Die Neue Rundschau*, LXII, No. 1 (1951), 21-37.

Seidler, Manfred. "Strukturanalysen der Romane *Der Prozeß* und *Das Schloß* von Franz Kafka." Diss., University of Bonn, 1953.

Seidlin, Oskar. "Franz Kafka—Lackland. An Austro-German Jew from Bohemia," *Books Abroad* (Norman, Oklahoma Press), XXII, No. 3 (1948), 244-46.

———. "Hermann Hesse: The Exorcism of the Demon," *Symposium* (Syracuse, N.Y.), IV (1950), 325-48. [analogies between Hesse and Kafka]

———. "The Shroud of Silence (Kafka, Rilke, Hofmannsthal)," *PMLA*, LXVIII, No. 2 (1953), 45 ff. Also in *The Germanic Review*, XXVIII, No. 4 (1953), 254-61.

Seyppel, Joachim H. "The Animal Theme and Totemism in Franz Kafka," *MLA: Literature and Psychology* (New York), IV, No. 4 (1954), 49-63. Also in *American Imago*, XIII (Spring 1956), 69-93.

Slochower, Harry, ed. *A Franz Kafka Miscellany*. 2nd ed. New York: Twice A Year Press, 1946. See in particular his article "Franz Kafka, Pre-Fascist Exile" [pp. 7-30 of this vol.].

———."The Limitations of Franz Kafka," *American Scholar* (New York), XV (1946), 291-97.

Spann, Meno. "The Minor Kafka Problem," *The Germanic Review*, XXXII, No. 3 (October 1957).

Spilka, Mark. *"America:* Its Genesis," *Franz Kafka Today*, ed. Angel Flores and Homer Swander. Madison: University of Wisconsin Press, 1958.

Stallman, Robert W. " 'A Hunger Artist,' " *Franz Kafka Today*, ed.

Angel Flores and Homer Swander. Madison: University of Wisconsin Press, 1958.

Storz, Gerhard. *Sprache und Dichtung.* Munich, 1957. [pp. 201-204 deal with stylistic investigations of *The Trial*—direct and indirect discourse]

Stumpf, Walter. "Das religiöse Problem in der Dichtung Franz Kafkas," *Orient und Okzident* (Leipzig), No. 5 (1931), 48-63.

———. "Franz Kafka," *Die Furche* (Berlin), XVIII, No. 3 (1932), 249-62.

———. "Franz Kafkas Werdegang," *Die Schildgenossen* (Augsburg), XIV, No. 4 (1935), 351-66.

———. "Franz Kafka, Persönlichkeit und geistige Gestalt," *Die Fähre* (Munich), II, No. 7 (1947), 387-97.

———. "Franz Kafka. Der Mensch und sein verlorenes Einst," *Literarische Revue* (Munich), III, No. 5 (1948), 281-84. [deals with "In the Penal Colony" and "Investigations of a Dog"]

Susman, Margarete. "Das Hiob-Problem bei Franz Kafka," *Der Morgen* (Berlin), V, No. 1 (1929), 31-49.

Swander, Homer, "*The Castle*: K.'s Village," *Franz Kafka Today,* ed. Angel Flores and Homer Swander. Madison: University of Wisconsin Press, 1958.

Tauber, Herbert. *Franz Kafka: Eine Deutung seiner Werke.* Zürich-New York: Oprecht, 1941.

Thurston, Jarvis. "'The Married Couple,'" *Franz Kafka Today,* ed. Angel Flores and Homer Swander. Madison: University of Wisconsin Press, 1958.

Toulmin, A. G. *Humor in the Works of Kafka.* Somerville College, Oxford, 1951.

Tyler, Parker. "Kafka and the Surrealists," *Accent* (Urbana, Ill.), VI (Autumn 1945), 23-27.

———. "Franz Kafka und die Surrealisten," *Das Lot* (Berlin), II (1948), 75-82.

———. "Kafka's and Chaplin's 'Amerika,'" *Sewanee Review* (Sewanee, Tennessee), LVIII (1950), 299-311.

Ulshöfer, Robert. "Entseelte Wirklichkeit in Franz Kafkas 'Verwandlung,'" *Der Deutschunterricht* (Stuttgart), VII, No. 1 (1955), 27-36.

Urzidill, Johannes. "Rede zum Ehrengedächtnis Franz Kafkas," *Das Kunstblatt* (Potsdam), VIII, No. 8 (1924), 250-51 [funeral oration in Prague on the occasion of Kafka's death]

———. "Franz Kafka, Novelist and Mystic," *Menorah Journal* (New York), XXXI (October/December 1943), 273-83.

———. "Personal Notes on Franz Kafka," *Life and Letters Today* (London) (September 1944), 134-40.

———. "Recollections," *The Kafka Problem,* ed. Angel Flores. New York: New Directions, 1946.

———. "Franz Kafka and Prague," *The Germanic Review,* XXVI, No. 2 (April 1951).

———. "Meetings with Franz Kafka," *Menorah Journal* (New York), XL (1952), 112-16.

———. "Begegnungen mit Franz Kafka," *Neue literarische Welt,* III, No. 2 (1952), 3.

———. "Kafkas *Briefe an Milena,"* *Neue literarische Welt,* IV, No. 5 (1953), 6.

Uyttersprot, Herman. *Eine neue Ordnung der Werke Kafkas? Zur Struktur von "Der Prozeß" und "Amerika."* Antwerp: C. de Vries-Brouwers, 1957. [cf. the replies made by Max Brod, Willy Haas, and H. S. Reiß (see above in this Bibliography)]

Vašata, Rudolf. *"Amerika* and Charles Dickens," *The Kafka Problem,* ed. Angel Flores. New York: New Directions, 1946.

Vietta, Egon. "Franz Kafka und unsere Zeit," *Neue Schweizer Rundschau,* XXIV, No. 8 (1931), 565-77.

———. "The Fundamental Revolution," *The Kafka Problem,* ed. Angel Flores. New York: New Directions, 1946.

Volkmann-Schluck, Karl Heinz. "Bewußtsein und Dasein in Kafkas *Prozeß,"* *Die Neue Rundschau,* LXII, No. 1 (1951), 38-48.

Vordtriede, Werner. *"Letters to Milena*: The Writer as Advocate of Himself," *Franz Kafka Today,* ed. Angel Flores and Homer Swander. Madison: University of Wisconsin Press, 1958.

Wagenbach, Klaus. "Franz Kafka. Eine Biographie seiner Jugend (1883-1912)." Diss., University of Frankfurt a.M., 1957. [this has since been published: Bern: A. Francke, 1958]

Wahl, Jean André. "Kierkegard and Kafka," *The Kafka Problem,* ed. Angel Flores. New York: New Directions, 1946.

——. *Petit histoire de "l'existentialisme," suivie de Kafka et Kierkegaard. Commentaires.* Paris: Club Maintenant, 1947.

——. *Equisse pour une histoire de "l'existentialisme," suivie de Kafka et Kierkegaard.* Paris: Arche, 1949.

Waismann, F. "A Philosopher Looks at Kafka," *Essays in Criticism* (London), III (1953), 177-90.

Walker, Augusta. "Allegory: A Light Conceit," *Partisan Review* (New York), XXII, No. 4 (1955), 480-90. [deals with Kafka's allegories and "The Burrow"]

Walser, Martin Johannes. "Beschreibung einer Form. Versuch über die epische Dichtung Franz Kafkas." Diss., University of Tübingen, 1952.

Walter, Siegfried. "Die Rolle der führenden und schwellenden Elemente in Erzählungen des 19. und 20. Jahrhunderts." Diss., University of Bonn, 1951.

Warren, Austin. "Kosmos Kafka," *The Kafka Problem,* ed. Angel Flores. New York: New Directions, 1946.

——. " 'The Penal Colony,' " *ibid.*

Webster, Peter Dow. "Arrested Individualism or the Problem of Joseph K. and Hamlet," *American Imago,* V, No. 3 (1948), 4-23.

——. "A Critical Fantasy or Fugue," *American Imago,* VI, No. 4 (1949), 3-15.

——. " 'Dies Irae' in the Unconscious, or the Significance of Franz Kafka," *College English* (Chicago), XII, No. 1 (1950), 9-15.

——. "A Critical Examination of Franz Kafka's *The Castle," American Imago,* VIII, No. 1 (1951), 3-28.

Weiskopf, Franz Carl. 'Franz Kafka und die Folgen. Mythus und Auslegung," in his *Literarische Streifzüge.* Berlin: Aufbau, 1956.

Weiß, Ernst. "The Diaries and Letters," *The Kafka Problem,* ed. Angel Flores. New York: New Directions, 1946.

Weiß, T. "The Economy of Chaos," *ibid.*

Weltsch, Felix. "Freiheit und Schuld in Franz Kafkas Roman

*Der Prozeß," Jüdischer Almanach auf das Jahr 5687.* Prague: 1926/27.

————. *Religion und Humor im Leben und Werk Franz Kafkas.* Berlin-Grunewald: F. A. Herbig, 1957.

Wiese, Benno von. *Die deutsche Novelle von Goethe bis Kafka. Interpretation.* Düsseldorf: August Bagel, 1956. [pp. 325-42 deal with Kafka and "A Hunger Artist"]

————. "Der Künstler und die moderne Gesellschaft," *Akzente,* No. 2 (1958), 112-23. [deals with "A Hunger Artist" and "Josephine, the Singer"]

Woodring, Carl R. " 'Josephine the Singer, or the Mouse Folk,' " *Franz Kafka Today,* ed. Angel Flores and Homer Swander. Madison: University of Wisconsin Press, 1958.

Zangerle, Ignaz. "Die Bestimmung des Dichters," *Der Brenner* (Innsbruck), XVI (1946), 112-20. [corresponds to the article cited below, "Der Dichter und das Kreuz"]

————. "Der Dichter und das Kreuz (Rilke, Trakl, Kafka)," *Das goldene Tor* (Baden-Baden), III (1948), 413-26.

Zimmermann, Werner. *Deutsche Prosadichtungen der Gegenwart.* Düsseldorf: Schwann, 1954. 3rd ed. published in 1956. [deals with "In the Gallery," "An Imperial Message," and "Before the Law"]

# Index of Kafka's Writings

# Index of Personal Names